ALOYS FLEISCHMANN
(1910–1992)

A Life for Music in Ireland
Remembered by Contemporaries

D0348138

Also by Ruth Fleischmann

Catholic Nationalism in the Irish Revival: A Study of Canon Sheehan 1852–1913, Basingstoke (Macmillan) 1997

(Ed.) *Joan Denise Moriarty – Founder of Irish National Ballet: Material for a History of Dance in Ireland*, Cork (Mercier Press) 1998

ALOYS FLEISCHMANN
(1910–1992)

A Life for Music in Ireland
Remembered by Contemporaries

Edited by
RUTH FLEISCHMANN

MERCIER PRESS

MERCIER PRESS
5 French Church Street, Cork
16 Hume Street, Dublin 2

Trade enquiries to CMD DISTRIBUTION,
55a Spruce Avenue, Stillorgan Industrial Park, Blackrock, Dublin

ISBN 185635 328 1

10 9 8 7 6 5 4 3 2 1

Printed in Ireland by Colour Books Ltd.

CONTENTS

ACKNOWLEDGMENTS

About 160 people have helped to make this book possible: to them I express my grateful thanks. At the same time, I apologise to the many people whom I have not been able to contact who would have had much to say on the various aspects of Aloys Fleischmann's work presented here. (I intend to undertake a study of his life, and would be very glad to obtain further information from anybody who knew him in any capacity).

I am grateful to Her Excellency the President of Ireland, Mary McAleese, for having graciously granted me permission to reproduce the speaking notes she used when she launched Aloys Fleischmann's *Sources of Irish Traditional Music* in University College Cork in January 1999. I also thank the Minister for Education and Science, Micheál Martin, and Alderman James A. Corr for permission to reproduce their tributes to Fleischmann broadcast by Cork Radio in 1992.

I thank Aosdána for permission to reproduce the Fleischmann membership proposal by Gerard Victory; the Royal Dublin Society for permission to reproduce the citation for Fleischmann's Honorary Life Membership, and Trinity College Dublin for permission to reproduce the citation for his Honorary Doctorate in Music. I thank Rev. Dr Benedict Cullen, OFM Cap., Archivist, for permission to reproduce the article by Frederick May published in *The Father Mathew Record* of 1949, Capuchin Publications Dublin; Eve O'Kelly, Director of the Contemporary Music Centre Dublin for permission to reproduce Ita Beausang's Fleischmann obituary published in *New Music News*; Rev. Tom Hayes, editor of *The Fold*, for permission to reproduce Rev. Dr James Good's Fleischmann article published in *The Fold*; Garland Publishers of New York for permission to reproduce Mícheál Ó Súilleabháin's Preface to Fleischmann's *Sources of Irish Traditional Music*; Aengus Fanning, editor of the *Sunday Independent*, for permission to reproduce Mary Leland's Fleischmann obituary; Colin Scott-Sutherland for permission to reproduce his review of Fleischmann's *Piano Quintet* CD; Phyllis Doolan for permission to reproduce her late sister Bridget's tribute to Fleischmann broadcast by Cork Radio in 1992; Gerald Y. Goldberg for permission to reproduce his late wife's tribute to Fleischmann broadcast by Cork Radio in 1978; Mrs Geraldine Victory for permission to reproduce her late husband's assessments of Fleischmann's compositions broadcast by RTE in 1992; Helen Shaw, Director of Radio, RTE, Cork Radio, Dan Collins and Donna O'Sullivan for permission to reproduce extracts from radio interviews on Fleischmann of 1978, 1980 and 1992. I thank *The Examiner* for permission to reproduce photographs; I thank the editors of *The Examiner, The Graduate UCC, The Irish Times, New Music News* for publishing my letter about this project.

For invaluable assistance I thank Virginia Teehan of the University Archive UCC, Lucy O'Donoghue of the UCC Graduates Association, Katherine Weldon of the President's Office, Eve O'Kelly of the Contemporary Music Centre of Ireland, John Fitzpatrick of the Cork Choral Festival, Carol Acton, Sister Rosario Allen, Séamas de Barra, Ita Beausang, Máire Brugha, Sister Miriam Buckley, Catherine Burns, Canon Jerram Burrows, Nicholas Carolan, Michael Casey, Mary Connole, Patricia Cox, Joseph Cunningham, Dan Donovan, Theo Dorgan, Emelie Fitzgibbon, Monica Gavin, Ryta Gleeson, Gerald Goldberg, Richard Goodison, Catherine Dower Gold, Philip Graydon, Tom Hamill, Nóirín Hurley, Oliver Hynes, Florence Jansen-Linehan, Axel Klein, Lola and Cáit McDonnell, Seán Mac Liam, Dermot McLoughlin, Mary Martin, Adrian Munnelly, Conn Murphy, John A. Murphy, Orla Murphy, Marie Nevill, Máire Newton, Máire Ní Mhurchú, Tomás Ó Canainn, Shane O'Connor, Cherry O'Keeffe, Hugh O'Kelly, Maigread Ó Murchadha, Máirín O'Rourke, Moira Pyne, Seán Teegan, Alison Walsh, Máire and Michael Weedle, Harry White, Patrick Zuk. I am grateful to Gráinne Delany of the Faculty of Linguistics and Literary Studies at the University of Bielefeld/Germany, who did the scanning, and helped with the deciphering of handwriting and transcription of tapes.

This book has been a family undertaking. Very special thanks are due to my sisters Anne and Maeve, to my brothers Neil and Alan, and to my husband Rainer Würgau.

RUTH FLEISCHMANN, MARCH 2000

Introduction

This book is about a musician of German ancestry whose people had emigrated to Cork in the 1870s, and whose life was dedicated to promoting a culture of music in Ireland. Though without 'a drop of Irish blood in his veins', Aloys Fleischmann became more Irish than many Irish people were, being a fluent Irish speaker, spending decades studying Irish folk music, and a lifetime seeking to improve the cultural quality of life in the provinces. During his 46 years as professor of Music in University College Cork he tried to build the foundations and create the institutions necessary to develop music nationwide, from primary to third level education. Many of his compositions reflect his concern to create a specifically Irish form of modern music. He worked right up to his death at 82 completing a major research project on traditional Irish music. He thus undertook the sort of work on Ireland's unique musical heritage which scholars had done for the country's language and literature at the beginning of the twentieth century.

Many of the scholars and artists who at that time had helped to preserve the nation's heritage and to create a sense of Irishness regarding language, literature and history were also to some extent outsiders, people like Douglas Hyde, W. B. Yeats, Synge, Lady Gregory and George Russell being of Anglo-Irish settler origins. Fleischmann was imbued with the tradition of the movement that they embodied: the Irish cultural revival. When he was born, Ireland was still under British rule. He had personal recollections of the Troubles. His father was interned as an alien when he was six. He was terrified one evening in 1920 to see British soldiers with blackened faces on the roof creeping past his attic window to raid the house next door. Militant Cork republicans with an interest in the arts, such as the MacSwineys, the MacCurtains, the Stockleys, were friends of his parents – but so was Lord Monteagle, a musician from an Anglo-Irish family. He thus learnt early on that the arts can form bridges between people of very different persuasions. His youth coincided with a time of decisive change. He was eleven when Ireland became independent; he began his studies in University College Cork at the end of the first decade of the Free State; he was doing postgraduate studies in UCC when de Valera won the elections of 1932. Six months after his arrival in Munich to study at the Academy of Music and the university, Hitler's Nazis came to power: 'Aryans only' notices soon began to appear on campus. He had the privilege of being taught composition by Joseph Haas, of attending lectures given by Thomas Mann, of hearing music

11

by Richard Strauss, Bruckner, Schönberg. Nevertheless, the situation in Germany and the offer of a university post in Cork brought him home in 1934. It was during his formative time in Munich that he discovered where he belonged: in Germany he found his Irishness and resolved to spend his life in the small place where he had grown up. There he was to work with others to try and generate a richer cultural life; this he believed was essential if the city was to cease to be a place from which gifted people had to flee in order to develop their talents.

One such person who had left Cork was Fleischmann's friend, the writer Seán O'Faoláin. He believed that Fleischmann was deluding himself with his hopes of being able to open up the enclosed world of the south. Fleischmann argued in a letter of December 1948 that he suspected Cork was no worse than the average English or Russian town of its size, and that in Cork one might indeed find 'more diversity, and sense of humour'. In his reply O'Faoláin wrote:

> Cork is as you say just like any provincial town anywhere: a bit nicer in fact being so beautifully placed, and in itself a lovely little hole. When I lived in it I used say, 'How can anybody who has ever lived here leave it?' Of course I was kidding myself. Once I got out of it I could be honest with myself. But why do I say these things to you. – I'm only annoying you, and why should I do that? ... It can't be done, you incorrigible dreamer. You're only kidding yourself. Sit down, dear Aloys, and write *beauuuutiful* music, and pitch the whole lot of them to hell's blazes: now and again have a rare (very rare) promising student out; play music for him or her; gas; expand; talk to him about Germany and France and Italy; go for extended holidays abroad; take what Cork offers – a certain grace of face, good pubs, good dogs, good walks. But for Jasus' sake stop thinking it's anything but (as you say) any old provincial town anywhere in which any man of talent would break his melt. Your da struck me as one of the sanest men in Cork – playing his organ, training his fine choir, walking out the dog, probably going to the flicks, and not bothering his behind about *uplifting* Cork. You're a plain lunatic I tell you. And a dear fellow.

During his youth, Fleischmann had not been as cut off in Cork as one might imagine. Through his knowledge of German he was able to read books not available in English, and he had had contact with people of imaginative vision such as Daniel Corkery, whose original and stimulating insights into Irish culture and European literature fed his mind. Fleischmann's stay abroad had allowed him to get to know a part of the continental world outside Ireland, taught him to appreciate what his own small country offered and inspired him to try and make that more European.

The diversity of Cork's cultural life increased in the 1950s. The period after the Second World War had been the most dismal one since the founding of the state. The economic direction taken was not effec-

12

tive: unemployment and emigration were wreaking havoc and the country seemed blighted. In an attempt to halt this decline, Seán Lemass founded the Tóstal festival which he hoped would revitalise every town and village in Ireland. It had a dramatic impact in Cork, anticipating in cultural terms the opening towards Europe which was to bring economic development from the 1960s.

Music served as a bridge builder when from 1954 choirs from the North began to participate in the Cork Choral Festival at a time when virtually no contact existed between the two parts of the island. But the bridges were not restricted to Ireland. The citizens of Cork met and sometimes made friends with people from Eastern Europe whom they hosted in their homes; choirs and folk dance groups attended the Festival year after year despite problems with commissars, clerics and censors inside both the iron and green curtains that weighed so heavily on their respective communities. During the 1950s some of the world's best orchestras were heard in Cork, audiences for which had been built up through concerts given by the local amateur players of the Cork Symphony Orchestra. First-rate dancers appeared in Cork every season, in the context of the local ballet production put on by Joan Denise Moriarty, the valiant pioneer of dance in Ireland. Performance, active participation in the arts and service to the community were seen by Fleischmann and Moriarty as the essence of cultural life. Theirs was not the approach of giving people what they want to hear: they sought to make it possible for the audience to appreciate excellence. The expe rience of the Cork Choral Festival has vindicated this standpoint. Fleischmann believed that it is one of the essential human needs to find self-expression in the arts: through them people can achieve an awareness of what life can be and through them find a source of strength in coping with its vicissitudes. He believed that if the state was to fulfil the duty laid down in the constitution to 'cherish the children of the nation' it must ensure that the imagination as well as the understanding of all citizens be fostered and stimulated, as creative ability is the essence of the human kind and its development a basic educational right. Ireland's splendid folk heritage in song, story and poetry was for him evidence of the rich natural endowment of the Irish. This was the philosophy of the Irish Revival, refreshed with a new draught from one of its original sources: European romanticism, which he had encountered during his studies both in Cork and in Munich.

Fleischmann saw himself as an educator in his university post. In this matter, too, he disagreed with Seán O'Faoláin. In a radio broadcast on Cork of 1948, O'Faoláin had called University College Cork a fourth-rate institution – Fleischmann wrote to him:

Objectively speaking the reference flattered us – if the greatest of the continental universities be taken as first-rate, we would probably come in the tenth or eleventh category, ahead only of some of the American and colonial colleges. But to refer to a body as fourth-rate implies either that it should be first-rate, and isn't, or that it thinks it is first-rate, and isn't. In both cases the implication is unjust. A small college set in a relatively poor and uneducated agricultural community, lacking in grants and endowments, with a spoiled and twisted tradition (from godless ascendancy college via hyper-nationalism to hyper-religiosity), we cannot hope to be more than a little better than what we are, nor are any of us under any delusions as to the deficiencies of our set up. Supposing you were referred to in a broadcast as a fourth-rate novelist, would you not feel that the reference was somewhat gratuitous? And if Balzac or Chekhov be admitted as first-rate, the classification might not be unduly harsh.

O'Faoláin retorted that UCC was not fourth-rate, but useless, indeed 'a fraud'. He listed professors who were boring, ignorant, unsuitable – and he deplored most of all that some of them regarded themselves as teachers. One he described as being:

... a monster as a professor: a sweet old lady no doubt. Do you know what she used to do? – She used to *teach* us. Sacred Heart – teaching in a university!!!! You know, grammar and syntax and this and that and Oh! and Ah! and groans. And everybody said she was marvellous: because she *did* teach the little ducks, spoon-fed them, breast-fed them, predigested their pap for them. Aloys. A university is a university, as Gertrude Stein might say. Anything else is nought.

O'Faoláin regarded scholarship, personality and a cultured ambience as essential requirements for a university teacher. The accounts given by those of Fleischmann's former students who have contributed to this book suggest that they regard him as having been a good professor in these terms. However, they all highlight that he taught them in the sense deplored by O'Faoláin, that they were instructed and given a firm grounding in the craft of music. The BMus course was designed to allow the average student capable of disciplined application to attain the degree. The exceptionally gifted determined neither pace nor content of the course and they were expected to acquire solid foundations whatever their hopes and aims. O'Faoláin's viewpoint is that of the individualistic creative artist struggling against the restrictions imposed by mediocrity and ignorance. Fleischmann's agenda was to seek to create structures through good music-teaching nationwide which would foster talent broadly, thus creating conditions favourable to the exceptionally gifted.

It was an uphill struggle. The remarkable flowering of the arts in Cork today is the result of a long haul by many people. The contributors to this book seem to agree that in the field of music, the prime mover from the 1930s to the 1980s was Aloys Fleischmann. But individuals can only have such an impact if they have the gift of bringing out the talents and energies of hundreds of others whom they inspire and win over for their cause. Such individuals must be able to perform a sort of loaves and fishes miracle, liberating hidden resources in others, which are then shared and made productive. Some of the character traits which can generate such charisma have been portrayed in this book with affection and respect by Fleischmann's former students, colleagues and friends. Among the characteristics singled out are his deep love of music and his ability to impart that to others; his personal example of unflagging service to the cause; his courtesy and modesty in dealing with people of all sorts and stations; and his humour.

He encountered much opposition in his many crusades; his attitude towards adversaries was determined by a rare insight: the ability to distinguish in a controversy between the person and the issue. That meant he could remain on cordial terms with people whose policies and courses of action he deplored and was vigorously combating. This was confirmed to me recently by one of the people with whom he had serious conflict. Perhaps the bitterest disappointment of his life was the Arts Council's withdrawal of funding from Irish National Ballet, an undertaking for which he had prepared the ground since the 1940s together with Joan Denise Moriarty. He considered the Council's decision a gross error of judgement, a damaging blow to the arts in Ireland and a crass example of cultural discrimination of the regions perpetrated by an unaccountable public institution. The chairman of the Council at that time was Adrian Munnelly. He has told me that after the cessation of funding to Irish National Ballet, he continued to have close contact and friendly personal and professional relations with Fleischmann despite their differences over the withdrawal of support for the Cork Choral Festival and Cork-based Irish National Ballet, indeed that he had 'great affection for him'.

Fleischmann's presumption of the integrity of his opponents was not a tactical trick: he never spoke ill of them as people, though he would wax eloquent on their woeful views and policies. Even in the few cases where he personally was subjected to mean-spirited behaviour and indignity, he continued in the interest of the issue at stake to cooperate with those who had injured him. He never discussed with the family what this cost him: we found awe-inspiring the strength of character which enabled him to stand above and disregard personal hurt in the service of the greater good.

His strong sense of mission did not give rise to any notions of grandeur as to his own role: he saw himself as a servant of his cause, not as a prophet. When speaking in public of himself he made a point of underlining his ordinariness. For instance, when asked on a radio interview about his experience as a composer, how he coped if a composition was not well received, he spoke of the disappointment and self-doubt that ensued, but went on to describe it in terms of a man who puts a bet on a horse that doesn't win. The image is not that of the Misunderstood Artist, but of the common man who has taken a risk and lost out.

One of his teaching aims was to impart his own sense of mission to his students: he could not envisage his graduates regarding their profession as music teachers as a mere livelihood. On a radio programme produced by Donna O'Sullivan after his death, an unnamed student said of him: 'He always asked those of us who were from the country not to stay in the city where we qualified, but to return home and give children back something of what we had got from him: to present music to them in a manner that would give them a love for it ... and bring the excitement of the whole thing to children.'

His sense of duty prevailed until the end. An image of him remembered by his daughter Maeve illustrates this. After his wife's death in October 1990, he lived alone in the big old house with the stream running through the garden and under the kitchen. The house had been flooded several times, and one tempestuous night in winter after a week of heavy rains, his daughter came up around midnight to check how high the stream was. She found the entire house in darkness, but from the back lawn saw a light in the study: the solitary desk lamp illuminated the dome of her father's head as he sat engrossed in his work, oblivious of the lateness of the hour, of the raging storm, the torrential downpour and threat to his home. During his last weeks, his powers of concentration prevailed over exhaustion, nausea and intense pain. The frail figure sat at the dining-room table, the large volumes of collected folk music piled up around him, checking the print-out of his magnum opus, *Sources of Irish Traditional Music*, although he was almost too weak to move the heavy tomes, and every movement caused him agony. He was proud that his fulfilled and happy life remained a working one – until three days before his death.

It is no coincidence that the Irish song he chose for the audience to sing at his last children's concert in February 1992 was *Amhrán Dóchais*, the Song of Hope. The text is by the Cork Celtic scholar of Danish ancestry, Osborn Bergin, one of the founding members of the Gaelic League; the music was Fleischmann's own arrangement. The song – which he believed would make a far better national anthem than *The Soldiers' Song* – can be read as a personal farewell and an expression of what he stood for:

Slán go deó le brón is buirt,
Slán gan mhoill d'ár gcuimhne duairc,
Canaim laoithe dóchais i dteangain bhinn na Fódla
'Gus seassaimís go beomhar ós comhair an t-saoil!

Farewell forever to sorrow and care
Farewell at once to bitter laments.
Let's sing a song of hope
In the sweet tongue of our forefathers
And stand bravely before the world.

(*Maidean i mBéara agus Dánta Eile,* Dublin 1918)

1: FLEISCHMANN THE PROFESSOR

ITA BEAUSANG NÉE HOGAN, UCC Music Graduate, Acting Director of the Dublin Institute of Technology. This is the obituary she wrote for the journal of the Contemporary Music Centre of Ireland (New Music News) *in September 1992.*

The proverbial visitor from Mars who might have dropped into Cork's North Cathedral on the morning of 23 July 1992 would be excused for wondering what kind of person had inspired such a gathering. The presence of so many civic and academic dignitaries suggested a tribute in honour of an important public figure; the beauty of the liturgy and richness of the music indicated an artistic connection; young and old from all walks of life thronged the cathedral, their attentive faces reflecting the dignity and solemnity of the occasion. Time seemed suspended as the Requiem Mass progressed, punctuated by moments of grandeur and emotion. Afterwards, the procession moved into the courtyard under a canopy of umbrellas. There was no sense of hurry as people gathered and talked, reluctant to bring the ceremony to a close. Although they mourned his passing, there was palpable pride in celebrating the life of Professor Aloys Fleischmann, Freeman of Cork, of whom it may truly be said: 'They will rest from their labour for their deeds will follow them.'

From the litany of his labours it is obvious that Professor Fleischmann presided like a colossus over the Irish musical landscape. As teacher, composer, conductor, academic, campaigner and organiser, he influenced successive generations from the 1920s to the 1990s. The words indefatigable, tireless, dynamic, extraordinary, recur in the many tributes published and broadcast since his death. Yet perhaps the most amazing aspect of his personality was his simplicity in coping with the multiplicity of his activities. Although he was constantly busy, he never gave the impression of not having time for other people.

My first childhood memory of Professor Fleischmann is in the Cork Opera House, as conductor of the Cork Symphony Orchestra with the Cork Ballet Company, of which he was co-founder with Joan Denise Moriarty. His name was already familiar to me as one of my father's colleagues in 'the College'. I was also taken to concerts in the City Hall conducted by him, but on those occasions there was no ballet, to my regret.

In retrospect I realise what Herculean efforts it must have taken to combine the talents of the professionals and amateurs of varying standards who made up the Cork Symphony Orchestra. The programmes included not only standard works but also first performances of music by contemporary Irish composers. His own compositions also featured; one unforgettable experience was a performance of *Clare's Dragoons* for baritone, war pipes, choir and orchestra, during which Joan Denise Moriarty made a dramatic entrance into the Aula Maxima, red hair flying, playing the war pipes.

The Cork Orchestral Society, founded in 1938, was an early example of Professor Fleischmann's gift for galvanising community effort through loyal and hard-working committees. Cork business and professional people who supported the society were dubbed 'vultures for culture', but it was no mean feat in the days before sponsorship to host concerts by visiting orchestras such as the Vienna Philharmonic and the Boston Symphony, in addition to local events. This organisational flair was to be fully realised in his mammoth task as Director of the Cork International Choral and Folk-Dance Festival for 33 years from 1954 to 1987.

I first met Professor Fleischmann officially in 1953, when I became one of three first-year Music students at University College Cork. At that time the Music department was housed upstairs in a cluster of rooms on the ivy-clad East Quadrangle. These included a small lecture room, a practice room and, from 1956, the Bax Memorial Room. Arnold Bax, a life-long friend of the Fleischmann family, had been extern examiner in Music to the National University, and had died in Cork. The punctual arrival of the Professor was heralded by his swift steps up the stone stairs. Cars were as scarce as Music students, and he was a familiar sober-suited figure travelling by bicycle and later by motorcycle to and from his home on the other side of the city.

Lectures were delivered formally from a closely-typed set of notes, even when, in second year, I was the only student in the class. As in other faculties the age of specialisation had not yet dawned, and he taught the whole course (with the exception of Irish Music, for which the lecturer was Seán Neeson). He was equally at home in practical and academic subjects, embracing all aspects with enthusiasm. I recall with pleasure his distinctive voice with its slightly pedantic pronunciation, and the quizzical expression which greeted some strange progression in a harmony exercise.

His score-reading at the piano was remarkable, especially as he was by his own admission no pianist. I particularly remember his zest in presenting intricate scientific details of the course in acoustics, and his masterly classes in analysis. His unique method of analysis, in which wit and erudition were combined to reveal the innermost secrets of the music, later reached a wider public when his analyses of commissioned works became an enthralling feature of the seminars on contemporary choral music held at UCC from 1962 in conjunction with

19

the Choral Festival.

As a working composer he encouraged creative activity among his students. Part of the examination in orchestration consisted of a concert, or 'Orchestral Evening', held in the Aula Maxima, for which the Cork Symphony Orchestra was drafted to rehearse and perform arrangements and original compositions by students. Compositions by the young Seán Ó Riada were first heard at these concerts, which were conducted by the students themselves with varying degrees of proficiency. Afterwards everyone adjourned to the college restaurant where a decorous tea was provided.

Music also played a part in university life through the activities of societies, such as the Choral Society and the University Art Society, which had been founded by Professor Fleischmann in 1931. In the 1950s the Art Society was active in organising lectures and recitals by visiting celebrities, which were attended by students and members of the public. The Choral Society gave many successful performances over the years, but on one occasion incurred sharp criticism from the Professor for putting on *The Mikado* instead of something more worthy of a university, such as a Monteverdi opera.

At the beginning of each academic year a massed choir was recruited from all faculties to sing at the so-called 'Red' Mass, held in St Mary's Church, Pope's Quay, to celebrate the beginning of the academic year, and attended by students, staff, and civic authorities. Several rehearsals were held by Professor Fleischmann in the Aula Maxima, and any students who joined for frivolous motives soon realised their mistake, as no time was wasted and they were cajoled into singing by the conductor. Student choirs were also assembled for other ceremonial occasions in the Honan Chapel, with Professor Fleischmann directing from the Victorian harmonium.

By the time I was a post-graduate student the Music department had begun to expand. The student population explosion, with a corresponding increase in the number of staff, resulted in a thriving department, in which Professor Fleischmann continued to be the driving force. His example inspired music graduates long after they had left UCC. My contacts with him continued after I left Cork to live in Dublin. On the rare occasions when his music was performed in Dublin he seemed mildly surprised to meet expatriate Corkonians who attended. I was fortunate to work as his research assistant for the Royal Irish Academy *New History of Ireland* and experienced his precise attention to detail and his prompt response to queries. His greatest research project, *Sources of Irish Traditional Music*, the monumental index to the published collections of Irish folk-music, completed during his terminal illness, is his final legacy to music in Ireland. His correspondence was legendary: letters from all over the world were answered by return of post, typewritten by himself with the characteristic signature at the end. Christmas cards usually featured a print of Cork or a drawing by a Cork artist.

Aloys Fleischmann the campaigner revelled in fighting indifference and apathy for the cause of music. For the man who climbed Mount Brandon on his eightieth birthday there were no insurmountable obstacles. When I heard him speak so eloquently at a public meeting in the Mansion House, Dublin, about the disbandment of RTE performance groups as a result of the 1990 Broadcasting Act, I remembered a campaign which he had fought in Cork over thirty years ago. Then, as a result of concerted efforts, the Radio Éireann String Quartet was established and based in Cork. Now the RTE Vanbrugh String Quartet was one of the groups whose future was in jeopardy. The wheel had come full circle.

It is appropriate that the survival of the Vanbrugh String Quartet has been guaranteed for the present through the generosity of the Governing Body of UCC. Indeed, the university has proved a worthy setting for Professor Fleischmann, through financial support and the provision of facilities for such events as the annual seminar on contemporary choral music. The city of Cork too has cherished her adoptive son and recognised him as 'one of her own'.

His appointment to Aosdána brought him a national platform from which to express his concerns about the future of music education in Ireland. His was not an elitist approach. After all his years in music he was a realist who took situations as he found them. He knew that music must be accessible, and of course high standards were also his aim, but he was a pragmatist. His last letter to me, written ten days before his death, made no concession to his illness. In it he referred to the importance of encouraging appreciation of music in the school curriculum. As I was away I did not receive the letter until the day after the funeral. I welcomed it as a symbol of the indomitable spirit of an incomparable man.

> To seek through the regions of the earth
> For one his like, there would be something failing
> In him that should compare.

(Shakespeare, *Cymbeline*, Act I Scene I)

ANITA O'CONNOR (CORK), UCC *Arts Graduate. Her memories of Aloys Fleischmann were recorded by Anne Fleischmann.*
I took Music as a minor subject for the first year of the Arts degree simply because I appreciated it. Aloys Fleischmann was a wonderful professor. I realised after I had left college that that man had taught us not

only music, but also English, history, and some German. He used to explain what was going on in the world of whatever composer we were dealing with and what effect that had had not only on Mozart or Beethoven, but on the Irish as well.

He was 28 when I began and he had no rooms in which to teach. Patrick Merriman was president of UCC at the time: he didn't see any reason to set up a Music department. So we had classes in the Observatory whenever the Physics department wasn't using it. Aloys Fleischmann gave us as much time and put as much thought into those lectures as he would have done for a great big class, though there were only two of us – the first two to do Music as a subject for the Arts degree.

He was a most eligible man, of course. I can still see him striding with verve across the quadrangle, and if you met him he was vivacious, effervescent. He had a wonderful manner: that was how he gathered everyone around him in forming the Art Society and the orchestra. We students had a most interesting social life. Professor Stockley of the English department and his wife, Professor Mary Ryan of French, Professor Hogan of History and the Fleischmanns all gave evenings at which they opened their homes to us: we often read plays or acted them.

When he started the orchestra there were practices in the Aula Maxima of UCC. His very regal looking mother would come and sit there with her score. The Music students would attend rehearsals to listen and learn: if we chatted or even whispered she would hear us: one glance from her and we would desist. But she would sometimes stop him during the pieces, pointing out for instance that an entry had been wrong. I was surprised that he took it from her, because he was very sure himself of what he wanted from the orchestra. But he was invariably patient and polite, though once or twice he reverted to German, and may then have been a little more forthright! But she was great: she came all the way up to listen to what he was doing and she encouraged him.

I knew Aloys Fleischmann senior very well. He was the organist in the cathedral and was a quiet retiring man. He used to teach singing in Farranferris, but he was too timid for the boys up there, who weren't interested in music or who thought that a choral class was good for fun. He took me up to the North Chapel, the North Cathedral, a couple of times and played the organ for me. He once gave me a book of Yeats' poems: *The Wild Swans at Coole*. He was great with the cathedral choir: the men loved him. He had a fine mind.

There were such colourful characters among the students. Edward Sheehy, who was to become a writer, was a good friend of Aloys

Fleischmann's. Ned's brother Michael Sheehy did Arts with me. Michael had intended to go into the church but, as he told me himself, after he advocated the reading of Oscar Wilde, they said goodbye to him. His sister Eileen married James Stack of the Little Theatre Society.

After college I lost touch with Aloys for a while: I started having children, which curtailed my activities. But when he started the Cork Choral Festival, I sang in a choir and worked with him as a driver or receptionist, meeting and minding adjudicators and composers. I remember once, another helper and myself were driving the Dublin composer Gerard Victory to his hotel when he said to somebody with him: 'You know, Cork is really amazing: we don't get this treatment anywhere else!' And they asked whether we did this all the time, perhaps professionally. I remember saying 'Good God, no! We'd only do it for Aloys Fleischmann.' Another time I minded the renowned Danish composer Vagn Holmboe and his artist wife Meta, who were great collectors of trees. They dug up some gorse bushes to take back home and I felt like saying 'Lord, you'll be sorry, because they will spread everywhere.' I took them down to Fota to show them some real trees and they were delighted with the place. It was so interesting meeting such people and I was very glad to be able to help in this way.

The Choral Festival meant a lot to us all and we learned a great deal. One of the first things was how to dress as a choir. Very early on we had an Italian choir who appeared on stage dressed in black and white; the skirts were all the same length; they had their scores beautifully done up in one colour and they had been taught to hold them properly. We learnt that lesson from them. Soon very many foreigners came to the Festival and they had to be invited to stay in our homes. That was another novelty for Cork people. And then the schools were brought into the Festival, which was wonderful. A whole new world was opened up to us.

The choirs improved amazingly from one year to the next. A nun brought a choir from Fermoy which progressed by leaps and bounds, so much so that you'd be waiting for her to come on stage with them to show how the piece for their competition should be sung. The Festival encouraged church choirs and choirs in towns, and choirs started by the Irish Countrywomen's Association. It gave them the courage to enter for the competitions as they got very good assessments from the adjudicators who would both praise and indicate how they could improve the weaker points.

I never remember Aloys being cross. He could be frustrated and even depressed, but he didn't show it for long. If there was a crisis, he would lean back and say 'Oh my goodness, what am I going to do?' But somebody would always come up with some answer. You see, he did so much work himself: he was one of those people who always came well prepared to every meeting, who kept in touch with what every committee was doing – he never just delegated.

Only once did I ever see him somewhat frustrated, in a funny little way. It was with Professor Dan Corkery. We were talking of place names, and of Irish names and their translations. Aloys said what his name was in Irish, but Corkery took a different view. It was the first time I saw Aloys being quite adamant about something. But there was no nastiness in the way he held his ground: it was an academic argument, and he and Corkery were very good friends.

He gave Joan Denise Moriarty great backing: without his orchestra her ballet company would never have done such wonderful performances. Adapting the music to the dancers must often have called on his patience. At rehearsals his orchestra would be doing fine, but sometimes the dancers weren't and everything would be held up. But he never got cross.

He had a very nice circle of friends: there was Seamus and Maigread Murphy, the Neesons, and for instance Seamus Kelly, who became Quidnunc of the *Irish Times*. He was working in the ESB here in Cork at the time and he managed to study English with Corkery. I would keep a place for him at lectures because he was sometimes late if he had to dash up from town from his job. Seamus was brilliant. He kept up his interest in the Cork ballet and in the orchestra after he went to Dublin. All those people were drawn into Aloys' work.

In conclusion I was going to say that we all adored Aloys, but you don't adore anyone but God, so the nuns taught me. We were devoted to him. His only weakness could be that he might perhaps have driven his family crazy by concentrating completely on what he was doing. His strength was that he never spared himself. He kept going, despite all setbacks and he was very good at encouraging people. In his illness he was hard on himself. I remember him attending a recital of the Vanbrugh Quartet when he was dying. He sat there throughout, determined to back them up by his presence though it must have been agony for him. He never complained.

EILEEN BARRY NÉE O'DONOVAN (LISTOWEL, CO KERRY), UCC Music Graduate, Piano Teacher
Aloys Fleischmann was dedicated to bringing great music to the people of Cork. Before I began to study music I had often attended concerts given by the Cork Symphony Orchestra, which the Professor had founded and conducted. I remember one concert in particular given at the Aula Maxima in 1945, which included the dramatic *Clare's Dragoons* with Joan Denise Moriarty playing the war pipes, as well as the

Professor's song for UCC 'Where Finbarr Taught', which the audience was invited to sing. I was a member of the choir that sang in the ballet *The Golden Bell of Ko* put on in 1948 by the Cork Ballet Company to music by Professor. As there was no room for the choir in the back of the stage of the old Opera House, we sang up in the 'gods'. Pilib Ó Laoghaire conducted the choir, which he had just founded – Cór Cois Laoi. The ballet was a most colourful work and everything went off very well.

I first met the Professor when I, Pilib Ó Laoghaire and the Capuchin Father Augustin O'Brien started on the first year of the Music degree course in UCC in 1947. His mother, Frau Tilly, was my piano teacher for several years, and I studied the organ with his father. Professor did all the lectures except for those on traditional Irish music, which were given by Seán Neeson. We found all the classes very interesting. Pilib had to give up after the first year as he couldn't at that time play an instrument, and his choir wasn't accepted on its own. He graduated much later. Father O'Brien also gave up after the first year, as he was sent to America by his order. I took singing and piano for my practicals. The training in harmony, counterpoint, form and orchestration was of much use to me in my work with choirs afterwards as I arranged many suitable airs for them. I also ventured into composition and had good results – and of course Professor Fleischmann was always ready to vet my work. I taught the piano in the Cork School of Music, and privately after I had left Cork.

MAURA LAWLOR (TRALEE, CO KERRY), UCC Music Graduate
I was lucky to be a member of the UCC Choral Society during 1945-7 when we sang in the chorus of Handel's oratorios *Saul* and *Judas Maccabaeus*. Professor Fleischmann was a gracious and hardworking man, dedicated to his profession. I consider myself lucky to have been instructed by him in choral music: he was so easy and pleasant to work with in class.

JAMES SHINE (DUNGARVAN, CO WATERFORD), UCC Graduate
In the early 1950s when I attended University College Cork, or 'College' as it was then described by students and the general citizenry of Cork alike, it was a rather different place from the institution that exists now. The main difference was one of size both in terms of numbers of students and the physical extent of the campus. The student body hardly exceeded one thousand and the campus was enclosed in the block encompassed by the south channel of the Lee, Donovan's Road, College Road and Gaol Walk, with generous open space within the area. Both these factors gave college and student life a sense of inti-

macy which would be impossible in the current state of development and probably meant that we had more knowledge of personalities and faculty members outside our immediate academic interest than is the case nowadays.

Another important difference from my point of view was the Honan Hostel, on campus, now sadly demolished to make way for other developments. The Hostel housed about thirty-five students, mostly impoverished undergraduates, of whom I was one. No doubt students still would describe themselves as impoverished, but looking back on those days I think that we had the edge in terms of absolute absence of cash. In fact our acquaintance with the cash economy hardly existed, and the notion of including money in a student budget to enable participation in the pub culture, as the USI now does, would have seemed as exotic to us as many of the half-baked philosophies which we debated on the front steps of the Hostel. Such debates had the merit of being free entertainment, and our search for such was diligent.

Thus, when around this time a series of free public lectures was organised by Professor Fleischmann, the purpose of which was to introduce classical music and the great composers to a wider audience, I and some of my companions in the Honan decided to give one of them a try, particularly as the lectures were in the Dairy Science lecture theatre, so close to hand. The subject of the first lecture, illustrated by recordings, was the Overture from Beethoven's music to Goethe's *Egmont* (opus 84), and I for one, although totally ignorant of classical music, the extent of my acquaintance being a few operatic arias sung by John McCormack and Peter Dawson, was totally captivated by the power of both the music and Professor Fleischmann's analysis of it. My recollection is also of a large audience, equally appreciative. I cannot recall in any detail the subject matter of any of the other lectures (I think the *Eroica* may have been one), but I do know that for me it was the beginning of a lifetime of pleasure derived from classical music.

Subsequent to these lectures we students became aware of informal 'musical evenings' in the Staff House to which a few of us managed to gain admittance. Again, these were conducted in the main by Professor Fleischmann, and while bashfulness at my ignorance prevented me from risking more than a nodding acquaintance with him, when I look back with pleasure on those formative years in 'College', his face is one which comes to mind.

For all my subsequent listening to classical music for pleasure I never acquired sufficient critical competence to comment on the Professor's capacity as a composer or teacher of music, but for me at least he had the gift of communicating his enthusiasm for his subject, which is not always the case with eminent academics, and for engendering a desire to explore it on one's own at a pace which made it all pleasure and no pain!

SISTER HILARY HURLEY, UCC Music Graduate, Lecturer at Mary Immaculate College, University of Limerick
Professor Aloys Fleischmann, lovingly called 'Prof' by his many graduates, was a man who made a deep and lasting impression on me. During my time in Cork, in the early 1960s, UCC couldn't boast of a very elegant Music department. That never prevented a prolific output of work from the same building, and I certainly enjoyed each aspect of music as it unfolded in his capable hands.

I always felt that Aloys Fleischmann treated each member of his class with respect and sensitivity. I recall occasions when I had written music that did not reach the standard required and, which I now know, would have been frustrating for one of his talent, his comment never went further than – 'Surely, Sister Hilary, you didn't mean to write those chords?' In modern parlance 'I got the message' and hoped my next attempt would produce more harmonious sounds!

He was an indefatigable worker himself and did demand work from his students. A sight familiar to us all was to see him coming to College on his moped and we knew that, no matter what time of day it was, he already had accomplished many other tasks. He appeared to be part of so many aspects of life in Cork and when he spoke, one discerned that his interests were worldwide. Side by side with all of that he produced so many creative works. One wonders how he had so much energy. For me, approachability marked his personality – a praiseworthy characteristic for any teacher. Here we have an example to follow.

Professor Aloys Fleischmann I miss you. You were an inspiration and source of encouragement for me. You have gone to receive your well-earned reward for all you did in life. Thank you, Prof, for who you were to me and to so many others.

> Deep peace of the running wave to you
> Deep peace of the flowing air to you
> Deep peace of the quiet earth to you
> Deep peace of the shining stars to you
> Deep peace of the gentle night to you
> Moon and stars
> Pour their healing light on you
> Deep peace to you

(Traditional Irish Blessing)

MAURA MCAULIFFE NÉE JOYCE (CHARLEVILLE, CO CORK), UCC Music Graduate, Music Teacher

My music education with 'Prof' began with an explanation of the etymology of the word *music* and a series of definitions given down the centuries. We discovered that in the sixth century BC Confucius saw music as the heart's response to the world, that Aristotle believed music and ritual were conducive to proper conduct, we heard the views of Plato, St Augustine and Beethoven. And that Samuel Johnson had defined music as being 'of all noises, the least disagreeable'. Most of these profound statements went completely over our heads – we were in our first week of 'Uni', beginning a whole new life of fun and freedom. What Confucius or Plato thought of music hadn't the slightest impact on us. It's funny how interesting it seems twenty years later. Our first year of counterpoint with Prof brought us through terminologies for harmony, counterpoint, form structure and colour. Counterpoint exercises filled up manuscript books, and every week we waited with baited breath for the return of the corrected manuscripts – would the verdict be a *good*, a *fairly good* or a *very good*? One week the excitement in the Music department was tremendous: Prof had lost a bundle of exercises – they had fallen off the back of his motor-bike on his way to the department, and he hadn't noticed until he got there. Prof travelled everywhere on that motor-bike: he arrived every day with his helmet in his hand, books under-arm and saluted everyone with : 'Good morning, Miss Joyce' or 'Good afternoon, Mr Daly'. Everyone was addressed in a formal manner, yet everyone knew that Prof had a deep and personal interest in each one of us. I can still remember being called into his office and being reprimanded for not concentrating in class! Neither did we dare to miss a lecture, as he immediately checked on our whereabouts.

Our harmony lectures took us through rules and regulations, structures and chords, culminating in third year with our own sonata movements and fugues. Lovelock's harmony book caused many a nightmare over those three years, yet we all ended up with a solid understanding of harmony and counterpoint, which unfortunately seems to have disappeared from a lot of undergraduate Music courses nowadays.

Our history course began with our famous textbook Grout: *History of Western Music*, a name which still sends little shock waves through me. 'Grout' haunted us for three years also: it was like a living person, introducing us to the state of music at the end of the ancient world right up to the twentieth century. As I browse through my Grout now, I find dried pressed flowers, postcards and autographs – memories of a world gone by.

In our form and orchestration class, Prof introduced us to all the various instruments and their sound capabilities. Our scoring techniques developed from a string orchestra in first year through to the full symphony orchestra in third year. Each of us had to orchestrate a composition of our own choosing, culminating in an end-of-year concert with the Cork Symphony Orchestra. The poor members of the orchestra spent weeks rehearsing our efforts – patiently trying to make sense of badly written and badly structured scripts, confused and nervous students, and an irate Professor trying to coordinate the whole experience. We bribed each other to play percussion parts to enhance our works – I can remember at one rehearsal holding the cymbals and waiting for my cue to clash them. When my moment finally came, I actually fell and created uproar – Prof was not impressed. All went well on the final night however – the orchestra played valiantly through each score, we conducted to the best of our ability and Mrs Neeson sat in the audience and actually wrote a critique of our efforts for the following day's *Cork Examiner*! I was accused of having a 'frozen shoulder' – to this day, I have very little confidence in my conducting capabilities.

I joined the Cork Symphony Orchestra in my first year – in the back row of the second fiddles sitting next to my friend. We were so proud to be part of Prof's orchestra! We rehearsed in the Maltings every week. We played for the ballet in November. I should say we played for some of the ballet – Susan and myself spent most of our time trying to look at the stage from the orchestral pit, trying in vain to see what was going on above us. Meanwhile Prof conducted us with his own panache and style – regularly losing his conductor's baton, which would go flying through the orchestra and hit some poor player on the head.

Our spring performance was always connected with the Choral Festival. To this day I associate April/May with Prof dressed impeccably in his tails, the Choral Festival concerts, the Festival Club and the City Hall filled with daffodils. The Festival Club in the Metropole showed us another side to our beloved Prof – the Prof who danced all night with each and every one of his women students, the Prof who was full of fun and wit and humour, the Prof who endeared himself completely to each of us.

I remember the excitement amongst us when Prof was declared a Freeman of the City – we conjured up endless possibilities for him, free parking, free concerts, free food and more. He agreed with us that such privileges would be convenient when it came to parking his bashed-up car. He often declared that he could park it anywhere without ever worrying about a parking ticket – and that is exactly what he did!

Our most memorable night with Prof was just before our final exams. He had built up a tradition of inviting all his third year Music students to his house for a party before we all went our separate ways. He was best at telling ghost stories about Arnold Bax – I was so engrossed in this story-telling that I shrieked hysterically when he announced that the chair I was sitting in was still regularly visited by the deceased Sir Arnold!

My post-graduate year was spent studying the music of Erik Satie and Les Six under Geoffrey Spratt but Prof kept a constant eye on my progress throughout the year. He actually retired that year and my fondest memory of my UCC days was of presenting Mrs Fleischmann with a bouquet of flowers at Prof's retirement function. I was chosen as I was his youngest graduate – an honour I greatly appreciated.

MICHAEL WEEDLE (CLANE, CO KILDARE), UCC Music Graduate, Music Teacher
When I left school I spent the next three years of my life in a surveyor's office in the South Mall but I kept up my piano with Tilly Fleischmann and, after a year or so, changed over to organ with Aloys senior (the 'old man' as everybody affectionately called him). When I was 21 I could take office work no longer and went to College to do a BMus.

I found out quickly that Prof had scant regard for college bureaucracy. Music students had to take a modern language, with a First Arts exam after first year and lectures without exams thereafter. I opted for Irish because I was good at it. The authorities said 'It is not a modern language'; Prof said: 'It's spoken in our Gaeltachts; of course it is!' So I did Irish. But, having got my exam, I thought it would be lovely to do German now. Officialdom said a change was out of the question; Prof said the whole point of the rule was to give his students as broad an education as possible; so I did German for the rest of my time.

In those days (I started in 1951) the Music department was tiny. When I was in first year there was one third year student, John Reidy (later to be Seán Ó Riada), one second year, Fr Anthony Sanusi (a Nigerian, who later became a bishop) and there were actually six of us first years: the late Bridget Doolan, who became head of the School of Music, Máire Ní Bhriain (married Gearóid Ó Cleirigh in the Diplomatic Service), Mother Dolores O'Keeffe, a Loreto nun from Fermoy, Pat Sullivan, a teacher in the 'North Mon', Harry McKearney, a Kiltegan clerical student and myself. We were of course extremely fortunate because it was the nearest thing to individual tuition as we all stood around the piano and everybody's work was played and discussed by all. Harmony and counterpoint were done on the blackboard with all contributions and suggestions teased out by the whole class.

Prof made me secretary of the Art Society in first year and for this I found him a very hard task-master. When there were concerts in the Aula Max I seemed to spend all my time in and out of town to businesses, the *Examiner*, 'Glen House', College, fighting with the bureaucrats about requisition forms and licking stamps – he wouldn't hear of having letters franked, because unless individually stamped, they would be thrown in the dustbin. But he gave me other jobs for which I have had every reason to be grateful all my life. Every St Patrick's Day there was an Irish Mass in the Honan Chapel and I had to train the choir and play the harmonium. It was at this stage that 'the old man' gave me one of the best pieces of advice I have ever had; he said: 'A choir is like a dog – it knows if you are afraid of it!'

One other job was like a nightmare at the time – in his own ballet, *The Golden Bell of Ko*, there is a choir in the wings singing very otherworldly music in thirteen beats to the bar and this, of necessity, in darkness. I had the job of conducting the choir. I had to stand on some sort of box with Máire Ní Bhriain shining a torch on my score and hope for the best. It was in the old Opera House and went well every second night and moderately on the other nights. The only consolation was that, the music being unusual, Prof and myself were probably the only people in the Opera House who knew whether it was right or wrong. But you can well imagine that conducting a choir never again held any terrors for me.

Our extern examiner was Sir Arnold Bax. Being an organist, I had to meet Prof and Sir Arnold in the North Cathedral for the performance part of my practical, but since score reading, keyboard work and so on would be more easily done on a piano, we all piled into my father's old banger and headed off to College together. The informality of the whole thing didn't strike me until long after. Talking about Sir Arnold, he and Prof were driven on some kind of outing by a taxi driver from Passage. Maureen Corkery (Dan's niece) told us that the Passage man kept saying afterwards 'Two barmy oul' lunatics'. Presumably the conversation in the back of the car was about something other than the Cork hurling teams the Sars and the Bars or Christy Ring.

TADHG COTTER (BANDON, CO CORK), *UCC Music Graduate*
I am just one of the many, many students who passed through the Music department of UCC in Professor Fleischmann's time; I do not want to repeat what countless others will have said, so I will limit my account of him to two aspects which struck me particularly.

One thing that I remember him for is his wonderful and quite daring sense of humour. He often told jokes during lectures or made humorous comments which were usually quite risqué, and he seemed

31

to take note of who understood them and laughed at them. His limericks at the annual department dinner were also quite daring.

Another recollection I have of Prof was the last time I saw him. The incident may seem trivial, but it illustrates his integrity and generosity. It was on the Cork train waiting to leave Heuston Station in Dublin. I had arrived early and had a seat whereas Prof arrived late and was making his way down the train looking for one. In deference to his age I offered him mine, but he refused it, and although I pressed him repeatedly to accept, he went on his way.

He was one of the finest people I have met in the course of my life: a very generous-spirited man, extremely intelligent, hard-working, and a person of great integrity.

Richard Goodison (Cork), UCC Music Graduate

I admired Professor Fleischmann with a sort of reverential awe when I was a child and teenager; when I came to study Music in his department I got to know him as an admirably courteous professor, teacher and composer, but also as a kind friend who gave such wonderfully good example. I find it humbling to think of his achievements, his extraordinary energy and strength of will.

Professor insisted that every BMus novice study one other Arts subject in first year. Students were thus made aware that there were arts other than music: this helped to balance the students' academic diet and to broaden their outlook. As there was a possibility that I might go to Italy later on, Professor suggested that I study Italian. I did so. It was one of the most rewarding experiences of my life.

At the time when I attended College, the number of Music students was increasing, but Professor still continued to give individual attention to each person. I believe that when examination time came around we were judged not merely on our performance in the examination but on the quality of our work and progress throughout the year. This was just. I worked hard enough throughout my years at the Music department, but due to illness I missed several months' class tuition in my last year. While I had to try to catch up, I found the examiners justly understanding. One of them was Denis Arnold, the authority on Gabrieli and Monteverdi.

One very exciting event came at the end of third year in College. This was the conducting examination. Each student had to arrange for full orchestra a piano piece by one of the great composers or alternatively to compose an original work for full orchestra and then conduct the Cork Symphony Orchestra in a public performance of the work before a packed Aula Maxima. This was a great if nerve-testing experience. One felt one was really making music. As there was not enough time for adequate rehearsals with a large number of students, performances were not always perfect, but the amazing amount of hidden talent that became manifest was wonderful and the concert extremely enjoyable. Our gratitude is due to the hard-worked Cork Symphony Orchestra for taking part and for their patience.

For personal reasons I did not take up a musical career after I graduated, but returned to a former position in the civil service. I think Professor was disappointed and I was told later that he had exclaimed to some class: 'Imagine, one of our graduates went to work in the Income Tax Office!' However, my spare time and holidays were given up to musical activities including the sharing with others of the appreciation and enjoyment of music, so my education was not in vain. I am still very grateful for it. When in 1978 Professor was made a Freeman of Cork city, I was in London on holiday and sent him a card congratulating him and detailing the musical events I was attending. He wrote me a very courteous and encouraging reply in which there was no expression of recrimination whatever.

I was greatly impressed by the funeral service organised for him. The weather was most inclement, but the torrential rain only reminded me of the burial of poor Mozart; and the indomitable spirit with which the choir sang the motet at the graveside was typical of the soul being celebrated. Two little things happened that proved significant to me. Very often when I met Professor at a concert or a recital he would offer me a lift home in his car. After the funeral mass at the cathedral I was on the lookout for a lift to the cemetery. Standing alone in the rain I was spotted by Mr O'Connor, the undertaker, and soon found myself ushered into a large limousine in which I travelled in style all alone as far as St Finbarr's Cemetery. I smiled inwardly, thinking of Professor's many previous kindnesses. Afterwards the driver drove me home and on the way the second incident occurred, which may have been just a coincidence, but which again made me think. Approaching St Luke's Cross on Wellington Road, the car came to a standstill. Something was blocking the progress of the traffic. As we waited, two young boys ran past on the pavement: one dropped something and returned to pick it up. I was reminded of an incident which had happened in that exact spot when I was a young boy. I was running along with the usual impatience of youth to get somewhere in a hurry and as I careered by, I half-collided with an elderly man coming in the opposite direction using a walking-stick. I stopped to apologise, and was given a far more effective lesson in good manners than any outburst of offended rage could have achieved: the elderly man turned in my direction, raised his hat politely to me, and then continued on his way. That gentleman was the Professor's father.

Sheila Duffy, née McDevitt (Leixlip, Co Kildare), UCC Music Graduate
My memories of Professor Fleischmann are nothing but happy and full of gratitude. I first met him in 1958, when I was a young nun of 22 years, totally unsure of myself and completely in awe of university and indeed of the Professor. There were only about five of us in that First Arts / First Music class, so none of us could escape his continuous assessment of our progress. We did not realise then how fortunate we were!

'Prof', as we called him, made music accessible to all. He would play our 'sections' on the piano, wincing visibly at the dreaded fifths and octaves, and gleefully hammering out our unintentional discords. 'That's the punishment!' he would say. I never saw him lose his patience. I remember one episode in particular. Prof had to attend a staff meeting and, rather than let us off our lecture, he proposed that we harmonise one of his 'lugubrious' texts: something like 'Deus meus adjuva me'. We decided to surprise him with a polyglot, polyphonic effort, so we applied our dubious linguistic skills with Spanish, Irish and English texts, all woeful in more ways than one! Then we scampered off home, before the staff meeting ended. Later that evening Prof phoned me at the convent. 'Aren't you the little scallywag!' he said. 'I came back from my meeting and saw – darkness. Then I found the monstrosity on the board!'

'Were you not impressed?' I queried.

'Impressed! With fifths and octaves all over the place, not to mention the bad grammar! Wait till I see you all!'

He called me another time into his office to give me some 'fatherly advice' as he said. I had been having trouble with my right arm and hand; he suggested I go to London to see a specialist who had cured his wife. Needless to say, that was out of the question; but I have often wondered if he then had some inkling of what was in store for me, as my health continued to deteriorate until I finally left the convent in 1971. Incidentally, that same office was accessible to us Music students. We could go in and pick out records and play them at will in the music room. How many of the UCC lecturers and professors would have thus catered for their students?

I remember Prof calling out to Ardfoyle, and propping his bike near the convent door. He had hoped that I would do an MA degree in African music, but that was not feasible. When eventually I went to Nigeria, we got involved in producing biblical musicals in the parish church. I wrote to Prof describing one such pageant, thanking him for all he had taught me and for opening my soul to music. He wrote back, sending me a really lovely letter. I met him again at a graduates reunion in 1976 or 1977. I was with my husband Peter. 'Well, I cannot get over this girl', he said, his eyes twinkling. That was the last time I saw him.

Prof was a wonderful teacher – 'exceedingly good', as he would say, at co-relating the arts, and putting everything in a historical perspective, asking us for instance: 'What was happening in Ireland when Mozart died?' He was a gentleman to his fingertips and one of the greatest influences in my life.

SISTER TERESA WALSH (THURLES, CO TIPPERARY), UCC Music Graduate, Music Teacher
The city of Cork has always held a favoured spot in my heart as has the Music department of UCC and when I heard of the death of the late Professor Fleischmann my thoughts turned naturally to those trouble-free days of study in UCC.

Professor *was* the Music department and epitomised for me the hospitality and friendship that I experienced in the city. He was also the fire behind the many musical initiatives of Cork. He did everything in his power to cajole and encourage his students to learn and to become truly committed to the cause of the development of music in the country, to which he dedicated his life. His commitment to the task in hand was truly commendable as was his encouragement to those with obvious talent. His work ethic was such that there could be no complaint of lack of interest in any of his students; in fact, from our perspective he erred on the other extreme. His generosity of spirit and fairness to all was obvious in the respect he showed to each person with whom he had dealings. His desire was that his students should pass their exams and he did everything in his power to ensure their success.

As a Christian he epitomised values of commitment, dedication and hard work and was therefore a wonderful example to all who came into contact with him.

SISTER NUALA REIDY (FERMOY, CO CORK), UCC Music Graduate, Music Teacher
I did my BMus degree at UCC with Prof (as he was affectionately known to us) from 1971-1973. I loved him, and although very average both academically and musically, I understood and enjoyed all his classes. He was first and foremost a gentleman. He treated all of us the same and encouraged us all the way, no matter how weak we were – and I was weak. He taught rather than lectured us and corrected our exercises as if we were in secondary school, marking them from Fair to Excellent – I seldom received the latter! I always felt we were part of one big family of which he was the father. He jollied us along when we got depressed and kept us on the straight and narrow when we

showed an inclination to stray! We had an annual party in different hotels, which was a highlight. He always had great stories and jokes and we used to have a highbrow singsong with canons and rounds.

I will remember him especially for helping me in the summer of my BMus. He corrected my exercises every week. I posted work to him and he posted it back to me with helpful advice and comments: something way beyond the call of duty. I have no hesitation in saying I owe him my final exam.

There is no doubt but that it was he who began the musical education of teachers in Ireland. He trained so many of us and taught us how to teach by his own excellent and joy-filled classes. If I learned one thing it was to be a bright, interesting teacher even with my limited ability. I know my classes are fairly enjoyable – thanks to him.

I would regard Professor Fleischmann as one of the most influential people in my life. He was a teacher by example first and last. He was a superb musician, clever, intelligent, amusing – but with all that a compassionate and kind human being. I count myself extremely lucky to have been a student while he was in charge of the Music department.

MARY HOGAN (LONDON), UCC Music and Arts Graduate
I was Professor Fleischmann's student from 1973 to 1977. I did a BA/ BMus in English and Music. 'Prof' was popular with his students: he was a calm and steadying presence. My mother, who had known him over many years, told me that Alfred O'Rahilly, the President of UCC, once said to her that he had been 'rounded like a pebble', by the stormy seas which his parents represented, if I understood my mother correctly.

I was most interested in the practical side of music, especially the piano, so at the time I did not greatly enjoy studying harmony and counterpoint. Ironically, in recent years I've taken to setting poems by Shakespeare and Yeats to music, and the training has come in very useful. I got an Honours BMus in 1977.

Finally, I would like to express my great admiration for the Professor's composition, *Songs of Affection*. My sister Ita and I once sang it in the City Hall and it was an experience I treasure.

REV. PAT AHERN (TRALEE, CO KERRY), UCC Music Graduate, Founder of Siamsa Tíre – The Folk Theatre of Ireland. His memories of Aloys Fleischmann were recorded by Anne Fleischmann
I was ordained in 1957 and sent to Tralee as a young curate. I had been promised by my bishop that when I was ordained I would be sent out to Rome to do music as I had a great interest in it, which very few of

the Kerry lads in Maynooth at that time had. When I had been ordained, the bishop came to me and said: 'I promised that you could go to Rome to study, but there is an old man down in Tralee, the Dean of Kerry, the parish priest, and he has no choir. He's just finished renovating his church. Would you ever go down to him for a year and get a choir started and then I'll send you out.' I went down, started my choir and a year passed, two years passed and ten years might have passed and I would still have been there. So in 1959 I went to see my bishop. He said to me: 'Look, you're not going to get to Rome, but would you consider going to Cork to Professor Fleischmann?' I have a cousin, Pat O'Sullivan, who had also been with Professor Fleischmann; he was full of praise for the course, so I was keen to do it.

The Professor was most welcoming. I'll never forget his wonderful smile, which always indicated that he was pleased to see you. Even that day when I met him for the first time he was full of encouragement and kindness: he made me feel totally at ease. I didn't realise he was going to give me an audition there and then: I got a little piece of music to arrange, to harmonise. I had done only very little music at college in Maynooth; I had taken up the piano late in life and I had done a little harmony.

I went to Tilly Fleischmann to study the piano. She had the same winsome smile as the Professor. She was very like him in many ways. But she was a woman of steel behind the smile, as any of her pupils will tell you. I played a few things I had done in Maynooth for her. The first thing she said to me was very encouraging: she told me that I was very, very musical. That removed a lot of the fear I had. But then she said: 'You have to start now from scratch.' And so I did. We got on very well, I think because she took great pity on me having to travel all the way from Tralee. I went up and down in the one day, twice a week: a distance of 75 miles. She realised that this was a great sacrifice, and I think she had visions of me climbing over mountains to come into Cork.

I didn't achieve more than an adequate standard on the piano, but what I learnt from her was musicianship: how to interpret a piece of music, and phrasing. I am very grateful to her for that: it has always stood to me. But I also remember being afraid of her classes. She had a way of making you feel guilty if you hadn't worked hard enough for the week, which for some strange reason we feared. That's not taking away from her great kindness, but she had that knack of being able to get at you, though it was always in the interest of encouraging you to try to play better. If you played well, then you were fully praised.

She took me up one day to meet her husband, Aloys Fleischmann senior, the visit having been arranged a couple of weeks before. She went away and left us together up in the attic. He told me he liked to be up near the stars. When I was coming away he foraged and found a few pieces of music, his own compositions, which I have to this day. I still use one of them with the choir here locally: a Christmas carol.

I found it very difficult to keep up with all the work we had to do – I had to do my full-time job in Tralee as well. I envied the others being able to give all their time to music and being able to attend other functions. I missed out on many things. For instance most of the students used to get a chance to play in the orchestra, even if it was only drums or triangle. I was raised with the traditional fiddle, which Professor allowed me to play as part of my practical.

The Music department was small at the time I was there: there were seven of us. The Professor was most charming and helpful and took a great personal interest in his students, which he kept up even after we graduated. I would say that composition was his first love: he encouraged us to be composers. I had been in the choir in Maynooth, where we had sung a lot of the old masters and I had a grasp of how that music should sound. We had to do that period, the sixteenth century, as part of the course, and I loved it. He paid me a great compliment one day. When he was playing my exercise he said: 'My goodness, that's wonderful. If you go on like that you'll be writing Masses!' That was a great feather in my cap. But he encouraged everybody: anything that you did well was always acknowledged and praised. But like his mother, he was never slow to correct you and be firm with you. He was very much the traditionalist, I suppose: he believed in the traditional method of harmony and counterpoint and teaching students the basics. There was one girl in the class who was a bit experimental: she did all sorts of new things. He wouldn't agree with her at all and yet he would admire the fact that she was ambitious and enterprising. But he would pull her back to the basics and make her learn the rules.

I had a great experience in the final year. I specialised in choral conducting and prepared a choir here in Tralee, which I brought up to Cork with me for a recital in the Aula Maxima of the college. My parish priest, the Dean of Kerry, came with me. He was an unusual character, an aristocratic type, who always wore a long black coat; he was quite proud that his boy, his curate, was now performing in the university. The Professor – like Frau Tilly – knew him and had always been very taken by him; they sat beside him during the concert, which went well. We had worked very hard at it in Tralee; I loved choral work and had the tradition from Maynooth, so I think I scored fairly high in that area. I feared for other areas like history, though, where I hadn't had enough time to do much work.

It was a very full course, which gave me all I could do to cope with: it was wonderfully wide, covering all aspects of music. I felt, in hindsight, it was a blessing in disguise that I went to Cork rather than being sent out to Rome, where I would have got a much more limited training, as the course would have been confined to church music and chant. But in Cork there was a great sweep of the whole broad spectrum of music and I was deeply grateful for that.

The Professor encouraged us to compose. Later on I wrote a Mass with an Irish text and had it published. I sent a copy to him and he wrote me a lovely, gracious letter. He thanked me for giving him the privilege of seeing the work. Imagine that coming from my professor! He praised everything that he could praise, but he never gave unqualified praise – he also had a few critical constructive comments, which were all valid. I wished that I had had them before I published the Mass.

He took the keenest interest in the students who did anything after graduating, and never failed to give encouragement. He would often give private tuition to somebody who needed it. His greatest strength was his wonderful personality: kindness personified. He was always so gracious and charming, with a lovely beaming, approving, welcoming smile. And there was his great capacity for hard work. He was hard on the orchestra at a time when music wasn't as organised and tuition wasn't as advanced – the string instrument players were often a problem for him. But he would keep going regardless and he would work and work and work.

I graduated in 1962 and it was shortly after that I started working on a concert at Siamsa. What I had learned from him was invaluable to me. I began to arrange the music that we played and sang: I could not have done that without his training. He used to invite Siamsa up to the Choral Festival quite a few times and always came around afterwards full of praise. If Professor liked it, that was all I needed to hear: that was the kind of regard we had for him. The last time I saw him was when he came down for the opening of our newly built Siamsa Theatre in Tralee in November 1991. That wasn't long before he died. He was very busy with his collection of Irish folk music and was telling me all about it with the same enthusiasm that he had always had for music, and which he passed on to so many of his students.

ANGELA O'MAHONY (CORK), UCC Science and Music Graduate
When I went to university in 1943 to study Science, I joined the Choral Society, and that was my first encounter with Professor Fleischmann. As there were not enough UCC singers, he recruited from outside the university, and the Aeolian Choir was formed. Our first work was *Saul*

by Handel in which the Cork Symphony Orchestra participated. It was an arduous task for the Prof because quite a lot of the choir were unable to read music. However, it was a great success.

This was followed by *Judas Maccabaeus* and many more oratorios. Prof did a work based on *Clare's Dragoons* for a Thomas Davis concert in the Cork City Hall. It was a very difficult task to learn it – but it was a memorable performance. Joan Denise Moriarty played the pipes, entering from the rear of the concert hall: very impressive.

In 1977 I again went to UCC as a mature student to study Music. That was when I really got to know Professor Fleischmann. He was a wonderful person to work under. We had a broad spectrum of every aspect of music. He was a thorough gentleman – I never knew him to lose his temper. He never addressed any student by their Christian names: it was always Mr and Ms. We had a counterpoint exercise every week and were graded. One student got a P and exclaimed – 'Oh I got a pass!' To which the Prof replied: 'P is not for pass: it's for Poor.'

I was privileged to be in the last BMus class he had before he retired in 1980 and I qualified the same year. As our final year exam was not held until the autumn, he was available right through the summer if we needed any help.

To me and I'm sure to many many more, Professor Fleischmann was a wonderful man, always in good humour and loving his music. Ar dheis Dé go raibh a h-anam.

MÁIRE WEEDLE NÉE GARVEY (CLANE, CO KILDARE), UCC Music Graduate
In my time at UCC with the highly esteemed 'Prof', we were a very small group in First Music – there was Bernard Geary, now composing and teaching in Dublin, Olive Murphy the harpist, now teaching in Texas, and myself. We got an excellent grounding in harmony, counterpoint and keyboard work. He carefully checked our weekly exercises and encouraged all kinds of extra-curricular musical activities, such as attending concerts in the city or at the university. He hoped to turn out fully rounded students, not merely bookish graduates. For this type of education I am eternally grateful to him, as I had come up to Cork in 1950 from a country town and had never heard a symphony orchestra.

I always found the Prof a reasonable man to deal with – he was understanding and sympathetic when necessary. However, Madame Tilly Fleischmann, his mother, with whom I studied the piano for five years, scared the wits out of me. On one memorable evening when it was pouring rain and I had acquired a Morris Minor (part owned with two brothers) I offered the Prof a lift down to the city as he was on a bike. He graciously accepted, but as we passed the Erinville Hospital he said: 'Perhaps you could risk second gear, Miss Garvey?' I had just learned to drive and was on my maiden voyage up to College!

ESTHER GREENE NÉE DUNNE (KILLARNEY, CO KERRY), UCC Arts and Music Graduate, Music Teacher. Her memories of Aloys Fleischmann were recorded by Anne Fleischmann
The Death of Frau Tilly Fleischmann
Professor Fleischmann, like his mother, was a wonderful teacher, who worked with his students beyond the call of duty. After the lectures, we young students would be drained, and would be dragging ourselves home, but he would be bounding off, running up three stairs at a time to an orchestral rehearsal, organising the chairs first before the practice, which lasted until late into the evening.

Professor's mother, Frau Tilly Fleischmann, had an enormous impact on my life. When she died, I felt as bereft as if I had lost a family member. Let me tell you the story of how the Professor's wife and myself found her. It was on 17 October 1967: I was teaching at Scoil Mhuire in Cork, and during a free period in the afternoon I got a sudden very strong impression of Frau Fleischmann, and felt that she wanted me. I just had to go up to her house (which was not far from the school) to make sure she was all right. I found the door closed, which was most unusual, as she always left it open in the afternoons for her pupils, and nobody answered the bell. I was just about to go to Seamus Murphy, who lived a few doors further down the terrace, when Mrs Fleischmann drew up in her car. A student had phoned her to say that he had not been able to get into the house for his lesson.

Mrs Fleischmann had a key, and when we went in, I thought I heard the piano upstairs. In the drawing-room I found everything prepared for the lesson: Frau Fleischmann's long black velvet cloak with the silver clasp was folded over the chair, the cat was on the hearth-rug, the fire was lighting – but there was no sign of Frau Fleischmann. It was in the kitchen I found her. I'll never forget her dignity in death. She was lying on the floor, straight, as if she had felt it coming on her. She had finished her lunch. Her purse was open on the table – and even at such a moment I marvelled at how orderly everything was. It looked to me as if she had been looking for her tablets. Her face was extremely peaceful, her clothes were arranged, down to her ankles. It was as if she had known death was coming, and she was not going to be caught in an undignified pose.

Mrs Fleischmann stayed with her while I went down to Seamus Murphy, who wept when he heard the news. In the meantime, Mrs Fleischmann had got in touch with Professor. Seán Ó Riada happened to be in the Music department too and he arrived at the house before

Professor did. He had had a great relationship with Tilly, though she had often told him off when he was being impossible. He stood at her feet, the tears streaming down his face, and said: 'Oh Tilly, you bloody woman, what did you go and do this for?'

Then the Professor arrived, and I made to leave, but he put out his hand to stop me. He stood at her feet; a look of great sorrow passed briefly over his face; he gave a very deep sigh – and immediately the control set in: absolute control. I wanted to say: 'Professor, please cry!' but I just left the kitchen. He was obviously deeply upset. Ó Riada, the Celt, was able to bawl and roar, but Professor's German side prevented him from giving vent to his emotions. I was so sorry for him.

A Sister of Charity arrived to lay Frau Fleischmann out. I got towels and a basin of water, as requested, but the Sister said to me afterwards: 'What a fastidious lady! There was very little for me to do.' She asked what Frau Fleischmann was to be laid out in and suggested the Dominican or Franciscan habit. I couldn't imagine Frau Tilly in either, and suggested the blue and white of the Children of Mary. When the two undertakers arrived, the Professor and Seán Ó Riada lifted Madame Fleischmann from the floor and laid her in her coffin in the front living-room. She looked magnificent in death.

I was about to go home but Mrs Fleischmann wouldn't let me. She could be very kind. She put me into her car and said: 'You're worn out and in shock. I'm taking you up to the Glen for supper: you haven't eaten all day.' So we all sat around the beautiful dining-room table in the house, the Professor trying to carry on as usual. He was very pale, but that was the only sign of his suffering. I was unable to sleep that night, and sat up writing letters about the extraordinary experience.

Frau Fleischmann was laid to rest in St Finbarr's cemetery beside Herr Fleischmann, close to the great Sir Arnold Bax – for whom she had such respect and affection and whose very difficult music she interpreted so well – and not too far from the Republican plot, where the Fleischmanns' friend Terence MacSwiney is buried.

SISTER DE LOURDES KEANE (CORK), UCC Music Graduate, Music Teacher
It is with great respect and deep gratitude that I write of my professor, Aloys Fleischmann. I have rarely, if ever, met anyone of such high standards in his work, expectations, teaching and encouragement of his students, even the less talented. He demanded a lot and we always tried to meet his requirements.

He was a person of great nobility of character, a gifted musician, composer, conductor, and single-minded in his dedication to all that was good and beautiful in the world of music.

I think we owe him a deep debt of gratitude for the high standard we now enjoy at the Cork International Choral Festival. He would not lower those standards, despite a lot pressure at the time.

He was a beacon of light to the artistic life of Cork and his name will always be spoken of with respect.

RYTA GLEESON (CORK), UCC Music Graduate
My first introduction to Music studies at UCC was very pleasant: the senior students gave a concert at Professor Fleischmann's house in Oileán Rua or Hop Island in Rochestown – a lovely old house with a long drive leading up to it. I thought my three years would be filled with a succession of such treats. We did of course have some more musical afternoons hosted by the Professor, but they were usually in the university.

There were only two of us in the class: Annette Rohu was the other girl, and both of us did ballet. Sometimes before a lecture we would practice turns, etc., on our 'blocks' – of course one day Prof opened the door and was nearly sent flying by two ballerinas! He tut-tutted a bit, and his mouth twitched, but he said nothing. Lectures were very pleasant, and we never missed one (we had made a pact) so no one would have an advantage from a solo lecture. Prof had his hands full with us as we were very different students. Annette was a performer – Feis Cheoil – and was a great music reader. I had a good ear: Prof used to test me to try and catch me out, but I would invent things rather than read. Our extern examiner was Sir Arnold Bax, who was a great friend of the Fleischmanns. Professor's mother, Frau Tilly, was my piano teacher and she would sometimes talk to me about Bax during my lessons: about his great love for Ireland, the revolutionary poetry he wrote under the name Dermot O'Byrne, his friendship with Yeats and his love affairs.

I'm afraid I was not too serious a student. I got engaged in my second year and married five months after qualifying. I wasn't encouraged by my parents to look for a job during those five months. But Professor had his own ideas. He set me to work doing a little research for him on music in medieval Munster, so I got permission to go to the archives up in the Clock Tower of UCC to look for items of interest. Professor would join me sometimes to see how I was getting on. Many times I got sidetracked by some hilarious and often ribald material, which was embarrassing when the Professor saw it too! The report was eventually published in the journal of the Cork Historical and Archaeological Society in 1965.

EVE O'KELLY (DUBLIN), UCC Music Graduate, Director of the Contemporary Music Centre of Ireland

Aloys Fleischmann and my father (the late M. J. O'Kelly, Professor of Archaeology in UCC from 1946 to 1982) both started out as part-time professors in UCC and it took some years before the College authorities could be persuaded that there were sufficient students of their respective subjects to justify full-time posts. All their lives they were easily recognisable figures around the campus as being the last two members of staff to persist in wearing academic gowns. They always had the same characteristic chalk-marks on the lapels, from clutching the gowns oratorically as they lectured.

Formality and tradition were important to Aloys Fleischmann. No matter how well known his students became to him over their years in the Music department – and even long after they had left and attained a position of their own in the world – they remained 'Miss So-and-so' and 'Mr So-and-so'. First years always found this a little intimidating but I suspect he found it infused his lectures with an element of drama (always the sign of a good lecturer, in my view). There was a kind of rolling relish, a ring, to the way he would utter your name to ask a question or pass some comment on your work, which no mere Christian name could ever express. Much could be conveyed by a rising or falling inflection, accompanied of course by raised eyebrows, a hand clutching the gown and that characteristic habit of rocking back on his heels. 'Miss O'Kelly? Consecutive fifths in your harmony exercise again?'

He was a great dancer too. At the annual Music Dinner he made a point of dancing with every female, by the end of the evening leaving the rest of us on the sidelines exhausted. No matter what the music was doing, *he* danced the waltz and twirled his partner around the room very stylishly. Of course any form of popular music from the twentieth century (including the entire spectrum of jazz) was anyway apostrophised as 'jungle music' and was greatly to be deplored, but he was prepared to indulge us in the milder forms for the annual 'do'.

Many are the tales about his exploits on the famous motor-bike (need I say he refused to wear a crash helmet?) so I won't add to them, but I can testify that it really is true that our harmony and counterpoint manuscript books came back splashed with mud sometimes following some contretemps on a wet day. When he was finally persuaded to get rid of the motor-bike (or maybe it gave up the ghost?) he graduated to a car and was an equally erratic driver.

The last time I saw him, not long before he died, we met on the train from Dublin to Cork. He had been up for the day for something and I now realise, although I didn't know this at the time, that he was already ill. He insisted on giving me a lift home from the station even though I was going to a completely different part of the city. I remember being amused, but not surprised, to find that he had left his car parked all day on the busy road across from the station, on double yellow lines and with all the doors unlocked. He was the one who was surprised that anyone should think there was anything unusual about this.

He was a supporter of the Contemporary Music Centre from its foundation in 1986, writing to my predecessor to wish him success in the 'Gargantuan task' he had undertaken. In response to a request for information some years later it is regrettable to note that his reply was, 'As for articles on my music, there is hardly anything worth recording'. In the same letter (to Bernard Harris, dated 28 February 1990) he referred to a review of his *Piano Quintet* by the composer Frederick May which appeared in 1949. May apparently described the *Quintet* as 'erudite' and some of it, 'tortuous and obscure'. Fleischmann commented that at a forthcoming performance in Dublin (24 June 1990) the work would no doubt 'not be found learned or obscure but just 'old hat'.

In the light of the above it is nice to note that the library and archive collection of the Contemporary Music Centre now provides very much better information on Aloys Fleischmann and his music: scores, recordings, articles and press clippings, concert programmes, interviews and talks by and about him. After all his battles for music in Ireland, it's the least we can do.

The Contemporary Music Centre is Ireland's national archive and resource centre for new music. It contains the only comprehensive collection in existence of music by Irish composers: The Contemporary Music Centre, 19 Fishamble Street, Temple Bar, Dublin 8, Ireland. Email: <info@cmc.ie>

CATHERINE FOLEY, UCC Music Graduate, Lecturer in Ethnochoreology at The Irish World Music Centre, University of Limerick
From 1974 until 1977 I studied for a Bachelor of Music degree under Professor Aloys Fleischmann at University College, Cork. Having studied classical music at the Cork Municipal School of Music, and Irish traditional music at home with my father, it had long been my ambition to study for my BMus degree with Professor Fleischmann. This was due to the knowledge I possessed, coming from Cork, of Professor Fleischmann's reputation. It was said at that time that the Music degree under Professor Fleischmann was the hardest programme at the university, but a great one. The western classical music tradition was represented by Professor Fleischmann while the Irish

traditional music tradition was represented by the late Seán Ó Riada, followed by Tomás Ó Canainn and Mícheál Ó Súilleabháin. With my bi-musical background, I knew this was the place for me. Besides, on a personal level, my brother Joe had been a boy chorister in Professor Fleischmann' s father's choir at the North Cathedral, Cork, so I felt quite comfortable and proud about the idea of studying with Professor Fleischmann.

My memories of Professor Fleischmann are vivid. He used to say that he was training us all to be pioneers. He certainly did! The music programme designed by Fleischmann was broad in that one was expected to be competent in most areas of music education. Consequently, during my period of study in Cork, great emphasis was on harmony and counterpoint, together with morphology, orchestration, history of music, opera (with the late Charles Lynch), music aesthetics, acoustics, and Irish traditional music. Our annual evenings conducting our own orchestrated pieces with the Cork Symphony Orchestra were cherished memories and valuable experiences. During my later years of teaching music at first, second, and third levels of education, I always felt pedagogically equipped.

Professor Fleischmann was a teacher par excellence. He was fair in that he treated each student with the utmost respect and referred to each student in a formal capacity and was never on first names terms. I never heard him raise his voice or ridicule or criticise another student. And, as with all fine teachers, he had a keen sense of humour. In addition, he was an encouraging teacher. He knew I was an Irish step dancer and encouraged my dancing along with my music. In 1977, he invited both myself and fellow student, Aidan O'Carroll, to dance at the Cork Choral Festival, then organised by Professor Fleischmann. This was a memorable and enjoyable experience for both ourselves and our fellow students as it added another dimension to our music experiences in the department.

This encouragement and acceptance of dance within the Music department acted as a catalyst for me later in life when in 1988 I completed the first doctoral thesis in the world on Irish traditional dance within the international discipline of Ethnochoreology in London. Today, I have designed and teach both the Master's course in Ethnochoreology, and that in Irish Traditional Dance Performance at the Irish World Music Centre, University of Limerick. These are the only programmes of their type in the world and it is often that I have reflected upon the pioneering spirit of Professor Fleischmann when he established the BMus degree in Cork those many years ago.

To all who had the privilege of studying with Professor Fleischmann, it was clear that he was passionate about his life's work. He excelled as a supportive voice for classical music in his teaching, composing, researching and organisational abilities. He loved and was committed to his work in music. Within the Music department, he was first in and last out each day. His work for the university, together with that for the Cork Symphony Orchestra, the Irish National Ballet Company, and the Cork Choral Festival are hallmarks of, and continue to be witnesses to, the quality of his commitment to the arts. We will be forever grateful to him.

Long may he live in our memories!

Canon Donal O'Driscoll (Cork), UCC Music and Arts Graduate, Former Lecturer in the UCC Music Department
A Cherished Memory
In the early 1960s I studied for the BMus degree in UCC under Professor Aloys Fleischmann and later worked under his guidance as a part time lecturer in Aesthetics in the Music faculty. I greatly admired and respected him for the following reasons:

• his cornucopia of musical knowledge and his qualities as an excellent teacher, a fine composer and a brilliant orchestral and choral conductor;

• his wealth of erudition revealed itself in his interest in the other arts, in literature, in science, philosophy and theology. As well, he had a particular interest in the socio-economic aspects of national life, which he expressed in occasional letters in the national press;

• his rich personality, so authentically real and genuine, which expressed itself in a temperament always affable, courteous, tolerant and positive in outlook;

• his profound religious awareness as a well-informed devout Catholic, very conscious of the truth that in God we live, move and have our being.

We, his friends, were really delighted when his native city Cork, mindful of the Professor's accomplishments and contribution to its cultural life, conferred on him the great honour of the Freedom of the City.

A cherished image of Aloys was his boundless energy exhibited not alone in his many professional tasks and duties but also in his physical mobility, swiftly ascending and descending stairways with flying toga and in some dare-devil motor-scooter riding!

Yes, it was my great privilege to have shared some of life's experiences with him. Surely the good Professor must now be sharing heavenly glory with the saints and angels in the celestial choirs singing that hymn of God's glory – Holy, Holy, Holy Lord God of Power and Might, etc. Perhaps Aloys has been given a prestigious conducting job in one or more of these choirs! For him – as for St Augustine –

'music flowed into mine ears and the truth poured into my heart.' Yes, music lifted his soul, winged it with sublime desires and fitted it to bespeak the Deity.

Requiescat in pace.

STEPHEN JARDINE (SALT LAKE CITY, USA), UCC Music Graduate
I had only brief contact with Professor Aloys Fleischmann. This took place during the latter part of 1978 and on through most of 1979. I was an American who had been accepted to study in the Masters of Music programme at University College, Cork. I had come to study Irish traditional folk music. I met Professor Fleischmann on my first day at the college: my main recollection is of him wearing a tattered black professorial gown and his arriving at the college in the morning riding a motor-cycle.

Being from the United States, I knew nothing of how individuals were seen in the community or by their colleagues at the college. I had very little contact with Professor Fleischmann until near the end of my stay in Cork, when I was called into his office with regard to a review of my thesis.

As a preface to this encounter, I would like to mention that participation in university level education here in the United States is often determined as much by a desire for education as by a process that screens out and then allows only the top academic performers. In my own case I believe that a *desire for education* would be the appropriate label. It has also been my observation that there are significant differences in emphasis and approach between the two educational systems of the United Stated and of Ireland.

To return to my thesis: I entered Professor Fleischmann's office to encounter a somewhat intense interrogation with respect to the thesis I had written. Professor Fleischmann pressed me on a number of points about grammar. One point in particular involved gerunds. I really did not know what a gerund was. I remember Professor Fleischmann grilling me with regard to the use or misuse of gerunds. I also remember my frustration level building as well as the Professor's. I'm not sure now, almost 30 years later, how long this interrogation lasted. Perhaps it lasted 30 minutes or perhaps an hour. Professor Fleischmann was probably stunned. I was certainly frustrated.

Then Professor Fleischmann seemed to mentally pause. Finally he asked me what I intended to do after finishing up in Cork. I told him that I intended to return back to the United States and seek employment or additional schooling for employment – probably as an accountant. He then asked me why I had come to study at Cork. I told him that I had played traditional folk music for a number of years and that it was very interesting to me and that I had just wanted to come to study more about it. He then said to me something like 'You just came here to study because of a love of Irish traditional music. Is that right?' I told him that was correct. At that moment all the dynamics of the last frustrating hour changed. Professor Fleischmann never discussed the issue of gerunds with me again – either that day or any other time after that. He seemed to understand where I was coming from. I later tried my best to improve the grammar of my thesis. I was eventually awarded a Master of Music degree with second honours. But I have always remembered Professor Fleischmann's kindness to me that day.

SISTER MIRIAM BUCKLEY (CORK), *UCC Music Graduate, Abbess of the Poor Clare Monastery*
Memories in a Monastery
1968, the year of my Leaving Certificate, was the first year of the free grant for third level education. It was assumed by my parents that a BA in languages would be my choice. However, my heart was set on something else – something I hadn't studied either for the Intermediate (as the Junior Certificate was called then) or the Leaving Certificate examinations: music!

Having given up the piano at twelve years of age and scratched away on the violin in the school orchestra, my practical and theoretical musical standard was almost nil. An interview with the Professor of Music in UCD ended abruptly with the advice to come back when I would at least have Leaving Certificate standard. Down I went to Cork on the train, with *Moonlight Sonata* piano music under my arm (I couldn't play it!) for an appointment with Professor Fleischmann. I was made welcome. He said the *Moonlight Sonata* was about the required standard for first year, but that the lack of Leaving Certificate music was a problem. I interrupted: 'If I could just have a chance, I'd really kill myself practising.' Professor gave me an ear test and then told me I could try. I could have hugged him!

With the invaluable help and advice of Bridget Doolan (may she rest in peace) I began piano and violin lessons in the Cork School of Music. At home in Waterford at weekends and during summer holidays, I took violin and viola lessons from an elderly German violinist, Hermann Gebler, who had played in the early days in the Cork Symphony Orchestra under Professor Fleischmann. Professor was amazed to hear Hermann was still alive and very pleased that I was taking lessons from him in return for my mother giving him his dinner every day.

Eventually Professor Fleischmann invited me to join the Cork Symphony Orchestra. This was a most enjoyable challenge. He was held in tremendous respect by all the players, who marvelled at his extraordinary energy and dedication. To my question one day during a break as to where he got all his energy, he replied: 'Sugar!' Another day, he arrived for rehearsals with his arm in a sling. He had injured his finger dreadfully while using his lawnmower, but life had to go on, no matter what!

And yet, there was a kindness about him which allowed him to be sympathetic in moments of human need. He would always make allowance for me when nervousness prevented me from performing as I should have during practical exams. An incident occurred during my degree year which I will never forget. One afternoon, Professor asked to see me. He wasn't in his usual breezy form.

'What's this I hear about you playing with some group?'

Immediately, I knew he was referring to my playing 'blue-grass' fiddle music.

'How could you do this to me?' he asked, obviously annoyed and upset.

I risked the reply: 'Because I like the sound of it.'

'Well, it's either one or the other,' he stated authoritatively, which left me in no doubt as to what he meant. And that was the end of my wayward 'blue-grass' adventures, although to this day, I still love the sound of it.

At the time, the episode affected me deeply. It wasn't just a question of musical aesthetics, but the question, 'How could you do this to me?' It was like something my father would say to me. And there was something father-like about the Professor, which in no small way helped to bring out the best in his students. He knew how to encourage, correct and challenge, because his standards were high. So, I settled down, 'back on the right track', secretly amazed at his concern for me personally, his utter sincerity and his passionate concern for the cause.

My musical dream came true when in 1972 I graduated with a BMus degree, feeling enormously indebted to Professor Fleischmann. Having signed on for post-graduate studies and secured tutorial hours in the Music department under the Professor, I began to feel unsure about the direction my life was taking when, out of the blue, 'the call' came. Some time later I made my way into the Music department and knocked on the secretary's door where Marion Murphy and Professor Fleischmann were talking together. I said: 'I've something to tell you: I'm going to be a nun, in the Poor Clares.'

Utterly stunned, he said: 'My goodness, Ms Buckley, that's very noble of you.'

I can remember thinking to myself: 'If beauty lies in the eye of the beholder, then here's a deeply spiritual man.' Then, resuming his professorial role, he said something about the appalling situation of church music and that maybe this was my chance to improve things. Marion, in her inimitably humorous way, said: 'Professor, if you're so worried about the state of church music, why don't you become a monk?' We all laughed heartily.

One day in July 1976, in my Poor Clare postulant's dress, I was summoned to the visitors' parlour to see Professor Fleischmann and his wife Nancy. It was one of those special moments. We chatted for about half an hour, during which it transpired that Nancy was related to the foundress of the monastery – Sister Marie Dwyer, daughter of Walter Dwyer. Before leaving, Professor said to me: 'I can see you're extremely happy.'

I said: 'Professor, maybe I wouldn't be here but for you.'

As she left, his wife told me something characteristic: that they were on their way to Kerry but had to return to the house to collect the Professor's forgotten swimming things!

Every Christmas I sent Professor a card and always received a short acknowledgement, with his usual 'good to know you continue happy and fulfilled'. A fortnight before he died, I sent him a note assuring him of the prayers of the Poor Clare Community. His reply indicated a deeper appreciation than usual of the power of prayer. He spent some time not long before his death in the Bon Secours Hospital next door to the Monastery. I felt it was not just coincidence that I happened to be so near him at that time. The bond between Professor Fleischmann and those who loved and admired him reaches out into eternity – his spirit lives on in those whose lives he touched and shaped and enriched. On behalf of them all, and on my own behalf, I pray: 'God rest and reward his noble soul', and on Professor Fleischmann's behalf, in the words of St Clare I pray:

May you be blessed, O Lord, for having created me!

DECLAN F. TOWNSEND (CORK), Composer, UCC Arts and Music Graduate, Lecturer at the Cork School of Music
Without the encouragement and trust of W. E. Brady, Bernard B. Curtis and Aloys Fleischmann I might have been a Dominican priest rather than a musician. As a teenager I seriously considered the former. However, having been invited at the age of 14 by Professor Fleischmann to play in the Cork Symphony Orchestra (leader: W. E. Brady – my violin teacher) and then encouraged by Bernard Curtis and the Prof to take music as an Inter Cert subject I was seduced into the notion of a career in Music. In the early 1950s there were very few string or wind

players in Cork who progressed beyond the grade five level in exams and I was very much a *rara avis*. The director of the School of Music and the professor of Music at UCC persuaded my very reluctant mother to allow me study for a BMus – but not unless I took a BA as well, so that I would have some prospect of getting a job.

It is difficult now to realise what a revolutionary and risky step I had taken. When I entered UCC in 1955 I was one of a class of three. In 1958 an unprecedented five students graduated with a BMus and in 1959 there were only two of us.

Encouraged on all sides I threw myself into musical life in college, playing chamber music, organising lunchtime recitals (an unheard of idea in 1957) and conducting a string orchestra and the Choral Society. I discovered an ambition within myself that recognised few limits because I failed in none of the ventures I tackled. No matter what I tackled or performed 'the Prof' was always present and his presence was a constant at every venture undertaken by any of his undergraduates – or graduates. He might not have approved of light music, of operetta or revue, of even céilí-band-style playing of Irish music but he attended everything.

As a teacher he was mediocre; as a professor he was superb. The distinction is important. A good teacher proceeds from the known to the related unknown, anticipates the difficulties students may find in grasping concepts and discovers ways around these difficulties. The Prof, being phenomenally gifted himself, recognised no difficulties and expounded on every subject on the degree course with equal erudition. Luckily for us students, Bernard Curtis, J. T. ('Jock') Horne and George Brady understood the mysteries of harmony, counterpoint and fugue and were prepared to teach us the mechanics of these disciplines so that we could keep in touch with the mysteries of harmonic and formal analysis which were being expounded in the university. The Prof had one ambition for his students and it was this: all graduates of University College Cork would have some acquaintance with every, and I mean every, branch of music being taught at university level in these islands. Where other universities, Dublin, Durham, or Oxford might produce fine specialist composers, historians, etc., UCC was producing graduates who specialised in nothing but knew something about everything – and who could play an instrument to a fairly high level. Uniquely in the country, Aloys Fleischmann was teaching undergraduates who would be employable in secondary schools or as specialist instrumental teachers. Together with Bernard Curtis he had founded the Music Teachers Association in order to improve teaching standards and raise public consciousness of the importance of music in cultural life in general and in education in particular. The

MTA, led by the Prof, was largely responsible for the slow, gradual growth in acceptance by the Department of Education of the inclusion of music in the secondary school curriculum, not just for talented players but for all students. It is quite astonishing that one who himself would not have been a success in a classroom should have been so successful in providing people who have been outstandingly successful teachers. He had a vision and he was sufficiently charismatic and awe-inspiring to either cajole or intimidate Department of Education personnel, school principals (and even some bishops) to go part of the way to sharing that vision.

It is difficult to assess how good a practical musician he actually was. I never knew him when he conducted choirs. As an orchestral conductor he was technically quite poor. Amateur players require three things of a conductor – a steady pulse, a clear, unequivocal indication of down and up beats and clear directions regarding entries. In each of these areas he was undependable. Professional players hate conductors who talk too much – they rely on the stick to indicate phrasing, balance and dynamics. The Radio Teilifís Éireann orchestra played well for him, despite his deficiencies because, as one player told me, 'he is such a nice man'. Whether he was a good conductor or not is, however, somewhat irrelevant as without him it is unlikely that regular orchestral concerts would have become a feature of Cork musical life.

It is, I think, unfair to those who preceded him to suggest that he was the first to establish an orchestra in Cork. The Cork Philharmonic Society Orchestra did exist, though on an irregular basis, both George Brady and 'Jock' Horne being sometime conductors. What Aloys Fleischmann brought was stability, a place to rehearse, 'respectability' through its association with the university and, of course, the benefit of his professional training in Munich, his phenomenal energy, his openness to new music, his scholarship, his indefatigable determination and his considerable organisational skills. It took an exceptional person to combine all these talents and, ignoring all setbacks and criticisms, to remain as conductor of Cork Symphony Orchestra for so long. Knowing how much of himself he put into the maintenance of what he had created, I often cringed in embarrassment at the ill-mannered, cavalier attitude towards rehearsal shown by so many players over the years.

I never heard him actually play as a solo pianist or as an accompanist so I do not know how sensitively he played. I only heard him as an illustrator of particular harmonic sequences, as a player of our harmony and counterpoint exercises, as a score-reader and, at such time, he was quite unmindful of tone quality and refinement – he was simply using the piano as a tool. He was a phenomenal sight reader and his ability to reduce a complex orchestral score to music for two hands was awe inspiring. In such circumstances, however, one could not guess at the level of his sensitivity to music. Nor could one guess by listening to performances by the Cork Symphony Orchestra. An amateur orchestra which survived only because of his persuasive powers and was peopled, in part at least, by players whose technical skill was often over-stretched by the programmes he chose, did not allow a fair assessment of the musicianship of the conductor.

The breadth of his scholarship is, however, undeniable. He was the antithesis of the present day iconoclastic specialist. Whether the subject was medieval church music, Baroque organ music, Romantic orchestration or contemporary compositional techniques, he could hold his own in debate with any specialist. His interest in Irish music was lifelong. Again, it is difficult to assess whether this interest was wholly cerebral partly driven by a sense of national pride (he was intensely proud of being Irish and proud of our heritage of song, story, dance, myth, etc.) or whether he genuinely loved the folksong and dance music of Ireland. I suspect that he genuinely admired the craftsmanship of well made tunes and, taking pride in our heritage, applied his vast knowledge to the *Sources of Irish Traditional Music,* which will be his lasting monument, out of mixed sentiments of love and duty.

Perhaps it is the latter which was the single most important motivator of this complex man who could sympathise with people but not empathise. There was his duty towards his students – he never cancelled a lecture or failed to correct assignments. Civic duty led him to found and chair the Cork Orchestral Society and the Music Teachers Association, to lend his unstinting support to Joan Denise Moriarty, the Cork Ballet Company and Irish National Ballet, to be one of the instigators of the Cork Film Festival and Cork International Choral and Folk Dance Festival. And national duty led him to write cogently and passionately to the newspapers regarding what he perceived to be wrong in Irish society – be it poor taste, lack of support for the arts, unfair standards of musical criticism, national greed or insufficient support for music in education. This sense of duty may have been his principal driving force. It was certainly a sense of duty which influenced his early compositions. He was firmly on the side of those (few) composers who saw Irish art music deriving its inspiration from Irish roots rather than those who looked to Europe and the exciting experiments going on there. Even a cursory glance at his list of compositions will reveal this determination to be an Irish composer, with an Irish voice, rather than a European composer who lived and worked in Ireland. Of these early compositions it is, I think, his *Trí hAmhráin* which impresses me most. It reveals an original voice, distinct in idiom from most of his contemporaries. The songs are passionate and quite beautiful. It is a pity that his compositional output is so small. In view of all the other things he did, it is remarkable that he actually found time to compose.

Despite the admiration which must be evident in what I have written, he disappointed me in many ways. The first instance was when, at a public lecture, he quoted findings from my MA research without attribution, without telling me that he was going to do so. Although this was, I discovered, not uncommon in scientific research it came as a shock to me to find that one whom I admired and trusted as a research director could be so unmindful of the feelings of a young graduate.

My greatest misgiving regarding him, however, is in connection with his lack of faith in his own graduates. From 1960 onwards, the intake into the UCC Music department grew bigger each year. It became obvious that a whole-time professor and a part-time lecturer in Irish Music were insufficient to run the department. Many very talented people had graduated under his tutelage and some had gone on for further study. I am just one of those whom he encouraged to study for higher degrees. Yet, unlike his colleagues in other departments, he did not employ us as demonstrators or tutors. He denied us the opportunity of entering Academia, of growing in scholarship so that we could realistically compete for academic posts. Even though he encouraged my research towards the PhD (following which I was to be his nomination for the proposed Chair of Music in University College Galway) he could not find a part-time post for me in UCC. Seán Ó Riada, who had made a national reputation with Ceoltóirí Chualann and written successful film scores, was the first of his graduates to be employed in UCC. This lack of trust in his own graduates was compounded when UCC employed English graduates as lecturers. They, naturally, brought a different perspective and seemed to undermine his own self-belief. One instance will illustrate his apparent lack of trust in his own graduates. John C. Murphy, a piano teacher in the School of Music, one of UCC's brightest graduates in his understanding of harmony and harmonic analysis, was employed as an assistant lecturer in UCC. As conductor of the Ladies Choir of the Cork School of Music and the City of Cork Male Voice Choir he had won several prizes at the Choral Festival. When he proposed starting a choir in UCC the Prof would not sanction it, as one of the English lecturers had a choir – Pro Musica Sacra – in operation. However, another English lecturer was given permission to start the UCC Choir and Orchestra within the same year! These British-trained academics, specialists mostly, appeared to completely undermine his self-belief, while ostensibly flattering him. It was sad to watch, as I became increasingly the recipient of many stories of double-dealing, both from him and from undergraduates and graduates alike during the 1970s and 1980s.

I had been constantly consulting him as a researcher into, first, the origins of Irish dance music, later into the value of the choral arrangements of Irish folksong, and finally on the subject which became my doctoral thesis: choral folksong. Having taken the revolutionary step of totally changing my field of research (after eight years of increasingly diffuse chasing after clues) I embarked on a project that was close to his heart. Although I was unaware of his attitude when I began studying the choral folksong arrangements of nationalist composers Kodaly, Bartok, Holst and Vaughan Williams, it gradually became apparent that he empathised with the philosophy which inspired my research – we were of one mind regarding a truly Irish school of composition. He was a superb director of research, allowing me academic freedom yet remaining ever vigilant regarding the side roads down which I might have travelled. At the writing stage his command of language was enormously helpful, preventing excessive claims, insisting on clarity of expression and remaining ever conscious of the underlying case which I was proposing. Many, many times, however, I was frustrated by the over-stretched schedule he imposed on himself. There were times when I had to wait for weeks for a consultation. Some of these took place late at night in the Choral Festival office, others in Glen House early in the morning. His directorship of the Choral Festival, together with the self doubt planted by his imported colleagues, in fact delayed the submission of my thesis by at least six months. He could not decide on the best way of presenting a particular set of tables and feared that the extern examiner would object to the particular presentation on which he and I agreed. He had come to rely on one particular English lecturer for advice and the prevarication of the latter, combined with the demands of the Choral Festival administration meant that my thesis went 'on the back burner' and I missed the deadline for submission. In the event, we used the already agreed method of presentation and Dr Harrison approved the award of PhD, pronouncing the thesis worthy of publication without any alteration, vindicating our decision. He was really pleased for me. I was his second PhD and his first, Ita Hogan (now Beausang) was the first to be awarded a PhD in Music by the NUI. Why he had not encouraged others down the road of scholarship I never understood.

Neither did I understand why he did not teach composition. Patrick Zuk was, so far as I know, the only student he ever taught the art and craft of composition to and this only happened after his retirement from UCC. John Reidy, Bernard Geary, Michael Casey, Garry Crowley and John Murphy all showed talent and originality, yet this master of analysis, and he was in my experience without peer, never actually taught them to compose. He taught the nuts and bolts of the craft at undergraduate level but never pursued it with any of the truly gifted people he taught.

I suspect that I will never truly forgive him a hurt/humiliation which he could have prevented. In 1978, having competed at the Cork Choral Festival as conductor of various choirs for 14 years, my choir, the Cork School of Music Choir, won first prize in Competition B, for National Choirs. Dan Donovan announced the result but was contradicted, on stage, by one of the adjudicators. The trophy was then presented to Father Seán Terry, conductor of a Fermoy choir, as if they had won. Aloys Fleischmann, director of the Festival, Lord Mayor Goldberg, the other adjudicators and other members of the Festival committee sat on stage, knowing that a mistake had been made – and did nothing. It was the responsibility of the Director to publicly correct the error. He did not. Privately, he met my baffled wife and me in the body of the hall and told us that Father Terry's choir had not won. Privately he sent a message to the Imperial Hotel requesting the return to the City Hall of Father Terry and the trophy. In the Council Chamber of the City Hall the trophy was awarded to me but the *Cork Examiner* published a photograph (on the following morning) of a jubilant Father Terry being awarded the trophy by Lord Mayor Goldberg. While a brief letter from the director, recounting the facts as he saw them, was subsequently published in the *Cork Examiner*, the damage had been done. He never acknowledged his own culpability in the affair and I'm afraid I lost my absolute trust in him.

In summary, then, I will always thank him for the fact that I have had a rewarding career in music. I recognise his greatness as a national figure in the promotion of music in Ireland. I acknowledge his stature as an academic of outstanding ability but, as a man, I found him distant, over-formal, self-deprecating and not always generous in his treatment of people.

MICHAEL CASEY (DUBLIN), Composer, UCC Music Graduate, Former Assistant Head of Music Services in Radio Teilifís Éireann
I attended UCC from 1961 to follow Fleischmann's BMus course, where I got to know him very well and spent a lot of time in his company. I was flattered to think that he considered me to be one of his brighter pupils. He generously organised scholarships and a studentship for me.

He was always very unhappy about my activities in the world of 'pop' music and probably felt that these were not in keeping with the dignity of a university Music student. He tried to persuade me to give up playing in showbands, but I declined. I think that he genuinely felt it would affect my musical tastes. We disagreed on this and a number of other things. Years later he asked me to lecture to his students on 'pop music'. Was he trying to tell me at this stage that he had changed his mind on the whole business? I have often wondered about this.

In common with many of his pupils, I was dragooned into helping out during 'his' annual Choral and Folk Dance Festival held traditionally in the City Hall in Cork. When I was asked to be an adjudicator recently, I felt very comfortable being there but also privileged and flattered to be invited to hold that position. This Festival, which he had founded, was one of his favourite projects. He threw his heart and soul into it. The energy he brought to it was phenomenal. Indeed the energy he brought to all of his projects was never anything less than whole-hearted. I think one of his regrets was that he did not have anywhere near enough time for composition, which did not come easily to him. Does it come easily to anyone? The seminar on contemporary choral music was his special love and he was really in his element in dissecting, analysing and discussing the various compositions. After he ceased active participation in the Festival, many thought that it would cease with him. But the Festival had become such a part of the fabric of the arts in Cork that it had developed a life of its own. It is still a regular part of the Cork 'tourist' year and it is renowned throughout the world.

Another of his 'babies' was the Cork Symphony Orchestra, and of course I was dragooned into playing the double bass and percussion in that group. His persuasive powers were such that he could induce amateurs, semi-professionals and professionals to work together with some playing for nothing, others for a modest fee and yet others for the 'normal' concert fee. That entry in the *Guinness Book of Records* detailing his association with the CSO gave him an enormous quirky pleasure.

One of the most difficult tasks that I had to perform in my years of orchestral administration in RTE happened in 1981 during the production of the ballet *The Táin* in the Abbey Theatre in Dublin for which Fleischmann had written the music. He had insisted on conducting the work himself against all advice, with the result that the committee of the RTE Concert Orchestra came to me to complain that they could not follow his direction. They liked the man and respected him but they had the utmost difficulty in following his beat. I asked him to come in to my office to discuss the situation. He came immediately and I had to tell him plainly of the problem. The matter was simple:

we would have to get another conductor or cancel the performances completely. He agreed to let Proinnsías Ó Duinn conduct the ballet. He was really very gracious about the whole matter and he thanked me for handling the problem so gently and positively. It was something I hated having to do but perhaps it was better coming from me than anyone else.

The Prof had a great, dry wit. On one occasion we were talking together in the foyer of the City Hall in Cork during the interval of an RTE Symphony Orchestra concert when two of the male dancers with the professional ballet company (Irish National Ballet) came up to us and without so much as a 'by your leave' addressed the Prof: 'Professor, as you well know, we are two practising homosexuals and we are very disappointed with the scene here in Cork!'

To which the Prof replied: 'How long have you been in Cork?'

'Two weeks,' came the answer.

The Prof responded: 'Two weeks! Ah, I think you have to give Cork a chance!' and he glanced at me in great amusement, the laughter dancing in his eyes.

His classes were always interesting and he had the great gift of handling effectively small groups of students with widely differing abilities. I don't imagine any of us felt that we were being neglected or short-changed in any way. I asked him many questions and although I am sure that he must have found it a distraction, he never was anything but courteous. I remember distinctly to this day his answers, which were hardly ever void of an element of humour, preceded by that mannerism of his of hissing before responding as in hidden laughter. Once I asked him why it was that Mozart towered head and shoulders above his contemporaries, who were all writing music in the same Mannheim style such as Cherubini, Boccherini or Salieri. He looked at me benignly and said: 'Dear, dear, Mr Casey – I was hoping that you would have been able to tell *me* that!' On Brahms, I quizzed him on the significance of the chorale interlude in the introduction to his first symphony. His answer: 'Presumably Mr Brahms thought it a good idea at the time.' I also questioned him on the provenance of the rules of harmony and counterpoint. He explained that these so-called rules were the crystallisation of the practice of the last two hundred years or so and that I was always welcome to do what I like with them – provided, of course, that I knew what I was doing! Once when he commented adversely on a harmony or counterpoint exercise of mine, I pointed out that Bach had done exactly the same thing on many an occasion; to which he replied: 'Mr Casey, when you reach the same facility that Bach had with his harmony and counterpoint you can do very much what you like: and then you won't be coming here to UCC for lessons!'

We shared an antipathy to the music of *My Fair Lady*, which was current when I was a student. He described the music as badly crafted and full of musical solecisms and we delighted in bringing examples to each other's attention as we discovered more and more of them in the vocal score. Contrariwise we shared a great admiration for the score of Delibes' *Coppélia*: 'a wonderfully crafted piece, full of imagination and inventiveness' was the verdict. We also shared a hatred of piped music in public places. Even today, every time I complain about its invidious presence, I think of the Prof's slightly worried reaction to my dogged insistence that the music be turned down, or better still, turned off altogether.

I was asked to conduct a shortened choral-verse interpretation of William Walton's *Facade* in 1964 for a guest appearance by the Montfort Singers at that year's Choral Festival. He expressed his doubts and his unhappiness to me about the success of the performance as the music is quite difficult for professionals to bring off let alone a bunch of amateurs. I tried to assure him that I would have no trouble in conducting this work. His reply was: 'It's not you I'm worried about: it's the players!' I remember him coming up to me after the first performance of the Montfort Singers' production of *The Music Man*. He was very fulsome in his praise of my conducting and told me he was impressed by the tightness of the ensemble and the absence of accidents which seemed to have been a feature of first-night performances of musicals in Cork. I thanked him and told him that I had insisted on having not the customary one but two band calls. He observed: 'I hope that the fashion you have started will soon catch on!'

There are many such incidents, as there are bound to be in such a lively relationship as we shared, which are hidden from my memory by the passage of more than thirty-odd years. One particularly embarrassing moment for me related to one of his student presentations that he held annually in the canteen in UCC known as the 'Rest'. I was to conduct the performance of a piano piece by Mendelssohn which I had orchestrated. When I mentioned to him that I had invited my parents to the event, he became very upset, saying that it was only he had the right to invite people. I offered to pay for their tea and biscuits but that seemed only to upset him more. My parents attended in any event and we never discussed the matter again. He probably felt that he had made his point sufficiently.

He had amongst his possessions an incomplete clarinet dating from the end of the eighteenth century. It was missing the barrel and the mouthpiece. To my eye it looked to be about the same size as a modern Eb clarinet. I found the required pieces of the present-day instrument and after a bit of elementary carpentry I was able to get them to fit the older instrument. Hearing the instrument played gave him enormous pleasure.

During his declining years he hardly ever missed an artistic event in Cork, especially if it were ballet or an art music concert. The last time I saw him was a few weeks before he died when I had to help him into the Aula Maxima in UCC for an RTE Vanbrugh String Quartet concert. He was really very frail by then and found it frustratingly difficult to get around.

The city of Cork mourned the passing of the Prof much in the way they would honour a national hero and there are few I am sure who would disagree with such treatment. He brought music to a city that, without his sheer commitment and tenacity to get things done, would probably not have had anything near the amount of activity and standards of the arts that Cork possesses to this day. I am grateful to him for all he gave me.

PAULINE MACSWEENEY (CORK), UCC Music Graduate, Music Teacher
I came to the UCC Music department as a first year student in 1973. My initial reaction to Professor Fleischmann was pure terror of this Victorian figure in his black gown, who addressed all the students formally, and called each of us in turn to the blackboard to fill in the next harmonic progression in front of our class mates. But the terror subsided as the weeks went by and he quite quickly became 'Prof', a fatherly figure for whom we felt much bemused affection.

He was constantly unintentionally making us laugh. He was like some cartoon character, racing off on his motor-bike, falling off podiums, running around with his black gown and wisps of hair flying behind him. He could be deliberately funny, too. On one occasion while he was conducting for the ballet, his glasses fell off and he couldn't read the score, but the orchestra valiantly played on. The following night, coming up to the same section of the music, to the horror of the orchestra he let his glasses fall again – but this time, with a big smile, he took another pair out of his pocket.

The basis of his teaching was a rigorous training in harmony and counterpoint. In counterpoint we worked through the five species and in final year wrote compositions in five parts. We handed in exercises weekly which were returned, corrected in detail, and marked *Fair*, *Good*, or *Very good*. It must have been a huge workload for him. I'm afraid I, and I suspect many others, approached these more as mathematical than as musical exercises. However, I do have an abiding love of contrapuntal music, which may partly relate to that experience. I think I've had more pleasure from listening to and playing Bach's '48' than almost any other music.

61

The more interesting subject on his course however was orchestration. In the first year we could either compose or arrange a piece for string quartet, in second year for wind and string, and in third year for full orchestra. In our final year we wrote out all the parts, had one or two rehearsals and finally a public concert where we each conducted the Cork Symphony Orchestra playing our 'work'. This was a very exciting and unique experience for young music students and demanded a lot of work and patience from everybody concerned, not least from Professor Fleischmann.

The other really stimulating musical experiences during my years at UCC were the inspired lectures on opera by the pianist Charles Lynch and the rehearsals and performances of Handel's *Messiah* and Bach's *St John Passion* with Christopher Stembridge. We were a very fortunate generation of music students to have experienced those men and I feel a lot of credit is due to Professor Fleischmann for having had the vision and flexibility to appoint two performing musicians who could communicate to us students in a non-academic way.

Although the BMus course was a very conservative one, we did have some exposure to contemporary music through the commissioned works for the Choral Festival – attendance at Professor's lectures and analyses of the new works was more or less compulsory for the students. I remember also that he organised a group of us to go to Dublin to hear a concert of music by Messiaen and we actually met the great composer himself.

After my BMus I did a Master's degree on organs and harpsichords: Professor was very supportive, on one occasion even driving me to see an organ. He also went to a lot of trouble to have part of my thesis published in the journal of the Royal Irish Academy and he always had time for any of my problems or questions during that time.

Perhaps Professor Fleischmann's most important and lasting legacy to Cork and to Irish musical life is the Choral Festival and I feel sure that the exceptional quality and quantity of choirs around the country at the present moment is to a large extent due to his dedication to choral music throughout his life. Like many hundreds of other former students, I remember him with gratitude and affection.

NOEL O'REGAN, UCC Music Graduate, Senior Lecturer in Music, University of Edinburgh
The name of Aloys Fleischmann was already somewhat legendary when I first met him in Galway around 1969. In an age when senior academics enjoyed a status closer to Parnassus than they do now, the triumvirate of Boydell, Fleischmann and Hughes (professors of Music

in TCD, UCC and UCD respectively) represented to a young school-boy from the west of Ireland in the early 1960s a sort of musical pantheon, to be approached, if at all, with the awe otherwise reserved for bishops! It was, of course, a respectful age and something of it continued to hang around Professor (or Prof as we later always referred to him among ourselves as students or graduates – and continue so to do) through the 1970s. He always used surnames, prefaced by Mr or Miss, the tone of voice alone indicating the level of approval, disapproval, or intimacy which he intended. This may have represented an equivalent of the German polite form of address: his German name certainly added to the mystique which surrounded the man and his office, as of course did his musical lineage which, it was whispered, led back (through his mother) to Liszt.

My earliest meeting with him both reinforced the aura of respect and revealed the kindly courtesy with which he unfailingly met people from all walks of life. He came to give a visiting lecture to the University College Galway Music Society of which I was a committee member, and we entertained him to dinner afterwards. I'm afraid I don't remember the topic of his lecture; what has stayed in my mind was his proselytising zeal for music education in the west of Ireland and, in particular, his insistence that it was high time UCG had its own Music department. This was a theme to which he was to return often thereafter, saying that he had long done his share of training students from west of the Shannon to be future music teachers; it was a task which properly belonged to the province's own university. This sense of responsibility for the training of Ireland's young musicians and its future teachers was a leitmotif in his life's work and probably represents his most important contribution. It was something he shared with Anthony Hughes, though their methods varied. The UCD Music department kept its numbers of degree students low, insisting on keeping high standards; at the same time Hughes introduced a teachers' diploma which provided a more basic academic foundation for those not able to read for a degree. Fleischmann was more pragmatic, always willing to take a risk on a student and keen to have as many as possible take degrees in order that they might spread the good word further afield. He could be very persuasive with Mother Superiors, for example and, if they didn't always send their most musical nuns to study for the BMus, Fleischmann felt that at least those who came could be trained to the best of their ability and go back to their schools armed for battle in the cause of music. All this must have given him and his colleagues some heart- (and ear-) ache at times but it was eventually to pay off, at least in terms of numbers. By the 1970s UCC had become the most populous Music department in the country. Critical mass had been reached and interesting things could begin to happen.

When in 1971 I accepted a postgraduate scholarship to study Chemistry in UCC, the attraction of moving to Cork was as much my perception of its active musical life, dominated as I imagined by Aloys Fleischmann and Seán Ó Riada (who sadly died just before I made the move), as it was UCC's new Science building and the equally legendary Prof F. L. Scott with whom I was to work in Physical Organic Chemistry. At the time I looked on music as a hobby and Chemistry as a career; that things were to change was in no small measure due to Fleischmann's capacity to encourage working teachers and others to do part-time Music degrees. When, in the case of my own group, the number of such part-timers was not sufficient to form a viable class, he decided to re-schedule the full-time classes for late afternoons and Saturday mornings so that we could continue to attend. His poor colleagues were also persuaded to go along with this, though the Saturday morning sessions were quietly dropped after the first year. I continued to juggle full-time laboratory work on antibiotics (at the Pfizer Chemical Corporation in Ringaskiddy) with counterpoint and harmony exercises, and revelled in escaping from the laboratory at 3.30pm to attend classes in the Rectory on Western Road. It must be said that Pfizers were equally accommodating in allowing me lots of flexibility, even when it became obvious that the end result would be my moving out of Chemistry.

I enjoyed the family atmosphere in the Rectory, something which had not been so prominent in the larger Chemistry classes of my first degree. Fleischmann did much of the teaching himself, especially in harmony and counterpoint. His teaching was very much in the Fuxian tradition of species counterpoint and followed a rather technical approach to chromatic harmony which had one resolving complex chords without any particular context, for example. It seemed somehow removed from real music and when, on later going to Oxford to do a PhD, I took counterpoint classes with Bernard Rose at Magdalen College, it was a bit of a shock to be expected to produce Palestrina-style counterpoint and stylistic Bachian fugues. At the same time Fleischmann could be an inspiring teacher, especially in his third-year history course on nineteenth and early twentieth century music. His choice of set works was excellent and these have remained firm favourites over the years. A recent performance of Mahler's First Symphony by the Royal Scottish National Orchestra under Alexander Lazarev left me very moved, not just as a result of the stunning excitement of the music and the playing, but also because of so many memories it inspired of my final BMus year. As a university teacher myself I now realise the huge amount of work Fleischmann put into marking our exercises. I also appreciate and pass on to my students his pragmatic approach: 'always do your work with a pencil in one hand and a rubber in the other' he would admonish – and very sensible advice it was too (though these days one has to substitute the word 'eraser' for 'rubber'!). I also now know the pitfalls of lecturing on a topic on which one is less than up to speed. I remember affectionately Prof's attempts to explain to us the basics of acoustics without really (or so it seemed to a somewhat cocky scientist) having mastered the concepts himself. That he nonetheless thought it worth trying to cover acoustics was typical of his approach: he recognised its importance and, in the absence of anyone more qualified to teach it, would do it himself.

As student numbers grew, he did have the opportunity of bringing in other members of staff. In choosing colleagues (in so far as the choice was his) he did not look for clones of himself: rather the opposite in fact. This could sometimes lead to tensions within the academic family, not all of them creative. Students of my generation could occasionally find themselves pulled between opposing ideals or conflicting personalities. Dealing with these was a useful part of the learning process. Becoming aware of different approaches to the discipline helped make us more critical as students and not always prepared to accept what we were told. Tensions could arise in the hothouse atmosphere of the Rectory and perhaps Fleischmann was not always sensitive to these or (more likely) did not quite know how to respond. I remember a rather acrimonious general meeting of staff, students and alumni (which was held on an annual basis) where some of these tensions boiled over and a few of us second-year students expressed our dissatisfactions with aspects of the course. For Prof this airing of dirty linen in public was unseemly and he afterwards admonished us for being disruptive and even revolutionary (it must be said we were pretty unlikely revolutionaries!). The lack of a staff-student council (now seen as an essential part of any university department) meant that we lacked any other forum for airing our views. I'm sure that to Fleischmann, used as he was to deference and to acceptance by students that their teachers knew best, this must have been troubling. His older certainties were disappearing and he felt it incumbent on him to defend them wherever possible. It is to his credit that he never seemed to hold our public intervention against us. It is also to his credit that he didn't, at least as far as we could judge, try to interfere in his colleagues' teaching. Having been instrumental in bringing to UCC a number of highly talented, but very diverse, individuals as staff members he generally let them get on with it, allowing each to fashion courses and extra-curricular musical activities according to their lights. This cannot have always been easy for him; he had been used to controlling everything and may not have realised that, in the wider scheme of things, these new influences would work well. From this distance I know how fortunate we were in those years in having access to the breadth of experience available in the UCC Music department. It was an exciting place to be and, on the whole, provided the stimulus necessary for students to develop their own talents, both musically and intellectually.

Music is a unique academic discipline in the level of contact which music-making can provide between staff and students, much of what is learned and retained comes, not through formal lectures or tutorials, but in the nitty-gritty of orchestral playing or choral singing, above all in rehearsal. In all of this Fleischmann was tireless, as a conductor, administrator or simply as an enabler, in creating a department where such involvement was accepted and expected. One of the highlights of his course was the opportunity offered to each student to orchestrate a piece and then to conduct the Cork Symphony Orchestra in its performance, not just once but in both second and third year. With Prof's fatherly but owlish presence just behind the student's right shoulder, this was at once a frightening and exhilarating experience; the opportunity to hear and have to conduct one's own orchestration was invaluable and something all too rarely offered in Music departments. We pitied the members of the orchestra but clearly their own strong commitment to their founding conductor saw them through – and they must have shared in his enthusiasm for educating future teachers and musicians. Other opportunities which Fleischmann provided were in connection with the Cork Ballet Company or the Cork Choral Festival. This last saw the man at his most energetic, dashing from City Hall to University to Festival Office, taking a seminar here, a rehearsal there or a reception somewhere else. For those, like myself, with a passion for choral music the Choral Festival was a highlight of each year, providing a stream of memorable visiting choirs as well as a platform for our own performances. It was certainly his most constant achievement.

My last meeting with Prof occurred in an unexpected way sometime in the late 1980s. On entering the music reading area of the old British Library deep in the bowels of the British Museum building I saw him sitting there, absorbed in a printed collection of Irish and Scottish tunes which he was researching for his beloved index. We were both in a rush, trying to get some work done quickly before leaving London and so there wasn't time for more than a short conversation. I should not have been surprised to see him there but the context was certainly not one I had associated him with. The British Library and all it represented of historical research was my territory and it seemed as if Fleischmann had strayed into it. At the same time we were now closer to being equals in that august room than we had ever been before, which was strange for both of us I'm sure. I wish we had had more time to talk then. He had never been very forthcoming to his students (other than a very select few) about his major research project, which was a pity. My own instincts towards musicology were nurtured by others, Christopher Stembridge and David Wulstan in particular.

It was as if Fleischmann didn't quite take his own research seriously – and yet he obviously did and thankfully brought it to a conclusion before his death. As I was not a composer, nor overly enthused by analysis, I missed much of what he might have had to offer. As a historian I regret that he didn't find the time, or perhaps the motivation, to do more writing or historical research into Irish music.

What of his overall legacy? Others will be able to offer more informed comment on his compositions. His index of printed Irish tunes must ultimately prove immensely useful and some of his early writings on music in Ireland, as well as his encouragement of younger scholars to take up the topic, are valuable. Certainly he was of huge importance for Cork, for its cultural life and its self-image in the difficult years before the era of the Celtic Tiger. In its heyday his Choral Festival represented all that was best in the city, both to its inhabitants and to those outside. In a sense it was for all this that he had been brought into the world and groomed from his earliest years. Since it was his destiny, it is perhaps a pity that Cork was not a bigger theatre, a more substantial centre capable of throwing out greater challenges. Cork could be very cosy, and something of a cocoon to those who made a success there. Good things could be achieved (and undoubtedly were) but the challenge to greatness was rarely thrown up. It was a pity too, I think, that Fleischmann had not spent longer abroad before returning to UCC. My own experience of having moved and stayed away has made me see the advantages of having to make one's mark in a foreign place. But then I haven't returned to put something back and, in Fleischmann's eyes, that might have seemed less good. His sense of duty drove him to give of himself unstintingly in the cause and, if this led to a certain dilution of his talents and standards, it meant that the widest possible constituency benefited. I certainly gained a very sound musical formation from him, and from his colleagues in the Cork Music department, something for which I will ever be profoundly grateful.

RENEE MCCARTHY AND DENISE MURPHY, *UCC Music Graduates, Music Teachers*
We have many happy memories of the music scene in Cork from the mid-1960s to 1980. Like so many other musicians we owe a great deal

of our musical education to Professor Fleischmann, who was at the centre of everything to do with music in the city at that time.

He had such a sense of humour that studying under him at UCC was fun, playing in the symphony orchestra a great pleasure and working with him on the committees of the Orchestral Society and Music Teachers Association was a delight. His enthusiasm for every aspect of musical life was infectious and we were very grateful to receive so much encouragement from him for the Suzuki Programme which we set up under the directorship of the late Mr Bernard Curtis.

But the most outstanding image has to be of him charming everybody around him into doing all that had to be done to make the musical event being undertaken a great success and in the process he managed to make one feel that nobody else could do it just as brilliantly, which was really great for one's confidence.

CONN MURPHY (CORK), UCC Music Graduate, Music Teacher
I knew Aloys Fleischmann quite well, as teacher and mentor, from about 1970 onwards, and he is one of a very small group of people, along with my mother and my first school principal, who influenced the direction of my life. As a schoolboy, I had learnt the piano from the wonderful Mary Ring O'Brien in Macroom, and I did not know then that one could do a degree in Music. I got to know Prof initially rather at second hand while I was at UCC studying science (1966–70): because I was very keen on music, I became involved with the Choral Society and matters musical, and one of my best college friends was a Music student. I still remember with pleasure my first ever symphony concert in 1967 in the City Hall with the Cork Symphony Orchestra conducted by Prof.

Subsequently, I managed to work through to a BMus in 1975 – that was only possible because Prof arranged almost all the lectures in the afternoons to facilitate the small bunch of school teachers among his students. For that privilege I am still grateful. They were some of my best years, although I was under severe pressure, teaching maths by day and doing harmony exercises until the small hours! Our mentor was frighteningly businesslike. I recall a student who sat beside me in class remarking that Prof's work rate must be about 110% at everything he did, far ahead of any average which we, unscientifically and perhaps optimistically, put at about 67%. But Prof also wanted his work to bear fruit. I remember when he first welcomed me as a student, he made the (very non-pc) remark that he always tried to have men in the BMus course – in the world of 1971, women graduates would not all continue at work whereas men were obliged to!

The Cork Symphony Orchestra, inspired and led, patiently, by

Prof for so long, gave us Music students the really marvellous opportunity of conducting a real orchestra. For my BMus I recall – with some awe even now – taking the orchestra through my own arrangement of my grandmother Kelleher's two favourite Irish songs. I was proud and pleased. And it was only possible because Prof had made it so.

After 1975, I helped to run the Music Teachers Association, and got to know many musicians. I like to think that he found me useful and reliable. The Association was another of Prof's projects. Over its sixty years, it did much to promote music in education. In the early days it arranged concerts throughout the south. It always tried to offer professional advice to music teachers. Prof was very aware that private music teaching was unregulated and unevenly available, and attempted to have appropriate registration and regulation introduced nationally. In this he was not successful. He resigned as chairman when he retired from UCC, and the Association continued to attend to the concerns of its core group: the private music teachers. Other aspects of its previous work had been taken over by new agencies, most notably by Cumann Náisiúnta na gCór for the provision of choral training and advice, and by the Post-Primary Music Teachers Association for the teaching of Inter Cert and Leaving Cert Music in Schools. In 1997 the MTA had a small celebration in the Aula Maxima at UCC to mark its sixtieth birthday. In 1998 it was replaced by a Regional Music Teachers Association.

In April 1980, together with some other students, I organised a retirement function for Prof. We tried to write to every graduate of UCC Music, and also established the initial Fleischmann Prize Fund, which still continues.

Thank you, Prof, for everything!

JOHN B. POWER (DUBLIN), UCC Music Graduate, Director of the Defence Forces School of Music
'Mr Power – you are incorrigible'.
How often I heard that remonstration during my three years as a student in the Music department of University College, Cork. The Professor, holding his throat in that peculiar way of his, always delivered it with a vague hint of amusement and anticipation. It was usually provoked by my unorthodox explanation of some harmonic device and by my attempts to relate the particular usage to the world of pop, jazz or film. The ensuing class discussion would elicit much bluster from the Prof while he proceeded to rail against what he considered to be 'not serious music'. However, we suspected that his indignation was not really in earnest and that he appreciated the diversion which incidents of this type allowed.

I first came across Professor Aloys Fleischmann at a lecture in the Imperial Hotel. The subject of the lecture was Richard Strauss' tone poem *Till Eulenspiegel*. I had just begun to study Dentistry at UCC and I attended the lecture in the company of a first year Music student – Mícheál Ó Súilleabháin. Although I had an interest in music, I did not have any momentous expectations for the night ahead. I was completely overwhelmed by the enthusiasm, clarity and involvement with which aspects of the work were revealed by Professor Fleischmann. He moved between tape-player and charts – all the while explaining details of form and orchestration. By the time the lecture ended I had begun to think that perhaps I should expand my knowledge of the classical music repertoire. I enrolled as a piano student in the Cork School of Music and attended as many concerts and recitals as possible. By the time I returned to university after the summer of 1970 my interest in matters orthodontic had taken second place to music. By Christmas it was time for a decision. I arranged an interview with Professor Fleischmann with a view to abandoning Dentistry and pursuing a musical career.

The interview demonstrated the practical side of the Professor's approach. In fact his advice was almost fatherly. He explained the precarious nature of the musician's life and pointed out what I stood to lose monetarily by giving up such a secure profession. It was obvious to him that I had 'burned my boats' by then. Having satisfied himself that I had some musical aptitude he agreed to take me the following year.

My memories of the Music department on the Western Road are all happy ones. Classes in those years were small and the atmosphere was warm. And at the heart of it all was the Prof. Arriving on his scooter. Bounding up the stairs. Corrections to strict counterpoint exercises. Octaves and fifths. The dreaded red pencil. Chalk-dust. Groups around the piano marvelling at his score-reading abilities. The old-world formality and courtesy. And always calm and patience.

In retrospect, I think that the attribute which I admired most in Professor Fleischmann was his kindliness. He was concerned for the individual and made allowances for my shortcomings. In later years our paths crossed infrequently. When we did meet he appeared to have lost none of his enthusiasm. He was still the Prof that I remembered – offering advice and suggestions. Ever interested.

His influence on my life has been considerable and in some intangible way which as yet I am unable to absolutely define, that influence goes beyond the purely musical. He seemed to belong to another time. A chivalrous and less self-centred time where certain things had a value beyond money and where obligation and duty were paramount.

ROBERT WELCH (COLERAINE, NORTHERN IRELAND), Poet and Writer; UCC Arts Graduate, Professor of English at the University of Ulster
I see him looking round the door of the Arnold Bax Memorial Room in the Music department at UCC. Bax's white bust staring into the umber shadows of this treasured place. We are gathered for our theory lesson, given by Seán Ó Riada. Fleischmann, the professor, is a somewhat remote figure for us, first arts students, taking Music. A swift presence, like a tremor on the air, a lightness.

Air. He wore a capacious overcoat of some waterproofed stuff. It was heavy, with cuffs and epaulettes of some kind, if memory serves. It was an airy coat, but protective, also, which he needed for the scooter. Buoyed up by the slipstreams of the air, he'd putter on his scooter up Summerhill in those days when roads and streets would be trafficless for minutes at a time.

Silence. That was part of his tonality. A form of silence that acted like a reminder of what was easily overlooked. A nurturing silence. Not a weight, or a hesitation. An urgent pressure to be, to be there, to make the instinct cohere to the moment. A presence.

When you entered that domain, those environs of the Bax room, the Music department, there was a sense that here there operated, as stricture and support, the institutions of law. Laws of form, laws of order, laws of music. No parallel fifths, however alluring that moody progression of sound. Laws rooted in the order of things themselves when they are as they are. Observe the laws of form, which are those of being itself, and wonder occurs: Bach waking up on a morning with the world in his head. The laws of the air, the laws of the slipstream, of moving bodies conforming to gravity defying the tendency, innate to us all, towards stasis, passivity, surrender.

Where does energy come from? What propels, impels, pushes, so that it must be realised or something falls away inside. It was visible in the flowing dance of his movements as his bodily charge animated the realisation of the music's laws, second by second, when the Cork Symphony Orchestra drove through his *Clare's Dragoons:* breathless vigour, the panting of horses, blood, victory sensed. For a moment, the great lord of death disregarded, as all that matters is the onward rush of life itself as it surges against fate.

From this silence, scrupulously conserved, from this adherence to the laws of being, from this onward rush, all seeking, all open: the quietness of his children, the sheer beauty of his daughters.

MARY HORAN (CAMBRIDGE, ENGLAND), UCC and Cambridge Music Graduate
There is a tendency, when reviewing the events of life as they recede into the distance, to lose a sense of perspective: the brighter things take

on a halcyon hue, the memory of which sustains us through many vicissitudes, while the less felicitous things somehow seem more intractable, bestowing retrospectively a hard-won wisdom that ensures a calmer maturity. Life as an undergraduate Music student at UCC in the mid-to-late 1970s had all the vicissitudes of mythical student existence. But looking back now, most of that past seems brightened by the memory of the special presence of Professor Aloys Fleischmann – the focal figure of student musical life at UCC – and the ambience of intense musical endeavour which he created.

Kindly, gracious and light-hearted, he was practically without exception respected and loved by all. In his habitual mien he was the epitome of the beleaguered and unworldly professor: begowned, and always in a hurry to fulfil the daunting set of tasks that comprised his daily ritual. But behind this abstracted exterior was a man of great dignity and courteousness who seemed to uphold an ancient code of chivalry. One of his endearing characteristics was that of quaintly addressing everybody in formal terms; no student surname was unknown to him. In his teaching he adhered to rigorous pedagogical standards with a fierce resolve. Weakness – in the sense of inability to produce impressive work – he always tolerated, but absence from lectures or the non-submission of the weekly compositional assignments in harmony and counterpoint – which he personally corrected and graded – elicited admonishments for long afterwards whenever one happened to cross his path! To the callow and arrogant undergraduate, it was not immediately evident that a much greater principle than the attainment of contrapuntal mastery underpinned his zeal: that what he really wished to inculcate was discipline – the steady and regular application to the materials in hand necessary for the accomplishment of any goal, scholarly or artistic.

In attempting to capture something of the essence of that unique time and place, it is well to describe the setting. The Music department was housed in the Rectory, a large Victorian house across from the College gates. Lacking the architectural grandeur of the main university buildings it had, nevertheless, a distinctive character and a congenial atmosphere. It is true to say that it owed much of its character and distinction, as well as its historical musical associations, to Professor Fleischmann. Over the years he had turned it into a conducive place for study, filling its pleasant and spacious rooms with pianos, while preserving its salient structural features and form. It seemed to have reached its zenith in the mid-1970s: the time when growing staff numbers and administrative demands would require the conversion of music rooms into offices was still some years away. The memorable visit of President Erskine Childers in the autumn of 1974, when he was shown about with pride and delight by the Professor, was a tribute to the place and to Professor Fleischmann's achievement in giving outward form to his vision of an institute of learning of the most enlightened kind. Enshrined at the heart of the building was the Bax Memorial Room. Legend had it that Sir Arnold Bax, who had acted as extern for many years, died suddenly in Professor Fleischmann's home after a day of examining in the Music department. Subsequently, some of his manuscripts were offered to the university on condition that a memorial room be established in his name. These manuscripts and other memorabilia – old pipes and an assortment of brushes and snuff boxes, as well as notebooks containing his literary efforts – were on display in this room. The centrepiece was the grand piano which Bax had bequeathed to the pianist Harriet Cohen; and on the wall above the piano was his death mask (cast by the sculptor Seamus Murphy), and a number of framed photographs, including one of Cohen and Ralph Vaughan Williams at the inauguration. In the 1950s and 1960s such luminaries as Edmund Rubbra, Arthur Bliss, and Benjamin Britten paid official visits. Music students had access to this hallowed place at all hours; overlooking the Mardyke and beautifully lit with the western evening light, it was a peaceful and inspiring place to work.

The other eminent presiding spirit in the Music department was the late Seán Ó Riada, whose memory had been honoured by the inauguration of a lecture room in his name. For those of us who arrived just a few years after his death in 1971, when the mythology surrounding him had grown to heroic proportions, there was a palpable sense of having missed a vital piece of Irish musical history in the making. Still, it was thought-provoking to consider that the composer of the music for *Mise Éire* had some twenty years earlier countenanced the self same harmony exercises that were our constant fare, and none too willingly it seemed!

Composition – traditional harmony and species counterpoint, progressing to canon and fugue in the final year – was central to the degree course. Considerable emphasis was also placed on orchestration, and the development of keyboard and conducting skills. But despite the predominantly practical nature of the course, lectures on the history of music and the repertoire, both classical and vernacular, were concentrated and wide-ranging. Professor's lectures, which he delivered in eloquent declamatory tones, were vivid, rich in classical reference (he had a special affection for Greek and Celtic mythology), and enlivened by anecdotes. The development of critical acumen was a central concern. He relished the beauty of the masterpieces and chose recordings of the finest interpretations by conductors such as Knappertsbusch, Furtwängler and Klemperer to introduce them to us in their noblest form. He sometimes illustrated short excerpts or harmonic sequences on the piano with an exquisite sense of nuance and cadence. While he was partial to all the late Romantics – Mahler, Elgar, Strauss and Bruckner, in particular – Wagner was held in the highest esteem. Woe betide the student who ventured into the *viva voce* for the BMus degree without a perfect recall of the leitmotifs of *Tristan*!

The training of teachers was essential to Professor Fleischmann's vision of the cultural role of a university musical institution. His mission was to send skilled, well-informed professionals out into the remoter parts of the country to instruct and enlighten. Music, he believed, could improve society: it developed the intellectual faculties, increased the learning abilities of children, and occupied people in a constructive and socially binding way. The success of his efforts to propagate music in provincial Ireland could be witnessed at the annual Choral Festival, when for a week in the spring former students from all over the country convened in Cork with choirs of their own. It was gratifying to see these choirs, often newly formed, or of a parochial nature – performing cheek-by-jowl with acclaimed choirs from cities such as Budapest or Tel Aviv, and competing to the highest international standards.

A highlight of the Easter term were the seminars on commissioned works which were held in conjunction with the Festival. Again, we were aware of the venerable tradition which underpinned this event: of the fact that among the past contributors were such figures as Darius Milhaud, Zoltan Kodaly, Egon Wellesz, Boris Blacher and Edmund Rubbra. The seminars took place in the Aula Maxima, and had, since time immemorial or so it seemed, followed the same procedural form: the commissioned work was performed by a choir of the composer's choosing, and subsequently subjected to minute and dispassionate analysis by the Professor. He seemed to have the gift of getting to the core of a piece. While the composition was being dissected at the piano, the composer – by now, like Eliot's Prufrock, 'sprawling upon a pin' – might disagree with the reading, or, as was often the case, admit that although he could now recognise the patterns or underlying schematic devices that had just been identified, he was in fact unaware of them when composing. Audience participation was welcomed, and on many occasions generated debates of the utmost relevance to the technical and aesthetic problems surrounding the composition of music in the twentieth century.

Professor's retirement in his seventieth year was a source of sadness for those who remained in the Music department. His departure to a remote room in 'The Maltings' was lamented by all whom he had encouraged and inspired. There he continued his research on the index of Irish folk music, in progress since the 1950s. True to form to the very end, he completed his magnum opus, *Sources of Irish Traditional Music – 1583-1855*, shortly before his death.

Níl agam ach guidh le h-intinn éagnaigh
Chum aingil is naoimh bheith síor da aodhaireacht.

ADRIAN GEBRUERS (COBH, CO CORK), UCC Music Graduate, Director of Music, St Colman's Cathedral, Cobh, Lecturer in Carillon, Music Department UCC, President of the World Carillon Federation
A Twinkle in the Eye
Of the many memorable aspects of Aloys Fleischmann's personality, the one which remains most vivid for me is his wry, almost mischievous, sense of humour. The whimsical look was never far from his gaze, the twinkle in the eye was very much part of the persona. Indeed, I sensed this central characteristic of the man long before I had met him for the first time. I remember my father returning from meetings of the Advisory Committee of the Cork International Choral Festival and regaling my mother with detailed accounts of how Aloys would bring the members around to accepting his choice of set pieces for the various competitions. It was obvious that Dad had a sneaking admiration for anyone who could thus triumph in a group of such independently minded musicians and still send everyone away feeling satisfied with the outcome. But then his diplomatic and organisational skills were justifiably legendary.

An essential part of that look was his spectacles. Indeed, we owe a debt to the unknown optician who always seemed to supply Aloys with glasses just that little bit too large, for he turned this apparent inconvenience into a genuine tool of expression! Any student who was ever at the receiving end of the professorial stare directed over the top of those ill-fitting frames could vouch for the veracity of this fact. One such occasion in particular stands out in my mind. Though normally the most punctual of people, a delayed flight from London had caused the Professor to be late for our lecture. At that time, UCC's Music department was located upstairs in the east wing of the quadrangle, now part of the administrative block. While not large, the lecture room would have been more than adequate in size for the small numbers reading Music in those days but for the fact that the space was also home to a grand piano. This instrument had belonged to the composer Arnold Bax, whose pianist friend Harriet Cohen had donated it to the Music department; it was thus considered something of a relic. To while away the time until the lecture eventually began, one of our class started vamping on the piano popular ditties of the day. Suddenly, the professor appeared silhouetted in the doorway like some figure out of Velasquez. The four words he uttered are forever seared into

75

our collective memories: 'And on Bax's piano!' And yet, even then, me thought I detected a slight sparkle in the eye!

A story concerning his early days at UCC is almost certainly not apocryphal, since Aloys himself was known to occasionally recount it. In the absence of permanent premises, the Music department was forced to occupy a series of temporary locations. This most unsatisfactory state of affairs finally came to a head one evening when the Professor and several students were accidentally locked into the Aula Maxima by a porter, unaware that they were occupying a corner of the hall! But for the climbing skills of one of the students, they could all have ended up spending the night incarcerated. Aloys was now more determined than ever to resolve this situation without any further delay. His search for suitable premises eventually brought him to a circular edifice close to the south-western perimeter of the college, in fact the observatory. Finding the door open and the building unoccupied, he ventured in to discover a small but adequate space for his needs. The necessary arrangements were promptly made. Several weeks later, a lecture was suddenly interrupted by the arrival of the professor of Physics at the door. Pointing a finger quivering with anger at the centre of the room, he demanded: 'Where is it?' The gentleman was enquiring for his seismograph. Unaware of its scientific significance, Aloys had unceremoniously removed this 'pole stuck in the ground' to make room for a piano. 'You wouldn't mind,' he quipped many years later, 'but the thing registered a major earthquake every time a bus passed along College Road!' And so, once again the Music department resumed its nomadic existence.

There was never any hint of malice in his dealings with others even if he viewed them, as indeed he surely did himself, as part of an idiosyncratic cavalcade of life. In truth, the Professor was a gentleman to his fingertips. And I can never recall seeing him at any formal musical function other than in full evening dress, down to the patent-leather shoes. This he obviously felt to be the minimum of courtesy due to the performing musicians.

In 1958, the organising committee of the Cobh International Carillon Festival commissioned two compositions from Aloys Fleischmann. Though these were his first works for carillon, it is a measure of the man that his *Toccata* and *Nocturne* were soon to become an established part of the repertoire. In later years, when I met Aloys at concerts in the Cork City Hall or elsewhere it gave him great satisfaction to hear of the latest performance of one of these pieces in Ottawa or New York or wherever. 'You know,' he once commented, 'little did I think that those two carillon compositions would turn out to be among my most performed works'.

It was in the Aula Maxima at UCC that I saw him for the last time, a little bit more fragile now. A few years later, in the same venue, I gave the dedicatory recital on the Music department's new carillon practice console. Naturally, a Fleischmann carillon composition was included in the programme. And as, thanks to the wonder of modern computer technology, his *Nocturne* rang out on the Cobh Carillon in the hallowed space of the Aula, it didn't take much to imagine the Professor sitting down there in the front row … and, yes, with that unmistakable look on his face.

2: The Educator of Teachers

Joseph Leake (Cork), UCC Music Graduate, Founding Director of the City Music College Outreach Network Cork

As a young schoolteacher in Dublin it seemed to me that every musician I met had studied with 'Prof' – as Professor Fleischmann was affectionately known to his students – and the general consensus was that the UCC Music department was the only place to study music.

Having written to him in early 1979, I was invited to be interviewed in Cork. I met him downstairs in the department: he was cheerful, friendly, businesslike and – in a hurry. 'Follow me', he said and disappeared upstairs. By the time I reached the landing, he was gone. I tried a number of doors and finally located him in the upper office. After a few words about my career to date I was admitted to study in UCC – no forms, no complications: just simple, straightforward and sensible. A slight hitch with the Admissions Office – they had no record of me – was instantly sorted by a call from Prof.

The UCC Music department had been run by Prof since 1934 and in 1979–80 – his last year – it was very much Prof's department. We were well looked after. The whole atmosphere there reflected him. His formal mode of address was the normal form of address from one student to another. Even now when I meet someone from my student days, we will often greet one another with mock formality and laugh over the good times. Fun, hard work, certainty, security – a real family atmosphere – characterised the ambience. Humour was one of Prof's great teaching tools. He used it to great effect after playing the slightly confused academic which allowed him to maintain strict control of his department and its students without appearing to do so. His lectures to us were often hilariously funny, always informative and often inspiring. He told us one day that his job was to train us to bring music to the general public. We would as it were 'spread the good news'. One day 'mischievously', and no doubt with tongue in cheek, he raised the ire of the mainly female music class by stating that he preferred to teach his two male students because the females would get married and give up their careers. There was uproar. He was highly amused. Nobody took offence. In fact shortly afterwards just before Christmas 1979 Prof was waylaid on the upper landing by a sizeable group of his female students and under some 'mobile mistletoe' hugged and kissed. He loved it. Prof's successor, Professor Wulstan, told me that Prof was very reluctant to retire. We were all very reluctant to let him go. We knew it was the end of an era. He *was* the Music department. Perhaps it was because he practised so fervently what he preached, i.e., writing, conducting, teaching and promoting music that he inspired so many people. You were in no doubt that you were in the presence of greatness and yet he was always so completely unassuming.

When Kay O'Sullivan and myself founded City Music College, Prof immediately wrote a letter of congratulation and support. Whenever we met he always addressed me by name – how did he remember all his students' names? – and wanted to know everything about my musical endeavours. I had the privilege of working with him in the Opera House when he conducted *The Fairy Queen*, a ballet based on Purcell's music, in 1985. I trained and conducted the choir for it. As ever, he was a pleasure to work with and got the best out of the singing group.

My two last memories of him were seeing him running along the Opera House bridge and dodging the traffic on the quay: he must have been at least 80. The last time I saw him was in City Music College as he was running up two flights of stairs. He was not in his traditional navy but wearing a lovely sports jacket. I congratulated him on how well he looked.

He is fondly remembered by generations of his students for whom life would have been much poorer without him. Many of them will be teaching well into the twenty-first century. His Choral Festival still flourishes. Indeed his contribution to the musical life of Cork is such that it is surprising there is no permanent and fitting memorial to his memory.

Ar dheis Dé go raibh a h-anam.

FLORENCE LINEHAN (ASTEN, HOLLAND), UCC Music Graduate, Music Teacher

> Had I the heavens' embroidered cloths
> Enwrought with golden and silver light ...

Often as I dwell on these lines, I find myself back in Cork as a student in the lecture room in the Music department, Western Road, with Prof (as we affectionately knew him) having handed back our homework, standing in front of the class, his left hand holding the front of his ageing gown, chalk in his right hand, his head to one side in anticipation of the next progression, we studying the possibilities. The exercise would be written on the blackboard and would be completed one by one by the class. The atmosphere in the class was always warm and amicable, kept vibrant by the witticisms and exchanges between teacher and class. After sometimes intense speculations about the possibilities and discussions about the impossibilities, the completed work would be sung by the entire class. Then someone would slip quickly downstairs to put on the kettle and return immediately to work until it was time for one of the class to suggest a break. And he would retort in a mischievous tone that we had too many breaks and they were 'far too long'. One of the class would bring him coffee and a chocolate gold-grain. And he'd protest about being spoiled. We'd happily go for our break but Prof never had a break. During that time he was available to students and as always there was never enough time.

Aloys Fleischmann, 'Prof', was an inspired man, a kind of Renaissance figure. A *carpe diem* man. He had a vision, a dream to be realised. He wanted to educate – *educare* – to lead his students in the discovery of music which he would define chuckling, quoting Johnson, as 'of all noises the least disagreeable' and – as Plato defined it – 'the movement of sound such as will reach the soul and educate it in virtue.'

The study of that 'movement of sound' would keep us fully occupied from now on, inspired by his dedication and discipline. We gradually began to realise that Prof was no ordinary professor. We could see that he always had lots to do. Yet he seemed to get energy from his work instead of losing it.

We discovered in those years how much his students meant to him. And we learned from each other how much he stood by his students in time of illness and trouble. He was more than an imparter of knowledge. He was a kind of father figure who believed in getting the best out of each student. He was critical but challenging and had a strong sense of humour to keep things in perspective, was quite absent-minded and could be very entertaining. He invariably corrected each student's homework twice a week. He knew the piano teacher of each student, had time to listen to each student play during the year and followed their progress with interest and often with witty or pungent remarks. He would turn up to recitals and concerts and sit among his students and chat with them as often as with other friends and acquaintances.

The Choral Festival was one of the highlights of the year bringing many musicians to Cork. This was when boundaries in music – if ever there had been any – melted away. 'Sine Musica Nulla Vita', as the canon goes which he often used in his audience participation. For UCC the highlight was the seminar in the Aula Maxima. This is where Prof revelled in the analysis of the commissioned works and the discussions that followed. Many a composer sat 'aghast' at what Aloys Fleischmann discovered in his work, not least the late William Walton who found it most intriguing and added to the conviviality with his quick wit. The atmosphere was one of welcome and belonging, even to the undergraduates who often found themselves out of their depth. Of course Professor knew that. It wasn't a problem to him. He would never use such a situation adversely. We were simply expected to be there! Prof was a highly disciplined man, unselfish, utterly unmaterialistic, above pettiness, had authority and exuded at the same time a childlike trust and simplicity.

He was always indebted to anyone who helped him in this great task he felt called to. Whether towards student, graduate or willing hand, he was motivated by respect and gratitude, and showed it. As young graduates many of us helped out and were in turn helped out by older experienced graduates in the Music Teachers Association. This group did excellent work in promoting standards in the teaching of music in all fields. Prof worked together with his graduates who organised courses for all types of musicians, bringing expertise from home and abroad to continue the education of teachers and students.

In my schooldays we had been fortunate to have a fine musician as music teacher. There we learned the basics of music literacy. Music was first sung, then played. For a young musician the aim was to open a score and be able to sing the music without accompaniment. This could be achieved by learning to listen, aural training; and that began by singing and knowing how to write down what one sang: first melody, then bass and gradually the other parts. Then came elementary harmony lessons. Although we didn't do music as an exam subject we had well-structured teaching on a 'sound' basis, if I may be permitted a pun. Good teachers will imbue their students with a love for their subject, a curiosity to explore further, an enthusiasm that demands energy and that repays in turn, and a good sense of criticism which ensures a constant growth. Our teacher was a recent graduate who had all those qualities.

In the 1960s the results of the work being done by Prof and his graduates from UCC were continuing to bring music to schools all over the province. Choirs sprang up in schools; children stayed on after school to practise singing, in choirs, in duos and trios. Schools began to see the value of music in the lives of their students; children discovered the riches of singing, sang songs at home and passed on the songs to others. I remember my sister singing a setting of 'The Lotus Eaters' with some friends. Their school choir was going in for the Feis. They loved the song, sang it tirelessly and taught it to others, complete in parts, for fun, which brought us all into further contact with the poem. Those girls loved their teacher, who was a gifted musician also imbued with the ideals of her Professor. And there were many such graduates. Not all the graduates went into teaching. Others went into research and we would often hear of their work from Prof, as many of them kept up correspondence with him. He found it all so stimulating.

Prof's whole life had been immersed in music in all forms but

81

song was one of the deeper veins. This was made apparent to me on telling him of a forthcoming recital of *Frauenlieb und Leben*. He told me of his mother's great love for Schumann and went on to describe the song cycle *Lied* by *Lied*, finishing by saying 'I'll bring the score to the recital, my dear, and we can share it.' And he did.

He would often recall seeing Richard Strauss in the Conservatorium in Munich during his student days. He loved the works of Strauss, not least his *Lieder*, and would bring them to life at the mention of any one of them, so deep was his admiration and understanding. The music of Vaughan Williams too had a place in his heart, as did that of Arnold Bax, both friends of his and his dear wife Anne. We would often listen to stories he told about the lovely times with these two great people, their interests, and their holidays together with the family.

When it came to his own compositions Prof was very modest. He once asked me to sing some songs of his so that he could record them. They were to be performed but the singer had 'found them rather difficult to read', so he recorded them to make it easier. He had a way with words which was the essence of courtesy, and always tinged with humour. His ballet *The Golden Bell of Ko* was performed during my student days and some of us sang in the chorus. That was a wonderful experience, musically, socially, aesthetically, from the practices to the last performance. But the experience I mostly associate with Prof, as teacher, composer, Irishman, was when he conducted *Song of the Provinces* and I sang in the chorus. It was an unforgettable experience to stand there with friends and be part of this great work. 'I found in Inisfáil the Fair' the beautiful melodic line, the rich colourful orchestration, the choir made up of people from all walks of life and trained by a gifted, dearly loved musician and graduate, the late John Murphy, the Cork Symphony Orchestra, which had existed for so many years under Prof's direction and with whom my mother played as a young violinist: all of this and a packed City Hall to listen and enjoy. This wonderful event was surely education.

But the one who caused this event to happen would turn up as usual next day at the Music department, the homework corrected and ready to return with comments. He would be as cheerful as ever, have a list of things to be done immediately (no time to waste). He would continue to follow his muse with an inbuilt stoic discipline, ever courteous and respectful to all his students, the 'Misses' and 'Misters,' as each had his title. They would be there waiting, ready to listen. There was no place for pomp.

The year would go on. The Graduates' Ball would take place in December where Prof would be the life of the party with games and limericks and lots of fun. Concerts would take place; exams would be taken before Extern Professors. There would be so much to be discovered, so much to be proved in research. The cycle continued. ...

These are just some of the myriad memories I and no doubt many of my fellow graduates cherish of our Professor, Aloys Fleischmann, who contributed distinguished public service to Ireland and Munster in particular. A man of intellect, vision and discipline, of high moral values coupled with a vulnerable naivety. We loved him dearly.

> But I, being poor, have only my dreams;
> I have spread my dreams under your feet;
> Tread softly because you tread on my dreams.
>
> (W. B. Yeats)

SISTER ROSARIO ALLEN (CORK), UCC Music Graduate, retired Music Teacher of the South Presentation Convent Cork. Anne and Ruth Fleischmann recorded the following conversation.

I had been a primary teacher for twelve years when my community decided they wanted somebody to do a degree in Music, and I was the chosen one, though I had only done grade 5 of the Royal Academy long ago and taken music at the Training College. When I went to UCC to be interviewed by Professor Fleischmann, I was terrified he would ask me to play. But he didn't: he was very nice; there was no question about his not accepting me. He would never discourage anybody and if he could help, he would.

It was new to me to be studying, to be going out on the street, to be attending orchestral practices in the evenings. He corrected our harmony and counterpoint at the keyboard. He'd be reading my bit of music and then he'd say: 'Sister, did you mean this?' And then his hands would go down and play something awful. And I'd say: 'No, Professor, I didn't mean that.' And he'd say: 'Ah, you meant F sharp, didn't you?'

I hadn't, of course. But he was so considerate about our feelings. The lectures were grand. If you frowned because you didn't understand something, he would always explain to you. He didn't have to often, because he knew what we were able for and he came down to our level.

The course went on for three years, which I enjoyed immensely, though I didn't have as good a foundation as I should have had. But Professor catered for that. He didn't mind, as long as you were doing your best and did your homework. Once when I was sick and wasn't able to go to College, I thought it would be a good idea to do extra counterpoint exercises at home. Poor Professor sat down at the piano and began to correct them. When he came to about the fifth one, I suddenly realised that I was putting work on him. But he did not say a word.

83

After I had got my degree, he asked if I would be on the committee of the Music Teachers Association. You were never commanded; it was always: 'Would you be so good as to ...?' He fascinated me. He'd be there at the meeting with a whole lot of music teachers, and he was the chairman. He was so interested and so anxious that music would be improved in the schools. He wrote letters to the principal of every school, and he would go to the Teacher Training Colleges to see whether the students were getting the proper training to teach music. He particularly deplored the fact that boys weren't being taught the subject in schools, and that music wasn't compulsory. He had the facts: that only so many per cent were being taught music, which wasn't an examination subject. Then when music and musicianship did become an examination subject, he pointed out that the pupils didn't have to have any background in music, that the course was geared to suit the listener rather than the performer. Some schools were doing very well, and he was always advising the principals. You'd think he'd nothing else to do. He might come to a Music Teachers' meeting at 7 o'clock, and at 8 he'd say: 'I must rush away now – we have a rehearsal for the ballet.' But when he was dashing out the door, if you wanted to ask him something, he'd listen to you. I don't know how he kept his mind concentrated: he was a remarkable man.

I was invited to be a member of the Choral Festival committee to represent the schools. Professor was such a good chairman, most agreeable to everybody, taking everybody's ideas; and even when people weren't so nice, he was able to manage them very pleasantly. He was always a gentleman: I never saw him ruffled. I'm sure he mostly knew what the best procedure would be, but he always listened to everybody, never putting himself or his ideas forward. He might give his reasons why something should be done, but he never insisted.

There was no children's competition at the Choral Festival for the first few years. When it did come, I put in a choir: there were very few school choirs at that time. But then the Schools' Competition grew and grew, and soon choirs were coming down from Dublin and other parts of the country, and very excellent choirs too. Professor would make sure to put in an appearance in spite of all he had to do at College. Whether you had success or not, he'd always write to thank you. He aimed high, but what I admired about him was his willingness to encourage if he saw people were really making an effort or if he saw that they had improved.

Our choir also performed for the ballet; Professor was very appreciative of that, too. We did Humperdinck's *Hansel and Gretel*: we were the gingerbread children singing, and there was an echo choir, so there were about ten of the children backstage – terrified. It was their first time performing in the Opera House. I remember the secretary of the Orchestral Society, Sheila Goldberg, writing afterwards to thank the children who, she wrote, 'not only sang like angels, but behaved like them too!' She didn't know that I was going around making sure they did. Later some past members of our school choir were in other ballets with adult choirs: for example the Polovtsian Dances from *Prince Igor* by Borodin. We joined Cór Cois Laoi that time because they needed more sopranos. Many years before that Pilib Ó Laoghaire had invited some South Pres. girls to join with Cór Cois Laoi in singing *Clare's Dragoons*, with Joan Denise Moriarty playing the bagpipes, in the City Hall.

The Professor did a lot to help improve the standard of church music. When Seóirse Bodley and Fintan O'Carroll and other eminent people were writing Masses, I asked him one day whether he would write a Mass. Though he said: 'Nobody would sing it', he did write one. He sent it to me in August 1972 with a note: 'I am almost certain you won't like it, and that – except for the Kyrie and Agnus Dei – it will be too troublesome for your choir. However, it is the best I can do.' There was a P.S.: 'Hope you will accept the dedication!' He was so humble: would I 'accept' – sure I was delighted! In September he sent me another hymn, and wrote: 'I meant to write something simple and straightforward, but it turned out quite differently to what I expected.' There was a P.S. this time about some hymns I had got from England, which I myself didn't think were very good, but I had sent them to him for his opinion: 'Am returning those hymns. What deplorable rubbish!'

His was a very difficult Mass. He told me it couldn't be simple. I had meant he should do a congregational Mass, but he composed it for juvenile or ladies choir. And I had the temerity to teach it to my children! He came along to the rehearsals, and of course he put the finishing touches to it. It was produced in our chapel; Christopher Stembridge played the organ – that will give an idea of the high standard: nobody else could have played that accompaniment. Professor conducted and we were squashed up in the little organ gallery, but he didn't mind. After that performance on Ascension Thursday 1973, I got a letter – he was always thanking you for everything. He said:

> I feel I must write, first of all to thank you most warmly for your kindness in putting on my mass, and the endless toil which this must have involved; and secondly to praise you and the girls of your choir for having mastered its difficulties so admirably, and for having succeeded in giving such an effective performance. I was quite astonished at the very favourable reactions, even of the most critically-minded people present, and having grave

doubts as to whether the mass is as well written as it could have been, I feel the enthusiasm must have been primarily due to the conviction of the performance, due in turn to the hard work which you and the girls put into it, and the remarkable feat of their singing it from memory. The whole service was a memorable experience, and I cannot thank you sufficiently for it, or the delightful hospitality which we enjoyed, both during and after! Please thank all your girls most heartily again for me.

He was so grateful to the children when he'd come for the rehearsals of anything we did, whether it was the ballet or the Mass. There would not be a move out of the girls: they enjoyed it immensely, even though they might be standing up on stools for maybe half an hour, but they were intelligent enough to see what the man was giving them. It was great music. The choir loved it: you would hear them singing it around the place later on. I remember Christopher Stembridge being surprised that children could sing it. But I couldn't have done it if I had not gone to College with the Professor, if I hadn't been his pupil. I wouldn't have dared, and I wouldn't have been able to read such complicated music. There was one bit in one of the hymns, where thirds were to come in on a B flat, and I never really was sure of it myself. But – they had it. Now, maybe I would hit the note on the piano just to help them in the beginning, but they could do it. And if they couldn't, Professor would get them to do it. I don't know how he managed it, but they always did it for him.

The *Mass for Peace* was easier. It was in unison. There were two other schools involved, St Vincent's and Saint Aloysius. He performed the *Mass for Peace* twice: in 1977 and in 1978. And again he wrote to thank me, as usual putting all the praise on the children instead of on himself:

> There seems to have been a very favourable reaction. Please thank your girls most heartily, and tell them that I have heard most enthusiastic reports of their singing from the most diverse quarters.

When the Presentation Congregation was celebrating the bicentenary of Nano Nagle's death in 1984, one of our sisters, Sister Déaglán de Paor, composed a poem 'A Naino Nógla' and she asked Father Pat Ahern of Siamsa in Tralee to put it to music. I thought the words and the music were great, but I wanted the Professor's opinion. He wrote:

> I think the hymn really excellent. It proves that pure pentatonic and the *sean-nós* are still very much alive. ... I would not like to see a note of it changed. The accompaniment will be important, and I would be most interested to see this – if I might have the privilege. I congratulate you on having secured such a fine and dignified hymn in the authentic Irish tradition for your bicentenary.

86

Then came a PS giving one tiny point of criticism: he'd let nothing go, but the praise came first and foremost. He wrote an accompaniment himself for the hymn.

He pointed out to us the inadequacies of some of the music which was being produced, and of some of the older hymns, like 'Oh Mother I/Could weep for mirth'. It nearly killed him altogether when they started having songs in church like 'Michael Row the Boat Ashore'. He gave us lists of the good hymns that we knew, which was very helpful. And then there was a competition announced for a hymn for Knock. He wrote a *Magnificat*, sent it to me and wrote:

> I fear it doesn't read easily, or smoothly, but it's the best I have been able to do. Would you ever look through it, and if you can suggest emendations which would make it more acceptable, I would be deeply grateful.

The humility of the man. He then came down to see me and played the *Magnificat* on the piano in our convent before he sent it away, as he wanted me to say what I thought of it. I had the audacity to suggest that one syllable would be better on a different note. And he took it and thanked me! I'm sure that's what he meant himself, but just had not written it that way. I had learnt from him the importance of detail, and he had done it in a hurry. But I couldn't believe it when he made the change immediately. Only two people had submitted Magnificats in Knock, and the adjudicators couldn't say which was the better, so it was a draw. I came home full of enthusiasm, hoping to teach it and have it performed, but that was not to be! I was very disappointed. But I still have it and it will be performed sometime, please God.

And then one day I met the Professor's daughter Maeve and asked how her Dad was. She said: 'Looking his 82 years.' I hadn't talked to him for a while: I hadn't dared encroach on him. The last time I saw him was some weeks before he died: that was at the concert in the Aula Maxima of UCC when his songs were performed – I always went to his concerts. I was at the funeral too, of course. I remember it rained dreadfully: even the skies were weeping.

At the UCC graduates' dinner organised for his seventieth birthday and retirement we sang Beethoven's canon 'Noble Be Thy Life'. I had suggested it: we had done it in the Training College long ago and I had kept the music. I felt this was really right for him: 'Noble be thy life, helpful and kind, yea kind, yea kind'. Noble was his life indeed, and he was most helpful and kind to all who had the good fortune to study and work with him.

JIM HORGAN (FURBO, CO GALWAY), UCC Music Graduate, Vocational Music Officer, Music Teacher. This account was recorded and transcribed.

I went to University College Cork in 1972. I had been studying accountancy at the Technical College and finding it heavy going working long hours all day, and then having to study more at night. It seemed a good idea to go to university to study there. My sister was in the College Madrigal Group and as they were looking for a bass I joined, although I wasn't a Music student. I was in good company with Mícheál Ó Súilleabháin, Nóirín Ní Riain, Seán Dunne, Sister Maura and many others. That was when I got to know the Music department. It was in some ways a bit frightening. It had all these rows of piano-practice rooms out of which poured glorious sounds of Mozart, Chopin, Debussy. I half expected Beethoven to walk out the door or Franz Liszt; but the people who had been making all this marvellous music were just gifted teenagers. It was a magic sort of place to be. It was also very successful at the time.

The Professor was very clever socially. He set up a common room with a little kitchen off it, where we could make coffee – that was something no other department had. Everyone got to know everybody else; in fact, students from other departments often came into the Music department for the coffee, so it was really the ideal university situation. I found myself very attracted to it.

I gave up Commerce and decided to try Music, because I had been in and out of the department at lunchtime for a whole year. However, I had never seen Professor Fleischmann. When I wrote to him, he invited me in for an interview. He dealt with me very sensitively, very politely – and very speedily. It took him about two minutes to discover I had a good ear; he saw at once that I was unable to sight-read, and he found out I had only done a small number of junior piano grades. But he said that he would take me on if I could get myself up to Leaving Certificate standard by September (this was June). He had assessed me thoroughly, applied himself to the problem, and made a decision all within five minutes. This was typical of him: he combined politeness, sensitivity, speed and great efficiency.

I started studying Music in September 1972 – there were no Beethovens, no Franz Liszts about the place: but many sensitive young people. The lectures were quite difficult, but always very pleasant: highly efficient and thorough, never intimidating in any way, and always great fun. In first year we had three hours of class on Saturday mornings. During the week, the classes were from three o'clock to six: this was to facilitate a substantial number of primary school teachers who wanted to take degrees in Music. Each of the sixty or seventy students did a harmony and counterpoint exercise every week: that meant

120 exercises to be corrected week after week by Professor. Never once during my time in the department did he fail to return our work at the next class, and he never missed a mistake.

The department was like a large, happy, extended family in which everybody worked very hard. Everyone was most dedicated: I never heard money or careers discussed; conversation always centred around some aspect of music. So, in the academic sense, it was an excellent department. But Professor was not an academic exclusively. Having searched high and low, he found a young lecturer called Christopher Stembridge, who was an organist and keen on performance. Professor set him the task of mobilising the whole department, which he did with great speed and efficiency, and formed a group called Pro Musica Sacra. Not only had he the whole Music department in it but musical people from all other departments and even outside the university as well. He made an enormous success of it. Pro Musica Sacra performed works of the highest quality. In first year, we did Bach's Cantata *Singet dem Herrn*, which has an 8-part chorus with orchestra. So the Music department was very active, with performances of all kinds all over the place undertaken by the orchestra, Pro Musica Sacra, the College Musical Society – which at that time was under Mícheál Ó Súilleabháin – the Madrigal group and a new Irish music group under Tomás Ó Canainn. In my first year in College, I think I was on stage twenty times. The Cork International Choral Festival has to be mentioned too in this context: from second year on, many students were conducting their own choirs and entering for the Choral Festival competitions as well.

I won the Rural Choirs Competition at the Choral Festival with the Kinsale Choral Society in 1975, and I was still celebrating at 3 o'clock in the morning when I met Professor. I was a bit embarrassed, so I offered him a drink out of the Cup straight away, as I couldn't think of anything else to say. He had a quick drink and said: 'Just the man I was looking for – you have your conducting exam tomorrow night at 8 o'clock.'

I said: 'I haven't finished my orchestration yet!'

'All right,' he said, 'come in at 9am and we'll do it together.'

So I did, and we got it finished, and I took the exam that evening. He made no concession to tiredness or to celebration or to anything else: you had to work.

Professor had a scooter: he loved dodging in and out of the traffic, because he hated any kind of waste of time. He'd come in on the scooter, make a little illegal run-up by the side of the department, and park the bike there. When he broke the windscreen once in an accident, he couldn't get a proper replacement: the newer screens were all too short. He would sit upright, totally straight-backed on the scooter, as a German would, and the normal windscreen only reached to his chin and let the wind go straight into his face. So he bought a big sheet of perspex, and he asked me if I would try to fit it on. I mobilised some of the Music department students; we got the complete works of Palestrina, made a sort of bridge with it on the floor of the common room; we steamed the perspex, and we all sat down on it on top of the complete works of Palestrina to shape the perspex into a curve. Then we fastened it on to his motor-bike and up it stood, straight as a die: he sat up behind it, also straight as a die, and off they went!

When I came close to taking the BMus exam, it was a boom time in Ireland. Schools were employing more music teachers in towns and there were Vocational Educational Committees where they had never been before, who were also taking on Music graduates. But it was becoming obvious that the new jobs were being quickly filled and that future graduates would be facing job shortages and a career crisis. Since as far back as 1954, Professor had been meeting Vocational Educational Committees with the intention of starting rural schools of music. Graduates had been trying from about 1954 to become active in this field, often with disastrous consequences for themselves. I know of people who were later to become distinguished in other fields of music who suffered huge hardship trying to work in VECs all day and then try to start schools of music in the evenings, working double shifts. The only school of music which worked was Pilib Ó Laoghaire's, so it was clear that rural schools of music could function, given the right support.

When I qualified Professor asked me if I would take on the job of staffing a rural school of music for the Waterford VEC. I accepted. I came from a business background: I had been a factory manager before I went to college; I was 30 when I left college. The Professor invited a delegation of the VEC to the university for an official reception. Some of the students played for them; Francis Waters' lovely madrigal group called Madrigal 75 sang, and Professor gave a talk on Irish music. We were then welcomed to the Cork School of Music by the Director, Miss Doolan. John Fitzpatrick brought us to see the Rural School of Music, which had been set up by Pilib Ó Laoghaire; in Cobh we were introduced to a teacher giving brass classes with great success. So we had seen the full range and at their next meeting, the VEC agreed to establish a school of music along the lines I was proposing. They already had a school of music, which gave mainly tin whistle, and accordion classes, music for céilí dancing, to get more people involved. Their main aim had been to promote the Irish language.

So in 1976 we set up the school of music, and started in Tramore,

Dungarvan, Ring, Old Parish, Cappoquin, Lismore; later on in the Comeragh Mountains, in Cool Na Smear and Kilbrine among others. At this stage the problem was to find enough teachers. So I went to the Music department in Cork and found excellent people who agreed to come down to Waterford and teach. But they had lectures in College in all kinds of subjects. I had to go to Professor and say 'I can start the school of music; I can enrol about 1,000 pupils, but I can't get enough teachers.' As usual, within a minute he came up with the solution: that they would have no lectures in the Music department on Thursdays, which meant the students would be free to go out and teach. This was marvellous. It meant I could go to Cork on Wednesdays, pick up the teachers, drive them down, give them bed and breakfast in my cottage in Ring and the next day drive them to the various centres. I also had to go to Cork on Saturdays to bring down music teachers. And I even went on Mondays as well to bring down a violin teacher for all the parish schools. At that time I was travelling 1,000 miles a week, every week, at my own expense, to build up the school of music.

The Professor was fully behind it. He had contacts in the Department of Education. At this stage, Peadar Killian was now Chief Inspector of all subjects; he had been a Music Inspector, so his dream had come true: he was at last in a position of power to do something about music. He had discussions with Professor Fleischmann; he came down and inspected my classes for a whole week. He sent me on courses for school orchestras during the summer months and was prepared to back the scheme to the hilt. At this time they discovered a similar project in Connemara, and one in Dundalk, which they also backed.

So within a short time, the Vocational Education Committee and Peadar Killian in the Department of Education sanctioned enough money to buy County Waterford instruments for a full orchestra. We bought 16 fiddles, a number of cellos and the traditional side-drums; we bought uilleann pipes, piano accordions, button accordions and brass. Schools of music now were being seen as a reality in rural Ireland: setting them up seemed to be a real possibility. After a few years our school of music had something like 1,000 children on stage every year. We were doing this with part-time teachers, bringing people down from Cork, from universities, supplementing the local teachers; but obviously it wasn't possible to continue like this: we needed full-time people. So Donal Kelleher, the Chief Education Officer, spoke to Professor Fleischmann and to as many influential people as he could and eventually Peadar Killian stuck his neck out and said: 'Advertise three full-time jobs'. We advertised in all the newspapers – but nobody applied for the jobs: nobody was interested in travelling the country from place to place to teach music. And so the unique opportunity was lost. Through the 1980s we were faced with financial cutbacks in government. Annually things got tighter and tighter, until eventually all VEC teachers had to teach ordinary VEC classes – and that was the end of the school of music as we had planned it.

The financing of schools of music outside the VEC system was extremely difficult. The school year for music teaching is very short: with summer holidays, Christmas holidays, Easter holidays, bank holidays and church holidays are taken out, what remains are three ten-week terms a year. That is a very short working year for anybody. The working day is also short. Children are in school until 3.30, so music teaching can start from around 4 p.m. and go on at the most to maybe 6.30 or 7.30. Another problem was the one-to-one teacher ratio which was expected in music teaching at that time – and still is today to some extent – which makes things very expensive indeed. The VEC rate at the moment is something like £18 an hour, which means teachers could live well enough for three ten-week terms, but then they face 22 weeks of unemployment. Another problem is the huge drop-out rate. You could expect maybe 30% to drop out after the first term alone. And if the music lessons went on into the month of June and the weather was fine, you could find yourself having a very lonely existence at the piano. Even with parents paying up to half the cost, a large subsidy would still be required.

However, there were some hopeful signs on the horizon. Mr Simpson in the north and Dr Bradshaw in Trinity were introducing us to the new Kodaly philosophy. This was a large body of methodology from Hungary, which makes music teaching possible in larger classes both in music schools and in primary schools. Another factor that gave rise to a lot of hope was the popularity of traditional music. This was becoming almost world-music and classes were springing up all over the country. Because it was folk music, it was possible to start on things like the tin-whistle, where you could teach maybe 20 or 30 at a time. It developed on to accordion classes, where you could take three or four at a time; and with the traditional fiddle you could also take large numbers in the early stages. So things began to look up.

However, a lot of research needed to be done on how to make the best use of this new methodology and this very significant feature of Irish music. So, working with the Irish National Teachers' Organisation in Waterford, we ran summer courses for primary school teachers, brought in Dr Holden from England and Dr Bradshaw from Trinity, and got more than 100 teachers on each of our INTO summer courses. The primary schools were benefiting enormously from the new methodology in Waterford; I was getting a great opportunity to study it, to try out the Kodaly method and traditional music together and to develop a methodology. However, it takes about eight years to get from Junior Infants to Sixth Class, so our research took all of that time.

It became clear to us that the Kodaly method is excellent and matches very well with traditional music. It is of enormous benefit to the primary school system to have good traditional music, excellent singing and sight-reading. Thus the technical side of music – all the reading and writing – and the oral work could all be done in school, which would be a tremendous help to the schools of music, because the children would already be musically literate before they get an instrument at all. So the future seems to lie in a greatly enhanced primary school system using traditional music as a mother tongue and moving on from there into a school of music. I am now working on an MA thesis with Professor Ervine in the Education Department of University College Galway. I wish Professor Fleischmann was alive to take the work a step further, but at any rate his spirit of energy and enthusiasm is still the driving force behind everything for me. So perhaps the story isn't finished yet.

Finally: a word about that driving energy. Professor's wife a number of times stopped me at concerts and asked whether I could do anything to stop him working too hard. She said that some day he was going to drop dead and be found somewhere, as had happened to his mother. At this time he was over sixty-five and driving himself incredibly hard. But I don't think he could have been stopped. It must have been like a dream come true for him to have this wonderful department working as well as it was after a whole lifetime's work. He told me himself that he worked very hard all his life, but that he always felt tired. People think that his tremendous energy came naturally to him. In fact, however, he was often exhausted, but never gave into it: he believed in that sort of discipline.

CANON G. H. J. BURROWS (DUBLIN), *retired Headmaster, Rochelle School Cork*
I regret that I am unable to furnish a full-length sketch of Professor Aloys Fleischmann, whom I remember with appreciation. In fact, in our severally busy lives he and I seldom met. Nevertheless, it is with pleasure that I write these few lines. I feel honoured to be associated, as a friend and contemporary, with this highly esteemed fellow-citizen of Cork, who shared with me the same year of birth, 1910.

Though our paths seldom crossed we shared a common area of interest, namely the introduction of the young to their cultural heritage. This was my vocation as a schoolteacher; this was part of his vocation as a professor of Music. We educators found a great ally in Professor Fleischmann in our concern to awaken interest in the heritage of music. Amid the claims of the musical world at a higher level

Aloys never neglected an opportunity to introduce the younger generation to the wealth of music which awaited them.

Aloys went to much trouble to arrange with visiting orchestras additional concerts for schools on the mornings after their public performances in the City Hall. At these informal concerts for schools he would give a running commentary, mainly explanatory, thereby stimulating the interest of the students. He had the gift of rapport with the young and I admired his skill in gaining their attention. I can still remember him introducing the bassoon, whose very name was music in itself, as it rolled off his tongue.

I remember, too, his courtesy and helpfulness whenever I would have occasion to arrange seating for students or friends attending concerts. Professor of Music though he was, minor details were never too trivial for his attention.

Cork was proud of its professor who held the chair of Music in its university for nearly fifty years. As a citizen of Cork I, too, held him in high esteem. I admired not only his musical ability but also the simplicity of his personal life. I well remember, for example, that, however severe the weather, he would be seen facing the elements on his scooter.

Aloys and I met for the last time at the Requiem Mass for Charles Lynch, the pianist, in September 1984. Aloys helped to shoulder the coffin and some of his friends were anxious lest he would over-strain himself. It was my final glimpse of him doing a good turn for some one. Now he himself has departed from this earthly scene. We are the poorer for his passing.

CANON GEORGE SALTER (CORK), Rector of St Luke's Parish
Soon after my arrival in Cork in September 1951 as Curate of St Luke's Parish on the north side of the city, I became acutely aware of the presence of Professor Fleischmann. I had, of course, heard of this man of music before I came to Cork and was fully aware of the contribution he was making to the music life of Cork. With the launching of the Cork International Choral Festival, which was largely spearheaded by him, ably supported by a willing band of helpers, I soon got to know him well. Being chaplain of the Actors' Church Union in Cork for over 30 years, this made it possible for me to have access to opera, theatre and choral performances in our city. Having a living interest in the Irish language and our Gaelic culture, Professor Fleischmann and I often had interesting discussions on this exciting subject. It was a great joy that he pursued this deep interest in Irish culture over the years and brought a great deal of it to reality in the performances of the Irish Ballet Company in co-operation with Joan Denise Moriarty. We had

numerous discussions on church music and he was always advocating high standards – such standards were the hallmark of his performances with the Cork Symphony Orchestra. He supported the idea of the availability of churches for the performance of sacred music by visiting choirs and this brought a breath of fresh air into our churches in Cork from the 1960s onwards. We saw the expansion of the department of Music in University College, Cork under his direction and its moving to new premises on the Western Road. Above all for me, my memory of him will be his sheer courage and determination in initiating the Cork International Choral Festival and bringing it to a position of recognition worldwide. Cork is justly proud of Professor Fleischmann as a Freeman of our city.

COLUM Ó CLÉIRIGH (DUBLIN), UCC Music Graduate, retired Senior Lecturer of Music in St Patrick's College Drumcondra
Shortly after the end of the Second World War news came to my hometown of Clonmel that a famous professor from University College, Cork was coming to give an illustrated lecture on music. I was then eleven years of age, with little interest in school except for my music classes; my teacher, Nellie Reidy, suggested that I should attend the Fleischmann lecture.

Clonmel was a town which boasted of two thriving choral societies, an amateur dramatic society, which ran many plays and brought a variety of theatre companies to the town – it was one of the first theatres in Ireland to show Beckett's *Waiting for Godot*. The enthusiastic young director Brendan Long, later editor of *The Nationalist* newspaper, was a great collector of Wagner's music and a fan of Fleischmann's. Famous musicians had also visited Clonmel in the past: Franz Liszt, for example had stayed at Hearn's Hotel, owned by the famous Italian Bianconi, who ran the first horse drawn buses in Ireland. Now it was, so to speak, the second coming with the Fleischmann arrival. His mother Tilly, as I discovered later, had been a pupil of Franz Liszt's last pupil Stavenhagen.

Fleischmann had a magical, warm clear voice. We were all split into groups and for the first time I learned what a canon was. We sang a German hunting round, simple but great fun. At one stroke he had the full attention and practical involvement of his audience. This for me was my first lesson in a practical approach to teaching and learning. It has sustained me throughout my teaching life. The magic and beauty of the German language was the next treat on the menu. It was his account of *Lieder* singing as he translated for us the very fine Richard Strauss song, Op. 27 No.4 'Und morgen wird die Sonne wieder scheinen': I was totally bowled over. I had never heard anyone make such musical sense, and in such an unawesome manner: music became so accessible in Fleischmann's hands.

I felt that as a mere schoolboy I had no place there and was about to leave when Brendan Long asked me if I would like to meet the Professor and have a cup of tea. They were discussing some aspects of the *Leitmotif* in Wagner's operas. I stood in awe with my cup dancing a jig on the saucer from nervous tension coupled with the fact that I had no idea what type of animal or instrument a *motif* was. Then came Fleischmann to the rescue; all kindness and curiosity to know what my interest in music was since I was the only schoolboy present. I found it so easy to talk to him: he was just like a friendly uncle with a genuine interest in helping to open new doors of perception. When I returned to school, I took a totally new interest in both English and Irish poetry, because of those *Lieder* songs. I took part in all our musicals and theatre productions and read everything I could find in our local library concerning opera and the lives of the great composers.

I continued my musical studies, took some diplomas in music and became a teacher at the local high school. In 1954 the first International Choral Festival was announced as part of a nationwide Festival called An Tóstal. This Choral and Dance Festival, the brainchild of Professor Fleischmann and others, is still going strong after nearly 50 years. I've only missed one Festival in all that time. To Fleischmann and Pilib Ó Laoghaire I owe my commitment to and love of choral music. I next met Aloys Fleischmann when, with others, I helped to bring the Cork Ballet Company to Clonmel. During a walk to show them to their hotel Fleischmann asked me if I had any interest in doing a BMus degree at UCC. This man was totally dedicated not just to music, but also to music education and its position in our school system.

The Prof, as he was affectionately known, was a very practical musician in all respects. But there are ample stories about how very impractical and even naive he could be about mundane matters. He expected everyone to be diligent and totally adaptable like himself, and where there was a will there were always many ways. He called me to his office one Christmas just as I was about to go home for vacation. 'My dear man, would you ever be so kind as to help me to deliver this bass drum to the City Hall? I need it for *Cinderella* tonight, and by the way here's the xylophone: would you take it to Clonmel? I need you to play it for the ballet.' All said in one breath. Well, we took the bass drum: me as pillion rider on his scooter, with drum, which proceeded to slip under a bus but was retrieved by Prof while I held the scooter. I then took the train to Clonmel with my great big xylophone, to be met by a taxi driver who said: 'Man! aren't them quare blocks of kindlin' to be bringin' your poor mother for the fire, an' they all tied up with ropes too? Ha! I think that aul' university is doin' strange things to yer head.' I still have the programme to prove that I was once upon a time the xylophonist for the Cork Symphony Orchestra.

Prof's music course at UCC was a broad course which helped to form the basis for a sound knowledge of most aspects of music. In addition to harmony, counterpoint and music history there was also orchestration. He insisted that each year we would arrange or compose for the local symphony orchestra. Not alone that, but we had to get up in the Aula Maxima and conduct for an audience, sometimes with cacophonous, eerie results and somewhat frayed tempers on the part of the players. I had once written a highly florid solo passage for violin at presto speed with quirky bowing, which was to be played by the leader of the orchestra, Dorothy Foley. We were doing the run through rehearsal and I was conducting. She suddenly stopped; in her somewhat shrill high-pitched voice, ignoring me completely, she said: 'Look here now, Professor, does this fellow think I'm a Yehudi Menuhin or something?'

The Professor: 'Oh! but my dear Miss Foley, I think he is a bit nervous!' and then to me: 'My dear good man, would you ever be so kind as to drop that an octave and perhaps take it at a slightly slower pace, if you don't mind, just to see if it's an improvement?' I was none too pleased that my masterpiece was being butchered. A most tactful and persuasive man, he always sought to calm troubled waters.

We were the only third level college in the country for many years that had such a course. Also added to this was a course and examination in physics, i.e., acoustics. and in the final year aesthetics and musical criticism. Thus we were prepared to go out to schools with a certain informed sense of music education. He also selected extern examiners of international quality and academic standing. I had that fine English professor and composer Sir Edmund Rubbra for my finals. Other examiners were Sir Arnold Bax, Sir Michael Tippett, Roman Vlad and many other famous composers and academics. Apart from his very interesting lectures, he had a profound knowledge of and interest in many types of literature in many languages.

He had some 'blind spots' – jazz for instance. He once said to me, when I showed a particular interest in that genre of music, that it was music from the whorehouses of New Orleans! Both myself and other students had regular rows with him on this topic. I also felt that he was concerned with having a more vocational rather than academic approach to his students. However, it should be said that this sprang from his utter commitment to producing good general teachers rather than an elite small group of academic high flyers. This was a very necessary service to the country's schools. I can now say this quite authoritatively, having been an examiner of the Leaving and Junior Cert. practicals for many years. Most of the best performing choirs in all four provinces were taught by teachers who were former students of Fleischmann's. Of course, many of us who were interested went further afield to other universities and institutes of higher learning to pursue post-graduate studies in specialist areas, and mostly with the Prof's approval and sound advice. In later years he produced his fine crop of home grown postgrads.

It was Rubbra, Fleischmann and Ó Laoghaire that directed me towards music education studies in England and choral studies at the Zoltan Kodaly Pedagogical Institute in Kecskemet, Hungary and to the Ferenc Liszt Academy in Budapest. Here I felt I had come full circle since studying piano with Prof's mother Tilly. Later when I became senior lecturer in Music at St Patrick's College in Drumcondra, I founded the International Kodaly Society in Ireland, running two international three-week seminars in 1983 and 1985. Professor Fleischmann was most supportive on both occasions: he gave lectures and brought his entire staff.

He took a paternal interest in all of his students, even to the extent of being concerned about their health and general welfare. He was most patient and kind; even having to give a mild rebuke to a student seemed to upset him. When the Prof died, I lost a true friend.

The late BRIDGET DOOLAN, *UCC Arts and Music Graduate, former Director of the Cork School of Music, on Donna O'Sullivan's Cork Radio Programme on 29 April 1978*
When I first met Professor Fleischmann I had come up to University College Cork from Waterford to do an Arts degree with Music as a subject in first Arts. So I went along for interview to Professor Fleischmann, as I did to all the other professors of the subjects I was taking and, before many minutes had passed, Professor Fleischmann had encouraged me to do a double degree. From then on his enthusiasm and his encouragement meant that Music, instead of being just one subject among many, came to be the dominant subject during my time at university.

It was first of all his own infectious enthusiasm, his tremendously wide-ranging knowledge and his ability to be interested, not alone in what he was teaching, but in the development of every student he had. Now admittedly at that time we were a tiny department: I think in the year before me there was just one – the late lamented and very great musician Seán Ó Riada. But in my year we were five, quite a vast number for those days. For each of us the Professor had the ability to draw out of us what was best in us. His wide-ranging knowledge meant that he could present the earliest music – Ockeghem, Obrecht – and the most modern that we would come in contact with at that time – Schönberg, Hindemith – and convey the same enjoyment and enthusiasm for all of them. One never came away with a sense of personal prejudice in him for any particular branch of music.

He was a very young man to be professor. I spoke of his infectious enthusiasm, and must also speak of his energy. We've all seen the evidence of this in the Choral Festival, the Orchestral Society, and all the manifold things that he has got underway here in Cork. I remember if we were sitting waiting for a lecture – which we were very rarely doing, as Professor was usually there on the dot – but if we were and we heard footsteps coming, we always knew if it was Professor, because he was running, he was taking at least three steps at a time.

You notice I call him Professor. That was something which came out very soon in my time at University College Cork. I had other professors; I was taking an honours course in French and in English, and I found my lecturers and professors there also very stimulating, but there was only one person whom one called *the* Professor, and that was Aloys Fleischmann.

The late BRIDGET DOOLAN on John Quinn's Radio 'Forum' in April 1980
It is a difficult assignment to sum up a lifetime's work in a few words. But I would say that Professor Fleischmann's basic achievement is that his graduates are to be found in every field of music education in the south of Ireland, in fact throughout the land. His degree course is arguably the strongest in the country. I think his aim has been to educate specifically for the teaching profession and for this he has set up a course which produces graduates who can teach in secondary schools. The instrumental tuition taken outside the university is also covered by graduates. In fact in institutions such as the Cork School of Music almost fifty per cent of the staff have degrees from University College Cork.

But it is I think on the secondary level that his main contribution has been: there he has succeeded in flooding the market with graduates. In the primary sector he has always encouraged primary teachers to come and take the degree course, believing that a teacher, even in a non-specialist area such as primary school, will give a better music class if they are graduates and have a full academic training, and in this he has succeeded admirably. So I think without him there would be virtually a desert; it is really due to this one man that music in education, certainly in Munster and in very many schools throughout the country, is in a very healthy state.

I first met Professor Fleischmann in 1974 when I applied to do Music as part of first Arts at UCC. I had qualified as a primary teacher and was teaching full-time at North Presentation Primary School. I hadn't studied music in school for the Leaving Certificate and had only studied piano to grade 5, but not during the final year at school, and not in the Training College. So before the audition I had a few lessons from a student to prepare a piece to perform. For harmony, I bought a book to find out what chords and triads were! Another student friend of mine helped me prepare for the harmony assessment. I really felt I had very little chance of being allowed to study Music, and was amazed when Professor Fleischmann said he was prepared to give me the chance. I feel that anyone else or any other college would have totally dismissed me. At the end of first Arts, Prof invited me to study for a BMus. I am so grateful to him for the three years that followed, which were the most exciting musically, and the most enjoyable years of my student life.

One characteristic which impressed me so much about Prof was the regard in which he held each student. Whether you were a brilliant musician or a mediocre or very inadequate student, he treated everyone equally and with total respect. Even though he never addressed any student other than formally, and this could have made the Music department quite a cold and impersonal place, the opposite was true. The Music department had a family atmosphere and was a really happy environment. Prof was always in good humour as he zoomed about the place, taking a few steps of the stairs at the time, and then tearing off on his motor-bike, without a helmet! (I had a motor-bike too and spent quite some time admonishing him on how irresponsible it was not to wear a helmet: a useless exercise!). He always seemed in a hurry and, at the same, had plenty time for his students. He was always totally charming, disarming and very dignified.

Professor Fleischmann was very encouraging of any of our efforts at music-making. He would always try to find something encouraging to say after a concert. If the performance left a lot to be desired he was never disparaging but would talk about the musical composition rather than the performance. I remember every time I conducted my rural choir at the Choral Festival, he was always the first person to meet me at end of the stage steps to shake my hand and say 'Well done!' It amazed me that a man in his position and with his commitments not only kept track of our musical efforts but took the trouble to recognise and encourage our efforts.

The state of music education in Ireland was of great concern to Professor Fleischmann. He was utterly committed to improving the situation at all levels but particularly at primary level. He felt that to make any impact on the music education system, one had to start with primary schools. This was the reason he went to such great lengths to accommodate primary teachers who wished to study Music, by organising lectures after school hours and also on Saturday mornings. How he got the full-time students to agree to this I'll never know, but then again it was impossible to refuse him. His causes always had the noblest of motives and his arguments were so plausible that one couldn't refuse.

I worked with Prof on the Board of Cumann Náisiúnta na gCór, during which time we got permission from the Department of Education to run a pilot scheme. This scheme allowed a number of primary teachers who were very successful at teaching music to visit other schools (at the schools' request) and demonstrate teaching techniques to the teachers in their own classrooms over a period of several weeks. Eventually the 'trainees' would take over the class, as their confidence grew and the visiting teachers would act as advisers. This scheme operated in Cork for two years. Prof was so enthusiastic about it. When the report on the scheme was completed he actually took it with him on a visit to President Mary Robinson and placed it on her desk. He never tired of knocking on doors and endlessly pursuing those who had the power to make a difference, in an effort to improve music education and make music available to all young people, so convinced was he of its benefit to the development and advancement of the human mind.

Professor Fleischmann's commitment to choral music speaks for itself in the wonderful success of Cork International Choral Festival. There is no doubt that it would not have survived the many years of financial difficulty were it not for his infectious enthusiasm and his refusal to see anything other than success and survival. In the early 1980s I joined the Artistic Board of the Choral Festival. My main area of involvement is in organising the schools competitions. To see the increase in numbers of school choirs and adult choirs throughout the country and the huge improvement in the standards of singing over the years is quite amazing. Prof would be so proud of the achievement. He has left a wonderful legacy to choral singing.

I find it hard to speak of Prof in anything other than superlatives. I know I speak for all the students in my time when I say that we all looked on him with huge admiration, awe and respect. The truth is we all loved him and we were all the better for having known him. He had a major influence on our lives. He was an absolute gentleman and I am so grateful that our paths crossed.

VERA KENNY NÉE JONES (CROOM, CO LIMERICK), UCC Music Graduate, Music Teacher

I first met Professor Fleischmann – forever afterwards to be known only as 'Professor' or 'Prof' – in 1957 when I attended my first lecture as a student in the small Music department situated above the president's quarters in UCC. I had heard stories of the aloof seers who lectured to their students from their God-like heights, so it came as quite a shock to see the young, vibrant, energetic man who bounded into the room and who taught, not lectured. Prof was an excellent teacher, one who inspired and encouraged, but he was quite a hard taskmaster and expected all given exercises to be done, indeed more than once I missed a good party because these exercises had to be handed in the next day, which necessitated, for me at least, long hours of hard work. I wish I had kept some of them – each time I was hopeful that they would be returned with few corrections, but each time they were returned covered with red marks and gentle remarks such as 'but how could you write so many augmented fourths?' or 'you must hear your work, my dear!' How could I confess to him that I found it difficult to hear the harmonies in my head? If the truth be known, I was not a great musician and might not have managed the course had it not been for Prof's guidance and constant help. In later years I tried to model my teaching on his – the occasional joke, the endless patience and the determination to keep the standard as high as possible. I also tried to pass on to my students the love of music which he had passed to me.

After I left College I was out of Ireland for a few years and so had little contact with UCC or the Music department there. I returned to Ireland in 1966 and Prof came to visit me. I never knew, nor asked, how he had discovered that life was difficult for me then, but he arrived and offered me his panacea for all ills – hard work. I was to do a Master's degree in Education, taking an aspect of music as my thesis. When this fell through, he cajoled me into writing a book for teaching music to students at primary school level. It certainly was hard work, but I must confess that I loved it. I made some good friends through it and felt a sense of achievement that gave me new confidence as a teacher and as a person.

During the late 1960s and early 1970s great thought was given to music in education and a syllabus was put in place for secondary schools. Needless to mention, Professor was very involved in this and I was delighted to find that he was agreeable, indeed anxious, to listen to the views of teachers, mine included. We sometimes met and discussed, for long periods of time, what would be suitable and good for the syllabus and I'm proud to say that some of my ideas were incorporated into it. I felt very strongly then, as I still do, that we need an educated audience, and Syllabus B of the Leaving Certificate gave just that. I still thank Professor mentally when I meet former students at concerts and I see their enjoyment and enthusiasm.

At this stage I was teaching in Limerick and the highlight of our year was the class outing to the ballet in Cork. The students loved it and loved to go back stage to meet the dancers and sometimes Joan Denise Moriarty and of course Professor. He was always unfailingly kind and generous with his time and answered all their questions with great courtesy, though he must have heard the same questions many many times. During this time he sometimes took time out from his busy schedule to visit my family and me. We sometimes went off to a local beauty spot or historical site. I had a romantic, slightly vague notion of the history of these places, which did not please him. 'How could you know so little about your own county, my dear?' He even went so far as to buy me a book *Portrait of Limerick* by Mainchin Seoighe, which still has pride of place in the sitting-room, but we did not come to an agreement on our ideas and I confess I still cherish my dim twilight of myth and legend to his preferred daylight clarity of facts and figures.

Once I accompanied him to Galway: he was giving a lecture in the university there and was kind enough to include me in the outing. We stopped at Coole on the way there. It was not then as tourist orientated as it is today, but we loved it, saw the autograph tree and walked to the lake. I said as much as I could remember of 'The Wild Swans at Coole'. The beauty of the place, the sense of history and the lovely music of the poem make that day forever a cherished memory.

As the years passed and Prof got older and my responsibilities broadened I saw less of him. We met occasionally; one of the best meetings was a reunion here in Limerick organised by Deirdre Hanley – a past pupil of mine and a graduate of the Music department of UCC. I think Prof really enjoyed himself that night. There was the inevitable singing of rounds and canons and, as there was a large group of alumni, there were many stories of college escapades and cherished musical memories of embarrassing or funny moments during lectures, orchestral practices or social gatherings, all of which brought home to me again how charismatic this man was who, seemingly so easily, gained the respect and love of such diverse people.

When I heard of his death I could not bring myself to go to Cork. I wanted something more personal. I went to Lough Gur – the scene of one of our trips and as I stood beside that lake I bade my own private farewell to the Professor I had known – musician, teacher, gentleman and friend.

AIDAN O'CARROLL (TRALEE, CO KERRY), UCC Music Graduate, Director of the Kerry School of Music and Performing Arts. This was recorded by Anne Fleischmann.

When I went to University College, Cork I had to decide between studying Music or Mathematics. I had the good fortune to be able to turn to Father Pat Ahern, who of all of Dr Fleischmann's students made perhaps the greatest impact on me, musically and theatrically. But he was reluctant to steer me in any particular direction, so I went to UCC none the wiser. When I went in to register for the degree course madness prevailed, and I put down Music. At the first meeting with the staff in the Music department, Aloys Fleischmann made an entrance not unlike Dracula, with cape flying, larger than life. He was very kind, very paternalistic, and most active movement-wise, thus keeping students alert all the time. We got straight down to work. I was overawed by the presence of people who had had an ideal musical upbringing, whereas I had just come out of the mountains with an immense interest but very little formal tuition in music.

He recommended that I should take piano lessons from Mrs Geraldine Neeson. When I attempted to play the Chopin *Nocturne in E Flat* for her, which now most ten year olds have in their repertoire, she said: 'Well, there's no doubt about your musicianship, but you don't know how to play the piano. Would you like me teach you?' It took nine solid months until I could eventually say to her with sincere humility: 'I am now ready to start learning.' I eventually came to a point after a number of years of study when Aloys Fleischmann advised me to consider a career as a concert pianist. Once I had picked myself up off the floor in shock I said I would be prepared to try. I did so over a year while I was doing my postgraduate work, but it was not for me.

When I did the first section of my final exam I was very involved with Siamsa Tíre and was scheduled to go with the company to America to do a concert tour standing in for the principal dancer, who was unable to travel – normally I was the second dancer. That meant I would have to take on the responsibility of the tour with 32 shows in 28 days. Prof allowed me do my practical examination before the other students to make that possible. I worked myself to the bone during the summer, and I was the first male undergraduate to get a first class honours degree. He was always totally and utterly engaging. We knew that there were about ten other things on his mind all the time, but his lectures always started on the hour and finished on the hour; there was never five minutes taken for something else and I have no memory of him ever leaving the room to accept a phone call. He was meticulously fair, especially when students had to be made to repeat.

All our exams were in September so those who did not pass had to repeat the year. We had to do up to twelve exams, including practicals, but it never seemed to bother us. He was always so helpful, so sympathetic to those students who he knew he could not pass. I do not know of any of them who came out feeling that they had been wronged.

Behind his formality, there was enormous humour. There was a nun in our year who took the whole class under her wing and would remonstrate with Prof if she thought he was setting too much work – he set work once a week for harmony, once a week for counterpoint; there were analyses and essays to be written and reading was expected. He would enter into mock negotiations in front of the class with great humour and eventually a compromise would be reached, leaving everyone happy. Everything was done theatrically. There were no demeaning encounters with students: never in public and I have never heard of any happening in private. He had a fatherly talent. There were thirty in my class: a very happy class. He always made sure that there were no tensions among the students. We knew there was always going to be fun in his classes so nobody would dream of missing them.

I do not think he was ever a trained dancer, but his energy was tremendous. He could transfer his weight up and down the stairs extraordinarily rapidly. One of my most vivid impressions was of how he could get from one place to another in a room while one would still be looking at his first position. I have never forgotten the expression that would come over his face when he was suddenly inspired with a thought, perhaps by something that had just been said. It was as if he was looking at light. Scientists and psychologists say that intelligent people constantly need light to stimulate the processes. It was striking how he would look into the distance in a room of thirty people for about five seconds and then something very significant would come out.

The fact that he had been trained in Germany, that he had studied where Richard Strauss taught, was exciting for us and lent his views an immense authority. He was rigorous in his teaching. His teaching of the Fuchs system in counterpoint was one of the most important influences on me during my time in UCC. His insistence on harmonic analysis from a traditional point of view gave me a rigour and a discipline in approaching all music: I feel deeply indebted to him for that. It is fashionable nowadays to dismiss the Fuchs system, but I think that anybody who wants to know anything about music should be conversant with it.

The other outstanding memory for me is Joan Denise Moriarty and the Ballet Company. I first came across Joan Denise many years before meeting Prof. She was fascinated by Siamsa because she was approaching the same artistic issues but from a different angle and standpoint. She was extremely gracious. She did not see the more rural and arguably authentic base of what Siamsa was doing as a threat to her. I know that she was very supportive of Father Ahern: I think it was she who helped to secure us an invitation to perform in the Opera House, which we did for the best part of a week to packed houses. We were all invited over to her studio in Emmett Place. I have a lasting memory of this extraordinary woman, of a face that even a great artist could not have sculpted or chiselled to show the pain of life: those enormous eyes, constantly engaged in a search for light; the head always raised, not in arrogance, but because of the ideas she was aiming at high up out there. She was remarkably elegant, and thin as a lathe. We were shown the dance studio and the costume rooms. I thought they were among the most beautiful things that I had ever seen. She was one of those people who stood apart: she was always with you, but always detached, preoccupied.

I did not meet her again until I was in my first year at UCC in 1973. That year I had for the first time heard the National Symphony Orchestra play at the City Hall and was utterly overwhelmed. Not long afterwards I went to a performance by the Cork Symphony Orchestra with the Cork Ballet Company and saw ballet dancers for the first time. I had never heard such music before; the beauty, economy and expressiveness of the movement made an indelible impression on that boy from the bog. In the mid 1980s I hounded Joan until she established a ballet school in Kerry in 1987 with her teacher Sinead Murphy. There are now 300 students attending at three centres.

I think that in Joan Denise Moriarty and Aloys Fleischmann there was an extraordinary meeting of minds, of aspiration, of inspiration. They were thrown together by a happy accident of time, of place, with similar perspectives, aims and ideals. I have never seen a collaboration like it: it was one in which there was not a trace of opportunism on either side. I was fortunate enough to have been constantly in their company for about six years: their unique spiritual bond was to me deeply impressive, indeed awe-inspiring. Joan was a most remarkable woman. I continued to have a direct association with her right up to the time of her death. Even when she was in considerable pain she was always so gracious, but also remained uncompromising with regard to discipline and standards. She was a very strong woman. If at the time she founded her school it was regarded as a sin to be a formidable woman, then she was a very grievous sinner. I found her utterly inspiring.

Watching Prof was a lesson in interpersonal management, in people-skills. If in a particular situation he saw that the course he was on was not going to get him any further, he would immediately change tack and do something unexpected, something that would take people off their guard and suddenly make them realise just how pompous, conceited or officious they were being, and yet he would let them down without any humiliation. He was also a tremendous fighter. I know that from what he told me himself and what I have heard about his extensive correspondence, his letters to the Pope and to so many other authorities. Sometimes one has to make a bit of a fool of oneself to make a point, and the disregard for protocol that comes with age was quite deliberate: he was an awesome master at that.

He was always acutely conscious of the needs of music in Ireland. He told us students we would achieve most by going back into our own communities. He warned us of the difficulties that would lie ahead: of the apathy, the outright hostility to attempted change and to any perceived interference, whether by the Department of Education or other institutions. He told us there was a good fight to be fought out there, and to go and do it. Many graduates were inspired by him, many of them highly talented people who chose obscurity in the knowledge that they could make a far greater contribution by doing so. I meet them occasionally, teachers who are doing tremendous work in their own schools. But it is not outreaching into their immediate communities as it could do, and I believe that it is now time to create a model that can be replicated around the country. We have tried with the Kerry School of Music and Performing Arts to bring music and dance into the communities. I wish this were happening everywhere because it would transform the face of music in the country. At the moment there are about fifteen hundred people availing of our services. It is probably the largest privately organised performing arts school in the country. I think Prof would be pleased.

It is unfortunate that so few of his works are available. I love some of those I managed to find. I remember hearing his *Cornucopia* performed live from the National Concert Hall on RTE and was astonished by the sheer capacity for invention, for organisation and calculation of effect. I thought that it was a remarkable work. I believe that in time we will hear more of his compositions. Boydell and Fleischmann and others made a massive but quiet contribution to music. I consider it is time that their work be re-evaluated on its own terms but also in a historical context. The recent development of contemporary music owes much to the Music Centre in Dublin, which is doing an immense amount for awareness of compositions and supporting composers in their work. But there is a danger that in bringing forward and platforming so many composers, and in making contemporary composition a living issue, the work of previous generations of composers may simply be recorded, archived and put away on shelves. Aloys Fleischmann's place is guaranteed as a composer and as a highly prominent person within the music life of Ireland in the twentieth century. His impact has been enormous: I do not think that it can be overstated.

SÉAMAS DE BARRA, Composer, UCC Music Graduate, Lecturer at the Cork School of Music
Fleischmann's teaching and the content and structure of the courses for the BMus degree at UCC were originally shaped in direct response to the very poor state of music education in this country generally in the 1930s. Shortly after his appointment as acting head of department in 1934, he published an important article detailing the shortcomings of the music profession, focusing in particular on the indifference of the Department of Education to music as a subject, and on the general incapacity of music teachers, many of whom were unqualified. Standards were appallingly low, and Fleischmann concluded that 'if any uplift is to take place it must begin with the teachers, the children and the schools.'[1] This was indisputably sound. Unless there are firm foundations, it is pointless to aspire to any higher levels of attainment. It is worth remembering that in the 1930s in UCC there were long periods when there were no undergraduates in Music. It could hardly have been otherwise. There was virtually no teaching that could have brought students up to the level of even a modest university entrance test. Fleischmann saw his appointment as an opportunity to do something practical about this where he could, and to attempt to tackle the problem at the root. Progress was slow however, and it was difficult to break out of the vicious circle of inadequate teaching perpetuating inadequate teaching. Many of his earliest students were in fact already qualified teachers who had some aptitude for music and whom he persuaded to undertake to study for the BMus degree, often on top of already heavy professional commitments. Their pioneering enthusiasm can only have equalled his persuasiveness. Gradually the situation improved: a handful of competent and dedicated teachers meant that the number of suitable applicants began to rise. Writing in 1945 Fleischmann mentions that there were twelve undergraduates currently studying Music; in 1974, when I was in first year, there were about seventy.

Of course Fleischmann has been criticised for designing a degree course the principal purpose of which was supposedly to produce teachers, to the neglect, it is usually implied, of academic scholarship. And enough of Fleischmann's graduates did become teachers for the criticism to appear plausible. It is in essence however a misrepresentation. Fleischmann's clearly stated view was that 'university education opens the mind to the subject as a whole and provides the proper background for later specialisation',[2] and it was in accordance with this view that his undergraduate programme was designed. If it is true that in reality this later specialisation for the most part did mean teaching there were good reasons for it, among them employment opportunities for the graduates. And it would be disingenuous not to acknowledge that Fleischmann certainly expected most of his graduates to enter the teaching profession. But this was essentially incidental. Fleischmann's object was to equip his students with a solid general competence, as thorough and as broadly based as possible. This he rightly felt could be the only 'proper background' for good teaching should his graduates choose to become teachers; and presumably he found it difficult to imagine any more adequately suitable background to good academic scholarship. To open the mind to the subject as a whole was, in short, to present the student with possibilities, the subsequent choice of direction depending only on the inclination, aptitude and ability of the individual as well as on opportunity.

This insistence on 'proper background' must not however be taken to imply undergraduate courses of nebulous content or vague generality. On the contrary, central to the degree programme were the specific technicalities of traditional compositional discipline. 'By undergoing a three-year course in composition, the student acquires an insight into the structure of music which is denied to those who have not actually mastered the rudiments of composition themselves,' he wrote.[3] Species counterpoint up to five parts, sixteenth century vocal counterpoint, invertible counterpoint, canon and fugue together with the usual study of harmony, form and orchestration were the undergraduates' lot in my day. My own students today find it hard to imagine how we could have acquired sufficient technical skill to sit in an examination hall and compose a fugue on a given subject in three hours. These studies were supplemented by studies in conducting, various forms of keyboard work, acoustics, the history of music and Irish music. This is the disciplined education that Fleischmann himself received from Lacy in UCC and from Haas in Munich, and it is worth recalling that up to about 1970, with the sole exception of Irish music – for which there existed a long-established independent lectureship – he taught every course himself. Such an education is now largely a thing of the past. The solid is unfortunately replaced by the nebulous, the specific by the vague, and consistency and continuity have given way to the haphazard, by which no disciplined technique can ever be acquired.

Fleischmann had an exceptionally good rapport with his students. The atmosphere in lectures was almost invariably good humoured and work was done without undue solemnity. Students were always addressed formally of course, and he in return was always addressed as 'Professor'. In the current climate of spurious intimacy when it is assumed as a matter of course that one will be on first-name terms with everybody, even with total strangers, this would probably be understood as inimical to easy relations. But it was nothing of the kind, and it would be nonsense to suggest that any of his students might have been intimidated by it. He was a courteous man in an old-fashioned way, and this mode of address was a natural part of that courtesy. But it was more: without strain or stand-offishness it allowed him to maintain an appropriate and necessary distance, and ensured that his good-humoured relations with his students never acquired that confusing personal dimension that can so bedevil the objective assessment of work. The result was that his students considered him to be a fair-minded man. They trusted him and however highly he may have thought of the work of particular individuals I cannot recall there ever being the slightest suspicion of favouritism. He did however tend to get bees in his bonnet about some students, I believe, although I never witnessed this personally. It was very difficult to get him to change his initial impression: if a student made a slow start at the beginning of first year and failed to produce, say, counterpoint exercises for the first few weeks of term that poor unfortunate, in spite of all subsequent efforts to redeem himself, was for ever after associated with irregular work. Fleischmann would pounce on him and exclaim: 'You'll be sunk! You haven't done a tap for weeks!' All protestations would be in vain. But there was usually a twinkle in his eye and one was never really sure whether he meant it or not. I suspect not. Just as one was never sure whether his legendary *double entendres* were innocent or deliberate. Some of them were decidedly *risqué* and as the class hooted with laughter he would assume his best bewildered expression. On the whole we tended to doubt if he was quite as innocent as he contrived to look especially as we were perfectly well aware of his fondness for reading naughty limericks at the annual Music department dinner, a performance that by popular request had long become obligatory.

It has been said that Fleischmann was more concerned with bringing the poorer students up to scratch than with getting the best out of the better ones. This is possibly true. Better students might have been encouraged to achieve more, I suppose, if the tempo had been set to match their ability, but it would have been at the cost of leaving others to flounder. This is always the problem with classes as opposed to the teaching of individuals. And given the very varied musical backgrounds of prospective undergraduates the problem here was more

110

acute than it might otherwise have been. Fleischmann's pragmatic approach was no worse than others I have seen and indeed better than most. He established and endeavoured to maintain a general standard and his principal objective was to ensure if possible that all students reached it. He did not feel the need to worry about students of ability. They were not harried if they defaulted on routine work which he knew they could do and he clearly expected them to have the initiative to explore beyond the confines of the course. I do not know what more he or anyone else could have done under the circumstances. As I myself went to college primarily to learn as much as I could about music and only secondarily to pass examinations and obtain a degree, this suited me admirably. My preoccupations however never seemed to coincide with what happened to be on the course and he must surely have had misgivings about some of my work. But he never said much. I do not imagine he can have exactly approved, but he was always encouraging, if in oblique rather than in direct ways. One particular instance of this comes to mind. As a second year student I was bold enough to object in class to his use of the term 'modulation' and adduce what I thought were cogent reasons for my view. He disagreed and reiterated his own understanding of the term, which was the traditional one. But his disagreement had nothing dogmatic about it. In fact I believe he was pleased that I had thought the matter out for myself, and it became a sort of running joke for two years. 'We will now modulate to the subdominant, if Mr de Barra doesn't mind,' he would say. Later he gave me a book, which I still have, called *Challenge to Musical Tradition* by Adele T. Katz. 'You should read this,' he said, 'you will be pleased to know that Miss Katz agrees with you.' A gesture that conveyed his attitude better than any words could have done. Needless to say he never missed an opportunity to allude to our opposing viewpoints: 'And so we find ourselves in the key of the mediant minor, *pace* Mr de Barra, *and* Miss Katz!'

The study of orchestration is one subject that is less than satisfactory from the students' point of view if they do not have an opportunity to hear some kind of performance of their efforts at scoring. Without this, the subject hardly leaves the realm of paper work and is of minimal value. As a student in Munich, Fleischmann himself was 'furious about the fact that Haas taught us orchestration but we never heard anything we scored.' Characteristically he determined to do something about it: 'I instigated my colleagues to organise an evening at which our scores, which we had done specially for the occasion, would be played by a group from the Academy conducted by us.'[4] Later he also determined that his own students in Cork would have the benefit of hearing what they had written, and by the time I was an

undergraduate the Cork Symphony Orchestra had long been annually at their service. Not only was this therefore one of the most enjoyable but also one of the most useful parts of the BMus course, the subject happily leaving the lecture room for the concert hall and obliging
the students to put their theoretical knowledge to the immediate practical test.

One had the choice of either arranging a suitable piano piece for
the specified orchestral forces, or of composing something of one's
own, and many students who might not otherwise have done so were
thus encouraged to attempt original work and to gain the invaluable
experience of seeing the entire process through from initial inspiration
to eventual public performance. Naturally one had to produce a full
score on which one was assessed for the purposes of the examination.
But one also had to copy a full set of orchestral parts, the practical discipline of knowing how to lay out and organise orchestral material
being considered a basic part of one's training. As a left-handed copy-
ist I confess I found this part of the business somewhat trying and it
was only with difficulty that I managed to produce material in some
way adequate. Once this was done one then rehearsed the orchestra in
one's work and in culmination, conducted a public performance. Inadequacies and errors were of course mercilessly exposed in rehearsal
as one player perhaps failed to cope with the idiosyncrasies of one's
handwriting, and rehearsal time was wasted in explaining what one
meant, or, most humiliating of all, as another perhaps pointed out that
such and such a note was not available on his instrument. Lessons so
learned are unlikely to be forgotten! Fleischmann, always an encouraging and tolerantly amused presence at one's left elbow as one stood
on the podium, would peer into the score at the offending passage and
say 'Aren't you a terror!' as one blushed with mortification and departed to undertake the necessary revisions.

When I was an undergraduate the orchestration course, taught by
Fleischmann himself, was spread over three years, the first year students studying the technique of stringed instruments and scoring for
string orchestra. The procedure in first year was that those students
who had completed a score which Fleischmann had both seen and
passed would distribute the parts on the stands of the string players
during the interval of one of the Cork Symphony Orchestra's regular
rehearsals. Fleischmann would bring the rehearsal to an end twenty
minutes or so earlier than usual and the wind and brass players would
depart. A trembling first year would then be summoned to the podium to stand in front of the strings and to conduct his work, trying to
relate as best he could the sounds that emerged from the orchestra
with the sounds he had imagined as he penned his score. In second

year the woodwind instruments were added to the strings and the students gave a public concert of their productions. This was a relatively minor affair mainly attended by the first years who wished to see what was ahead of them and by the third years who wished to take the measure of the up-and-comings. Parents, piano teachers and a handful of other interested and supportive parties swelled the numbers.

But the big event was the third year concert. This was held in the Aula Maxima of the college and drew a large audience. It was always an occasion of considerable excitement, increased of course by the usual flurry of last minute activity, as absolutely final alterations would be made to the orchestral parts. The fact that this was an examination not only in orchestration but also in conducting seemed to fade out of consideration in the nervous anticipation of performing. The event was reviewed in *The Cork Examiner,* which of course made us all feel that we had arrived. The late Geraldine Neeson, the newspaper's music critic, was usually tactful, often encouraging and, perhaps most importantly of all, never failed to mention everybody.

The orchestra for which we wrote was now complete with the addition of brass and percussion, and indeed anything else the individual student could think of which he could persuade someone to play for him. I remember playing the piano for several colleagues, and everyone seemed to take turns to play some percussion instrument or other. This latter activity took place under the watchful eye of Annette de Foubert, the orchestra's timpanist, who supplied the various instruments and who assisted the neophyte percussionists to count their bars rest correctly – a very tricky business for the inexperienced – and to come in on time. Looking back I wonder if we can ever have conveyed adequate thanks to the gallant band whose members voluntarily put their time and talents at the disposal of the BMus students in this way. It must certainly have taxed their patience if not frayed their nerves to play in one evening twenty or so different pieces (twenty-three in my degree year) from twenty different sets of parts of varying quality under twenty different student conductors of varying ability. But they did it with great good humour and were the means by which one of the least tangible of subjects was transformed into a valuable practical experience.

Of course many undergraduates played in the Cork Symphony Orchestra, but even for those who, like myself, did not play an orchestral instrument Fleischmann usually found a job. We were drawn into the circle of his activities. Each year for example the orchestra presented a full-scale evening symphony concert, preceded that morning by a concert for school children. At this Fleischmann would usually present an analysis in simple terms of one of the works on the programme with the orchestra playing excerpts to illustrate the points he made. Then there would be a performance and we, the extras, would have to stand behind the players and hold aloft at the appropriate moments enormous cards bearing the legends 'first subject', 'transition passage' and so on, to focus the children's attention on the unfolding structure as they listened to the music.

The point is that connections such as these, however slight, with the Cork Symphony Orchestra or through the orchestra with the Cork Ballet Company or with the Cork International Choral Festival meant that it was more natural for music students in my time to face out towards the city rather than in towards the college. We could not but be aware of the Music department as a centre of activity which radiated out into civic life through Fleischmann's committed involvement with the music and culture of Cork. And through this, even in small ways, we began to become involved ourselves. It was all extra-curricular of course. We were willing volunteers. But I sometimes think it was in fact one of the most profound aspects of the education he gave us: by silent example we learned of high-minded idealism, generosity of spirit and dedicated commitment to the community. In my experience Fleischmann never once drew attention to the work he did in this way. He simply did it. And the lesson could not have been taught in any other way. Some students may possibly have missed all this: there are always a few who keep their heads down and think only of examinations. For those of us who became aware it was an inspiration and, long after the details of lectures have inevitably faded from the memory, it is what remains.

I was in fact Fleischmann's very last student in UCC. He retired in April 1980 but remained as acting head of the department until the following September when the appointment of his successor was to take effect. His final duty as professor of Music, beyond his extended term, was to oversee the completion of my MA degree that October. I saw him quite often during the summer of 1980 and he was clearly distressed about relinquishing his department. It seemed to me odd at the time that he had not anticipated his eventual retirement more practically and had no likely successor, one of his own graduates perhaps, groomed and waiting in the wings. But unfortunately it does not seem that he was a man to entertain such eventualities. His break with the department was complete. Not with the College of course: he was made Professor Emeritus and was facilitated to some extent in the completion of his work on the *Sources of Irish Traditional Music*. In my naivety I thought it sad however that there seemed to be no question of his being invited back even as an occasional guest lecturer. There was in evidence no awareness of what his achievement had been in virtually creating and building up the department, and there was certainly no tactful understanding that retiring from the chair of Music might have been for him much more than simply retiring from a job.

The new policy was one of discontinuity. Not everything changed overnight naturally, but the desire to dissociate the new department from the old was unambiguously indicated. Its existence of course could now be taken for granted and it was neither necessary nor convenient to acknowledge either the circumstances that shaped it or the considerations that determined the structure and content of the courses, let alone the possibility that any of them might still obtain. The state of music education in Ireland is, I suppose, unlikely to be a matter of any great moment to career academics from elsewhere whose only serious commitment is to their careers, and the important contribution to its improvement that Fleischmann saw the department making simply became irrelevant. For many of us who were present during this period there was a curious feeling that the Music department was being detached from the living context that defined it and doomed to continue its existence *in vacuo*.

If this had been all it would have been a pity certainly, but unfortunately it was accompanied by a scarcely concealed contempt both for Fleischmann personally and for what the BMus course had been. Even now after all these years I find myself wondering why this should have been necessary. Changes, yes, by all means – one would have expected them. Even far-reaching changes. But the students were clearly given to understand that they were being emancipated from the outmoded and the second rate. It was impressed on those unfortunates who had almost completed their studies that their degrees were virtually worthless as one year in the new department could not, it was suggested, redeem two years in the old. The students were emphatically unimpressed by this, and indeed became acutely unhappy about the direction some aspects of the degree course had begun to take. For all the inflated talk, there was simply nothing to show that could in any way justify the regrettable belittling of Fleischmann's work. There was no new vision to replace the old. All that happened in fact was that the haphazard replaced the coherent. The students became very disillusioned, and as successive heads of departments brought no improvement, a serious discontent festered under the surface for ten years.

Fleischmann was undoubtedly disquieted by the nature of some of the changes to the course and in particular by the erosion of what he would have considered necessary technical training. This was not due to any personal pique at alterations to his degree programme. It was because he knew what the detrimental long-term effects would be for music education. It was entirely characteristic of him to approach the successive heads of department directly and to remonstrate with them, pointing out what he saw as the possible, indeed likely consequences of their policy. Seeing that a larger issue was at stake he was quite prepared to pocket his pride. One can only imagine how he was received, and his intervention certainly made no difference. When in 1991 an outgoing degree class finally and formally drew the attention of the president of the College to their dissatisfaction with the course they had just completed Fleischmann was hurt and disturbed by the suggestion that he was in some way behind the protest, that insidious outside influence had been brought to bear on these graduates who would otherwise have been perfectly content. The suggestion was absurd of course, but for Fleischmann it was a final unpleasantness. Sadly, he had no reason to modify his views about what the Music department had become by the time he died.

3: The Campaigner

The late SHEILA GOLDBERG while Lady Mayoress of Cork was interviewed on Cork Radio in 1978 by Donna O'Sullivan when Fleischmann had been made Freeman of the City

DO'S: Aloys Fleischmann has been described as a born leader, a man who gathers willing helpers and exudes the kind of energy that drives everyone and everything before it. Constant *aide-de-camp* over the years is Sheila Goldberg, who with many others helped in the early difficult years of organising.

SG: It was an uphill fight in spite of the fact that he had many willing helpers. There was always this question to begin with of money. There was never enough money to do anything, and he himself would go out and go around to the various firms and the various people and get money. He had to start from this very basic thing. And this is something I am sure nobody ever associates with him, but he is the most fantastic fundraiser I have ever met.

DO'S: A man of this calibre must also make great demands on those who work around him, as you did – was he a demanding person?

SG: Yes, I think it's true to say he was, but he always did it in such a way that it never seemed to be demanding, and you were always glad to do it for him because he was so sincere about the thing, and he worked so hard that you felt you had to follow his example. You always had the feeling that you must do whatever he asked, that you couldn't possibly let him down because he only asked you to do something that needed to be done and that was worthwhile. He never asked you to do anything that was superfluous.

DO'S: He seems to be an ideal combination of industry and imagination, which is rare.

SG: He is both these things, but then as I said to you before, he is a very rare man.

DO'S: But the Prof is modest in the extreme. It would be unfair to describe him as the man behind so many cultural movements in the city: he is in there, pulling more than his weight with unflagging spirit. Our city officially holds him in high regard, for his remarkable achievement conferring on him with love our greatest honour.

SG: But then this is a very remarkable man we're talking about. His single-mindedness and sincerity and his unbelievable stamina and determination – these, together with his very fine mind and industry and his great humility and modesty, make him one of the most versatile and extraordinary men of our time.

The late COLM Ó HEOCHA *President of University College Galway; from a letter to the editor of July 1996*

I held Aloys Fleischmann in high regard for his many contributions to music education in Ireland. In fact, I feel somewhat guilty in that during my twenty year term as President of University College, Galway, I did not succeed in having a department of Music established. Aloys Fleischmann visited me shortly after my appointment to urge me to have a professor of Music appointed, and he told me that I was the third president of UCG that he had urged to provide an academic music education for the west of Ireland. Unfortunately, I was not successful in raising the necessary funding for the project. I am also pleased to put on record my admiration for the work of Joan Denise Moriarty; as a member of the Senate of the National University of Ireland, I gladly supported the motion that she be conferred with an Honorary Doctorate.

MAIRTIN MCCULLOUGH (DUBLIN) *former Chairman of the Arts Council of Ireland*

I am happy to set down this account of the Aloys Fleischmann I knew and respected. I acknowledge that what I offer is not very profound yet it will, I hope, reflect those qualities which demonstrate his integrity, his enthusiasm and his very lively interest in public affairs – especially where they impinged on the world of music.

I suppose my first encounter with Aloys was during the early days of the Music Association of Ireland, of which the late Olive Smith was the driving force. He represented, I recall, Cork interests thereon, always in a refreshing and go-ahead manner. François D'Albert (violin) and the late Charles Lynch performed some of Bax's compositions to mark the anniversary of Arnold Bax's death (he died in Cork in 1953). Aloys was at the centre of the local organisation, giving powerful assistance, as always, to ensuring a successful occasion. I believe that this was an MAI occasion, as was the subsequent visit of the celebrated London String Quartet, led by Douglas Cameron (cello). Later in the life of the MAI, I approached Aloys regarding the possible award of an Honorary Doctorate by UCC on Olive Smith, who was an indefatigable and powerful advocate in the cause of music. He did his best in this regard, but I think he found that the National University of Ireland (NUI) ruled the 'politics' of such issues and that he, in Cork, would not have sufficient 'clout' to accomplish a favourable decision. Olive's own university, TCD, awarded her an Honorary Doctorate in Music some years later, in recognition of her trojan work.

Also in the MAI days, there was a monthly journal produced. One of the critics thereon published some scathing, savage and unjust reviews. Aloys took grave exception to these – as did I – so he penned his own trenchant response, deploring the destructive nature of these reviews and questioning the competence and fair play of the author. Being in full support of Aloys' views, I wrote subsequently to the Editor indicating that I fully accepted all of the points made by him. Aloys, being an authoritative figure in the musical life of Ireland, was to be respected in such matters.

On another occasion, Aloys wrote (it *might* have been in *The Catholic Standard*) a splendid article in which he fiercely criticised the musical quality of some of the hymns sung at Catholic services, describing them (I seem to recall) as trite, banal and meretricious. While this went down well enough with those who knew their music, it was a brave statement to make in holy Catholic Ireland! Yet there weren't many who could argue with him given his status of professor of Music at UCC and a leading expert in his field.

Of course, Aloys' greatest claim to fame was his energetic association with the Cork International Choral Festival, which he had, in fact, established. His enthusiasm and dedication to its success bore fruit when it soon became a festival of international repute. He will always be remembered for his magnificent and tireless commitment to one of the most important musical events in the Irish calendar. He invited me (as then chairman of the Arts Council) to open the Festival in 1985 or 1986. He kindly met me at Cork station; he purported to drive me to a pre-Festival reception, but en route he forgot which hotel we were to go to! This, I thought, was a delightful touch of the 'absent-minded professor', so a phone call to another hotel put us on the right track. And, I have to add, he was a bit absent-minded too when driving the car, albeit one on loan to the Festival, courtesy of Ford's.

Also during my tenure as chairman, the Arts Council decided to appoint a popular music officer, i.e., we were giving recognition to pop music as an art form. (I confess that I wasn't altogether happy with this decision, but had to accept that it was an expression of our youth culture.) Aloys was outraged! He wrote me a scathing letter, denouncing the Council's ignorance and irresponsibility. He could see no way that pop music could remotely be treated as an 'art form', demolishing it as barbaric, hideous and certainly not musical. It was truly a brilliant letter from one who was unafraid to speak his mind on such topics.

Finally, my admiration grew for Aloys with his readiness to enter into any fray, even if it was outside his world of music. I remember his many contributions to affairs of wide public interest, writing many letters to *The Irish Times* on a variety of general subjects. This demonstrated his nimble and alert mind; and he was always refreshing in what he had to say.

Altogether, I reckon, a man of many parts, fearless in the opinions he expressed and patently honest in his dealings with others.

MICHEÁL MARTIN, *Minister for Education and Science, in 1990 Lord Mayor of Cork, on Donna O'Sullivan's Cork Radio programme of 22 July 1992 after Fleisch-mann's death.*
As a younger person, I did not know Professor Fleischmann as inti-mately or as personally as the other members of this panel: Alderman Corr, Geoffrey Spratt, or John A. Murphy, but I can bring a young per-son's perspective to it. I came on Council in 1985, and I suppose the deliberations of the Arts Committee since then have been on events and festivals and topics which the modern generation take for grant-ed. When one looks back at his achievements one can appreciate what enormous initiative and energy he must have had to be a founding member of the Symphony Orchestra, of the Choral and Folk Dance Festival – and today's generation take all of those for granted. Like-wise his academic achievements: the Music department of University College, Cork is one of the foremost now in the country, a tremendous product – again he was a major pioneering influence on its develop-ment. We have to thank him for leaving a wonderful legacy both in the academic and in the wider cultural field. And what I can remember as a member of the Arts Committee is what John A. said: that he com-bined temperateness with passion. He wrote frequently to us individ-ually on a wide range of issues, most recently on the Opera House: it was not so long ago that he wrote to me, giving his own particular per-spective on it and urging me to take a certain course of action. I don't want to go into the merits of the issue, but it really illustrates his total commitment to the city, and to the artistic and cultural institutions of the city. His energy and his civic-mindedness is something that will always be remembered.

RICHARD WOOD (CORK), *Director of the Fota Foundation, Member of the Cork Orchestral Society*
Aloys Fleischmann was a fearless fighter for the causes he espoused, and apart from his beloved music, one of those causes was the fight to save Fota Island from the banal and destructive plans of developers, and its preservation as a great ornamental estate for the people of Cork.

Aloys was quick to appreciate the cultural and ecological value of this estate, and its potential as a place of relaxation and instruction. He was more outraged than most when its owners and, it was thought, guardians, his very own place of work, University College, Cork, re-vealed that it had secretly done a deal with an unknown English developer to dispose of virtually all the Island for conversion to an 'exclusive' golfing and leisure resort. The College argued firstly that it needed the money, secondly it was not in a position to maintain the estate, and thirdly that commercial activity as proposed would 'save' the place by converting its landscaped parkland to a golf course, adding a 100 bedroom hotel to the house and siting this hotel in the walled gardens so that it could overlook the world-famous arboretum, and by building four hundred 'lodges' in the Island's woodlands.

The crassness of this proposition was lost on no one except those in authority, and an outcry resulted. Few members of the staff at UCC openly supported the widespread opinion of the general public with one or two honourable exceptions. They seemed to take the view that discretion was safer than valour. Eventually corporate Cork asserted itself, not wishing to allow the opportunity of such a development to slip through its fingers, regardless of the location chosen for it. The close ties between the College and the business community, so strengthened in recent years, no doubt bore fruit, and the evidence of this was to be found in the sudden volte-face by the local press, which had been loud in its support for Fota and all it represented, but at a certain point began to sing the praises of the developers and their plan. (It is worth noting, more than ten years later, that the economic activity promised is confined to one golf course and a clubhouse).

It takes a strong man to stand up for a cause he believes in against such a united and powerful background, but Aloys had such strength, and had it in plenty. When he was asked by the Fota Foundation, which was spearheading the campaign to save the Island, to act as one of its patrons, he accepted the position without a moment's hesitation.

He was the ideal patron. Not only was he a Freeman of the City, but his extraordinary commitment to the cause of music was known to everyone. He was a familiar figure dashing through the traffic on his scooter at all times of the day and night on his way to the College, to private lessons, to meetings, to rehearsals, and to concerts. Though he was an intellectual giant, far better read and more educated than virtually any of his contemporaries in the city, he was self-effacing in company and at meetings, even of the Cork Orchestral Society, where I was able to observe him for some years. He was deferential to the ideas of others but could skilfully draw out the best from all contributions. His respect for everyone was enormous, and equal: he never made anyone feel inferior, indeed his praise for even the smallest service was warm, perhaps occasionally extravagant. People loved him for these qualities. This was in sharp contrast to our opponents, the College and the developers. We could not have found a better person. (I cannot, however, allow that statement, true as it is, to pass without mention of the late Councillor Gerry O'Sullivan, Lord Mayor of Cork at this time who consented, as Lord Mayor, to become our other Patron. His vision of the value of Fota to the people of Cork was as clear as that of Aloys, and was in sharp contrast to the vast majority of local and indeed national representatives at the time. In fact, so disgusted was he at the College's actions that he became the first and only Lord Mayor to resign from its Governing Body).

Fota Island has now, alas, been mutilated beyond repair. Attitudes towards it have, however, changed with changing personnel, and some now in authority would like to put the clock back. The value of the example shown by Aloys is gaining wider recognition and as public life reveals itself to have been more decadent than was ever imagined, the example of someone who was entirely selfless, without guile, and totally dedicated to excellence and the good of his fellow men is something that is of inestimable value to our view of ourselves and our health as a nation.

May he never rest in peace –
may his spirit remain with us as an example
ever urging us on to do greater good!

THE VANBRUGH QUARTET – GREGORY ELLIS, ELIZABETH CHARLESON, SIMON ASPELL, CHRISTOPHER MARWOOD: *Artists in Residence, University College Cork*
We were introduced to Professor Fleischmann at our first concerts in Cork as the RTE Vanbrugh Quartet. The sheer strength of his personality, boundless enthusiasm and indefatigable spirit were a legend in Cork, and we were privileged to have had his support and friendship from the beginning of our residency. However, the origins of our debt to Prof, as he was fondly known, go back several decades, to when he instigated a move to create a professional, performing group resident in Cork. After much petitioning and haggling, this idea became reality as the RTE String Quartet, and were it not for his commitment, we would not now be holding one of Europe's finest chamber music residencies.

Some of our most vivid memories of Prof include an evening we spent at his home, where he introduced us to some of the work in stained glass by Harry Clark, and entertained us with outrageous stories from his years as Cork's premier music maestro. He showed us around his house, with enthusiasm leaping up the stairs three at a time (apparently, he climbed Mount Brandon on his eightieth birthday, and when someone asked him why he chose to do such a crazy thing at his age, he replied characteristically: 'Bravado!'), and told us about the time they were flooded and he had to go fishing in his living-room for scores that were about to float out of the window down the stream.

When we ran into difficulties with RTE because of a misfiring Broadcasting Bill, Prof together with Geoff Spratt and some Cork politicians took the train up to Dublin to lobby RTE, and wrote vociferously in the press, lampooning the cuts. Two or three years later the bill was revoked and we were reinstated. It was an extraordinary feeling as a musician to have one's corner defended in this way so vigorously, even though we realised what was at stake was not just our own jobs, but the principle of having a professional, performing, music group living and working in Cork. What was quite awesome was Prof's guts for a fight, and that for a man in his 80s.

It is clear that Prof's musical personality influenced countless young people as each year he gave a concert in the City Hall conducting the Cork Symphony Orchestra. With the Vanbrugh Quartet he conducted Elgar's *Introduction and Allegro for Quartet and Orchestra*, to tumultuous applause from the hundreds of kids who had been bussed in for the concert – it was to be his last one. So many adults from all walks of life have fond memories of these concerts, and have mentioned this to us over the years, from garage attendants to bank clerks.

We are also grateful to Prof for a fine piano quintet which we recorded for Marco Polo with Hugh Tinney. Like his personality, the work is fiery, witty, uncompromising and with loads of bravura.

Sadly, we were on tour when Prof died, and only heard about the funeral upon our return. We have clearly witnessed the end of an era, yet Professor Fleischmann has certainly left an indelible mark on the cultural heritage of Ireland as a whole and on Cork in particular.

FRED O'CALLAGHAN (DUBLIN), retired Director of the Army School of Music
As a teenager I began to attend the concerts at Dublin's Capitol Theatre, given by the Radio Éireann Orchestra under Captain Michael Bowles. It was probably through these that I was first made aware of the composer, Aloys Fleischmann, and came to hear such works as *The Humours of Carolan, Clare's Dragoons* and the overture *The Four Masters*.

Although, having already chosen a musical career, I was full of dreamy ambition, the thought that I might one day be on friendly terms with this man would, I am sure, have made my head spin. But of course when after a few years I met him, I was immediately put at ease by his characteristic person-to-person directness. It was not in his nature to be either aloof or patronising.

During the time that I was Instructional Officer in the Army School of Music, I was occasionally dispatched south to take over the Band of the Southern Command, should it happen that its regular conductor was away or indisposed. The pleasurable aspects of these interludes were sometimes enhanced by Professor Fleischmann, who tended to

accord me visiting musician status and – his perpetuum mobile existence notwithstanding – would take it on himself to welcome me to
Cork. This would take the form of, say, inviting me to supper at his
home or to the opera at the Palace Theatre or to a concert at UCC with
students conducting pieces orchestrated by themselves.

I can see now that the source of his information about my arrivals
and departures was probably the grapevine within the Command
Band. The band was accepted as an integral part of Cork's musical life
and Aloys knew individual members very well. He relied heavily on
their participation in the Cork Orchestral Society activities and even
had a friendly arrangement with the barracks, whereby he would go
to the bandroom for preliminary rehearsals with the instrumentalists
concerned. A considerable anecdotal lore developed around these col-
laborations with 'the Prof', which in no way reduced the respect felt
by the bandsmen. How could they not respect this learned man who
took them so seriously and dignified them by habitually putting
'Mister' before their surnames when addressing them?

It doesn't seem to be widely known (though I have it directly from
Aloys himself) that, had the great Colonel Fritz Brase had his wish,
Aloys Fleischmann might have become an army band conductor.
Brase, who was on visiting terms with the Fleischmann family, met the
young Aloys there and, obviously impressed, could see great prospects
for him as an army musician. He wasn't sure whether Aloys' German
birth might be an impediment to his entry to the army, but for the rest,
the colonel was so carried away by his own enthusiasm that he left the
house, oblivious to the possibility that the enthusiasm might not be
shared by his young listener. Some time later, Brase was pleased to report that he had consulted the appropriate authorities and that the
matter of non-Irish birth was not in fact a problem. Poor Aloys now
had the unenviable task of tactfully explaining to the well-intentioned
colonel that actually he planned a different future for himself.

Once when I was conductor of the Army No. 1 Band, finding that
we were due to be in Cork for a few days, I offered to do a lunch-time
recital in UCC, and got a very positive response from the Professor.
The programme I proposed consisted mainly of wind band classics by
composers such as Holst, Vaughan Williams and Grainger. But to these
I added as a sweetener a short piece called 'Encore Blues'. This title
seemed to put Aloys slightly on his guard, but I assured him that this
was tongue-in-cheek writing – quite a sophisticated little composition.
The event was memorably successful, and the general mood and sense
of rapport were very rewarding for the band.

Trying to uphold musical standards in an army set-up poses ongoing problems – not necessarily of the army's making. Linked to

these was the long struggle to get a fairer deal for the army bandsmen, who, as I liked to put it, suffered from the joint handicap of often being regarded within army circles as not being real soldiers, whereas the musical world outside was slow to recognise them as real musicians. I found these aspects of my work very wearing and not surprisingly my frustration sometimes peaked. At one such point I turned to Aloys and found myself, by appointment, at his rooms in the Music department on Western Road. He welcomed me and, of course, gave me his full attention. In no time my problems were also his. I could not myself be more indignant than he became on my behalf. How could he help, he wondered? Should he write to ... ? But even if he went no further, he had already helped and I departed feeling renewed, understood and supported.

Although he was ever ready to take up a just musical cause, I don't believe he really relished campaigning. In a letter to me, early in 1986, he dealt with the purpose of his writing in a few sentences, but added, before signing off: 'I am dreading the confrontation which now looms with the Arts Council, and which may well erupt into full-scale war, since the future of the Choral Festival is at stake. If we lose out it will not be for want of effort'.

I had the privilege of serving with him on adjudicating panels at various times. On reaching the discussion and decision stages, it could be no surprise to anyone that Aloys, with his fabled analytic powers, would have already formulated certain important considerations. But what, in retrospect, I find most striking was his ability, whether as chairman or member, to state his views with clarity and conviction, but without that sort of finality which could preclude useful debate or disqualify the views of his colleagues – to which, needless to say, he listened with unfeigned interest.

I must have been just one of countless people who could see that Aloys' vast contribution to music and to cultural life in Ireland was not duly recognised, particularly outside Cork. The Royal Dublin Society has for some years now been selectively honouring individuals who have served the community with great distinction, by conferring on them Honorary Life Membership. In 1990, I felt it was high time that the name of Aloys Fleischmann should be entered on this list and (being myself a member of the RDS Council) made a few exploratory approaches. I was encouraged to set out my case in letter form to the committee concerned, and I quickly got down to the task. 'How,' I asked, 'can one synopsise the career of this great man who this year marched past his eightieth birthday as though it were just another milestone in an ongoing, well-planned journey?' And I included in the letter a chronology of his more important achievements, in which connection I had consulted Dr Geoffrey Spratt. I own to feeling some personal satisfaction when eventually I heard that the committee had accepted my recommendation. But it was a safe bet, I suppose.

Meanwhile I had asked permission of Aloys to include his overture *The Four Masters* in a Dublin Orchestral Players' concert which I was to conduct in March, 1991. He graciously consented and lent me his own manuscript score, which enabled me to make copious adjustments to the library score which I had borrowed. Not only did he attend the performance in the Royal Hospital, Kilmainham; he also sat out a final rehearsal, saying scarcely a word but continually smiling his encouragement. True to form, he sent a letter from Cork (dated 24 March – the day after the concert!) thanking me for 'putting on my overture' and praising the performance. He enclosed a copy of his lecture 'A Key to Sources of Irish Traditional Music', which he referred to as 'a small memento, which explains what I have been up to for years, and for another year or two to come'. Sadly, it was to be one year rather than two. But that, to use his own phrase, was 'not for want of effort'.

JOHN O'CONOR (DUBLIN), Pianist, Director of the Royal Irish Academy of Music. The following reflections were recorded by the editor.
When I was still at school, I remember going to record recitals in the Goethe Institute, because there was so little live music going on in Dublin. The Symphony Orchestra gave about twelve concerts in the Gaiety Theatre, which were called the Subscription Series. These were often then repeated in the City Hall in Cork, and sometimes in the Savoy in Limerick. The Symphony Orchestra also gave free concerts in the Francis Xavier Hall, which was often used for bingo. There was no glamour in going there: the people who did were there for the music – in spite of the dreadful seats. The acoustics there weren't nearly as good as in the City Hall in Cork either, which everybody agreed had the best acoustics in Ireland.

Aloys Fleischmann insisted that the Symphony Orchestra went to Cork, and always drummed up audiences for it. Everybody admired him for his tenacious fight with RTE. He was a very stubborn man, determined to get his way, which is the only way to get things done. I remember years ago, when I was running the first International Piano Competition in Dublin, Fanny Waterman, who directs the Leeds International Competition, was over on the jury. She had been interviewed by the *Irish Times*, and asked me: 'What's feisty? That's what they say I am!' I said that a feisty person was somebody who fights tooth and nail for what they believe in and keeps on going until they get it.' I could say the same thing about Aloys Fleischmann. He fought tooth and nail to have RTE place the Concert Orchestra in Cork, and when they wouldn't do that, he got the String Quartet. He was prepared to keep going, to fight on till he had it. The splendid string school in the Cork School of Music is there thanks to him. But in 1990, the fight had to be taken up again when there was a big pull-back in RTE. The minister had put a cap on the amount of advertising RTE was allowed, and therefore there was less money to go around. RTE decided to scrap the National Chamber Choir and the String Quartet. Thanks to the determination of a lot of people in Cork, including Aloys Fleischmann and University College Cork, the quartet was saved. That is an invaluable resource: they are a wonderful quartet. They have an international career, but they are also committed to playing all around the country: they have travelled everywhere in Ireland. They promote Irish composers, and they are running the marvellous Bantry Festival, the West Cork Chamber Music Festival.

The first time I went to Cork to perform I had been invited by Bridget Doolan to play at a lunchtime recital in the Crawford Art Gallery. That was the first time I met Aloys Fleischmann. I was in awe of him, because everybody involved in music in Dublin spoke of him and Charles Lynch as the two people who did an enormous amount to put Cork on the map for music. There were a few people around Ireland who took that sort of initiative. There was Willie Watt, who started the Waterford Music Club and John Ruddock who was running the great series in Limerick; there was Tom Walsh in the Wexford Opera Festival. Often in places like that it's one person who is prepared to keep going. In Cork, there is no doubt about it, it was Aloys Fleischmann. He was involved in the ballet too of course, with Joan Denise Moriarty. (My wife is from Cork; she did some ballet with Joan Moriarty when she was a child, and she studied at the School of Music with Bernard Curtis.)

Things have changed enormously for music since my early days in Dublin. A Music Diary used to be kept in McCullough Piggott's music shop. Charles Acton in his role as music critic of the *Irish Times* would lambaste anybody who would dare to put on a concert when there was another one on. So if you were going to plan a concert, you had to go to the Diary first. Nowadays there are sometimes five or six concerts on some nights, and it's impossible to get to everything. The young musicians have much better chances these days. When I was a child, to win a prize at the Feis Cheoil in Dublin was the ultimate; nowadays the students are looking towards international competitions and international careers. When I was a boy the only Irish musician abroad that I know of was Hugh McGuire, who was playing the violin in London in a string quartet: there weren't any other Irish musicians abroad having an international career. Of the pianists, Veronica McSweeney was doing most of her work in Ireland; Charles Lynch only played in Ireland after the Second World War; of the violinists, Geraldine O'Grady only played in Ireland. Of the singers, Bernadette Greevy was beginning to make a name for herself around the world, but there weren't really any other Irish singers around. Now there are Irish singers in many of the world's opera houses. With regard to pianists: I am making a career, Hugh Tinney is making a career, Barry Douglas is making a career; we have this new young man Finian Collins, who just won the Clara Haskell Competition in Switzerland, and you can see the standards of the young ones coming up.

In my day, if somebody went abroad to study, they went to London and they often disappeared without trace, or the string players played in an orchestra, the pianists either got married abroad or came back and taught. But nowadays there are probably at least 50 Irish musicians between the ages of 20 and 25 studying at major conservatoires around the world. That's a considerable number for such a small population. And it's thanks to the push that a lot of people gave to music in that era. When I was a child, classical music was still very much the foreign music; and it wasn't felt, as it is now, that we could be as good at it as the rest of the world: we can play classical music the same as anybody else. But you have to realise also there was awful pressure on Irish people. A year after I decided to base myself in Ireland, in 1976, Fanny Feehan wrote an article in *Hibernia* saying: 'What a pity John O'Conor didn't make it – he had to come home.' That was the attitude. It hurt very much at the time. I hadn't broken in to America at that stage, but I was going to Japan and to Europe quite regularly and I'd won two international competitions.

I encourage people to come back, because I think living in Ireland is fantastic and we need the people who have achieved something to return and give it back to the Irish people and also to stir up the Irish people. Look at Mícheál Mac Liammóir: he could have had a career anywhere in the world, but he chose to come here, and what an influence he was on everybody else! Aloys Fleischmann fought tooth and nail to get the string quartet – the Academia Quartet came from Romania with their spouses and started teaching in the Cork School of Music and just look at the influence they have had! Now of course it is just taken for granted that there is an excellent string school in Cork.

When I was going abroad to study, Tony Hughes was professor in UCD; he knew one teacher in Vienna, and he advised me to go for the Austrian government scholarship. But when I was due to go, we discovered that his friend was in America for the year, so we had no contacts. Now, if one of my students wants to go abroad, I can pick up the phone and contact friends in any major music conservatory: the head of piano in Vienna, in London, in Helsinki and so on around the world. Those connections help the young people enormously. It's a completely different world now musically. The young people coming up don't realise it: they have different expectations, which means they have to work to a higher level.

There is also a big difference in the amount of business sponsorship which has become available over the past fifteen years or so. Gradually the arts are being looked at by businesses as being a regular possibility for sponsorship. But there is a lot to be done in the schools. In every country around the world these days, it is becoming more difficult to get classical music made into a regular part of the curriculum. It's very depressing in a lot of places. Sir Simon Rattle talks about it in England: that he despairs of what's happening. I speak to colleagues in Germany who despair that even in Germany music is being taken out. After the war one of the first things they rebuilt were the opera houses – that mightn't happen now! Even in Austria, music is not necessarily part of the school curriculum. I think that happened earlier in Ireland than anywhere else. There was a big down-swing. There were enlightened people like Peadar Killian in the Department of Education, who did a lot to foster music. But gradually over the years there was a whittling down of the number of music inspectors. It used to be that anybody who wanted to become a primary schoolteacher had to pass in music, and that is no longer the case.

But I see a lot of hope recently because in the last five years, since I've been working with the Department of Education, I've seen a huge swing towards recognition that you must give a broad education to people and not just scientific, not just mathematical, not just computers. You have to give them something else because people need other things for life: otherwise you don't expand. I think there will be a huge change in music education within the next ten years.

RAYMOND WARREN, Composer, Cambridge Graduate, Professor of Music at Queen's University Belfast 1955-72, now Professor Emeritus of Music at Bristol University
My First Meeting with Aloys Fleischmann
Aloys Fleischmann was a man of many parts, any one of which, given his seemingly limitless energy, might have sufficed for a normal career. There was his work as a composer and as a conductor and his extraordinary achievement in setting up a major and, in some ways, quite unique International Choral Festival in a rather unlikely place (readers from Cork must please note that I did not say unsuitable!), unlikely if only on account of its remote location in continental terms: and furthermore not only setting it up but also directing it with im-

mense success for some 40 years. But he was also a distinguished academic, both as a teacher and a writer on Irish music, and I thought I would build these short reminiscences around this side of his work. There will be others who will remember him better than me in this as in the other areas, but this is where I probably got to know him the best; and, as it happens, many of his qualities as an academic became evident on the very first occasion I met him, in the spring of 1959. This, then, is a snapshot of some of his concerns, and some of the things he was doing and thinking in mid-career.

The occasion was a symposium at University College Cork on the subject of the organising and teaching of university music. At that time I had been just three years in my first post as lecturer at Queen's Belfast; among the others there were Anthony Hughes, who had only recently been appointed to the chair at University College Dublin after the long tenure there of John F. Larchet (another of the great names in Irish music) and Brian Boydell, who at that time hardly had a post at all. He was desperately trying to persuade the authorities to set up a proper internal Music department at Trinity College, Dublin which, despite its long association with music over several centuries, was really little more than a body conferring external degrees. There weren't any other Music departments in the country then and so I suppose in a sense it was appropriate that Aloys should have taken the initiative to get us all together, because he'd held the chair in Cork for 25 years and was much the best established person to do so. Even so, the initiative in actually getting round to doing it was typical of the man.

Aloys got the enterprise off to a characteristically warm start by meeting two of us from our Dublin train and it soon became evident that the warmth of his personality was matched by a very clear and penetrating mind. When, later, I learned of his academic background, I realised that he integrated into his musicianship both the practical skills (in his case in composition and conducting) which he had formally studied at the Akademie für Tonkunst in Munich and also the systematic musicology studied at the university there. Such an integration was attempted, not always successfully, by the English universities at that time, but not on the continent, as the divided institutions at Munich show. What made Aloys so interesting to an Englishman like me was that he had arrived at this composite musicianship in his own way and from a quite different direction than that of my own Cambridge background. I think that he brought a certain Germanic sensibility and attention to detail to bear on his analytical thinking and sometimes this led to criticisms of him. I recall, to jump ahead some 10 years for a moment, his giving a lecture on Debussy's quartet, and in the audience was Seán Ó Riada, a musician for whom Debussy could do no wrong, and who was rather scathing of an approach, too Germanic in his view, which saw a formal weakness in the fact that in the first movement, the second subject in the exposition is not recapitulated. Personally I was inclined to accept Aloys' general assumption that this particular work of the composer's early period does in so many ways fall into the French nineteenth century 'classical' tradition that it is fair enough to examine it as such. He was, incidentally a very clear lecturer: efficient too in that he could illustrate his points by playing from the score at the piano with a facility that made it sound like a straightforward piano piece. He did the same thing from a microscopic orchestral score of *La Mer* to illustrate a point of harmony.

Back to the 1959 symposium. I was struck by his approach to two problems which were rather different from anything I had met personally. The first was the very poor quality (in those days) of music education in Irish schools. His response was to tackle both symptoms and causes: the former by instituting in his department a carefully worked out course in techniques and history beginning in the first year with very elementary things; the latter by advising, and indeed cajoling the schools all over the south of the country and so establishing a relationship with them which was quite unique in my experience. He said that he saw it as a prime function of his to train well-qualified music teachers for the schools and then for him to go round the schools and authorities persuading them to appoint such teachers. He seemed to be taking on a whole regional project virtually single handed.

The other problem for him at that time was how to integrate Irish traditional music into a university curriculum, the difficulty being not only how to give academic credibility to an area of music which at that time had been subjected to comparatively little academic scrutiny, but also how to pitch the standards so as to be commensurate with the more highly academicised 'European' components. What he did was again pragmatic: on the one hand to think through what were the best analytical techniques for studying the genre and to encourage performance of as high standards as possible in relation to what he regarded as the best traditional practice; on the other hand he initiated musicological investigations so as to create the best background resources for systematic study. This being my first opportunity to talk to university musicians in the south (for Ireland in those days was much more isolated than it is now) I was interested to note that none of those at the symposium from the National University questioned the important place given to this part of their curriculum. Their country as an independent entity was still only some 30 years old and it went without saying that promoting its indigenous music was a perfectly natural contribution they should make towards the realisation of their national identity. In this Aloys was as enthusiastic as anyone and I would argue now that his most enduring single achievement, even more important than his historical writings, may well prove to be his catalogue of the printed sources of Irish traditional music, a massive work of scholarship which he didn't quite finish in his lifetime (it has since been completed and published) and which is an important resource for those working in the field. However his undeniably great enthusiasm for the subject didn't prevent his showing some impatience and frustration at the too rigid regulations designed to promote Irish studies in his university. These meant, for example, that he was not always free to appoint to his staff those he thought to be the best. I have a letter from him dating from the 1970s in which he writes: 'Our recent advertisement might have meant expansion, but though we had a field of 18 candidates including a DMus and several PhDs, I fear we made no appointment since the statute which lays down that Irish music must be covered is not workable. We will have to create a junior post instead.'

Looking back on it now, I don't think Aloys' initiative in setting up the symposium (and his clear headed chairing of the sessions) led to any tangible results at the time, though they did set up friendly relationships between the various departments which were to bear fruits later. This is particularly true of relationships with my own department at Belfast which were not helped by the uneasy political climate of those days. There were actually long standing historic ties between the universities at Belfast and Cork because they were founded at the same time in the nineteenth century as twin colleges in the old Queen's University of Ireland. Aloys knew this of course and also knew, when he invited us symposium delegates to a public event on the last evening, the Bax Memorial Lecture, that there was a somewhat similar endowment in Belfast. There the benefaction came from the estate of Hamilton Harty and had helped to fund our chair in Music and also funded (regrettably only in part) an annual H. H. concert to include one of his works. The problem for us in Belfast was that almost all Harty's works used an expensively large orchestra.

Cork had handled things better. Bax, who was of course a much more important composer than Harty, had been a personal friend of Aloys and had left his library of scores and some other artefacts to the university. These were housed in a special Bax Memorial Room, which Aloys had showed us round – very knowledgeably, as one would expect. After the lecture, which was given that year by Ivor Keys, who had been the first to hold the chair in Belfast but had by then moved on to Nottingham, we were invited into the Bax room for drinks: among the fifty or so there were the German Ambassador, the Lord Mayor of Cork and the pianist Harriet Cohen, who had been closely associated with Bax. Aloys was the perfect host on such occasions, making conversation easily as he moved round the room introducing people. The reception was clearly going very well when it was interrupted in a most dramatic way. Harriet Cohen, looking up at a certain trophy fixed to the wall above a case of orchestral scores, suddenly shouted out 'Aloys, Aloys!' He was at the far end of the room at the time but being a small man and quite quick on his feet he soon filtered through the suddenly hushed assembly to see an accusing finger pointing upwards; 'There's worm in Arnold's cricket bat!' The delightful incongruity of decay in such a symbol of Englishness was not lost on the Irish people there, and certainly not on Aloys himself. After all, the same Bax had been so sympathetic to the Irish cause at the time of the uprisings earlier in the century that he had written patriotic Irish poetry (in Irish) and the general view was that he'd never have been offered the post of Master of the King's Music had His Majesty's advisers at the time been able to read it! And so to my growing appreciation of Aloys' personal qualities was added the realisation that he could keep a perfectly straight face, as he reassured Harriet that the bat would be properly treated. We had a good laugh about it afterwards, and I'm sure he did get the bat treated – he was a man who got the small things right as well as the big!

4: THE ORGANISER

(1) The Cork Symphony Orchestra

LOUIS MARCUS (DUBLIN), Writer and Film-Maker, UCC Arts Graduate, Member of the Cork Symphony Orchestra
When you contemplate the state of classical music in Ireland today, with its multiplicity of symphony, chamber, college and youth orchestras, its string quartets and choirs – to mention only some of its vibrant life – it is hard to believe that in the early 1950s the Irish musical scene was a virtual wasteland. But it was. And one of the pioneers who struggled in that wilderness with vision and determination was Aloys Fleischmann.

The challenge was difficult enough in Dublin. But in Cork it was truly daunting. While the city had a long-established affection for the popular operas with their succulent arias, its attitude to classical music was dismissive. As someone said to my violin teacher, Willie Brady, in contempt for the symphonic repertoire, 'What Cork likes is a good tune!' Aloys Fleischmann set out to change that. And he had the mettle for it.

As a boy, living round the corner from University College Cork, I would often notice him as a striking figure on his way to lectures. He sat stiffly upright on a weirdly motorised push-bike that left a rasping echo along the Western Road, his briefcase slung from the crossbar. He was clearly oblivious to the possibility of ridicule at a time when people sneered easily at the unconventional. And the image remains with me as a symbol of the man – single-minded, indifferent to popular prejudice, and very efficient.

Of course, he enjoyed a certain licence in the climate of that time. As an expert on classical music he was expected to be eccentric. And then, though quintessentially a middle-class Corkman, he was of German parentage – another guarantee of oddity.

I saw little of his father, a quiet tubby man who was an organist and choirmaster, though I remember one celestial evening when he conducted a choral programme of Palestrina in the Honan Chapel of UCC. But Frau Tilly Fleischmann, the Professor's mother, was altogether more colourful. Reputed to be a living link to Liszt, she exuded an aura of Habsburg musical *gravitas* that was both anomalous and exciting in the Cork of the time. Tall and slim, she would waft into the City Hall for the rare symphony concerts in a long black dress, trailing a diaphanous scarf and a strong whiff of Vienna. Her piano students found her rigorous in the cause of music. One talented girl I knew was upbraided by Frau Tilly for contemplating marriage. 'But what about your career?' To another student she fulminated that Cork people had flocked in trains to Dublin to see a mere football match when they wouldn't cross the road to hear a concert. It was actually an All-Ireland Hurling Final, and I could sympathise with the sporting enthusiasm. But I knew what she meant. I got to know Aloys himself when, as a schoolboy, I joined the violins of the Cork Symphony Orchestra, which he conducted, and played in it for about seven years through my college days until I emigrated to Dublin. The brass and woodwind came mostly from the No. 2 Army Band, stationed in Cork, and as professionals they didn't need to join us until the last few rehearsals. But apart from a few local teachers, we strings were rank amateurs and had to be coached once a week for several months before a performance.

We met every Monday night in the Aula Maxima of UCC, walking up the winding avenue, leafy in early autumn and lamplit in winter, to the great Gothic pile of the college. Most were women, and many of them were elderly. As the cold began to bite in the draughty cavern of the Aula Max the older ladies would wince, and car rugs began to be tucked around rheumatic thighs.

Very few of us seemed to practice our parts between rehearsals so that Fleischmann was confronted with the same mistakes and shambles week after week. I used to wonder at his patience and the unfailing courtesy of his remonstrations. How could a man of his musical sensitivity go through this continuing torture when he could sit at home listening to the world's great artists on gramophone records? But Fleischmann seemed determined to make live classical performance a reality in Cork despite the obstacles, a vision that has since been fulfilled.

As the annual concert approached, things somehow fell roughly into place. And when we were joined by the professionals of the brass and woodwind, the exhilaration would grow. For us amateur music-makers the experience of performing, however raggedly, the masterworks of the concert repertoire was an experience not to be missed.

We gave two programmes a year. One, coming up to Christmas, was a symphony concert in the City Hall with a visiting soloist. And it always included a new Irish work, conducted by the composer. One year it was the turn of Frederick May. Being rather deaf, he was not to conduct but would be required to take his bow from the stage after the performance. Alarmingly, as the hour of the concert approached, there was no sign of the composer. I learned later from the sculptor, Seamus Murphy, with whom Freddie was staying, how the crisis was solved. Frau Tilly determined to find him, and Seamus, knowing the composer's personal predilections, suggested that she might try the pubs on the docks which sailors frequented. Quite unabashed, Tilly called a taxi and sallied into a succession of waterside dens until she discovered Freddie, dragged him into the car and had him in the City Hall in time to take his bow.

Our other annual outing was to play for the Cork Ballet Company in the Opera House and, after it was burned down, in the City Hall. The great satisfaction of this was that you got six whole nights of performing. And, of course, there was all the colour of the ballet. Even more than orchestral music, ballet was an utter anomaly in Cork. When he heard of the company's formation, Frank O'Connor scoffed that you couldn't have ballet in his native city as there were no Commissars for the ballerinas to sleep with! Yet this delicate art attracted a host of Cork practitioners. Perhaps one might have expected it to appeal to girls. But even at a time when men dreaded being regarded as cissies, it had a loyal bevy of male dancers too.

This improbable flower was the work of yet another visionary who matched Fleischmann's inability, or unwillingness, to contemplate failure in attempting the impossible – Joan Denise Moriarty. She was too tall to be a successful ballerina herself, though she was splendid as an ancient Irish warrior-woman in *Macha Ruadh*, a ballet she created to Fleischmann's own music. But she whipped her charges into an annual week of dance and music that judiciously skirted the more demanding classical repertoire and successfully exploited their real gift for comedy and mime.

In the lead up to a ballet week, we were joined by the dancers for the last few rehearsals in the Aula Maxima. To those of us whose knowledge of ballet was confined to the film *The Red Shoes* and the colourful novels of Brahms and Simon, this was a rare encounter with the exotic. These creatures in their black leotards seemed to belong to a rarefied world. And the fact that some of the ballerinas' thighs were thicker than those in a Degas painting, or that they were called Mary or Philomena rather than Natasha or Svetlana, did nothing to destroy the magic. The aura was completed by the elaborate formality with which Fleischmann and Joan Denise would address each other during the regular stoppages for adjustment of tempo or breakdown in a difficult passage. 'I wonder, Professor Fleischmann ...' Joan Denise would call from the depths of the hall. 'Certainly, Miss Moriarty', Fleischmann would reply. There was a breath of the Bolshoi on the Western Road.

Remarkably, the ballet was a popular success in Cork and we played to full houses. I suspected rather meanly that the women in the audience came mainly to revel in the glamour of the costumes while their husbands, dragged there reluctantly, could at least enjoy in that pre-miniskirt era the rare sight of so many girls' legs. But for the participants, it was a heady experience. I shall never forget how, when the heavy curtain rose for the second and third acts, its backdraught would waft across the orchestra a pungent aroma composed of stage-dust, grease-paint and human sweat.

One year it was decided to take the ballet on tour. That is, we were booked for a two-night stand in the Town Hall, Killarney. It was not a success. The audience on the first night consisted of a handful of people from whom the proverbial word of mouth must have spread through the Kerry town. On the second night, there was one local in the cheap seats at the back and, in the dearer front row just behind the conductor's podium, a corpulent American whose enthusiasm was more vocal than one would have wished. 'Great stuff, Prof', he would roar as Fleischmann drove the orchestra into a rapid passage. 'Lash into 'em, Prof', he shouted, jumping up and down and clapping his hands in excitement. At moments like that, one's heart sank for the future of musical art in Ireland.

There was one other occasion that one would wish to have been spared. It was the custom that the morning after our annual symphony concert in the City Hall a repeat performance would be given for the schoolchildren of the city. At one of these, the audience was to be addressed at the end of the programme by a Department of Education Inspector of Schools.

Standing beside Fleischmann's podium, the visiting dignitary spoke at length and exclusively in Irish. He launched a savage attack on the kind of 'foreign' music that had been played, so unsuited to the native soul, and extolled the traditional musical riches of the Gael. At one point he looked at Fleischmann, smiled at the audience and said, 'Tá sé ceart go leor. Ní thuigeann an Gearmánach mise'. (It's all right. The German can't understand me.)

Fleischmann stood impassively through this tirade. When the Inspector had finished, he bowed politely to the speaker beside him, turned to the audience and announced in a firm voice, 'Seasagaigh suas, a pháistí, agus canfaimid Amhrán na bhFíann.' (Stand up, children, and we'll sing the National Anthem.) Then with a flourish of his baton, he launched the orchestra into the familiar tune. The face of the troglodyte on the platform beside him got redder, and redder, and redder.

Little did the Inspector of Schools suspect, nor would he have understood, that Fleischmann was engaged in major, long-term research on Irish traditional music that has since been published to some acclaim. And there were other quiet services that he performed in an endless effort to advance the standards of music. One of these, in which I was involved, was to bring the strings of the Cork Symphony Orchestra to the Music department of UCC one night a year to allow his students to hear what their compositions would actually sound like. We squeezed into a large drawing-room, and afterwards we were treated to tea and cake.

Between our variable abilities to sight-read, and the students' tyro efforts at conducting, these sessions no doubt fell somewhat short of those at the great European conservatoires. But the important thing was that they took place at all. Fleischmann was doggedly building a musical infrastructure for Cork. And after years of struggle, he succeeded in persuading Radio Éireann to employ a professional string quartet and have it based in that city. The performers had additional duties as teachers, and from that flowed the blossoming that has since made Cork a centre of high excellence in string playing.

Years later, when I served with Aloys Fleischmann on the Cultural Relations Committee of the Department of External Affairs (as it was then called), I came to realise that his work for the growth of music extended beyond Cork to the whole of Ireland. For a man so serious about his mission and so beset by obstacles, he was unexpectedly cheerful and good-humoured. And he had his own brand of droll wit. Once, when we were about to tune for an orchestral rehearsal, he asked me to strike A on the grand piano that was almost inaccessible behind heavy furniture. But I managed to reach the note by turning my violin bow upside down and hitting the key with the nut. 'Ah,' said Fleischmann with a twinkle, 'I didn't know you could play the Hammerklavier!'

But he was quite devoid of a Rabelaisian sense that could spot, and take steps to avoid, the *double entendre*. In the giggly uneasiness about sex among students in the 1950s, stories were eagerly retailed around college of the Professor's unwittingly ribald remarks in composition class about the characteristics of the flute or the horn. And in front of nuns, too! He was equally uncomprehending of our amusement one night at orchestral rehearsal when the predominantly female strings insisted that he hadn't given out the parts for the national anthem the week before, when he equally insisted he had. 'Now, ladies,' he said, polite but stern, 'when you go home, be sure to search your drawers!' Such was the innocence of the 1950s.

All in all, he was one of those rare and ultimately seminal figures who dragged Ireland in various fields from the swamp of its post-independence complacency to a real sense of international standards. That he did so with such imperturbable patience and personal charm makes him an object of both admiration and affection to anyone who knew him.

SISTER MARIE COLLINS (CORK), UCC Music Graduate, Music Teacher

I had been a late starter: music was an idea for the future, for my retiring years perhaps! The piano and organ had been my instruments and now, here I was, a mere sixth grader in the 'fiddle', taking my place among the second violins in Professor's Symphony Orchestra! It was a suggestion from my teacher that it would be a good idea if I could gain admittance: it would give me confidence to play with experienced musicians. So, in I went, without any test piece from Professor, through symphony concerts and many ballet performances, not to mention the greatest highlight of all – playing in the Gaiety Theatre, Dublin, where we staged *Swan Lake* to an enraptured audience, or so it seemed! All praise to my dear friend Marie, who never hinted at the 'sour' notes coming from time to time from my direction. Should Professor ever detect any disharmony emanating from our quarter, I had already forewarned him that I was the culprit!

From the word go, I never ceased to marvel at the wonderful gifts with which this man was endowed. Setting music aside, it was evident that everybody in the orchestra loved and respected him to a high degree. 'Prof' was their hero, beloved by all. First and foremost, he was a true gentleman, belonging to a courtly era. To address members of the orchestra by their first names had no place in his book. Indeed his memory for names was phenomenal. Respect emanated from him and evoked equal respect in return.

If patience is a virtue, he surely excelled in this quality. It was tangible! People arriving late on occasion, or perhaps not turning up at all so that vital instruments were missing, should have provoked an impatient outburst. Not his reaction. Crossing his arms on his chest, he would raise an eyebrow, pull a face and nodding his head would say: 'Let's carry on' – a lesson for many of us to learn! His reaction was similar when, on occasion, hired music sheets were forgotten or lost when due to be returned. He was the loser, having to pay the fines.

The Sunday afternoon rehearsal for the opening night of the various ballets has to be recorded. There were three focal points. We, the orchestra, tuned up in the pit. The dancers were all ready in the wings, whilst Miss Moriarty with a small entourage ensconced themselves in the auditorium. The overture out of the way, Professor stood poised awaiting the 'green light'. Act One had taken off and gallantly we responded to our conductor's baton. Alas! not for long. The sudden and pained voice of Miss Moriarty calling: 'Profess-or-r-r' reached our ears, signalling that all was not well. Clearly our sympathies lay with our conductor during the ensuing debate. We were either too fast or the dancers too slow. Nods, smiles and winks for the orchestra as Professor indicated that we return to bar fifty-four.

After three hours of rehearsal, during which we experienced 'red lights' followed by 'freeflows', we were all set for the opening night's performance. Not surprisingly, all went well, ending with Professor mounting the stage, joining hands with the Ballet Company to great applause and curtain calls, which he indeed merited. Miss Moriarty rarely took a bow. The amount of work involved with the production probably left her spent.

> How poor are they
> that have not patience!
> What wound
> did ever heal
> but by degrees?
>
> (Shakespeare)

Professor's unremitting dedication to hard work was remarkable. How true the maxim 'One man sows, another reaps'! How well it applies to 'Prof'. To quote from an interview with two noted sisters, members of the orchestra for fifty-eight years: 'He opened up a whole new world for them and for many others who were privileged to hear him tell the stories behind the classics, so as better to perform them in concert.' His dedication and hard work was evident in the way he personally prepared the venue for the weekly practice, arriving early, clearing chairs and tables, and placing music stands so as to ensure that everything was in readiness for the arrival of the musicians. Furthermore, he was again at the helm after the two-hour practice, to replace all furniture, leaving the place in its pristine state for next day's occupants. On one occasion it was noticeable that he limped badly. The story emerged that he had broken an ankle earlier in the afternoon and yet he never complained, standing for the entire practice.

No marks for naming the composer of the *Surprise Symphony*! On the fortieth anniversary of the formation of the Symphony Orchestra, we had a celebration. My contribution was a cake – a beautiful cake, the product of the culinary genius of a friend, replete with a musical clef on top of white icing and bearing the usual congratulatory scripting for such an occasion. Professor was intrigued by the work of art. Here lay the big 'surprise' for me. I had never envisaged that Professor, so entrenched in the world of music, could succumb to the mundane level of being bewitched by a fortieth anniversary fruitcake! Ever after I arrived on his doorstep at Christmas time with a cake of far less grandeur, which he welcomed with the wonder of a child. His good wife was wont to remark: 'He'll husband that most carefully and only very special visitors will be treated to a slice!'

Professor was conscious that music for leisure was the trend for the future. Hence his indefatigable effort to promote choirs, instrumental listening and appreciation of music in the schools at all times. He maintained that it sharpened the intellect for the study of other subjects. After he had founded the Cork Choral and Folk Dance Festival, choirs sprang up all over the country to participate in the senior and junior competitions available on the programme. Foreign choirs and dancers opened up a new era for many who would never have had the experience of same. The US, Europe, England and Wales intermingled with each other and our own Irish choirs in the City Hall, made radiant for four days with flowers and flags to greet the competing nations on their arrival. Preparation for the Festival entailed much hard work, co-operation from many willing bodies and the provision of accommodation for visiting choirs from abroad. Sunday night was memorable for choral and dance farewells, prize-giving and the great finale from the combined choirs on stage rising to a great crescendo – signalling the close of a great week. For 'Prof' and his loyal helpers remained a hefty debt to be defrayed. 'Having sown in tears', he never let monetary matters 'dim the star he followed'. How beneficial for us that this Festival, his initiation, continues under a new leadership and happily fewer financial worries!

I sat beside him on the balcony on his last appearance at the matinee for senior schools' choirs in competition. To me, he looked thin and worn but he gave no hint that anything was amiss, applauding the various choirs as they came on stage with his usual vigour and appreciation. He left early saying he had to meet his daughter, arriving from Germany. In no time, he was back on stage presenting prizes and certificates of merit. I marvelled at this man whom nothing could deter from keeping the music going.

During the following weeks, news filtered through that Professor was ill, seriously ill, some said. Nobody could conceive that the end was in view. Early in July, I decided to call on him before going to Donegal on my annual retreat. I found him working on his book, a compilation of material on Irish music begun thirty years previously, which he needed to complete against time. His daughters, like ministering angels, were with him and withdrew for a while. Though very weak, he was most welcoming and merely commented that the diagnosis wasn't good. I had brought along a violin for his little grandson who had begun taking lessons. Smiling, he drew the bow across the strings. To me, it was the last reveille! Sadly, I rose to leave, promising to remember him in my prayers. Indeed, I had a short letter from him while in Donegal wishing me a happy time and as usual thanking me for the visit.

Like the prophets of old, he could foresee where the future lay, that music would occupy a phenomenal place in the world of today. His students and their students again would carry the flag wherever they went, filling the leisure hours for many with music, 'heavenly music that vibrates in the memory.' Professor was one of those who marched to the tune of a different drummer. His dedication to duty, his hard work and patience in adversity, his humanity and great pride in his family and his palpable concern for the way the world was going are but some of his qualities that merited for him the greatest honour this city could bestow on anybody: Freeman of the City of Cork!

Ar dheis Dé go raibh a h-anam!

We are all but tenants.
And shortly
the great Landlord
will give us notice
that our lease has expired.

(Joseph Jefferson)

Mary Collins (Cork), UCC Graduate, Member of the Cork Symphony Orchestra, the Cork Orchestral Society, the Choral Festival Committee
My first contact with Professor Aloys Fleischmann was when, in secondary school, I wrote to him asking if he could include music as a subject for the entrance scholarship to University College, Cork. He wrote back to say he would be delighted to do so, and so music joined the list for the entrance scholarship. In subsequent years I often wondered how many students took the subject, as I soon learned that it was a much-neglected one in schools.

To help remedy this situation the Professor introduced the schools concerts in the City Hall. Before his own Cork Symphony Orchestra concert, he gave a performance for the schoolchildren in the morning, so that it served as a dress rehearsal for the evening. The children came from a radius of twenty miles or more, as well as from city schools. The City Hall was always packed. Each piece was preceded by a short explanatory talk and the children were encouraged to take an active part in the proceedings. They enjoyed it enormously and learnt that making music could be fun.

When the RTE Symphony Orchestra came, they performed for the children on the morning following their evening concert, and had a special shortened programme, as a full symphony concert would have taxed the concentration of the youngsters. They held the first performance at 10 o'clock followed by a break for refreshments for the orchestra, and then a new group of children trooped in for a repeat show. Sadly these schools concerts were discontinued in recent years – surely a step backwards, musically speaking.

But to get back to UCC. Some of the most enjoyable moments there were spent rehearsing in the Professor's choir and playing in the orchestra. Things were never dull when he was at the helm. I remember the cocky medical student who thought his interpretation of a piece was superior to that of the Professor! The Prof told him: 'I'm open to correction in one matter only, that of the Irish language, and I would remind you that in all other matters pertaining to the music I am the sole arbiter'.

One evening there was a concert in Fota House when the resident peacocks struck up a rival performance on the lawn outside. They hadn't reckoned with the Professor, who immediately gave chase and added enormously to the enjoyment of the evening. I don't remember what the concert programme was, but I do remember the Flight of the Peacocks.

After more than fifty years of conducting, he could still be amazed at the lack of knowledge of the audience: 'If I don't keep my arms in the air continuously,' he would say, 'they'll clap'. On one occasion when the clapping came in the middle of a phrase, he remarked afterwards in astonishment: 'Wouldn't you think they'd recognise a half cadence?'

At his funeral service in the North Cathedral, I saw many young people crying – a true sign that in him we had had a Man for All Seasons.

ALISON WALSH (CORK), *Member of the Cork Ballet Company, the Cork Orchestral Society, the East Cork Choral Society, the Cork Choral Festival Committee*
Miss Moriarty decided to put on a night of ballet in the Opera House in 1947 and I was one of the many members of the cast for *Vltava*. I was twelve. We practised in many dirty dusty halls on Sundays. Then we were told that Professor Fleischmann and his orchestra would be there the following week and that we would have to be very well behaved. Other than that we were, that the performance was a great success, and that a Government Minister in evening dress sat in a box in the old Opera House while we twirled and sashayed as a river, I have no further memories. But we made history.

The following year I was part of the *Nutcracker Suite*, being a soldier in Act One and a flower in Act Three. Again it was rehearsals in filthy halls and coming home fit only for deep cleaning. Then the Professor and the orchestra came one Sunday to the Central Hall. We were very much in awe of him, and all the more so when we were told that he wrote the music for *The Golden Bell of Ko*, performed in 1948. It was about a Chinese bell-maker who failed to get a bell finished in time and faced execution, but was saved by his three daughters who sacrificed themselves for him. At that time I was attempting to play the violin with appalling results and having lessons from the late Billie Foley. She sat next to Willie Brady, leader of the orchestra. One night the three girls jumped as usual into the fire to save their father, and three others ascended to heaven. But they got stuck half way up – Heaven must have been full that night and there they swirled half way to eternity. Meanwhile Mr Brady through looking at the stage lost his place, so did a number of others in the orchestra, but all kept on playing and lost 11 bars somewhere. But all finished on time and the Professor, who had written the work, said it was 'excellent playing'!

That same year *The Faery Queen* was performed in the City Hall and we, the lower members of the chorus, were given rooms on the third floor of the City Hall in which to change. There was a corridor outside so we younger ones pounded up and down, skeiting as we called it. The orchestra also changed there. Now I was a tall girl – almost five foot ten and well built. This night I was pounding along the corridor as usual in my stage costume when little Mr Brady came out of his room; I bumped into him, knocking him over; then I picked him up, dusted him down, apologised and asked if he was all right. He looked at me in total horror. Meanwhile Miss Moriarty and the Professor were standing nearby, discussing the performance, and had seen the whole incident. The Professor tried to hide behind Miss Moriarty, who seemed very cross. She gave me a lecture but I suspected that her crossness was a cover for her amusement.

I then changed schools and study took over so although ballet continued, I was in no more major shows. But our school used to attend the Professor's children's concerts for schools in the City Hall. By now the Professor had become part of our family's Lares and Penates. My brother's school also attended the concerts. The Professor would ask certain members of the orchestra to demonstrate their instruments and each one's capabilities. Invariably some boy in the audience – and it was always a boy – would say 'a saxophone, surr' when a huge brass one was shown, and then the Professor with infinite patience would explain why it was not a saxophone. This occurred at every concert and we used to look forward to it as an annual tradition. Non-musical friends who attended the concerts played cards, chess, did their homework and on one occasion a group of boys let off a stink bomb in the boys' toilets! I remember attending one concert of some famous visiting foreign orchestra who played movements from some grand work. We waited to the end to applaud and gave them a standing ovation. That night the orchestra repeated the work to an adult audience who ignorantly applauded at the end of the first movement. We, the schools audience, were very pleased with ourselves.

144

I was a member of the Orchestral Society for a number of years and reached the giddy heights of being the secretary in charge of refreshments. The Prof lived only for music, to such an extent that the normal everyday world hardly impinged on his consciousness. On one occasion I tried to explain the amount of time it took just to buy three dozen cups. He was not aware that all china had to be washed before it was first used. On another occasion I was overseeing a mid-morning snack for a rehearsing orchestra. I said we'd serve tea and biscuits; he said no: coffee and sandwiches. I said no: tea – cheaper and easier as there was no need for cream; and biscuits – no preparation or washing up of plates, etc. Again he was amazed.

The Choral Festival and its continued strength is a tribute to him. Every night saw him in his seat on the left of the front row downstairs, ready to leap up to congratulate someone and thank them for their contribution. For many years we – the patient audiences – put up with long, high-brow works with late running concerts because the Prof could not find it in his heart to curtail things. Kevin Breen used to tell a story of some IRA man who was about to take to the stage to make a speech. Kevin called the Prof over and asked him to talk to the man, meanwhile the guards were informed. In the middle of the Prof's discussion about the concert the police nabbed the man, leaving the Prof amazed: 'But he was so attentive – you mean he was in the IRA?'

Whenever he used to be at a loss about what dance team to have we would suggest a) a certain group from the south of Ireland – they came once, and mercifully once only, and were excruciatingly dull; b) a group of English male dancers who wore bells on their knees: they were equally dreary if more vividly dressed than the unfortunate Irish group; c) a group of Turkish male dancers – these came from the East End of London, were unprepared to perform, came on stage and had a confab as to what they would do, broke down during the attempt and in their spare moments off stage they used to pinch the rear ends of girls. They were shipped off very quickly. The Prof was horrified when he was told about their carry-on.

We had a great twenty-fifth anniversary celebration of the Choral Festival in the Metropole Hotel. First there was a lovely meal, then a concert, choir, group and individual items. We gave the Prof a present of a silver baton, and he was very chuffed, but I believe he lost it the following week. I heard that he lost or mislaid many of the presented items he received down the years.[1] We ended up with a wonderful dance.

There was so much fun, gaiety and friendliness engendered by the Choral Festival. I remember being abroad once in Bulgaria with some English people. We met with some locals who asked where we were from, so the English people said: 'London'.

'Yes,' said the locals.

'Cork,' said I.

'Oh, you have a great singing Festival there: my friends went last year.'

The English I was with were quite miffed. I remember well the final year for the Prof as Choral Festival director. He got two standing ovations and forgot to play the National Anthem.

I was a member of the East Cork Choral Society and in 1985 there was a celebration in Cloyne Church of Ireland Cathedral for the tercentenary of Berkeley, the philosopher, and the Prof wrote *Time's Offspring* for choir and augmented orchestra. It was a modern work and we were used to singing oratorio. We ploughed on with it, parts in Latin for which our Latinist insisted we use the more modern pronunciation. We did some of our rehearsing in Midleton College with Patrick Zuk. Then the great day dawned and the Prof arrived to conduct a rehearsal with Patrick at the piano.

Most of the choir members had never met the Prof. It was late spring and he wore a white suit and black shoes that were not matching. He upscuttled us as he required that we sing the work twice as fast as we had rehearsed it. Then we had to change our Latin pronunciation back to Roman usage, which pleased us. It was an augmented orchestra, someone said that the Prof had invited anyone who had ever played in the orchestra to perform, so the sound was huge. The work started when Canon Mills, a Church of Ireland clergyman, had to introduce the piece to the accompaniment of the orchestra. But no one could hear him. We missed our cues and then sang flat and sharp if we could be heard at all. I knew the Prof, so I had the temerity to tell him that we could not hear the note cues for our entries. During a break the Prof rearranged the seating of the orchestra so things were a bit better then. He actually took home *all* the scores – and it was an augmented orchestra – and he re-scored the entire work for the following week. What patience. Patrick Zuk in a recent interview has also paid tribute to the Prof's patience and attention to detail. Our next rehearsal of *Time's Offspring* was an improvement but on the big night, the performance in Cloyne Cathedral before a 'distinguished audience' was well below our best. But as no one had ever heard the work previously, criticism was muted. There were physicists and atomic scientists in the audience as there had been Berkeley 300 celebrations in the US and in the UK, on the continent and in Cloyne. Actually, although the piece was very modern, I liked several aspects of it quite a lot.

We are all unique, but the Prof had a very special quality of kindness, infinite politeness. He was patient, always remembered everyone's name, gave time to each person and had an old world charm that was totally sincere. Everyone who knew him had their own special story, and they were myriad, because he was who he was and had all of these warm, kind qualities and always expected the very best from everyone. People did things for him: sold tickets and programmes, showed people to seats, put up with a lot – because they loved him. I seldom saw him annoyed: once with an incompetent person in the orchestra for the Berkeley celebration, and he was once disgruntled with me over a gaffe, but he was a supremely gracious, courtly man. We were all very fond of him and would do anything for him. He had great charm and always saw the best in everyone. He was of another age and I don't think much of the ugliness of modern day life really impinged on him. We were so fortunate in Cork to have had him and Miss Moriarty at the same time. They brought music, colour, life, a feeling of the exotic, a richer canvas of romance to so many – and this touched all kinds of people from all social backgrounds. It was an honour to know them.

JIMMY HYNES (CORK), Member of the Southern Command Army Band and of the Cork Symphony Orchestra
My first opportunity to work with the late Professor Fleischmann occurred in the autumn of 1975. I was invited to play in the orchestra for a production by Cork Ballet Company at the Opera House. It was my first time playing with the orchestra and, being a percussion player, my task was to play bass drum and cymbals. I remember at that performance being overwhelmed by the power and enthusiasm the 'Prof' generated throughout the orchestra.

As a member of the Army Band I found the 'Prof' held us Army lads in high respect and indeed he would often make this obvious at rehearsals. We Army lads often had the 'Prof' visit us in the bandroom in Collins Barracks. He would arrive on his famous motor-bike, less the helmet of course. I always looked forward to those special rehearsals, and can recall many hours of great enjoyment, both musical and jovial, listening to the great wit and appreciating the character of the Professor.

Throughout the twenty years I had the honour of working with him, his great love and dedication to music was something I always admired. My musical education and playing experience were truly enriched by having the opportunity to play under his baton. The people of Cork and Ireland were surely lucky to have had the 'Prof' in our midst.[2]

May he have a well-deserved rest in peace.

MICHAEL MCCARTHY (CORK), Leader of the Cork Symphony Orchestra Cellos
Professor Fleischmann was one of the best-liked, most hard working
people involved in the Cork music world. He was a man who could
cope with all emergencies that came his way when it came to putting
on a performance. While on many occasions there were volunteers
who were delighted to help, there were times when Prof did everything.[3] He was always full of energy, and he had the same respect for
everybody in the orchestra, whether they were professional or amateur.

In his time he had to cope with a bomb scare in the Cork Opera
House during a ballet performance, which was a costly event, and one
or two car crashes. The motto: 'The show must go on' always prevailed and he therefore made Cork a splendid place for music lovers,
music makers, professionals and amateurs alike. He is greatly missed
and has not been replaced.

Of course it goes without saying that the man was a gifted musician and conductor and wonderful when it came to ballet productions.
His students are now teaching all over Ireland and in many parts of
the world. I am sure that there are many people who live in Eastern
Europe who remember the times they came to Cork for the Choral
Festival, and found it a place which made them very welcome. Cork
can be proud of all that Professor Fleischmann did for music and for
the city.

JOE RUSSELL (CORK), Member of the Cork Symphony Orchestra. His memories
were recorded by Anne Fleischmann.
My mother taught me the piano from the age of three or four. I began
to learn the violin at the age of seven, then I took up the cello at fourteen and became quite crazy about the trumpet when I was sixteen. I
knew Professor Fleischmann from the time my mother used to play
the viola in the orchestra: I used to go along and practice with her sometimes. So he knew I played the trumpet; he needed a trumpet player
and I said I'd do it. I played from 1979 to about 1987. I played for concerts and for the ballet in the Opera House, which was great fun. You'd
rehearse with the company and get to know them afterwards.

He was very tolerant of the players – I suppose he had to be with
an amateur orchestra. It was difficult to get them together, difficult to
co-ordinate them. As far as playing was concerned, he was mighty tolerant of mistakes. If something went badly wrong and it kept on being
repeated, then he'd get angry. Some of the brass instruments were just
too loud, but with these instruments it's very difficult to make a nice
sound and not play it loudly. He had a job on his hands, but he did it.
At the end of the day everyone managed to pull together and every-

thing went well. But a lot of effort went into getting it that far. I was up at his house in the Glen a couple of times in winter practising with some of the other players. The drawing-room was very cold and damp: there was only a small heater and a piano, which I think was out of tune. We were a group of three or four and we'd rehearse for an hour or two, in the hope that we would get it right when the moment mattered. It improved our playing, I have to say that. We also rehearsed in other places, but what I remember is Glen House. I had been there before when I was about twelve as I was a playmate of Alan Fleischmann's: we used to have fun there. One day part of the ceiling fell on the trumpet players, but I wasn't responsible for that. One of the others must have raised his instrument a bit too high and done the job!

The Professor had a focused dedication. He was able to address people so well, with such camaraderie. He had command of the situation, a natural command. And he kept going until the very last. I remember seeing him conduct in the Opera House and thinking he looked frail. That was about a year before he died.

LIAM NOLAN (CORK), Member of the Southern Command Army Band and of the Cork Symphony Orchestra
Professor Fleischmann conducted the Cork Symphony Orchestra for more than fifty years. For twenty-five of those years I played first trombone with the orchestra. We played twice annually, or to be more precise three times: there was a symphony concert in the spring, a ballet with the Cork Ballet Company in the autumn, and at the Cork Choral Festival the orchestra usually contributed a short piece at the opening ceremony.

During my time with the orchestra we tackled most of the standard repertoire, and most of the classical ballets. This was possible with a largely amateur orchestra because at the helm we had a man of seemingly limitless energy, of great single-mindedness, and a determination that I have not witnessed in any other person I have encountered.

I am a member of the Southern Command Army Band and Professor Fleischmann drew most of the woodwind and brass wind players from that organisation. It was a practice of the Professor's to hold many rehearsals in the Army bandroom prior to a forthcoming concert, and although there were only seven or eight players involved, he approached those rehearsals with the same vigour he would have applied had the full orchestra been present. No detail was overlooked. The rehearsals normally lasted two hours with a short break. The break was for the players' benefit; the Professor would have preferred none.

The Professor was a lot more than merely a very hard-working man. In my opinion he was a first-class musician, a composer of note, an educationalist, writer and scholar. He possessed a remarkable memory, and although the orchestra numbered in excess of sixty members, he never forgot anybody's name, and he would refer to members very formally as Mrs, Mrs or Miss as the case might be, or regarding members of the army band, according to rank. For trombonists there are often long periods of rest during the course of some works in which one is obliged to count bars, and if despite all the activity going on, one missed an entry the Professor would glare down, letting the player know he had an all-hearing ear.

It was evident to me that music was this man's life; he seemed to devote all his time and energy to its cause. I will remember him as a gentleman and a scholar who enriched my life and am grateful that I was fortunate enough to have known and worked with him.

MÁIRE NÍ CHEALLACHÁIN (CORK), UCC Music Graduate, Member of the Cork Symphony Orchestra, on Donna O'Sullivan's Cork Radio Programme after Fleischmann's death in July 1992
Everybody knew the name of Professor Fleischmann; even as children involved in music in Cork we had an image of him as the god of music in our particular sphere. On meeting the man when I began my studies at university, I was very much in awe of him, as we all were. But very soon we saw the human side of him and though the awe remained, the feeling that he was an authority figure, we very quickly came to have affection for him, which grew over the years. Coming out of university four years after having started there, you felt you knew the man as a person, and I'm sure that yesterday there were many tears shed because he wasn't just a professor: he was somebody most special, whose influence went very deep. Also at that time, I became a member of the Cork Symphony Orchestra, which is an amazing institution. Many people have been members of the Symphony Orchestra for forty years; it was very unusual in that you had people there from all walks of life and from all over the county. He did want to achieve a certain amount professionally but I always felt that what he wanted to do with his life was to improve the community, create a community spirit, and this was very much brought across to us, his students. He wanted his standards, but what he wanted was for us to make an impact in society. And I think if you look around, all around Ireland, in any town you go to, you will find graduates of Professor Fleischmann. They may not be specialising in any particular thing, but they are influencing society in choral societies, orchestras, etc. If you look at the choirs coming to the Choral Festival for the competitions

every year, you have the people who have been students of his.

His sense of fun was quite amazing, because he had such an austere exterior; but the Music department parties were really something to be looked forward to and something to be talked about afterwards for a long time. He was the most marvellous dancer, had a most fantastic sense of fun and was the best person at playing musical chairs that I ever encountered. I have memories of him coming out after Cork Symphony Orchestra rehearsals, trudging along carrying the big tuba. He would always do this sort of thing: would set up the chairs for the orchestra, would bring the tuba home for the player – and on going to find his car would perhaps go to the wrong car, because these things didn't really matter to him.

SIMON O'FLYNN (CORK), *Viola Player of the Cork Symphony Orchestra. His reflections were recorded by the editor.*
I joined the Cork Symphony Orchestra in response to a formal note from the Professor, because my mother and my aunts played in it. I remember my first rehearsal well, because it was the first time I was called Mr O'Flynn. I must have been around 17. I thought Professor had mistaken me for my father.

He knew exactly what he was going to do at every rehearsal and exactly what time he was going to spend on any given piece. Everything was structured: there was progression that you could see and be happy with. When we got to the Aula Max for the rehearsal, everything was laid out. Only years later did I understand that he had done most of the preparations himself, having arrived at least an hour earlier. He was magic to be with. Everything was taken seriously, but in such a way that it was not dour, but always humorous. The rehearsals were occasions in themselves.

To get an orchestra functioning is the most complex matter. It is not a mere question of getting 50 players. You have to get so many first violin players who have the capability to play the violin at that standard. Then you have to get so many people content to play second fiddle, which is a political trick of the first order. It is no good having people in the second violins who can't play: they are just as important at the first, but they seem to have a bad name. And then you have to get viola players, who are always cranky, having been thrown out of violin classes as children and taken up the viola as a last resort. You will invariably not get the players in the quantities that you want them: one season you could be awash with violin players and have no cello players and no viola players. Putting a professional orchestra together is far less difficult than an amateur one, because you are paying these people to do it, whereas to get an amateur orchestra functioning just for a season is a mammoth undertaking. You need players with a special type of talent: they must be prepared not to be a genius and to offer the kind of commitment that will go through rain, floods and flu to get to rehearsals. I rarely missed a practice, but if I did, I always got a phone call wanting to know why. If Professor hadn't done that, the orchestra would have petered out. It was not at all unusual to get a call from him before eight in the morning, or close to midnight. My wife used call me to the phone saying: 'Either your business is on fire or has been broken into, or else it's Professor Fleischmann!'

The other thing I got a sense of over the years is that there was no compromise made just because we were an amateur orchestra, players who have other things to do with their fingers and minds during the day; never was it used as an excuse that he was conducting an orchestra of players of differing abilities and of mixed professions and trades. The great works, the difficult ones, were undertaken, as if we were a full-blown world-class symphony orchestra. I often found myself in a strange situation. People knew me as a player, but they also knew me as a butcher and quite often after the concert, they'd come up and say: 'Lovely, lovely, that was very nice'. But by the following morning I had undergone a metamorphosis, changed my feathers so to speak, and was safe to approach. I used to get the other side then. They'd come into my business and say 'My God, that was terrible!' I never tried to justify anything. I used to always chuckle inwardly, though, because they were comparing us to the record they had at home, or had got from the library, of the London or the Berlin Philharmonic and had found we weren't quite as good as that. Of course, we weren't – local musicians from Cork, who had all the limitations of rural Europe. But we were now being compared to the best orchestras, being actually put into the same bracket! It was the ultimate success really.

It was Professor who did it. I don't know how many times it was said during the first or second rehearsals: 'This is too difficult, we'll never do this. The man is mad: this is way out of our league.' We'd have chickened out of it. He had the courage to walk out on the stage in front of an amateur orchestra and do these colossal works. I have played under professional musicians and they all say the same thing: 'It'll be a disaster!' That's part of the theatre. It's like being on the high wire of a circus without the net under it. The net is taken away when you are playing with amateur orchestras: if things go wrong, they really do go wrong. He took on a huge commitment and he carried it through.

One day Professor found out that my daughter, Sarah, played the viola with the National Youth Orchestra and of course he wanted her to play in his orchestra. So soon she got a formal note inviting her to come. She accepted because her grandmother, her grandaunts and her father were in the orchestra. I remember after the first rehearsal she said: 'Do you know, he called me Miss O'Flynn! Doesn't he know my name?' And I told her my story about being called 'Mr O'Flynn' when I was 17. It was then I realised how long it had been going on. So at one of the concerts three generations of my family played together: my two aunts, Cissie Howell and Kitty Bresnan, myself and Sarah. That shows the role the orchestra had in my life and my family's life.

We almost regarded the orchestra as a family. We were among the players who seemed to be there forever, who had almost become statues in the orchestra. My mother and her sisters were in it right from the beginning: I don't think they missed a single year. They would have travelled through civil wars, pestilence and plague to get to rehearsals. They went because they enjoyed it. At that time, a woman's role was in the home. They couldn't go to the pub, there was no television, and the radios that were available had very bad reception, so this was a wonderful opening. They got to know the repertoire. They used to take it very seriously and practised daily to get the music right. And that was through pregnancies, and minding large families and through illnesses at a time when every sickness could have killed you. Maybe it contributed to their longevity.

But if we felt the orchestra was our family, we also felt we were the Professor's family. I never got the impression during rehearsals that there was any other interest in his life apart from us. He had this tremendous power of focus and language. There was not for one minute a deviation from the task on hand. For example, once in the Maltings he slipped off the podium, hit the back of his head as he went down and collapsed motionless on the floor in front of the whole orchestra and choir, blood streaming from his wound. There was absolute silence. Mr Jerry O'Connor – who was Secretary at the time – jumped up, followed by Mr Nicholas Waters, his assistant. One of them began to whisper an Act of Contrition in Professor's ear, just in case. It certainly brought him around: he sprang up, jumped back on the podium and said 'Come on: letter A, letter A!'

I remember one other dramatic event. We were playing in the Opera House doing the ballet *Coppélia*, which has an important viola solo, 'La Paix'. I was an adequate player maybe, but not a soloist, so the Professor brought in a professional player. The gentleman incidentally used to bring his dog to rehearsals; it was constantly scraping at the floor because there were rats underneath. An orchestral pit is the place where one is closest to electrocution. There are wires everywhere, because each stand has a bulb with 240 volts, quite enough to kill you stone dead. All the wires trail along the floor, but nobody cares: they trip over these things all the time, being utterly absorbed by the music. Mr de Reyghera's solo came up: a tense time. He began beautifully and was about two or three minutes into the solo, sitting on the edge of his seat, rocking away, the cable underneath. It wasn't long before his seat cut the cable, a shower of sparks came from under the chair, all the lights in the orchestral pit went out and everything went dead, except the solo. He knew it so well he didn't even realise the lights had gone. I consider that a triumph.

Music and theatre are like that. You are very close to disaster at all stages. It is a bit like flying. Once you have taken off, you know you are going to have to bring down the aircraft: you hope you will land safely, but you might crash. It is the same with playing music. Once you start the piece in performance, the piece must progress. You are now flying, and you must make sense of the music, must bring it down safely. For anything to happen in between to stop it would be a disaster. Amateur players can get distracted, we are perhaps only half concentrating, are too aware of our inadequacies, are not used to the stress of performing and so on. But if you avoid disaster, and accomplish the task, you get an extraordinary feeling of exhilaration. You have sailed so close to the wind and you have got away with it one more time.

It can be almost like a trance. I still wonder why I do it: after all, I need not play, I need not perform! Why do I put myself in the arena where I court disaster? But you enter into another world with music. We have all seen young boys or girls going through the streets with music blaring in their ears. In my opinion, there is something in our brain that you can unlock with music. The fact that I am a musician has helped me survive in business, because it brings me another way of thinking. But once you have unlocked a certain area of your psyche, you want to enter it again and again: it can become addictive. It can be almost like a drug and it can hurt, it can indeed destroy. You have to be strong with music, otherwise it can gallop away with you and rot you to the core. You have to be able to wrestle with it. Like everybody else, I would love to be able to make a living from it, to play every day. You begin to study it when you are six or seven and it eats into your emotions. Before you come to the use of reason, the adult use of conscious reason, your emotions are now rushing you along, through music. What if you want to be a concert pianist and you don't have the fingers, or the hands, or the money to do it? Do you go on the dust heap? Are you forever more dissatisfied?

The Professor had the courage to stand up and face the public with us amateurs. His neck was on the line: if the whole thing had collapsed, it was he who would have had to creep off the stage. He need never have done it. I suppose he was addicted to it just as we all were. Of course he also knew that unless you perform music, you don't understand it. It is easy enough to do things properly in rehearsal, but when you get out on stage, a whole different set of pressures come on. You must move differently, you must think differently, you must concentrate, you must forget everything except what you are doing.

Music is the only thing I'm afraid of. I find it has much in common with flying. Everything else you have in your mind has to go. You focus on one thing and one thing only. When you come back from flying, you are almost reborn because you have spent an hour or half an hour with an absolutely clear mind. It doesn't matter whether the bank manager is running after you or anything else. Your mind has been scrubbed clean for a while. Once you have rested, you can cope. Music does the same. When you are playing Mozart or any of the great works, you just cannot think of anything else. It's quite impossible: there's too much going on.

Everybody in an amateur orchestra is always playing to the best of their ability. I consider musicians should get great credit just for turning up – it's so easy to stay back and watch and not expose yourself to criticism. It's the safe way to live. But to get up and *do* it, despite the restrictions: that is success! We didn't crawl around and say: 'We won't do it because we aren't good enough.' That would only have been an excuse for doing nothing. We said: 'This is the way we are doing it! This is us!' It was almost an act of faith in humanity itself. I know how lucky I was to have lived through the magic that was the Cork Symphony Orchestra and the Ballet.

MARY ELIZABETH BULLARD (UPPER BASILDON, BERKSHIRE), UCC Graduate, Leader of the Cork Symphony Orchestra 1986–1991
I had the greatest respect for Professor Fleischmann, and working with him was an honour. I first met him when I was just twelve years of age and was singing in the South Presentation Convent Secondary School Choir. I recall rehearsing his Mass for a performance in St Francis Church in 1978; my recollection is of a rather tall, imposing man for whom we performed sections of the Mass. We were in awe of him.

Two years later he invited me to join the Cork Symphony Orchestra – his orchestra. Absolutely thrilled, I went along to rehearsals at the Maltings, an annex of University College, Cork, on Monday nights, where I found a group of enthusiastic people, not all professional musicians, varying in age considerably. At just fourteen years of age, I was the youngest member. There were fascinating and rather colourful characters among them. I remember Prof's baton: it was made of metal, and really heavy – quite a weapon in fact, and I suspect responsible for many a dent in conductors' stands.

Prof had an old-world charm, and always addressed people formally. Even during moments of agitation during rehearsal, he still retained his reserve. Stories abound in Cork about hilarious incidents during performances, such as one about a violinist playing away enthusiastically, blissfully unaware that his desk partner's hairnet was dangling from the tip of his bow. I recall also hearing about the journeys to and from rehearsals when Prof drove some of the players. One or two of them swear that the car tore along on two wheels on occasion, but this did not happen at any time when I was present.

I was constantly amazed at the speed with which the Prof himself moved, however, and at his energy. It seemed to be endless. As a college student, I worked with him for a time on his book *Sources of Irish Traditional Music*. He had a little office on the top floor of the tall Maltings building. On at least three occasions, I recall him running, yes, running up three flights of stairs, two steps at a time, to the office on top. In fact on one of those occasions, he grabbed me by the arm to assist me – I reached the top gasping for breath, whereas he quietly entered his office and sat down to work, seemingly unaffected by the exertion. Rumour had it that he would climb over the eight-foot gates if he had been working late and they had been locked.

I enjoyed every minute of my time in the orchestra – with one single exception. I will never forget one ballet rehearsal, for one of the last ballet weeks directed by Miss Moriarty and Prof. The orchestra was missing one or two key players that evening, but those present were working in earnest. One dancer had a tantrum and yelled at Prof that the music was disgraceful. He was not a guest artist: they always knew how to behave; in fact he was the only dancer I ever heard treat Miss Moriarty or Professor without courtesy. I was deeply incensed and seethed with rage at having to sit there in the leader's seat and witness such a childish outburst, such an insolent attack on a dear friend and a great man. As long as I live, I will never forget the professor's response: he apologised. I am not sure how I managed to find enough composure to finish the rehearsal without going for the dancer's throat: it felt like a personal onslaught.

In 1991 I went through an extremely painful time personally and I decided to take a year away from Cork in order to find inner peace. I found it very difficult to say goodbye to Professor, and I cried. I returned to Cork some months later and decided to call on him at home. Prof's daughter Maeve opened the door to me, and when I asked to see him, she showed me into the drawing-room. To my consternation,

I saw him laid out in his coffin. As I had been away, I had had no idea he was ill. I remember sobbing uncontrollably: this great gifted man had gone, and I had been too late to say goodbye. I touched his face gently. An acute sense of loss and of despair stayed with me for quite some time. Even now as I write, I am moved to tears recalling the shock of the last time I saw him.

Rest in peace Professor – you are forever in my heart.

(2) The Cork Ballet Company

DOMY REITER-SOFFER (TEL AVIV, LONDON), Dancer with Irish Theatre Ballet from 1959–64, Choreographer to the Cork Ballet Company and Irish National Ballet up to 1989. These memories were recorded in Hong Kong.

I first heard of Professor Fleischmann from Joan Denise Moriarty when she engaged me to dance with the Cork Ballet Company for *Petrouchka* and *Les Sylphides*. For some reason I visualised him as a very stout, dour, difficult person – perhaps because everybody called him 'Professor Fleischmann' and nobody seemed to call him 'Aloys'.

Some weeks after I had arrived in Cork I was told that we would be rehearsing with the Cork Symphony Orchestra. I arrived quite early at the City Hall, wanting to warm up. When I went in I saw a man with glasses wearing very simple clothes arranging all the chairs and the music stands, and taking a broom in his hand to clean away some dirt. Thinking that he was the janitor, I asked whether the rehearsal was here, and he said yes it was. He said that nobody had so far arrived and that he was not expecting them yet as they were always late. 'But I am here', he said. When I asked who he was, he told me he was Aloys Fleischmann. I could have fainted on the spot. Here was a wonderful musician doing all these odd jobs in order to make the ambience for a rehearsal!

And he was quite right about the orchestra: by then the dancers had arrived, Miss Moriarty had arrived, all of us were ready for rehearsal – but there was only a trickle of musicians coming slowly in. We had to start the rehearsal on time, because we had to finish within three hours, and five or six musicians had not yet arrived, because they were all working. As the rest drifted in gradually, all he did was to look up to God, so to speak, as if to say: 'Here we go again.' This man put up with a lot throughout the years that he was the conductor of the orchestra: people coming in and out, arriving late, people not coming as they were sick – but he managed years and years of making music in this small city under very difficult circumstances.

The other thing that struck me all the years I knew him was that he was very gracious; and he always called people by their surnames:

Mr or Mrs. He was part of my life at that time, being on the board of directors of Irish Theatre Ballet. We used to go out quite a lot and also converse a good deal, but he still called me Mr Reiter, which was very strange to me. Many years later when he sold his car, or his car went bust, he started riding a motor-cycle. Once after I was at dinner with Miss Moriarty and him, he insisted on taking me home – Miss Moriarty's hair I think stood on end! After a petrifying motor-cycle trip to my hotel, he said to me: 'Now you can call me Aloys!' I think he had a marvellous sense of humour, though few people saw that.

Another thing which was so special about him was that he cared: he loved the people he worked with. That was very apparent during the orchestral rehearsals. He exuded love and attention and patience, and patience, and patience. Where I or any other conductor would have lost their temper hours before, he was still nurturing, pushing, trying to get some of these musicians to play correctly. And he was still so polite, still calling them Mrs This and Mr That and saying: 'Oh, Mr This, if you only do this and this, it will be all right.' He had the patience of a saint.

And he supported all the arts. Cork was his city and he wanted, very much like Miss Moriarty, to help to foster a wide culture there of such high standard that the city would be proud of it. Every time I created a ballet, I asked him for advice about the music. He was very patient and wonderful to work with, because he was very exact. In a way too much so – he would say for example: 'Oh, but you can't cut here because this is a passage which is very important in this piece of music!' And of course he was always right.

He was very proud of the dance company, as he was very proud of the orchestra. He felt this work for the arts is a part of life like eating, like drinking, like breathing. I once asked him: 'How is it possible to conduct as well as teach, as well as doing such an enormous amount of work and composing on top of everything else and writing?' He said to me: 'It's the need to do all of these things. If you want something, you have to find time.'

He used to come a lot to rehearsals; he wanted to show that he cared. In times when the ballet company was in the depths through lack of money and problems with the Arts Council, this naturally translated to the dancers and some of them were feeling down. But he would appear during rehearsals, he would talk to the dancers, especially the new dancers who came to the company from abroad, he would be interested in where they came from, where they had studied, and this was very important for a young dancer coming to a new company. When he conducted for the ballet, he would ask were the tempi right. He would say: 'I prefer the tempi being so, because that's the way the music should be.' But if it was impossible for us, we would speak to him about it, and he was always ready to compromise, though without going so far as to compromise the music.

I remember when we were doing *Oscar* [*a ballet choreographed by Domy Reiter-Soffer based on Oscar Wilde's life to music by Bax*] and he told me Arnold Bax was a close friend of his family, that he used to come to Cork a lot. He had wonderful stories about Bax. He said he was delighted that his music was being used for Irish National Ballet, because it was time for it to be heard. He came to rehearsals and was very encouraging throughout. At that time of course Miss Moriarty was no longer director of the company, but he still cared, he still wanted to be there for us.

After Miss Moriarty died I called on him at home. He was very upset, but he didn't show it. He put questions about how I was doing, what I would be doing in the future and what was happening in my life. It was I who should have been asking what was going on in his life, but here he was talking about me. He was the most unselfish person I have known.

One performance with the Cork Ballet Company I will always remember. My father had died just two days before the premiere and I really didn't want anybody to know. Needless to say I was most upset, but there was no one to take my place, so I couldn't go back home. He must have noticed that I was down, and after one of the dress rehearsals, he came to me and put his arm around me. He was not a tactile person: I had never seen him hug anyone or kiss anyone before, as friends do. He said: 'I know you're upset, but you're doing the right thing, and I'm with you.' And after the premiere there were lots of flowers. He brought me a beautiful note, saying an artist belongs to the whole world, does not belong to any creed, colour or country, and there was a rose with this note. It made me feel so good.

He was a very modest man, and appreciative of anybody doing the slightest small thing for him. He did tons of things for others, but he himself had no expectations. He only wished and hoped that people would be better in their jobs, and make better music and he tried his best throughout. I'll remember him forever and always.

JOHN ROBERT WHITTY (DUBLIN), *retired Official of the Department of Finance*
Some time in the early 1970s the then Minister for Finance asked me to look into the question of making a grant from public funds to the Irish Ballet Company (later to be called the National Ballet Company). I did so and, with an assistant, interviewed representatives of the Ballet Company. We explained to them the conditions attaching to such a grant, namely that the money would be spent solely on the expenses

of the company, that the authorised sum would not be exceeded and that annual audited company accounts would be provided.

When these terms were accepted, I reported accordingly to the Minister and he, I believe, mentioned the matter to the Government. The agreed grant was provided for in the Miscellaneous Expenses Vote, which was passed by the Dáil every year until the Arts Council took it over, after which it was absorbed into the annual vote for their body.

In subsequent years, I met the National Ballet Company on a number of occasions. As Aloys Fleischmann was a member of the board, I got to know him quite well. My colleagues agreed with me that he was probably the 'toughest' member of the board, especially where the amount of the annual grant was concerned. Needless to say, he always wanted more as the activities of the Ballet Company expanded but it was our job to keep the grant as low as possible. The inevitable compromise was usually grudgingly accepted by Aloys. There was never any acrimony at these meetings and the company always stayed within the agreed grant.

I had a great respect for Aloys Fleischmann and regarded him as a friend. I knew he could be trusted completely with any aspect of our negotiations and all relevant matters would be discussed with him (and indeed with the other board representatives) in complete confidence. It was always very clear that his main concern was with the musical side.

I last saw him at the funeral of Joan Denise Moriarty and was very sad to hear of his death some time later.

M. NEWTON *on behalf of the late* PATRICIA O'REILLY (DUBLIN)
On behalf of a friend, the late Patricia O'Reilly, I would like to record what she told me of her brief collaboration with Joan Denise Moriarty and Professor Fleischmann, in line with what I believe she would have wished.

At the time I knew her, in the early 1960s, Miss O'Reilly was employed in Dublin as part-time secretary to Mr Justice Price, in connection with his research in the field of Celtic Studies. In this capacity, she spent a considerable amount of time at the Dublin Institute for Advanced Studies (Institiúid Ardléinn Bhaile Átha Cliath) at its original address in Merrion Square: an environment which contributed further to her long-standing interest in early Irish history and mythology.

In this context, she mentioned to me that in the late 1940s she had sent Professor Fleischmann and Miss Moriarty her libretto for a ballet based on the story of *The Children of Lir*, hoping they might find inspiration in the ancient 'swan' myth. Miss O'Reilly had made the contact knowing of their interest in Irish culture: she had attended the first performance of Professor Fleischmann's *Clare's Dragoons* in 1945, at which Miss Moriarty played the war pipes; and she was also aware that in 1948 they had produced *Puck Fair*, a ballet to music by Elizabeth Maconchy.

She told me that although she had not expected any recognition, she was subsequently invited as a guest of honour to the opening night of the ballet at Cork Opera House in May 1950. Miss Moriarty, Professor and Mrs Fleischmann had made extensive arrangements to receive her, leaving her in no doubt as to the value of her contribution.

In old age, Miss O'Reilly recalled with pleasure the welcome and hospitality she was accorded in Cork. What had given her particular satisfaction was the meeting of minds and the opportunity to evaluate and discuss the interpretation of her original concept. She was further gratified to find that *The Children of Lir* had marked the beginning of a sustained interest in traditional Irish literature, which was to lead Miss Moriarty and Professor Fleischmann to create several other ballets based on Irish legends, among them *Macha Ruadh*, *Lugh of the Golden Arm*, and the *Táin*.

ANNE MARIE MURRAY (CORK), *Member of the Cork Ballet Company*
Professor Fleischmann was a very dedicated and determined man, passionate about the arts. The Cork Ballet Company danced every year to music played by his orchestra: what a privilege it was to perform to a live orchestra! We would rehearse from about August through to early winter with tapes and Professor would come to the Studio in Emmett Place and sit quietly to get a feel for the flow of choreography and performance. He would see straight away that we could not perform the cygnets in Act 2 *Swan Lake* to the same tempo as the music on the tape, as it was played by some major world orchestra. Miss Moriarty would shake her head in exasperation if we complained in any way: she expected us to dance to the highest levels, always.

We had rehearsed so much by the time we came to hear the orchestra for the first time that we would invariably get an enormous shock. I clearly remember the wet, dark, dreary November evenings in a vocational school up in Togher in Cork. We would arrive early, always disciplined by Miss Moriarty. The costume ladies would be set up in a classroom and would have us trying on our flimsy, filmy pieces, pinning and unpinning, while we shivered in bare skins. The rehearsal room was probably the gym or assembly hall. It was most unsuitable for ballet dancing because underneath the lino covering was concrete, which would shatter your shins and cut to your toes, if you dared to go on pointe. Of course Miss Moriarty expected us to be on pointe and to rehearse as if we were on stage.

How differently was Professor's orchestra treated! Arriving early, the Professor, with his incredible, electric energy, would start to put out rows of chairs for his orchestra. I suppose we should have helped him, but Miss Moriarty kept us very busy with costumes, warming up and rehearsing. Professor would always put out the chairs himself; it was rare, in my experience, to see a member of his orchestra arrive early to help him. He would be busy, flying here and there, arranging seating, music and stands. Then he would take his place next to Miss Moriarty to talk through with her his concerns and plans. They were a good partnership. They were both very inspirational people and very determined: they really believed in the creation of performance and its future for Ireland.

While we were working, Professor's orchestra would start arriving: they never began a rehearsal as a group, but Professor never abused them. We used to watch in awe as he politely acknowledged each latecomer. He was always a gentleman. Heaven help any dancers who would have dared to arrive late – they would have got a very different reception from Miss Moriarty! But the gentlemanly tolerance had drawbacks: poor rehearsal attendance could mean slow progress with the music. It could happen during the first rehearsals that you would not recognise your solo when it was played, especially if we were doing a difficult work such as Prokofiev's *Cinderella*.

Professor always showed absolute concern for the dancer. He was what could be truly called a team player. He had the whole performance in his head; it seemed as if he had a vision and he knew where each part fitted. The dancers were important because we were the ones who brought the music alive, we interpreted the music and were its visible manifestation for the audience. He would always replay a piece for a dancer, even if Miss Moriarty became impatient and wanted to move on. At the end of the piece he would ask you: 'Well, Miss Gordon, was that to your satisfaction?' Even if it was not and you were shaking in your pointe shoes and wondering whether it was ever going to sound right, you had to acknowledge Professor's concern, care and enthusiasm with a smile and a big thank you.

During the performance itself, Ballet Week in November, we used to find that the orchestra would play faster and faster as the week progressed. Professor was always approachable. Miss Moriarty did not like the dancers to make suggestions about tempi. Behind her back, I would, at the request of the others, ask Professor if he could slow down a piece such as Act 2 *Giselle*. He never made you feel uncomfortable and was always very caring. But it could happen that the piece to be slowed down was in fact sped up, and all Professor could say, almost sadly, was: 'I tried to get them play it at a slower pace, but they took no notice!' Once I remember dancing a solo in *Sleeping Beauty* on the opening night with no sound from the solo instruments and only the orchestral accompaniment as background. Luckily we were so well rehearsed by Miss Moriarty that I danced on as if nothing was wrong. Afterwards Professor came to tell me that the soloists had not turned up! He had such patience.

Professor took a great interest in all of our activities, not only when his orchestra was involved. He would attend our own performances that we called 'dance-ins', when we created our own choreography, put it to music and performed it. He was enthusiastic, generous and gave us much praise and encouragement. He was so pleased when he saw what the dancers could create; he was always looking to talent and how it could flourish. Without Professor, Miss Moriarty might not have been able to create the companies she did, as he was also tirelessly involved in raising funds and support. We might never have had the chance to dance in the Opera House, season after season, with professional dancers, to some of the best music in the world. Professor Fleischmann and Miss Moriarty made it all happen!

Muriel Large (Eye, Suffolk), *Administrator of Scottish National Ballet, Administrator of Irish National Ballet 1973–88*
My first sighting of the Professor was in the Cork Opera House. I looked down from the circle to see a solitary man in a crumpled raincoat in the orchestra pit trying single-handed to cope with the spacing of his seating plan for the players, the lighted music-desks and piles of orchestral parts for distribution before the evening's rehearsal. I didn't realise at the time how typical was this picture, and how representative of all the detailed organising and unglamorous chores which fell to his lot. He was one of the least pretentious men I have ever known.

In public, Professor Fleischmann spoke with ardour and sincerity, and his letters to the press were justly famous. One felt he should have belonged to the age of 'knights in shining armour', who were always prepared to charge into battle to right a wrong and see justice done. A devoted friend and adviser to Joan Denise Moriarty (and Vice Chairman of Irish National Ballet from its inception) he continually supported her while championing her cause – ballet in Ireland – together with his other campaigns for government recognition of the arts in general and music in particular. Looking back, one perceives just how deeply he was enmeshed in every kind of arts activity, but his genuine enthusiasm preserved him from any feeling of resentment that his necessary presence and participation would be taken for granted.

In private, his gentle and courteous manner overcame many a problem with his university students, and he could be a charming and erudite companion at table. Cork was indeed fortunate to benefit from the Professor's lifetime of service in the arts, and finally recognised this by honouring him with the well-deserved Freedom of the City.

DONN MCMULLIN (CARRIGALINE, CO CORK), Manager of the Irish Ballet Company 1973–1976
My first contact with Professor Fleischmann was shortly after I had been appointed in 1973 to the position of General Manager of the recently formed Irish Ballet Company (later to become Irish National Ballet). From then on I used to meet him at our regular board meetings. There were, of course, other meetings in those early days of frantic planning for our first season. During that time, the Professor would often drop into the offices in Emmett Place for various consultations with Miss Moriarty, Miss Muriel Large, the administrator and myself. These contacts remained consistent until I left the company in 1976 to take up a position as General Manager at the Everyman Playhouse. During these three years, I got to know the Professor very well at least on a business footing. His main interest and considerable input was centred on the musical and artistic aspects of the company's affairs. I felt that he found the business side of things somewhat puzzling and at time confusing. Though by no means a hard-headed businessman, his acute insistence on artistic excellence and full recognition of the attendant demands on human resources which these strict criteria imposed on all concerned, ensured that a consistently high standard of performance was maintained. On this, he was totally at one with Miss Moriarty.

For myself, I found him to be the epitome of a fast-vanishing courtesy and charm. On opening nights or other important occasions when the company invited special guests, he always made a special point of seeking them out and ensuring that they were particularly cared for. He was a shy, retiring man, reluctant to draw attention to himself, and almost dismissive of his own achievements. In this he was decidedly unworldly. On the other hand, he was in the forefront when it came to recognising the talents of others, and was totally sincere and quick in expressing his praise and encouragement. In essence, his gentle manner, soft voice and warm smile made him the perfect gentleman of the old school. His passing has left the world of the arts very much the poorer.

MONICA GAVIN (CORK), *Member of the Cork Ballet Company*
Dancing to the Professor's Music

The main contact of the Cork Ballet Company with Professor was through his music for the ballet. His first ballet, *The Golden Bell of Ko*, performed in the Opera House in 1948, was part of a programme at which my mother introduced me to the wonderful world of Joan Denise Moriarty's Cork Ballet Company and Professor's Cork Symphony Orchestra. The ballet was about a bell-maker, whose three beautiful daughters sacrificed their lives in order that a golden bell could be completed for the local mandarin. The music created a marvellous Chinese atmosphere and the finale, when the daughters threw themselves into the furnace and their spirits rose to the heavens, causing the gold bell to appear out of the fire, was theatrically and musically brilliant.

In 1951, Professor and Miss Moriarty produced a short ballet, *An Cóitín Dearg*, with libretto by Micheál Mac Liammóir. It was a 'boy loves girl' in Connemara story. His mother intervenes and each go their own way to America, where they make good and return home. They only recognise one another when they put aside their American finery for her red petticoat and his báinín, and everyone joins in the final country dance. This work went unnoticed by me. I remember seeing the programme which consisted of *Suite Classique* by Debussy, *Valse Triste* by Sibelius, *Coppélia* Act 2 by Delibes, and *Hungarian Fantasy* by Liszt, but not a thing about *An Cóitín Dearg*; the competition was pretty strong.

Describing his music in a radio interview when he received the Freedom of Cork, Professor said he wrote 'in a rather terse and austere style based on Irish folk songs – not too esoteric: fairly diatonic'. My first experience of dancing to his music was the Irish ballet *Macha Ruadha*, a lusty tale of Irish folklore. Having strained muscles, ligaments, etc., trying out roles as Macha's women warriors, I landed my first part with Cork Ballet Company as one of five grey-haired Druids. Professor's music was difficult. We stood behind our stone altar and counted 5, 8, 13, 11, etc. Our prayers to the gods for a successful result to the battle between Macha and Cimbaeth and their fearsome warriors brought forth white smoke from the altar every night – except the gala night attended by President and Mrs Seán T. O'Kelly. They were seated in the box at stage level, in the old Opera House, looking straight at us. The fuse failed and not a wisp of smoke appeared. The dramatic score added to the warlike atmosphere of the ballet and yet a soothing lullaby, introduced by the harp, changed the mood to a quiet, calm section before the final battle. This programme with *Coppélia*, the first full-length ballet performed by the Cork Ballet Company and the Cork

Symphony Orchestra conducted by Professor, was critically acclaimed by the press, and very well received by the audience.

The Cork Choral and Folk Dance Festival, which began in 1954 as part of the Tóstal celebrations, presented a whole new challenge to Professor, as chairman. He introduced foreign choirs and at once transformed what had been a boring, repetitive competition for Irish choirs, opening up a whole new world of choral music and strange and wonderful sounds. His boundless energy enabled him to keep in touch with the concerts in the City Hall, the office where catastrophes were averted, the seminar in contemporary choral music set up by him at University College, Cork where specially commissioned works were performed, analysed by him and discussed. These works were subsequently performed at the Festival. He had to meet eastern European conductors, and their commissars, who were anxious to collect the subvention promised by our wheeling and dealing Professor to enable brilliant choirs and dance groups to travel outside the 'iron curtain'.

It was inevitable that a Folk Dance Group would be formed from the Cork Ballet Company to take part in the Choral Festival. The first performance in 1957 was *The Planting Stick*, with music by Professor. This was a completely new venture, combining ballet movements with Irish step dances, taught with great patience by Miss Moriarty, who was herself a champion step dancer. The costumes, based on the clothes worn by the Aran Islanders, where Miss Moriarty spent many holidays, consisted of red tweed skirts, black poplin shirts, cream crocheted shawls and heavy black cotton tights, made specially by Sunbeam Wolsey, and which, when later worn on tour, would stand on their own!

The Planting Stick, composed for string quartet, flute, harp, percussion and mixed-voice choir, was a work dance portraying the planting of the potato. The boys, in their tweed pants and Aran jumpers, used the long sticks to dig furrows, make a hole for each potato, close the furrow; the music for this section was staccato and strong. The girls entered with lunch, wrapped in napkins, and danced to a lively, melodic and – for Professor – catchy reel. The group danced together and finished with the boys holding the sticks, in the shape of a farm gate, and the girls looking over it. The dance was a happy one, the music was a pleasure to listen to, and the red petticoats are still being used by girls from the J. D. Moriarty School, when they carry the International Flags for the Opening Ceremony of the Choral Festival, over forty years later. Thankfully, the black cotton tights are long gone!

The *Táin*, a ballet based on the cattle raid of Cooley, was the last collaboration between Professor and Miss Moriarty, and was performed in 1981 for the Dublin Theatre Festival. This work was the result of much agonising, consulting, but according to Professor, no compromising by 'her ladyship', as she 'guided' the composer, in certain sections, towards a satisfactory blending of music and dance. The resultant dramatic production was the best work choreographed by Miss Moriarty to Professor's exciting score, played by the RTE Concert Orchestra and danced, with great enthusiasm, by the very talented members of Irish National Ballet. The set and costumes of blue, silver, reds and browns, designed by Patrick Murray, completed a first class production. It was a great disappointment that the *Táin* was not performed after the Dublin Festival.

The Professor always arrived early for rehearsals and rushed around putting chairs and music stands in place for the orchestra. The Aula Max in University College, Cork with the paintings of the presidents of the college looking down on us, had an old-world atmosphere of floor-to-ceiling bookcases. We danced on points around the knotholes on the well-worn floor, while Professor sang the parts of absent members of the orchestra. When something went wrong with the music, he apologised saying 'I'm awfully sorry – we'll take that again – from No. 24: Mr W. you never came in', this with his hands crossed and a lugubrious look on his face.

When guest artists arrived, sometimes just in time for the dress rehearsal, it took a lot of patience and diplomacy on all sides to work out an amicable agreement on the timing of certain movements. The conductor had to take his cue from the male dancer, when he came on stage for his solo variation, with possibly an arm movement or a step to commence his dance; on other occasions the dancer would wait for the music; this could sometimes produce stalemate. As the years went on, Professor remembered to look at the stage, to slow down for jumps and lifts, to speed up for turns, although one ballerina was heard to gasp: 'he's gone mad' as she pirouetted down the rake, across the front and up the other side of the City Hall stage.

He loved parties, organised games for ballet Christmas parties, danced with the ladies at the Choral Festival Club and swung them off their feet. He did everything with enthusiasm. He really enjoyed his trips away with the Folk Dance Group, on two occasions to Germany: in 1956 Wewelsburg Castle in Westphalia, where Himmler had entertained his generals during the war, and which was now the centre for an International Youth Dance Festival. Professor was in his element, acting as manager and interpreter to the group. This entailed chasing up lost luggage and a special flagpole, which had been lent to us by the Irish army, and which was left on the train when the group, with baggage and props, got off. The second German visit was in 1966 to Berlin, where the performance was attended by Dr Willy Brandt and to Dance Festivals at Deidesheim and Dillenburg. Professor was a great help to Miss Moriarty when the group attended the Dijon International Folk Dance and Wine Festival in 1961 and again in 1965. The programmes for the various concerts had to be altered to fit the time allowed for the competitions and they must have done a good job because on both occasions we won prizes for presentation, costumes, dancing and Miss Moriarty's striking appearance playing the war pipes at the parades on the streets. Professor was invited to conduct his *Clare's Dragoons* at a concert in Dijon some time later.

Speechifying came easily to him, from welcoming Miss Moriarty and the Ballet Company to the first orchestral rehearsal each season, to delivering major speeches at symphony concerts, at final nights of the Choral Festival and ballet seasons, with capacity audiences at the City Hall, Cork Opera House and Gaiety Theatre Dublin. On these occasions he would deplore the lack of official support and funding for music and dance.

Professor attended a number of functions at the Studio, Emmett Place. He retired from the Music department, University College, Cork in June 1980 and was presented with a pair of gauntlets for his bike. He had quite a reputation as a driver! He transported various large musical instruments in his moderately sized car and on one occasion a drum got dislodged from the car boot, as he was driving up Mahony's Avenue; it rolled down the steep hill and conveniently ended up outside a small shop, where the owner looked after it until it was claimed. He regularly carried a double bass and a number of sometimes-reluctant passengers in the two-door car. His escapades with musical instruments were legendary.

In May 1984, on the occasion of the golden jubilee of the Cork Symphony Orchestra, an inscribed cut glass bowl was presented by Miss Moriarty on behalf of the Cork Ballet Company. The performances of the orchestra were always attended by Professor's wife, Dr Anne Fleischmann, and family, and his mother, Mrs Tilly Fleischmann, a pianist of note, who always dressed in black, and who frequently attended ballet rehearsals at the Aula Max.

Miss Moriarty and the Ballet Company celebrated Professor's eightieth birthday in April 1990 when he was presented with a dress-shirt, bow tie and handkerchiefs, and a special cake at a party in the studio. On the same day two years later, the company showed the video of Richard Collins' production of *Cinderella*, cut the birthday cake for Professor, and toasted absent friends, the late Richard Collins and Joan Denise Moriarty.

The Professor and Miss Moriarty had a major involvement in the lives of the citizens of Cork. They inspired a great number of people to leave their humdrum lives, even if only for short periods, and achieve satisfying, uplifting, weird, marvellous, but never dull, theatrical and musical experiences. We shall not see their like again.

MILO LYNCH (CROSSHAVEN, CO CORK), Member of the Cork Ballet Company
I first came to know Professor Fleischmann via the Cork Ballet Company and Joan Denise Moriarty, with whom he collaborated in that remarkable venture. I particularly remember his exquisite and very formal politeness, and his essentially unassuming personal style, cycling around Cork with briefcase dangling from his handlebars, wearing a heavy tweed belted overcoat.

When Diaghilev began his work with the Russian Ballet, he had the advantage of working with professional dancers, choreographers and musicians such as Stravinsky, Cocteau and Leon Bakst. He also had a cultured and sophisticated audience. Aloys Fleischmann and Joan Denise Moriarty had to undertake their work for Cork under very different circumstances. I have a vivid memory of a public meeting in the City Hall with all the city's aldermen and TDs on the platform. The professor described how the arts were funded in Europe, and particularly in Germany, where he said that orchestras and bands were funded from the rates. Fleischmann had both the courage, the wisdom and the particular skills needed to win the support of a considerable array of disparate people who patronised and financially helped the Ballet.

SINEAD MURPHY (CORK), Member of the Cork Ballet Company, Teacher at the Moriarty School of Ballet
I was a student in Miss Moriarty's Ballet School for eleven years, and one day in February 1987, Miss Moriarty invited me to train as a ballet teacher in the school. I was stunned because to be invited to do anything by Miss Moriarty was a privilege, but to be invited to teach was something awesome. I accepted and started on a journey to what have been the happiest years of my life.

One of the most memorable moments of my teaching career was my very first day. When I arrived at the ballet studio, Miss Moriarty presented me with flowers and a gift – an ornamental owl attached to which was a note saying the owl would always watch over me. To this day, the owl travels everywhere with me as one of my lucky charms. Accompanying the flowers and the owl was a card wishing me luck with my new life and welcoming me into 'The Family' – a card I will always treasure.

When I was teaching in Tralee and Killarney Miss Moriarty would often accompany me on the train journey there. I loved those times.

We would sometimes talk for hours or just sit looking out at the beautiful scenery. I often wondered what she was thinking during those times. In the evenings we would either be invited out for dinner or dine with each other. Miss Moriarty was like a child when the menu was presented to us and she was trying to decide what to order. I loved being with her and always felt proud in her company; it was very special to think that she had chosen me to teach in her school and constantly gave me encouragement.

It was through my contact with Miss Moriarty that I got to know Professor Fleischmann. The first thought that comes to mind when I think of him is that he was a 'gentleman'. The word personifies him in more ways than one – he certainly was a gentleman – and he treated everybody who came into contact with him with the utmost respect. My parents were very interested in the arts and from a young age I was taken to the Opera House in Cork on a regular basis. The annual ballet week in November was one of the highlights of my year. As a pupil of Miss Moriarty I was proud to be in the audience, but the elegant gentleman in evening dress caught my attention as much as the dancing, scenery and costumes. I grew up learning about the work Professor Fleischmann did during his life, but I suppose I was too young to understand and appreciate his dedication to his work. It was not until I started working as a teacher for Miss Moriarty that I fully appreciated the work that Professor did. I remember when I first performed with Cork Ballet Company being in awe of the man with the baton. Sometimes I think he worked harder than we did. He would arrive at the rehearsal hall and set out the chairs and music stands, sort out sheet music and greet us all with a friendly 'good evening'. He always addressed me as Miss Murphy and made me feel so special. He worked tirelessly to get the tempo correct for us dancers and when all that hard work was done – at 10.30pm in the evening – he packed away instruments, music stands and made sure the hall was as he had found it. No task was ever too great or too small.

When I began teaching, Miss Moriarty and Professor involved me in the rehearsals, probably because some of the children from the school used to dance in the productions. It was then that I really became aware of the hard work and dedication that both of them applied to the preparation of everything they did. When Miss Moriarty became ill in August 1991 and was hospitalised during rehearsals for *Cinderella*, I became further involved in the production and organisational side for the Ballet Company. I always had the utmost respect for Professor but during those difficult rehearsals – knowing Miss Moriarty was seriously ill in hospital – my admiration for him grew and grew. I think we could all see he was upset that Miss Moriarty was ill and we all knew that he was seriously ill himself, but with his true professionalism he worked tirelessly to make sure the production would be a success. Many times when I visited Miss Moriarty in hospital, Professor was already there discussing the production and he would then dash off to other commitments. It made me tired just to look at him, but he loved his work and 'No, I cannot do that' was a phrase I hardly, if ever, heard him say. When Miss Moriarty died his energy was amazing. He organised her funeral and at once began planning a tribute production of *Giselle* for November 1992. It is hard to imagine that such a sick man would have the time and energy to even think about such a task. That just goes to show what a giant of a man he was. Sadly, Professor did not live to see the plans for the production come to fruition, but the Ballet Company and the Symphony Orchestra carried his plans through and the production was a great success.

All through the rehearsals and the show, I kept thinking if only they were both alive to see how the show was coming together and how successful it was eventually. I continued with my teaching examinations after they died, and last year I was awarded the fellowship of the Imperial Society of Teachers of Dancing (ISTD) and have been invited to become a classical ballet examiner. I only wish they were both there to share the achievement with me.

I learned so much from Professor during the years I spent with him and I am glad that in the last few years of his life I really got to know and appreciate such a remarkable, kind, gentle and disciplined man, who was totally dedicated to music and dance – his life.

After Miss Moriarty's death, I wanted to remember her as I knew her in life and that was as a very special lady. The night of her removal was one I will never forget. As I was driving away from the church I saw a sad and lonely figure standing motionless and gazing into the distance – it was James N. Healy. That picture will stay with me for the rest of my life because it reminds me so much of Miss Moriarty herself. Even though I remember her as a warm and loving person she also came across to me as a person who had endured much loneliness during her life. I think this loneliness made her the special person she was, because you could not help but love her. I loved her like my grandmother. We had a very special bond and I feel that the bond has not been broken by her death.

(3) The Choral Festival

ROYAL DUBLIN SOCIETY Speech Made in Honour of Aloys Fleischmann on the Occasion of the Award of Honorary Life Membership granted on 27 June 1991
1991 is the sixtieth anniversary of Aloys Fleischmann's graduation from University College Cork. In 1934 he was appointed Acting Professor of Music at University College Cork and was appointed to the Chair two years later.

From 1935–1936, the University Orchestra, under his direction, gave one or two concerts each season as part of the Art Society's programme. It was his policy to include a work by a contemporary Irish composer in each programme. In 1937 his own *Trí hAmhráin* for tenor and orchestra appeared. In 1939, the orchestra became the Cork Symphony Orchestra.

Perhaps the most famous of the projects to which Professor Fleischmann dedicated himself, with characteristic flair and enduring fervour, is the great Cork International Choral Festival. Associated with it is the annual Seminar on Contemporary Choral Music, to which the bulk of Irish composers have contributed.

Where, with all this, he found time for writing and composing is a matter for wonder. Right through the years, he has continued to be composer, as well as teacher, conductor, trainer, organiser, analyst and researcher.

In recognition of his outstanding contribution to music in Ireland, and for being an accessible, patient and sympathetic listener with time for other people's ideas and problems.[4]

MOIRA PYNE (CORK), Member of the Cork Orchestral Society, Cork Choral Festival Committee
How is it possible to add to what has already been said about that exceptional man, Aloys Fleischmann!

My first contact with Aloys was through his cousins, Frieda and Pat O'Malley-Williams, who were schoolmates of mine. Through them I got to know his parents 'Onkel Aloys' and Frau Tilly. Pat and I went to German classes in those days and joined 'Onkel Aloys' for coffee and German conversation afterwards. He talked a lot about his gifted son then but it was a long time later that I personally came across Aloys through the Cork German Society of which I was a founder member and Honorary Secretary in the 1950s.

Also in the 1950s the Cork International Choral and Folk Dance Festival was established as a part of Tóstal Ireland – a great Festival of Ireland, set up by Seán Lemass to promote our country internationally in the depressed years after the war. Aloys was appointed Festival

172

director and really threw himself into this project, supported by a very efficient and powerful committee of well-known Cork citizens, with the Lord Mayor as president. Aloys was already well known in musical circles in Cork as professor of Music at UCC and conductor and founder of the Cork Symphony Orchestra and Cork Orchestral Society – all of which he had built up to promote music, of which there was at that time very little.

Perhaps the Choral Festival offered the greatest possibilities as he had a pretty free hand in its organisation, aided by an interested, capable and indeed dedicated group of people. Aloys travelled abroad from time to time seeking choral and dance groups from many faraway countries, including the Eastern Block countries, little known to us in those days. This project was not only exhausting but even slightly dangerous then, but Aloys managed to collect a remarkable variety from places as far away as the USSR, Bulgaria and the Baltic Countries, Estonia, Lithuania, Latvia, etc. These were a great novelty for Cork audiences at that time, before television, as well as forming unexpected and welcome links between so called political rivals of those days. We had and still have a marvellous catering group, who provided three meals a day for a number of our guests. This was necessary then on account of the financial position of the Eastern Block countries, who were artistically a great asset to the Festival but who had very little – if any – currency so we had to lay on accommodation – bed and breakfast in private houses, if possible – for many of them. There were serious difficulties with language, etc. Our host families were marvellous and volunteered this service over the years, organised, of course, by a special section of our committee. One of my lasting memories of the time, at the height of 'the cold war' was seeing at mealtimes at a table a mixture of US and Soviet choir members all happily 'fratting', exchanging little gifts, the flags of both nations on the table. This Festival of ours blended most unlikely combinations of states and lifelong friendships were formed. Aloys himself was instrumental in bringing these groups to Cork where they were received by the Cork people, who tried so hard to welcome them – and all this at a time of international stress and misunderstanding.

Aloys had by now also set up a seminar of contemporary choral music at UCC where three composers: one Irish, one English and one from another country or even continent, e.g., the US, were chosen to perform a special work, first performance to be at UCC and also to be presented at the Choral Festival centre of concerts, the City Hall, Cork. To this mostly unknown and sometimes exotic music the audience had to be initiated – not always willingly, but here Aloys really demonstrated his amazing talent and knowledge, for this became and still is an integral part of the Festival programme. Some of the greatest names in contemporary music took part, such as Sir William Walton, Boris Blacher, Darius Milhaud, as well as the Irish composers Brian Boydell, Gerard Victory, Seóirse Bodley, Seán Ó Riada, Aloys Fleischmann himself and many, many other well-known people. This was a great opportunity for our own Irish composers to meet these people informally and to mix with them freely in Festival time. All this was organised and put on by Aloys too, who already had more than enough work with the Festival itself, but this exceptional man seemed to thrive on all this activity.

I had been on this Festival Committee myself almost from the setting up of the project. But now Aloys did me the honour of roping me in to help him more, so I became his 'Man Friday' with various duties and a title such as 'Administrator'. The number of competitors, composers and so on was growing so fast that we had to set up various sub-committees in charge of sections, such as a Reception Committee to arrange accommodation, transport and meals for literally thousands of participants. This is a real success story and the members of these committees have contributed a great amount to the success of the Festival – all choirs are met and greeted on arrival in Cork, conducted to their accommodation, each group is provided with a Reception Officer, if possible somebody with a knowledge of the group's language, who would stay with them during their time in Cork and solve any problems.

As well as this there was also the whole responsibility of staffing the concert venues, the staging, stewarding – all the routine jobs of running a theatre. In all literally thousands of willing volunteers were recruited, wonderful people who sometimes even took part of their holidays voluntarily to carry out these commitments. Naturally Aloys was the driving force behind all this and my job was to try to see it was carried out as well as possible – not easy when so many people were involved, but Aloys jollied us along and worked so hard himself that we happily carried out his ideas, if sometimes with certain misgivings. But he was always polite, courteous and we were dedicated to him. I often say that in those days my main concern was 'to stop things happening to him' for he was impulsive and sometimes looked for the impossible. He often told me I was 'very sensible' – he seemed to trust me and almost always discussed arrangements and suggestions with me. We sometimes disagreed but he was always polite and understanding so this arrangement worked very well for many, many, years. I loved the Festival and greatly enjoyed working with him – it was a wonderful experience and I would tell his wife Anne that he and I had a 'love/hate' relationship, which greatly amused her. She was incredibly supportive of him, defended him like a lion when necessary and made many useful and successful suggestions.

During this busy and eventful period, Aloys also somehow found time to organise the Cork Symphony Orchestra as well as four concerts a year in Cork by the RTE Symphony Orchestra on tour and several extra concerts by, for instance, the Vienna Philharmonic Orchestra, Boston Symphony Orchestra, Bamberg Symphony and many others. Also he was organising and promoting the Cork Ballet Company, which later became the Irish National Ballet, putting on several original ballet productions, with its director, Dr Joan Denise Moriarty. How all this was possible I cannot imagine. His standards in music as well as in everything else he touched on were very high and he filled in his life span with an incredible number of promotions of all kinds. He was always to the fore in supporting all artistic endeavour such as the proposed Sculpture Park in Cork and art exhibitions in Cork, of course with the help of fellow art lovers.

Apart from this serious side of his character he was great fun to be with and seemed to attract unwittingly minor disasters such as unexpected little accidents like losing vital music and exam papers, which blew over a bridge in Cork having been only loosely secured to the back of his scooter; the saga of the large drum that broke free from the boot of his car to bounce down Mahony's Avenue to be rescued and safely stored for him by a local businessman; or the time when, running along the street to collect a musician off a train at the station and, not paying attention to the terrain, he didn't notice excavations in the footpath and fell down into a deep hole, but turned up later in the Aula Max, UCC rather the worse for wear and bloodstained, and still wanted to be at the recital. On that occasion I had to order him to go home. He was somewhat crestfallen but did as he was told! He once turned up for the Festival opening on stage in the City Hall wearing one black and one brown shoe with his dinner jacket. His secretary then told him to go home to get the correct shoe, which he did in a great hurry, but then rang her at the office because he had already forgotten what he went home for. Even though we found this amusing, it was kind, sympathetic amusement for we all really revered him and understood his little mishaps.

He was a kind and understanding friend. On the death of my husband, he was a tower of strength, ringing up every evening to enquire if I was all right, offering help of all kinds. I miss terribly his great friendship and solidarity now that he too has passed on.

He was so simple and unassuming while honours were being loaded on to him – the Freedom of the City of Cork, the appointment to Aosdána, the ultimate in representing the arts, and many other honours of all kinds. But he was basically a humble man and devoid of intellectual snobbery, yet in his search for artistic perfection he was a hard taskmaster. (When asked what quality I personally might have contributed, I always say 'endurance'!) He will always be remembered by his colleagues and friends in the music world as well as by his many dedicated and willing co-workers. I am grateful to have known Aloys for he was an inspiration to us all and I will always remember the privilege and experience of having worked with him. This little quotation from the German would seem to sum Aloys up accurately:

> Immer höher muss ich steigen
> Immer weiter muss ich schauen.
> Ever higher must I climb
> Ever wider must I view.

JAMES CORR (CORK), on Donna O'Sullivan's Cork Radio Programme after Fleischmann's death in July 1992
You know, as well as being an accomplished academic and musician, Professor Fleischmann was also quite a humble man. If I can just describe one little incident: I remember coming in here into the studio in 1983 or 84 about a week before the Choral Festival to talk about the fringe activities of the Festival – the choirs singing in banks and the folk groups dancing in the streets, and various things like that. We came in to Stevie Bolger's afternoon programme, and as we entered there was loud rock music echoing through the studio, and Professor looked at me in amazement. I'm sure Stevie won't mind me telling this: Stevie was sitting behind his table there keeping time to the music, and the minute the music finished, he said: 'Well, Professor, what do you think of that?'

And Prof said: 'I thought 'twas dreadful.'

And as we went down the stairs afterwards, he said to me – he was always very polite when he was referring to people: 'Was I a little insensitive to Mr Bolger?'

And I replied: 'You know, you were really.'

And he said: 'I think in future you should do these interviews yourself, because I put my feet in things.'

He really was a very humble person.

And he infected us all with his enthusiasm to make sure that whatever happened, the Choral Festival would go ahead. Let me tell you a story that I think is typical of the man. In 1983 I had just begun looking after the finances of the Festival. I met him shortly afterwards and asked what the situation was like. He said: 'Ah, not too bad.' But I suggested we should go to see the bank manager. The manager was glad to see us and told us he was worried about the Festival's over-draft, which amounted to £15,000 – a lot of money at that time. He indicated that things could not go on like this, that he could not toler-ate such a debt. The Professor paused and then said: 'I have just fin-ished paying for my house – you can have the deeds as security.'

The manager was clearly taken aback. He said: 'No, that will not be necessary. But try to keep the overdraft down.'

I said to the Professor afterwards: 'You're a terrible man: you might have lost your house!'

'Ah,' he said, "twould have been all right.'

Now, who else in Cork would have done that?

Jim Horgan (Furbo, Co Galway), UCC Music Graduate, Vocational Music Officer and Teacher.

The Cork International Choral and Folkdance Festival was started by Der Breen and Professor with the Tóstal movement in 1954. It quickly grew to be one of the major cultural events in Ireland; its success was due to a large extent to the very high standards set by Professor, both standards of performance and of adjudication. A panel of two highly respected international adjudicators and one leading Irish musician were chosen each year. The success was also due to the work of Pro-fessor's friend, collaborator and co-conspirator Pilib Ó Laoghaire. The sheer number of choirs in the south and the incredible standard of singing cajoled out of these choirs by Pilib and his staff of conductors was described by Professor as the bedrock on which the Festival stood. They were both justifiably proud of the idea that one of the most important cultural events in the country should have come from real grass roots. The ordinary people of the south, from small church choirs and small rural choirs were coming together, achieving the highest standards and performing on stage alongside the best choirs from all over the world. The standards of Irish choirs of course continually improved with years of participation in the Festival. It was Professor's wish that this increasing standard would be brought back into the communities all around the county as a rising tide floating all musical ships. I believe it was this idea of his that the work of the university, through the Choral Festival, should filter down and influence the grass roots, the community, that distinguished Professor from many other academics of his time.

The contribution of the Festival to the Irish language was and con-tinues to be considerable. Pilib and the Professor were both fluent Irish speakers. All Irish choirs had to sing one of their competition pieces in Irish. This for decades kept thousands of people in touch with the lan-guage at a time when they might not otherwise have heard a word of

Irish from one year to the next. It also created a demand for arrangements of Irish songs. Almost every Irish composer and arranger over the past 45 years has had songs published in Irish. The net result is a staggering collection of material now available in the library of Cumann Náisiúnta na gCór. This I consider to be something of a national treasure.

HUGH O'KELLY (CORK), former Vice-Principal of the Christian Brothers College, Member of the Cork Choral Festival Committee
I came to Cork in 1951 and was one of the fáilteóirí [hosts] of the Choral Festival from about 1956 for about a dozen years. I soon began to see what an enormous organisational task it was. One example of the attention to detail that was required: when Professor Fleischmann received the programme offered by a choir, he used to take the score in one hand and the stop-watch in the other, and would stroll through his office, through the landing at 15 Bridge Street, perhaps Mary O'Leary's office, and back to his own, humming or lilting all the time; he had to attach an accurate duration time to each item in the proposed programme.

There were some marvellous fáilteóirí. Sonia Werge had learned Swedish from her father. She had a great sense of humour: she could be soaked with the rain, frozen with the wind, starved with long hours, overworked – yet she always came up full of bounce. A number of us did a bit of extra language learning. I was told one year at a preliminary meeting that, in addition to my Germans, I would be looking after an Italian choir: the Gioacchino Rossini Male Voice Choir. So I bought an Italian phrase book and worked out how to say things like: 'Your guest-house is here; breakfast will be ready at 8am; at 10.30 a girl will come and walk with you to the rehearsal hall.' Before the end of the Festival, one of the Italians asked me where I had learned my good Italian, which made it all worth while! – That particular group never ceased to wonder how the flowers blooming around the City Hall could survive Ireland's dismal climate.

What exactly an amateur choir was could be a matter for debate. When I was in the boxing club in University College Dublin in 1941, my coach was Frank Cooper, who in 1934 had won the Police Welter Championship of Europe in Berlin. He told me: 'The Germans and all the Eastern Europeans have a totally different idea of "amateur" to what we have.' I felt it was unfair that genuinely amateur choirs from Dublin, Cork, Northern Ireland and Britain were thrown into the ring with rigorously professional groups from the Communist block and western Europe. Willi Träder's Berlin choir, for instance, which won the principal award in 1956, was made up altogether of musicians who earned their living conducting choirs and/or teaching music. Groups like that could be very dismissive about local choirs: I remember a German male voice choir being quite furious that the first prize was awarded in a competition to an Irish choir that had allegedly sung the whole of the main item half a tone flat.

It used to also annoy me to see that a great fuss was made, both by the general public and by the fáilteóirí, of choirs from Romania, Hungary or the like, whereas the smaller choirs were almost ignored. There was, for example, a ladies' choir from Plymouth, a choir from Bangor in County Down, and a choir from Naas: they had no language problem, they could find their way around, and therefore very little was done for them. But they came again and again, they raised their own travel funds, they were the backbone of the Festival. The Festival could not have been run on the people from the East, who milked it for what they could get out of it and then were heard of no more.

The Prof was always concerned about the lack of music in most boys' schools. However, the school I taught in – the Christian Brothers College – was one of the better ones in that respect. In 1951 under Brother K. C. Meers it became the first school in Munster to bring in a full-time music teacher – the late Michael O'Callaghan. He had a violin class of 25 pupils. We put on the *Mikado* – a great favourite with schoolboys: they have only to learn the *-ado*, as every schoolboy can act the *Mik* without being taught. After the Christian Brothers purchased a carpet shop next to the school, Brother Meers had a fine stage built. However, the orchestral pit had to be limited to an area between two reinforced beams in order to keep the auditorium from falling into the bicycle shed – the pit was not big enough for a grand piano. Principals after Brother Meers cut down on music, and the two professional music teachers, Michael O'Callaghan and Declan Townsend were lost to Christians by principals making them teach other subjects besides music.

Although I am illiterate musically, and all my 'education' carefully protected me from ballet, I had the greatest respect for Aloys Fleischmann: he combined the most courteous, considerate and warmly friendly personality with his musical genius.

GORDON SPEERS (PORTADOWN, NORTHERN IRELAND), *Musical Director of the Portadown Male Voice Choir*
My first experience of the Cork International Choral Festival was back in 1965 when St Mark's Parish Church Choir from Portadown, of which I am still a member, competed there.

I clearly remember being somewhat overawed by the vastness of the City Hall, fascinated by the very cosmopolitan gathering, and the superb singing of the most complex music by composers I had never heard of will stay with me always.

It was a few years later that I returned, this time with Portadown Male Voice Choir under conductor Jack Braid. One of the set pieces being *Clic Clac Danse Sabot* by Poulenc. What a challenge: difficult music in a foreign language, an international panel of adjudicators, a huge audience, an atmosphere that was electric – but we rose to the occasion and won. To say that there was jubilation and celebration would be an understatement.

One couldn't help but be impressed by the superb organisation behind the Festival or by Aloys Fleischmann, whose brainchild the Festival was.

I have returned many times since with Portadown Male Voice choir as their Musical Director. We have been victorious on a number of occasions but win or lose we were always given the most wonderful welcome by the people of Cork. In 1986 when the choir was celebrating its sixtieth anniversary a visit to the Festival was considered a must and as on a number of occasions we received a standing ovation from a packed City Hall.

The choir were the first recipients of the PEACE award, which at that time was awarded to the choir who, in the opinion of the adjudicators had, through music, made the greatest contribution to peace and understanding. When Dr Brian Boydell announced that the adjudicators were unanimous that the award should go to Portadown Male Voice Choir, again a packed City Hall erupted with applause, standing and cheering, an experience that moved many to tears in choir and audience alike. Little wonder then that the Cork International Choral Festival has a very special place in the hearts of our choir members.

It is our intention to return to the forthcoming Festival safe in the knowledge that win or lose we will be part of something very special, will hear some wonderful performances, broaden our musical experiences and renew acquaintances with the lovely people of Cork.

All this has been made possible by the man who started it all: Aloys Fleischmann. I salute his memory.

STEPHEN WILKINSON (SALE, CHESHIRE), *Composer, Conductor, Adjudicator at the Cork Choral Festival*
I have happy and significant memories of the Cork Choral Festival. The whole atmosphere of the Festival was warmth itself, and genuine interest, not just in the City Hall, but out in the city.

It was my privilege to attend three times. The first was to conduct the BBC Northern Singers in the première of Walton's *Cantico del Sole* in 1974, a Festival commission. It came to me in the composer's MS, reasonably legible but I found it best to transcribe it all for safety and we worked hard at it both conscious of the honour of being entrusted with launching a work by a very distinguished composer and finding it no mere *pièce d'occasion* but a notable addition to his not very extensive *a cappella* output.

As a bonus we were also invited to première Aloys' own *Poet in the Suburbs* to words by John Kinsella, a lively and engaging work – though distinctly contemporary in its demands on the singers! It was very self-depracatingly offered to us but accepted with alacrity. I hope we brought it off; he certainly seemed genuinely pleased.

A feature of the Festival was of course the seminar that followed the performance of a commission. I recall that we gave another performance of the work at the seminar to start the ball rolling. The ball then rolled, but not for long. The initial comments from the house were not entirely to the composer's taste. Walton announced with unassailable authority: 'It is a very beautiful work and it had a very beautiful performance.' That was the end of the seminar. If that was a disappointment at least it was good to hear that he was pleased with us for he never said a word to me directly. (I had hoped for a brief exchange, for we had both been choristers at Christ Church Oxford, and I would have liked to know if the Choir School was as appalling in his, much earlier, day as in mine.)

My second visit was in 1980 with my amateur choir (which at 80 I still conduct) to première *Siberia*, John McCabe's fine setting of a poem by James Clarence Mangan. I seem to recall that both performance and seminar passed off well on that occasion. It was certainly a very happy one often recalled with pleasure by the participants.

And the third visit was in 1985 to adjudicate – always a stressful experience for me – I never felt I had the authority of the Delphic oracle. There were indeed some stunning performances but what I chiefly recall were my fellow adjudicators Gerard Victory, and James Wilson from both of whom I subsequently commissioned works.

Which returns me to the thought of the Festival's own commissions, an outstanding creative achievement of which I am sure Aloys must have been justly proud. I certainly had no problem some 10 years ago in putting together two full broadcast programmes of them with the Northern Singers. I packed in conducting the choir in 1992 (after almost 40 years) but the tapes might just possibly be still in existence. Sadly I'm not in touch with the Festival now but I much hope the commissioning continues. It has certainly done much both for music and for Cork.

MÁIRE NÍ MHURCHÚ (CORK), former Head of Radio Programmes Radio Teilifís Éireann
I first heard the voice of Professor Aloys Fleischmann when I attended my first symphony concert as a young schoolgirl, after my family moved to Cork. I have never forgotten his impassioned plea for an 'Orchestra for Cork' and this need was voiced again at each succeeding concert.

Professor Fleischmann didn't get the orchestra he so badly wanted, but instead – a string quartet. He was full of praise for the musical richness each successive RTE String Quartet brought to the city, not alone in public performance, but also for the expert tuition given to so many pupils in the Cork School of Music and elsewhere.

Our paths did not cross until I joined RTE. The hour-long Choral Festival programme transmitted on the final night of the Festival was one of the musical highlights of the year from the studios. All of the set pieces performed by the competing choirs in the preceding days and nights, as well as many non-competitive works, were pre-recorded. As director of the Festival, Professor Fleischmann had a huge workload. I often hesitated to approach him for information, because he always insisted on securing the relevant details himself to ensure that I received them. Because the time span was so short between the release to us of the adjudicators' results and the actual transmission of the programme, this special co-operation was invaluable.

The benefits of the early Choral Festivals should never be underestimated, because they provided such a valuable platform for choirs from all over Ireland as well as those from further afield. The Eastern European choirs, in particular, derived such pleasure, not alone from participating, but also from sampling the generous hospitality of their Cork hosts. Their hard-currency travel expenses were severely limited or, in most cases, non-existent.

Again in the early years, audiences were rather slow to savour the unfamiliar choral works, but with astute programming – interspersing these with more popular pieces – the concert-goers were most effectively musically educated!

In 1987, Professor Fleischmann's marvellous memory was a tremendous help when researching for the special programmes and an exhibition to mark '60 years of broadcasting from Cork'. Not alone was he able to identify many old photographs, he was also able to provide actual copies of programme sheets. It seems he retained not one or two, but up to five copies of each important document.

Our final contacts were made by telephone. His interest and energy never flagged in putting forward by way of letters to the papers his concern for music-making in the city. His calls, seeking clarification of different points usually came around 11 o'clock at night. I didn't mind in the slightest the late hour, due to his exquisite politeness at all times and his desire to ensure that everything he wrote or spoke was totally correct.

CHARLES HENNESSY (CORK), Member of the Arts Council of Ireland. This was recorded by Maeve Fleischmann.

Before the Tóstal was begun in the 1950s, there was very little going on in Ireland in the way of culture. There were the occasional visiting opera companies, there was the cinema, and there were the Abbey and the Gate theatres in Dublin. The Tóstal brought dramatic development. It galvanised the whole country into life, it permeated the whole country: every village had its Festival and for the first time business was involved in culture. This provided the starting point for the work of the Professor.

I first met Aloys Fleischmann when I was a young solicitor being trained in the office of my late partner, James W. O'Donovan. Professor used to come in regularly for endless hours of meetings, and what I remember is his extraordinary courtesy to me as a young student. I was always 'Mr Hennessy'. James O'Donovan was on the board of the various Ballet Companies for decades, and I think there was a great deal of discussion and argument at those meetings, whereby each could be exasperated by the other. They reminded me of two stags with antlers entwined! But they never seriously hurt one another: I think one won one battle and the other another. But I do know from James O'Donovan that he had a colossal respect for the Professor.

The Choral Festival was an occasion for crises every half hour: you were dealing with choirs coming from all over the world, there were language difficulties, feeding them and even trying to get them on the stage were major undertakings! I remember counting one night: it took nearly a quarter of an hour to get one group of 97 up on stage! Then programmes used to run late, and everybody who had travelled any distance naturally wanted to have their piece performed nonetheless. But I never saw him panic: he was always in control, and he must have been under extraordinary pressure.

His main strength I think was this driving passion he had particularly for music, but also for dance and for everything cultural. He was interested in the theatre, in literature, in every aspect of the arts right across the board. And it was a passion which was absolute, I would say without fear of contradiction: a dedication and a devotion of the time he had been given on this earth to his passion, which he served morning noon and night, day in day out, year after year. It was quite an incredible performance. I was going to say: Cork should never forget him – I can say positively: Cork will never forget him.

His weakness was that he could be quite impossible in the pursuit of that passion. There were times when common sense would be over-ruled, when he just would not see that something could not be done. It did not often happen, but there were times when he gave a whole lot of energy to something that did not materialise. I think he believed that the rest of mankind thought exactly as he did – and let's be honest: they didn't and they don't!

My abiding memory is of his extraordinary gentlemanliness. When I say 'gentlemanly' I use the word in the sense of 'mannerly', 'respectful', of having a sense of ethics within the profession: his honesty, his integrity – these were features I admired in him. And his constant militancy as far as the arts were concerned. You could only describe it as militancy at a time when the arts were very much the poor relation. The arts were ignored by politicians in those days. They only began to see that the arts were important when they woke up to the fact that there are votes in the arts, that there are now so many people working in the arts and earning their bread and butter. Something I have always passionately believed in is that artists must be paid. But at that time artists were expected to put up with not being paid. People were expected to give very demanding lectures and to pay for their train fares themselves into the bargain! So he came in at a time when it was a completely uphill battle, and he succeeded. In other words, he laid the groundwork for the success of the artist in Irish life. Irish artists are now recognised and not only recognised for their talent, but are also being paid for having that talent and for devoting their time to the pursuit of that talent. And the Professor, like J. B. Kearney, was one of the forerunners of that development. He was a wonderful man and I was very proud to have known him even in a very small way.

VIVIAN RYAN (CORK), Secretary to the Cork International Choral Festival in 1980, on Cork Radio April 1980
He's a very energetic man, and he expects you to be the same. Other than that, he's not really demanding: he's very reasonable, very interesting to work with. He has ten times more energy than I, and always will have I think. But he allows you to work in your own time, and as long as you get the job done and, of course, get it done properly, he doesn't really interfere with you.

He puts an awful lot of work and energy into the Choral Festival. The whole of the programme rests with him, and the putting together of it, which is a very tricky job. Even at the slackest part of the year, he comes in every day for approximately half an hour, and then at the busy time, he's here morning, noon and night, including weekends. The Easter weekend just gone now he was here every day I think. So if you were to tot it up, it would horrify most unions. But he doesn't think in those terms at all, and he doesn't think about remuneration or anything like that.

If things go wrong, he's only deflated momentarily. And he always looks at once for the solution, and usually finds it, usually finds a replacement. He never panics. Sometimes I wonder how he can be so enthusiastic about the thing when he's been doing it for so long. He's been doing the bulk of it since it began in 1954; he's always done the programme, even though he wasn't always director, and he still seems as enthusiastic and interested as I presume he was in 1954.

VALERIE KILLEEN (CARRIGALINE, CO CORK), Secretary to the Cork International Choral Festival in 1987

I first met Aloys Fleischmann in 1985 when I went to work for the Association of Irish Choirs. However, it was not until 1987 (which was Professor's last year as director of the Cork International Choral Festival and the year when the Association took over the running of the Festival) that I really got to know him well. As secretary of the Festival, I used to have to do all of Professor's typing for him. He would dictate letters on to tape regarding the Festival, which I would then type. In theory, this arrangement should have worked perfectly well. However, in practice, this was not always the case. Quite often Professor would turn his dictaphone off half way through dictating a letter and forget to turn it back on again, while at other times he would completely forget to turn on the dictaphone while dictating a letter, leaving me sitting there with just a blank tape to listen to! He also had the annoying habit of coughing into the dictaphone whilst dictating. This could be quite hard on the hearing.

Filing was another problem area. Professor would regularly take letters from the files and forget to put them back. When challenged as to their whereabouts, I would be quickly told that I was 'a silly goose' and that, of course, the letters were there. I very soon learned that, if I was to maintain any control over the filing at all, I would have to create a duplicate set of files unknown to him. This worked well until the day that he discovered the second set of files (safely hidden behind my desk – or so I thought) and so foiled my cunning plan to outwit him!

I remember vividly the first time I made Professor a cup of coffee. Having handed him the coffee cup (which, I should explain, was only a very small cup) he then, much to my amazement, proceeded to heap copious spoonfuls of sugar into it. I often thought afterwards, when I made him a cup of coffee, that it would be a whole lot easier if I were just to pour the coffee straight into the sugar bowl and have done with it!

One of the most interesting days of my working life while secretary of the Choral Festival was the day that Professor brought into the office his collection of index cards with details of all the pieces of music he had collected for his great life's work on the origins of Irish traditional music. The previous week, in the course of conversation, it transpired that he did not have a copy of these, so it was arranged that he would come into the office and I would photocopy them for him. This he did; it took a whole day. I can remember standing with him in the small photocopying room of our office in the Old Model School, as it was then. And, while he sorted the index cards into their proper order, I carefully photocopied each one. During the course of the day we talked about everything under the sun, from the meaning of life to rock 'n roll, and back again. I was amazed at his ability to talk so knowledgeably on so many diverse subjects. He even told me that day that he had a keen interest in the paranormal and regaled me with several ghost stories. He said that, in his opinion, many ghosts chose to haunt certain places simply because they were happy there in life and so wished to remain there in death, which to my mind seemed a fairly sensible explanation for such things.

In conclusion, if you were to ask me what impressed me most about Professor Fleischmann, I would have to say that there were two things above all else. Firstly his ability to make everyone he came into contact with feel at ease. There is a line in Rudyard Kipling's poem 'If' that springs to mind when I think of Professor 'Or walk with kings – nor lose the common touch'. He treated all people alike, regardless of their station in life, or so it seemed to me, be they musician or non-musician (such as myself), academic or non-academic. And secondly, his ordinariness – something which I considered to be quite extraordinary, given all of his great achievements in life. Both of these qualities I found very endearing in him, and in my eyes they more than made up for his frustrating little habit of dictating half or none of a letter on to tape, not to mention playing havoc with the Choral Festival's filing system. Being the Choral Festival's secretary during 1987 was certainly nothing if not challenging!

MICHAEL DAWNEY (POOLE, DORSET), Freelance Writer, Arranger and Composer
We owe a great debt to Aloys Fleischmann. In the European context, what he achieved was remarkable. He explained to me in 1974 why music had not been a priority for the Republic of Ireland, whereas literature had always commanded more support; the Republic simply did not have the resources from which to finance a strong musical system. However, he believed that the spirit and genius of the people might triumph over these material constraints. One of the strengths of

southern Ireland is that its former geographic isolation has given the region a wonderful vital folk music tradition. The classical tradition of art music has had less chance to develop, although Cork was in the past a great international centre. Aloys told me that in 1938 he was offered an assistant conductorship of the Radio Éireann Orchestra. The president of University College Cork, Alfred O'Rahilly, advised him to take the post, as 'there was no future' for him in Cork. But Aloys stayed there, and was to make the city become a meeting place for musicians such as Arnold Bax, E. J. Moeran, Charles Lynch, Seán Ó Riada and others.

Aloys' greatest legacy, at least that which affected most people, is the Cork International Choral Festival. My interest was aroused when I reviewed some music linked to the Festival and later wrote a feature on the Festival itself for the English Catholic magazine, *Church Music*. I enjoyed Festivals in 1974, 1975 and 1976. Aloys directed the Festival with great energy and was assisted by a vast range of helpers. Choirs from all over Europe and the USSR found their way to Cork. Folk music and dance featured: Irish step dancing was juxtaposed with other styles from abroad. One must pay tribute to the wonderful charm, kindness and hospitality of the people of Cork, who organised everything with great enthusiasm. Formidable practical difficulties were overcome, e.g., the logistics of programming hundreds of singers in dozens of choirs on to the City Hall platform and other venues, so that all could be heard over five days. On any one day you could hear choral music, if you wished, from 10am to 11pm. The city went *en fête* for the duration of the Festival, generating a unique atmosphere!

The most valuable part of the Festival and Aloys' most tangible achievement was that a fine range of small-scale choral music was commissioned and performed. There were many successes. Lady Dorothy Mayer and various business companies paid for the commissions. Every year three or four composers were commissioned, usually including an Irish, British and German composer. In the 1974 Festival works were commissioned from Sir William Walton, Boris Blacher, Roman Vlad and Brian Boydell. Walton and Boydell were awarded honorary doctorates by the National University of Ireland. It was customary for the commissioned works to be analysed at a seminar in UCC, Aloys analysing the pieces. A Walton masterpiece, his splendid setting of the prayer of St Francis of Assisi, was performed by the BBC Northern Singers. I could not think of a more sublime setting of the words attributed to St Francis. It was a coup for Aloys to have persuaded Walton to compose it. Sir William vacillated about attending, but finally appeared at his seminar. He was sceptical about analysis. He said teasingly of his piece that he 'regarded it as a very fine work'!

He left the analysis at that and us bemused. Brian Boydell's *Mouth Music*, performed by the RTE Singers, also proved very interesting with ingenious, novel vocal effects. In 1975 it was suggested that there should be a competition for composers: Aloys asked me to draw up the rules. In 1976 it attracted many entries; one of the adjudicators was Adrian Cruft. I was fortunate to win joint first prize with Jane O'Leary for a setting of Ó Riordáin's *Siollabadh*.

As for Aloys' varied, impressive and moving compositions, I was happy to be able to write about them in the *Composer* magazine and talk about them in an RTE broadcast. It would be good to hear more of his compositions, and those of others of his generation. In England we live in a kind of museum or heritage society, where musicians seem only to perform the same standard pieces from the past and neglect living composers. If given the chance, the public often really enjoys new music, but because performing organisations are overly concerned with money, few new pieces enter the repertory. Aloys' energy and enthusiasm made him able to do much. He often praised people who had 'done so much for Irish music'. That phrase can now aptly be applied to him.

CARA O'SULLIVAN (CORK), Singer

My earliest memories of Prof are quite distinct. My late father, Donal O'Sullivan, was involved in various committees for the Cork Choral and Folk Dance Festival. From Christmas through to the end of April (when the Festival began), the phone calls became longer and more frequent, they were usually from Prof. By mid-April he would call at any time during the night. We were never alarmed by these late night calls. Mum knew there was no one lying dead somewhere: it was Prof. He always apologised for the disturbance and then got stuck into whatever thorny problem had been heaped on him from some far flung country: a choir in a broken-down bus coming from Czechoslovakia in trouble at some border, a folk dance troupe loses its dancing shoes en route from Russia – the problems were endless but Prof would call my father as well as many others during the night, in order to find solutions to near impossible situations.

My father worshipped Prof. He was spoken about in almost reverential tones in our house. If anybody dared to speak against him or was disrespectful, Dad would give the poor misfortunate a lash of his tongue, which was sharp enough – that I have on good authority.

I was unlucky enough to perpetually lose out on birthday parties, as my birthday always fell in the middle of the Festival. For years, as a child, I was convinced Prof put the Festival on at that time just to spite me. Dad took his annual holidays during the Festival in order to give it all his attention. Mum went to the city hall for the competitions, so I was on my *rothar* when it came to a party. However, at thirteen, I finally plucked up the courage and (very politely) asked Prof if there was any possibility he could change the timing of the Festival, as every year it clashed with my birthday. Prof apologised for the inconvenience and explained the timing was out of his control. An hour or two later, he met me at the Stardust (Grand Parade Hotel) Club, which helped feed all the visitors, and produced a box of chocolates, and asked everybody – it seemed like millions – to sing 'Happy Birthday'. The secret grudge I held against him seemed to melt away and anyway, I decided at thirteen, it was time to start forgetting birthdays!

My own personal experiences with Prof were in the last four years of his life. They were few enough really, but quite formative. As I began to develop as a singer, Prof would often appear in the audience, and it caused waves backstage. It seemed he put a stamp of approval on the concert or recital, simply because he bothered to turn up. Afterwards, he would come back to meet the performers. He would stick out his hand, congratulate all concerned and leave. None of your air-kissing business. His old-world formality and courtesy was such a change from the usual verbal flatulence that pervades the performing arts.

He quietly encouraged me over the years – with the help of his pupils, Séamas de Barra and Patrick Zuk – to learn unusual and interesting songs for recitals. Patrick was enormously helpful to me, and together we gave memorable performances of songs, including Prof's own composition *Trí hAmhráin*.

Our debut recital at the Aula Maxima UCC was the last time Prof heard one of his works, as he died shortly afterwards. I have continued to sing *Trí hAmhráin* with other accompanists and also with orchestra, in Europe as well as in Ireland, but that was a special night and a memorable occasion. My most treasured possession is a signed copy of his songs, which he gave me only a few days before he died. As my late father called him – 'A gentleman and a scholar'.

John Fitzpatrick (Cork), UCC Music Graduate, Director of the Cork International Choral Festival
The name 'Fleischmann' meant very little to me prior to attending University College, Cork to study Music in the late 1960s. I had studied with Bridget Doolan, the highly regarded piano teacher, in the Cork School of Music. Bridget referred frequently to Frau Tilly Fleischmann and her reputation as an excellent piano teacher whose technical and stylistic approach to piano playing directly derived from Franz Liszt. But I knew nothing of either the work or personality of Aloys

Fleischmann, the man I came to know as 'the Prof' in the ensuing years.

In the late 1960s the Music department was housed in the President's House in a corner of the quadrangle. The staff was very small, just Professor Fleischmann and Seán Ó Riada, and the accommodation and facilities could best be described as charming and intimate. With the introduction of free university education by Donagh O'Malley the overall numbers in the college increased over the next few years. A dramatic increase in the numbers of undergraduates studying Music resulted in an early move of the Music department to 'The Rectory', near the college gates on Western Road, and must have increased dramatically the Professor's workload.

My initial impressions of the Prof were those of style, personality and character. He was full of physical energy, always in a hurry, stairs taken two a time and always at a run; a fine looking person whose presence immediately lit up a room; sartorially elegant if in a dated and slightly Edwardian style; gracious and well-mannered in his dealings with everyone; very formal and old fashioned in the way every student was referred to as Mister, Miss (never Ms!), Sister, Father, etc.; an excellent and interesting lecturer, his lectures being delivered with his hands in position on the front of his coat lapels (a characteristic pose with which I became very familiar), a serious academic of quite obviously very high intellectual ability; yet a man blessed with a great sense of humour and mischief in his dealings with his students; a fine human being who never contrived to be anything else but himself.

All his students will remember his Heinkel motor-scooter and the way he drove it for years without recourse to helmet or particular concern for his own safety. On one eventful day the class' efforts in counterpoint were returned embellished (probably improved!) with an overlay of car tyre marks. This resulted from a skid on the train tracks which, at that time, traversed Brian Boru and Clontarf Streets linking the two railway stations to each other, his subsequent fall off the scooter, the distribution of the scores over the street, where they were run over by the Cork traffic and their collection by our esteemed Professor to ensure their immediate return to his students. This physical stoicism was again seen when he arrived to give a lecture with his finger bandaged. He had just previously nearly lost the tip of his finger on the blade of the lawn mower, had had it attended to, but came to class as there were students waiting and lectures to be given!

Over the many years I knew him he never denigrated his students, orchestral members, fellow board members, or Festival volunteers. Yet the simple address of 'Mr Fitzpatrick', 'Miss Murphy' was pregnant with meaning and sufficient for the recipient of such attention to know exactly where they stood. I only saw him angry once. At all other times he was the essence of old world civility and gracious-ness. I respected his honesty and integrity hugely. His qualities of sin-cerity, honesty and charm were obviously genuine and, coupled with his wide range of achievements at local and national level, were the principal reasons he was loved and respected by all. Even if he had not achieved as much as he did he would still have engendered the same love and respect.

One particular story he told in a self-deprecatory way related to a visit he made to Tig Kruger in Dún Chaoin while on holiday in Kerry. The host having heard that there was a noted and important musician in the pub, introduced Professor Fleischmann to the assembly and requested him to play something on the fiddle, which was there for just such a purpose. 'I'm sorry, but I can't play the fiddle', said the Pro-fessor. Kruger then requested him to play a tune on an accordion that lay to hand. 'I'm sorry,' said the Professor, 'but I can't play the accor-dion!' In growing exasperation he was then requested, at the very least, to sing a song ('Abair amhrán'), to which the professor replied: 'I'm afraid I don't sing!' Kruger's response was: 'So this is the kind of person we have as a Professor of Music in the university – a man who can't play a fiddle, or accordion and can't even sing a song!'

One of the highlights of my year as a student of the Music depart-ment was in attending the seminars on contemporary choral music organised by the department in association with the Cork Inter-national Choral Festival. These were held in the President's Drawing-Room, featured the Radio Éireann Singers and their conductor Waldemar Rosen. The intimacy of the venue and its close proximity to the gardens created a wonderful atmosphere. The composers commis-sioned to write works were in attendance, their works were analysed by the Prof and much discussion ensued. It was the first realisation I had that all composers were not dead and consigned to the history books for the specific reason of study and exams.

It was here that his formidable intellect made itself obvious. He sat at the piano and presented analyses that were thorough, interest-ing, elucidatory and understandable. These analyses were interspersed with practical demonstration on the piano of particular aspects of the work. It was here that I became aware of his deep knowledge of liter-ature and the arts in general. It was also where I heard him converse in German for the first time and remember being conscious of his wider range of attributes. The important aspect of these seminars was firstly in providing a platform for the presentation and performance of contemporary choral music by composers of international reputation to audiences who had little experience of contemporary music and secondly, featuring Irish composers as commissioned composers long

191

before any Music Commission Schemes existed. It is the prime reason that audiences at the Cork International Choral Festival are so educated and open to listening to new music. His vision in seeing the importance of such a platform and his integration of the works into the nightly gala concert programmes is still an integral part of the Festival.

His involvement with the Cork International Choral Festival (or the Cork International Choral and Folk Dance Festival as it was originally termed) from its inception in 1954 and its subsequent development as a Festival of truly international proportions is one of his major legacies to the musical life, not just of Cork, but of Ireland. The Festival was central to the development of choral music in Ireland and provided for many years the only competitive platform to which Irish choirs could aspire. Many choirs were formed expressly with the ambition of competing at the Festival. The Festival also featured marvellous international choirs whose musical styles, vocal sounds and choral repertoire had major influence on the development of Irish choirs and Irish choral music. It was here, for example, that the choral music of Zoltan Kodaly was heard and became a staple part of the repertoire of Irish choirs long before its discovery by European choirs. The Professor was particularly successful in attracting a number of the great Bulgarian choirs like the Rodna Pesen Choir from Bourgas and the Morski Zvoutsi Choir from Varna to Cork in the 1970s. Choirs as varied as the Bulmershe Folk Choirs from England, the Wartburg College Choir (Iowa) from the USA and the Via Nova Choir (Munich) from Germany delighted audiences in Cork also. It was particularly apt that Cumann Náisiúnta na gCór (The Association of Irish Choirs) was initiated at one of the Festival's opening ceremonies.

Prior to the collapse of the various socialist regimes in central and eastern Europe he introduced Cork audiences to the quite stunning displays of folk dancing from these areas. The athletic physicality of a group from Georgia and the Voronezh Group from Russia, featuring stately female dancers who seemed to float over the stage, will remain long in the memory. These groups were fully professional and consequently their standards were of the highest order. He did have his failures also! One in particular comes to mind. A group of Limbo Dancers, whose performance was very entertaining but more suited to the particular stimulating atmosphere of a night club in Soho, performed one night to the obvious embarrassment of the Professor. The group was on the first plane back to England the next day due to his immediate intervention. He presided over the Festival in a benign and dignified way at both committee meetings and the Festival itself and was very conscious and appreciative of the input of all the volunteers who helped to make the Festival a success. His choral compositions, both

Aloys Fleischmann's grandparents – Alois and Magdalene Fleischmann, Dachau, c. 1890
[painter unknown]

Aloys Fleischmann's parents, Aloys and Tilly, Munich 1905

Aloys Fleischmann as a child in Western Road, Cork

Aloys Fleischmann with Tilly Fleischmann and Máire McSwiney in Bavaria, 1931

Aloys Fleischmann, c. 1930

Aloys Fleischmann and Anne Madden on holiday in Grúig, 1939

Aloys Fleischmann's wedding to Anne Madden, 1941

Aloys Fleischmann with his parents at his wedding in 1941

Aloys Fleischmann with son,
Neil, 1945

Aloys Fleischmann as Auditor of the Arts Society, 1931, with [l. to r.] J. J. Horgan, Coroner; Dr Thomas Bodkin; Prof. Stockley; Prof. Corkery and Prof. Porter

Aloys Fleischmann with Ken Macken, wife Anne and Joan Denise Moriarty, 1950s

Aloys Fleischmann with his wife Anne, 1957

Aeolian Choir, Honan Chapel, University College Cork, early 1950s

Aloys Fleischmann with Leon Goosens, wife Anne, Sir Adrian Boult and Sen. J. Dowdall

Rehearsal with Cork Symphony Orchestra, Aula Maxima, University College Cork

With Mrs Vaughan Williams, wife Anne, Harriet Cohen; Ralph Vaughan Williams and Prof. Seán Teegan

Cork Ballet Company brings The Nutcracker *to Dublin, 1973; with Hilda Buckley, Joan Denise Moriarty, Lavinia Anderson, Aloys Fleischmann, Andrea Weinberger, Michael Glendinning, Helen Starr, Michel Breuil* [photo courtesy of The (Irish) Examiner]

Aloys Fleischmann with President Childers, Music Department, University College Cork, 1974 [photo courtesy of The (Irish) Examiner]

Aloys Fleischmann with his wife Anne and Finbarr Crowley, 1975

Aloys Fleischmann with G. Y. Goldberg, Lord Mayor, at presentation of Freedom of the City, 1978 [photo courtesy of The (Irish) Examiner]

Aloys Fleischmann in a jocular mood, 1980 [photo courtesy of The (Irish) Examiner]

At the seminar on Contemporary Choral Music, University College Cork, 1981
[l. to r.] Kieran O'Gorman (adjudicator), Albert Bradshaw (adjudicator), Noel Kelly
(adjudicator), Dr G. K. Spratt, Philip Cranmer (adjudicator), Aloys Fleischmann, Prof.
Raftery (vice-president, UCC), John Buckley (composer), Peter Erdgei (adjudicator),
Sven-Erik Bäck (composer), John Kinsella (adjudicator), Prof. David Wulstan, University
College Cork, Wilfred Josephs (composer)

Fiftieth celebration of Cork Symphony Orchestra, 1984, with Lord Mayor and President
Hillary

Family gathering, 1988; Aloys Fleischmann, with his wife Anne and children –
Anne, Alan, Ruth, Neil and Maeve

Aloys Fleischmann accompanying grandson, Max in 1990

Aloys Fleischmann in a pensive mood [photo courtesy of The (Irish) Examiner]

Son Neil, at the launch of Aloys Fleischmann's magnum opus, Sources of Irish Traditional Music, *University College Cork, 1999; with President Mary MacAleese, Mícheál Ó Súilleabháin and President Michael Mortell* [photo courtesy of The (Irish) Examiner]

accompanied and *a capella*, are a testament to his understanding of the voice and its use in a choral context and must have gained from his involvement with the Festival. It was only recently while researching a particular project in the Contemporary Music Centre that I came across an *Anthem* and a series of *Fanfares*, which he apparently had written for the Festival. It is particularly fitting that the Festival's major international competition is now called 'The Fleischmann International Trophy Competition' in his honour.

Coda: Some cameo memories of the Prof and the Festival are of:

- the opening night when his introduction of the illustrious members of the stage party without recourse to notes was particularly impressive
- his valiant efforts at encouraging the members of the audience to join in the singing of the round: *Viva la Musica*
- the way he sat in the front row of the Front Parterre in order to be close at hand to individually thank the conductors and choir members of visiting choirs for coming to Cork
- his encouragement of young conductors such as myself when we made our first tentative steps on the stage of the City Hall
- his willingness to allow me as a young conductor to look for music in the collection of scores that had accumulated over the years in the Festival office
- his invitation to me to become a member of the Festival's artistic board when still very young was again characteristic of his continual support for young musicians
- his enjoyment and participation at the Festival Club.

JEAN SHERIDAN HEALY (CORK), Journalist and Writer
I suppose I can claim to have known Aloys Fleischmann for more than forty years but that would not be strictly true. The knowledge I had of him was limited to that of 'the Professor', the urbane academic with whom I became acquainted through the decades at countless press briefings and fund-raising appeals on behalf of the Choral Festival, the Cork Ballet and Irish National Ballet Companies and also through controversies on matters of music such as his stand on the awful unsuitability of the words of the National Anthem to our times.

His handling of the press and of his committees were always object lessons in good communication without the need for today's professional public relations people. With his pleasant voice and manner he would woo us from initial blasé detachment into willing cooperation and even the sharing of his enthusiasm with whatever he was involved in. This was usually the need for publicity or the acquisition of more money and more patronage from business, more visible support from the city as a whole, and all in the great cause of Music.

I came to appreciate that this was a man of extraordinary single-mindedness whose whole life was so motivated and enriched by music that he made it a personal crusade to involve everyone in Cork and far beyond in his own enjoyment and appreciation of the best of it without regard to what it would cost in time, energy, comfort, possessions or money. For him, it seemed, life without a well-spring of music would be only a half-life and because it was so genuine, his idealism was infectious.

If this, the public man, was the side of Aloys Fleischmann that I knew – really the only side – I could in truth claim him as an old and loved family friend by inheritance since he and my late husband, Joe Healy, were friends and colleagues from their early student days in University College Cork. They were alike in many ways: unworldly, naturally courteous, lacking in guile but rich in a sense of humour and irony – and they had style.

They also shared a knowledge of Irish as well as of several European languages and had the experience, probably rare among students then, of post-graduate study in Germany during the momentous years between the two world wars, Aloys in the German Academy of Music and at Munich University, Joe as a student of Celtic Philology and German under Professor Mülhausen, who later became a high ranking Nazi and spy, who featured in the book *Hitler's Irish Voices* about the part played by G 2 Irish Intelligence during the war.

Only a few years separated them so that they also had the same memories and experience of an earlier UCC, which in size, numbers and attitudes bore no resemblance to the present one other than in the fine grey stone buildings around the Quad.

Sometimes, in conversation, they would slip naturally into German or drop names that carried resonances which newer staff could not understand; old stories such as that about 'Alfie and the Nun'. This was about an earnest and naïve nun student who requested that a table be set apart for her colleagues in the Student Restaurant in accordance with their Holy Rule. To this, the President, Alfie O'Rahilly, shook his book and said 'THIS is our Holy Rule and while you are a student here, you must abide by it.'

In such little, inconsequential things, friendships are formed and also, I suppose, the sharing of the same rites of passage through academic life. Following their studies in Germany they got Masters degrees, Doctorates, lectureships and professorships: Aloys earlier to become the youngest ever professor in UCC at twenty-six years of age and the longest serving at his retirement.

In time our children became contemporaries and formed friendships with each other, and when the Choral Festival was launched, it was inevitable that Joe would be commandeered to act as interpreter and translator for Spanish, German, Portuguese and other visiting choirs.

Like so many others in the city, it was through the Choral Festival rather than the university that I came to admire and know Aloys. Here I could watch him at his most deeply involved; stretched flat out physically and mentally under real pressure before, during and after performances from keyed-up conductors, uncomprehending foreigners, over-worked staff, the threatened disruption of programming by transport or accommodation delays, by ruffled feathers over protocol, by the effects on choirs of family tragedies back home, even by the great international tragedy which occurred during the Festival of 1986 when a beautiful choir which had travelled from a town near Chernobyl heard the dreadful news of the nuclear power station disaster there.

Looking back now through old Choral Festival programmes from the first humble one on plain white paper, without a cover, to those which followed on glossy paper, their impressive covers with reproductions of old and new views of Cork, I became aware, in retrospect – though not at the time – of the political and diplomatic minefield which Aloys and the Lord Mayors of the time, with the Council and Committee, had to negotiate during the worst years of the upheavals in the North of Ireland. In programme after programme I can see that big choirs which had sung in Cork in the Festival's first decade returned again and again and even into the tragic 1970s, the recurring names of such as the Portadown Male Voice Choir, the Clarence Singers from Belfast, choirs from Derry, etc., competed in harmony in the City Hall.

For the 'times that were in it' that in itself was an exercise in reconciliation, unappreciated, but real. In its way it underlined the achievements of Aloys and of Dermot Breen – its first Director – when the Choral Festival was first launched as part of An Tóstal. (Cork continued to use the original purple Tóstal flag long after every town and city in the country had ceased to fly theirs.) In vision, talents and energy, the Fleischmann/Breen combination had the qualities of endurance.

Previous to this Aloys was perhaps not very well known outside academe, other than as a supporter of young artists, writers and musicians and as conductor of the Cork Symphony Orchestra, which subsequently played for the Ballet Company. His was the influence responsible for visits to Cork of such international figures as Yehudi

Menuhin, the Boston and Hallé Orchestra, etc., but for all the cultural prestige which such gala occasions conferred, they were often regarded as elitist, out of touch with the consciousness of the average-to-low-income public.

In establishing the Choral Festival, Dermot Breen tapped into his instinct for what Cork needed, and wanted, in colour and stimulus during the sad, drab, emigrating 1950s, while Aloys with his crusading spirit saw it as the route towards familiarisation with good music in the natural cradle of the schools, then through local and church choirs and ultimately to higher national standards in churches and cathedrals all over the country. And so they came: school children from Donegal to Kerry, to make beautiful, thrilling sounds unlike anything they got from the Top Twenty or the local disco – they had been made acquainted with the difference.

I asked an industrialist, now in his fifties, who was at school, later in UCC during the first decades of the Festival, what he felt about it. He gushed with praise. 'One just cannot convey what it meant to us then. What people now forget is that Cork was only getting back on its feet after the shortages of the war and the heavy emigration. Because money was tight for almost everyone, things weren't happening so it was dreary and insular. But the Tóstal started and then developed into the separate Film Festival and Choral Festivals and for these weeks the city was really transformed – and I think we were too. It was a sort of revelation to us of how really insular we had been. We had people from eastern and western Europe, from the United States and the Caribbean in gorgeous costumes stepping and twirling and leaping in dances totally different from ours; glorious singing and the great cheering and excitement when the winners were announced on the closing night. It was unforgettable.'

This man was one of the many who used to go down to the quays in Cork to see the Choral Festival visitors sail home on the *Innisfallen* – Cork Airport had not opened then – and there was handkerchief waving, tears and promises to write and to return and send photographs. Compared to today's musical events it all seems so innocent and far away but the singing and the songs were both uplifting and sophisticated and that the results filtered through is evident to anyone who listens to the Sunday morning and Easter services recorded by RTE, even from small rural churches.

From the annual, unrelenting anxieties of its committees to stretch budgets to achieve the near-impossible, such as getting a choir of 60 or so Polish miners or Russian steelworkers to compete, and be accommodated, to the less obvious ones of how to balance the pure entertainment side of the Festival, with Aloys' ideal of it as a means of getting acquainted and educated into the best of great music, was a miracle of inspiration and organisation.

It was a measure of his reputation and academic stature that Aloys succeeded in getting powerful – powerfully rich – international companies to give him their patronage for the commissioning and performance of new works from eminent new composers world wide.

Twice daily in the Aula Maxima of University College Cork during the Choral Festival, seminars were held in advance of the first performance of the works and I think that it was there Aloys Fleischmann was at his happiest; visibly glowing and excited as he and his scholarly contemporaries and participants analysed and dissected, praised or criticised the new works, sometimes with such spirit and violence that he needed to steer them into calmer waters.

Though musically far out of my depth, I would sit enthralled at his grasp of the composers' intent, aspirations and achievement. At the finish and on a day which had begun at 7am and would probably end in the early hours of the next at the Festival Club, he would be constantly waylaid for more views, more information.

There must have been many occasions when he was tempted to, or actually showed natural impatience, or even 'savage indignation' but I never witnessed it, never saw evidence of it. After meetings or seminars I would see him rev up his motor-bike and with his briefcase on the carrier, he phut-phutted through Patrick Street, weaving his way, unrecognised, through the traffic to his home in Ballyvolane, there to change into immaculate evening dress for the night's performance in the City Hall.

From my comfortable seat on the balcony I became familiar with his routine down below in his accustomed chair in front of the stage. I used to cogitate about his schedule in a mood like that of the poor scholar in 'The Deserted Village' – how did one small head, one slight frame, carry all he knew and had to remember? When did he have time to eat, to placate the temperamental, to converse with composers, conductors or with the eminent judges he coaxed from home and abroad to listen for almost a full week to choral singing and to mark papers by the light of a little green-shaded lamp beside them in their balcony seats? The answer lay in his motivation, drive and intellect backed by a highly polished and utterly dependable organisation.

I once heard the valet of Frank Sinatra describe in a radio talk the routine for dressing the singer before a concert. It was a performance in itself, with a staff in attendance and it seemed to take hours. First Sinatra stood on a table of a certain height, then the pristine white shirt was slid over his shoulders, then each leg in turn slipped without creasing into the trousers, perfectly pressed where they ought to be, and so on with shoes laced, bow tied, cuffs linked and handkerchief peeping. So, how did Aloys, without valet or staff or time, achieve the same effect and always arrive punctually accompanied by his wife Anne or daughter Maeve, or both, to take his seat and, by his presence, confer both dignity and scholarship to the occasion?

To its eternal credit, Cork's City Fathers and without exception, its public and its commercial and business interests, formally acknowledged the exceptional contribution made by Aloys Fleischmann by making him a Freeman of the City in April of 1978. The only son of German parents, it is impossible to think of anyone else of his stature who became so absorbed, so enmeshed in Irish sentiment, language and tradition, who so richly deserved the honour.

5: The Colleague

(1) Remembered by Non-Musician UCC Staff

Rev. James Good (Turkana Desert, Kenya), formerly Professor of Philosophy at University College Cork
A Tribute to Two Fleischmanns:
Fleischmann Senior

The elder Fleischmann was organist and choir-master in St Mary's Cathedral, Cork for a long lifetime. Through his teaching of church music in St Finbarr's Seminary, Farranferris, he influenced several generations of priests, giving them an appreciation of Gregorian Chant and of church music in general.

We youngsters of the Seminary classes in the late 1930s did not perhaps get far beyond the simpler hymns of the Holy Ghost Hymnal. But Herr Fleischmann (as we generally called him) did his best to over-ride our boorish ways and instil in us a feeling for the beauties and joys of classical church music.

There was a memorable occasion in the Seminary when the students were barred from their once-a-term film in a city cinema due to an outbreak of measles. Herr Fleischmann announced that he could provide a replacement: a performance by the Cathedral Choir. So, barred from our favourite cowboy shoot-outs in the Savoy or the Palace, we sat in silence through several hours of four and eight-part harmonies and pretended we were enjoying them. It would have hurt Herr Fleischmann to give the impression that he was less entertaining than our cowboys.

The elder Fleischmann's wife Tilly was a gifted musician in her own right, bringing to her many pupils in Cork the long tradition of German piano music associated with Liszt. Like her husband, she believed perfection was not just something to be vaguely aimed at; it was something that had to be attained through endless hard work.

When 'the Herr' died (Tilly referred to her husband by that title) the Cork sculptor Seamus Murphy was commissioned to design his gravestone. Through some misunderstanding the letter s was omitted from the surname. Tilly declared that the Herr would never rest in peace under a headstone which misspelled his name. So the name had to be re-carved and the omitted s restored to its rightful place on the stone.

Professor Aloys
Much has been written of Professor Aloys Fleischmann. I knew him as a colleague on the staff of UCC. He brought honour and fame to his university and to his city for his many contributions to their musical life.

A friend in Cork asked me to say Requiem Mass for Professor Aloys soon after his death. I did so in a tin-roofed church in the heart of the Turkana Desert. In the course of the Mass, I suddenly recalled that Aloys and myself had a brief controversy over church music. We crossed swords (in the *Fold*) over the proper place for the choir at Mass. I held that all the congregation should be encouraged to sing, while Aloys held that a small, properly trained choir should provide the music. As the sweet sounds of four-part harmonies provided by the parish choir were wafted out over the sands of the Turkana Desert, I realised that Aloys had got his wish – a very select and well-trained choir providing the music, at least at his own Requiem Mass in Turkana. He had the last word in the controversy.

Both father and son will surely feel at home, enjoying the music of the heavenly choirs. It would hardly be blasphemous to suggest that either father or son might not be incapable of conducting the angelic choirs if called on to do so.

May their gentle souls rest in peace.

TED NEVILL (CORK), Lecturer in Geology at University College Cork
My first meeting with Professor Fleischmann took place under unusual circumstances. It was in March 1959 and I had just arrived in Cork to take up a lecturing post in Geology at University College. Searching for rock outcrops for teaching purposes, I took the car down a narrow road in the Glen on the north side of the city. The road came to a sudden end at a spread of gravel at the back of a house and on the gravel there were stacked hundreds of short orange draining pipes.

I was turning the car to make my escape when I inadvertently touched the pile; down came the pipes and, rolling all over the place, they hit together and made a musical sound. The not unpleasant note from this earthenware alerted the professor, who came rushing out in astonishment, not at what I had done to his pipes, but at the pleasant sound the humble artefacts were capable of producing.

MÁIRE MULCAHY NÉE MACHENRY (CORK), Emerita Professor of Zoology and Animal Ecology at University College Cork. This was recorded by the editor.
I first got to know Aloys Fleischmann when I was in school, through the school concerts. I only realised a couple of years ago how lucky we were, when I heard an interview on the radio with a woman who or-

ganises music in Galway. She was making the point that Galway had no music school, no chair of Music in the university and as a result there had been no music there. It was only then I realised: in Cork we had a School of Music, we had Aloys Fleischmann, we had the Orchestral Society, we had the orchestra, we had the Choral Festival, we had the Ballet Company. We were utterly spoiled – but we took it all for granted, because we assumed everybody had it!

At the schools concerts we heard most of the programme that would be played that evening, with explanations. Aloys Fleischmann was the ultimate enthusiast. He would always introduce a number of the instruments, would get people to play a little bit, so that we could hear the sound of the individual instrument outside the orchestra. Every year he used to hold up a wind instrument and every year somebody would say it was a saxophone! That was the only time I ever saw him irritated.

There was always an essay competition held in connection with the concerts: I remember I once wrote an essay about the associations which came into my mind when I was listening to the music. I bumped into him sometime after that, and he told me: 'I really enjoyed reading your essay, but it wasn't on what was expected for the essay competition, so you didn't win a prize. But I really enjoyed reading it.' I was about 14 or so, and this made me feel about ten feet tall. He was that kind of a person: he went out to people, no matter who you were. He shared his enthusiasm. And I now realise he must have ploughed through close to 500 essays, probably single-handed.

I also remember him through the Ballet Company. I went to ballet classes for nine years and that included dancing in the ballets that were put on for the public every year, with music by the Cork Symphony Orchestra. I enjoyed it thoroughly. I made great friends through it. What it left with me more than anything was a subconscious awareness of orchestral music, which I hadn't known I was acquiring: it was a wonderful education without one ever realising it was an education. I was in the Czech Republic this year at a meeting near the Vltava river: I remembered Smetana's wonderful *Vltava* music from the time it was done by the Ballet Company.

Later when I began working in College I was conscious of Aloys Fleischmann being one of a small group who was very aware of the College environment at a time when the most awful buildings were going up. He and a few others ploughed a lonely furrow trying to get people to be more sensitive about their environment. I became a member of the Academic Council as a lecturer. There, when he had something on his mind, nobody would stop him from raising it. Presidents would rule him out of order, but he'd still get his spoke in! He wasn't being discourteous: if he was concerned about something, he felt he had to speak out, and he did.

I remember when he 'retired', he was given a room in the Maltings. Our department was moved there, on a temporary basis for a year – something like 28 years ago. We were in two buildings, in one of which the floors sagged, and the higher up you went, the more they did so. You had to watch where you were putting your feet because you'd trip over the slope in the floor. (A couple of years ago, we were told we had to get out of that building before the end of the month because it was going to fall down). Aloys Fleischmann was given an office which had no phone at the top of that building. He would get his phone calls into the Security Desk in the ground floor hall of the second building, somebody would go to the bottom of his stairs and shout – and he would come racing down the steps, bound into the Security Office, take his phone call and then bound back to his office, up the stairs again two at a time. And if he bumped into you on the way, you got a big smile and a friendly word. He was full of beans. I will always remember his smile.

I think the most remarkable thing about Aloys Fleischmann was his combination of enormous persistence and enthusiasm. He would never give up on anything. We all know how difficult it is to get anything going – and he not only got things going, but he kept them going. We've suffered in Cork since he died, may the Lord have mercy on him. But I feel tremendously fortunate to have been able to grow up taking all he gave us for granted.

JOHN P. TEEGAN (CORK), *Emeritus Professor of Chemistry of University College Cork*
Some Recollections (Largely But Not Wholly Non-Musical)
Aula Maxima, UCC, Wednesday, 17 May, 1944 at 7.15pm
I was a second-year Science undergraduate. Aloys Fleischmann was Professor of Music, and on that evening he conducted the strings of the Cork Symphony Orchestra with two soloists in a programme which included Handel, Grieg, Mahler, Larchet and Mozart. It was over half a century on, when I had become familiar with Mahler's music, that I realised how far-seeing and up-to-the-minute Aloys was to include that beautiful *Adagietto* from Mahler's Fifth in a concert way back in 1944, when Mahler's music was hardly known in Cork.

I had never heard of Aloys Fleischmann and I have forgotten how I came to be there – probably dragged along by some enthusiastic co-student, who was trying to round up an audience for the occasion. Having been reared on a thin diet of recorded opera, this was my first orchestral concert and I enjoyed it. It was to be the first of many, many

evenings (and afternoons) of classical music given not just by Aloys'
own orchestra – the Cork Symphony Orchestra – but by many international orchestras, the visits of which were organised by the Cork
Orchestral Society founded by Aloys. It may have had its committees,
presidents and patrons, but Aloys was the real power.

But, to come back for a short while to my undergraduate years, I
learned that Aloys' professorship was a part-time one – and the money
small, that he gave his lectures in the College's astronomical observatory, in which there was inadequate lighting and no heating and many
noisy disturbances from the nearby men's and ladies' clubs, to which
I am sure I frequently contributed. I also heard of a series of public lectures on music he was giving at the time, so along I went. To hear and
see Aloys lecturing was an enervating experience – the dynamic figure
now talking, now at the piano, now at the gramophone, now pointing
to a projected slide. It was just great, and the music – Beethoven's *Eroica*,
Smetana's *Ma Vlast*, Rimsky-Korsakoff's *Scheherazade* and much more.
Aloys had started me on a life of musical appreciation.

Others far more expert than I will write of Aloys' great contributions to the musical and artistic life of Cork, but I just had to write the
above few lines to highlight what he did for me, a chemist, whereby
all chemists, in fact all scientists are regarded by and large as philistines.

When I returned to a lectureship in University College, Cork in
the 1950s, the Music department had mercifully moved to a better home
in the Quadrangle, and it was in those years that I met Aloys. The
common denominator was the College Art Society (which had been
founded by Aloys himself in his undergraduate years), of which he was
president and the student members selected me as their staff representative. Then there was the Cork Gramophone Circle (now long
since defunct) in the affairs of which I became involved. Although Aloys
was not a member he contributed the occasional brilliant illustrated
lecture. I was also a regular visitor to the College's music library, which
was housed in the Music department and Aloys was always most
helpful.

In the years to come our paths would cross in a number of very
diverse ways (some of which are related below). We would become
friendly in a sort of formal way. I don't think that we ever called each
other Aloys and Seán and of course we didn't always agree with each
other but my admiration would never wane for this completely
unselfish man, who put music before all else, music in the College, in
Cork and in Ireland. In the College community a man like Aloys, who
would doggedly pursue what he regarded as best and would not easily take 'No' for an answer, inevitably caused eyes to be raised to heav-
en and one often heard: 'Fleischmann again' or: 'the man's impossible'

or: 'he's a typical Prussian'. On one occasion, when he was being particularly 'difficult', I heard one high-up in the College hierarchy say: 'you know, Fleischmann would make as good or as bad an engineer as a musician!'

I suppose nobody in the College now remembers his composition of the 1940s *Where Finbar Taught – A Song for University College Cork for Choir and Orchestra*. Not by any means one of his better compositions but worthy of a revival in the Aula Max, where it received its first (and only!) performance.

The First Bax Memorial Lecture
The First Bax Memorial Lecture was given by Ralph Vaughan Williams in the Aula Maxima on 15 October, 1955. His subject 'Some Aspects of English Folk Song' was illustrated with gramophone records. This presented a problem for Aloys as to where he could obtain equipment suitable for a space the size of the Aula Max. He knew that I was involved with the Cork Gramophone Circle and that the Circle had suitable equipment. Could I borrow it for the occasion and, furthermore, operate it? After much to-ing and fro-ing we got the equipment up from town to the Aula Max, where it performed magnificently with me in the 'driving seat'.

After the lecture the platform party withdrew to the adjacent Council Chamber. I had a record of some of RVW's music and I wanted him to autograph the sleeve so I followed timidly into the Chamber where a photographer was arranging for a group picture. Aloys said to me: 'Do please join in'. When I politely declined and made for the door Aloys pleaded: 'But you must: we have three ladies and only two men!' And so the young chemistry lecturer found himself sitting on RVW's left. Aloys was on his right and the three ladies (Ursula VW, Aloys' wife Anne and the pianist Harriet Cohen) standing behind. I felt I had arrived – thanks to Aloys.

But that was not the end of the story. Seventeen years later my wife, Maura, and I were at a recital at the Royal Festival Hall in London. On the second floor there was an exhibition commemorating the centenary of the birth of RVW and amongst the many photos of great celebrities was the one taken in the Aula Max, fully annotated. Was I flattered!! In 1971 Oxford University Press published *Ralph Vaughan Williams: A Pictorial Biography* by John E. Lunn and Ursula Vaughan Williams, and there again was the Aula Max photo. In the caption Fleischmann was spelt incorrectly and I was promoted to professor!

On the Dublin Train
Aloys and I often met on the morning train to Dublin. Both of us

would have reading/writing to do, so we would agree to work as far as Portlaoise and then for the rest of the journey chat over a cup of coffee. One morning somewhere in the 1960s Aloys was enthusing over the fact that the Music department now had a second full-time member of staff, the recently appointed Seán Ó Riada; by now his own professorship had become full-time. Yes, this had all kinds of advantages, amongst which was the fact that he (Aloys) could go to Dublin for a day with an easy mind knowing that the fort would be looked after in his absence. As we alighted from the train in Dublin I spotted Ó Riada alighting from the carriage in front of ours. I just could not resist the temptation of pointing him out to Aloys. 'Oh!' he exclaimed, 'the bounder, the bounder!' He raced off ahead of me. Whether he caught up with Ó Riada and, if he did, what transpired between them, I shall never know.

Some years later again somewhere between Portlaoise and Dublin he was congratulating me on my election to membership of that august body, the Royal Irish Academy, of which he was then a longstanding member. I expressed the view that I thought the Academy was very Dublin orientated, and those of us who lived outside the Pale could not afford in terms of time or money to attend its meetings on a regular basis. Said Aloys 'I agree fully with you, but I find Academy House, central as it is in Dawson Street, very convenient for leaving a bag or a parcel until I am ready to go for the train'.

A Second Floor in the Aula Maxima
The mid 1960s saw a sharp increase in student numbers and no government funds to relieve the chronic space shortage. Somewhere about 1966–67 wind of the word got out that a proposal was coming before the Governing Body to put a second floor in the Aula Max at a level equal to the top of the bookshelves. This would double the floor area and access to the upper floor would be no great problem. It was understood that the president of the day and the 'clerk of the fabric' were all for it. After all a second floor had been put in the adjacent library with great success and admiration. To a handful of us (non-Governors) this was a preposterous philistine plan to utterly destroy a beautifully proportioned hall.

Aloys took it on himself to raise the matter under Any Other Business at a meeting of the Academic Council. Of course the chair tried to rule him out of order as it was a non-academic matter, but when a few of us chimed in that it was academic the chair grudgingly gave in. Aloys was at his 'non-music' very best (he was one of the most articulate speakers I ever knew) making a great case for not proceeding with 'this piece of desecration'. Of course one could almost hear the establishment saying: 'Fleischmann just wants it as it is for his concerts'. At the same time one could feel support for Aloys growing. The chair decided to kick for touch and suggested waiting 'until we see what the Governing Body has to say on the matter'. This was agreed *but* ne'er a word was ever heard again about a second floor for the Aula Max, thanks largely to Aloys.

The Aesthetics Committee

What was known for a long time as the New Science Building was completed about 1971. It has been regarded as something of a monstrosity even by some of those who were beneficiaries thereof. One day Aloys walked up the Gaol Walk from Western Road and what he saw appalled him.

The north end of the Science Building was a rectangle of dull grey stone and glass with all kinds of rectangular excrescences, including a chimney stack, towering above the beautiful classical portico and front wall – both in Cork limestone – of the former gaol. The contrast was and still is shattering. His remedy was a rather daft one: plant a line of trees between the two and in time the north end would be invisible. For a number of sound reasons this was impossible. In fact there was no solution and a quarter of a century has not dulled the jarring effect on the eye. But Aloys kept on fighting and finally authority, in order to get him off its back, did what it always did: namely set up a committee with a vague remit about maintaining good standards of taste and encouraging a sense of art in the College. The membership comprised Aloys as Chairman, Dr J. B. Kearney, Mr P. Vernon and myself. Of course Aloys was the driving force. It became known as the Aesthetics Committee and was frequently sniffed at and even made fun of. During its lifetime it acted as a useful watchdog on buildings and modifications thereof and it encouraged the acquisition by the College of works of art.

It died when Aloys retired but by then it had done its job. Twenty odd years on, new buildings on the campus blend well with the older ones. The College has acquired a worthy collection of paintings and works of sculpture adorn the grounds – all due in no small part to the Aesthetics Committee, but in particular to its chairman.

The Appointment of Aloys' Successor to the Chair of Music

Some of us knew that it would be impossible to find another Aloys, to which some others said 'Thank Heavens for that'. Anyway, all the motions for the filling of the chair were gone through and I found myself appointed Chairman of the Assessment Committee, which would make its recommendation on the short listed candidates to the relevant College bodies. The committee comprised four experts in the subject – two from outside the College and two from within and a non-expert chairman who would preside over the interviews and ensure that each interviewee got fair treatment. It was a long hard day and the experts were unanimous in their recommendation. I knew that Aloys was going to be bitterly disappointed. I also knew that I was going to be the one to tell him. We had arranged (all highly irregular of course) beforehand that I would phone him that night and had previously sworn him to secrecy. That was the hardest phone call I ever had to make. When I told him he just said 'Thank you' and hung up. I did not blame him.

The Room in the Maltings

When Aloys retired he asked if he could be given a room in the Music department to continue his work on Irish music. The president of the day refused point blank to grant his request. In fact he refused to give him a room anywhere, as space was at a premium. But Aloys kept knocking knowing – as most of us did – that if you keep knocking long enough, authority will ultimately give in just to get you off its back and Aloys got some kind of a room one floor up in a library store in the Lee Maltings.

It was a rule that, for security purposes, all College buildings had to be vacated by midnight. The particular security men in charge of the Lee Maltings from time to time had some difficulty in shifting Aloys. One night, when the man on duty opened the ground floor door, a large rat ran out from the stacks and scuttled along the passage way. The man threw his large bunch of keys and a heavy book-end and shouted 'Get out you b——t——' An apologetic voice came from the floor above 'I am just coming'. (I was told this story by the head security man of the time at the Maltings).

Aloys Fleischmann as I Perceived Him

I hope that some aspects of Aloys' personality, as I saw them, come through in what I have written above. He and I were not close friends and I was never deeply associated with him in any of his great musical undertakings. I always enjoyed the many which I attended. I could see that he was a man of boundless energy. He never wasted time chatting to his colleagues after a meeting. He just dashed off to whatever was next on his crowded agenda. His visits to the Staff Common Room were very rare and when he did come it was generally to 'catch' some particular colleague. At social functions he appeared to be somewhat ill at ease. A single glass of wine would be his limit and small talk bored him.

He was formal in his dress and address – always a suit of clothes even on ordinary working days and always 'Mrs', 'Dr', 'Professor'. When he addressed his students individually it was always 'Mr' or 'Miss'. I don't think that he possessed any sense of humour whatever. If one told him a joke it went flat and I don't think I ever saw him laugh.

Nora Brown (Cork), UCC Graduate, Retired Librarian of University College Cork

It was in the autumn of 1945 when I enrolled as a first-year Arts student in University College Cork. One of the more exciting aspects of this process was choosing two clubs or societies. I joined the Choral Society, where, for the first time, I experienced that tremendous energy which could weld amateur singers, many of whom like me, were poor sight readers, and an orchestra, in its cradle days, into a fairly acceptable performance of music which was totally alien to our culture. We were swept along by this dynamic enthusiasm, even as we struggled with the difficulties presented by the score of *Samson*, and in the following year of *Judas Maccabaeus*. The professionalism of the principals – Rita Lynch (Soprano), Maura O'Connor (Mezzo-Soprano), William Penny (Tenor) and Richard Mason (Bass) must have been some consolation to Professor Fleischmann's musical sensibilities. Only a man of his determination to lift musical standards in Cork could have succeeded in these ventures.

Some eight years later, Professor Fleischmann assembled a special choir from college members and other choirs in the city to form the Aeolian Choir, for the performance of Borodin's *Polovtsian Dances* with the Cork Ballet Company, together with his own composition for ballet, choir and orchestra, *The Golden Bell of Ko*. It came to the dress rehearsal in the Opera House. Strange sounds were emanating from the brass. The maestro brought the performance to a halt and enquired, 'Mr ..., I don't think that you're playing what's in the score'. A timid voice replied: 'I forgot my music, Prof.' It was unforgivable of course. We were delighted by the conductor's reaction. He gave vent to a torrent of anger, which I can still recall to this day, because it was so unlike Professor Fleischmann's calm and patient manner, in spite of all the difficulties that he had to overcome.

For the *Polvotsian Dances*, the choir was in costume on stage, at first lying prone, while the members of the Ballet Company were supposed to dance airily around and over us. We were not so confident in their skills that we could 'sleep', but kept one eye open until we rose to sing that delightful music.

The choir was off stage in the wings for *The Golden Bell of Ko*. We needed to read the score but found ourselves in complete darkness, and had to rely on memory to interpret the music. We got through it mainly, I think, because the Professor had the gift of inspiring a choir and orchestra to give the best performance of which they were capable.

Another memory from those days was singing in his work based on that rousing tune *Clare's Dragoons*, when the audience was startled by the bagpipes, as Joan Denise Moriarty made a striking entrance from the back of the City Hall.

Professor Fleischmann's love of choral music led to the foundation of the Choral Festival, which did so much to widen our appreciation of European and American music, and to make Irish music known to a wider audience. I joined Cór Cois Laoi in 1954. The Festival became the focal point of our year. Competition was really keen as we listened with deep interest to the performances of the foreign choirs, the Guinness Choir and the Cork School of Music Choir. Every point was earnestly debated before and after the result. It was so encouraging to see newly formed choirs coming from many parts of Ireland. The mixture of singing and dancing from several European countries, so eloquently compered by Dan Donovan, was a new experience for Cork audiences. One of the most interesting musical developments which emanated from the Festival was the establishment of Music graduates who specialised in choral singing in many counties in Ireland. Cór Cois Laoi was the instrument for their final examination. I recall our conductor, Pilib Ó Laoghaire, forecasting that choral singing would lead to the development of instrumental music, and he has been proved right.

As a member of the library staff in UCC, I discovered that Professor Fleischmann's activities were not confined to musical performances. He was a real academic, deeply interested in the origins of Irish music. Frequent visits to the inter-library loan section over a number of years, where the late Paddy Ahern drew on Irish and foreign resources to produce photostats of the earliest Irish tunes, culminated in the publication of his unique reference work, *Sources of Irish Traditional Music*, which will be utilised as long as scholars are interested in Irish music. The Departmental Music Library, which I attempted to restore to order on a few occasions, also brought me in contact with Professor Fleischmann. It took me some time to realise that the stock was being freely used as demonstration material for lectures, and as practice material for students, making it quite impossible to maintain the kind of control which prevailed in the main library. The Professor was so apologetic when items could not be located, but we both knew that it was a hopeless situation until a library assistant was appointed. The Cork Symphony Orchestra had permission to practice in the Aula Maxima, which at that time housed the Modern Languages and Ancient Classics' collections of the library in locked presses. Open access was unheard of until late in the 1970s. French books were in great demand, but were frequently barricaded in by rows of music stands and drums. So Professor Fleischmann and I engaged in a friendly but persistent dialogue to move the offending stands at sufficient distance to allow for the doors to be unlocked. It is consistent with his unfailing courtesy that he finally succeeded in training the orchestra to move their paraphernalia to a mutually satisfactory position.

When I recall Professor Fleischmann, my impression is of a person who never stopped working, who was constantly active in all forms of music, in administration for the Choral Festival, in academic research, who could cope with all kinds of contingencies and overcome them. He was a man with a mission, to bring Ireland into the mainstream of music, and to develop her own musical heritage. The Professor must have experienced tremendous satisfaction when the two strands were brought together in the work of his pupil, Seán Ó Riada.

MARY MOSS NÉE MANNING (CORK), UCC Graduate, formerly Secretary to the President of University College Cork
My memories of Professor Fleischmann go back to my student days, to the Commerce Faculty, when UCC was still small enough to get to know staff and students of other faculties. The Professor, who had founded the Art Society in his student days in 1931, encouraged us to enjoy good music and culture. We joined in choral work in concerts, oratorios, etc.

Quite a few years later I got to know the Professor better when I was President's Secretary. The Music department was over our offices in the East Wing, and we were treated to piano music around examination time and occasionally a small choir would burst into song.

The Professor was tireless in his work, and always rushing from lectures to orchestral rehearsals, meetings and so on. He was utterly dedicated to UCC, his students, and the city of Cork. I hope we did not take him too much for granted. I was not in Cork during his later years, but was glad to hear he had been given the Freedom of Cork City. Very few deserved the honour more.

For my own part, I will always be grateful for his public lectures on music in UCC and in the city, and for his concerts. Because of him I enjoy music so much now. I am glad I knew him.

When I arrived at the department in June 1973, Professor Fleischmann was away on holiday and Geoffrey Spratt had just been appointed. He and some of the final year students took the record library apart and re-catalogued all the records (long-playing vinyls) and this library was in my office. We all had great fun and I learned as they worked.

The Prof worked at home in the mornings; I would ring him at 09.15, my start time; he would be there (probably up since dawn), give me my work for the day and I would have it ready when he came into the office around 3.00pm, when he usually had a lecture in term-time. On his way, he would call to the Festival office and check in there on the Festival work. He was never late for a lecture. He told me once that in the beginning he had to force himself to teach: that it would not have been his chosen occupation. He would slide in on the motor-bike (the Vespa had died by the time I started), slipping on the cobbles on wet days, right the bike, scoot in, grab his gown and off into class. In the breaks, he would come to the office. Some days, he just did not want to do anything, but I used to goad him and he would say: 'My dear, you are a bully!' in the nicest possible way.

He used to always give money to the winos (street alcoholics): they came regularly and he gave regularly. This irked me because they also came when he was not there and when maybe I would be there alone. When they wanted money they were dangerous.

People used to often come into the department with soaked and dirty music manuscripts which would have fallen off the back of his bike and ask whether they were the Professor's. It is a measure of how he expanded Music as a subject that if music manuscript were to be found in the street today, it would not be the obvious thing to bring it to UCC's Music department, then *the* centre of the subject, as nowadays there are so many others as well.

One time during a summer, the staff all took off on a picnic: Geoffrey Spratt and Vivienne, Nóirín and Mícheál Ó Súilleabháin, myself and Prof. Off we went down around Oysterhaven and Kinsale. He ran up hills and dragged us (I've a mark on my right foot to this day) over ditches, up on to cliffs and made us swim when the tide was in. We had some good laughs – he was full of life.

The Christmas Dinner was an event he looked forward to. He would insist that only classical music, Strauss waltzes, etc., were played and he would waltz the girl students around all night and never tire. Once, when one of these functions was held out of town and I was one of those travelling in his car to the dinner, he told us ghost stories to shorten the road. He said his family thought their home, Oileán Ruadh or Hop Island House, was haunted by the ghost of a former owner, a colonel who had been killed by the IRA during the Troubles. Prof said his three-year old daughter Ruth had seen this man, calmly asking at breakfast who the stranger was that she had met on the stairs. The Prof told us that there were numerous uncanny occurrences in that house.

For some of the time I was there, Charles Lynch gave piano master classes to the students. He was very grand, without a penny: he would come into the office and ring up O'Connors of Northgate Bridge and order a taxi to take him home. They used to send Mercedes Benzes and limousines and never charged him anything!

One day the Prof arrived into the office after an Academic Council or Arts Faculty meeting, which were then held in the old Council Room, behind the Aula Maxima. When I looked at his coat, there seemed to be something not quite right, but we carried on and after a while the phone rang. It was Tim O'Leary, the attendant in the Staff House. 'Would Fleischmann have taken the wrong coat, girl?' said Tim. Prof had gone by this time and nothing more could be done. When I rang him the following morning, he told me that his keys would not work in any of the locks: he was frantic and couldn't understand it. So I told him that Tim thought he had in error taken a coat belonging to somebody in the History department. Prof asked that his coat be brought down to the Music department; but the staff member from History would not let go of it until he had got his own one back. Tim thought this was hilarious. For the record, the Prof's coat was in much better nick than the other one!

SUSAN SAYER, Director of the Teaching Development Unit at University College Cork
I arrived at UCC in 1981 when Aloys Fleischmann was already gone from that institution and my first awareness of him was entirely second hand. It is all the more surprising, therefore, how very strong and enduring my sense of him was, and how much of an active 'presence' he was in my life, so that I felt that I knew him much more than was occasioned by the few times that we actually met.

My first career was in music, earning my living in the USA as a lecturer in composition and theory and harbouring pretensions of spending my life as a composer. Naturally when I arrived in Cork, I was still very interested in music – especially in the Music department at UCC in case I could make any useful working connections with it. To my surprise, despite his absence, Aloys Fleischmann still loomed large in the UCC picture. The UCC Music department was undergoing significant changes of policy and practice under the leadership of Aloys' successor and the new leadership felt the need to justify its weak, ineffective and increasingly unpopular efforts by decrying what

212

came before and blaming former colleagues and students of Aloys' who remained on the scene for many of the problems arising. The atmosphere in the department was generally troubled and, to the satisfaction of many, that head eventually managed to gain a professorship elsewhere and left the scene.

A second new regime soon followed. I recall from that source blame for the discontent and lack of success of further new policies being placed on what was termed the 'inferior quality' of incoming students – i.e. they were not capable of appreciating or making good use of third level education in Music. It was explained to me that this was the legacy of Aloys Fleischmann who, although he had for a long while been 'Mr Big' of music in Cork, had failed to make sure that the content and standard of local second level music training was sufficient that the students would be adequately prepared to profit from the more 'modern' approach and up-to-date training now offered at third level.

Today there is a third successive regime in the UCC Music department but times have changed significantly both within and without the university. 'Market' considerations have become paramount in education (as in most other spheres of life) – not merely within the Music department but college-wide, nationwide and internationally. The current new head is largely of the new breed, in tune with matters of marketing, image and public relations; whether sufficient attention is now devoted to issues such as curriculum coverage, performance standards, acquisition of technical knowledge, etc., is a matter for debate. Moreover, the formal complaints to the college of recent years by UCC music students about the inadequate training they were receiving have finally disappeared from view and been forgotten. Thus the College is happy enough that all is well.

During all this time, of course, I heard about the 'Fleischmann regime' from former students and colleagues of Aloys who were less than satisfied that the changes in the Music department had constituted an improvement. From time to time they described to me, in almost loving detail, the items of curriculum, the teaching methods and the high standards, as well as the personal idiosyncrasies that Aloys had brought to the task. Over the years no doubt there was an increasing factor of rose-tinted spectacles in those reminiscences, nevertheless the respect for what had come before was genuine and deep and led the individuals concerned to have experienced a serious sense of loss. Thus it was that Aloys was real, powerful and important to me before I ever met him face to face. Eventually I met Aloys himself and became acquainted with other aspects of his work – at first most notably the International Choral Festival and, later, most importantly some of his compositions. My sense of him grew accordingly and was amplified by a number of personal conversations that I was privileged to have with him either at public functions or occasionally in a private social setting.

Interestingly, the Cork School of Music in 1996 began a third level degree course of its own and it remains to be seen whether this will present a serious challenge to the student intake of the Music department at UCC. Even more interesting is the fact that while the influence of Aloys Fleischmann at UCC is now near to zero, the top leadership and one or two individuals at the Cork School of Music still represent former colleagues and students of Aloys' whose sense of him and what he represented remains very much alive. Whether or not, however, the top leadership can resist the extreme and increasing pressures towards education as a commercial enterprise and keep alive any of the ideals and standards that came before remains to be seen. In the short run the odds are against it. What will happen in the longer term – e.g., whether there may be a swing back towards individual competence and skill as educational values in which the memory of Aloys Fleischmann and his work will help to lead the way – I of course can't know. But I can hope, and I know there are still a few others around who share that sustaining expectation.

ANNE HESKIN (CORK), Retired Secretary to the President of University College Cork
Naturally I had heard of Professor Aloys Fleischmann long before I joined the administrative staff of the President's Office at University College in May 1961. I am not in any way competent to pass judgement on his great musical achievements. However, I am well aware of his tremendous contribution to the musical life of the university, the city of Cork and indeed to the nation as a whole. He was well known internationally also for his great musical achievements – as teacher/mentor, composer and conductor.

I got to know Professor Fleischmann well over the years. He was always a very courteous gentleman, even when he was annoying us in the office. He was forever in a hurry, which I guess was not so surprising, as he had so many things to do, practically all at the one time. One of my strongest memories is of hearing him pounding up the stairs outside our office to his own office, which had been located overhead in the Staff House for some years. In those days he was well known around town, whizzing in and out of traffic on his scooter.

The ordinary day to day way of life and the running of a house seem to pass him by. He did not appear to realise that the necessities of life had to be paid for. I remember hearing, at one stage, when an increase in salary was mooted for the academics in College, that he said no such increase was necessary, or deserved!

Professor Fleischmann was the bane of the lives of all administrators with whom he came in contact. However, all knew his worth and respected his sincerity. They never failed to assist him where possible. He was never one to take 'No' for an answer and was forever seeking to override the refusal of the use of the Aula Maxima for extra rehearsals for his Symphony Orchestra which had not been pre-booked at the beginning of the season. Indeed, permission might as well have been given upon the initial request, as he invariably got his way, even when the Aula had been set up in a particular way for examinations or other specific functions. He would keep his promise of having all the desks and chairs back in their correct order for the following morning's activities and would lead his band of helpers in replacing them after the rehearsals. No task was ever too menial for him, provided it enabled him to get his orchestral or other musical work done.

As director of the Cork International Choral Festival he used to bring some of the visitors to meet the President each year. Again, confusion reigned beforehand until matters were taken in hand by some of his superb helpers, most notably Mrs Moira Pyne. She was the soul of discretion and somehow managed to get everything running smoothly in the end.

Though I understand Professor Fleischmann was a great hill walker, climbing to the top of Mount Brandon on his 80th birthday, music was his life. He worked at it right up to the very end of his long and fruitful life, never sparing himself.

Ar dheis Dé go raibh a h-anam.

JOHN A. MURPHY (CORK), Emeritus Professor of Irish History at University College Cork, former Member of the Irish Senate[1]
Aloys Fleischmann, Colleague and Friend

As a first year UCC student in 1945–46, I enrolled in the College Choral Society. For the purpose of performing Aloys Fleischmann's memorable Clare's Dragoons extravaganza for the Thomas Davis centenary, our group became a component of the huge Aeolian Choir (so named by Aloys himself, presumably), an ad hoc amalgamation of a number of city choirs. I remember vividly a rehearsal of the work, complete with orchestra and Joan Denise Moriarty's war pipes, in the Aula Maxima, the ceremonial heart of the College. I recall the flamboyant President Alfred O'Rahilly roaring his bravos from the gallery while the young conductor maintained his customary composure and urbanity.

Nearly half a century later, in June 1992, as his wheel of life was slowing to a stop, I saw him for the last time, on two successive nights in that same great hall, scene of his erstwhile triumphs. Frail and terminally ill, he had come from his sick bed to attend a Cara O'Sullivan/ Patrick Zuk recital which included some of his own songs. On the following evening, he was there again, this time to say goodbye to the Vanbrugh String Quartet whose continued location in Cork he had struggled so hard to maintain.

On that 1945 occasion, I admired him from afar, as it were, being an anonymous albeit lusty contributor to the sound of that great choir. Some years before his death, when we were colleagues of long standing, I happened to mention my long-ago humble role in *Clare's Dragoons*. He arched back his head, in a characteristic gesture, to have a better look at me before expressing his disbelief; 'My goodness, surely not! You were much too young!' Such ingenuous flattery endeared him to me further. Not so flattering perhaps was his assumption that, as a colleague, you were as knowledgeable as he was about arcane aspects of the institution. 'You know, of course, that there is a large cavity under the floor of the Aula Maxima? You didn't know that? My goodness!'

Meetings of the Academic Council were sometimes tedious and tortuous and since Aloys had umpteen things to do, attendance must often have vexed him sorely though he did his best to conceal his frustration. His relationship with academic administrators was far from serene. He had a somewhat cavalier attitude towards regulations if they seemed to conflict with the interests of the subject and of his students. I remember occasions when the College Registrar (who understandably had his own priorities) would sternly reprimand Aloys for what was alleged were his anarchically flexible attitudes to deadlines. The Professor of Music would sit there with an urbane expression of injured innocence, mildly outraged that anyone would consider him unreasonable or uncooperative.

Though he and I were colleagues for a long time, our first contacts were acrimonious. In the course of a contribution to an *Irish Times* supplement on Cork, where I surveyed the city's social and cultural scene in the mid 1970s, I half mischievously suggested that ballet often teetered on the verge of the ludicrous, that it was doubtful 'if it should be done at all unless it is done superbly' and that it tended to be 'a class cult for the daughters of the socially pretentious'. I (light-heartedly) added insult to injury by asserting that set dancing would be a more appropriate and realistic preparation for the rigours of Irish life. The Prof (than whom nobody could be less pretentious) was understandably incensed at such provocative snipings directed at a major cultural undertaking of his, and a testy debate ensued in the correspondence columns of *The Irish Times*. In retrospect, realising the daunting obstacles in the way of the whole ballet enterprise, I became aware that my 'ballhopping' was somewhat misguided and irresponsible. *Mea culpa!* Issues of common concern later drew us together. Everyone knows of Aloys' absorbed involvement in the extra-mural cultural scene but few are aware of his wider civic interests. He was not only concerned about official neglect of the arts, and curriculum downgrading of the humanities but he was distressed about northern violence and the sickly economy of the 1980s (professors should take a ten percent salary cut, he told his unresponsive colleagues!). He worried about poor Cork attendances at visiting National Symphony Orchestra concerts, and he was keenly aware that social and geographical apartheid resulted in a cultural comprehension gap in our society. To a small extent, I was able to give voice to some of these concerns in Seanad Éireann where I represented National University of Ireland graduates for several years. On one occasion, he was characteristically appreciative of some advice offered him in connection with an article he sent to the *New York Times* and in October 1991 he was excessively grateful for background historical information I was able to provide for some of his tune titles.

I was greatly honoured when Aloys proposed me for the honorary position of president of the Cork Orchestral Society. Perhaps I appreciated even more his invitation to join him in climbing Mount Brandon to celebrate his eightieth birthday. This remarkable happening apparently originated in an earlier, uncompleted Brandon attempt by his father to mark *his* seventieth birthday. He was accompanied on that occasion by young Aloys, who was determined there would be another day! (As a young teacher, I knew Aloys senior to see. He conducted the North Cathedral choir and had been one of that interesting tribe of German organists who secured appointments to Irish Cathedrals in the early years of the twentieth century just in time to be interned when the Great War broke out.)

On a squally Easter Monday 1990 I joined the Prof's family and two priest friends to pay homage to Kerry, to St Brendan and to the ancestral Fleischmanns. The conditions on Brandon summit were arctic but the octogenarian Aloys took the whole thing in his nonchalant stride. Back at the Casán na Naomh base, we gratefully supped from the coffee flasks, and divested ourselves of our rain-gear. 'But,' I exclaimed, 'you're wearing a collar and tie and ... a suit!' Surprised at my surprise, he rejoined 'But what else should I be wearing?' Later on, he surveyed unflappably the bustling bank holiday scene in Paudie O'Shea's pub in Ventry (when had he last been in a hostelry?) and politely expressed his preference for an apple juice.

As a musician and composer, Aloys Fleischmann enjoyed the esteem of his peers and indeed was laden with academic honours. He *could* have stayed within the walls of musical academe, devoting himself exclusively to creative research and dynamic teaching. But he was committed to the principle of gown serving town, the UCC Music department in his time being pre-eminent in this regard. He gave generously of himself to the people of Cork, enriching their lives immeasurably and, by so doing, becoming the most significant Corkonian of his time. German by ancestry and birth (going to Munich to be born, so to speak), Aloys Fleischmann's intense allegiance was to Ireland – and to Cork. He fought tenaciously for the city's place in the cultural sun, not out of sentimental provinciality or anti-metropolitan bias, but because he wanted his own people to experience the best. Because his genetic background was different, he did not evince that Gascon-like volatility and excitability which Ernie O'Malley noted of the Cork character. Rather did Aloys display an equable temperament, sustained by a single-minded sense of discipline and commitment which made frustration (experienced in dealings with officialdom) all the more disappointing. When he felt passionately about the iniquitous Broadcasting Act, for example, he expressed himself in a characteristically composed manner – *suaviter in modo, fortiter in re.*

His impressive public service was founded on his secure and certain sense of himself as an academic. From his appointment in 1936, when he was hailed as a new star in the college firmament, to his (semi!) retirement in 1980, he was first and last the 'Prof', the quintessential professor. He was a vigilant watchdog on the aesthetics of campus buildings. He was frequently influential in the drama of college politics, both on stage, so to speak, and behind the scenes. In retirement, his recollections form an invaluable part of the college's oral history archives. He was, above all, committed to high academic standards and sought an appointments system which would be above reproach, would not involve canvassing and would be free from any suggestion of nepotism or personal influence. (He wrote about this in the *University Review*.)

His concern was that the UCC Governing Body, as traditionally constituted, could not be trusted to operate a disinterested and objective appointments system, and he spoke from disenchanted experience. In his view, the National University federal framework, with the final say being left to the Senate, was a vital (if not universally dependable) safeguard. Hence his dismay at any suggestion that the constituent colleges of the university might become autonomous and be the final arbiters in the matter of appointments.

Some ten days before his death, he wrote to me expressing his deep concern about all this, and I would like to think that I was able to reassure him that the contemplated provisions for autonomy at

Cork and elsewhere (eventually enacted in the 1997 Universities Act) would guarantee those high standards of academic appointments which he so ardently desired. That he should be preoccupied with academic and scholarly matters on his deathbed, testified to a remarkably disciplined and stoic temperament.

I particularly treasure that last letter, even as I imagine him bounding up to some celestial podium and vigorously conducting angelic music of his own composition. I am also very glad that I regained my footing after the balletic stumble long ago, and went on to become his friend.

VIRGINIA TEEHAN, Director of the University Archives, University College Cork
The Fleischmann Archive – A Unique National Resource
The Fleischmann family transferred the Fleischmann Archive to the University Archives at University College, Cork in 1993. The archive is a unique, irreplaceable resource which the university is privileged to care for.

The function of the University Archives is to professionally care for the institutional records of UCC and those associated with the university. It is appropriate that UCC should be given responsibility for the Fleischmann Archive and thus continue the lengthy association between the Fleischmann family and the university. The university provides a natural home for this wonderful collection.

It is not the objective of this paper to outline in detail the content of the archive. It would not be possible in the available space. The aim of this paper is to explore the value and potential of the archive.

Contexts
A dedication to music – its composition, performance, academic scrutiny and enjoyment as reflected in the life of Aloys Fleischmann, his parents and grandparents, overwhelmingly define this archive. However, its broader context is shaped by generations of one family, who initially emigrated to Ireland from Germany in the 1870s. This background provides the framework which informs the unique characteristics of the collection.

The preservation of family records and many photographs of family and friends dating from the start of the twentieth century symbolise the careful protection of a past by generations of one family. Newspaper reports of Fleischmann's father's, production of nativity plays in the artistic community that was Dachau, Germany, in 1904, and many other scrapbooks, letters, postcards and photographs from this time and place are fascinating historical and social documents. Letters home to Cork from Fleischmann's father while a prisoner of war in the Isle of Man during the First World War are equally unique items. The music manuscripts containing music written by Fleischmann senior for the prisoner of war camp orchestra dated 1917 and 1918 are poignant records of another life. Such materials record the dramatic impact on family life which political events can dictate. These intimate family records bear testimony to the small, somewhat peripheral, groupings of non-nationals living in Irish provincial cities, such as Cork and Limerick, in the early decades of the twentieth century. These extraordinary music manuscripts, letters, postcards, scrapbooks, newspaper cuttings and photographs evoke a sense of displacement from one's cultural origins in an adopted country.

The Fleischmann family was at the centre of musical and cultural activity in Cork. Aloys Fleischmann senior succeeded his father-in-law as cathedral organist at St Mary's Cathedral; his wife Tilly (Maria Theresa Mathilde Swertz) was an acclaimed musician and pianist in her own right. Both were lively participants in the musical and social life of the city. Individually they had an major impact on musical developments and teaching in Cork for many decades of the twentieth century. Their work and subsequent legacies are fully recorded in the archive. The relationship between son and parents is a strong thread running though the personal papers. The preservation of letters to Tilly Fleischmann from Richard Pfeiffer and Professor Kellermann upon the birth of her son to the inclusion of records relating to the administration of their estates after their respective deaths demonstrate this theme. Aloys Fleischmann's letters to his mother and father, while a student at the Staatliche Akademie für Tonkunst at Munich University (1932–34), are those of a son whose interests and passions were exclusively artistic and in the main, musical, deeply enjoying the rich cultural environment in which he was placed. The rapidly changing, volatile, political landscape which surrounded that environment is rarely mentioned. The letters that Fleischmann wrote from Munich represent, within the context of this collection, a revisiting of cultural origins – origins which influenced the impact that the Fleischmann family had on Irish musical, artistic, and cultural life throughout the twentieth century.

Scope and Content

The Fleischmann Archive is physically large, containing approximately 350,000–400,000 individual items in a variety of media formats: letters – typescript and carbon copies, manuscript; music manuscripts – the original scores of both Fleischmanns' compositions; photographs – black and white, colour; newspaper cuttings; posters – Cork Ballet Company, Cork Symphony Orchestra, etc., line drawings and colour;

tickets; complete series of performance programmes; flyers for performances; degree parchments, certificates, diplomas; miscellaneous cards including birthday cards, Christmas cards and mortuary cards; books, government reports, university calendars; sheet music (much belonging to Fleischmann's father); tapes – video, audio (cassettes and reels, music recordings and recordings of interviews, lectures including Thomas Davis lectures); records; conducting baton, spectacles, academic robes, scrapbook and slides.

There are over 2,000 photographic prints in the archive, many taped and video recordings of performances, radio and television interviews given by Fleischmann and others such as Joan Denise Moriarty. The final draft *Sources of Irish Traditional Music 1600–1855*,[2] Fleischmann's seminal research project as recorded on magnetic tape for printing, is also included. The archive spans the period 1890–1992/93.

A major part of the archive contains records which document Fleischmann's work as professor of Music at UCC (1936–1980) and as head of a vibrant, colourful academic department, producing a growing number of graduates, including such distinguished musicians as Seán Ó Riada, Nóirín and Mícheál Ó Súilleabháin. Also present is information on the teaching of music – lecture notes, examination papers, material on the setting of standards and creating of curricula, the running of a university department and involvement in university politics. Efforts to develop the musical and cultural life of the College are well recorded, as is the establishment of the Art Society by Fleischmann in 1931 as an undergraduate student. As a member of UCC staff, Fleischmann and other colleagues established the House Advisory Committee in 1975 that grew into the Visual Arts Committee in the early 1980s. The archive records in detail Fleischmann's many skirmishes with the College authorities in meeting his objectives in this area. The archive strongly confirms John A. Murphy's opinion, as expressed in his history of UCC:

> From the beginning, Fleischmann was concerned to advance music and the arts in the wider community beyond the walls, and over the next five decades his energetic contributions to the musical life of Cork probably constituted UCC's single most valuable service to the city. He promoted the professional interests of music teachers and organised lively summer courses in the college, raised a storm when he condemned the use of tonic solfa! As founder of the Art Society and the Cork Orchestral Society, he was already being nationally acclaimed at thirty as a 'young and gifted live wire.'[3]

Fleischmann's research work is well represented in the archive and in particular reflects his ongoing work in compiling *Sources of Irish Traditional Music c. 1600–1855*[4] (a major research project which lasted from

1954 until Fleischmann's death in 1992) and his contribution to *A New History of Ireland*.[5] As well as comprising a record of this academic work, the archive also reflects Fleischmann's work as a composer. His varied body of work is regarded as representing a significant contribution to Irish music. Fleischmann maintained close contact with his contemporaries, particularly in the field of music in Ireland, but also in broader cultural terms. The archive reflects this and contains a large amount of personal correspondence between Fleischmann and such composers as Arnold Bax, Jack Moeran, Fred May, Brian Boydell, Ina Boyle and Elizabeth Maconchy as well as fellow academics and friends, for example, Joan Denise Moriarty, Seamus Murphy, Seán O'Casey, Paul Kont and Seán Ó Faoláin, Harriet Cohen, Eilís Dillon and Jeanne Sheehy amongst others.

Fleischmann's participation in Irish cultural discourse is reflected, through correspondence with taoisigh, senior politicians, and membership of organisations such as the Arts Council, Aosdána (Ireland's state sponsored academy of creative artists), the Cultural Advisory Committee and the first Broadcasting Advisory Committee. Evidence of this commitment to Irish cultural developments is contained in the archive through extensive materials outlining his involvement in a range of activities such his rôles in the establishment of the Cork Symphony Orchestra (1934); the Cork Orchestral Society (1938); the annual Cork International Choral and Folk Dance Festival (Director, 1954–1987); the Cork Ballet Group/Company (1947–92) Irish Theatre Ballet 1959–64, Irish National Ballet 1973–89); The Irish Music Teachers Association (1935); Irish Church Music Association; Cumann Náisiúnta na gCór (1982); Cork Music Festival (1940); Cork Film Festival (1953); An Tóstal; Cork 800; Annual Carol Concerts, Feiseanna Cheoil and his membership of the Royal Irish Academy. Aloys Fleischmann was closely involved with the ballet company set up in Cork by Joan Denise Moriarty: they had a lifelong fruitful partnership in dance and music. Fleischmann's public profile is represented though the texts of many of the public lectures and speeches that he presented throughout his career contained in the collection.

This archive distinctively proclaims the personality of its creator over a long period, his individualism, the controversies, for example, in 1964 when republicans opposed the Earl of Rosse opening that year's Choral Festival and the bitterness over the Arts Council's axing of the Irish National Ballet Company in 1988, are all part of the archive. Fleischmann's singular determination to achieve his aims is evident throughout the collection. The organic way in which the archive was created and naturally grew directly mirrors a very meticulous approach to work. This attention to detail and the recording of his work in an organised manner is, ironically, juxtaposed with many personal eccentricities, for which he was well known. The organisational nature of the arrangement of this archive by its creator greatly enriches its quality as a primary source.

Professional Protection
This archive is a resource of national importance. It requires professional archival skills to ensure its permanent protection and realise its full potential as primary source for research. Processing the archive is central to the protection of its individual character. Professional archivists in UCC are currently listing the archive. Only when this list is complete will the potential of the archive be fully evident. As a means of protection for this valuable archive and in adherence to professional practice, the archive has been closed to public scrutiny until the listing process is completed.

The objectives of the listing process are to ensure that the unique integrity of the archive is preserved. Listing or describing the archive results in the compilation of a descriptive list, which is the most fundamental finding aid, produced for the archive. The descriptive list will be made available in traditional print and electronic format. It will also be available through the World Wide Web and is being done in a manner that conforms to international descriptive standards. In this list:
- each individual item (independent of media format) is described in an appropriate, accurate manner, there are approx. 300,000–400,000 individual items in this archive;
- the relationship between items is clearly established;
- the overall system of arrangement is clarified;
- the nature, acquisition, and appraisal of the archive is explained.

The final descriptive list will permit users to:

- browse through the contents of the archive in a manner which reflects the way in which the archive has been created;
- judge the evidential value of the items it contains;
- assess the integrity of the archive;
- understand its implications as a primary resource.

From a professional archival perspective, the descriptive list is an important security mechanism because:

- it identifies items precisely and notes their size, characteristics etc.;

- its compilation results in the systematic numbering of all items in the collection and thus prevents possible theft or loss;
- it allows the archivist to identify detailed conservation requirements and evaluate their priority in an appropriate manner;
- the absence of a descriptive list would mean that should any part of the archive be lost or destroyed its existence or contents would never have been recorded.

When the descriptive list is finally produced the archive will be opened for public use.

Potential Use

This archive will be of interest to a range of users. The university archives is committed to ensuring that it will be made accessible in a manner which maximises its potential as a unique national cultural resource. The listing work outlined above is being conducted in a manner that utilises all available professional and technical options in an innovative manner. Furthermore, the rapid developments in scanning technology and other media offer exciting opportunities which the University Archives wish to exploit and thus make this valuable archive as widely accessible as possible.

Independent of the format of availability there is no doubt that the archive will be of interest to a wide range of scholars and individuals. It will be of particular use to those interested in twentieth century Irish music and in Ireland's social and cultural history. The archives' reflection of Cork's social and cultural life make it of special relevance to local historians.

Summary

The Fleischmann Archive is a complex collection comprising the records of the life and work of Aloys Fleischmann (1910–1992). The Fleischmann family was at the nexus of Cork activity in orchestral music, choral music, chamber music and dance. The archive demonstrates a collection of material by one family who had a profound influence on Irish cultural life. It gives a perspective on the social, educational and cultural life of Cork City from the 1920s to the 1980s. The material contained in the archive provides an insight into formal music education in Ireland and into the world of amateur musical activity as evidenced by Cork at that time. During the period of the archive, the Cork Ballet Company, the Cork Symphony Orchestra and the Cork International Choral Festival flourished. There is evidence of contact with international musical influences, as illustrated by the invitation of foreign orchestras to play in Cork. During this time, Cork became the recognised centre for musical training and activity in Ireland. There are not one but two major schools in Cork producing a formal education in Music – UCC Department of Music and the Cork Municipal School of Music – Cork is a magnet for learning the profession of musician. In the archive there is continuous evidence of the act of musical creativity and its performance.

Significantly, this archive acts as a demonstration of how culture in the new state was operated. The politics of culture is shown by contact with the Arts Council, government departments, senior politicians and clerics and records the increasing formalisation of the administration of Irish culture over a long period.

The archive is versatile, containing images both still and moving, text – letters, diaries, postcards, research materials, administrative records, and sound. When the archive is completely catalogued and made fully accessible to the public it will re-shape discourse on culture in the new state, furthermore it will add a new dimension to Irish musical/social and cultural studies.

(2) Remembered by Musicians

JOHN MILEY (DUBLIN), Clarinettist
While I was not one of Professor Fleischmann's students, I have a very pleasant recollection of him.

Between 1948 and 1952 as an amateur I was principal clarinettist in the Dublin Orchestral Players and the only clarinettist in the county playing concertos and chamber music. Aloys Fleischmann was present in 1951 when I had considerable success with the Mozart Clarinet Concerto with the DOP. I tried unsuccessfully to get an audition with the RTE Symphony Orchestra (which had a vacancy for a clarinet) and meeting Aloys Fleischmann at a DOP final rehearsal early in 1952 I told him of my problem and that I was contemplating emigrating to India. He told me he was on a Broadcast Guidance Committee and would try to do something. Believe it or not, a week later I was summoned to the office of Fachtna Ó hAnnracháin, RTE's Musical Director and offered the job of second clarinet in the Symphony Orchestra. I did not take it as the day before I had signed a contract to go to India and felt honour bound to carry it out.

I hardly spoke to Aloys Fleischmann afterward but the whole episode showed what a kind and enthusiastic man he was and his determination to see that what was right was done.

Aloys was a priceless gift sent to us in Ireland. His contribution to Irish musical life, particularly in Cork, will never be forgotten.

LINDSAY ARMSTRONG (DUBLIN), Cor Anglais Player, former Director of the Royal Irish Academy of Music

On any occasion when I met Aloys Fleischmann, he was extremely kind and friendly to me, and on at least two occasions I was a guest at the family home in Cork.

On the musical side I remember a particularly happy collaboration when he conducted – in the 1960s – a Francis Xavier Hall concert in which I played the cor anglais solo in Sibelius' *Swan of Tuonela*. Aloys Fleischmann was a most distinguished figure in Irish musical life. His influence was immense and will live long after him.

PATRICK RING (DUBLIN), Singer

Long before I ever met the late Professor Fleischmann, his reputation was well known to me and I was aware that he was a high profile figure on the Irish music scene, widely known and very highly respected. He was not merely an academic but someone who was in the very front line fighting for music's rightful place in Irish society.

My first personal experience of Professor Fleischmann was at the Cork Choral and Dance Festival – his own brainchild – and its continued success to this day is a monument to his inspiration. He held open seminars at the university for the introduction of newly commissioned choral works for the Festival. His analysis of these new compositions was thorough, informed, painstaking and revelatory, often leaving the composers at a loss for words. In the evening he would sit in the front row in the City Hall for the first performance of the new work.

My impression was a man of complete dedication and integrity in his attitude to music, not for any personal kudos, but solely for the welfare of something more important than such considerations.

Work for the advancement of music in Ireland was and is an uphill struggle all the way and I don't think it has ever had a more tenacious and doughty champion in its cause. After all, he could have had a more serene and easy existence if he had settled for university life, but he obviously felt a very strong desire to spread appreciation of music as widely as possible. He took on politicians and the powers administering music in Ireland or, if necessary, a critic who needed to be chastened, as he so memorably did on one occasion.

He was of course a fine practical musician as pianist, composer and conductor. I had the privilege of being conducted by him in a fine performance of Handel's *Messiah* with the RTE Symphony Orchestra and Our Lady's Choral Society.

As a person, I always found him gentlemanly and charming, if rather formal by Irish standards.

The last time I saw him was at a meeting in the Mansion House,

Dublin, in 1990. This was held in an effort to save RTE's Vanbrugh String Quartet and Chamber Choir from disbandment. I thought the Professor was beginning to look physically frail, but his contribution before a sizeable audience was by far the most eloquent and powerful of the whole afternoon. I need hardly say that the String Quartet and Chamber Choir are happily still in existence and thriving.

I don't know of anybody who cared so much for Ireland's music or who worked so tirelessly in its cause. My respect and admiration for the late Professor Aloys Fleischmann is absolutely unqualified.

BETTY RUSSELL (CORK), Pianist. This was recorded by Anne Fleischmann.
My family decided to come back and live in Ireland in the 1950s after Ceylon had become independent. When we were still in Sri Lanka, somebody who knew we were going to move to Cork told us about the Fleischmanns, and said that they were known far and wide because of their musical talents. When I arrived from Sri Lanka, a family friend, Vi Dwyer, took me to the musical events in Cork right from the first week. We went to one of the rehearsals of the Cork Symphony Orchestra: that was the first time I met Aloys Fleischmann. I played the viola as well as the piano, and had played in symphony orchestras in Colombo when we were there. I was recruited at once. Aloys was the most amazing man. I don't know how he put up with some of the people in the orchestra. Nobody arrived on time: they came when it suited them. I don't know how he managed to get anything out of them, but he did and there were concerts once every year. He would never lose patience with any one particular member of the orchestra, but he did sometimes get a little agitated if something wasn't right. That is one of the things I remember about him most: his extraordinary patience. And his mind was so brilliant.

I also remember driving with him in his car, and I was terrified. I was playing the Khachaturian piano concerto in Fermoy and I thought I would not be able to perform if the journey went on like that. He wasn't a terribly good driver: he drove pretty fast and pretty erratically. He would be conversing deeply with you and have half an eye on the road. I asked him to please slow down and to pay attention to the road, which he did.

I had given solo piano concerts in Australia, and had played with professional orchestras and broadcast when I was living in Perth. But I was also used to playing with amateur orchestras from my time in Ceylon. I'm terrified of playing in public, but he was absolutely marvellous. He brought me through it: it was the most wonderful experience and I actually enjoyed it. I don't think I would have played with any other conductor except him.

227

I studied the piano with his mother, Tilly Fleischmann, who was remarkable. I was very fond of her and I learnt a great deal from her. However, at the beginning it was a bit difficult adapting to a new teacher – traumatic in fact, because she had her own very definite ideas, and nothing else was any good. So I had to try and marry off together my technique and her technique. It worked extremely well. I'd always had trouble with my memory and with learning new music, and that's where she was most helpful. I learnt the hard way, the really hard way. She said if you can do something properly then you won't be nervous. As a pianist she was very good. I was at her last two recitals. She was intent on being able to pass on the Liszt tradition of piano playing and when I came along she felt she had someone who would carry it on after her.

But I just wasn't dedicated enough: every so often I would give up the piano, but would then come back and start again. One day I finally put music out of my mind. I ceased going to concerts, I ceased doing anything. All of a sudden I could just see no sense in working myself to the bone, when I felt I wasn't getting any further. I was really terrified of playing in public. From that day on I never opened the piano. Or rather, I stopped until my little grandson came along, when I began to teach him. However, we used to continue to host Orchestral Society recitals here in Dunkathel House, and then the Radio Éireann String Quartet lived here. I liked having musicians around, having the house alive with music.

PROINNSÍAS Ó DUINN (DUBLIN), Conductor of the National Concert Orchestra
I met Aloys Fleischmann on many occasions both in Dublin and Cork but never purely socially. He always struck me as extremely energetic and enthusiastic about his profession as a composer and educator. I have always admired the manner in which he manipulated every possible opportunity to further the artistic life of Cork and that he succeeded in doing so over such a long career in a city that could be both incestuous and fickle. He explained to me at one meeting that he was hyperactive and required only a few hours sleep! !

The first time I saw him was when, as a young boy, I attended a symphony concert in the Phoenix Hall in Dublin when he conducted a concert of the music of Arnold Bax. I am sure that would have been in the 1950s. That was the only time I saw him conduct. Apart from *Táin*, I have only conducted one or two small pieces of his for orchestra and one for choir. Another piece I heard many years ago was his *Clare's Dragoons* for orchestra, choir and war pipes: I can still remember the dramatic impression it made. The *Táin*, of its nature, was theatrical and, as I recall, contained many moves I would have consider-

228

ed influenced by Sibelius and, perhaps, Vaughan Williams. My impression of the smaller orchestral pieces was that his writing was always practical if a shade too cerebral.

At the time of the Dublin Theatre Festival in 1981, I was in hospital recovering from an operation on the inside of my nose. (I had suffered some breathing problems in the preceding years since I returned to the country, especially when combined with hay fever). I was visited late in the week by someone from the Music department of RTE to see if I would be well enough to take over the final rehearsals in two or three days time of the new ballet as a problem had arisen during the preliminary orchestral rehearsals in the studio. The performances were to run for a week in the Gaiety Theatre. I distinctly remember my first thoughts and concern was regarding the Gaiety, where I had been Music director many years earlier. It was always a very dusty place – something that never endeared it to me but which concerned me more just then, given the nature of the little operation!

Knowing that the composer had been scheduled to conduct, I questioned the nature of the problem as I did not wish to offend anyone if I agreed. It was explained to me that whereas Dr Fleischmann obviously knew his score, he did not have the conducting technique to convey his intentions in the allocated rehearsal time. (I never addressed him by his first name because he was my senior. It was drummed into me as a child that this was correct etiquette unless the senior party expressed a wish to be called otherwise!) This message was confirmed to me by the orchestra leader at my first rehearsal. I hope the experience was not too embarrassing for Aloys Fleischmann and that he was reasonably happy with the result.

As a foot note I should explain that whereas Dr Fleischmann had considerable experience conducting, it was largely with students. In fact he told me on one occasion that he frequently had to rehearse his woodwind players individually and then section by section, etc. This would have meant a very different pace and technique than the one required by a professional orchestra who sight read the music (more or less) and who depend on following the expression of hands and body language. What they do not want is to be stopped too often, which ruins the flow or structure, or to be spoken to at length with explanations rather than read the intentions through the conductor's hands. Very few musicians who conduct students or amateurs succeed in the professional arena because of the very different techniques required for both. Those who do appear to have the occasional success usually do so at the expense of very lengthy, costly and trying rehearsal sessions.

Aloys Fleischmann was always kind and courteous to me and always enthusiastic about progressing the arts.

KEVIN ROCHE (DUBLIN), RTE Producer, former Member of the RTE Symphony Orchestra

I was always very much aware of Aloys Fleischmann's stature as a composer, of his importance in musical education in University College, Cork and of his dedication to the musical life of Cork. I had met him from time to time over a period of thirty years or more, but got to know him when I became 'second–in–command' to Fachtna Ó hAnnracháin in Radio Éireann. However, our relationship was always very formal: we were always 'Professor Fleischmann' and 'Mr Roche'.

I had actually played under his baton in performances of his *Clare's Dragoons* and his ballet *The Golden Bell of Ko*. The former was in Dublin's Phoenix Hall around about 1949–50. The music calls for a war piper to make a dramatic entrance at the climax of the story and to march from the back to the front of the hall playing heroic music. The piper on this occasion was none other than Joan Denise Moriarty, and she made her entry at the appropriate moment. But she had fractured a leg a short time before and it was encased in plaster. Which meant that she had to throw the leg out sideways with every second step as she marched down the hall. It reduced the whole scene to farce and the audience fell about.

The Professor had a problem with the Radio Éireann Symphony Orchestra when he conducted *The Golden Bell of Ko*. He actually accused the orchestra of not following his beat – in fact, of playing late, i.e., after his beat. In response, the more vocal members told him what was wrong with his beat. The problem is a difficult one to explain in mere words. The best analogy I can think of is this: visualise somebody throwing a ball forcefully to the floor, so that it bounces up again. Regard this as the conductor's down–beat, which is the most important beat in a bar of music. All professional orchestras play the first note or chord of the bar at the split second in which the ball hits the floor and rebounds. This technique enables the players to play exactly together. But the orchestra which Fleischmann conducted in Cork was not professional: it was a mixture of students, part–timers and teachers. They were accustomed to playing just as the down–beat started, i.e., just before the ball hit the floor. I am assured by a friend of mine who played in the Cork orchestra that they rarely managed to play together. So when Fleischmann accused us in the Radio Éireann Symphony Orchestra of playing late, the orchestra told him how it should be done. The problem was never resolved and I dare say it still existed in later years when there was a disagreement with the orchestra over his conducting of his ballet the *Táin*. Proinnsías Ó Duinn stepped in for him.[6]

I also met Fleischmann a few years later at the Cork International

Choral Festival, when I was assigned to record the many competitions and other performances, from which I produced a series of radio programmes. I was aware that he had been mainly responsible for the inauguration of this highly successful Festival. It was one of the many events which were initiated in different parts of the country, around the late 1940s or early 1950s, as a result of *An Tóstal* (the Pageant), a project dreamed up by *An Bórd Fáilte* (the Tourist Board). The events differed in format and content in different towns and cities. Most of them died out after a year or two, and the Cork Choral Festival is one of the very few still surviving. My recollection is that the standard of performance of the Irish choirs varied a great deal, but the best of them were very good indeed. There were choirs from the UK and a great many from the countries of the Eastern bloc, as it was called in the days of the 'Iron Curtain'. Some of these choirs were very large and their musical standards were superb. The extraordinary thing is that they arrived virtually penniless and the people of Cork provided accommodation and food for them. I was not involved in the actual organisation of the event but my impression was that it was excellent. Some Irish dance teams put on a non–competitive performance in between the choral competitions, and I remember a remark made by a European adjudicator who was seeing Irish dancing for the first time, and whose command of English was not the best. He confused the words 'virtue' and 'virtuosity', and he said to the audience: 'Never have I seen such virtue in the legs with so little movement of the body'. Obviously that was in the days before Riverdance!

I always had the highest regard and respect for Aloys Fleischmann, as a person, as a composer, as an educator, and as an organiser of many musical projects.

UNA HUNT (DUBLIN), Pianist, Music Graduate of Queens University Belfast and of the Hochschule für Musik in Vienna, Lecturer for Piano in the Cork School of Music 1981–1989
Professor Fleischmann was already an elderly gentleman when I met him in the early 1980s. I remember clearly his gifts of optimism and single-mindedness, qualities which I think are of great importance to musicians, because it is never easy, especially in arranging performances of new works. I was aware of his name of course long before my arrival in Cork in 1981. He had already achieved legendary status all over Ireland, even among the musical community in Belfast where I grew up. One of the first to welcome me to Cork, he immediately asked me to give a recital for the Orchestral Society soon afterwards. Having never even been close to the city before the year I joined the staff of the School of Music, I had co-incidentally taken part along with

other musicians from north and south of the border in a tour for the then Cooperation North just a matter of months previously. On that occasion I played for the first time in the hall at the School of Music and remember meeting the Professor, who was most courteous, making a point of introducing himself.

The Professor was always interested in the latest musical project that occupied my time and as such was what I would consider to be a genuine enthusiast. While I had a warm and friendly relationship with him, it was also quite a formal one: I always called him 'Professor' and he always referred to me as 'Miss Hunt'. He was quite a pragmatist, as indeed one must be as I mentioned earlier, ever searching for opportunities to have his compositions performed. At one point I remember him appearing in the staff room of the School of Music, resplendent in motor-bike helmet and accompanying regalia to ask me to take part in a very special project. It was to perform *Le Balai de Plume (The Feather Mop)*, a work for solo piano, written in 1970, which he had in fact planned to have performed on an earlier occasion. It was intended to be a kind of skit on music theatre and in addition to playing the piano required dressing up and a certain amount of 'clowning around' from the performer. As the visual aspect to the piece was so important, he had succeeded in interesting RTE in having it televised. The good Professor considered that I had the necessary wherewithal to cope with those additional performance requirements. In fact he declared that no one else could possibly do it!! We shall never know the truth of it for he retrieved the score to make amendments and some time later told me that the performance had been postponed. I believe that the score of *Le Balai de Plume* is now also missing, so sadly we may never be able to see a performance of the work.

In the summer of 1990, the Professor asked me to play his *Piano Quintet* with the Vanbrugh String Quartet. The first performance was to be in Dublin followed by a performance in Cork at the Aula Maxima in UCC. We were to share the concert with Madrigal 75. The *Piano Quintet* was, I believe, written during the 1930s and had not been performed in its entirety since Professor Fleischmann's mother had played the piano part in its first performance in 1939. I have vivid memories of exhaustive rehearsals for this work with the Vanbrugh Quartet. The ensemble was difficult and it took some time to get a good grasp of the work, but the Professor was quite clear and uncompromising about what he aimed to achieve. At the end of the day I think we gave two pretty good performances, particularly I recall in Cork, where I remember a lot of interest in the *Piano Quintet* at the time.

My other memory of working with the Professor, was for a performance of Saint Saens *Concerto no. 2* with the Cork Symphony Orchestra, which he conducted and which was performed in a varied programme at the City Hall on 21 April 1988. This was a work I had wanted to perform for some time and the Professor embraced the idea wholeheartedly. He never seemed deterred from tackling a work by technical or any other problems. At times he rehearsed with many of the orchestral members missing, but made the best of it. That's why I say with conviction that he was always the enthusiast when it came to music, the performance was what mattered and he always managed to get the best out of everyone on the night.

JOHN GIBSON (CORK), Composer, Pianist, Lecturer at the Cork School of Music
I first got to know Professor Aloys Fleischmann as a legend rather than in person. I was a Music student at University College, Dublin from the late 1960s to the mid 1970s and we heard about the atmosphere in the university in Cork where Professor Fleischmann taught large numbers of happy students with a renowned zeal and enthusiasm. This was all rather very much in contrast with the situation in UCD. However, that is a story for another day. Suffice to say, the situation in Cork seemed to be ideal for encouraging young musicians and composers.

I came to live in Cork in 1982, having obtained a lectureship in Piano at the Cork School of Music (with Professor Fleischmann on the Assessment Panel). Before this time I had got to know the Professor at various concerts during the successive Twentieth Century Music Festival held in Dublin at Trinity College and other venues throughout the city during the late 1960s and 1970s. I always found him to be very energetic and unfailingly courteous and friendly. He had an immediate rapport with young people (I was young in those days!) and expressed a great interest in young composers. When I came to live in Cork I, of course, met him on numerous occasions, e.g., after concert receptions in the City Hall, when the National Symphony Orchestra visited (then the Radio Teilifís Éireann Symphony Orchestra) and regularly in the Green Room when he came to congratulate artists from home and abroad on the success of their concerts. I remember being due to give a recital for the Cork Orchestral Society (which he had founded in 1938) with the Cork singer Deirdre Crowley and having to call it off due to illness. On my return to health, he met me and was most sympathetic.

I remember also playing the Liszt transcription of the *Liebestod* (by Wagner) for a ballet workshop organised by the Irish National Ballet. It was choreographed by Jonathan Burnett, a wonderful energetic dancer. The Professor was most complimentary and explained that his mother, Frau Tilly Fleischmann, had often played the piece. She had of course been a pupil of one of Liszt's last pupils, Stavenhagen.

I have vivid memories of the Professor conducting ballets (in the

233

Opera House) and orchestral concerts in the City Hall. He was always vigorous and energetic and rumour had it that he supported both ventures often with his own money. Other memories include him riding a motor-cycle around Cork until late in life. Also full of joy at the launch of the successive Cork International Choral Festivals where he was renowned for garnering support from the corporate sector. I remember him analysing a choral piece as part of the Contemporary Choral Music Seminar at UCC. He was able to simplify the dense new music in the most cogent fashion. It must be mentioned that the Cork Symphony Orchestra, Cork International Choral Festival, Cork Orchestral Society created a vibrant musical life in Cork and Ireland at a time when virtually nothing happened without the Professor's involvement. And of course he founded all three.

I had the good fortune to play his *Suite for Piano* at a concert in the Aula Maxima of University College, Cork, which was very effective and written by him at a young age. I also turned pages for Hugh Tinney when he performed the *Piano Quintet* with the Vanbrugh String Quartet also at the Aula. I'm delighted to see a CD of this work by the same artists is now available. Both works have hints of Irish music with a very coherent treatment of ideas and like the man himself are full of energy and excitement.

I had the honour of playing (with John Godfrey) Mozart's *Double Piano Concerto* on the 60th anniversary of the first performance of the Cork Symphony Orchestra (conducted from 1934 to 1992) by the Professor. On that occasion the same concerto was played by Tilly Fleischmann and Geraldine Neeson.[7] There was in the audience in 1994 some of the original members of the orchestra. It is fair to say Professor Fleischmann contributed enormously to the cultural and social life of Cork in particular and, of course, Ireland.

Professor Fleischmann was a larger than life character. Being a Dubliner, I can't help comparing him to the Italian Michele Esposito who lived and worked in Dublin from 1882–1928. He, like Professor Aloys, organised concerts, conducted orchestras, examined, taught, composed, etc. How fortunate the musical lives of Cork and Dublin were to be enriched by these wonderful dynamos of music. I, in my turn, am the musical grandchild of Esposito (having been taught by his star pupil Rhona Marshall) and am lucky to have known, in person, Professor Fleischmann and to have been inspired by his example in Cork.

Ave atque vale.

Máire Larchet (Dublin), formerly Principal Viola Player in the Radio Éireann Symphony Orchestra

I first met Professor Aloys Fleischmann when he used to visit our home, to have discussions with my father, who was then Professor of Music at University College, Dublin. On days when he would be invited to lunch, my mother would be anxious that everything would be ready on time, because she knew that as the clock struck one o'clock, the doorbell would ring, and there he would be, bringing his Germanic sense of punctuality into the rather more relaxed and casual atmosphere of our home. Even after a lifetime in Ireland, he never lost his cultural traits of punctiliousness and formal good manners.

Some years later, as a member of the Radio Éireann Symphony on tour, I would be invited to visit his house in Cork. There I would receive the warm hospitality of his attractive, clever and witty wife, Dr Anne Fleischmann. His five children would be there, and the house would be alive with activity and hustle and bustle.

As an orchestral player, I often took part in performances of his compositions. I remember the *Four Masters Overture*, the Chinese ballet *The Golden Bell of Ko* and especially *Clare's Dragoons*. This latter was a large scale work, of great originality, scored for full orchestra, choir and war pipes. It had a very stirring and dramatic climax, when the piper, Joan Denise Moriarty, would appear from the back of the auditorium, clad in saffron kilt and buckled shoes, and would march up to the stage playing the pipes, whose penetrating sound could be heard above the combined choral and orchestral forces. For performers and audience alike, this was an electrifying experience, never to be forgotten.

Professor Fleischmann's contribution to the development of music in Ireland has been immense. He had vision, great knowledge, a wide culture and dynamic energy. He also had the gift of inspiring others with his enthusiasm, which must have enabled him to initiate and sustain so many musical activities in Cork over many, many years. His achievements richly deserve to be remembered with gratitude and admiration.

Gerard J. Larchet (Dublin), Engineer and Horn Player

Firstly, may I say that I knew Aloys Fleischmann for a very long time, over forty years. I first met him in my parents' home where he was a regular visitor: I can recall driving him to Heuston Station to catch the Cork train on numerous occasions. I think he saw my father as advisor, senior colleague and friend. I am familiar with most of his compositions although I never had the opportunity to play any of his orchestral horn parts during the nine year period in which I enjoyed the practice of two professions, engineering and horn playing.

Apart from Fleischmann's achievements as composer, etc., I will always remember him for his enthusiasm and for his great kindness. One example of the latter was an occasion during the first prolonged bank strike, I think it lasted six months, when I found myself with my two young sons caught in Cork city overnight with a smashed car windscreen, a wallet full of cheques but no cash. I phoned Aloys from the Silver Springs Hotel and explained my predicament. Within half an hour, he appeared on a bicycle with enough cash to see me through the night.

I was in the audience for the first performance in Dublin of *Clare's Dragoons*. The venue was the Capitol Theatre (originally and before my time the 'Scala') and I remember it very clearly. Joan Denise Moriarty and bagpipes marching up the centre aisle from back of the stalls. A most exciting piece. That and his *Four Masters Overture* I consider his finest orchestral works – they are original, well constructed and a pleasure to hear.

SHEILA LARCHET CUTHBERT (DUBLIN), *formerly Harpist in the Radio Éireann Symphony Orchestra*
The contribution made to music in Ireland by the late Professor Aloys Fleischmann is incalculable. As composer, teacher, conductor, scholar and campaigner, he spent his life in its service.

I came to know and admire his compositional skills during my years as a member of the RTE Symphony Orchestra, and before that, when I attended the first performance of his inspirational work *Clare's Dragoons* with its sensational entry of a very young Joan Denise Moriarty, playing the war pipes!

In spite of onerous commitments to the university and to Cork, Professor Fleischmann found or somehow 'made' time to travel quite frequently to Dublin to attend Council meetings of the Music Association of Ireland and to fearlessly plead the cause of music in the 'corridors of power' or wherever else he thought it necessary to do so.[8] His efforts in support of the Irish National Ballet and Cork Ballet Company, as music director and conductor, are legendary and a testimony to his determination and dedication to this beautiful art form.

In 1956 he edited a scholarly book *Music in Ireland*[9] which is a very valuable reference and research document. I have reason to be personally grateful for his prompt and generous response when I invited him to contribute a composition to *The Irish Harp Book*, of which I had been appointed editor. His charming 'Dance' movement from the ballet *An Cóitín Dearg* is now known to and played by many harpists both here and abroad.

236

It was my privilege to have been invited to perform what I believe was Professor Fleischmann's last composition – *Games,* a song cycle of verses by the Serbo–Croat poet Vasco Popa, set for mixed choir, percussion and harp. The work was composed for the Cork Choral Festival in 1990 and performed by the BBC Singers under their conductor, Simon Joly, the percussionists James Hynes and Noel Heraty, and myself. Though heavily involved in the preparation of his monumental *Sources of Irish Traditional Music,* he travelled to Dublin on two occasions to talk through the work with me in advance of the rehearsals with the choir. When discussing his harp parts with me, he would always say: 'I'm afraid this is very difficult!' – and invariably, it was true!

It was a pleasure to have known Professor Fleischmann.

PHILIP MARTIN (CALNE, WILTSHIRE), Composer, Pianist, Member of Aosdána, Fellow of the Royal Academy of Music, London
My appreciation of Aloys Fleischmann knows no bounds. I first met him about 1980 when I gave my first piano recital in Cork at the School of Music. His energy and enthusiasm for everything was the first thing to strike me. He took me that afternoon to lunch at the university, where we inspected the Harry Clarkes at the University Chapel. He then took me to a most memorable Patrick Collins exhibition at the Crawford Gallery. We followed this by 'ringing the bells of Shandon', and I collapsed in a heap back at the School of Music whereas Aloys was still as fresh as a daisy and ready for more. I needed a rest as I was performing that night!

I witnessed this same enthusiasm and boundless energy every time we met subsequently and he had always something to comment on after my concerts – he became a regular 'fan' of mine. He later invited me to write a piece for the Cork International Choral Festival and flabbergasted me by analysing my work in front of a large audience at the university. I learnt things about my piece that I never knew!

I loved him dearly and always loved to see him coming. My first piano Trio is dedicated to him with love and admiration for his wonderful musicianship and endearing personality.

BRIAN BOYDELL (DUBLIN), Composer, Emeritus Professor of Music at Trinity College, Dublin
I first came to know Aloys Fleischmann in the mid 1940s as a fellow composer and as an inspiration to me in my efforts to further the cause of music in Ireland: for he had already done so much before me, particularly in the field of education. We also shared the responsibilities of organising and conducting the amateur orchestras in our respective cities.

Early in 1948 I was involved along with Freddie May and Edgar Deale in founding the Music Association of Ireland. Aloys was an obvious choice as a member of our Council: indeed his enthusiasm and selfless devotion to our common cause was not only an inspiration to all of us, but his unbounded energy in lobbying government departments and official bodies was of tremendous value.

During these early years of mutual support our friendship grew and expanded to include our families. When Aloys came to Dublin he often stayed with us, as I did at his home in Glen House when I visited Cork. I soon realised that he was so wrapped up in his musical mission that he had little awareness of the mundane practicalities of life. This was delightfully illustrated when our two young children placed a realistic rubber fried egg on his breakfast plate. He continued vainly cutting away at this object throughout most of the meal while he discussed his plans for the day. It only dawned on him after much futile effort that it was a practical joke. His other-worldliness was sometimes alarming. I remember following him in my car as he careered through the busy Cork traffic on his motor-scooter, with sheets of what were no doubt important documents fluttering into the gutter from the briefcase behind him. How he survived on his scooter was a miracle, for the rules of the road meant nothing to him.

Although he may have been unaware of familiar practicalities, he frequently displayed his remarkable ability at solving practical problems in the organisation of musical affairs. How else could he have run the orchestra, founded the Choral Festival and organised the university Music department – in addition to so many other achievements? I think that he was happiest in the midst of crisis: setting out in search of a lost Russian choir during the Choral Festival appeared to be his most stimulating form of entertainment.

His outstanding ability to analyse new music in a constructively critical way was demonstrated each year at the seminars he instituted on contemporary choral pieces commissioned for the International Choral Festival. His insight into new music, even that which was quite alien to his own style of composition, was particularly impressive. I soon came to regard him as the only critic of my own music whose freely offered judgement was always of positive help.

Besides his very many achievements and the warmth of his friendship one must record his great sense of loyalty. As an example, I remember his old friend the pianist, Charles Lynch, running out of money in Kenmare and being unable to pay the hotel bill. Aloys organised a collection on his behalf and having collected a suitable sum drove all the way to him with it to help him out. Charles, whose mind inhabited a world even more distant from mundane life than Aloys', paid his bill and then promptly ordered a taxi to drive him to Dublin.

I owed so much to my friendship with Aloys Fleischmann that it was most satisfying for me that in 1964 the Senate of Dublin University welcomed with enthusiasm my proposal that his outstanding contribution to music in Ireland, both as a composer and administrator, should be recognised by the award of an honorary Doctor in Music.

JOHN BUCKLEY (DUBLIN), *Composer, Graduate of the Royal Irish Academy of Music, Member of Aosdána*
Aloys Fleischmann – A Personal Recollection

Amongst my most treasured possessions are the twenty-eight letters I received from Aloys Fleischmann over a thirteen year period between 1979 and his death in 1992. The letters cover a rich and diverse range of themes of both a personal and public nature. The Cork International Choral Festival, the Irish Ballet Company, choreography, Aosdána, University College Cork, The Association of Irish Composers all loom large amongst the correspondence. Many letters offer invaluable advice and critical appraisal of my own compositions. In their broad scope of reference, their wealth of detail and their constant generosity of spirit, they serve as a reminder of one of the greatest figures in the development of music in modern Ireland.

The nineteenth century saw virtually all musicians of ability and ambition having to emigrate in order to sustain a professional career. In the early part of the twentieth century however, a number of Irish musicians decided to remain at home and attempt to establish and develop a native musical culture. Aloys Fleischmann played a seminal role in this movement and his contribution to the development of the current thriving situation is of the utmost significance. As early as the 1930s he identified the total lack of any tradition of musical composition, the lamentable and haphazard state of music education, the general indifference to music and a lack of awareness of its importance as the kernels of the problem. He then set about transforming the situation 'with determined action', to use his own characteristic phrase.

His commitment to the development of music in Ireland was wholehearted, sustained and incapable of being deflected. He applied vigorous pressure on all organs of state to improve the conditions for music and to enhance the professional status of musicians. Indifference and downright hostility to his aspirations merely strengthened his resolve. He didn't merely wait for others, however, to do the work but became actively involved in the establishment and development of new musical and cultural institutions. His legacy in this area is nothing short of the miraculous: the Cork International Choral Festival, the Cork Symphony Orchestra, the Irish Ballet Company, and his role on Toscaireacht of Aosdána, to mention just a few.

His numerous publications, especially his editorship of *Music in Ireland* (1952), and his monumental pioneering work *Sources of Irish Traditional Music*, the thematic index to the published collections of Irish folk-music, all raised public awareness of the importance of music as part of the cultural fabric of the country. His legendary status as professor of Music at University College, Cork and very significantly his fine body of original compositions all attest to a man wholly engaged in the practical implications of his intellectual and philosophical aspirations.

His work as professor of Music at UCC has left a lasting impact on the Irish musical landscape. Generations of his students have become music teachers, academics, performers and arts administrators to the great enrichment of Irish musical life. His courtesy and generosity to his students is well known and his memory is held in admiration and affection by them. While I never had the privilege of attending his lectures, I got an insight into his work as professor when I applied to UCC to do an MA in composition as an external student. With unfailing generous support and enormous patience, he led me through the labyrinthine process.

He was a marvellously incisive music analyst and critic, his seminars on the newly commissioned works each year at the Cork International Choral Festival being a particular revelation. He would frequently demonstrate points of harmonic or structural significance, much to the surprise and delight of the composer, who might often be unaware of such detail. In these seminars he displayed a great ability to get to the core of the music and highlight its essential character.

I feel very privileged to have had the benefit of his advice and insights on my own compositions even though I was never formally his student. His advice, encouragement and criticisms would be offered after concerts, after hearing broadcasts or after listening to tapes if he couldn't attend the concert. His criticisms were always to the point and offered in the spirit of constructive debate.

As a composer, Aloys Fleischmann left a distinguished body of work across a wide range of genres. His style drew on the broad European mainstream tradition coloured with elements of Irish music. He combined dramatic flair and energetic drive with a sense of lyrical reflectiveness. Amongst my personal favourites are *Cornucopia* for horn and piano or orchestra, an aptly titled work of rich and colourful musical ideas, *The Táin* , an epic response to the Celtic saga and *Games,* written for the 1990 Cork International Choral Festival.

Of the many personal recollections I have of Aloys Fleischmann, one stands out. In a pub after a lunchtime concert, my six year old daughter (who probably shouldn't have been there in the first place) proclaimed herself to be hungry. Before I had time to respond, Aloys had given her half his sandwich. It was a gesture wholly characteristic of this most generous spirited of men.

CHRISTOPHER STEMBRIDGE (CAMBRIDGE AND PFITSCH, ITALY), Organist and Cembalo Player, former Lecturer in the UCC Music Department
I first met Aloys in August 1969, over thirty years ago. The previous summer I had given a recital in Dublin and travelled to Belfast for an interview for a position as organist (in a Catholic Church – as a non-Catholic in Belfast in 1968!) At the time I held a full-time organist post in Munich. Gerard Gillen advised me against Belfast and told me there would be an interesting job coming up in Cork. In July 1969 Gerard wrote to Aloys about me. Aloys' idea was that a part-time lectureship at UCC be supplemented by teaching organ at the Cork School of Music and serving as organist at the North Cathedral where his father had officiated for so many years. However, Cork sounded even less promising than Belfast in Aloys' reply to Gerard Gillen:

'It is indeed kind of you to have thought of suggesting a suitable applicant ... but alas, we are the most conservative, if not retrogressive diocese in the whole country, and if I know His Lordship the Bishop of Cork, there would be no question of his appointing an Anglican ...'

I was planning a cycling holiday in Ireland and a few days after receiving the above, sent on to me by Gerard, I arrived in Dublin. There late one night I met Aloys – he had just been to a reception at the British Embassy during the Horse Show. A few days later on my cycle trip I made it to Cork where he showed me the department and the North Cathedral organ. Back in Munich my composition teacher, Harald Genzmer, who had been the official Choral Festival composer some years previously, encouraged me. 'Fleischmann is the most amazing analyst,' he said. 'He sees all kinds of things in a work that a composer would never imagine were worth analysing.'

But it was June 1971 by the time interviews took place and I was a little alarmed on arrival in Cork to discover that there was no question of discussing the supplementary work at the Cathedral or the School of Music. A couple of weeks later a letter from Aloys reached me in London: 'Alas, I have most regrettable news,' it began. Apparently he had nearly lost a finger by trying to sort out his lawn-mower. But, typically for him, the 'regrettable news' did not refer to his finger, but rather to the fact that his inability to attend an Academic Council meeting had led to discussion of my possible appointment being postponed until the next session. A further letter in September, however, informed me that as Seán Ó Riada was too ill to teach, arrangements would be made for me to be appointed to teach full-time temporarily in the department. I expressed some misgivings since, being a practising musician, I felt I did not want to be tied up full-time in university work.

In fact Seán had died by the time I arrived in November. Anne collected me off the boat early one morning and whisked me to an Irish breakfast before a roaring fire at Glen House. I had no option but to attend Aloys' performance at the Opera House that very night and began lecturing the next day! The students seemed to be under the impression I was German. A month later I gave my first organ recital in Cork. Aloys was most complimentary and I remember the first alarming experience of travelling pillion on his motor-bike, overtaking a double-decker bus on a bend going up to St Luke's. He presented me with a copy of the *Táin* which I still treasure. At Christmas I was invited to the Fleischmann's; in those first years if I stayed in Cork for Christmas I was invariably invited to the Fleischmanns. Once a friend from the Munich avant-garde music scene came to give an informal lecture during the holidays. It was not Aloys' thing at all and he was very puzzled by it; nevertheless we were all invited round to his house for a party afterwards. There was always warm hospitality.

He repeatedly asked me during the first weeks to make any suggestions about changes that might be made to the course. But when I did suggest anything he often came up with a cast-iron reason for leaving things the way they were. He gave me the impression that I was free to do things my own way, but when he once caught sight of exercises I had written out, based on Schönberg's pretty traditional *Harmonielehre*, his disapproval was immediate: 'But that's not Victorian harmony!'

I could see there were new things to do and the first thing was to see about getting an organ for UCC. I pointed out to Aloys that my lectureship had been advertised as a 'lectureship in music including church music'. 'An organ!?' he said, 'We don't even have money to buy books and records for the department.' This, to put it mildly, was something of an exaggeration and in fact the college was willing to consider the purchase of an organ which was installed in St Mary's, Shanakiel in 1973. I think Aloys somewhat resented the fact that it was not his idea – although at an early stage he had driven me to Macroom where we had both examined a positive organ that somebody thought might be for sale. He never found the time to come and see the college organ during installation (his wife, Anne, did!) and also declined to speak at the ceremony after the opening recital. This was rather sad.

I soon discovered that the 'other work' outside the university envisaged by Aloys to supplement the part-time lectureship had been a figment of his imagination. He had never discussed it with anybody either at the Cathedral ('We have our own organist' they told me) or at the School of Music – which did not even possess an organ. ('I don't really know why you came to Cork' were the words with which the affable Bernard Curtis greeted me!). I had no choice but to accept the situation and function as part of the quasi family set-up that was Aloys' world. I suppose I felt a little resentment at this, but with the passing of years I have reason to be more than grateful for the way that things worked out. A part-time university lectureship is a dream for a musician who wants to be part musicologist and part practising musician. Ironically, Aloys could never understand that. He thought I was most unwise – not to mention ungrateful – when I turned down the offer of a permanent full-time lectureship. As it is, I shall be eternally grateful to him for creating the part-time one which I held for 20 years. We had rather different ideas but both enjoyed putting a lot of energy into working with the students. My approach was naturally a lot less formal than his and my long hair and refusal to wear a gown must have irritated him enormously. On the other hand I was able to teach what I wanted to teach in my own way for the most part. There was tension but tolerance. Criticism but respect. Once after a bitter argument I was talking to a former student. 'Ah well,' he said, 'at least you're not fighting each other with gamps like he did with Seán Ó Riada.' In spite of everything I think there was a generally humane and relaxed atmosphere in the department.

Denis Arnold, Professor of Music at Oxford and external examiner for the NUI in the early 1970s once said to me: 'I enjoy Cork! Not that the department is a happy family. In fact, like most families, it's fairly unhappy.' It really was like that. Aloys was a father figure that the students understandably adored most of the time. Lively and energetic – Brian Boydell referred to him as 'Flashman' – he would bound up the stairs four at a time to his office. If you had a request that appealed to him he would act impulsively without giving it a further thought. ('I'll get on to the president about that right away so', or: 'I'll get Mr So-and-so to do that so.') But it was not always easy to talk to him. I suppose there was a kind of shyness. A very gifted final-year student who was becoming rather apathetic – I think the general standard was too low to make any demands on her – came to talk to me; she had tried to talk to him about her problem and he had merely suggested that she should see a psychiatrist. This advice seemed to me to be quite out of place. (In fact well over half the members of her class were seeking psychiatric help at the time if I remember correctly – a reflection of the lack of student counselling facilities in the UCC of those days.)

While Aloys shied away from private discussion, he would happily air his views in print and challenge anyone to argue with him. Thus a bitter discussion with his UCC colleague in Irish History, John A. Murphy, was carried on in the correspondence columns of the *Irish Times* and not, as John A. suggested might be more appropriate, 'in his local or mine'. Or when I was invited to write an article for the *Irish Press*, Aloys never commented on it to me but penned his own article in reply. He would telephone – sometimes late at night – or write to me rather than try to discuss a thorny question face to face. On one occasion I was hauled over the coals for not wearing a tie at first-year practical exams. (I would have liked to help create a more relaxed atmosphere on these occasions; Aloys' formality did not seem to be very helpful to the students.) His attacks were not malicious. He obviously felt the need to maintain a formal front and not lose his professorial dignity. He wanted the department to be like that too. On the other hand there was at least one occasion each year – the department Christmas Party – at which he would love to let his hair down.

Each year – normally in the second term – some Sunday evening was set aside for a grand discussion of department affairs. All undergraduates and staff as well as a good number of graduates would attend. Each class would choose a subject for discussion. These occasions were of course good, though perhaps more often than not Aloys would be vigorously defending the status quo. One year led to some bitterness. For a long time the Music department had been out of step with other Arts subjects in not holding all its exams in June with the opportunity to repeat in September. Aloys maintained that Music was a special case and that some papers should be held in June while the students should prepare the rest over the summer and sit them in September. This was quite hard on many. Not only did they have to swat during the whole vacation (many needed to work then to earn something), they also had to repeat the whole year if things went wrong as there was no chance of an autumn repeat. The final-year class chose this matter as their topic for discussion at the annual meeting. Eventually Aloys agreed that it would be discussed in the coming weeks. However, he refused point-blank to budge. After a while I suggested that the students write to the Arts Faculty. They did this and their request was granted and in future all the exams were held in the summer with repeats in the autumn. Aloys was furious with me for aiding and abetting and did not speak to me for months. He also gave no annual party for the students that year. (He normally invited all the fresh graduates to his house.) This was rather unfair since the outgoing class had raised the topic for the future good of the department; they themselves were too late to benefit from the change.

He was therefore a loner and a fighter. He fought for what he personally believed was right – for what he considered the well-being of the department vis-à-vis the College, for music education against society's apathy, for Cork against Dublin centralisation. His untiring effort to make things work was amazing. I remember being shocked on going to the Maltings before an orchestral rehearsal to find him putting out all the chairs single-handed. He had obviously never believed – perhaps never wanted to believe – that others would help. He perceived his mission for music as an uphill struggle; he would battle alone. He had difficulty in appreciating the efforts of those who did not see things his way. It seemed so natural for him to expect loyalty not only to the department but also to his other activities. In my first year I happened to be in Dublin on the final day of the Choral Festival. I spent what was then a small fortune and took a plane back in order to be present at the closing ceremony. Absence would have been unthinkable!

His early compositions had shown promise but of course he was hopelessly out of touch with the modern world. He did not however shy away from complex writing. (I can remember finding the organ – part of his Mass far from easy to play when we once performed it in the South Pres.) He once lent me a tape of an impressive symphonic movement that had been recorded by South West German radio. The performance of his ballet *The Golden Bell of Ko* was also memorable. His strong point was orchestration. That was something he tried hard to impart to the students, giving them the chance to conduct their own efforts. Musically many of the results might have been questionable, but the exercise was often probably a successful stimulant of the imagination.

As far as the department was concerned he had made up his mind at an early stage that he wanted above all to produce schoolteachers and he never considered changing the courses that he taught. He did not regard reading as a priority and indeed rather devoted any time outside teaching to his many other musical activities. (I seem to remember a student who had once missed some lectures being able to swat them up by using notes that her mother had made when the same course had been taught in her day!) On the other hand he was punctilious in spending time and trouble correcting student exercises. Most will remember the wodge of exercise-books perched precariously on the back of his motor-bike; I think they fell off on more than one occasion.

When my initial period of temporary full-time work had ceased and I was simply part-time I asked Aloys whether I might consider spending part of the year in Oxford as a graduate Music student. His reply was positive. 'But,' he added, 'of course I'm afraid the president will never agree.' I saw the president the next day and was told that if it was all right with the Head of Department it was fine by him. At that point Aloys changed his view and tried to block my intended course. The Dean of Arts took up my request and when a committee decided that I could go ahead, Aloys was hurt and even threatened to resign. Fortunately a compromise was agreed, but from that moment on I was to be something of a persona non grata.

I moved to Oxford, continuing to lecture part-time in UCC, moving back to Cork in 1981 when David Wulstan – senior lecturer under Aloys – took over the chair. The department changed direction a little and produced one or two fine scholars. The 'foreign' leadership was balanced by a new and vital Irish presence on the staff in the form of Gerald Barry. My own work continued much as it had under Aloys. But after David Wulstan's brief stay and Carolyn Lee's interregnum (she had also served under Aloys) the department was to alter considerably. It was then that I began to see my early years in Cork in perspective: in spite of differences with Aloys, our sometimes strained coexistence had in fact been a very productive one.

I last met Aloys in January 1991 when we lunched together in the School of Art. I told him I had handed in my resignation – 'After all these years?' he seemed surprised. We chatted about lots of things – including the department. And after all those years we seemed to be standing on fairly common ground.

GEOFFREY SPRATT (CORK), Director of the Cork School of Music, Lecturer in the Music Department of University College Cork 1976–92, Founder-Conductor of the Irish Youth Choir and Fleischmann Choir of the Cork School of Music, Director of the Cork International Choral Festival 1988–93, Chairman of the Association of Irish Choirs and Cork Orchestral Society
When the [Cork] Examiner asked me to write the obituary for 'the Prof' which it was to publish on 23 July 1992 – two days after his death – I attempted to summarise what might be regarded as the key facts about his life and achievements before describing the seven-men-in-one I thought Aloys Fleischmann had been. The difficult task was trying concisely to detail the highlights of a myriad of distinguished appointments, awards, contributions and services, but there is no need to do that again now as others will have woven them, and so many more, into the rich tapestry which is this book. The relatively easy part was to relate how I had experienced him as a remarkable phenomenon of seven men in one.

The passage of nearly a decade has allowed for much reflection and I find that I miss him even more keenly now than I did at the time of his passing. Aloys lived through an era in Ireland when a handful of classically-trained musicians had to be like the craftsmen of medieval cathedrals. Wondrous and lasting monuments were created through the sweat and toil of those who, metaphorically, hewed raw blocks of stone and fashioned them with little more than their bare hands. But Aloys was not just a craftsman in this sense, he was also the cathedral architect – but one who not only had the vision to conceive, but also the ability to lead every sort of craftsman by example. As every aspect of classical music in Ireland continues to lurch from crisis to crisis – as it has done for more than a decade now – hardly a day passes when I don't pause to ponder on how he would have focused his bullish courage, unfailing energy, unparalleled and always practical experience, superior intellect, and profound wisdom to address the issues which arise from the AIDS of classical music: the combination of a lack of national music policy and standards, a lowest-common-denominator syndrome, and a climate which not only allows for, but actually encourages self-aggrandisement. It is not that the seeds were not germinating even in the 1980s; when the *full* story emerges about the demise of the Irish Ballet Company – and a combination of the Freedom of Information Act and a legally preordained period of time will ensure that it eventually does – the arts world will have to live with a legacy of Haugheyesque character by way of a prelude to more and worse ...

For the obituary in 1992 I wrote that:
'Aloys Fleischmann was at least seven men. He was an inspirational teacher who created a university Music department in which students learned how to learn, and the vital need to project their love of music with an enthusiasm that helps keeps its study alive. He was a distinguished and multi-faceted scholar whose contributions are to be found in a wide range of journals, books and encyclopaedias. The fact that only four days before he died he managed to finish the project on which he had been working for more than 30 years – the *Sources of Irish Traditional Music 1583–1885* – was little short of a miracle, and evidence of the single–mindedness of purpose that was a characteristic strength. He was a composer whose output bears the hallmarks of craftsmanship and individuality, and speaks directly to performers and audiences alike. He was a conductor who often directed the RTÉ orchestras in years gone by, and whose 56 uninterrupted years at the helm of the Cork Symphony Orchestra earned him a place in the *Guinness Book of Records!* He was a tireless administrator, not just of his university department, but of institutions like the Cork International Choral Festival and the Cork Orchestral Society – both of which he founded to fur-

ther his vision of music for a great university city. He was a tireless crusader who waged effective campaigns on behalf of a myriad of causes in the city and on a national level. He was a family man who, together with his wife Anne, raised five children – two sons and three daughters – who have all distinguished themselves in their respective fields. He was a friend to countless people – always willing to help them in any way he could and never too busy or full of self-importance to care. Above all else, though, he was a truly wonderful human being who enriched the lives of all those who came into contact with him and were not too arrogant themselves to recognise his greatness.'

On reflection, perhaps that actually describes nine men in one – even if the final two characteristics to a large extent made possible his success as the first seven.

The intervening years have not resulted in my feeling a need to revise my view or express it differently. Time has allowed me, however, to form the view that if Aloys had channelled more of his time and energy into composition then Ireland might have had a composer of truly international stature whose music would have been played and heard throughout the world in the 1940s, 1950s and 1960s. If the world had discovered that music in Ireland existed before it formed the mistaken, but understandable opinion later on that it is a low-grade mishmash of classical / traditional / popular elements, classical music in Ireland might not be suffering as badly as it is at the start of a new century. What is urgently needed is a comprehensive contextual appraisal of his compositions; such would go far beyond the scope of a volume like this, but – hopefully – people like Séamas de Barra and Patrick Zuk will produce it in due course. Nevertheless, if he had devoted himself to composition, so much of what was achieved for classical music in Ireland over a period of nearly half a century might not have been. In addition, countless people (and, remember, the contributors to this volume only represent a small fraction of the unquantifiable corpus), would not have benefited so immensely, in so many different ways as they did because Aloys was who he was, when he was, and – if nothing else – sacrificed so much of himself for the good of so many for so long. Some will say that this was a form of selfishness – thankfully the majority will know that this would be an unworthy misinterpretation of a truly great man.

TOMÁS Ó CANAINN (CORK), retired Lecturer in Engineering and in Irish Music at University College Cork; Uilleann Pipes Player
I first met Aloys in 1961, when I joined the staff of UCC. I had already heard of him, of course, when I was in Liverpool University, where we had research students from Cork, who regarded him as a local legend.

He was very encouraging when I sought permission to sit in on his harmony and counterpoint lectures and on Seán Neeson's Irish music classes. I think Aloys was tickled to find that a member of the engineering staff had such an interest in music. 'Philistine' was a favourite word of his when referring to the general scientific staff of the College, though he did grant honourable exceptions!

My wife Helen and I would often meet him at evening concerts, when either his own orchestra or the RTE Symphony Orchestra played. In fact, you could be sure of finding him at almost every concert of those days, either as organiser, conductor or listener. He would always greet you with: 'Aren't you very good to come!'

We had a big night of celebration in the Vienna Woods Hotel in 1963, when Seán Neeson retired and Seán Ó Riada took over as Irish Music lecturer, having been head-hunted, as it were, by Aloys. I remember the Prof telling me that Seán Ó Riada had been the most naturally talented Music graduate of the department. I have to say, though, that Seán was not at the top of Aloys' list of hard workers.

Work was of first importance, in his view. I remember him telling me that he worked really hard at school in St Finbarr's College, Farranferris. In his own words: 'I was a devil for work – a swatter – and not very popular for that reason'. His results were proof of that: three firsts in Ireland in the Leaving Certificate examination, as well as a second, which would have been a first as well, only that the fellow who got first had a 10% bonus for doing the examination through Irish!

Such personal details I only discovered by probing him for an article I was writing about him in *The Cork Review*, just before his death. It was typical of the man that he insisted on reading the proofs, in case he had said anything which might be hurtful to someone else – all this at a time when we both knew he was dying.

Aloys' predecessor as professor in UCC was Frederick St John Lacy, who had been appointed lecturer in Music in 1906, basically because he was a singing teacher, with whom the wife of President Sir Bertram Windle had studied. She recommended him to her husband. Things were simpler then!

According to Aloys, Lacy complained to the president in 1911 that no student had yet signed up for Music, because he was only a lecturer – not a full professor. The president promptly promoted him to a professorship and he eventually got his first student, who graduated in 1916. Aloys himself graduated with a BMus in 1931 and an MA in 1932. He spent a couple of years studying in Munich and came back to succeed Lacy as professor of Music in UCC in 1934.

I started doing the BMus part-time with Aloys in 1968. He was the most conscientious lecturer I ever had and would go to any lengths to get his musical message across. He was a firm believer in the old-fashioned virtues of rigid classical harmony and counterpoint, extolling the advantages of its inherent discipline. He was the complete musical all-rounder and we put our hands and minds to everything musical. He was a gospeller for music, of course, and saw his graduates as disciples who would change the face of Irish musical education,

I was talking recently to Mary O'Callaghan, another mature student in our class, who remembered, more than anything else, the Prof's kindness and helpfulness to her, when she came as a primary teacher to enrol for the BMus. Timetabling clashes with other departments were smoothed out with a few quiet phone-calls from him and in no time at all she saw the whole world of music opening out before her. She remembers Aloys talking to her about his worries for another student and his suggestions as to how that student could be helped. Most saw only the Prof's formal exterior: those who were having difficulties experienced his kindness.

His formal mode of addressing students was well known. While I was a student of his I was always a very formal Dr Ó Canainn and he insisted on having homework done well and submitted on time. I was very conscientious in my first year, but I have to admit to a certain laziness subsequently. I remember his pretended horror when Mary O'Callaghan suggested a new formal name for me – Dr Dolittle – after I had appeared yet another day without harmony homework to show him. I think he enjoyed the occasion.

It was only when I became his colleague, lecturing in Irish Music, after the death of Seán Ó Riada in 1971 that he began to address me as Tomás, my wife Helen always remained Bean Uí Chanainn to him.

I remember him being very pleased, a short time before he died, at an excellent performance the BBC singers had given of a new work of his *Games*. What seemed to surprise him most was the ease with which he had composed the piece. I remember him saying: 'You'd imagine that at the end of my days now, I'd find it harder and harder.' With typical modesty he attributed his musical success to the excellence of the poetry he was setting.

It is only in retrospect that one appreciates the cultural dynamo that was Aloys Fleischmann. He was continually encouraging, cajoling, pressurising others, so that it is a wonder he had any time left for his own work, which was considerable. I remember the time he was due to conduct a concert of the National Symphony Orchestra in Dublin, but on the previous evening he decided that his lawn needed a quick mowing. Unfortunately he got his right hand badly cut by the mower's blades, as he tried to clear it. We all assumed that was the end of his concert, but he didn't see it that way. He had the right hand in a sling next day and conducted the Dublin concert with his left hand. Very few things kept Aloys from doing his duty.

When I think of him now, I see him as I often saw him in the early 1960s – an upright figure on a motor-bike, weaving expertly through the evening traffic of a busy MacCurtain Street in Cork. He is in that traffic now, but somehow not of it. As he looks out over his thick glasses, I know he is thinking of music or ballet or that night's rehearsal with his orchestra or, more likely, the next move in his ongoing struggle with the Philistines. There is always something to be done or a battle to be won! The traffic behind him is still stalled as he accelerates up Summerhill North, his gauntleted hands on the handlebars guiding him to the Glen and home.

6: THE SCHOLAR

HER EXCELLENCY PRESIDENT MCALEESE at the Launch of Fleischmann's Sources of Irish Traditional Music *in University College Cork 8 January 1999[1]*
Launching a book is one of the most pleasurable tasks which occasionally falls to me as President. The book we are launching this evening has a very special role in Irish cultural life, and I would like to express my thanks and appreciation to the Irish World Music Centre for inviting me to launch *Sources of Irish Traditional Music*.

Traditional music has always been an intrinsic part of our culture. From the earliest times, the joys, sorrows and everyday life of the Irish people have been reflected through our very rich heritage of traditional music. It has passed from parent to child, generation to generation, in a line which stretches back many centuries.

We have long been renowned for the wealth of poetry and writing that this country has produced to international acclaim. Perhaps, however, in times when literacy was confined to the fortunate few it was in traditional music that ordinary people could best express themselves. It is a language that carries across nations, accessible regardless of literacy skills or education, a form of expression that has provided an ever more important link to the past, as the Irish language itself was eroded.

It is also a form which Irish people brought with them wherever they went, and which immeasurably enriched the musical development of the New World. In my visits to the United States and Canada in particular, I noticed that the rich cadences and rhythms of traditional Irish music very obviously form the bedrock of the musical tradition.

There was a time in this century when it looked as if the popularity of this priceless heritage was declining here in Ireland. I am delighted that this trend has been reversed. In recent years, we have seen Irish traditional music receive the acclaim it deserves, both at home and across the globe.

The richness of our traditional music owes much to its resilience and adaptability. It has not remained static, but draws constantly on new influences as each successive generation adds its own spin. Whatever the variations, however, traditional music continues to draw on the rich well of tunes from the past. Without a knowledge and appreciation of these roots, it could not survive and develop.

That is why this publication is of such importance. Not only will it ensure that our more ancient tunes and melodies are kept alive, it will provide a rich source of inspiration for our young musicians to draw on. It is a wonderful piece of work, the culmination of over forty years of research led by Professor Aloys Fleischmann. Professor Fleischmann, sadly no longer with us, showed an extraordinary level of devotion and energy in compiling the almost seven thousand tunes included in this work, accompanied by an analysis of structure and tonality and detailed notes. It is the largest publication of any kind on Irish traditional music, bringing together all traditional tunes recorded in Irish manuscript and printed collections, together with related material in Scottish, Welsh and English collections and in eighteenth century ballad operas.

All but a few of these sources are out of print, so this vast body of folk music – generally acknowledged to be one of the finest in the world – was in danger of being lost. Bringing these sources together for the first time provides invaluable reference material for both future research and performance. It enables us to map the evolution and change in traditional music in Ireland up to the middle of the nineteenth century and revives many airs that had fallen out of use in the living tradition.

Professor Fleischmann is vividly recalled in the affectionate tribute paid by Mícheál Ó Súilleabháin in his preface to the book. Who else would have embarked on a work of such monumental proportions? – a project which must truly have been a labour of love, working on it as he did after his retirement and right up until his death in 1992. His achievements are truly exceptional – as Professor of Music at this university from the age of twenty-four, for a period of no less than forty-six years, he inculcated a love of music in generations of students. His legacy to this city is no less remarkable. He not only founded the Cork Symphony Orchestra, but also served as its conductor for fifty-six years, an achievement which earned him a well deserved entry in the *Guinness Book of Records*. In his spare time, he co-founded the Cork Ballet Company and was founder of the Cork International Choral Festival.

However remarkable his achievements, Mícheál Ó Súilleabháin's preface underlines the fact that this was not a solo run. The project had its beginnings in the 1950s, as a student project of Annette de Foubert, a graduate of Fleischmann's department. In the 1960s, he formed a team to continue the work, consisting of Seán Ó Riada, Pilib Ó Laoghaire as well as Annette de Foubert. Marie Neville assisted with the project and Mary Bollard and Nóirín Ní Riain were part of the team in the 1970s. Their work was continued by Helen Walsh and Sarah Collins in the 1980s, with Nicholas Carolan acting as consultant to the project from 1988 onwards.

The person who gets least credit in the preface, and perhaps next

to Professor Fleischmann deserves the most, is undoubtedly Mícheál
Ó Súilleabháin. Perhaps he is too modest to sing his own praises, so it
falls to me to do so. Having spent over 20 years contributing to the
project, the unenviable task of completing the work and acting as sub-
editor, fell his way. It is a mark of his dedication that even after moving from UCC to Limerick, he continued the work to the more glorious than bitter end. We owe him a great debt of gratitude for his dedication and perseverance.

Were it not for a number of dedicated collectors of Irish folklore
and poetry in the nineteenth and early twentieth centuries, much of
our rich heritage in the written word would have been lost. A similar
feat has now been achieved with our musical tradition. We owe an
immense debt to all concerned. It is uplifting to know that this heritage
is safe in the hands of dedicated researchers such as these. This work
will complement the dedication which Irish musicians have always
shown in passing their music to the next generation, devoting their
free time and energies in passing on their skills and knowledge to
younger musicians.

All that is left for me to do, is to again express my appreciation to
all involved, and to formally launch *Sources of Irish Traditional Music*.

*Mícheál Ó Súilleabháin, UCC Music Graduate, Professor of Music, Irish World
Music Centre, University of Limerick*
The Preface to Fleischmann's Sources of Irish Traditional Music
In October 1969 I found myself as a first-year undergraduate in University College, Cork seeking out the new location of the university's
Music department. The Old Rectory had been purchased by the university and was situated just outside the college gates on the side of
Cork city's busy Western Road. When I walked into the building that
wet Monday afternoon there was a bustle of student excitement. The
composer Seán Ó Riada, at that time a major national figure in Ireland,
was in his office on the ground floor, and Professor Aloys Fleischmann
was getting geared up to address his largest first-year class to date.
Twenty-two students, eleven male and eleven female, had turned in to
experience the unique almost family atmosphere of Fleischmann's department. Fired with his enthusiasm, we quickly learned that we were
to join the procession of pioneering graduates whose primary aim in
life was to turn the country around culturally by injecting carefully
metered doses of classical music throughout the second-level school
system in the most efficient manner possible.

For the next four years I experienced this truly extraordinary man's
dedication not only to his students but to everything he turned his
hand to. The course at that time was solid stuff – history, composition,

analysis, orchestration, the kind of fare he had inherited from his own university postgraduate student days in Munich. But he had developed all of this towards his own Irish cultural vision. Every student had the opportunity of hearing his end-of-year orchestration played by the Cork Symphony Orchestra with the frequently terrified student doing everything possible to put Fleischmann's conducting classes into practice in front of the ever-patient orchestra. This was a hands-on curriculum with the express intention of training Fleischmann's cultural foot-soldiers to get out there and continue the good fight.

A brilliant student himself, Fleischmann was the recipient in 1963 of the first Doctorate of Music awarded by University College, Cork. In 1934 at the age of twenty-four he had become Professor of Music at the university, a position which he held with unique style for no less than forty-six years. His term of fifty-six years as conductor of the Cork Symphony Orchestra – which he founded – won him an entry in the *Guinness Book of Records*. He co-founded the Cork Ballet Company and worked regularly with it for forty-three years, and he founded the Cork International Choral Festival, working tirelessly as its director for thirty-three years. Born in Munich in 1910, but raised and educated in Cork from early childhood, he was made a Freeman of the City in 1978.

His compositions always seemed to take a back seat to his social and educational activities, but the steady flow of works showed a growing and deepening maturity of style. Some of his best and most energetic youthful works were written in the two decades before his death in 1992.

While all this was going on, he always found time to give his students the rigorous attention which he himself demanded of them. Regular exercises in composition and orchestration were collected from every student several times each week and returned carefully annotated two days later, I never remember even one instance of a late returning of those manuscript sheets.

There was an endearing anachronistic quality at times about the man himself – and an occasional engaging eccentricity. Taking the stairs in the Old Rectory two steps at a time at breakneck speed, and leaping onto his battered scooter, he would sweep off downtown to the next rehearsal or committee meeting, his coat flapping in the wind. Once, the student manuscript exercises wedged on the back fell off on Patrick's Bridge, and the Professor was seen to stop the traffic as he dipped and bobbed through several busy traffic lanes rescuing the precious sheets. When he returned them to us next day, his red pencil markings were mixed with car-oil and tyre-thread markings. Triumph in the face of adversity was an everyday motivation for the Professor.

In his dress, and often in his manner, he was almost a late nine-teenth-century presence in the second half of the twentieth century. His formality was shot through with a controlled humour which at times to his students made him a larger-than-life caricature of himself. But the depth of genuine affection which all his students had for him was always palpable.

There was even more going on in that Old Rectory. The *Sources of Irish Traditional Music* project was moving into gear from its begin-nings in the 1950s as a student project of Annette de Foubert, herself a graduate of Fleischmann's department. In the 1960s Fleischmann formed a team consisting of a newly appointed staff member, the com-poser Seán Ó Riada, the choral conductor and the collector of tradi-tional song, Pilib Ó Laoghaire, and Annette de Foubert, who with thorough consistency handled the generation of the countless index cards until the project was lifted onto computer format in the 1980s. Ó Riada's tragic death at the age of forty in 1971 seemed to spur Fleisch-mann on with even greater determination to finish the work. The wealth of Ó Laoghaire's on-the-ground knowledge, of the song tradi-tion in particular, was lost with his death in 1976. Annette de Foubert was awarded an MA *Honoris Causa* by University College Cork in 1996 for her major contribution to the project.

When I took up the position as Assistant Lecturer in 1975, the office allocated to me was that which had been occupied by the late Seán Ó Riada. It was also the space where the *Sources* materials were kept. I was surrounded by a treasure trove of eighteenth and nine-teenth century collections – the very prints from which Ó Riada had accessed material for his revolutionary band Ceoltóirí Chualann in the 1960s. Laid out on a table in the corner were several large hand-made bindings of the sheets onto which Fleischmann had glued his many thousands of index cards. Checking a detail, he would fly through these creating a wind in the room as the huge sheets flapped like wind-mills. The pungent smell of fluid ink corrector was everywhere.

In my relationship with Fleischmann I found him casting me in the role which Seán Ó Riada and Pilib Ó Laoghaire had earlier filled. I was to be his link into the tradition on the ground. It was not the Pro-fessor's style to mix easily in the frequently laid-back indolent atmo-sphere within which many traditional music sessions might take place. As a result his interest rested more strongly on the tradition's products rather than its process. I still relish the memory of the countless hours spent with him in the frequently changing under-furnished and often cold rooms in a variety of peripheral locations at the university after his retirement as the project struggled to survive. Only his dogged determination kept it going through the long hours he spent attending to the minutest of details in every tune.

My increasing interaction with Fleischmann's work placed me in a position where I experienced the dedication and enthusiasm of a stream of students and colleagues of the Professor as he imbued them with his endless enthusiasm for the work. I must however single out two names here – Helen Walsh and Sarah Collins. These assistants to Fleischmann's work spent more time with him than any others after his retirement from his university duties in 1980 allowed him to concentrate almost full time on the *Sources* project. Their interest, respect, and dedication, not only to the work but also to the Professor himself, helped him though many difficulties in the final stages. As many of the rest of the team moved in and out at various times, Sarah and Helen maintained a continuity which grounded the enterprise with admirable efficiency.

In 1988, at the request of Professor Fleischmann, Nicholas Carolan agreed to act as a consultant to the project. For the next four years the proofs of the entire compilation travelled in segments from Cork to Dublin and back again, usually by post but sometimes delivered by hand to the Irish Traditional Music Archive, where the staff remember with fondness the Professor's whirlwind visits and lists of urgent queries. Since Fleischmann's death, Nicholas' expert eye checked many details and he played a vital role in the increasing teamwork which marked the final stage.

In 1990 the Professor climbed Mount Brandon in County Kerry to celebrate his eightieth birthday. Two years later, in the summer of 1992, aware of his approaching death, he completed a final session in his office location at the university and, armed with a plastic bag full of old Irish music prints, he insisted on walking to the hospital and checking himself in. When I visited him some days later he was sitting like a young boy on the edge of the bed with the music books spread across the floor like cultural maps. 'Where will we launch it, Mícheál?' His eyes were alive with the music which had occupied the deepest parts of his soul throughout his life. He died on 21 July 1992, having done a full day's work up to three days beforehand, despite great pain and nausea.

As Assistant Editor I was faced in 1992 with the task of completing the final checks and turning the gigantic opus around towards the printing process. When I moved to the University of Limerick in January 1994, the co-operation of the Boole Library at UCC allowed the entire Fleischmann collection relevant to the *Sources* to move to a prime location within the new Glucksman Postgraduate Resource Centre on the Limerick campus. Many of my postgraduate students at the Irish World Music Centre rallied around to assist in proof reading and the checking of what often seemed like an endless army of details. But it was one of these, Paul McGettrick, who emerged as the driving force behind the final three years of the project. With typical selfless dedication and admirable energy, Paul mediated in particular between the new computer format of the *Sources* and the project itself. That the work has appeared when it has is due in no small measure to his talents. Peter Flynn at the Computer Centre, University College Cork, was a constant source of encouragement and inspiration for Paul at all times.

It is fitting that it was Fleischmann's work which linked the research interests of University College Cork, and the new University of Limerick in this way. Cork has an international reputation for the way in which it nurtured the seed of Irish music studies throughout the years, a seed which continues to produce new growth with every year in the flourishing Music department which Fleischmann built up through a lifetime's selfless dedication. Limerick's growing ethnomusicology and ethnochoreology programmes continue to fan the flame of performance and research in oral-tradition music and dance, even while Cork consolidates and celebrates its widely admired music curricula and artistic educational environment.

From the initial personal research of de Foubert in the 1950s, the springing into life of Fleischmann's project in the 1960s with Ó Riada and Ó Laoghaire, and the work of the many dedicated research assistants who rallied round the project throughout the 1970s and 1980s, a great oak tree has grown in this the final decade of the twentieth century. It stands as a monument to a great citizen of Ireland, of Europe, and of the world as Irish traditional music breaks its ethnic bounds into the flow of a new millennium.

In it all, Fleischmann like a good cartographer has mapped the course of that tradition over three centuries. In doing so he has charted something at the quick of the Irish psyche which will undoubtedly prove to be a treasure house of information for future research and performance.[2]

DERMOT MCLAUGHLIN (DUBLIN), Artform Director, Arts Council of Ireland
I have a range of recollections of the late Aloys Fleischmann, all of them associated with Irish traditional music. My earliest recollection would have been no more than an awareness that there was, somewhere in the background, an enormous 'thing' being created, which would map out the history and sources of traditional Irish music. At the same time, I was aware of the more visible outputs of the late Breandán Breathnach through his *Ceol Rince na hÉireann* series and his important book *Folk Music and Dances of Ireland*, and many other pub-

lications that were appearing during the 1970s, 1980s and throughout the 1990s.

When I began work with the Arts Council in 1986 as Traditional Music Officer I came into contact immediately with 'the Fleischmann Project' and was soon to make acquaintance with the man himself. Up to the early 1990s, there was a lot of activity aimed at securing small amounts of funding, at regular intervals, to try to keep this gigantic project alive and I think that the willingness of funding organisations to contribute funding to the project was matched, if not exceeded by, the Professor's ability and ingenuity in creating reasons and rationales to explain why it would be impossible to refuse to support the project.

I had the pleasure of visiting his work station in Cork, as part of my work with the Arts Council and I will always remember the courtesy with which he dealt with everyone he came into contact with here in the Arts Council. I have a particularly vivid memory of a car journey around Cork followed by an extremely entertaining lunch and then a whirlwind tour through card index material, photocopies and other materials that were later to be transformed into the thematic index project.

Another more public encounter I had with him was as part of Éigse na Laoi, where I was involved in a presentation of traditional fiddle music from Donegal and from the Shetland Islands. One of the Shetland fiddle players, Davy Tulloch, was, and still is one of the more colourful and virtuoso figures in fiddle playing and he gave a suitably lively performance in Cork. At one of the events – the Ó Riada Memorial lecture that I was asked to deliver – Aloys Fleischmann asked some questions and made some very insightful points about the culture and practice of fiddle music. This certainly made an impression on Davy Tulloch, who always referred to the Professor after that as Professor Paganini, so astute were Fleischmann's observations on the subtleties of traditional music and its expression of the fiddle.

It is very difficult to give a vivid impression in so short a time of so energetic and farsighted an individual as the Professor. I will always remember him for his direct and forthright views, his admirable dedication to traditional music, and the quirky relationship that he seemed to have with that very same chaotic topic. Speaking both as a musician and as an administrator, all I can say is that he was a pleasure to deal with.

EIMEAR O'BROIN (DUBLIN), Conductor of the National Symphony Orchestra
My earliest recollections of Professor Fleischmann are of occasional appearances in Dublin, conducting some of his own works at Radio Éireann public concerts as well as of some broadcast talks on music

from the Cork studio. My parents (Dr Leon and Cáit Ó Broin) were in Cork and attended the first concert of the then Radio Éireann Symphony Orchestra outside Dublin on 18 September 1949 – conducted by Hans Schmidt-Isserstet, with Charles Lynch as soloist in Rachmaninov's *Paganini Variations*. The concert also included Beethoven's *Eroica Symphony* and the *Master Singers Overture* by Wagner. This concert was a landmark in the history of music in Ireland, not only for the remarkable quality of the performances all round but also for the arrangements at the Cork end, which were handled so professionally by Aloys Fleischmann and his team. I well remember the guests commenting on this and how Dr Isserstet was so appreciative of the capacity and attentive audience in the City Hall, including the 'Herr Bürgermeister', who had graced the occasion with his presence.

In 1952 I contributed an article on Count Plunkett's Collection in the National Library to a symposium entitled *Music In Ireland*, edited by Aloys Fleischmann and published by Cork University Press. I had researched this material from 1946-48, some of which formed the basis of a series of programmes entitled *Music by 18th Century Irish Composers*, broadcast by Radio Éireann in 1948. These included music by the Cork-born composer, Philip Cogan (1748–1833), who later became the teacher of John Field. It was my first experience of working with Professor Fleischmann and I found his interest, encouragement and enthusiasm most helpful as it was my first venture into print.

After I joined the conducting staff in Radio Éireann in 1953, my duties included conducting and introducing the Children's Concerts in Dublin and in the provinces. Those in Cork, at the City Hall, were always assured of capacity audiences at the two sessions at 10 and 11.45 hrs – up to 4,000 students in all. Once again, Professor Fleischmann was on hand to greet us and introduce the members of the Schools Concerts Committee, headed by the late Mrs Sheila Goldberg, who solved the many logistical problems in amassing so many pupils from colleges and schools in and around Cork.

Throughout the 1960s, 1970s and 1980s, he sometimes addressed the audience at the evening concerts, lamenting the creeping materialism that was a feature of the earlier 'boom' in a developing Irish economy and its rejection of the need to make space for the development of the finer things of the spirit. He particularly stressed the failure of the educational system to ensure the ongoing development and cultural formation in the life of the individual in modern Ireland – something no Minister for Education has tackled so far.

Whenever I conducted performances of his music, a letter of thanks and appreciation would arrive on my desk in a day or two – the last in 1988, after the National Symphony Orchestra played the

Overture to *Times Offspring* written to celebrate the tercentenary of Bishop Berkeley and first heard in Cloyne Cathedral in 1985. I enjoyed the splendid vigour of this music – so well crafted and reminiscent of Walton at his best. Once we discussed the possibility of making Cork a music and arts centre, modelled on Munich in Bavaria, albeit on a modest scale. We tried to identify the infrastructures that might be put in place and the possibilities of raising financial backing for the project from the state and regional interests. It is something that could be attempted in these more affluent times and one that would be a fitting memorial to this distinguished Irishman who was *the* intellectual force in Irish music in this century.

Marie Nevill (Cork), UCC Music Graduate, Research Assistant to Fleischmann
Even now it seems difficult to credit that 'the Professor' is not around, that one will not see his upright figure flying past on his way to the Maltings or to the university, stopping briefly (if he saw you) to ask why you were not at the previous night's concert or, if you were, to ask if you enjoyed it and to remind you that there was one the following week.

Not long after we came to Cork in 1951 at his request we attended one of the first concerts of the Choral Festival. We went with our seven year old daughter. There with about thirty other people, we listened to some local choirs. When I think that this was the birth of one of the most prestigious Choral Festivals in Europe I am lost in admiration for the perseverance and hard work of the man.

Some time afterwards I said to him at a College function: 'I play a little (who doesn't?), but I'd love to learn something about the structure of music.'

'Come to our lectures', the Professor replied. This amused me, but as any time he met either my husband or myself he asked when I was going to sign on, at last I did and began one of the most interesting and rewarding periods of my life.

He was a born teacher, very strict, assiduous in making us do our harmony and counterpoint exercises and learn our history of music, etc. We just could not have come into class without having prepared our work. Neither would any of us, during the five minute break, dare to slip out for a cup of coffee at the 'Rest'.

Though he was very strict, he never made anyone feel 'small'. He was an extremely sensitive man. As he went around the class making us call out the correct notes for the harmony of the tune he had on the blackboard, if one of us made a stupid mistake, he would 'cover up' and say kindly 'I'm sure you don't mean that, Mr/Miss ....' He opened a new world for us.

When, much to my surprise and delight, I got my BMus he persuaded me to write a book (with which he helped me) to cover the new course set by the Department of Education for Musicianship in the Intermediate Certificate. While doing this I saw a different side of him: his kindness, his accuracy and his wide knowledge of English. He had come first in English in Ireland and indeed in all his subjects in the Leaving Certificate at school, and had also got First Class Honours in English in his degree. He also helped me publish some works by George Manly Hopkins on the relationship between rhythm, music and poetry. He would transform my mundane writing into fluent prose.

After he retired, I had the privilege of helping him with the cross-referencing of his *magnum opus, Sources of Irish Traditional Music,* the two volumes of over 6,000 folk songs, showing their origins and variations, and which he gallantly worked at, in spite of great pain, until he died.

He was a deeply spiritual man. Once I asked him naively 'How do you compose? Does something outside yourself tell you what to write?'

He replied: 'In one of my works, the *Piano Quintet'*, I did feel I looked outside myself into another dimension.'

I think this is considered to be one of his finest works. When future generations assess the music written in the twentieth century his name will, I think, be foremost.

I remember how he climbed Mount Brandon on his eightieth birthday. He was dressed in a dark suit, a tie and wellingtons. He went quickly to the top, ate the Easter egg his beloved grandson had hidden for him, came down, went into his office, changed from his wellingtons into suitable shoes, took off his waterproof and was at a meeting promptly as always at 8.00 o'clock.

I'll close with words by Robert Browning which I think describe him:

> One who always held his head
> And marched breast forward
> Never doubted clouds would break
> Never held, though right was worsted,
> Wrong would triumph.
> Held we fall to rise, are baffled
> To fight better
> Sleep to wake.

TRINITY COLLEGE DUBLIN LAUDATIO delivered when Fleischmann was awarded an Honorary Music Doctorate in 1965
Our next graduate is a musician dedicated to his vocation, well-known, highly respected, much loved, Aloys Georg Fleischmann, Professor of Music in the University College of Cork, whom our southern academic sister honoured with the Doctorate of the National University a year ago. His compositions are eagerly heard and greatly admired not alone in Ireland but far beyond our shores throughout Europe and indeed in Canada. We recall with special appreciation and pleasure *The Three Sea Captains*, and *The Magic Fountain*, whose streams and strains seem to derive from the Muses' spring, Castalia itself. As conductor of the Cork Orchestral Society he is largely responsible for the high level of performance and lively interest in music which are turning Cork into the Pieria of southern Ireland. Indeed our whole country is enormously in his debt for the devotion and energy with which he has worked for the furtherance of the arts in general and of music in particular. He has never forgotten that, as the Greeks said, the uneducated are far removed from the Muses and the Graces, and that music is closely connected with an apprehension of the Divine. His right to speak with authority on musical matters has been recognised by his being invited to contribute to the standard works of reference in this field; it is entirely fitting that he should be the author of a symposium on music in Ireland which breaks new ground. We salute with gratitude and affection a champion of the arts, a gracious and gifted musician, a gentle and generous man.

SEÁN MAC LIAM, UCC Music Graduate, Lecturer in the Music Department, St Patrick's College Dublin
Aloys Fleischmann: An Appraisal of his Attitudes and Contribution to Music Education in Ireland
The earliest published writings of Aloys Fleischmann verify that he possessed, in every respect, a mind of his own time. On reading these works, I am amazed at the extent of his concern for the development of the Irish music education system and curious about how he came about this interest in the first place. After all, one could hardly describe his own musical experience in childhood as typically Irish. Born in 1910 of German parents, his mother, Tilly, had an international career as a pianist with a musical pedigree tracing its roots back to Liszt and Beethoven.[3] His mother's family had settled in Cork in the late 1870s; in 1906 his father, Aloys senior, succeeded his own father-in-law as organist and choir master in St Mary's Cathedral. Aloys senior was also a composer having studied under Joseph Rheinberger in Munich. The musical education young Aloys received at first hand from his

parents was considerably beyond the means of most parents of his generation. In University College Cork (UCC), he took his Bachelor of Music (BMus) degree in 1931 and his Master of Arts (MA) in 1932, after which he continued his musical studies abroad, studying composition and conducting at the Staatliche Akademie für Tonkunst, Munich and musicology at Munich University.[4] To fully understand his deeply held views on music education, one must appreciate this formidable musical heritage that he inherited and set this in the context of Irish society during the 1930s and 1940s, when many of his educational views were formed and first expressed.

Throughout my time as his student, I never heard him speak about his own experience of formal schooling in Ireland, although he sometimes referred to his meeting with Richard Strauss in Munich and other details of his student days in UCC. However, in an article published in 1971, applauding the child-centred objectives of the newly reformed primary school curriculum, he quoted Pádraig Pearse's words describing the 'murder machine' schooling received by the young people of his generation:

> There are no ideas there, no love of beauty, no love of books, no love of knowledge, no heroic inspiration. And there is no room for such things on the earth or in the heavens, for the earth is cumbered and the heavens are darkened by the monstrous bulk of the programme.[5]

My own earliest memories of Professor Aloys Fleischmann are also from the 1970s. Having spent most of that decade under his tutelage, I came to appreciate his formidable character and the dedication with which he applied himself to his job within the university, his responsibility to his students and his untiring efforts for developing music in the city of Cork and in the country as a whole. His considerable influence in this respect was in part due to his exceptional ability to argue his case convincingly both in verbal and in written formats. However, it was his energy of purpose, his extraordinary tenacity and his absolute belief in his own sense of what could be achieved, given maximum effort, that spurred all his endeavours for music education. His writings are energised with the same clarity and conviction about the importance of music in education, although the earlier examples up to the mid-century are fresher and more convincing in their relevance to that period.

As Professor of Music in UCC, he considered the education system to be a vital means of achieving the hoped for revival of music in Ireland. One of his earliest published articles entitled 'The Outlook of Music in Ireland' is a remarkable document reflecting on the standing of music in the Ireland of the mid 1930s together with proposals for achieving greater recognition and a better future for the musical arts. This article addresses the following three main points:

- the dichotomy between the popular and widespread Irish folk music tradition and the paucity of a comparable art music tradition here
- the diverse qualifications and mixed ability among instrumental music teachers throughout the country and
- the need to establish a common reliable standard in instrumental examinations and in teachers' professional qualifications.

Curiously enough, this article contains no mention of classroom music at either primary or post-primary levels.[6] A subsequent article published the following year expands on these points and challenges the conventional notion of Ireland as a land of song. He argues that instrumental training in Ireland failed to develop at the same pace as training in the other arts. Comparing the considerable training period and standards required in other professions and trades, he describes the membership of the music teaching profession as

> ... an El Dorado for young ladies covetous of pin money ... [who] with two months' experience or two years ... can warp and misdirect the minds of unfortunate children, nor will anybody be the wiser, for the public is not sufficiently educated or cognisant of standards to judge.[7]

One cannot help comparing this situation, as he describes it, with his own experience of music education. His description is perhaps a bit unfair and does not take into account the many teaching nuns whose musical standards and achievements remain undocumented and unrecognised in our social histories, or the fine church organists who, like his own father, provided a choral education to youngsters who otherwise would not have any opportunity or hope for even the minimum musical education. However, his broad point is easily verifiable and we have all known instrumental teachers with doubtful qualifications and even more dubious ability. In diagnosing the problem of bad teaching, he recognises the vicious circle that existed between its cause and its effect:

> Here, the most immediate issue is the problem of how to create an efficient body of music teachers, for in their hands lies the training of musician and of amateur, it is they who set the standard for the individual and the public alike. Yet the incompetence, the utter lack of responsibility in music-teaching in Ireland is such as no other profession or trade here would tolerate. Primarily this arises from the low standard of music which prevails all-round, but it can equally well be regarded as the cause.[8]

As a young academic, Aloys Fleischmann applied himself to the task of identifying an appropriate remedy for this problem. During the 1933–34 academic year, he estimated that approximately 14, 684 candidates submitted for music examinations in this state. More than half of these undertook examinations run by Irish examination institutions (Royal Irish Academy of Music, Leinster School of Music, Cork Municipal School of Music, etc.). Approximately 7,000 undertook examinations run by the English examining authorities (Trinity College of Music, London College of Music, Associated Board of the Royal Schools of Music, etc.). In the same year, however, there were only 22 students altogether taking the various music examinations at university level.[9] Serious music in Ireland was at a low ebb during this period but, with the appointment of Aloys Fleischmann as UCC's first full-time Professor of Music, it gained one of its strongest advocates. He considered the reform of music education pivotal in the reshaping of the musical *status quo* into what he hoped would be a new Irish *Ars Nova* period. To this end he rededicated his efforts in an almost heroic manner and through writing, lecturing, meeting civil servants and politicians, forming and addressing pressure groups, etc., he sought to bring pressure to bear where before there was little or no representation or even interest.

Apart from lobbying for a better deal for music in education, Aloys Fleischmann was never one to rely fully on others for deliverance. He first sought a ban on all imported musical examinations, not only because of their dubious and varied standards but because they resulted in a loss of earnings to native examining bodies and prevented the proper growth of an indigenous music education system here. He then tried to influence the setting up of an Irish University Examination Board in Music to create a fixed standard for all music examinations and to vet and validate teacher qualifications.[10] When this failed, he set out to rectify the situation within his own university and its immediate environment where he had most influence.

Detecting a poor response to his 1935 article, he founded the Music Teachers' Association in Cork the same year. The Incorporated Society of Musicians, founded in 1893, had previously included the interests of music teachers in its brief, but this organisation had ceased functioning in Leinster some years previously, leaving the Music Teachers' Association as the only professional organisation for music teachers at this time.[11] Its stated aims were the registration of music teachers and the promotion of protective legislation for the profession.[12] Its members included secondary school and some primary school class teachers, private instrumental teachers and teachers from the Cork Municipal School of Music. Attempts were made to forge links with the Dublin-based Music Association of Ireland, founded in 1939. However, the Dublin organisation only admitted teachers with professional qualifications and, since the Cork organisation was unwilling to abandon some of its very experienced, loyal but unqualified members, it remained largely confined to the southern region of the country. By 1950, the Music Teachers' Association had 109 members. Its president was Sir Arnold Bax and Aloys Fleischmann remained its chairman until his retirement, when he became president of the organisation. I recall his expression of disappointment on not being able to extend the membership of the Music Teachers' Association beyond the southern counties and, because of this, it failed to sustain its standing and influence in the long term, although it did provide considerable support for music teachers in Cork and surrounding counties at a time when there was little or no understanding of this need. During the early 1980s, however, most of the class teachers of music, feeling the need for their own representation at a national level, formed themselves into a branch of the Post-primary Music Teacher's Association, thus depleting the membership and influence of the original association. It was eventually wound up a number of years ago, after which the private instrumental teachers formed a new organisation to represent their own interests.

However, within the university where he had the authority and influence to realise his ambitions, Professor Fleischmann had more lasting success. Here he aimed to provide the appropriate educational standards for his new generation of properly qualified music teachers and to this purpose he designed, administered and taught a course of lectures, tutorials and practical skills that would, among other things, meet this need. Conscious of his obligation to fully educate his students as intelligent musicians, he included as a core value in the degree programme a sound academic training. To this, he grafted additional requirements that would distinguish his graduates from those of other universities. Apart from the study of acoustics (for some years taught by the Professor of Experimental Physics) in the second year of the degree programme, he also introduced a number of other courses with the specific intention of providing graduates with useful skills to enable them to understand and communicate their subject more practically. These additional skill-based studies were compulsory for all students but would have direct relevance to those students who would be preparing themselves for a teaching career. They provided opportunities to acquire a practical working-knowledge of the keyboard through improvisation, playing from figured bass, and from vocal and orchestral scores, training in choral and orchestral conducting, arranging Irish airs for various choral and orchestral combinations, as well as rehearsal technique. Involvement in the wider departmental interests viz. the Cork International Choral Festival, the Contemporary Music Seminar, the Cork Symphony Orchestra's concerts and rehearsals completed this very practical training. In addition, final year BMus students were required to specialise in one particular professional area that ensured students qualified as composers, musicologists, performers, conductors or teachers. Under his influence, a considerable number of students sought to specialise in teaching. Although he understood well the difficulties facing music teachers seeking full-time posts in secondary schools, with so few pupils capable of undertaking the prescribed programme, he nevertheless sought to ensure that trained teachers would be available in sufficient numbers to take up positions when the music syllabus became more open and accessible to the wider school-going population. In 1951, he writes that

> ... lack of adequate music teaching in secondary schools is bound up with economic and organisational problems. To become a full-time registered teacher of music in a secondary school, one must hold a University Degree in Music and a Higher Diploma in Education. There are four such teachers in the country ... but a new music course is to be included shortly in the Department's programme and with the goodwill of some enlightened principals throughout the country it is hoped that the number of full-time music teachers in secondary schools will begin to increase.[13]

Progressive reforms in the post-primary music syllabus during the second half of the century made his wish a reality. During this period, the number of second level music students steadily increased and by the 1980s, the position had considerably improved for young Music graduates seeking a career in education.

The comprehensive nature of the programme offered in UCC's Music department was not universally applauded. Its very breath presented the university with considerable timetabling problems, particularly for those students who were registered for degrees in other subjects as well as Music. Although students often found the time demands of the Music programme daunting, most understood the very distinctive opportunities it afforded and, in turn, UCC's music graduates were highly rated in the community and were especially valued in the schools because of their ability to engage school children in the various forms of practical music-making activities.

One has to marvel at Professor's commitment to teaching such a varied and comprehensive programme. Initially he had the assistance of one other staff member although, in later years, part-time staff greatly helped in the task. Indeed, nowadays, even generously resourced Music departments could not expect to teach such a full academic programme – harmony, strict and free counterpoint including double counterpoint at the octave, tenth and twelfth, canon and fugue, orchestration, the history of music from ancient to present times, form and analysis, Irish music, acoustics (in second year only), aesthetics and music criticism (in third year only) – in addition to the practical skills mentioned earlier. Of all the third year specialist options available, music education was the only one for which specific lectures were supplied. Fr Seán Terry, who introduced the Ward Method into Ireland in 1968, was contracted to train the students in this unique approach to classroom music; his course of lectures was available as an optional extra in all three years of the degree programme. This was complemented, in the final year, with an additional course of lectures on the theory and practice of teaching piano and voice.

Professor constantly criticised the exclusive use of the tonic sol-fa system of reading and writing music in schools because it was unwieldy when tackling more advanced music. He once told me that, as students progressed, those who had only experienced tonic sol-fa encountered great difficulty when expected to deal with staff notation. He considered training in tonic sol-fa to be bad practice, comparing it to language teaching where a teacher might introduce a second language through the medium of a third and inferior one, i.e., one not generally used for communication or the writing of literature. However, as a realist, he understood the dangers of confronting what was in widespread use in the schools, for fear of replacing bad practice with one that teachers are unable to implement. Writing of the 1971 new primary school curriculum in music, he says

> ... the exclusive use of sol-fa was abandoned a generation ago in the vast majority of English schools, and it is only now in the new curriculum that for the first time primary teachers in Ireland are instructed to combine sol-fa with staff notation from Class 1 on. That this will be done is again rather wishful thinking – how can it when 90% of the existing teachers do not know staff notation themselves! But at least the principle has been established ... [14]

His preference for the so called 'classical', structured approaches to teaching music literacy (i.e., Ward, Kodály, etc.) was based on the fact that they presented teachers with progressively sequenced materials and approaches that link both sol-fa and staff notation systems. This was his rationale for providing students with the opportunity to qualify as Ward practitioners. However, no single uniform approach to teaching notation could ever work in Ireland and, in the case of the Kodály and Orff methodologies, he must surely have realised that the differences in character between the Irish and mid-European personality and the strict disciplined attitudes required by pupils and teachers alike would create insurmountable obstacles to any successful implementation. However, in his writings, he continued to hold to the ideal.

Soon after his return from Munich in 1934, Aloys Fleischmann founded the Cork Orchestral Society with the primary purpose of providing orchestral concerts for the city. Like most of his musical projects, this too had an important educational dimension to its operation. Its Cork Symphony Orchestra also served as a practice ground for aspiring student performers and conductors and, occasionally, student compositions received their first performances under its auspices. It was his practice, as conductor of this orchestra for over 40 years, to encourage his students to attend rehearsals and he convinced his musicians to allow the students to sit among them so that they could learn at first hand about each instrument and how the orchestral parts should be written. Occasionally, often reluctant students were gently press-ganged into acting as deputy when there were absences among the percussion section. Each year, the orchestra undertook a special concert in the university's Aula Maxima during which each student, having previously been allocated rehearsal time, conducted their own prepared orchestration or original composition to an audience of their peers, staff and as many of their friends and family as could attend. These were always memorable and, for some students, daunting moments with Professor standing slightly behind and to the left of each student conductor, occasionally interjecting, politely correcting, praising and on occasion gently subduing rebellious musicians indignant at the sometimes eclectic *avant garde* nature of the music presented. One suspects that this was a task he thoroughly enjoyed – the master composer coming to the defence of his students' work. The orchestra also gave an annual concert for the city's school children with Professor acting in the dual role of conductor and presenter. One wonders about the lasting educational value of these musical encounters but I am sure that many Cork people remember as children their impact, even if the details of Professor's musical appraisals were somewhat over their heads. However, the evidence of his writings show that he himself understood their importance and their deeper significance in the lives of the children who attended his concerts. Writing about the success of the Radio Éireann Orchestra's school concerts on another occasion, he describes

> ... the children's wide-eyed wonder, their quick response and evident eagerness to learn the meaning of this strange, new language, shows how fruitful it would be to introduce them to instrumental music under more intimate conditions, and in rural areas where they would never have heard a violin properly played or even seen a cello.[15]

In explaining how music affects the individual and society he, unwittingly, reveals his own philosophy of music education, although he may not have recognised it as such at that time. If factual information supplies knowledge, it is the experience of live music that brings understanding and this, in turn, creates the need to repeat the encounter. He explains that

> ... music, being incorporeal, has a remote, elusive way of its own of getting at an inner world of meaning. Its very essence lies in the ever changing subtlety with which it can get inside the word, so to speak, and make the most hidden implications of an idea as clear as day.
>
> For all that, music is not difficult to access, though it must seem so to a community which conceives art-music as something strange and aloof. The appreciation of music, as of any other art, is not dependent on technical knowledge. No more is needed than to steep oneself in its medium, occupying one's mind with work after work, until the language appears co-ordinate, until the messages it conveys become pregnant with significance. But this presupposes manifold opportunities of hearing music, and the stimulation afforded by the presence of a vigorous musical activity. Without such activity a sympathetic public can never be expected, because it is the supply that brings the understanding and the demand.[16]

He also hoped that, by encouraging as many students as possible to enter the music teaching profession, he could create more understanding of music's value for the individual and society and that, through increased musical activity in schools, greater demand for music would eventually be engendered. With the benefit of hindsight, we can say that his hope has become a self-fulfilling prophecy.

After 1950, Aloys Fleischmann produced a number of publications that, among other things, attempted to assess the standing of music in Ireland.[17] To a certain extent, this may also have been his way of evaluating the impact on Irish musical life of his own efforts. *Music in Ireland; a Symposium*, with a forward by Arnold Bax, was one of his earliest and most comprehensive efforts at stock-taking. This book was for many years the standard work of reference on its subject and documented the condition of Irish musical life and the progress made during the first half of the century. Conversely, it also revealed the extent of musical neglect in the country during this period. The authors who contributed articles were among the foremost musical authorities in Ireland and leaders in their field. Having commissioned his authors, he persuaded the senate of the National University of Ireland to grant-aid its publication and this gave additional weight and importance to the work. In recent times, Professor Harry White writes that

> ... no other document has so comprehensively addressed the status quo of Irish musical life in any period ... Organised in three large sections ('Music

and the Institutions'; 'The Profession of Music'; 'Music and the Public') and prefaced with an historical survey, *Music in Ireland* surveyed the plural condition of music to one end: to establish that the general organisation of music in Ireland is much behind that of other countries. Fleischmann's strategy in this endeavour was novel ... he determined to list and describe every conceivable dimension of music making in Ireland. In this way, each subdivision of musical activity (education, professional organisation, professional training, performance, composition, broadcasting, Festivals, church music, the development of individual genres, the presence of music in major urban centres, musical societies, recital series, library sources and music libraries, registers of music teachers, dealers and instrument makers) was subjected to individual scrutiny, with the result that broad conclusions were substantiated by detailed evidence.[18]

In its conclusions, this influential publication drew attention to the two main obstacles to the development of music in Ireland during this period, viz., the poor state of the music education system and the failure of the authorities to financially support musical activity here.

Of course, as editor of *Music in Ireland*, Aloys Fleischmann was responding to the consensus view of things as perceived by the individual authors. There is some evidence to suggest that his own personal view of music education in Ireland by the 1950s may not have been as bleak. An article he wrote some months prior to the publication of *Music in Ireland*, sets out to challenge the absolutist and ungenerous position that music in Ireland was in a shocking state when, by his own reckoning, some measure of progress had been made. In reviewing the situation on the credit side, he first singles out progress made in the field of music education where

> ... class singing is now compulsory in primary schools, and four Organising Inspectors of Music supervise the work which is being done. The post of Inspector of Music for secondary schools was created three years ago, so that the numerous schools which have hitherto evaded music as an unessential and unwanted subject cannot with impunity continue to do so. By a recent order, the Minister has made it possible for instrumental music to be taught in vocational schools, a development precluded under the original terms of the Vocational Education Act. The Department of Education's Summer School of Music will shortly enter on its sixth session, and is having an appreciable effect, especially on school music. The establishment of an Arts Council has just been announced, to promote the knowledge, appreciation and practice of the arts, and with power to expend up to £20,000 annually.[19]

This article continues to review advances made in the country's general musical life that, even a decade previously, would have seemed unbelievable. However, his impatience at the slow pace of reform is also evident and leads him to speculate that 'it will take another century before we can hope to reach the level of the least progressive of other countries in Western Europe'. This frustration remains palpable when, writing the entry 'Music Education' for the 1968 edition of the *Encyclopaedia of Ireland*. Here he begins his discourse by noting that 'the leaders of education in Ireland have not yet been appreciably influenced by the radical change of outlook which has allotted to music a more prominent place in the school curriculum in England and in continental countries in recent years', although afterwards, he continues to praise the gains made up to then.[20]

His one publication devoted solely to music education was written in 1971. In some respects it is a disappointing piece of writing, reviewing older arguments, covering the full range of endeavours in music education here and including comparisons with other countries, most particularly Britain, Germany and Hungary. Here, the newly proposed child-centred approaches in primary education are of interest to him only to the extent that they contrast dramatically with the schooling experiences of his own generation. Similarly, he understands the new promise of a balanced curriculum to include a higher profile for the arts, and more specifically in his mind, additional time for school music. Notwithstanding this, one detects a lack of the freshness and confidence that characterised his earlier writings. Although his arguments cite several current experiments in music teaching, there is no awareness of the most significant studies and publications that were then beginning to impact on our understanding of the music curriculum and its appropriateness, nor does he mention any of the widely reported researches in the psychology of music education to aid his case.[21] These important studies and publications indicated that some curriculum music content was inappropriate and out of tune with the needs and interests of the general age group for which it was prescribed, although for some, given the rare combination of an enthusiastic and well qualified teacher on the one hand and a talented, well-motivated pupil on the other hand, it was demonstrably attainable. In drawing attention to the lack of an adequate system of music education in Ireland, Aloys Fleischmann always considered that the problem could be solved by providing all pupils with access to qualified teachers, sufficient study time and an engaging and incrementally-ordered music curriculum. Nowadays, studies in music education have advanced beyond this kind of rhetoric, nor is it true to say that pupil progress is necessarily related to an increase in study time. Failure in education is a multi-layered and complex problem, one that is not easily understood or rectified by the removal of financial or resource limits, as our attempts at reviving the Irish language demonstrate only too well.[22] It is not simply the adequacy or the quality of the supply that will ensure success but also its relevance to the individual's and society's needs. Many trained musicians fail to realise the extent to which society's musical needs change from one generation to the next. As they change, so too will individual needs and this will impact on the kind of music curriculum that is appropriate for each successive generation. In this respect the music curriculum can never be a prescribed constant but rather an ever evolving and variable list of musical requirements embodying social, economic and personal needs and standards. Aloys Fleischmann realised that, given the number of Irish taxpayers during the early 1970s, it was unlikely that, in this country, we could sustain the level of funding required to support the music education activities that were commonly available in other jurisdictions. What he failed to consider was the extent to which other educational interests, including other arts areas, were also demanding resources and change. In order to achieve any development, given the limited funding available, measured progress was all that was ever on offer. This still is largely the case today. Although we could never hope to match the international comparisons cited in his article, he continued to maintain this objective in the public eye; it is a tribute to his tenacity and drive that some considerable measure of success was achieved in this regard during his lifetime.

I have often wondered about the accuracy of his descriptions of music education in other countries. The Music department library in UCC had many such published accounts and he seems to have drawn upon these liberally without verification or first hand knowledge. Similarly his citing, in the 1971 article, of results of statistical tests conducted by the Hungarian Scientific Institute of Teaching is untrustworthy in several respects. Firstly, it is a partisan study in which the Institute is evaluating its own progress. Secondly, this document is a report and the 'scientific methodology' referred to is neither described nor made available even in the prime source for verification through scientific scrutiny. Thirdly and most important of all, the conclusion given is that, in communist Hungary during the 1960s, primary school children attending specialist music schools displayed 'a general intellectual development – quicker thinking, more concentration, more discipline, better co-ordination, increased capacity to memorise, and a wider emotional range'.[23] This is surely an unreliable claim; the only valid deduction to be made here, without the benefit of qualitative research measures, is that children who are good at music are also likely to be good at other subjects as well. It is not necessarily their study of music that improves their general level of intelligence but rather that intelligence effects pupil performance over a range of different subjects including music. In this respect, the study of music does not necessarily make brighter students, but it is more likely that bright students make good musicians.

One has to measure the deficiencies of the 1971 article against the fact the Aloys Fleischmann was not, in today's sense of the term, a music educationalist. Had he the choice, I suspect he would have preferred the life of a scholarly composer/conductor. Instead, realising more fundamental needs, he chose to occupy selflessly many different spaces in Irish musical life and one could not expect him to be fully *au fait* and up-to-date in all of them. However, on the positive side, the 1971 publication justifiably highlights blatant inconsistencies between policy and practice in Irish music education. Citing rule 20 of the then *Rules and Programme for Secondary Schools* requiring schools with no certificate programmes in music to provide an alternative singing programme on their timetable and submit this for approval to the Department of Education,[24] he rightly contrasts this with the false assertion in *The Curriculum in the Secondary School, Report of the Council of Education,* which was published in 1960, claiming that the number of schools in which singing is not taught is negligible.[25] In fact the report gave this finding because at that time there was no documented evidence to the contrary in the Department of Education's files, nor had any school ever submitted any alternative singing programme for approval to the Department or its inspectors.

Similarly, his reporting of statistics indicating the number of students taking the Intermediate and Leaving Certificate Music examinations makes interesting comparisons. In 1935, he estimated that a mere 55 students were examined in Intermediate and Leaving Certificate music. By 1961, the number of Leaving Certificate music students amounted to 75, i.c., 0.8% of the full cohort of Leaving Certificate students for that year. By 1971 he noticed a verifiable improvement in these numbers with approximately 3,000 students (i.e., 15% of the total cohort) sitting the Intermediate examination in music and he hoped that this would lead to a knock-on increase in the subject's popularity at Leaving Certificate level.[26] One wonders what he would have made of more recent statistics and, if this is to be the measure of progress, readers may draw their own conclusions.[27]

The number of Junior Certificate and Leaving Certificate music students expressed as a percentage of the total cohort sitting the Junior and Leaving Certificate examinations is given in the following table for the years 1988 to 1999:

Year	Examination	Number of music students	Percentage of the full cohort of certificate students
1988	Junior Certificate	10,816	18.0%
1988	Leaving Certificate	1,458	2.9%
1999	Junior Certificate	8,709	13.8%
1999	Leaving Certificate	2,995	4.8%

One of Aloys Fleischmann's most sensible and enlightened propositions, also chronicled in his 1971 article, was the County Music Organiser scheme. This was his attempt, here in Ireland, at replicating a scheme that was, by then, producing considerable results in Britain. He conceived his plan, with the blessing of the Department of Education, and the involvement of a number of County Vocational Education Committees. In return for scholarships, identified and talented individuals would, after receiving their musical training at UCC, undertake to return to their county regions to organise choirs, bands, music clubs, instrumental and other musical tuition, etc., as employees of the Vocational Education Committees. It was a bold and ingenious plan, one that particularly suited the practical mission of the Vocational Education sector, and could have been funded under their auspices without the need for additional legislation. In time, four county music organisers were appointed but

> ... they suffered continuous frustration: (1) because they were treated merely as teachers, some of them as itinerant teachers, not as organisers ... (2) because of the opposition of headmasters of vocational schools, who did not want music in their curriculum, and if they tolerated it at all, it was put outside school hours (in some cases after the buses had arrived to ferry the children home). As a result three out of the four resigned, and now only one is left to carry out a function which we had hoped would gradually spread all over the country.[28]

In apportioning blame for the scheme's failure, Professor Fleischmann singled out, in particular, the Department of Education for leaving the fledgling project without the necessary institutional support or encouragement. At present in County Cork, the country's only music organiser successfully takes responsibility for educating in music many hundreds of pupils as well as promoting a variety of musical events throughout the county. With this proof of its long term viability and success, it might be timely to revive this worthwhile idea.

I have always regarded the formal manner of Professor Fleischmann's interaction with people as the outward portrayal of his commitment to a classical order. His social as well as his educational values clearly stemmed from the philosophy of the enlightenment. Nowhere is this more clearly seen than in his attitude to new music. His composition students realised quickly that he was ill at ease with music that lacked clarity because it engendered audience confusion and, to his mind, this was not to be recommended. He preferred new music that maintained some relationship and continuity with past music, so that an educated audience could appraise its shape and, all the more easily, make comparative judgements as to its significance and value. However, he clearly realised the young composer's dilemma:

> A young man who has passed through his years of schooling and now masters his craft, cannot evade a momentous and somewhat bewildering issue. Either he has to choose the vocabulary of a pre-war generation, contriving to make it personal, or else he has to plunge into the principles of Schönberg or Milhaud and let loose a series of atonal or polytonal profundities on the astonished ears of a public acclimatised to Moore. Considering the anomaly of our present position, one feels inclined to favour the first and more cautious policy, for in seeking a new tradition, uncertain of our very footing, we must make good the breach with the past before we strike out apace.[29]

His attitudes to and understanding of Irish society were framed along similar lines to his educational and artistic perspectives. He believed in social order in much the same way as he required his composition students to write in an acceptable structure; and he lost no opportunity in his attempt to educate the public in his kind of social thinking. I recall, in particular, one of his many letters to the *Irish Times*, written during a period when the country was crippled with debt, inflation and unemployment. The substance of his message then was that public servants – and he was happy to include himself under that heading – and those with private means should agree to take cuts in salary so that the national debt would not be inherited by the youth of the country, thereby making it impossible for them to sustain a reasonable livelihood after they had completed their education. In his view, one's place in society involved particular responsibilities to its future, and he was concerned about the excesses of the present generation and their implications for those still in full-time education.

In his personality, Aloys Fleischmann exemplified many of the qualities of a great and successful teacher. He was not a reluctant teacher and possessed considerable communication skills and an infectious passion for his subject. It was he who first demonstrated to me the overriding importance of enthusiasm over teaching technique. In spite of this, it was well known that his lecture content remained broadly the same from one group of undergraduates to the next, so that it was possible for the more discerning student to be absent on occasion and to access the missing subject matter by consulting notes taken some years previously. However, such was his authority and conviction that students readily identified with the content presented, and absences were, as a rule, the exception. I don't think any of his students will forget his opening lecture to the first year BMus class. Here, he considered all the definitions of music and his sources ranged from the literature of antiquity through the many dictionary definitions to psychological and philosophical meanings as well as some eccentric ones designed to provoke laughter rather than understanding. This latter category are the ones that are most memorable, e.g., 'of all noise, the least disagreeable' (Samuel Johnson) and 'the brandy of the damned' (Oscar Wilde); but it was Beethoven's definition that obviously beguiled and enthralled the lecturer and received the most eloquent consideration and explanation, as indeed it had done in one of his earliest publications:

> ... Beethoven says, 'Music is the only incorporeal entrance into a higher world of knowledge.' The other arts arrive at this higher knowledge by a corporeal entrance – since their symbolism is related to the physical order – but music, being incorporeal, has a remote, elusive way of its own of getting at an inner world of meaning.[30]

Another standard Fleischmann lecture was on the profession of music. He always made his first year students aware that he regarded the BMus degree as a professional training with real employment prospects and, to this end, issued each with a resource pack of leaflets published by the Department of Labour. During this lecture session Professor reviewed the disparate nature of the profession and its many opportunities for employment. Although my resource pack has long since been lost, I recall vividly his overview of employment possibilities as instrumental teacher, performing musician, secondary teacher, broadcaster, songwriter/arranger, conductor, music critic, etc. He expected all his graduates to be able to turn their hands to many different musical tasks so that they could undertake various musical roles, if required.

This vocational approach to learning music, although not unusual in today's degree programmes, was out of place especially in the latter part of his stewardship of UCC's Music department. Furthermore, his overt encouragement of prospective music teachers sent mixed signals to those students who had other ideas or who had not decided on a particular career path. On occasion, disagreement was expressed regarding the nature and purpose of the degree and whereas he himself maintained an attitude to music education that encouraged everybody to make their contribution, I have never known him specifically to demand compliance. He was by nature a liberal and, whereas he might vehemently disagree with a viewpoint, he never sought to silence it. On the contrary, his department was the only one I have ever known to have an annual general meeting of students and staff. Students usually used these occasions to gain greater credit for course-work or to complain about excessive demands, unsuitable timetabling, etc. Professor was always willing to negotiate minor changes where a majority were clearly in favour. However, I have been present at a number of annual meetings when students directly challenged his accommodating teacher training within what was supposed to be a general academic programme. Given the all embracing, practical and comprehensive nature of the degree programme, it would have been easy for him to refute this claim, had he wished to do so. *Au contraire*, he always launched into a vigorous defence, claiming that teachers were the first and fundamental link in the chain by which music in Ireland would grow and develop. I have never known him to deviate from this value and, to this end, he not only encouraged students to teach but also accommodated serving teachers who wished to undertake degrees in Music within his department. Although I myself was a beneficiary of Professor's great educational plan, I understood the disaffected sentiments expressed about the timetabling. Lectures rarely began before 3.00pm, usually went on with just a short break until after 6.00pm and regularly included Saturday morning sessions also. Added to this was the arrangement whereby examinations were split between summer and autumn sessions to facilitate teaching students, thus denying full-time students the opportunity to earn money during the vacation period. As undergraduates, we were all more than a little grateful to the young student who naively complained about the possible effect of these hardships on her health, especially Professor's preference for lecturing at unsociable hours when students were least receptive. Rather than compromise his teaching students or his habit of holding two or even three lectures consecutively, he provided a self-run kitchen in the Music department so that students could sustain themselves for longer periods. This kitchen also enriched the social cohesion of the group and, in time, it became a focal point for musical discussions of all kinds. On occasion, we were joined by musically-minded students from other departments and it is well known that many a marital match originated there. Over subsequent years, Professor must have had occasion to regret this decision, especially when he had to hunt out students five minutes after the hour to attend scheduled lectures; but he was known to have confided to the department secretary that, unlike most of his professorial colleagues whose students could not be readily encountered between lectures, he at least knew where to locate his charges. Such memories exemplify the caring, happy and congenial learning environment he sought to create in his department, however testing his expectations were in other respects.

In hindsight, I now know that Professor's teaching style was uniquely his own and comprised a curious mix of both radical and conservative traits. In his teaching, he preferred drill and practice methodology as an initial approach to understanding, whereas, nowadays, educationalists prefer to emphasise the importance of understanding as a necessary adjunct to the acquisition of knowledge. In discussion, he readily defended the practical disciplines of music, stressing the importance of training as well as cognitive education. He had a scientific understanding of teaching, preferring to use the archaic term 'pedagogy' rather than 'education'. To this end he espoused, in his own teaching, a scientific strategy regardless of level or content difficulty. He considered that it was possible to teach music to everybody provided the materials were appropriately ordered and sufficient practice was given in its constituent skills. Knowledge, understanding and an artistic attitude would emerge from these connections in due time.

I don't think Professor Fleischmann liked the business of examinations much. He placed such great value on the process of developing professional skills and attitudes that he had only an obligatory interest in examination products and systems. Had he been allowed, I am certain that he would have rewarded student effort equally with the final examination outcome. He once described the methods of music education preferred in this country as negative and little more than 'a system of education by examination'.[31] In his 1971 article on music education, he castigates the status quo:

> ... especially in boys schools, [where] music and all extra-curricular activity is stopped after the First Year of Intermediate Certificate. This is a calamitous position, that just when our students are coming to some degree of maturity, any interests they have, any activities outside examination work, are cut off, and they are imprisoned within the walls of a stringent, cram-orientated results-system which has little to do with education in the broad sense.[32]

He further describes the charlatan attitudes of principal teachers who 'treat their schools as a sort of business based on examination results' because under no circumstances do they permit examination classes to be disturbed by allowing them to attend musical functions during school hours. This dim portrayal of boys schools is not very judicious or fair and my own experience would not fit his description. Whereas most boys schools rarely offered a reliable musical education, I have never known one to discourage its students from seeking it elsewhere, nor have I experienced situations where obstacles were placed in the way of musical pursuits especially where individual students demonstrated a genuine interest and talent. His poor opinion of attitudes in boys schools during the 1970s needs to be tempered by two arguments. Firstly, musical activities, other than pop music, would not have figured prominently as an extra-curricular interest of most secondary school boys at this time. Secondly, this period belonged to the age of meritocracy, when prevailing parental attitudes valued examination success as the key to an upward social mobility and better job prospects. The attitude of school authorities are always conditioned by social realities such as these, whether we like it or not. Paradoxically, a younger and more cautious Aloys Fleischmann approached this subject with greater balance twenty years previously. While reviewing the staffing arrangements for secondary schools in his 1951 article, he showed greater understanding of the school principal's dilemma in providing teachers for minority subjects such as music. He notes that the Department of Education's strict guidelines and pupil-teacher ratio are

> ... usually insufficient for purposes of staffing the school with general teachers and specialist teachers of essential or obligatory subjects. It would be expecting a great deal of the principals of schools to assign increments to specialist teachers of an extra subject such as music.[33]

That Aloys Fleischmann was a workaholic is a known fact and all who knew him could identify only too well its symptoms in his punishing daily schedule and work routine. It comes as no surprise, then, in his 1971 polemic on the poor standing of music in schools, he writes that

> ... the position has been considerably worsened for extra-curricular or marginal subjects such as music by the introduction of the 5-day week, because it reduces the space into which an already overcrowded curriculum has to be fitted leaving still less room for the liberal part of a supposedly liberal education. If industry and labour are aiming more and more towards a bigger return for less work and less time, why must education follow suit? No real student knocks off at the end of the fifth day, or at the end of the fortieth hour, and it is bad for him to have his curriculum compressed on the one hand, and on the other hand to be at a loose end for two whole days.[34]

Such a line of reasoning, credible as it might have been in the 1930s and 1940s, undermined the potency of his arguments in the 1970s when he was trying to convince Irish society of the importance of music, of its role in education and in the personal development of young people. Apart from this *faux pas*, there were other signs of his failure to keep abreast of modern social thinking, e.g. his ongoing and often vicious attack on popular music of all kinds, his disregard for Italian opera – obvious from its total neglect in lectures – and, more especially, his overt favouring of male and religious students because, unlike the younger lay female students who would inevitably be lost to marriage, they could be relied upon to contribute to music education full-time as their career. Happily, the passage of time has failed to substantiate this latter view and, paradoxically, the greater majority of musicians now teaching music in post-primary schools are lay and female. From a distance of over 20 years since completing my studies with him and, with the benefit of hindsight, I can recognise in many of these attitudes the natural cycle of human development from the radical and progressive tendencies of youth to the more conservative and regressive propensities of older people. Consequently, he should not be blamed for his failure to abandon older attitudes in favour of more modern ones, because such is the natural way of things; he was a man of his own generation, who took his measure from the values of past experiences, rather than what he would have considered to be the exigencies of vogue. In some respects, he embodied his own working definition of a good composition, i.e., 'not technically flawless but with sufficient energy and impact to allow us forgive its idiosyncrasies'.[35] In his case, it was his minor faults that forged the character as well as his charm.

As an advocate for the improvement of music in education, Aloys Fleischmann had few equals in his own time. 'Young people,' he wrote, 'who fail to come into contact with music in their school years are unlikely to develop a contact with it later, so that the schools are the crux of the problem.'[36] It is this view that fuelled all his efforts and he was never slow to seek meetings with anybody – politicians, school principals, public servants and the leaders of national bodies – whom he considered could influence the situation. Largely through his efforts and those of a few other pioneering contemporaries, music in Ireland has made considerable advances since the foundation of the state, a fact that does not go unnoticed in Harry White's summation of Aloys Fleischmann's legacy to Irish musical life. He writes:

> ... Fleischmann was to prove central to the reanimation of Irish musical ideas in the mid-twentieth century. Such figures did not register disaffection from afar; on the contrary, they were intimately involved with the development of a host of musical infrastructures – in education, in musical performance, in the emergent potential of sound radio – which conditioned their individual aspirations for Irish music. These aspirations centred upon musical composition itself, but the designation 'composer' appears inadequate as a description of their individual status ... given their influential commitment as ideologues of music in Ireland.[37]

NÓIRÍN NÍ RIAIN (DUBLIN), UCC Music Graduate, Singer
Pink Eternally: Remembering Aloys Fleischmann
This title – Pink Eternally – I take from a poem by America's great
spiritual poet, Emily Dickinson:

> But memory – like melody –
> Is pink – eternally.

A portmanteau word is one which telescopes or blends two other
words. And because my memory of Professor Aloys Fleischmann is
inextricably bound with melody, these two words – memory and
melody – merge to become 'Melory'. These 'melories' appear when I
enter the past time capsule which takes me back to Cork some thirty
years ago. Those years between 1969 and 1973 were a glorious, blessed
time-span of four years, chock-full of light-filled memories and
melodies. Memory inseparable from melody then – music inextricably
connected with existence and with the divine. And all of this enhanced
and heightened for me through the strong presence of the person who
stood at the helm, who steered the ship of the university Music department which sheltered me. That was Professor Aloys Fleischmann.

Someone who was sometimes father-figure. Sometimes, the cold,
tiresome professor demanding musical manuscript exercises, which
were almost invariably overdue. Sometimes, the empathetic examiner
hoping against hope that the miraculous might manifest itself through
and for you! But always, the shrewd, generous educator assuming the
true meaning of this role-word of being one who leads out, who brings
forth the latent potential in the heart of all in his path.

Two particular memories of Aloys as teacher appear which have
very different colours of melory. Firstly, I remember one particular
golden, autumn September late evening in 1977. I had just put the full
stop to a collection of wonderful *Déise sean-nós* melodies which I had
been privileged to learn from a fellow colleague of Professor Fleischmann in the Music department, Pilib Ó Laoghaire.[38]

Of course, the first person I wanted to 'come out' with, for what
was some three years of carefully transcribing these songs, was the
'Prof'. So armed with my manuscript and the various bits and pieces
of the forthcoming book, I turned up proudly armed with my *magnum
opus*. Well, my former Don took one glance at the title of my first sheet
and gasped in horror. 'But my dear Miss Ní Riain,' he tut-tutted me,
'surely, you mean Fore*word* not Fore*ward*?'

Off to a bad start. But all's well that ends well, because this same
irate man on that autumnal day went on to eventually write the introduction to the book. I will always be eternally grateful to him for both
his insightful exegesis on Pilib Ó Laoghaire and his endorsement of

this humble source of tunes.[39]

The second pedagogical memory takes me back to the Ó Riada Room on the occasion of my final practical Bachelor of Music examination. This room was a special space even at the worst of times, which this particular moment would have held for most students. This is because it was bounded on two sides by expansive windows overlooking fine oak trees. So, the natural light and the inbuilt perspective of the room always helped to heighten creativity and possibility. Well, at the *viva-voce* juncture of this academic scrutiny, the external examiner asked the imaginative question as to who my favourite composer was. I immediately replied: 'Well, there are two of them actually – Haydn and Grieg.' Now this seemed satisfactory to the peering board before me until I went on to add. 'You see, they're both so similar.'

'Really, my dear!' Prof horrifiedly broke in, acutely conscious that the Extern might assume that he had not sufficiently instructed us in the differences, cultural, chronological and stylistic, between the two composers. 'Can you, in Heaven's name, explain how?' he continued as he sat far back in his chair employing the familiar Fleischmannian affectionate idiosyncrasy of massaging his chin and scrutinising me carefully through black thick-rimmed spectacles. Very powerful, singular personal traits. Somehow, I managed to plausibly make my case. My argument incidentally was around melody once again, because I argued that both composers merged on the level of being superb melodists! I even managed to achieve an honours degree but most importantly afterwards it was an occasion of merriment between us both!

Other non-academic memories hark back to the Franciscan Hall in Dublin about 1971 when this same Professor, wearing the hat of conductor/composer this time, conducted his composition, *Cornucopia* single-handedly quite literally. Because earlier that day apparently, he had gashed his finger while mowing the lawn but insisted on conducting, one arm in a sling.

Then there were the many afternoons when I acted as 'dog's body' to the marvellous *Sources of Irish Traditional Music* which meant little or nothing to me at that time. It is only now, as I hold in my hands this inspired tome published recently, that I appreciate contributing towards this classic even in such a minutely, minuscule manner.

But my abiding memory of Professor Aloys Fleischmann lies in the realm of the prophetic! To set the backdrop to this, once again, Pilib Ó Laoghaire makes an appearance in this drama. On examining me in St Louis Convent Dundalk for my Leaving Certificate music examination, he, at once suggested that I should not pursue my intended

Law degree in UCD, but that I head for the Music department UCC. That, thanks to my courageous parents and Pilib's generosity, I did.

I came to UCC as a singer, steeped in popular music-hall style of songs like 'Somewhere Over the Rainbow', Gilbert and Sullivan operettas such as *Iolanthe*, etc. Yet lurking invisibly behind that tradition was a deep hankering for Gregorian Chant, which was the legacy of my childhood and adolescence. So, although I freely imbibed the classical singing techniques from the late Margaret Dillon from my first year, I was also captivated by the very different *sean-nós* singing, which I was simultaneously gathering from Pilib. Yet, my heart was later to find its true way through spiritual song.

But to return to the Professor, I vividly recall his comment on hearing me sing at the end of my second year. 'My dear (his favourite salutation to us, his female students,) you know, you sing in cathedral tone.' And right he was! But the timing was wrong then to really understand and pursue the inner message of his words.

Finally, I cannot remember Professor Fleischmann without reference to his noble, puissant wife, Anne. On the few visits to their mysterious, marvellous home in the Glen, I admired her greatly. Either as she graciously served us students a variety of Green Door cakes or later when we lived in Cork, when she summoned me up, out of the blue, to see her one October afternoon for afternoon tea. She was full of intuition and a person whose perspicacity and perceptions hit right to the soul.

HARRY WHITE, Professor of Music at University College Dublin
Polite Forms
I met Aloys Fleischmann just once. This seems a strange truth to concede at the outset of a memoir, but in fact we had corresponded so frequently prior to that occasion (and following it) that I am forced to think carefully, so strongly do I have the impression of having known him personally for a long time. To anyone with even a passing interest in the history of music in Ireland, and even more particularly in musical scholarship in this country, Fleischmann was an abiding presence. Those who did know him personally can attest far better than I to his extraordinary bearing. He was one of those people who somehow completes any gathering to which he belongs.

Others will have acknowledged in this book and elsewhere Aloys Fleischmann as a seminal figure in the modern history of music in Ireland. As an educator, as a composer, as a gifted practical musician, Fleischmann belonged to that generation of university professors whose brief was as wide as it was long. One thinks of Larchet in Dublin and indeed of Larchet's successor, Anthony Hughes. In Fleischmann's case, the sheer breadth of his activities was never confined to regional concerns: his sheer presence in Cork was undoubtedly a crucial influence on the well-being of music not only in the university but throughout Munster, but it is as a figure of national significance that I remember him here. He made Cork an international centre of choral music (among many other things), but he also entered a vital claim for the well-being of music and musicology in Ireland at large. One remembers his courteous interventions in the correspondence columns of *The Irish Times* in the later years of his life, but Fleischmann was a voice for art music in Ireland long before then. His whole career was committed to the development of music in Ireland, but in this memoir I should like to concentrate on his activities as a musicologist.

I can only speculate as to what his training as a musicologist in Munich must have been like. Born there but raised in Ireland, he went to Munich in 1932 partly to study conducting at the State Academy of Music and partly to read musicology at Ludwig-Maximilian University. Munich must have been an unnerving place in which to live and work, entranced as it then was by the spell of National Socialism: when I went there some sixty-five years afterwards as a visiting professor of musicology, the strongest impression of brutality and charm, of cosmopolitan largesse and parochial prejudice, indeed of international chic and a peculiar admixture of ultra-right conservatism, certainly unnerved me. Sitting one snowy afternoon in a cafe not far from Geschwister-Scholl-Platz, I was thinking of Fleischmann and how he must have regarded his native city in those disturbing days. I was also thinking about the Turks, whose presence in the late 1990s excited such repulsive sentiments (repulsive to me, at any rate) in one or two young, well-to-do musicology students of my acquaintance. I ventured all this to my drinking companion, who chairs the institute of musicology. 'It's shocking, I know,' he said, 'but it's hardly surprising. The Turks are the Jews of today.' This was not complacency on my colleague's part: on the contrary, he was at pains simply to register the unpalatable (if sporadic) fact of racism among the well-educated men and women in his charge. I wondered aloud what Fleischmann would have made of it: an affluent Munich woman in her late twenties, for example, vehemently defending the slogan 'Deutschland für alle? Nein! Für uns!!!!' as 'perfectly good sense'. Did he encounter even more vehement versions of the same brutal politics in his years in Munich? I suspect he must have done. But he returned to Ireland before the nightmare had entered its darkest phase.

Nevertheless, Fleischmann took at least two things from his musicology studies in Germany home with him. One was a passion for scientific exactitude in the matter of music history, a passion which was to abide. The other was a conviction, which may have been already inherent, that the first duty of a musicologist was to the music of his own country. In Fleischmann's case, this was Ireland for all practical purposes, and his scholarship and criticism thereafter centred upon the music of his adoptive homeland. As a conductor and indeed as a university professor, Fleischmann saw to it that the central European traditions of art music which were his birthright were inculcated in the musicians whom he taught and with whom he worked. But as a musicologist, his concerns lay elsewhere.

Three themes dominated Fleischmann's writings on music in Ireland, of which two were expressly musicological. In order, these might be characterised as a preoccupation with the place and perception of music in Irish cultural history; an abiding interest in music of the Celtic rite; and a scholarly interest in the provenance and dissemination of the corpus of traditional melody. Although each of these themes continued to occupy him right up to the time of his death, his published writings show that he pursued them more or less chronologically. Thus the early spate of polemical articles published in such periodicals as *Ireland Today* and *The Bell*, which began shortly after his return from Munich, display an acute concern not only with the (then) deplorable state of music education in Ireland but with the central cultural conflict that lay at the heart of Ireland's musical malaise: his argument that 'folk music' and 'art music' be regarded as 'two parallel streams', and that cultivation of the one did not necessarily promote well-being in the other did not augur much promise of a friendly reception in the Ireland of the 1930s and 1940s. Nor would it necessarily do so now, for that matter. But Fleischmann did not repine. If he remained persuaded that the nationalist claim upon the folk idiom inhibited the development of infrastructures necessary to the cultivation of art music, his response to this predicament was not further polemics but a magisterial survey, *Music in Ireland*, which he published in 1952. In this book, Fleischmann and his contributors made a powerful case for the rehabilitation of music in Ireland not by fulminating against the deprived *status quo* but by a systematic disclosure of that *status quo* in every conceivable dimension of the profession and practice of music. And not only music, but also musicology: Fleischmann was concerned to identify not only the impoverished condition of music sources but the want of research that then attended almost every aspect of Ireland's musical history, with the notable exception of folk music.

If, as I have argued elsewhere, *Music in Ireland* marked the beginnings of a professional musicology in Ireland, Fleischmann's brief did not rest there. Given his close association with Donal O'Sullivan, whose brilliant biographical study of Carolan was to appear some six years afterwards, it is not perhaps surprising to find Fleischmann himself increasingly engaged with the scholarly study of folk music, particularly with the question of musical sources. This preoccupation with sources, in fact, had already manifested itself in his earliest writings, including an important article on Irish sources of the chant which appeared in the prestigious *Zeitschrift für Musikwissenschaft* in 1934. Fleischmann, indeed, would maintain his interest in the music of the Celtic rite, an interest which culminated in his article on this subject which appeared in *The New Grove Dictionary of Music* (1980).

But it was the scholarly transmission and recension of Irish traditional melody which became for Fleischmann the central quest of his musicological career. There is some irony in this at first, given his brilliant identification of a creative impasse as between the dominance of the ethnic repertory in Irish musical affairs and the impoverished or confused concept of original composition, an insight sustained in his sympathetic and yet incisive article on Ó Riada which appeared after the composer's death in *Counterpoint* (1971). Nevertheless, Fleischmann's patient accumulation of source material rehearsed and tested in various learned venues (including the *Proceedings of the Royal Irish Academy*) must be understood, I believe, as a testament to his fundamentally positivist training as a musicologist in Germany. Given his own pragmatic temperament (in scholarly terms at least), and given especially the (literally) monumental traditions of retrieval and representation which were the bedrock of German musicology almost from its inception, it is less surprising than it first appears that Fleischmann should have promoted in turn the recovery of the ethnic repertory not in the anthologising spirit which had prevailed in Ireland since the publication of John and William Neale's *A Collection of the Most Celebrated Irish Tunes* (1724), but in the manner of a *catalogue raisonée* so dear to the traditions of German musical scholarship. Although *The Sources of Irish Traditional Music, 1583–1855* appeared some six years after his death, it testifies to Fleischmann's systematic application of the principles of German musicology to the music of this country. Fleischmann had always remained optimistic that these principles could be applied on a wider scale to music in Ireland (as witness his preface to Ita Hogan's *Anglo-Irish Music 1780–1830* [1966], a book which is deeply and impressively imbued with the same positivist spirit.)

My own debt to Fleischmann dates from the mid 1980s, when I began to think seriously about the condition of music in Ireland as the expression of some kind of unresolved cultural dislocation. Later still, when I published a survey of musicology in Ireland (1988), he wrote to me, offering congratulations, emendations and encouragement. Thus our correspondence began: always formal, always businesslike, always expressive of that polite form which no longer exists in English but which characterises so much verbal and written intercourse in German, even among colleagues (and sometimes friends) of very long standing.

And then I met him. Gerard Gillen and I had approached Fleischmann to launch the first book in the series *Irish Musical Studies* on 21 June 1990 in the board room of the National Concert Hall. When I arrived, Fleischmann was already there. We talked about the book, and he told me how much it meant to him that a book called *Musicology in Ireland* could at last appear: I told him in turn that without *Music in Ireland* the thing would have been inconceivable: one was a natural progression from the other. Then the photographer's flash went, and in the following day's *Irish Times* there was a shot of us both poring thoughtfully over the new-born volume. Over dinner afterwards, while we were absent-mindedly attended upon by waiters understandably intent upon Ireland *v.* Romania in the World Cup, I relished his subtle interplay of gentle courtesy and shrewd wit. And somehow, I felt the unmistakable impression of musicology as a worthwhile profession, embodied with adroit humour and a faintly ironic gravitas by the *Ordinarius* at my side.

In his last letter to me, several months afterwards, when, to borrow a phrase, 'he offered me the Du', I was immediately conscious of the rarity of that honour. 'Dear Harry', he began, and in parentheses: 'Surely we can dispense with the formalities by now.' The letter was signed 'Yours sincerely, Aloys'. Even now, I miss his presence in my life.

7: THE COMPOSER

AOSDÁNA: PROPOSAL FOR MEMBERSHIP by GERARD VICTORY October 1981
Aloys Fleischmann may justly be regarded as the doyen of living Irish composers – his extensive creative output dating from about 1933 to the present time.

His influence as an excellent teacher of composition has been very great. Among his pupils may be counted Seán Ó Riada, Bernard Geary and Michael Casey. He has been responsible in great measure for the development of contemporary Irish ballet music.

GERARD VICTORY (1921–1995), Composer, Director of Music, Radio Teilifís Éireann, on Donna O'Sullivan's Cork Radio Programme of 29 April 1978
Dr. Fleischmann developed a highly personal style of composition, which combined a great sense of the Romantic European tradition with a sensitive feeling for the essence of genuine Irish music. He was rarely, if ever, a simple adapter or arranger of Irish airs in periods when this seemed the obvious musical way of expressing Irishness. He incorporated Irish motifs and other thematic elements into a personal and highly international language. The choice of his subjects reveals his unending preoccupation with Irish roots, which he treated in ways at once novel and yet firmly linked to the great mainstream of Europe.

He has been the friend and guide of so many young artists and composers, including this speaker, indeed. Never have I known him, master of erudition as he is, to dogmatise over inexperienced young people. Never has he failed in respect for the individuality and uniqueness of young artists, however halting and uncertain their steps. The generosity of Dr Fleischmann somehow dictated that composition, in which he was so talented, would never distract him from the immense contribution he made towards vitalising the whole music scene in Cork and in Ireland.

GERARD VICTORY on Donna O'Sullivan's Cork Radio Programme of 22 July 1992 after Fleischmann's death:
Some of the other speakers have dealt with Aloys Fleischmann as a national figure, as well as being the centre-pin in Cork in regard to everything musical. But what I would stress most of all was the extraordinary generosity and kindness to other musicians. This has been mentioned already, but it extended much beyond Cork. I myself had the experience of being on the receiving end of it in no small measure, and indeed I probably would not be here speaking to you were it not

for Aloys Fleischmann and the encouragement he gave me to go on with a musical career back in rather disappointing days 35 or so years ago. He launched a number of young people into the compositional field; his performances with his own orchestra were quite exceptional in the amount of representation of contemporary works which he did – not easy with an amateur orchestra, and requiring enormous work.

But his own compositions were done in the midst of this unique, hectic and active career in other respects, organising and mustering the forces of musical Ireland, one might say, almost single-handed at times. He was able to write a long succession of works and what I think most remarkable is that he improved from a very good starting point right up to the end. He got better all the time. My happiest memories in very recent times were listening to two works of his: one the *Táin*, a ballet on the Irish saga. When I went to see it I was anticipating something quite different from what actually happened. It was a most sophisticated score; it struck me as having all the richness of Europe in the best sense of the word. It was not just Ireland, but every country, and the best of every tradition seemed somehow integrated in a brilliant way in it. It was extremely high-powered; almost overpowering, one might say, with very expert orchestration. And following that, in 1990, his *Games* was done at the Choral Festival by the BBC Singers, who came over to perform it. This work was written to a text by a Yugoslav writer: it is an extremely surrealist piece of poetry, brilliantly set to music in a way that went in another direction again and was immensely forward-looking, futuristic, one might say, and at the same time very direct and accessible. All his work has been like this and could appeal to wide audiences, I feel, in quite different ways: from *Clare's Dragoons*, a heartening Irish work taking the best out of a communal tradition with strong roots, ranging into this highly esoteric world which he could bring out so clearly. And all this was linked, as everybody has said, with a most humble personality. He never stood on dignity, even having received the highest possible awards, offices and accolades from all over the world, he used to go around up to a few years ago on a light motor-cycle, as I remember, through every weather in Cork, marshalling people and getting things done, utterly unconcerned with rainstorms and with any other obstacle. I think it was miraculous he happily survived those escapades on the motorcycle. But it sums him up for me: a person of immense humility and simplicity with this very rich imagination and deep understanding of every aspect and nuance of musical language and the musical world.

In Memoriam Aloys Fleischmann

Professor Aloys Fleischmann embodied so many remarkable qualities that really no adequate account of them could be given in a short tribute. From the moment I first met him, about forty years ago now, I realised that here was quite an extraordinary person. It was only with the passing of more years that I came fully to realise and assess to some extent just how formidable was his contribution to the entire musical life of Ireland.

My first meeting with him I recall was at a rehearsal of the Cork Symphony Orchestra, the remarkable amateur ensemble, which he developed with such loving skill over so many years. I remember finding him busily putting out the stands on the stage of the City Hall in Cork and personally sorting out the orchestral parts for the players. I thought at the time it was a little surprising that he was doing this, knowing his distinguished rank as a professor and scholar, and of course as conductor of the orchestra. I came to realise that all this was so typical of this marvellous man, who combined the highest musical scholarship with simplicity, a burning enthusiasm and a humility all fused delightfully together. At every turn one would receive a surprise of some kind from Aloys, however much one had got to know him. His analysis of the most complex musical score was always a delight, technically erudite and yet utterly lucid, to the point of being intelligible to the lay outsider as well as to the developed student. And how skilfully he could introduce humour into the most complex process, crystallising his remarks in a way that was unforgettable. I do believe his influence on several generations of students has penetrated for the better into very many avenues of Irish musical life.

His warm, ebullient and accessible personality disguised a little perhaps what was in every way a most profound psyche. This was revealed, often startlingly, in his compositions which, for over fifty years, covered a vast range of form and style. As in his teaching, his composition combined the highest scholarship with a voice that spoke to the world at large without exception. My first encounter with his compositions was hearing on Radio Éireann some time in the 1940s a performance of his ballet suite *The Golden Bell of Ko*. I remember being deeply impressed by the richness of the orchestration and the sumptuous oriental chording. This was the same composer who had launched his stirring setting of *Clare's Dragoons*, a work which transformed a patriotic ballad into a new and individual symphonic ambience which was irresistible. The catalogue became intensive covering almost every musical genre and never predictable, always taking an unexpected stylistic turn but always unmistakable in its personality, as recognisable in the music as in the man.

This was particularly so in his later years when most remarkably he stormed past new horizons, and showed new facets, which took us all unawares again. Among these later works were the ballet suite the *Táin* and, only two years ago, a most exciting choral work called *Games* for choir, harp and percussion. The *Táin* was a piece of incredible vigour with an expression of style that matched the archaic sombre saga perfectly and gripped its audience totally. *Games* was even more surprising. Invited by the Cork Choral Festival two years ago to write a work, he selected texts by a modern Yugoslav writer, Vasco Popa, which described a strange surrealist world with some ironic humour. Aloys seized on the essence of this work in a really uncanny fashion. He showed himself at the age of eighty to be a complete master of a highly contemporary idiom which had immense clarity, as always. However bizarre or surrealist the demands of the style might be, the result was always crystal clear and immensely moving emotionally in the excellent performance by the BBC Singers.

His work perhaps uniquely combined both an intense and recognisable Irishness and a totally cosmopolitan musical mind. He was an expert on Irish traditional music and, most happily, a vast catalogue of the totality of Irish traditional airs, which he had been compiling for many years, was completed just before his death. This background in Irish music he brought into many of his own works, but never in the form of a routine arrangement or a folksy style. In so many works it remained as a kind of foundation to his own imaginative voice, which transformed it into something very new and yet faithful to the spirit of its origins. Such works include the delightful *Three Songs* for tenor and orchestra of 1937, which added a touch of magic to three contrasting Gaelic poems, and the sensitive *Songs of Colmcille* of 1964, to words by Robert Farren.

An especial wonder was that such a creative and intense thinker was in another guise a person of such practical action and skill as a music organiser. He made the Cork International Choral Festival, starting in 1954, one of Ireland's extraordinary and outstanding events. It would be impossible to describe the energy he put into the creation and maintenance for so many years of this unique Festival. The fact that so many people contributed great skill and tireless industry to the accomplishment of this undertaking was a tribute to his own inspirational leadership, his own energy, and above all, the respect of everyone for his high talent and erudition – and awareness of his kindness and generosity.

On that score, he worked ceaselessly to encourage and reward emerging generations of Irish composers. The help he gave to so many could never be fully recorded. This was not just by such devices as commissions from the Festival, but by encouragement, both personal and practical in an unobtrusive but telling manner. I was myself the recipient of invaluable encouragement from Aloys at a very disheartening time. I know that this is only one of many instances where he stimulated and heartened so many people. The great sadness felt, I would say, by all Irish musicians at his passing is slightly tempered by the knowledge that his influence will continue to flourish in such a variety of ways: in the person of his many students, whom he inspired, and in the institutions he created and fostered. Also in that view of music and culture which he instilled into all of us, and which was so sincere, so vibrant, and so unforgettable.

FREDERICK MAY (1911–1985), Composer, Director of Music at the Abbey Theatre Dublin
The Music of Aloys Fleischmann (written in 1949)
Professor Aloys Fleischmann is a creative artist who has taken his subject sufficiently seriously to master the technique of his craft, and this is something so rare in Ireland, at any rate as far as music is concerned, that it is a matter for sincere congratulation. Both his parents are distinguished musicians, so that he had the great advantage of being brought up to reverence the masterpieces of the past and to understand that nothing could ever be accomplished without a thorough preliminary training in the mysteries of counterpoint, harmony and orchestration. He spent some time studying in Munich and, upon the completion of his academic training, he was appointed to the chair of Music at University College, Cork, a position which he continues to fill with great distinction, for he has proved himself an admirable teacher and lecturer. He is also very active as a conductor, and this has been of great benefit to his composition, because it has enabled him to become thoroughly familiar with the various problems of execution and interpretation that beset instrumentalists. For the past ten years or so his output, while not exactly copious, has been regular and sufficiently varied to prove that in Fleischmann we have a musician of wide ranging musical interests, and one who is by no means afraid of adventure and experiment. His works to date include a *Piano Quintet*, *Three Songs for Tenor, Voice and Orchestra*, a *Prelude and Dance for Orchestra*, a *Pianoforte Suite*, a suite for string orchestra, entitled *The Humours of Carolan*, an overture, *The Four Masters*, a song cycle, *The Fountains of Magic*, which is a setting for voice and orchestra of four poems all translated from the Irish by Frank O'Connor, and finally, *Clare's Dragoons*, a very ambitious setting of the poem of the same name by Thomas Davis. It is scored for baritone, war pipes, choir and orchestra and must be re-

garded as its composer's most considerable achievement to date.

To attempt a critical assessment of a composer who is still fairly young and in the full flow of creative activity is a virtually impossible task, but it is a service, both to him and to ourselves if one can make a tentative estimate of the pervading qualities of his music and see how they measure up to the standards set by other music which has come to find universal acceptance. The first and most vital question one has to ask oneself about any artist is: 'Has this man got a spark of what Beethoven called the divine fire in him or not?' If the answer is 'no' it is clear that all the good intentions in the world will not protect himself and his music from oblivion. I suggest that, in the case of Fleischmann, the answer to this question is a qualified 'yes'.

In order to elaborate this reply a bit further, let us look for a moment at two compositions which are as different as possible from each other, the *Piano Quintet* and the *Three Songs for Tenor Voice and Orchestra*. The *Piano Quintet* is extremely long and vastly complicated; it reads as if the composer had poured all his erudition into the writing of it. Strange rhythms fight and jostle each other, and not infrequently the harmonies become tortuous and obscure. But does all this expenditure of effort lead to any conclusion fundamentally so important as to justify the trouble taken to reach it? Speaking for myself, I do not think so, although others, of course, might hold a contrary view; but it is certain that this composer needs to be on guard against becoming the victim of his own learning, and forgetting the virtues of simplicity. When he forgets that he is a professor and obviously moved by some strong emotional impulse he can write music that is both moving and beautiful.

One of his finest works to date is undoubtedly the *Song Cycle for Tenor Voice and Orchestra [Trí hAmhráin]*; there is, by the way, another version available with piano accompaniment which has been published by An Gúm, and which well repays close study. All three songs are settings of Irish poems and Fleischmann, being an expert speaker and writer of Irish, found no difficulty in setting the poems in their original language; a serviceable English translation has, however, been made by the late Father Pat MacSwiney, of Cobh, so that the songs may be sung in either language. The first song is a setting of a poem by Turlough O'Carolan lamenting the death of the great general, Owen Roe O'Neill, victor of the battle of Benburb. The text of the second song is an adaptation by Mícheál Ó Murchú of an old French poem about a butterfly and a bee, who gaily discuss the business which each has to do. The third song is a setting, of another poem by Mícheál Ó Murchú – the piper has been away for many a year, the glens are silent, but when the sound of his pipes is heard again, echoing above the tread of marching feet, Sheila will know that her piper has triumphed, that the flag of victory is unfurled from the Suir to the Bann.

These songs combine remarkable lyrical beauty with deep intensity of feeling. The first and third seem to spring straight from the soul of Ireland and its historic past. The lament is built up from a throbbing ground bass and evokes an unforgettable picture of a nation in mourning, while the Piper, with his wonderful tenderness and love for Ireland, which is, of course, Sheila for the purposes of this song, and its mounting and evermore confident assurance of victory, is something that I defy any Irishman to listen to without a strange tugging at his heartstrings, springing both from the intrinsic beauty of the music and racial memories evoked by the poem. These three songs, and particularly the last, undoubtedly represent one of the highlights of contemporary music in Ireland.

Among the rest of his music, leaving aside, of course, *Clare's Dragoons*, the most noteworthy of his works are, it seems to me, his overture, *The Four Masters*, and his other song cycle, *The Fountain of Magic*. In its full-blooded opulence, and exuberant piling-up of masses of sound, the overture puts one in mind, more than once, of Richard Strauss, while *The Fountain of Magic* contains some beautiful orchestral tone-painting, illustrating first the mellow richness of autumn and then the barren numbness of winter; it concludes with a piece of rollicking good humour which proves that the composer can occasionally relax and enjoy the passing show, though his general mood is far from light-hearted. It is probable that both these works would produce a yet more satisfactory effect in performance if the texture of the music could be lightened somewhat. Vaughan Williams, when a composer with quite an established reputation, went to Ravel to try and discover how he might acquire greater clarity. Ravel is certainly not one of the world's greatest composers, but he was a master of taste; and now that he is dead and cannot any longer be appealed to personally for counsel, it might be a good idea if Professor Fleischmann would consider making a thorough study of as many of his scores as he can lay hands on – assuming, of course, that he has not already done so. To look at things for a short time through the eyes of this clear-sighted Frenchman might prove a most stimulating tonic. The supreme master and model where clarity of outline is concerned is Mozart; but then, I have no doubt that Professor Fleischmann is as fully conscious of this fact as I am myself. As for *Clare's Dragoons*, this work, like the *Song-Cycle for Tenor Voice and Orchestra* previously discussed, is inspired by intense patriotic feeling, and therein lies its strength. Both chorus and orchestra are used with an assured mastery,

and a picturesque and belligerent addition to the score is the employment by the composer of war-pipes, which make a striking impact
upon the eye as well as the ear. But compelling and imperious as are
the great choral climaxes, not to mention the triumphant vigour with
which the composer handles his forces, there can be no doubt, I feel,
that the most memorable passage of the entire work occurs quite near
the end, where the solo baritone, lightly accompanied by the orchestra, softly sings the following lines, the music swelling out towards the
end:

> Oh, comrades, think how Ireland pines
> Her exiled lords, her rifled shrines,
> Her dearest hope the ordered lines
> And bursting charge of Clare's Dragoons.

The poetry may amount to little more than doggerel, but it has
inspired the composer to another of those hauntingly evocative passages that sound as if they were written, not in the early 1940s of the
present century, but back in the dark travail of the penal days. Certainly, in this work, as in the three Irish songs, Fleischmann has managed to do something entirely original; he has become articulate for an
Ireland that is gone, or rather, he has given us in music a symbol of
what Ireland, her people, her history and the beauty of her hills and
valleys mean to each one of us. He has effected in sound a crystallisation and intensification of a feeling common to all Irishmen, and in so
doing he has secured for himself an honoured and a permanent place
in the musical history of this country.

(In: *The Father Mathew Record*, 1949, Capuchin Publications, Dublin)

JOHN KINSELLA (DUBLIN), Composer, former Head of RTE Music
I had a sporadic association with Aloys Fleischmann over a period of
approximately 25 years arising out of my position at the Music Department of RTE and my role as a composer. I found him most inspirational – on the one hand extremely kindly and on the other a man of
towering intellect.

I was on the receiving end of his campaigning for music in Cork.
This concerned mainly the maintaining of a string quartet there, and
while it was my responsibility to balance RTE's interest in this connection I always, in my heart, totally agreed with his point of view. Our
association was, in retrospect, positive. His initiatives are still bearing
much fruit in Cork and reflected in the country generally. The Choral
Festival is one obvious example. I and many other composers benefited through his commissioning, even though that meant facing the
rigours of his public analysis of these pieces – a task which he undertook

with kindness, total intellectual honesty and much genuine humour.

DAVID C. WRIGHT (ISLE OF WIGHT), Critic and Writer, who corresponded with and interviewed Aloys Fleischmann in 1990.
In addition to his untiring services to music, Aloys Fleischmann's contributions to the public service of the city of Cork and to Ireland in general were nothing short of phenomenal. He was a member of the Advisory Committee on Cultural Relations in the Irish Department of Foreign Affairs for eight years from 1955; first chairman of the Cork Sculpture Park between 1961 and 1989 and a member of the Irish Commission for UNESCO between 1962 and 1980. In his religious activities he was, for five years, from 1983 a member of the Music Advisory Committee for the Irish Episcopal Commission for Liturgy. One can understand why he was made a freeman of the city of Cork in 1978.

Yet for all this, how will he best be remembered? Will such memorials represent him merely as one who strove to give impetus to music education and to composition in Ireland which, in his words, is a country which, under a colonial regime for centuries, has had its own traditions swamped and was trying to start, virtually from scratch, to build up a new tradition from the second and third decades of this century?

Young Aloys had always been surrounded by music. His father was organist at St Mary's Cathedral in Cork from 1906 to 1962, and also taught at the Cork School of Music. He taught his son the organ and harmony, whereas Mrs Fleischmann taught young Aloys the piano – she had studied at the Royal Academy of Munich with Bernhard Stavenhagen, a pupil of Liszt. From 1920 to 1924 Aloys had violin lessons with W. E. Brady, who was to become leader of his distinguished pupil's Cork Symphony Orchestra. Many prominent musicians visited the Fleischmann household such as Herbert Hughes, E. J. Moeran, Harriet Cohen and Sir Arnold Bax who, as external examiner to the Music department, paid an annual visit each year for over twenty-five years, and in fact on one such visit died there in 1953.

Having taken his degree in Music in 1931 and his MA the following year in musicology with a thesis on *The Neumes in Irish Liturgical Manuscripts*, he went to the State Academy of Music in Munich until 1934. There he studied composition with Joseph Haas (1879–1960), in his time a well-known composer who had studied with Max Reger and, in fact, wrote his biography in 1949. Haas wrote operas and oratories and his chamber music was highly regarded. Fleischmann studied conducting with Dr Heinrich Knappe and musicology at Munich University with Dr Rudolf von Ficker (1886–1954), an eminent scholar specialising in medieval and sixteenth-century music; and with Dr Otto Ursprung (1879–1960), who had produced a *History of Church*

Music, complete editions of the works of Kerle and Senfl, and became well-known for deciphering the music of an Egyptian papyrus *Der Hymnus von Oxyrynchos*. Ursprung was very helpful to Fleischmann when preparing his first publication in a German music journal in the summer of 1934.

During his time in Munich, Fleischmann composed his *Suite for Piano* and a motet, *Illumina Occulos Meos*, which was sung by the Munich Cathedral Choir under Monsignor Ludwig Berberich at a service in the Cathedral in February 1934. Fleischmann had started composing juvenilia at the age of five and by about 1925 had written some songs and a string quartet. His urge to compose is understandable, as he grew up hearing Beethoven, Schumann, Chopin, Liszt and Debussy practised by his mother, as well as hearing Palestrina, Vittoria, *et al*, rehearsed and performed by his father's choir. His father had wished him to become a church organist as well as an academic musician and to succeed him at Cork cathedral, but Aloys had other plans, including concentration on research, composition and conducting. He had always been a resolute individual. It stood him in great stead. Back in Ireland he was appointed professor of Music at UCC, starting with two students; at his retirement from the chair in 1980, he had eighteen post graduate students and had produced in all well over three hundred graduates.

On his appointment in 1934 he had felt it essential both for the city and the Music department of the university to have a symphony orchestra. The best string players in the city, many of them professionals from the days of silent films, and wind players from the local army band were recruited and in March 1935 the first concert was given with an orchestra of sixty. This orchestra is now listed in the current *Guinness Book of Records* for 'durability'. This was also the year that saw the first performance of his *Trí hAmhráin*, a song cycle for tenor and orchestra, though with piano accompaniment only. It was composed under the pseudonym Muiris Ó Rónáin (Maurice Ronan). Being filled with enthusiasm for the Irish language and Irish poetry, he thought his German name inconsistent with his aims. His first work performed by professionals was the *Piano Quintet* given by the Kutcher String Quartet and the composer's mother at Clarence Hall, Cork in 1938. The same year saw his first broadcast: the orchestral version of his *Song Cycle* to Irish texts sung by Heddle Nash with the Radio Éireann Symphony Orchestra and the composer conducting, in Dublin's Gaiety Theatre. This is probably the first work of Fleischmann's maturity, although his *Suite for Piano* is impressive. Throughout his life his music was consistently tonal; he eschewed trends and reacted adversely to the prevailing fashions – firstly serialism; then the *Gebrauchsmusik* of Hindemith and the minimalism of today. He wrote some music in a diverting folk style and other pieces in a powerful but very personal style such as the superlative *Sinfonia Votiva*.

In common with Reginald Smith Brindle in England, Fleischmann had a staggering knowledge of music. He said that he had no favourite composers or works because he admired too many master works of every period. He was, however, deeply affected by performances of Mahler's *Song of the Earth*, Delius' *Sea Drift*, Berg's *Lyric Suite*, Dallapiccola's *Il Prigionero*, Bax's *Symphony no. 3*, Moeran's *Violin Concerto*, Messiaen's *O Sacrum Convivium*, Ligeti's *O Lux Aeterna* and Britten's *War Requiem*. As might be expected, he found little appeal in Gilbert and Sullivan, Bernstein, Steve Reich and John Cage or for that matter, Donizetti or early Verdi. To him Mozart is superb when inspired; Bach is 'as potent as the sea when properly played but dull when reproduced without expressive or emotional content in the manner of what Bax called "sewing machine music".' Beethoven he considered probably the greatest composer of all, Wagner a Titan of the theatre, Brahms he found always warm, majestic or serene. As for English music, Fleischmann believed that Britten brought 'fresh air and a new sense of wonder' into British music whereas he found Tippett seldom impressive. The works of Elliot Carter, Henze and Lutoslawski he considered intriguing.

He composed 'as he must'. His idiom changed over the years, having begun with a strong folk influence. He wrote for 'the public who are likely to be able to hear his work'. There is a waiting public beyond the Irish Sea and the Atlantic Ocean who should be introduced to the pleasing and aurally accessible music of this accomplished composer, who told me that he was not much affected by praise or criticism since the standard of criticism in his beloved Ireland was 'abysmally low'. He won first prize in a competition in 1953 with his *Four Fanfares* for An Tóstal and there are works commissioned for special occasions such as the overture *The Four Masters* (1944) for the tercentenary of the seventeenth-century Irish Franciscan historians; *Clare's Dragoons* (1945) for baritone, war pipes chorus and orchestra which was commissioned for the Thomas Davis and Young Ireland centenary and first performed in the Capitol Theatre, Dublin on 9 September 1945, with the war pipes played by Joan Denise Moriarty, founder of Irish National Ballet, who in her youth had distinguished herself at piping championships in Scotland and Ireland. This was the first time the war pipes had been used orchestrally, and the work was probably the composer's first public success; it was certainly one of the works that gave him most pleasure. After its first British performance with the BBC Chorus and London Philharmonic Orchestra under Maurice Miles on 27 June 1957, it was apparently suggested for inclusion in a forthcoming Promenade Concert, but rejected because the text was believed to be capable of giving offence to an English audience. The setting, to words by Thomas Davis, begins with an orchestral introduction which builds up into a magnificent march; there follows a 'battle section' in which the main theme is foreshadowed. Into this wonderful confusion comes the choir singing the first two verses. An interlude follows when the war pipes are heard off stage. The third verse is given to the baritone with the pipes echoing the refrain. The polyphonic fourth verse moves at a fast pace, while the last verse is begun by the soloist and continued by the chorus. For the final refrain the piper appears on the stage. The march ends the work in a vein of resplendent patriotism devoid of the pomposity that often disfigures attempts to give a boost to national pride. *Clare's Dragoons* is an impressive and absorbing work that should be enjoyed for its musical content alone. Its anti-English bias does not rule it out for English audiences, any more than one would rule out *La Traviata* because it involves prostitution, or Britten's *Death in Venice* because of its homosexuality, or Ligeti's *Le Grand Macabre* because of its use of strong language.

Fleischmann's *Poet in the Suburbs* was written for the twenty-first Cork International Choral Festival in 1974 and, incidentally, includes a brief aleatoric device to create a final climax. The work is imaginative and infectious. *Homage to Pádraig Pearse* (1979) was written to mark the centenary of the birth of the revolutionary leader executed in 1916. This, scored for mezzo-soprano, speaker and orchestra was first performed by Bernadette Greevy, Bill Golding and the RTE Symphony Orchestra under Colman Pearce at the Gaiety Theatre, Dublin on 18 November 1979. An impressive introduction leads to the first song which, like the fourth song, shows the dark way of life Pearse had chosen; the second song is both lyrical and strangely beautiful, whereas the third is playful but with allusions to the sinister secrets of his revolutionary activities. The narrator quotes Pearse on education denouncing the English education system in Ireland at that time as 'ruthless' and 'a murder machine'. 'Pearse on Nationality' speaks of the condition of the nation as spiritual and not material; it maintains that freedom is 'so splendid a thing' that it defies definition and that for centuries, it has been stifled in Ireland. The last song is the most moving poem of all recalling the ultimate sacrifice that many mothers made and were going to make. Whether this work would be acceptable to British audiences in the present climate is doubtful but, as music, as art, it is a moving piece full of interest, enhanced by the contrast of speech and vocal writing. The first three of Pearse's poems are in the Irish language, the last and the narration in English.

The Planting Stick for chorus, string quartet, flute and percussion was written for the Cork Ballet Company's performance at the International Choral and Folk Dance Festival of 1957 and is a good example of Fleischmann's folk style. *Song of the Provinces* dates from 1965 and is for audience, chorus and orchestra. The audience is required to sing a refrain three times, finally in a different time signature. The text tells of an Anglo-Saxon prince who visited Ireland in the seventh century and spoke well of all the provinces, extolling the virtues of each. Here is an eminently singable piece that captivates the listeners and causes them to feel something of the rich Irish heritage. *Tides* for mezzo soprano and orchestra (1974) successfully sets four poems by John Montague, displaying Fleischmann's expertise in vocal writing. But it is as an orchestrator that one has to admire his *Sinfonia Votiva* of 1977. It is in two movements, the first being an Introduction and Funeral March written in 1960 in memory of his friend, the writer and critic Edward Sheehy, while the second is a Bacchanal which follows the precedent of the funeral games of antiquity, and the merry-making which used to take place at Irish country wakes. The first movement was originally performed on 28 February 1961 in the Phoenix Hall, Dublin, with the composer conducting. He also premièred the complete work on 6 January 1978 at the Dublin Festival of Twentieth Century Music. The Introduction poignantly portrays the reaction and shock on first hearing of the death of a close friend; the frenzy of grief and the numbness of desolation. The Funeral March is deeply felt and moves to a prolonged climax. A trio follows in a nostalgic vein recalling precious memories. A stentorian trombone returns to harsh reality and the march is then resumed. The coda is both ominous and poignant and resolves into final quiescence. The Bacchanal begins with a percussion cadenza and conveys a sense of exhilaration; there is an amusing duet between two drunken revellers represented by the double bassoon and tuba. A reflective passage precedes the forceful recapitulation of the carousal. This is a powerful work, realistic and wholly convincing; it is all the more impressive because, while the anguish is clearly evident, it does not wallow; it is a work devoid of sentimentality.

How do we explain the fact that Fleischmann's music is largely unknown outside Ireland? Was he merely a very clever academic to be respected and remembered exclusively in Ireland? Are we to believe that his music would only be admired by the Irish? No, such a response is surely predicated on the implicit premise that the world still thinks of Ireland as a land of traditional music and rebel songs and will not accept that she is producing composers of real calibre. Nowhere is this more apparent than in the case of Aloys Fleischmann.

Aloys Fleischmann died on 21 July 1992. He will be remembered for all his many qualities. He loved the countryside and was quite an expert on birdsong. He loved to listen to silence and also the sea. Like Humphrey Searle, he had a wonderful capacity for friendship. He enjoyed life and loved dancing, even when he was eighty years old. On the day of his funeral in Cork Cathedral, the rain poured in torrents. It seemed to aptly typify universal sorrow at the loss of a fine musician and a truly great man.

PHILIP GRAYDON (DUBLIN), Music Graduate of Maynooth
Dr Ita Beausang wrote after Aloys Fleischmann's death in 1992 that he 'presided like a colossus over the Irish musical landscape'.[1] Fleischmann, along with fellow internationalists Frederick May (1911–1985) and Brian Boydell (1917–), comprised the vanguard in twentieth century Irish composition in the 1930s and 1940s who sought to evade the 'folk-music trap', epitomised by the music of C. V. Stanford (1852–1924), Hamilton Harty (1879–1941) and J. F. Larchet (1884–1967).[2] Instead, they sought to embrace the international Esperanto of modern music while largely resisting 'kow-towing' to the Irish Ireland influenced establishment in producing uninspired Irish traditional arrangements or derivatives of such music.

Fleischmann's pluralist views with regard to matters musical, which he expounded through the pages of Irish periodical literature from the 1930s to the 1950s, were symptomatic of an education divided between Cork and Munich.[3] However, initially his line was considerably softer than those of his compatriots; commenting on the position of music in Ireland in 1935, he wrote:

> We have on the one hand a tradition in folk-music, on the other hand a half developed art-music which is for the most part alien .... What we need is a Gaelic art-music which will embody all the technique that contemporary music can boast and ... be rooted in the folk-music spirit ....[4]

Fleischmann's youthful ardour for a 'Gaelic art-music' was, however, quelled by the late 1940s as his compositional *modus operandi* became increasingly dichotomous in nature. Although one is inclined to agree with Joseph J. Ryan's view that Fleischmann's more populist works 'tended to favour ... nationalist expression [and] had the effect of further moving [him] from outspoken criticism of what he hitherto considered the ascendancy of insular musical ideas and 'the upholders of traditionalism to a more median view ...' it is perhaps Axel Klein who posits a more convincing argument.[5] Aligning Fleischmann with other 'eclectics' such as A. J. Potter (1918–1980), Gerard Victory (1921–1995) and Seán Ó Riada (1931–1971), Klein asserts that the above are 'predestined to misinterpretation and misunderstanding by anybody hearing a single piece.' In Fleischmann's case, this was due to the fact that 'throughout his life he wrote a very understandable music, trying unsuccessfully to bridge the gap between the taste of the well-meaning friend of "light" classical music and that of the more discerning listener.'[6] It is in this sense that he came to 'don' two 'hats'; a fairly diatonic, populist style exemplified in orchestral works (with or without audience participation) that fulfilled commissions for public events, and were indicated by titles with 'Irish' connections, was counter-balanced by a more individual, detached and abstract voice found in the smaller-scale works which espoused modernism and cognisance of contemporary technique.

It is with acknowledgement of this dichotomy that one must approach his music. At the outset of his career, being of the opinion that his German surname was unsuitable to his nationalist aspirations, Fleischmann adopted an Irish pseudonym (Muiris Ó Rónáin) for his first major (similarly spirited) work the *Piano Suite* (Gaelicised as *Sreath de Phiano*) of 1933. Fleischmann persuaded its publisher, Chester, to print the performance directions in Irish, in addition to the conventional Italian. This rather strange arrangement baffled some in the music world, as he recalls:

> I remember on one occasion the composer E. J. Moeran ... said that English publishers had gone 'stark raving mad' – that ... Chester's [had published] a piece of music with Irish titles and directions. He said: 'How on earth could any publisher dream of producing something in the Irish language that nobody could understand?' He was so cross that I didn't like to betray the fact that it was I who was the culprit!'[7]

Axel Klein's comment in regard to the rhythm of the work as a whole, that 'one feels the jig sooner that one hears it', underlines the subtle influence of the folk-music style pursued at that time by his British contemporaries (Vaughan Williams, in particular, and his personal friends, Bax and Moeran) which informed Fleischmann's output for some years afterwards.[8] But it was the mythology, history and literature of Ireland that resonated more throughout his corpus; 'it seemed vital', he wrote, 'to delve into the Hidden Ireland,[9] and out of the heroic tales and romances to create an idiom which would express in music some of the essence of this rich untapped literary tradition.'

Fleischmann's wish in prose to 'tap into the literary tradition'[10] of 'the Hidden Ireland' was exemplified in music in 1937. While a certain amount of his early works expressed a conscious patriotism, they were 'never offensive but of a vigorous innocence which is peculiarly appealing.'[11] It is in this sense that one can consider the composer's *Trí hAmhráin* – (Three Songs) of 1937 on texts by Mícheál Ó Murchú, scored for high voice and orchestra, which allude both in sentiment and style to Irish traditional music.

Another of Fleischmann's early works to reflect the 'Irish' note was the *Piano Quintet* of 1938. However, the dropping of the Gaelic pseudonym for his first Irish premiere 'as himself', and the adoption of a more abstract form, also signified an increased catholicity of styles and influences in its make-up. As Joseph J. Ryan comments, the work is 'eclectic with a range of echoes from Stanford to Delius ...', while by complete contrast, Fleischmann's later 'modernist' works are fore-shadowed in the astringent harmony and fragmentary texture also found in the same movement.[12]

As Ryan posits, '[Fleischmann's] goal was ever to forge the uni-versal without repudiating the particular.'[13] This innate facet of his musical personality was also noted by Frederick May in an article in 1949. In discussing the nationalistic *Clare's Dragoons* (1944), he wrote:

> ... In this work as in the three Irish songs [*Trí hAmhráin*], Fleischmann has managed to do something entirely original; ... he has given us in music a symbol of what Ireland, her people, her history ... mean to each one of us. He has effected in sound a crystallisation and intensification of a feeling common to all Irishmen, and in so doing he has secured for himself an honoured and a permanent place in the musical history of his country.[14]

As his career progressed, his modernist 'hat' was increasingly worn; his elegant *Lament for Elizabeth MacDermott Roe* for string orchestra, 1946 (extracted from the four-movement *Humours of Carolan* (1941) and published by An Gúm, a government agency that circulated Irish music, especially folk-song), represents a synthesis between the 'Irish' modal style and the new, more cosmopolitan-inclined compositional disposition of his later works. One of the first clear examples of this lat-ter departure was the song-cycle *The Fountain of Magic* of the same year (based on Irish poems translated by Frank O'Connor) which in-cluded bitonal elements (i.e., the simultaneous use of two keys) and the use of varying metre while maintaining a semblance of traditional thematic development by use of short melodic and rhythmic units.[15] The composer's *Introduction and Funeral March* (1960), later appended by a third movement ('Bacchanal') and in this form renamed *Sinfonia Votiva* (1977), displayed a more serious, contemplative side of his com-positional character that contrasted with the many slight works for both professional and non-professional ensembles of the 1950s and 1960s such as *Song of the Provinces* (1965).

While the 1970s saw works such as *Mass for Peace* (1977) and *Omás don Phiarsach* (1979), it was exemplified by works such as *Cornucopia* for horn and piano, commissioned for the Dublin Festival of Twentieth Century Music in 1970. Presented in a version for orchestra a year later, the erudite wit underlying the broad interpretation of the work's title results in solo-writing of melodic and inventive fecundity befitting of the 'horn of plenty' in its title.

A further commission for the above-mentioned Festival was *Tides* (1973) a song-cycle for mezzo-soprano and piano that, like *Cornucopia*, was adapted for orchestra a year later but with the addition of a harpsichord. The first setting of four, 'King and Queen', portrays man as a ritual image; the use of harpsichord in this movement bespoke telling acknowledgement of its revival in twentieth-century music while lending a new and somewhat eerie quality to the orchestral colour.

Fleischmann's successful forays into ballet music in his collaboration with impresario Joan Denise Moriarty *(An Cóitín Dearg* [The Red Petticoat] and *Macha Ruadh* [Red Macha] of 1950 and 1955, respectively,) were crowned in 1981 by *The Táin* written for the Irish Ballet Company.[16] The composer once commented that he considered this work to be his most challenging and surprisingly – to him – most successful and popular orchestral composition: interpreting a mythological theme in terms of contemporary music, adding 'yet we filled the Gaiety with it for a week!'[17]

The broad wit that circumscribed the above-mentioned *Cornucopia* of the early 1970s was brought to the fore in Fleischmann's compositional swan-song, *Games*. Composed in 1990 (two years before his death), the piece was based on six poems by Serbo-Croat poet Vasco Popa translated by Anne Pennington, and was scored for choir, harp and percussion. Despite Fleischmann being an octogenarian at this stage, it astonished the audience at its premiere in Cork with, as Sarah M. Burn details, its 'virtuosity, vigour and vehemence.'[18]

In regard to Fleischmann's multifarious musical activities in general, one could contend that his compositional legacy would have been larger had he been able to focus his energies more pointedly; 'that he did not is due to his understanding of the larger obligation his generation had to create the circumstances in which modern Irish music could flourish'.[19] As de Barra adds: 'Aloys Fleischmann was keenly aware of his position as one of the first group of native composers to live and work in Ireland': '... how to be Irish in a larger European context [was] a question that lost none of its urgency' for him.[20]

CECIL HURWITZ (CORK), *Founder of the Cork PEACE Movement*
I came in contact with Professor Fleischmann in 1976. I had founded the Peace Movement in Cork in 1973, and in 1975 an association was founded in Dublin, called the Peace Week Association.

Each peace movement founded was invited to dedicate a week to Peace activities. Each peace movement was invited to prepare its own programme. My peace movement was called PEACE (Prayer Enterprise and Christian Effort). I devised a programme for Cork Peace Week. The week began with a concelebrated Mass for peace and reconciliation in Ireland and concluded with an ecumenical peace service.

I contacted the Professor and asked him if he would compose a Mass for peace. He was full of enthusiasm and he told me that he would be delighted to do so. Peace Week takes place annually in the month of March. The Professor composed the Mass, which was celebrated in St Francis' Church, Liberty Street, Cork in March 1976. He brought into the church the Cork Symphony Orchestra, and he had a choir composed of pupils from four primary schools in the city and county. The Mass was very beautiful indeed.

The Professor laid down the ground rules. He suggested that each composer's Mass should be performed for three years. A lot of work goes into the composition, and the congregation would need to be exposed to the new Mass more than one time. He also told me that every three years a different composer should be invited. He felt it would be a great challenge to the person who would compose the Mass.

Eight composers have written Masses for us: after the Professor it was Mícheál Ó Ceallacháin, then Declan Townsend, the late John Murphy (of the Cork School of Music), Angel Climent, David O'Sullivan and John Gibson. In March 2000 Marion Ingoldsby concluded her three years. Pat Killeen and Maria Judge have agreed to write the next two Peace Masses. Composing the Mass is a huge undertaking, and there is no financial reward.

The Professor, until his death, came to hear all the composers who had their Mass performed and he congratulated each one. On one occasion he said to me that the Peace Mass is one of the greatest liturgical occasions held annually in Cork.

COLIN SCOTT-SUTHERLAND (CRAIL, FIFE), Critic and Writer, Biographer of Bax. This is his review of the Fleischmann Piano Quintet CD Played by Hugh Tinney and the Vanbrugh Quartet

Aloys Fleischmann's *Piano Quintet* was written in 1938 and first performed by the Kutcher Quartet with Fleischmann's mother Tilly (a pupil of Stavenhagen) as pianist. The *Quintet* contains some powerful piano writing, here handled with magisterial assurance by the Irish-born pianist Hugh Tinney. The angular octave leaps of the opening quickly develop into a series of sectional mood-variations, the quasi-pastoral material hinting at things Irish, yet distilled through classical origins, and treated with considerable emotive power.

A gentle lyrical introduction on viola to the *Andante Tranquillo* second movement is not however so peaceful as it at first appears. There is a dark undercurrent of nostalgia that recalls, in the piano figuration, the mood of such pieces as John Ireland's second *Trio*, with its overtones of war – and develops into a restlessly protesting impetuoso central passage. The sombre mood returns and the movement ends in a kind of quiet resignation. In complete contrast the brief scherzo opens briskly in a folk-like mood. There is lots of melodic interest – a quasi-Irish violin melody, with much Delian dotted triple rhythm. The movement gradually slows into the final *Allegro molto* into which it bursts without a break. This has a driving tarantella-like rhythm (also heard in the first movement) and here again the opening octave figure of the work is prominent. A slower but dramatic central section leads to a resumption of the opening rhythm, and a broad modal theme in keyboard octaves ends the work.[21]

JAMES WILSON (DUBLIN), Composer

Thirty-something years ago, in conversation with the conductor Boyd Neel, I deplored the necessity that a composer has to extol his own work in order to encourage performances. Boyd looked at me and said: 'If you feel like that, then you're doing the wrong job'. I think that Aloys shared my difficulty; indeed he was far too reluctant to advertise his own gifts. Over the years I have had few opportunities to hear what he wrote. I remember the premiere of his witty *Cornucopia* for horn and piano at the Dublin Festival of Twentieth Century Music in 1970, and the occasion, many years later, when Aloys gave an illustrated talk on his work for the Ennis IMRO Composition Summer School. But he never encouraged discussion of his work.

Retiring as he was concerning himself, Aloys did a great deal to encourage other composers, myself included. His analyses of specially-commissioned works at the Cork Choral Festival were acute. And Aloys had the fairly uncommon attribute of being a gentleman. We first met one evening at the Gate Theatre about forty years ago. I was completely unknown as a composer, but Aloys treated me with the consideration that he would have given to one of the world's great musicians. At that time it seemed to me that the health of music in Ireland depended on three men, composers/organisers one and all: Aloys Fleischmann, Brian Boydell and Havelock Nelson.

Other people are better qualified than I am to speak of Aloys' work as a university professor and as begetter of the Cork International Choral Festival, where we in the audience had the chance to hear works specially commissioned from major composers. It is as a composer that Aloys most concerns me: through his music, one knows the man. I said that *Cornucopia* is a witty work. 'Witty' is something more than simply humorous; it implies an acute and sprightly mind at work. Every composition by Aloys that I have heard is excellently crafted. Listening recently to his *Piano Quintet* I noted the care given to the part for the viola; an instrument too often treated as a mere filler-in of middle parts.

This *Quintet* was the work of a young man; written in 1938, a lyrical piece, it inhabits the sound-world of Vaughan Williams and Rubbra. It has an energetic feel to it that occasionally results in writing that I find over-thick. A French composer would have written a more transparent score. In the settings of poems by John Montague, *Tides*, of 1973, the vocal line has the angularity that could be found in post-romantic composers of the European mainland.

To run a university Music department and an international choral Festival means a vast work-load. Had he been able to concentrate entirely on composition, I think that Aloys could have been a major composer. But then: many interested parties – composers, performers, students, listeners – would have been the poorer.

AXEL KLEIN (BONN), *Musicologist, Music Graduate of the University of Hildesheim/Germany*
Aloys Fleischmann: An Inspiration
I had only two meetings with Aloys Fleischmann, besides some correspondence, but these left lasting impressions on me and have influenced my work in a profound way. The second was during the Cork Choral Festival in March 1988. The first and most memorable one was on 8 November 1987 in Dublin, when the Project Arts Centre had been putting on a weekend of contemporary Irish music. During a late afternoon recital of song compositions by the Irish-American mezzo soprano Aylish Kerrigan and the composer and pianist Seóirse Bodley I heard the song cycle *The Fountain of Magic*, written by Aloys Fleischmann in 1945. In the small audience I noticed one elderly man sitting a little apart from the others, who sat probably as they had come in, in groups of three to five. I had never seen a photograph of him, yet I thought: 'This could be Aloys Fleischmann' and sure enough it was, as I discovered when I approached him after the recital.

I well remember my intense nervousness when I introduced myself as a music student from Germany who had just arrived two months previously and was about to spend a year at Trinity College Dublin. After all, before me stood the first living person I had ever met with an entry in the *New Grove Dictionary of Music and Musicians*! And he was not at all as larger than life as I had feared; quite the contrary:

I was overwhelmed by the kindness and warmth with which he welcomed me in Ireland and by the interest which he showed towards this German student with an interest in Irish (classical) music. Indeed his interest was such that he invited me to dinner straight away to a nearby restaurant in Dame Street and this was the beginning of a long involvement with Irish music which, I am sure, will last the rest of my life.

Our conversation lasted for about two and a half hours, half of which was in English and half in German. Up to then I had had little knowledge of Irish musical history, apart from what I had read in the *New Grove*, and knew less still about the various complications that prevented Irish music from making an impact on international musical life, to say nothing of the difficulties facing it in Ireland. We talked about music past and present, of composers and conditions, about Brian Boydell, Seán Ó Riada, Seóirse Bodley, about conservativism and modernism, traditional music and art music, differences between Ireland and Germany and about the long cultural conflict with England. This conversation with an experienced man of 77 years of age, who for decades had been very much an active part of what I was about to unfold, opened my eyes to the problems as well as to the possibilities of Irish music. Afterwards I was left with a conflicting feeling between despair and encouragement: on the one hand I now had an idea of what lay before me – a high and steep mountain with hardly a path to walk on – and on the other hand I was so certain that I would attempt the task.

Fleischmann put it to me clearly that Irish music needed documentation and an aesthetic assessment which could best be done by someone from outside. I knew what he meant. My year in Ireland (the academic year 1987–8) left me with the impression of a rich musical life, full of attractive and worthwhile music to be played and heard but, strangely enough, outside its own shores virtually nothing was known about it. If there had been two Aloys Fleischmanns, the other would surely have taken on the role of an international propagandist for the Irish cause; but he was the one and only Fleischmann concentrated on Cork and on Ireland, and he could not have done more. As yet the books on the history of Irish music were so few that one could count them on the fingers of one hand and between their publication lay many years. There was nothing on the music of the twentieth century, and this some thirteen years from its end! There were no recordings available, almost no published music. And I found it most shocking that some of my fellow students did not know what I meant when I asked about Irish composers. Things have changed in the meantime, thank God.

My book *Die Musik Irlands im 20. Jahrhundert* (1996) is a mixture of original research and an evaluation of existing material. Though it is as yet only available in German, I hope that it fills a gap in the documentation of Irish music and that it may provide some stimulus for others. That it was only completed when Fleischmann was four years dead makes me very sad, since it was he who encouraged its undertaking. Without his active interest and support and his positive example as someone who achieved so much against all odds, this study would not have been written.

Much has been said about Fleischmann the organiser, the professor, the educator, the musicologist, the man, and I am not going to add any more to this. What I feel is needed is a careful and thorough comment on his music. I believe that Fleischmann wished to be remembered primarily as a composer. In most of our correspondence after I had returned to Germany we exchanged views on compositions, *his* compositions. He wrote me a letter dated 24 December 1990, the first Christmas Eve after the death of his wife. I had sent him some questions, mainly on his music, in the course of the research for my book and other later writings, such as an article on him for the new edition of the German encyclopaedia *Die Musik in Geschichte und Gegenwart* (MGG). I think that in this special situation – Christmas and 'alone' among his children – he had a sense of finiteness and of looking back on his work rather than looking forward to what was to come. He replied: 'If you should be good enough to include me in an article, the works I would prefer to be judged by are the *Sinfonia Votiva, Poet in the Suburbs, Games* and the *Five Dances from The Táin*.'

I duly listened to this music and to many more of his compositions afterwards. I bought scores from the Contemporary Music Centre and some original published scores at the office of An Gúm, which they still sold for the designated price of the 1940s, now only a few pence. I copied tapes from radio broadcasts and directly from RTE. At first I could not make up my mind. I understood some of it (or believed so, I should say); I did not know what to make of other works. It took me some more experience to understand that what I had before me was a conscious dichotomy on the part of the composer between different approaches to composition. Now I knew why polite people rather said nothing about Fleischmann's music before having to say something unfavourable. They should have listened to other pieces!

I have argued elsewhere that throughout his creative life Aloys Fleischmann wrote two kinds of music.[22] One kind is that in which he stretched out his hand to those with little knowledge of the developments in recent musical history and who were to be catered for with well-made orchestral music as the better alternative to cheap musical entertainment or pop music of all kinds. This group of works includes his famous orchestral pieces with audience participation such as *Clonmacnoise* (1986) as well as some of the ballet music or choral music such as the *Song of the Provinces* (1963). There is a clear element of education in this music and he would not have written it had he been living in a central European metropolis.

The other component of his output is directed towards the more discerning listener with experience of international art music of the twentieth century. Many of these works are small-scale chamber music pieces or advanced choral music. Interestingly, two of the pieces he wanted to be remembered by are works written for the Seminar on Contemporary Choral Music: *Poet in the Suburbs* (1973) and *Games* (1990), at which he knew there would be a critical audience. The other two are orchestral: the *Sinfonia Votiva* (1977, incorporating the *Introduction and Funeral March*, 1960) and the *Five Dances from The Táin* (1982), a suite from the music to his last ballet, *The Táin* (1981). Significantly, none of the first type of work is mentioned among those he wished to be remembered for.

In addition, there is a gradual moving away from the influence of traditional music since the mid-1940s. This had been noticeable in his early success, the *Suite for Piano* (1933), published in London and recorded for LP by Charles Lynch in 1971. Although it is an original composition without quotations from actual folk music, Fleischmann uses typical melodic lines from traditional song and dance rhythms such as a jig in the fifth movement. Two more early Fleischmann pieces have recently been discovered by the recording media: the *Piano Quintet* (1938, CD of 1996 on Marco Polo 8.223888) and the *Lament for Elizabeth MacDermott Roe*, a separately published part of *The Humours of Carolan* suite for string orchestra (1941, CD of 1997 by Black Box Music BBM 1003). These are more mature works than the *Piano Suite* and the folk music influence is very subtle. It peeps through some melodic lines and a harmonic approach based on modal scales. For European ears the traditional aspect goes almost completely unnoticed – it is only with the knowledge of his Irish background that one suddenly discovers such traits. This at least was my experience.

In fact *The Fountain of Magic* of 1945, the piece I heard at that 1987 recital mentioned above, is among the earliest in his more European style. I included it in the analytical part of my 1996 study of Irish music. The piece, which I prefer in its orchestral version, makes a clear departure from a unified tonality. Though the first movement, *Winter*, is oriented towards B minor, Fleischmann uses many notes foreign to the scale. Some dissonant sounds originate from the simultaneous clash of two unrelated consonant chords, such as D sharp minor in contrast to a fourth chord based on C and G. There are many changes in the bar structure and the whole piece lacks conventional melodies. Though he avoids the sonata form, unity is achieved by the recurrence of small elements such as chromatically progressing chordal passages, descending scales ending on E flat and pitch repetitions using a semi quaver triplet with ensuing minim. These elements are to be found throughout the whole piece, but most often in the first movements.

There is not the space to illustrate my argument with many examples. But those who find contemporary modern elements lacking in Fleischmann's music, and who consider his role as composer but a minor facet of his life, should perhaps listen more closely to some chamber and small-scale choral music. In particular I would like to single out the works Fleischmann mentioned himself as well as *The Fountain of Magic* and *Tides* (1973). I am aware that there are works in his oeuvre with structural deficiencies – he sometimes has a tendency to lose his good ideas in the course of a longer work, some climaxes in orchestral music seem exaggerated and out of control. But there is surely scarcely a composer in the world without some individual weakness which one could make much of. At his best, Fleischmann's early folk-influenced oeuvre is on a par with that of his contemporary British counterparts and predecessors such as Bax, Delius or Bliss. In his more advanced later music he develops an individual voice in the European chorus of composers with the message that experiments are allowed in melody, harmony and rhythm but less so in form or instrumentation. This is a perfectly valid aesthetic point of view which deserves our highest respect.

JOSEPH RYAN (DUBLIN), Conductor of the No. 1 Army Band
It is indisputably early to attempt a full appraisal of the work of one who passed away within the decade but the fact that Aloys Fleischmann's life spanned the twentieth century and that he would have celebrated his ninetieth birthday in the opening months of the new millennium tempt one to at least some initial consideration of his singular contribution to the art of music in Ireland. Such an assessment is especially warranted as Fleischmann is a seminal figure in moving the nation to address its relationship with music. In conjunction with his academic colleague, John Larchet, Professor of Music in University College Dublin, Fleischmann set about the difficult task of reconciling the glaring discrepancy between Ireland's redoubtable musical reputation and its anaemic practice. Toward this end, he did much to champion the art, to popularise it, and to focus attention on the nature of music in a newly independent entity. It can be predicted that in

time, when distance affords more balance, he will come to be admired as a towering presence not so much for his original creativity as for his influence on the structure of music in this country.

Early evaluation means that objectivity is naturally clouded by personal recollection. In ways this is no bad thing. I cannot claim to have had long personal acquaintance having come to know him only in the last two decades of his life when he was already an established figure. It is indicative of his influence that I first came to know him personally through his involvement with the Cork International Choral and Folk Dance Festival. This was a characteristic initiative inaugurated in 1954 and it remains one of his most enduring legacies. It was characteristic in that it provided a focus for the most democratic and accessible form of music making: choral music. It drew together choirs from throughout Ireland and in doing so afforded them opportunity to hear some of the finest international exponents from various traditions. Its value as an educational experience and in fostering music in general would be hard to overstate. For all the charm and urbanity, Fleischmann had the political skill and innate perseverance necessary to bring such a project to fruition. One of my experiences of his determination concerns the Band of the Southern Command, the accomplished and permanent military band garrisoned in Collins Barracks, Cork that served over decades incidentally to provide a source of reed, brass, and percussion players for many of Fleischmann's ventures. I can recall one occasion when tasked, as visiting conductor of that band, to provide an opening recital for the Choral Festival in the City Hall; this was the subject of a late telephone call from the professor on the afternoon of the performance. Having warmly welcomed me to Cork and praised my willingness to undertake such a venture at short notice, he proceeded to request that I write a fanfare to open the evening. Such were his persuasive powers that not only did he get his fanfare but it was furnished in, what was for brass, the ungodly key of B major to suit the choral item that was to follow. Not for the first time had I the impression of encountering a steel fist within a velvet glove and, moreover, ultimately enjoying the experience.

As a senior academic with keen interest in Irish musicology he was generous and ever willing to talk about aspects of music in Ireland. Over the course of many conversations, I came to admire his enthusiasm and power of recall. While it is gratifying to know that he completed his *Sources of Irish Traditional Music*, it was undoubtedly a source of great frustration that he had not the time or health in his final years to complete other projects on which he was working.[23]

Notwithstanding what was stated at the opening of this article, it can be anticipated that in moving toward some interim assessment,

Fleischmann's contribution will come to be evaluated under three distinct headings: as a teacher, in the broadest sense; as a wily advocate with honed political skills; and as a creative artist with an individual voice. Some may balk at such categorisation or would wish to have his role as performer included especially for his long service as conductor with the Cork Symphony Orchestra. However, propagation and discrimination are uneasy partners; in his article on Fleischmann's ballet music, Séamas de Barra perceptively addresses the question of Fleischmann's performance standards:

> If ... he sometimes appeared vulnerable to the charge of being insufficiently discriminating it is because for him and for his committed contemporaries, in attempting to overcome the country's pervasive cultural inertia, any enterprise, no matter how tentative, was clearly better than nothing.[24]

Happenstance is a feature of life; and by its nature it does not readily conform to individual aspiration. In one of its manifestations, timing, Fleischmann might have considered himself especially fortunate to have had such a musical pedigree and to have returned from foreign study a large fish in a small pool to assume the chair of Music in University College Cork at the remarkable young age of 24. He repaid that trust with a lifetime of energetic application as both teacher and advocate. He popularised the art and saw it as his role to make music accessible; the balance between proselytisation and the maintenance of standards must have been an abiding pressure for him. In this respect his timing was not good; as one of the most voluble champions for music, much of the work necessary to install the foundation for a musical life fell directly on to his shoulders. It was not a task he shirked, nor even a thankless task; however, such concentration leaves little time for serious creativity and Fleischmann, like so many of his contemporaries, was, as a result, only an occasional composer. In this sense his timing was unfortunate: the very aspect for which he would most like to be remembered is the one that suffered due to the circumstances of the age. It could validly be argued that had he been possessed of an indubitably determined creative spirit he would have forsaken all other considerations in order to follow that star. Perhaps this is the *experimentum crucis* of true originality. The music of the occasional composer tends not to enjoy the longevity that is awarded with canonic status.

Fleischmann's background facilitated his adoption of a cosmopolitan stand regarding creativity. This minority view was trenchantly defended in numerous articles notably in the 1930s. It is interesting how the dominant musical issue of the time echoes the contemporary protectionist economic debate. In periodicals such as *Ireland Today*, Fleischmann argued against an insular view of Irish music contending that a newly independent people should demonstrate a confidence sufficient to take a rightful place in the broader European aesthetic. In practical terms Fleischmann was firmly against young composers becoming indentured to the concept of too obvious an 'Irishness', to what Bax called 'writing Irishly'.[25] In an early article Fleischmann asserted that it was far too easy

> to develop into an Irish composer by taking a few Irish airs and dressing them up in the conventional way, just as it is easy to pass off on stage as an Irish man by donning the kilt or the bawneen and speaking with a strong Kerry accent. How much more difficult it is to be Irish, intrinsically and organically, without any parade of the exterior trappings.[26]

Such opinion was not undisputed and led to open rancorous debate notably with Éamonn Ó Gallchobhair, who was to the fore amongst those who believed in the necessity to fashion a distinctive Irish style of music that relied on indigenous sources and that owed nothing to its European neighbours.

It is interesting to note how circumstance altered Fleischmann's creative perspective. This early trenchant anti-parochialism was tempered in later years following the success of works written with undeniably nationalist inspiration. It could thus be said that his prose writings and his early compositions were not consistent. His early works written under the pseudonym Muiris Ó Rónáin are quite consciously Irish in flavour. *Trí hAmhráin* (Three Songs) for tenor and orchestra with assorted Gaelic texts from Carolan and Ó Murchú is dedicated to Carl Hardebeck, an energetic collector and a true disciple of the insular focus. The first of the songs 'Marbhna Eoghain Ruaidh Uí Néill' (Lament for Owen Roe O'Neill) presages an abiding interest in the blind itinerant harper Carolan (1670–1738). Here Fleischmann employs a variation of Carolan's Gaelic text, an eight-line poem divided into two quatrains.[27] Fleischmann's penchant for mild dissonance with characteristic melodic decoration is evident through the set, the latter noticeably in the accompanying triplet figure in the second of the songs, 'Biogadh'. Another composition written under this pseudonym was the *Suite for Piano* (1933) which was published by Chester Music in 1935. The opening has characteristic drone fifths and fourths while the gentle second movement reveals Fleischmann's fondness for a good tune.

In 1938 Fleischmann again employed piano but on this occasion as the core of a much more ambitious and assured work. The *Piano Quintet* exudes a classical poise and confident conservatism. It was first given in April of 1939 in Cork by the Kutcher String Quartet with the composer's mother Tilly, a formidable and influential figure in her own right, on pianoforte. As with other of his early works, this is eclectic with a range of echoes from Stanford to Delius; this diverse approach is also evident in the variety of compositional device employed in the course of the piece. Conversational throughout, it is structured in four movements with a gentle Allegretto opening with initial octave leaps in first violin leading simply from dominant to tonic of the home *a* minor tonality. This closes securely after 34 bars on an open *a* chord and leads from there to a succession of moods, from a gentle Andante with a lyrical violin melody to a thickly layered central Impetuoso that again presents the unifying octave leaps. The Allegro scherzando shifts for contrast to a tonal centre of *D* and its rhythmic character is fashioned from the contrasting shifts of metre from three to two. The ensuing Allegretto is both playful and liquid with simple accompaniment. The final Allegro Molto introduces a theme in viola that owes much to the opening of the work. The sectional outlook is equally apparent here in the succession of fugato, lyrical melody of Irish character, and return to opening theme set high in first violin. The turn to the major mode is but momentary before the quintet concludes in the home minor.

Fleischmann's penchant for shifting harmonies by semitones while apparent is always within a tonal context that contrasts with, for instance, the approach of Frederick May in his fine *String Quartet* in c minor (1936). The variation principal employed gives rise to a sectional feel with continuing shifts in tempo and metre and yet the economic approach to thematic material and central axis of a minor ensures the unity of the work. While the work is not indentured to a specifically Irish programme, the linear writing and character of the initial variations invoke a distinctive spirit of place far more readily than does the May quartet. This can be heard in the first movement in the Quasi recitativo section where viola and cello combine to ruminate in an unmistakably Irish accent over held dissonance in the piano. In this respect Fleischmann's approach is at some philosophical remove from that of May: in more willingly turning inward with a linear design that is unmistakably Irish, he proposes consciously to represent the Irish condition; his goal was ever to forge the universal without repudiating the particular.[28]

The Humours of Carolan written in 1941 for string orchestra achieved sufficient acclaim to warrant the government agency, An Gúm, publishing the slow movement 'Elizabeth MacDermott Roe' in 1952. There was at this time a particular concentration on works for strings by Irish composers; one thinks of Arthur Duff in this regard, and the fashion reflects the strength of orchestral resources available at that time. Fleischmann's threnody is based on Carolan's air dedicated originally

317

to the eponymous daughter of Henry and Anne MacDermott Roe of Alderford in County Roscommon, being an influential family who were principal patrons to the harper. The free extension of the melody and pungent accompaniment provided by Fleischmann are character- istic of his method of reconciling a rich indigenous tradition within the broader European practice of art music.

A contemporaneous work within the same mode was *Clare's Dragoons* commissioned by the then Radio Éireann for the Thomas Davis and Young Ireland Centenary Concert to be given in the Capital Theatre Dublin on 9 September 1945. It is dedicated to Donal O'Sulli- van, who had devoted so much of his life to folksong collection and who, incidentally, provides the original air of Carolan's 'Elizabeth Mac- Dermott Roe' as number 83 in his two-volume work on the Irish harp- er.[29] *Clare's Dragoons* was the largest work to that date undertaken by Fleischmann and it betrays the same stylistic discrepancy with his ear- liest creative essays. This is a colourful setting of the five-stanza poem by the Irish nationalist apostle, Davis, and features baritone solo, cho- rus, orchestra, and ultimately a set of war pipes. Despite his earlier re- pudiation of direct folksong quotation, Fleischmann here skilfully inter- twines the central air throughout the protracted text. There is some- thing of the potboiler about this piece and its warm reception is whol- ly understandable. The introduction toward the closing climax of war pipes marching forward from the rear of the hall has a dramatic impact that is idiosyncratic and yet one that seems at odds with the gentle nature of its creator; it is just such a contrast that makes Fleischmann such an interesting study.

As with others whom circumstance dictated that the creative muse could only infrequently be indulged, Fleischmann's works are often a response to a commission for an occasion. It is from just such utilitarian beginnings that much of Fleischmann's finest work emerges. Notwithstanding the assignation as an occasional composer, and in- deed perhaps partly because of that role, he was not averse to rework- ing earlier material. Such an example is heard in his *Mass for Peace* (1977) which is essentially a recasting of an earlier Mass written for children's choirs in 1972. The later work was inspired by the estab- lishment of an organisation for peace on the island of Ireland that grew from the violence in Northern Ireland early in the 1970s. Fleisch- mann was the first in a series of composers commissioned to write a mass and he responded with a free and accessible interpretation of the form. He employs the ordinary of the mass with the exception of the credo and adds opening antiphon, responsorial psalm, and a commu- nion hymn 'As runs the thirsting deer'. This latter hymn is employed in both masses and is just one example of the motivic and stylistic relationship between the two works.

A similar accessible approach is evident in the short *Festival Song* (1978), a commission for mixed choir and orchestra for Fleischmann's beloved Cork International Choral and Folk Dance Festival. The text is supplied by John Montague, who had earlier furnished the four poems for the song cycle *Tides* (1973). The *Festival Song* is a bright joyful piece with orchestral fanfares leading to unison declamation of greeting for overseas visitors that opens to a fuller setting on the words 'Cecila and her harmonics'. This effective piece ends peacefully.

Fleischmann's abiding interest in ballet and his long collaboration with Joan Denise Moriarty, founder of Irish National Ballet, marks the finest example of a genre inspired by the occasion. This fruitful alliance grew from the first performances of *Clare's Dragoons* where the war pipes were played by Moriarty.[30] It is again telling how many of his dance inspired compositions are founded on Irish sources.

Here then is the record of a gifted man who experienced early success and dedicated himself to the promotion of his art. In doing so consistently he sacrificed the opportunity to complete the historical projects upon which he was determined and more crucially he forfeited both time and creative energy. The fact that he produced so many works is testimony to his imaginative proclivity. It is their quality and aptness for the occasion that attest a sure technical command and keen artistic discrimination. Despite an intermittent search for new creative personality, the majority of his work is cleverly wrought in a conservative style that is eclectic and always lyrical. Notwithstanding his early polemical certainty, he developed a musical signature that was recognisably Irish without resorting to pastiche.

PATRICK ZUK (CORK), *Composer, Pianist, UCC Music Graduate*
I must confess at the outset that I have found it no easy task to marshal my recollections of Aloys Fleischmann in a coherent form for the purposes of this article, so considerable and pervasive has been the impact of his personality on my own. In my mid-teens it was my good fortune to have the opportunity to spend two years studying with him privately as a composition student, the only one in fact that he ever taught on such a basis. This was after he had retired from UCC. I hope therefore that I am in a position to offer an unusually detailed account of his methods as a composition teacher and to give some wider impression of his attitudes to the craft of composition in general.

My first encounter with Fleischmann occurred when I was about fifteen years of age. A colleague of his, whose daughter attended the same school as I did, drew his attention to scores of mine she had seen. A request to see me followed. He looked through the scores and asked me if I would like to study with him. For two years thereafter we met for a two or three hour lesson every week of the academic year. With a generosity entirely typical of him – a quality to which I shall later have cause to return – not a single penny ever changed hands.

My first impressions – even allowing for the ready impression-ability of a schoolboy – were modified little in the course of subse-quent encounters. For all his formidable practical abilities as an organ-iser, Fleischmann's personality had a strange quality of remoteness, unworldliness even. His attire – which frankly bordered sometimes on the shabby – and the indescribably arthritic wrecks of cars he drove which seemed to trail rust in their wake, bespoke a pronounced indif-ference to material comfort and to the ephemeral vanities of marks of external eminence. In conversation his manner of expression was nat-ural and elegant; seemingly never at a loss for the right word, the lucidity of his discourse was the concomitant of a disciplined, pene-trating intellect. The breadth of his knowledge and command of his subject were at all times in evidence, as was his deeply personal and idealistic engagement with musical education. His aims in teaching were to impart a secure technical foundation, the techniques of disci-plined and informed critical thinking, a love and respect for the music we studied and to instil a desire for a wide-ranging general knowl-edge.

In the beginning I was naturally quite in awe of him – there was after all a difference of nearly sixty years in our ages. His rather quaint, old-fashioned gentlemanly courtesy quickly made me feel at ease and never at any time was I treated with anything other than kindness. His most severe censure and his exposition of even the most arcane mate-rial were leavened with his own highly idiosyncratic brand of salt wit. I can still hear him expostulating 'My dear man, you're a *terror!*' on finding some particularly ghastly solecism in an exercise. The effect of his manner I came to find captivating and quite endearing.

He began by initiating me into the rigours of strict species coun-terpoint, followed by eighteenth-century counterpoint, canon and fugue, the only solid foundation on which to build, he believed, if the student is ultimately to acquire a secure technique and a command of musical structures. He found it regrettable that these disciplines have been dropped from so many curricula at present due to current edu-cational fashions which were gravely misguided in his opinion. The study of counterpoint has the inestimable advantage of allowing the student to acquire in a systematic fashion an understanding of musi-cal logic and compositional resource that cannot be obtained in any other way. Even if a student's ambitions lie in the directions of schol-arship or performance rather than composition itself, the development

320

of practical understanding of the complex cultural artefacts of western art music is likely to elude him if these techniques have not first been mastered.

The understanding was implicit that this work was to be done with a meticulousness that extended even to the presentation of the manuscript. The mere avoidance of solecisms in part-writing was not enough: the aim was always to produce a musically satisfying result. The shape of the lines would be discussed, the appropriateness or clumsiness of the word setting, the possibilities of motivic working and the opportunities presented for the use of devices such as imitation. His own solutions to various problems that he would devise on the spot for me in a lesson for the purposes of demonstration were frequently ingenious and elegant.

This contrapuntal work was generally followed by analysis of scores – orchestral works and operas mostly – and a discussion of their instrumentation. During this part of the lesson, he would on occasion allow himself to digress. His abilities as a vivid raconteur were considerable – many students, I am sure, will recall his particular partiality to ghost stories – and our discussions of works by composers he had known intimately, such as Bax and Moeran, or by composers who had been commissioned for the Choral Festival such as Walton or Milhaud were enlivened by his recounting of anecdotes that could be by turns amusing or in some way illuminating of the music.

It was most interesting and instructive to discuss for example passages in a work where the composer had done something particularly fine and imaginative or where perhaps instead his structural sense had faltered. His analysis of orchestration was an aspect of our lessons I found particularly valuable. His sense of the orchestra, as one can judge from his own music, was colourful and imaginative and his long and varied experience as a conductor enabled him to make many practical observations on the secrets of truly effective writing for the medium.

These discussions would sometimes range quite widely at a tangent and we might have talked about literature, painting and other subjects. As a young person these conversations meant a great deal: then, as now, reading occupied me much but at that time I knew virtually nobody who shared my enthusiasms. Fleischmann knew several languages other than English and his knowledge of literature was wide. I remember one long discussion about the work of Verlaine, Rimbaud and Mallarmé, poets I loved at the time and of whose work I had made some settings.

The last part of a lesson was devoted to an examination of whatever piece I might have been composing at the time. It is really only now, some fifteen years later, that I appreciate the wisdom of his approach to this matter. As the reader may be aware, the teaching of composition since the Second World War has been a thorny business. The last century has seen the coming and going of many -*isms*, a great deal of stylistic flux and much uncertainty overall about any generally accepted criteria by which to make judgements of technical competence and artistic value. Advocates of various approaches anathematise each other in terms that can border on the virulent. It is not infrequent for compositions to be evaluated on the dubious basis of whether or not they conform to current critical fashions or to a particular subjective taste rather than on the basis of a more searching engagement which seeks instead to discern the technical achievement of a particular work. The approbation or disapprobation of many value judgements is seldom couched in anything other than nebulous generalities, concern with whether a work sounds 'contemporary' or not being one such common and particularly ludicrous instance.

Fleischmann was very reticent on the subject of contemporary music in my experience. I should say here that he never tried to influence me to write one way or another, least of all write in a manner that imitated his own. I did gather, mostly by reading between the lines, that he felt highly ambivalent about much that he heard. Only one instance comes to mind when he expressed himself more forthrightly in a conversation concerning the more *outré* experimental concoctions of the 1950s and 1960s. He regarded these with the utmost scepticism and saw them as being of nugatory artistic value. He also had very little time for music which was preoccupied with sound-effects and gimmicks of various kinds, feeling that this line of exploration was a cul-de-sac and that in the last analysis such procedures served too often to conceal a poverty of technique and imagination. The aggressive dogmatism and dismissiveness of the integral serialists repelled him; indeed to the end of his life, I gathered that he remained unconvinced by much serial composition feeling that the procedure was likely to degenerate into a mechanical method of note-spinning in the hands of the ungifted.

His own music, from his earliest period to his last, never abandoned tonality. But he regarded it as my responsibility to listen widely and to make informed critical judgements of my own about these matters. At the time I studied with him, much of what I wrote was naturally highly derivative. All young composers surely take their first steps in a similar fashion: one starts by imitating models, gradually assimilating and outgrowing their influence as one matures. I am profoundly grateful to Fleischmann that he never interfered in this natural process and allowed my development to take its own course. It is only possible after all to teach composition in a most circumspect and limited way. One can, of course, teach certain techniques such as counterpoint; one can discuss the practicality or impracticality of say, instrumental writing and other such sundry details, but he knew that one cannot teach a composer to be original. I am sure that Fleischmann would have been in substantial agreement with Schönberg's various dicta about the necessity to assimilate thoroughly the music of the past and to acquire a good general knowledge and sound traditional technical foundation before any really achieved and individual work is possible, as was emphatically the case in his own musical education. There is a danger that if a young composer is distracted prematurely by confusing and vague injunctions that he must at all costs be 'contemporary' – whatever that means in today's musical climate – before he has even acquired the skill and judgement necessary to write a musically satisfying counterpoint exercise, the result is likely to be a self-consciousness which may retard or even paralyse any individual creative endeavour. Fortunately Fleischmann did not adopt an unimaginative pedagogical method based on questionable postulates such as the avoidance of obvious consonances, for example, or which encouraged the slavish imitations of various clichés – sound effects and the like – or structural procedures culled from the practice of various contemporary composers.

He would rather discuss the principles by which the listener's interest could be maintained from start to finish of a piece and long-range continuity and coherence achieved. For example: was the thematic material distinctive and sufficiently contrasting in the different sections of a piece? Was any particular idea repeated too often so that tedium resulted or alternatively, was there too great an unintegrated proliferation of ideas? Were rhythmic patterns or climax notes repeated too often? Was there sufficient textural variety? Was the level of textural activation appropriate and logical in its particular context – and so on.

Fleischmann insisted on a thorough knowledge of the various instruments and their workings, emphasising the necessity for the development of one's aural imagination so that every pitch and timbre written was precisely calculated as to its effect. He had little patience with what he called 'notes orbiting in space' – that is, notes with no logical or structural necessity to be on the page. A finely nuanced sense of gestural resource appropriate to the particular context was thus developed.

Fleischmann was helpful far beyond the bounds of the professional obligations he undertook in teaching me. He felt it was vital that I should have the opportunity to hear work of mine performed in order to learn from the experience. To that end, he conducted two works of mine in performances given by the Cork Symphony Orchestra and also arranged for another two works to be performed by the then RTESO and the RTE Concert Orchestra. To this day I have no idea who paid for the copying of the orchestral material – a costly business – but I suspect strongly that he might have covered the cost himself. It would have been an entirely characteristic act of generosity, one that it affords me great pleasure to acknowledge in print all these years later.

My studies with Fleischmann lasted about two years. It was agreed that I would discontinue lessons when I started to study music at UCC. Unfortunately, I found my period of study there intensely disappointing and frustrating, particularly so since my earlier work with Fleischmann had been such a stimulating and positive experience. Standards in the department were in general low: many courses had a risible level of actual content and much of the lecturing was dull and ill-prepared. Such was the general feeling of apathy and disillusion that a substantial number of students from one particular class which graduated shortly after I did felt impelled to complain formally to the executive of the university. The attitude of the then professor to what I wrote was made abundantly clear in a number of dismissive remarks he saw fit to make in public and private. Nor did he show any interest whatsoever in my staying on in the department as a postgraduate student.

Troubling to attend lectures for much of the course was frankly a waste of time and it was not an atmosphere in which it seemed worthwhile to apply myself with much diligence. Resentfully, I did the bare minimum necessary to get by. Fleischmann naturally had been following my progress with interest. We met for supper one evening and he broached the subject: perhaps he sensed or had been informed that something was the matter. I distinctly remember how distressing he found much of the conversation that ensued. Fleischmann's sense of personal dignity did not permit him to express negative opinions about other members of his profession easily, but he was deeply saddened by what had transpired in the department since he had left.

I must emphasise that his reactions did not stem from personal chagrin: his was too generous a nature for this to have been the motivating force. His reactions stemmed rather from a deeply idealistic concern that graduates should be as well equipped and competent as possible to proceed into professional life. I consider myself highly fortunate to have been in the position of benefiting from the instruction he offered before a whole changing view of musical education rendered it obsolete.

SÉAMAS DE BARRA (CORK), Composer, UCC Graduate, Lecturer in the Cork School of Music

The Music of Aloys Fleischmann: A Survey

When Aloys Fleischmann left Cork for Munich in 1932 to study composition with Joseph Haas at the State Academy of Music he had the advantage of an exceptionally thorough training under St John Lacy. Lacy was professor of Music at University College Cork, the first appointee to a chair which had been created specially for him, and in preparing Fleischmann for the BMus degree he put him through his paces in the traditional compositional techniques: species counterpoint, free counterpoint and canon, and harmony, which included close attention to the treatment of Irish folk-tunes and the negotiation of the modes. As a result not only was the young Corkman in a position to do well in Munich but he could fault Haas' other students for their technical uncertainty: 'He didn't do species counterpoint with his class, with the result that the fellows with me were really hopeless – they had no technique', he recalled, adding characteristically that he thought species counterpoint essential for discipline.[31] Under Haas he continued to study canon in its more abstruse forms and pursued a rigorous course in fugal composition as well as a course in orchestration. There exists a substantial bundle of MSS from the Munich years which testifies to the diligence of these studies and in the sheer competence of its craftsmanship all the music that Fleischmann subsequently wrote reflects the technical assurance he acquired at this time.

He seems to have attempted very little original composition during this student period however. One song has come to light from his undergraduate years in Cork and there is a *Movement for String Quartet*, a private performance of which his father encouragingly arranged for him when he first arrived in Munich. It was in Munich too that he first had a work publicly performed. *Illumina Oculos Meos*, a motet for unaccompanied mixed-voice choir, which he completed in 1934 was sung by the Munich Cathedral Choir in February of that year. This is very much an offshoot of his studies and the most impressive thing about it is the easy fluency of its contrapuntal technique. But it offers no indication of the direction his music had in fact already begun to take.

The previous year he completed what was later to emerge as *Sreath do Phiano* (Suite for Piano). Considering this is his first sustained attempt at original composition it is a work of astonishing assurance. What is remarkable is its immediately distinctive voice and, considering the milieu in which it was written, the complete absence of contemporary central European influence. The style is diatonic and tersely modal and it is rather the accent of Irish traditional music that is

325

unmistakable. Its composition seems to have been a vital creative experience: 'I remember when I was writing the slow movement, feeling suddenly, for the first time, that I was groping into a new kind of world, which I had never sensed before. It was an extraordinary thing to be outside oneself groping into an inner world.'[32] And this experience was bound up with an intense realisation of his Irish identity. 'When I was in Munich,' he recalled, 'I was very homesick and had an enormous appreciation of everything Irish, much more than I had before I went there.'[33] It is not perhaps unusual for a sojourn abroad to sharpen one's sense of the qualities of ones native place. In Fleischmann's case this feeling appears to have been strong enough to be a permanent shaping influence on his music and indeed on his career as a whole. He realised, I think, what is in evidence in the music of the *Suite* itself and in virtually all his subsequent work that this inner world he speaks of, the source of his creativity, was inseparable from his sense of Irishness and that for him an authentically personal utterance could only be rooted in the culture of his country.

Although there was a certain amount of pressure to stay in Munich, Fleischmann did not entertain the idea. 'The Celtic pull was too strong', he said.[34] However favourable outward circumstances might have been, to have remained abroad would have left him nothing to say. Ireland was the defining context of his creative personality, depressing though the state of music here was, and the paradox of his career is that this context while allowing him to find an individual voice also prevented him from giving more than a fraction of his time to its development.

He returned to Cork in 1934 and was appointed acting professor of Music at UCC on St John Lacy's retirement. His acceptance of the post, shortly to be made full-time and which he held for forty-six years, he saw not merely as a job but also as a general commitment to the furtherance of the cause of music in Ireland. Circumstances were anything but encouraging and this commitment, often embattled, took a great deal of his energies. Composition could only claim a part of his attention and what is extraordinary is not that he did not compose more but, given the range of his activities, that he found time to compose at all.

Unquestionably he saw himself as a composer first and foremost however and, emphatically, as an Irish composer. His birth in Munich he always alluded to as an accident saying that his mother simply happened to be there on a concert tour, and he would have been irritated by any misleading reference to his 'adopted Ireland'.[35] He realised however that his German surname might be considered inconsistent with his nationalist aspirations and on returning to Cork he immediately set about finding a suitable Gaelic-sounding pseudonym under which to present his music. Advice was solicited. 'I think Maurice Ronan the best of the bunch,' suggested Daniel Corkery, 'but would Hugh Ronan be more euphonious? You won't find it makes much difference in the end'.[36]

So 'Maurice Ronan' it was, or rather the Irish language equivalent 'Muiris Ó Rónáin', and it was under this name that Chester published the *Sreath do Phiano* in 1935, Fleischmann in his nationalistic enthusiasm having persuaded them to print all the performance directions in Irish as well as the customary Italian. 'English publishers must be going crazy to start printing directions in an archaic language', E. J. Moeran told him, not realising who 'Muiris Ó Rónáin' was. But while there was as yet little music to show, he could of course only assert his Irishness by means of gestures such as these.[37]

It must not be thought that his view of what an Irish composer might be was in any way insular or parochial however. On the contrary, the problem as he saw it was in fact how to be Irish in a larger European context. 'What is needed is a Gaelic art-music,' he wrote in 1935, 'which will embody all the technique that contemporary music can boast and at the same time be rooted in the folk-music spirit'.[38] And the following year he amplified this by saying that 'such new expression, though breathing the spirit of the traditional music, need not have the remotest connection with its externalia in form or manner'.[39]

This was more than a positive programme: it was also intended to be a polemic in opposition to a feeling here in the 1930s (and indeed later) that the European art-music tradition was alien and that the musical expression of the Irish psyche could best be achieved by folk-music alone, or at most by arrangements or fantasias upon Irish folk-tunes. It is not that Fleischmann objected to the arrangement of Irish folk-tunes. He did not, in fact he himself produced an excellent set in the 1950s. Or that he objected to the use of folk-tunes by the composer when the need arose. Again, he did not. What he did object to was the assertion that a close adherence to folk sources was alone desirable, and that anything more was somehow un-Irish in direct relation to the degree of its departure from these sources.

Fleischmann reasonably and accurately pointed out that complex states of mind or feeling demand complex means of expression. Folk-music and art-music achieve different things and they should not be confused. 'A widespread cult of folk-music is an excellent thing in itself but it is also an end in itself,' he said.[40] 'One cannot expect of it [folk-music] to succeed in or to supplant that which is the realm of art-music, with its comprehensive forms, its power of sustaining and developing ideas, its wealth and profusion of expression and tonal effect. Such must be the resources of a music which is to keep pace with our spiritual and mental development in other spheres ...'[41] How exactly the spirit of traditional music might successfully be distilled into an art-music of sophisticated technical resource was a problem that Fleischmann with his love for and knowledge of folk-music on the one hand and on the other his thorough technical training in composition must have felt himself well placed to tackle. His experience in composing the *Sreath do Phiano* can only have indicated as much, giving him a glimpse of what might be possible.

But in attempting the creation of a distinctively Irish utterance this was one aspect only of the problem. There was another and in a clear reference to the position in which he now found himself he attempted to formulate it: 'A young man who has passed through his years of schooling and now masters his craft, cannot evade a momentous and bewildering issue. Either he has to choose the vocabulary of a pre-war generation, contriving to make it personal, or else he has to plunge into the principles of Schönberg and Milhaud and let loose a series of atonal or polytonal profundities upon the astonished ears of a public acclimatised to Moore.'[42] Fleischmann realised that not only did an Irish art-music have yet to be created but that the audience for it literally had to be created too: 'Considering the anomaly of our present position, one feels inclined to favour the first and more cautious policy, for in seeking a new tradition, uncertain of our very footing, we must make good the breach with the past before we strike out apace.'[43]

Fleischmann took his own advice and his next work after the *Sreath do Phiano* was very much a conscious attempt to show one manifestation at least of what this 'Gaelic-art music' might be like. The *Trí hAmhráin* [Three Songs] for high voice and piano, first performed in UCC in December 1935, were described in the programme note in the following terms: 'Seo dhíbh iarracht le Muiris Ó Rónáin ar dhántaibh Gaedhilge d'iompódh chun ceoil go bhfuil fíor-chor amhrán na ndaoine ann. Ní h-é seo ceol an tseana nóis, ámhthach, mar a tuigear dúinn, ach ceol ealadhanta an lae indiu go bhfuil sprid de'n tseana nós ann'. [Here is an attempt on the part of Muiris Rónáin to set Irish poems to music in a way that will reflect the true nature of the people's songs. This is not the old traditional music, however, as we understand it, but art-music of today imbued with the old traditional spirit.] The result is a remarkably successful realisation of his aims, the music being both immediately accessible and intensely personal. In an article published in 1949, one of the few instances of critical attention Fleischmann's work has received, Frederick May singles out the *Trí hAmhráin* for special praise. 'These songs combine remarkable lyrical beauty with deep intensity of feeling,' he wrote, '[and] undoubtedly represent one of the highlights of contemporary music in Ireland'.[44]

This view was endorsed by E. J. Moeran in a letter to Tilly Fleischmann, the composer's mother, a few years later. But Moeran had an important reservation. 'They are fine songs,' he wrote, 'and if Aloys gets them translated there might be a future for them of many performances. As they now stand, they haven't a ghost of [a] chance, until this country can produce an Irish speaking singer of culture and musicianship for all practical purposes they might be set to Fiji or Zulu texts ... It is very sad, but I do hope Aloys will eventually become more cosmopolitan.'[45]

While his enthusiasm to be an Irish composer could prompt Moeran to criticise his lack of cosmopolitanism, his ambition to do more than arrange folk-tunes or compose fantasias on them was likely to prompt others to criticise his lack of Irishness; while his composing music of any complexity whatsoever would undoubtedly alienate him from a public 'acclimatised to Moore', his pragmatic avoidance of the latest stylistic experiments was likely to stigmatise him as hopelessly out-of-touch. It cannot have been easy for Fleischmann to steer a course through these contradictory considerations and in the face of them to sustain a positive personal vision. But that is exactly what he managed to do, and in doing so to make a crucial contribution to the creation of modern Irish music. Any attempt to evaluate his work will have to take this fully into account. The style he evolved in the 1930s, his attempt to 'make good the breach with the past', was a completely convincing reconciliation of the demands of creative necessity with a clear sighted response to difficult and paradoxical circumstances. Not to acknowledge this can only result in a partial understanding of the course of his development and a distorted assessment of the nature of his achievement.

Fleischmann actually attempted, and failed, to persuade the English tenor Heddle Nash to sing the *Trí hAmhráin* in Irish. Consequently a serviceable translation was prepared and Nash performed them in English at a concert of music by Irish composers which Fleischmann conducted in Dublin in 1938 making it the first work of his to be heard on a national platform and to be broadcast. Not only did this important concert enhance the reputation he had already begun to earn as a conductor but it brought what was his finest work to date before a large audience and did much to establish him also as an emerging composer of national significance.

The final work of this decade and also the most ambitious is the *Piano Quintet*. This was completed in 1938 and first performed in Cork the following year by Tilly Fleischmann and the Kutcher String Quartet. Curiously it was presented under his own name although the pseudonym was in fact retained for a little while longer. It is Fleisch-mann's only substantial chamber work and, together with Frederick May's *String Quartet* of 1936, one of the first significant chamber works of the new Irish school. Fleischmann was fond of telling how its recep-tion was anything but friendly. 'Though conservative even fifty years ago', he wrote in 1990, 'it proved too "advanced" for the audience of its day, and evoked quite a hostile reaction in spite of its advocacy by the best English Quartet of that time'.[46]

In proposing the advisability of stylistic accessibility Fleischmann clearly never intended the wooing of the ill-informed and the igno-rant. The work makes no concessions to the incapacities of the public before whom it was first presented and this reaction can only have confirmed as correct his analysis of its difficulties with anything more than an obvious tunefulness. Even May found it 'extremely long and vastly complicated' and of the works discussed in his article it was clearly the one he liked least, although it appears he had not heard it in performance and based his evaluation on a reading of the score which, even with an experienced reader, does not always guarantee a clear imaginative realisation of a complex work.[47] There is undoubted-ly a prolixity of detail, and to this extent May's criticism is perhaps just. But more interesting is May's observation that 'he needs to be on guard against becoming a victim of his own learning and forgetting the virtues of simplicity',[48] and it is not unlikely that Fleischmann at the age of twenty-eight with his name now increasingly before a national public wanted to compose what could be considered a major work both in its import and in its dimensions. He certainly regarded it as the first work of his maturity. It is unquestionably a fine achievement, deeply-felt, thematically distinguished and technically impressive both in its structural control and in its handling of the medium.

In the 1940s Fleischmann consolidated his growing reputation. He gave the first performance of his new *Prelude and Dance* with the Cork Symphony Orchestra in 1940, and in 1941 he conducted what was to become in 1944, in its final version, *The Humours of Carolan*. This suite for string orchestra based on tunes by the seventeenth century Irish harper Turlough Carolan is an interesting attempt to connect the new Irish school with what there was of an extant tradition of composition in Ireland, much in the same way that Vaughan Williams and his con-temporaries in England looked back to Tudor church music and the Elizabethan madrigal. The difference of course was that Ireland had no such riches, such a tradition was in fact virtually non-existent, and Carolan was one of the few figures who produced music of any vital-ity. The music of 'such stuffed-owls as the eighteenth century Pale com-posers'[49] as Seán Ó Riada dismissed them, whatever its merits may be, had no particular qualities of Irishness to recommend it. Carolan's work alone was viable, and while principally taken up by Seán Ó Riada's Ceoltóirí Chualann and other traditional performing groups, Fleischmann's suite remains virtually a unique attempt to pick up these threads from the past and to link them with the newly emergent art-music. One movement of the suite, *Elizabeth MacDermott Roe,* was later published separately and much performed as an independent piece, Fleischmann finding it a very useful item when he needed something short of his own for inclusion in concert programmes.

Two of his finest works of the 1940s were composed in response to significant commissions. The tercentenary of the death of Mícheál Ó Cléirigh, chief of the four compilers of the *Annals of the Kingdom of Ireland,* known as the *Four Masters,* was celebrated in 1944. This national occasion was marked by a gala symphony concert (among other events) for which Fleischmann was invited to write a new work. He responded with an overture, *The Four Masters,* the most immediately appealing of the relatively few works he wrote solely for orchestra. An expansive sonata-form structure, it aims to recall ancient tales from the *Annals* and is, in its 'full blooded opulence and exuberant piling up of masses of sound',[50] a work of colourful pageantry and romance.

The following year there were also celebrations of national importance this time with a marked political dimension, the occasion being the centenary of the death of Thomas Davis, poet and founder of the Young Ireland movement. Fleischmann was again commissioned to compose a commemorative work and produced a brilliant and imaginative score which is unquestionably one of the key works of the period.

Clare's Dragoons, a setting of Thomas Davis' poem of that name and based on the vigorous martial air traditionally associated with it, was written for baritone solo, chorus, orchestra and, curiously, warpipes. This unusual addition to otherwise standard performing forces is due to his having seen Joan Denise Moriarty, a champion piper, hold her audience in thrall by a display of virtuosity at a concert of Gaelic music held at University College Cork in July 1939. Fleischmann was sufficiently impressed that now, six years later, he invited Miss Moriarty to perform his new work which had developed around the idea of an integral part for her instrument.

This invitation was to have far-reaching artistic consequences for Fleischmann. The story goes that in accepting it Joan Denise Moriarty seized the opportunity to overcome one of her greatest handicaps – the difficulty of providing adequate music for the ballet group that she had been training. There and then she struck a bargain: 'I will,' she told him, 'if your orchestra will play for my ballets'.[51] His agreement was to lead to a life-long involvement with the ballet as composer, conductor, and committee member, both locally in establishing amateur ballet in Cork, and nationally in the setting up of professional companies.

The public reception of *Clare's Dragoons* appears to have been somewhat muted at the first performance in Dublin in August 1945. Given the political significance of the celebrations the concert inevitably took place before an invited audience consisting of the president, taoiseach, cabinet, senate, dáil, judiciary and civil service. Fleischmann described it as 'probably the most philistine audience ever assembled in Dublin, most of whom had never been at a symphony concert before'.[52] The qualities of the new work were immediately recognised however by the discerning. Donal O'Sullivan, to whom the score is dedicated, wrote to Fleischmann the following day: 'Heartiest congratulations on last night's tour de force – for your *Clare's Dragoons* is nothing less than that! Not being a musical critic, I can't go into details. I can only judge by the effect on myself, and I was certainly thrilled as I responded to the changing moods; and the advent of the girl piper at the close provided a dramatic touch. It's a glorious tune, gloriously treated'.[53]

Clare's Dragoons ends with a stirring *coup de theatre* as the piper, who plays off-stage earlier in the piece, marches through the auditorium to join the other performers on the platform for the final climactic re-statement of the tune. And when the work was performed in Cork a month later it was a triumphant public success. 'It is one of the best works I have heard in Ireland,' wrote Seamus Murphy the sculptor in a letter of congratulations, 'I would not have missed it for anything'.[54]

The enthusiasm of the discerning amateur is confirmed by the judgement of the discriminating professional. '[It] must be regarded as its composer's most considerable achievement to date,' wrote Frederick May. 'Both chorus and orchestra are used with an assured mastery, and a picturesque and belligerent addition to the orchestra is the employment of war-pipes, which make a striking impact upon the eye as well as the ear'.[55]

May concludes his 1949 article by saying that in this work and in the *Trí hAmhráin* 'Fleischmann has managed to do something entirely original: he has become articulate for an Ireland that has gone, or rather he has given us in music a symbol of what Ireland, her people, her history and the beauty of her hills and valleys mean to each one of us. He has effected in sound an intensification of a feeling common to all Irishmen, and in doing so he has secured for himself an honoured place in the musical history of this country'.[56]

In just over ten years since the composition of the *Sreath do Phiano* and his return from Munich, Fleischmann had established himself as 'already an outstanding figure in contemporary Irish composition'.[57] Furthermore May's generous words indicate just how successful he was in fulfilling his aim to find an authentic voice for the Irish experience. The outward gestures of Irishness could now be dropped and Muiris O Rónáin slipped out of sight altogether. His style too began to open out and, while he remained true to his idea of what an Irish composer might be, the accent of folk music, one or two later works apart, became increasingly fainter.

Between *The Four Masters* and *Clare's Dragoons* Fleischmann had a second song-cycle performed. *The Fountain of Magic*, settings of four of Frank O'Connor's translations from the Irish, was completed in January 1945. There is some uncertainty about the date of the premiere which appears to have been a broadcast performance as what is described in the programme notes as the first concert performance took place in Cork on 2 March 1945. Although justly praised by May for 'some beautiful orchestral tone painting',[58] the work does not have the dramatic immediacy of the earlier cycle.

In due course Joan Denise Moriarty's Cork Ballet Group presented its first production with the assistance of the Cork Symphony Orchestra under Aloys Fleischmann. This was in June 1947 for one night only. But it was the beginning of a collaboration that was to last for almost fifty years, and writing for the ballet was to occupy Fleischmann's principal compositional energies for the next decade.

The response to this production was so enthusiastic that Fleischmann and Moriarty were encouraged to present a full week of ballet the following summer. For this Fleischmann wrote his first ballet score, *The Golden Bell of Ko*, and it is immediately clear that he had a natural flair for the dance: there is a precise and well-focused response to the demands of the scenario, and the music shows a talent for the vivid and colourful depiction of character and incident. In the evolution of his style the work is of particular significance in that it is his first score decidedly to exploit a freer approach to tonality and dissonance, having a greater angularity of melodic invention and pungency of harmonic idiom than any of his previous works. Based on a Chinese legend, the ballet is also the first work of his whose explicit subject is not in some way Irish, and it seems likely that an adequate response to the oriental theme necessitated a move away from his hitherto largely diatonic, often folk-accented style. He returned to Irish themes in his later ballet scores, as indeed in most of his subsequent music, but significant features of this stylistic expansion were to remain a permanent acquisition.

A second ballet *An Cóitín Dearg* [The Red Petticoat] was produced in Cork in 1951 as part of the Cork Ballet Group's fourth season. This was a collaboration with Mícheál Mac Liammóir who wrote the scenario and designed the décor and the costumes. Mac Liammóir's tale is of two young lovers, Colm and Nora who, thwarted in their love, leave the west of Ireland for New York. Here, unknown to one another, they are deeply unhappy in their new milieu of rootless if affluent cosmopolitanism. Eventually they return home and clothed in their New York finery they fail to recognise one another when they meet. But Colm changes back into his báinín and Nora into her red petticoat and, as Mac Liammóir puts it: 'nuair a fhilleas siad ar an tsimplíocht is dual dóibh annsin aithníonn siad a chéile agus an grá atá eatorra arís'[59] [when they return to the simplicity that is natural to them they recognise one another again and the love that is between them].

This parable of the dangers of gaining the world at the risk of losing your soul, and of the necessity of native rootedness was clearly of particular resonance for Fleischmann. Given his belief that an art will thrive only if rooted in its country's culture, creating its own particular expression of it, it is not difficult to imagine that his attraction to Mac Liammóir's scenario, apart from the splendid opportunities it afforded the composer, lay in the fact that it allowed him direct symbolic engagement with the artistic and cultural credo that shaped his career and informed the style and subject matter of his music. The outer acts of the ballet are set in the west of Ireland and depict a life which, if not by any means idyllic, is at any rate authentic. It is here, however frustrating their circumstances may be, that Colm and Nora finally realise they belong. The central act is set in New York, and Fleischmann employs the popular idioms of jazz (his antipathy to which was well known) to depict the rootless empty lives of those for whom there is 'nothing in the world but their money and their pleasures'.[60]

Macha Ruadh [Red (-haired) Macha], the third ballet for the Cork Ballet Company (as it had become in 1954), was premiered in 1955, and in the opinion of the press it was the most successful new work yet presented. Fleischmann's score, with its brash, clashing sounds as of ancient weaponry, is particularly evocative of the legendary past in which the ballet is set and a splendid example of the noble, heroic mode he excelled in.

This work also had a personal symbolic resonance. Authorship of the scenario is uncredited but it was probably written by Fleischmann and Moriarty in collaboration, and it tells the ancient story of a courageous queen striving against the odds who, ultimately victorious through sheer force of personality, establishes a great tradition. It is unlikely that a discerning audience could have failed to draw the parallel with both Joan Denise Moriarty's struggle to establish the ballet in the cultural life of the country and her hopes for eventual success, especially as she herself danced the title role.

In his final work for the Cork Ballet Company there is a wholly appropriate return to folk music as a source of inspiration, the last of Fleischmann's works to show this influence so directly. *Bata na bPlanndála* [The Planting Stick] was written for the Folk Dance Group, a division of the Cork Ballet Company which specialised in the steps and patterns of Irish dancing, and it was first performed in 1957 at the Cork International Choral Festival which had begun to feature the folk dances of different countries in order to vary the Festival's otherwise choral programmes. Described as a choral dance suite and scored for mixed-voice choir, flute, harp and percussion, it is an imaginative re-creation of one of the occupational mime-dances common in Ireland in the sixteenth and seventeenth centuries, and is based on the rhythmic movements used while planting potatoes with a special stick. Fleischmann discovered and uses one authentic planting-stick tune, and while the rest of the material is original it is modelled on the patterns of folk-song. He handles and develops this material with great skill, avoiding over-sophistication and without sacrificing interest maintaining the works essential simplicity. The result is a slight but attractive score, a period piece that manages successfully to distil in music something of the essence of the Irish rural idyll which influenced the work of so many artists here in the first half of the century.

Now, after ten years of almost complete absorption in composing for the ballet, one or two minor works apart, Fleischmann turned his attention as the 1950s drew to a close to a consideration once again of other significant compositional projects.

The first work of the new decade was the *Introduction and Funeral March* for orchestra completed in 1960 and first performed by the Radio Éireann Symphony Orchestra, conducted by the composer, in February 1961. A programme note informed the audience that although complete in itself it was ultimately to form part of a larger work which the composer hoped to finish shortly. Some sixteen years were to elapse however before Fleischmann came to add a final movement, *Bacchanal*, and the completed work as originally conceived was performed as *Sinfonia Votiva*.

A deeply-felt, personal utterance, the *Introduction and Funeral March* was composed in memory of Edward Sheehy, writer and critic and close friend of the composer's. It immediately made a considerable impression. In the view of *The Irish Times*: 'The pleasure of Aloys Fleischmann's conducting in the Phoenix Hall last night was enhanced by hearing this new work of his ... From the very beginning it is an immediately arresting work that compels one's attention and moves one greatly, as do only those works of art that have been written from inner compulsion'.[61] And after a second performance about a year later it was described as 'Fleischmann's deepest work to date, and one of the very best to have come out of modern Ireland'.[62] These notices set the tone for the critical reception of Fleischmann's new works during the 1960s, the period which marked possibly the highest peak of his reputation as a composer.

Fleischmann wrote to the poet Robert Farren in April 1964:

> Many years ago (I think it was as far back as 1948), I ventured to embark on a setting of parts of your fine poem on Colmcille, and I remember putting you to a great deal of trouble, including the writing of a special script. Then things went wrong – though I wrestled for many months I found it impossible to solve some of the problems which had arisen, or overcome a growing dissatisfaction with what I had produced. I still remember the pangs of guilt for having let you down!
>
> Recently I was invited to write a new work for a concert to be held in TCD in connection with the Bicentenary Celebrations of the founding of the School of Music there. Looking through a large pile of unfinished MSS I found your poem, and I was filled with the old enthusiasm, even as regards some of the sections I had completed. It occurred to me to ask whether you would give permission for a short work based on a few excerpts from your poem, as a sort of trial run for the original project.[63]

Robert Farren gave his permission and the 'trial run', *Songs of Colmcille*, was written for speaker, mixed-voice chorus and chamber orchestra. Fleischmann however never returned to the original idea of a large-scale work on the subject. And in the event, due to the difficulty of the score for amateur performance, a curtailed version only was presented at the concert in Trinity College as 'Three Excerpts from *Songs of Colmcille'*.

When the complete work was eventually performed in 1967 it met with an enthusiastic critical reception. *The Irish Times* critic Charles Acton wrote : 'I had the impression that this was the very best of all that I have yet heard from Aloys Fleischmann .... The music is enormously rich, as well as that it seems to marry completely the evocative words of Robert Farren'.[64] This view was unanimously endorsed. It was heralded as the 'highlight of the evening', and in the opinion of Michael Yeats: 'the main interest of last night's concert lay in the first complete performance of Aloys Fleischmann's *Songs of Colmcille* ... colourful and richly romantic in style, this music like so much of the output of this composer makes an immediate appeal to the senses. There is nothing cold or calculating about his method of composition: the sound he places before us is always warm and dramatic'.

Between the performances of the 'Three Excerpts' and the complete *Songs of Colmcille* Fleischmann conducted the premier of his *Song of the Provinces* in Dublin in June 1965. Completed in 1963, this was designed to provide an impressive finish to the final night of probably the 1964 Cork International Choral Festival. For mixed-voice chorus and orchestra with audience participation, and written in an immediately appealing style, it is perfectly tailored to such a gala event, the novel participation of the audience, which has to be rehearsed in its part beforehand, creating a good-humoured, festive atmosphere.

But the idea of including the work in the Festival programme had to be abandoned because, as Fleischmann later wrote when proposing the possibility of a performance by Radio Éireann, 'having approached some of the conductors of local choirs, I failed to get any co-operation, their main objection being that the writing is too difficult, and that they could not spare the time that would be necessary to master it'.[65] It was however included in the 1965 season of Radio Éireann Studio Symphony Concerts and Fleischmann, who conducted the whole programme, gave a performance of vigour and gusto, his rehearsal of the audience occasioning much hilarity.

'Aloys Fleischmann gave us a really exhilarating evening when he conducted the RESO at the St Francis Xavier Hall last night', wrote Charles Acton in *The Irish Times*, giving his opinion that 'Fleischmann's own work was a splendid end to the concert'.[66] *The Cork Examiner* reported that 'A tremendous ovation was given the first performance of Professor Aloys Fleischmann's new work for choir and orchestra *Song of the Provinces*', and continued, 'last night's audience, although taken by surprise, co-operated with such vigorous delight that it seems certain that this song is bound to be established in the choral repertoire of Ireland's orchestras and choirs – as well as those of other countries'.[67]

Comments like this last, although undoubtedly well-meaning and expressive of genuine enthusiasm, were so out of touch with the circumstances in which Irish composers were working as to be little more than empty pieties. It is worth remembering just what those circumstances were. Scores by Irish composers, with rare exceptions, remained unpublished, unpromoted and consequently, after the initial outing, usually unperformed. The question of becoming established in the repertoire simply did not arise. After all it is difficult, not to say impossible, for a work however brilliant to make its mark if it is allowed to fall into the void after the first performance. However favourable public and critical reaction may initially have been, there was no follow through. And Fleischmann was more fortunate than others in respect of subsequent performances, largely because of his own activities as a conductor. But it is worth noting that even a work as warmly received as *Songs of Colmcille* has not yet had a second performance although it is over thirty years since the complete work was first heard.

In July 1960 *The Irish Times* published a feature on Irish composers which takes *them* to task in this matter: 'it is clearly up to the composers themselves to market their wares and persuade us to use them ... but [they] seem singularly slack in seeking performance, commissions, liaisons with performers or publication'.[68] This is hardly fair. In Fleischmann's case, for one, it is demonstrably untrue. He was quite prepared personally to promote his own music, and did so as successfully as circumstances allowed. But the crucial issue is one of publication and professional promotion. English and other foreign publishers naturally gave full priority to composers of their own countries and there was little room for the work of Irish composers in their catalogues. The problem, as indeed *The Irish Times* acknowledged, was the 'virtual absence of an Irish publishing house'.[69] Virtual because the Government Publications Office, under the imprint of An Gúm, did in fact have a scheme for publishing music. It confined its catalogue largely to folk-song arrangements however, the works of composers who in Fleischmann's words 'could indeed do little more than add three fraternal parts beneath a tune',[70] and to other such compositions of a demonstrably *bona fide* Irishness.

An Gúm accepted two works of Fleischmann's and it is illuminating to consider the progress through the press of the second which eventually appeared as *Eilís Nic Dhiarmada Ruaidh* [Elizabeth Mac Dermott Roe from *The Humours of Carolan*]. Fleischmann left a summary of his dealings with An Gúm in this matter by which his frustration can be measured: 'Accepted 1950; March 1953 – ready to send for printing; Sept. '53 – first proof; Jan. '54 – 2nd proof; March '54 – 3rd proof; July '54 – copy arrived, without showing final proof. Many mistakes. No parts, though agreed; 1957 (*sic*) – no score, no parts and no reply to letter.'[71] It does not appear that *The Irish Times* was in possession of the full story !

A new generation simply did not have the opportunity to form any accurate assessment of the achievement of Fleischmann and his contemporaries. Their work was inaccessible. In Fleischmann's case this situation has persisted and while Charles Acton, as a critic of the older generation who would have attended many of the premiers, could write of a handful of Fleischmann's works as being 'part of the ordinary Irish musical literature',[72] Michael Dervan, as a critic of the younger generation, could comment after Fleischmann's death that he could 'make no such assessment, for that literature is not much heeded now by orchestral programmers at RTE'.[73] Indeed one could go further and say that the very phrase 'ordinary Irish musical literature' is itself little more than an empty piety when most of what has been composed since the founding of the state continues to remain indiscriminately ignored.

Although Fleischmann's reputation stood very high by the end of the 1960s, and critical opinion, such as it was, of his recent works was highly complimentary, there is no doubt but that he had become somewhat self-conscious about the direct, still basically diatonic mode of utterance that constituted the essence of his style. Already in 1963 in writing to Radio Éireann about *Song of the Provinces* he could feel it necessary to say, almost apologetically, that 'the style is, I fear, very conservative and intended for a popular occasion such as our Festival, but perhaps the participation of the audience would justify its inclusion'.[74] There is an implicit concession that the diatonic idiom is in itself somehow inadequate and requires special pleading. For the last work of the 1960s, a commission from the Dublin Festival of Twentieth Century Music, showcase for what there was of an Irish avant-garde, he certainly felt that the direct manner of *Song of the Provinces* would not do.

He seems to have experienced some sort of crisis of artistic conscience around this time. Of an essentially conservative cast of mind, he was decidedly unsympathetic to the more outlandish developments of the avant-garde. Nevertheless he became increasingly defensive about his own music, and about his early works in particular. It is not impossible that the change in his style evident from now onwards was due, partly at least, to a certain atmosphere of intellectual intimidation surrounding recent developments, to which he and others were to some extent vulnerable, and to the resultant feeling that he was behind the times. The intolerant dogmatism and sweeping dismissiveness of the leading avant-guard figures and their prophets was widely publicised after all, and it was with serialism, integral-serialism, aleatoricism, electronic music, and so on, that so much criticism and academic commentary seemed to be so favourably occupied. Greater figures than Fleischmann, Copland comes to mind, began to question themselves under this barrage.

Furthermore the question of what it meant to be an Irish composer, so urgent in the 1930s, scarcely seemed relevant in the 1970s. Times were changing. Cherished beliefs and values that had fuelled the long struggle for independence now came under the scrutiny of revisionist historians. Nationalism itself was made to seem questionable, and indeed for Irish intellectuals any overt expression of nationalist sentiment became something of an embarrassment. The whole of Fleischmann's compositional imagination however was bound up with the ideal of cultural nationalism. From the beginning, as we have seen, his declared ambition was to find an authentic voice for the Irish experience: 'to delve into the Hidden Ireland', as he put it, 'and out of folk song, out of the heroic tales and romances, to create an idiom which would express in music some of the essence of this rich untapped literary tradition'.[75] Such a project, so acceptable earlier, could only seem faintly ludicrous in the Ireland of the 1970s. Attitudes had chilled, and in an atmosphere that had become cynical Fleischmann found that a vital compositional criterion had become redundant. The style he had evolved to answer the need for a 'Gaelic art-music', although it was considered progressive here in its day, and had not of course remained static for four decades, now seemed dated. If the question of shaping a distinctly Irish utterance was to continue to remain of central importance to him, it was clear that a new mode of answering would be necessary.

He certainly felt it imperative to evolve some creative response to the new worlds of sound that were currently being explored. In the works of the 1970s the security of the diatonic manner has largely been replaced by chromatically based, freely dissonant harmony, essentially colouristic rather than functional, resulting in a much more fluid approach to tonality and a greater tendency towards chromatically angular melodic invention. Not that such tendencies were unprecedented in Fleischmann's work: as already discussed, a loosening of the diatonic style was to some extent in evidence since the 1940s. And while it could convincingly be shown, I think, that this late manner has its origins in the earlier music, and is to that extent a natural development of expressive necessity, its somewhat abrupt emergence at the end of the 1960s certainly indicates other causes too. 'I write as I must',[76] Fleischmann insisted, and while this is undoubtedly sincere it leaves undefined the exact nature of the imperative. And the indications are that this imperative was a dual one: whatever the internal necessity, he also felt an obligation to conform to some degree with the expectations of what 'contemporary' music should sound like or risk forfeiting all serious consideration. There was a fear, quite simply, of being thought hopelessly old-fashioned. The holding centre of his artistic personality was secure however, occasionally self-deprecating though he might be, and there were clear limits to how much recent technical innovation it could, or needed to, accommodate.

Fleischmann must also have realised that such stylistic 'advance' as he could in conscience embrace would, in the extreme politics of style that informed the discourse of the avant-garde, count for nothing. He could only accept that if in this view he was outmoded then he was in good company. What troubled him however was the critical appraisal of new works solely in terms of such politics. He certainly considered this both unjust and irrelevant in the assessment of the merits of new music, both on his own and on other's behalf. He deplored the fact that technical accomplishment and individuality of utterance could either be missed or so easily dismissed by critics who were busily trotting after the latest trends. 'Over the past few years,' he wrote, ' there is one kind of music which is almost certain to evoke an enthusiastic response, namely music which is written in an idiom which is at first hearing virtually incomprehensible. Though idiom is important one would have thought that the more vital factors, factors needing examination and assessment, would be the range, variety and depth of ideas, the validity of the structures and, above all, whatever the idiom, whether the music speaks with a distinctive voice'.[77]

Although this reads decisively as from one who knows his own mind, Fleischmann in fact remained both uncertain about the value of his earlier music (he always expressed surprise if one happened to allude to any of it favourably), and ambivalent about his position in relation to contemporary developments especially as reflected in his own recent works. The result is a curiously individual mixture of assertiveness and diffidence. It was quite characteristic of him unhesitatingly to pursue the possibility of a performance while at the same time modestly disclaiming the merits of the work in question. Revealingly, when asked in 1990 which of his works he considered his finest, he listed those composed in the 1970s on which presumably he felt his critical standing might ultimately depend. To the question which of his works gave him the most pleasure however he replied *Clare's Dragoons*.[78]

His attitude to what he called the 'antics of some of our avant-garde composers' partly resolved itself into irritated amusement.[79] He was simply unable to take them seriously, and was frustrated by what seemed their unquestioningly favourable critical reception. These feelings found an outlet in a send-up called *Le Balai de Plume* [The Feather Mop], subtitled 'essay for pianist-comedienne' and composed in 1970. 'For some time past I have been afflicted with a desire to parody avant-gardism and have finally delivered myself of the enclosed', he wrote when forwarding the score to RTE. 'It is I fear very irreverent [and] involves much clowning'.[80] Quotations from Stockhausen jostle with Liszt's *Second Hungarian Rhapsody* and the pianist-comedienne is instructed with choreographic precision in the manipulation of the mop. It never seems to have been performed. He hoped that it could be presented at the Dublin Festival of Twentieth Century Music, where it would have made its point most tellingly, and he subsequently tried to arrange for its performance on television. It was not intended to be anything other than a squib of course, though unfortunately one that never got a chance to go off.

The final work of the 1960s, already alluded to, was *Cornucopia*, a prelude and rondo for horn and piano completed in 1969 and performed at the first Dublin Festival of Twentieth Century Music in 1970. Like earlier works with piano accompaniment it was subsequently orchestrated and Fleischmann himself conducted the premier of this alternative version the following year. This bravura showpiece is assured in its handling of his expanded harmonic and tonal resources and can on the whole be considered one of the most successful of the later works.

But in *The Poet's Circuits*, a song-cycle for soprano and Irish harp completed in 1972, the nature of the medium immediately imposed stylistic restrictions. Fleischmann's problem was to accommodate the limitations of the Irish harp without reverting to what he now unsparingly referred to as his 'worst "folk-song" style'.[81] In his correspondence with Gráinne Yeats, for whom these settings of Padraic Colum were composed and who presented them at the 1972 Dublin Festival of Twentieth Century Music, he voiced his concern that he might not have been entirely successful in this. 'Herewith the last of the songs,' he wrote, 'I fear it is less good than the others, much more conventional. If you think it too much so for a Festival of Twentieth Century Music don't hesitate to confine the group to the other three'.[82] In the event only three of the songs were performed but, in spite of his misgivings, this was because the final song did not reach Gráinne Yeats in time.

With *Poet in the Suburbs* of 1973, although for unaccompanied mixed-voice choir, he felt no such restrictions. It was written for the BBC Northern Singers whose professional technique meant a freedom in writing chorally not normally afforded the composer. The work was occasioned by the twenty-first anniversary of the Cork International Choral Festival in 1974. Fleischmann, who as director of the Festival refused to entertain the idea of a commission, nevertheless felt that the nature of the event justified the inclusion of a new work of his own. 'The Festival creator and director happens to be one of our own distinguished composers,' commented Charles Acton in *The Irish Times*. 'It is absurd that his name should not appear on the list of works called forth by it. Unfortunately he adds to his many good qualities an obstinacy that could not [be] overcome. So this premiere is the closest one can come to what we want'.[83]

The work is a setting of Thomas Kinsella's wry look at the nature of the creative imagination, and Fleischmann's treatment underlines the poem's somewhat grim humour. The words are mostly delivered over and around parodistic accompaniment patterns which are derived from hints in the text and sung to nonsense syllables. This approach is entirely successful, at once setting the right kind of tone and allowing the light handling and clear enunciation of the text which is so essential if the piece is to make its proper point. It also affords continually changing textural interest the organisation of which is the structural basis of the work. The climax at the end, on frantic repetitions of syllables derived from the word 'tambourine', is not only a vivid illustration of the final lines which conclude the poet's catalogue of menacing obstructions to the creative act ('And there as usual lying last,/Helped along by blind Routine,/Futility flogs a tambourine'), it is also a rare example in Fleischmann's work of recourse to aleatoric technique.

The 'Song Cycle from *Tides*', settings of four poems by John Montague for mezzo-soprano and piano, was also premiered in 1974 at the Dublin Festival of Twentieth Century Music and, like *Cornucopia*, a version with orchestra was heard the following year with Fleischmann himself conducting.

It is interesting to note in passing the choice of contemporary poets, Kinsella and Montague, for these works. The bleak visions of one and the suburban banalities of the other are a far cry from the 'heroic tales and romances' Fleischmann had evoked earlier. This choice of course reflects his response not only to changes in contemporary music but also changes in contemporary Ireland. In a way that the poetry of, say, Padraic Colum could not, these texts obliged him to forgo the richly romantic style of the 1960s, while at the same time ensuring that such stylistic departures continued to have an Irish dimension. The new tone was unmistakable: 'Hard of outline, unusually unromantic',[84] Acton said of the *Poet in the Suburbs*, and he noted 'a starkness and vehemence to match the words' in *Tides*.[85]

It is interesting to note too a change of emphasis in the critical notices of the 1970s. There was a new idée-fixe: *Cornucopia* 'might have come from earlier in the century',[86] but *The Poet's Circuits* 'seemed idiomatic and present day',[87] whereas *Tides* represented 'a move into the later twentieth century',[88] and so on. Fleischmann's work had not hitherto been reviewed in such terms, and fascinatingly this change coincided exactly with the emergence of his later manner sharing the current general obsession with whether or not music sounded sufficiently 'contemporary'. And this was not confined to the newspapers. Composers reassured one another. In a letter to Fleischmann after the premiere of The *Táin* in 1981 Gerard Victory commented that 'there was great commitment in the music, and a highly contemporary flavour'.[89] Apart from the unintentional irony – the score incorporates long stretches from *Macha Ruadh* of twenty-five years before – the fact

343

that such a comment could even be made and intended as a compliment is absolutely indicative of the prevailing anxiety to be considered acceptably up-to-date.

If one includes both versions of *Cornucopia* and *Tides*, Fleischmann had six important premieres between 1970 and 1975. More, there was also a *Mass* for female voices performed in Cork in 1973. And other music was written, including *Le Balai de Plume*, which for one reason or another remained unperformed. This is not a bad showing for someone on whose time there were so many other demands. All things considered, his public profile as a composer was quite high. Nevertheless Fleischmann felt that he was no longer fairly represented in Radio Telefís Éireann's concert programmes. He wrote to Gerard Victory, who was Director of Music at RTE, in February 1974: 'I hope you will not mind my mentioning something which has dawned on me of late – that I have almost disappeared from RTE programmes, though revivals of earlier works by Fred May and Brian Boydell, for instance, are fairly frequent'.[90]

One result of this prompt was Gerard Victory's suggested revival of the *Introduction and Funeral March* of 1960, and Fleischmann took the opportunity to add the long intended third movement. This was finished in 1977 and *Sinfonia Votiva* was finally performed complete at the 1978 Dublin Festival of Twentieth Century Music with Fleischmann conducting the RTESO. An even more significant result however was RTE's commissioning of a new work for the centenary of the birth of Pádraig Pearse in 1979.

In accepting this commission for a work to commemorate possibly the most famous of modern Irish patriots Fleischmann was obliged to reconsider in the most direct way the nature of nationalist art, and it is interesting to see how he chose to respond to the challenge at this late stage in his career. Written for mezzo-soprano, speaker and orchestra, *Ómós don Phiarsach* [Homage to Pádraig Pearse] is a curious hybrid: settings for solo voice of five of Pearse's lyric poems, four in Irish and one in English, sit uneasily with passages for speaker from Pearse's polemical prose writings. Fleischmann makes no attempt to integrate the disparate forces as he does so successfully in *Songs of Colmcille*, and the overall effect is somewhat unsatisfactory.

What is fascinating however is how he avoids here the naively optimistic nationalism with which *Clare's Dragoons* could conceivably be charged. There is no attempt to explore the myth of Pearse's heroic self-sacrifice or to contribute to what by 1979 many might have been prepared to describe as the mythology of the 1916 Rebellion. The tone is personal rather than monumental (the use of solo voice, rather than chorus, is of course a means to this end), and the prevailing atmosphere is dark, elegiac and even menacing rather than triumphant. The weakest section is his treatment of the final lines of *The Mother*, a setting of which concludes the work: 'And yet I have my joy:/My sons were faithful and they fought'. Here the mood suddenly changes to one of defiance, almost of exultation, and it is revealing that this single attempt to strike the heroic attitude should be a serious miscalculation. The unselfconsciousness of *Clare's Dragoons* is clearly no longer possible. Undoubtedly the passage is designed to bring the work to a vigorous conclusion, but not only does it misrepresent the poem at this point, as I believe, it also fails in its structural purpose. It is too brief, almost perfunctory in fact, and does not carry conviction. In short it sounds forced and the effect unfortunately is one of bathos.

In their own terms the spoken sections, *Pearse on Education* and *Pearse on Nationality*, are successful in spite of the intractable problems such seemingly abstract subjects might appear to pose for the composer. But Pearse's highly-charged, emotive rhetoric lends itself well to musical amplification, and the vividly imagined orchestral background is one of the finest aspects of the score.

Fleischmann retired from the chair of music at UCC in 1980 at the age of seventy and among the many tributes he received was one from the Choir and Orchestra of the College who, together with the College Choral Society, presented a gala retirement concert which concluded with a performance of *Song of the Provinces*. Instead of the conventional presentation customary on such occasions the three performing groups appropriately commissioned him to write a new work for the same forces, including of course audience participation. It was ten years however before this new work was eventually heard.

In the meantime the first compositional project of his retirement years to be completed was *The Táin*, his final ballet score. Based on the *Táin Bó Cuailnge* [The Cattle Raid of Cooley], the twelfth century account of the exploits of Cuchulain and Queen Medb, this three-act ballet for the Irish Ballet Company is one of his most ambitious works in terms of length and organisation, and a late triumphant example of his personal response to the problem of shaping a distinctly Irish utterance. It was also his final creative collaboration with Joan Denise Moriarty, who choreographed it.

One particularly interesting feature of the score, as already mentioned, is its incorporation without strain or inconsistency of much of the earlier *Macha Ruadh*. Of his previous ballet scores this alone was never adapted in any way for subsequent concert performance, so none of the music had been heard since 1955. The extensive borrowings may have been partly a matter of simple expediency in the punctual completion of a large-scale work of course, but presumably

345

Fleischmann also felt that this music was too good to be allowed to languish in complete neglect, a revival of the ballet being most unlikely. The similar legendary-heroic world of the new score gave him the ideal opportunity to re-use the material, although his description of *Macha Ruadh* as a 'sort of preliminary sketch'[91] for *The Táin* is unfair to the integrity of the earlier work. His preparedness to return to earlier music in this way also indicates that whatever his anxiety may have been about the 'contemporary' status of his recent scores, it had now relaxed somewhat. And by and large this relaxation is reflected in the remaining works of the 1980s, although doubtless it was also influenced by their origins in commissions for amateur performers.

The Táin was premiered at the Dublin Theatre Festival in October 1981 and was an outstanding success. 'Joan Denise Moriarty has given us a work of which we can all be proud,' wrote Carolyn Swift in *The Irish Times*, 'unmistakably Irish in every detail. To Aloys Fleischmann's splendid score the story unfolds with all its comedy, ferocity and gallantry, gripping the audience from the moment the curtain rises'.[92] The company danced to full houses, and it was the opinion of the *Daily Telegraph* that 'the ballet has already established itself as the finest achievement of the Irish Ballet Company', and that 'it should take its place permanently in the repertoire'.[93] In the light of the subsequent fate of the Irish Ballet Company this sounds a little hollow, but the production was unquestionably a fitting climax to the long collaboration between composer and choreographer.

His ongoing conducting and organising activities apart, Fleischmann's attention during the 1980s was principally occupied by the *Sources of Irish Traditional Music*, a project on which he had been working for many years and which he completed a few days before his death in 1992. It is not surprising that consequently there was little compositional activity, and in fact he lived to complete just three more works.

In 1984 he received an unexpected commission from the Cloyne Literary and Historical Society for a work to mark the tercentenary of the birth of George Berkeley, philosopher and Bishop of Cloyne from 1734 to 1753. He responded with a cantata for chorus and orchestra which, like *Ómós don Phiarsach*, also includes a prominent part for speaker. The spoken texts, from Berkeley's own *Treatise Concerning the Principles of Human Knowledge* (1710) and *The Querist* (1730), are even less amenable to musical amplification than those of the Pearse work, but it must be conceded that having set himself such an unusual and difficult problem he solves it with ingenuity and imagination. *Time's Offspring* was first given by amateurs conducted by Fleischmann himself in Cloyne Cathedral in 1985, and it is a pity that, apart from the overture, this significant late work has never had a professional performance.

In 1990 Fleischmann celebrated his eightieth birthday. The Cork International Choral Festival, of which he had ceased to be director since 1987, commissioned him to compose a new piece for that year's Seminar on Contemporary Choral Music with which he at last entered the lists of the Festival's commissioned composers. It was in fact the second of two Fleischmann premieres featured at the 1990 Festival, the first being the performance at the gala opening concert of the work commissioned ten years before on the occasion of his retirement from the chair of Music at UCC.

This latter work, *Clonmacnoise*, completed in 1986, was felt to be a good occasional piece with many excellent moments having in particular a fine diatonic tune for the audience to sing. If not as distinguished as the earlier *Song of the Provinces* it was nonetheless very warmly received. It did not prepare the Festival audience however for the impact of *Games*, the new work, which was heard a few days later. Written for mixed-voice choir, harp and percussion, and brilliantly performed by the BBC Singers under Simon Joly, it astonished not only by its virtuosity, but by a vigour and vehemence extraordinary in any circumstances but surely exceptional in the music of an eighty-year-old man.

In *Games* there is not the slightest evidence of any diminution either of technical command or of creative vitality. Rather, if anything, is the reverse true. In fact Fleischmann spoke of a new fluency, describing it as 'the only work I ever wrote which gave me no trouble whatsoever: and you'd imagine that at the end of my days now, I'd find it harder and harder'. Adding with characteristic modesty, 'But this was the effect of the poetry, which I thought marvellous'.[94] The poems, translated from the Serbo-Croat of Vasco Popa, were a very unusual choice for him and certainly seem to have allowed him this late opening of new ground. It is good to think that such an expansion of vision should have been possible in his old age, although poignant that the work should also have been his last.

Aloys Fleischmann could no doubt have left a larger legacy of music had he directed his energies more single-mindedly. That he did not is due to his understanding of the larger obligation his generation had to create the circumstances in which modern Irish music could flourish. 'It is purposeless to talk or write about a musical revival,' he declared in 1936, 'unless determined action be the burden of one's theme. Without a decisive betterment of general conditions all hopes of a revival can be dismissed'.[95] This reads like a call to arms and in his teaching, his indefatigable organising, his willingness to sit on endless committees, his ceaseless prompting and provoking, he was certainly in the front line with those who led the assault on the inertia, indifference and ignorance in musical matters so prevalent in contemporary Ireland. While certainly not prolific, he did however compose steadily throughout his life. In spite of the many demands on his time and energies composing always remained an activity of central importance for him, and in the last analysis it is as a composer that his place in the history of music in Ireland will principally be due.

His reputation, at its highest from the 1940s to the 1960s, undoubtedly suffered an eclipse towards the end of his life. In changed circumstances he moved to the background of what was now deemed to be of moment in Irish music, and this must have been a considerable disappointment to a man whose work had previously been received with such enthusiasm. A new generation, while by and large respectful, had little real interest in what he had to say. And as the works on which his earlier reputation rested were virtually unknown, because unperformed, the significance of his achievement could neither be fully recognised nor appreciated. Lip-service, yes, possibly: although it is interesting to note how often his work is simply passed over when that of his contemporaries attracts comment. But as there has been no real assessment there can be no real understanding either of what his ambitions for music in Ireland were, or what his personal contribution to the realisation of these ambitions might be. And these ambitions were of the highest. Rightly he felt that in interpreting Ireland to itself music's role was both unique in that it articulated what the other arts could not, and essential in that this articulation was vital for self-definition. The clear apprehension of this dual importance of the role of music in the life of the country, and his own willingness to dedicate his energies to its promotion are the shaping factors of his career, and the source of the idealism that fired his creativity. 'It can be the composer's task', he wrote in the high-flown rhetorical style of his youth, 'to express the soul of that elusive entity in the nation's being, call it the '"Hidden Ireland" or what you will – it is yet in exile from its rightful place waiting, perhaps, the composer to place it there'.[96]

8: THE MAN

ELLEN CROWLEY NÉE MCSWINEY (DUBLIN), UCC Graduate, Piano Teacher
I knew Aloys as a child, and never met him again, except for a short encounter in college. During the First World War his father was interned in England, and Aloys' mother closed their family home and came to live next door to my family for most of the war years. We lived in No. 6 Brighton Villas, now taken over by the university. My sister and I were playmates of Aloys: we have very happy memories of those times.

There were no children living in the area, so Aloys had no one to play with except my family. Friends who came to birthday parties were Ivor and Joe Horgan and their sister Madeline, whose father, John J. Horgan, was a solicitor and member of the Cork Corporation. Another visitor was Sophie Stockley, daughter of the professor of English at UCC, whose mother was from Germany. We played mostly 'war games'. We made mud bombs in the garden, then picked sides, Germany versus Britain. We were all anti-British in those days. How could we be otherwise with a name like McSwiney? Germany always won, Aloys invariably having the best bombs.

One precious plaything which Aloys had was a red and white painted yacht with the name *Tilly* (his mother's name) on the side, carved by his father during his internment. We sailed it on the River Lee at the bottom of our garden. One day, when Aloys was called in to lunch, I begged him to let me play with it while he was inside. When I tried to pull it in, the string broke, and the yacht sailed off down stream, never to be seen again. When Aloys came out I was crying bitterly in a corner, but Aloys said it was 'all right'. He was more concerned at my distress than at the loss of the yacht. 'Coming events cast their shadows before': I often heard remarks made during his adult life about his sympathetic treatment of anyone in trouble with whom he had dealings.

Mrs Tilly Fleischmann was much admired for her courage in taking over her husband's position as organist in the North Cathedral. She also gave recitals and music lessons. The late Gerard Shanahan, a renowned pianist, was one of her pupils. She was a perfectionist and would not take on any pupil who did not practise. She practised for hours every day herself. We children rarely met her except as a gracious hostess at children's parties.

We missed Aloys very much when he and his mother left the Western Road towards the end of the war; my mother was in tears. I was a year ahead of him in UCC, but my only contact was as a mem-

ber of the College Glee Club, which he raised from amateur to professional standard.

MÁIRE BRUGHA (DUBLIN), Terence MacSwiney's daughter
Aloys Fleischmann's mother Tilly had quite an influence through her
music on my life and on that of my family – it was she who introduced
my mother (then Muriel Murphy) to the MacSwineys and in particular to my father.

My contact with Aloys Fleischmann was minimal, but two instances stand out. The first was when he and his mother were staying
in Munich in 1931 and came to visit me when I was living near
Garmisch. My aunt Mary MacSwiney, who was very worried about
my living abroad, used to ask friends who were visiting Germany to
try to look me up. I remember Aloys had just got his degree at a very
young age, and how very proud his mother was of him. I knew nothing of Ireland, not even where it was, and probably didn't take it all in.
But what did make an impression on me was how kind they were to
me to take me out for the day. A photograph was also taken of the
three of us, of which I still have a copy, me with my pigtails and little
Bavarian dress. It was the Fleischmanns' visit that brought my aunt
again in contact with me, and we started to correspond. I was brought
back to Ireland the following year, against my mother's wishes. There
was a subsequent case in the High Court in Dublin between my mother and my aunt for custody of me, which my aunt won.

The next time I met the Fleischmanns was after I had returned
home to Ireland. My aunts brought me to visit the Fleischmanns. As I
knew no English, this was a treat. While the old people chatted, Aloys
went to trouble to try to entertain me, which struck me as nice as he
was a grown-up young man – a university graduate. The last time I
spoke to him was at the funeral of Geraldine Neeson. The *Irish Times*
took a photograph of the two of us on the steps of St Patrick's Church
in Cork chatting to one another. We were unaware of this – days later
I was in a newsagent in Dublin and saw the picture on the front page
of the *Times*.

*PATRICIA COX NÉE O'MALLEY-WILLIAMS (COVENTRY), Aloys Fleischmann's first
cousin*
Whenever I hear Beethoven's Sixth Symphony, I immediately visualise Aloys on the podium in evening dress, conducting this wonderful music. I also clearly remember *Clare's Dragoons*, that lovely work of
his commissioned in 1945 for the Thomas Davis centenary, at the end
of which Miss Moriarty made a most magnificent entrance from the
back of the Aula Maxima playing the war pipes. But there wasn't a

great deal of contact between our closely related families. The person I saw most of and was most fond of was Aloys Fleischmann senior.

In all the 26 years I lived in Cork from my birth in 1921, I only ever remember Aunt Tilly (Aloys' mother) coming to visit us once, whereas her mother, our Granny Swertz, used to come twice a week. I don't think it was anything other than sheer hard work – Onkel Aloys with his Cathedral choir, practices, etc. and Aunt Tilly teaching. She was kind enough to teach my brother Arthur, and my sister Frieda and, for a short time, me, the youngest of the trio. She had many other very competent pupils and it was wonderful to be allowed to listen to them playing if we arrived early for our lesson. However, one day when I was nine, Aunt Tilly swept my hands from the keyboard, turned to Frieda and said: 'Take your little sister home, dearie, and teach her something useful like knitting, as she is not a pianist!' Funnily enough, I never minded, especially in later years when I fully realised her extraordinary talent and qualification. It must have been an endurance test to teach someone of that age who did not concentrate on exercises and simple piano pieces! However, I have played jazz by ear all my life and enjoyed it and, I am glad to say, so have my friends. I enjoy all sorts of music – from Scott Joplin to Wagner, American and English jazz, Gerschwin, Barber, Peter Krender. I love them all – Harry James, Louis Armstrong, as well as marches: German, British and American. So I was a bit of a pariah where the Fleischmanns were concerned!

But I used to love the soirées and receptions given by Aunt Tilly – especially if I were invited after a 'celebrity' concert or one of Aloys Junior's concerts at the Aula Maxima. Dear Onkel Aloys, an absolutely wonderful raconteur, used to keep the younger people spellbound with his ghost and other stories. His gorgeous accent and usage of English added to the general atmosphere. For instance one day he was telling us of the difficulty of getting on to buses: 'Mein Gott,' he said, 'they treated us like cattles!' He was a most charming and interesting person – Moira Pyne and I used to meet him regularly in the Savoy Cinema Coffee Lounge after our evening German classes at the then School of Commerce, and we had lots of chat and laughter. Violets were his favourite flowers. I remember bumping into him in town one day and he had a large bunch in his hand, which he sniffed from time to time as we chatted. A lovely man. My Dad thought the world of him although they didn't meet very often. Onkel Aloys was cathedral organist and choir master for almost half a century: I remember a piece of hearsay I got from my grandmother about him. That area was pretty tough when he first came to Cork, and apparently the local children used to catcall and shout names at him in the beginning as he made his way to his choir practices. But he completely disarmed them by rolling pennies down the road, which they would pounce on, fight over, forgetting all about him in the excitement. Sometime in the late 1930s he got himself a dog. He had a very gentle collie called Bran (after Fionn MacCumhal's hound) who used to accompany him everywhere. He loved this beautiful sheepdog, and was distraught when it disappeared one day. He put notices up in all the local shops, advertised in the newspapers offering a reward, and told the police. Eventually he learned that there was a dog answering to Bran's description in the Dogs' Home. So off he went, and came home with a collie which was not his at all, but he insisted it was, and kept it until it passed away in old age.

One reason why perhaps the Fleischmanns and O'Malley-Williams didn't really 'gel' was my grandmother's and my mother's interest in German politics. Granny Swertz was awarded the Iron Cross, Third Class, for her continued support of all things German. Although she really was quite poor, she always managed to give a small donation to the *Winterhilfe* fund and I believe she never changed her nationality, retaining her German citizenship till her death in 1945. Both she and my mother used to do what they could for the various German internees in the Curragh during the Second World War. Whenever I went to Dublin, from about the age of 19, I also met them and helped. We always seemed to be involved, even with escaped prisoners from *St Nazaire*, a renegade coaster ship, as well as with airmen, navy people, submariners, etc. You can perhaps imagine my absolute horror at the discovery of what had been going on in Germany during the war, when we heard about the concentration camps. I determined then and there never again to regard any nation as trustworthy.

GERTRUD BECKMANN NÉE RÖSSLER (DACHAU), *Aloys Fleischmann's second cousin*
My grand-aunt, Walpurga Maria Rössler, was Aloys' grandmother. She was a dashing girl of lively temperament, with a mind of her own, who fell in love with the local church organist. My great-grandfather, Walpurga's father, was a well-to-do tanner, who would not have reckoned with his only daughter marrying an impecunious musician. The organist went off to a place called Cork, where he got a post in the cathedral. He returned to Dachau the following year and proposed to Walpurga. She married him in 1880, despite the pressure no doubt exerted by parents and five brothers, and went with him to Ireland, where she had nine children.

Her second girl, Tilly, came to Munich to study music and often stayed with our family. True to family tradition, she also married a musician from Dachau, whom she took back to Cork with her. Her husband, Uncle Aloys to us, liked to visit our family. He would never tell us he was coming, but would simply arrive and knock at the window. Nor did he ever tell us when he was going, but would disappear without saying goodbye, always leaving some belongings behind, as if he wanted to be sure he would return. He was tremendous fun: we had some great escapades with him. He always had time for my sister and myself, would take us for walks, tell us good stories and he wrote some music for us too. Aunt Tilly was a tall, very beautiful woman, but she didn't have much interest in us children. Aloys, or Alfie as we called him, came to Dachau with his parents in 1931, and spent the summer there. He was much too serious for my taste, as I was by then a wild creature of ten. My mother took him to a ball once, but I think she had a hard time with him as he was a hopeless dancer. He could not take drink, either. Dachau is famous for the good beer brewed here, but Alfie didn't like beer. He once caused something of a sensation in that regard. They were having a meal out and a glass of beer was put in front of him, which he probably didn't want. What did he do but put sugar into it to improve the taste!

After he finished his studies in Munich, I didn't see him again until the 1960s. We got on very well from that time, although I was not the ideal companion for him, not being in the least interested in shrill modern music or bizarre painting, which he loved. But I let him do his own thing, and I think he enjoyed his holidays with us. For a very clever man, he was amazingly inept in ordinary matters. He took no interest in his appearance. He was forever getting lost, forgetting to get out of the train when he should have and ending up in the remotest corners at dead of night. We called him 'der irre Ire' – der Ire is the Irishman; add another r and it means 'the lunatic'. But we were very fond of him and greatly miss our quaint cousin.

LOLA MACDONNELL (BANDON, CO CORK), UCC Music and Arts Graduate, Music Teacher
I knew Aloys since we were children. My mother was a friend of Madame Stockley and studied the piano with Frau Fleischmann. Aloys and Sophie Stockley used to stay with us at Castlelack during the summer holidays. Castlelack was a great place for children and young people in the summer – there was the lake with a large flat-bottomed boat which could not capsize and there was a little island which we were always adding to with large stones. We were not allowed to use the boat without a grown-up and Aloys used to come with us. There was swimming, paddling and fishing. There was the farm and the mill. Nearby was the Duke's Wood. So it was an ideal holiday change from the city.

Aloys and Sophie were some years older than we were. When you are ten, fourteen is a much greater age gap than later in life. We four children were sent off to bed early even in long summer evenings while Aloys and Sophie stayed up with the adults in the drawing-room. We were furious and expressed our rebellion in noisy games upstairs. My mother would send Aloys to quieten us. I don't remember what he used to say but we all went quietly back to bed, happy and calm, for we all loved him. He was tremendously kind and had time for us unlike most boys of his age. He seemed very mature and joined with the grown-ups as an equal. I know my parents were very fond of him and loved to have him stay. He was interested in everything. I never remember him ill-tempered or selfish.

Later I knew Aloys when I was in University College, Cork – I was in his Music class. He was the same Aloys: kind, calm and conscientious – a great teacher, as all his students will confirm. We were five in the class and one of the members was Pilib Ó Laoghaire. At that time in the mid 1930s Music was not combined with other subjects as it is today, so very few people opted for that degree. We worked hard inspired by Aloys. It was important not to disappoint him. He made us do things we did not think we could do, like singing early motets at sight one voice to each part. He never criticised except to build up our confidence.

I was also doing an Arts degree and it was my great privilege to have Daniel Corkery as my English professor. There were two great qualities in Professor Corkery. Firstly he approached English literature from a Gaelic point of view. This was a slant which was not to be found in any of the background reading required of us. It was exciting and fresh. The other quality was a personal involvement. When Corkery introduced literature that he loved, he communicated his love to us and I, for one, have never lost it.

The Symphony Orchestra was newly in existence. After our lecture I would help Aloys to arrange the chairs and music stands for the rehearsals. All the players had their own places and Aloys was most careful about the arrangement. He was aware that some players might take offence if they were moved or demoted. This is an example, I think, of Aloys' care not to offend, to respect people's sensitivities and very sensibly not to prejudice his own projects, like the orchestra, by lack of attention to details that to others might seem unimportant. He avoided offending people. He was tolerant and courteous.

The orchestra, at that time, was a curious mixture. The Brady brothers, well known violin teachers in the city, were the leaders of the first violins and second violins. In the orchestra were some Brady students, schoolgirls with plaits, some college students who could play

354

an instrument, and various city instrumentalists. The wind section and percussion were supplied by the No. 2 Army Band in uniform. Because I had learned the harp at the Ursuline Convent in Blackrock I became the harpist. The harp score always has more rests than music and I always got lost. The music stopped and I would see Aloys looking at me with a pained expression. The Army sergeant who played the bassoon sat next to me. As he was used to counting bars he offered to count mine as well and give me a dig in the ribs when it was my turn to come in. It worked splendidly. The concerts took place in the Aula Maxima of the university and were very well attended. I remember especially one excellent concert with Gerard Shanahan playing the Grieg piano concerto.

I did not meet Aloys much socially as he was a professor – but from time to time he would come out to Castlelack and talk to my mother about his problems: the difficulties of getting support and funding and the frustrations he encountered. It was my brother, Liam, who suggested to him to get sponsorship for the Choral Festival. He was quite downhearted at times. He felt that he was fighting a solitary battle to bring music to the people of Cork. My mother was very fond of him and he had many good friends like Madame Stockley, who supported him and sympathised with his aims.

It was at this time too that the UCC Choral Society was born. Seán Neeson, who lectured to us in Irish music, called me into his office and said that he was starting a choral group. He sent me forth to get members. In a short time we had about 30 members and after Christmas we did a broadcast from the radio station in the women's jail. I shall always remember going up the stone stairs in that grim place. We sang 'Bán Cnoic Éireann Ó' and the 'Chúil Fhionn'. That was in the mid 1930s.

There were various musical circles in Cork. Madame Stockley would hold a soirée in her drawing-room and her pupils would illustrate the art of the *Lieder*. There were other groups also. But Aloys wanted to reach the city. He was intensely interested in all kinds of cultural development: ballet, painting, sculpture. He deplored the fact that music was not timetabled in the secondary schools. He was concerned that Irish culture should not be swamped by American and other influences. Irish culture and an Irish Ireland were at the heart of his efforts. I think his band of devoted voluntary workers recognised this and worked hard to help him achieve his aims. As we all know his achievement was monumental. Ní bheidh a leithéid ann arís.

MADELINE O'CONNELL NÉE HORGAN (CORK), granddaughter of UCC President Sir Bertram Windle, UCC Medicine Graduate. Her memories were recorded by Anne Fleischmann.

My father, John J. Horgan, became very friendly with Aloys' parents, Aloys and Tilly Fleischmann. Aloys senior had come to Ireland from Germany and became organist in the cathedral in Cork. Some years after that, the First World War broke out and he was in danger of being interned, Ireland being under British rule. It was my father who looked after him and as a solicitor was able to keep him safe in Cork for the first two years. But in 1916 he was interned as an alien. So that's how the friendship started. I remember he used to come a lot to our house, Lacaduv when I was a very small girl – that was after his time in the camp in England. He'd always come up and tell me stories, which were all about lions and tigers, and were told in his broken English; I was always terrified but enjoyed it. He was a most likeable man: very soft, very gentle. He loved to be busy doing all sorts of things and he looked very foreign with his unusual clothes and his gesticulations.

He was very close to my mother, who was a lovely person. She was a very good pianist. The other musician in the family was my aunt, Rita Horgan. She was Scottish and had come with the Carl Rosa Opera Company to Cork: that's how my uncle met her. She gave many recitals of songs composed by Aloys senior: she had a beautiful voice. I remember her doing *Madame Butterfly* and *Faust*. My mother was Bertram Windle's daughter. My father was very involved in politics, and used to advise Bertram Windle when he first came to Cork as President of UCC: that's how he met my mother. Windle's family were Irish Protestants; he studied medicine in Trinity and then got the chair of Anatomy in Birmingham University, where the anatomy school is still called after him. Then he was invited to come to Cork as President of UCC. He was very well thought of.

Everybody loved Aloys Fleischmann senior: he was especially popular with the musical women: with my mother and my aunt. He was the nicest man. His wife Tilly came across as if she was always acting a part. She used to wear long flowing robes: we children were a bit afraid of her because she was so much the *grande dame*. But she was a very good teacher and a good taskmaster. Both my mother and later my stepmother went to her for piano lessons and they had to work very hard.

Young Aloys, or Aloys Óg, as he was called in the family, was about the same age as my brothers Ivor and Joe. They were very wild. I remember Aloys chasing around the place with them: they used to have walking sticks which they used as swords. He had no brothers or sisters, but was part of our family until Ivor and Joe went to boarding school in Clongowes, and then that era finished.

I would think that Aloys was closer to his mother. His father would have influenced him quite a lot musically and in his way of thinking. Tilly was a dominant woman and old Aloys, as we used to call him, would sometimes take refuge from her, often in Lacaduv. They lived in Wellesley Terrace in a house that was full of books and pictures and had a definite atmosphere. Old Aloys was very much a loner, very much on his own, but with his music. I would say that he was very contented.

I met Aloys Óg again when I was in College, having been away at school until then. I don't think he had changed. I was the one person who would always pull his leg; he'd pretend to be very shocked but I never allowed him to get away with that because I knew him far too well.

I remember Joan Denise Moriarty dancing in the very early days. My husband St John knew her because they both came from Mallow, and he knew her growing up. I met her frequently and always felt that she was acting a part. She was a very gracious person, but not somebody you'd feel you wanted to get to know better. She was interested in the things Aloys was interested in and naturally they became friendly. Aloys' wife always invited Joan around to their house. Joan did tremendous work for ballet but I always felt that she was living a role. It may have had something to do with the uncertainty over her birth – it was well known in Mallow that her father was not Mrs Moriarty's husband. She was a kind woman, but very distant and dedicated.

I was in the same class in College as Nancy, as we called Anne Madden, whom Aloys was to marry. She called herself 'Anne' in college, but remained 'Nancy' to her oldest friends. We both did Medicine. She was two or three years older than the rest of us, because at school she hadn't done her Matric, the college entrance exam, and so she had to work for that first and learn Latin from scratch when she decided to study. She lived near me, and we'd go to college together; we were both members of the Art Society. I thought that she and Aloys were completely unsuited to each other. They had such very different backgrounds: she was Cork through and through, and Aloys wasn't. Personality-wise they were both intense, both took everything very seriously, both went for what they wanted. Aloys would go and do his own thing, and knowing him very well, I can say he was a selfish man. But then people who are into painting or music become like that because their whole lives are geared to the art. Maybe it was not selfishness, but single-mindedness.

357

Nancy was also a person who made herself. She didn't come from any medical background: she had to make her own way and become what she wanted to be, against a lot of odds. I don't think her mother would have encouraged her: there had never been a woman in their family who studied – they sat in their lovely houses and organised the family. Her mother was in a wheelchair towards the end of her life. She could be a domineering woman, like her daughter – both very definite personalities. Mrs Madden was also a very kind woman and I always felt at home in her house. Nancy was airy-fairy about lots of mundane things and I would often argue with her – she always loved an argument.

I was on the Committee of the Cork Art Society, which Aloys was head of, and the meetings were completely controlled by him. I used to throw in red-herrings just to annoy him, but he had a good sense of humour and didn't mind. He was like my own brother: I knew exactly what he was thinking. I was very fond of him.

ANNE FLEISCHMANN NÉE MADDEN (1912–1990) interviewed by Donna O'Sullivan on Cork Radio in 1978

D O'S: Somewhere behind every great man, there is a great woman. In this case, it is Mrs Anne Fleischmann, who could be said to have sacrificed her husband on the altar of art. She gives us a little insight into Aloys Fleischmann, the man behind the baton, as she recalls her first impressions of him.

AF: He was much more human than people were telling us and trying to have us believe. He was perfectly happy climbing into graveyards at two in the morning, and there was no false professorial nonsense attached to him.

DO'S: Married and at home, he was the father who enjoyed every minute of the time spent with his children, even if things didn't always go according to plan.

AF: They went down to Crosshaven at one stage visiting Miss Moriarty, who was staying with friends, and she had been given a cat that she didn't want to have at the seaside. I wasn't there, and she gave the cat to Aloys to mind and to put somewhere in Cork. And of course in the middle of the journey home, the cat jumped loose of everybody because it wasn't in a box; everybody got scratched, and the car went into a ditch. Aloys faints if he sees blood, but blood was pouring down the head of one of the children, so they had to go, cat and all, to the emergency unit of the hospital. But those things didn't often happen. There's a lot of the schoolboy in him still. He loves adventures, climbing down difficult places, doing things that can't be done. Difficulties are only there to be overcome.

DO'S: He's a very enthusiastic man, by nature, isn't he?

AF: I don't know whether you'd call it enthusiasm, but anything he does, he does with his heart and soul while that thing lasts.

DO'S: How does he manage to wear so many hats and to get so much done?

AF: By never stopping. Day or night. I think he has about six hours sleep and the rest of the day he's going flat out, following up all his bits and pieces.

D.O'S: Is that what keeps him young, and gives him the very young outlook on life which he still has?

AF: I don't think he has time to grow old. His mind hasn't grown old anyway. And he never walks upstairs: he always runs.

DO'S: In a life as crowded as his, does the Professor find time for his children?

AF: When pushed, when there's a real crisis. There was one time when Alan (the youngest) was still at Glenstal and had written home to ask if he could bring four fellows up for supper. So we said yes, and went to the match and when we came home we found to my horror that there were 34 boys and two priests. So I took the priests into the drawing-room and told my daughters to do what they could and the party went on. The school magazine wrote that the most exciting event of that term was being in Fleischmanns and hearing ghost stories told by Professor Fleischmann. He was always very fond of ghost stories; they inevitably come up sooner or later at a party.

DO'S: What does the Professor like to do when he's not working? Or is there such a thing as spare time in his life?

AF: He does a certain amount of gardening, because I don't and if he didn't do it, the place would be just chaos. So he keeps the garden in condition, cuts grass, and that sort of thing. He also cuts wood if he's put to it. But if he's really enjoying himself, he's climbing a mountain.

DO'S: How important is his work to him, or does he make a division between what is work and what is pleasure?

AF: No, he makes no difference. If he went to a film and laughed his heart out, he'd only have gone to the picture because it was necessary for him to be there. He never could admit to himself that he went because it would be fun to go.

DO'S: Does he never idle, then? Does he never waste any time?

AF: If he sits down for two minutes, he drops off asleep; he has that same capacity that his father had of having I think they call them catnaps: for ten minutes or a quarter of an hour. At any moment when he's not actually occupied with something, he'll go out like a light, even in the middle of a party.

DO'S: Mrs Fleischmann, do you think the Professor is very conscious of the work that he has done, and does he ever sit back and say: Well that was a good job and it was well done?

AF: No, he wouldn't dream of having time to think that anything was good that he had done. That's finished, and he's off on the next problem.

DO'S: He doesn't ever, ever clap himself on the back?

AF: The day the Choral Festival finishes this year, he'll be planning for his next big event, which will be the Playday of the students. Most people come home when their particular effort is over and say: 'That's great, I have a fortnight off now'. But nowadays he never even has one day free.

ANNE FLEISCHMANN NÉE MADDEN interviewed on 7 May 1980 by Dan Collins on the Cork Radio Programme Cork Man of Music *after her husband had retired*
AF: The private Aloys is quite different. When his students get into trouble, or get sick or vanish from class – and there are always one or two each year – he always follows them up. But we rarely see him. He's upstairs all the morning in his study doing his composition and things like that. He dashes his lunch. This year has been the worst of all. He has been out three times a week for lunch and only in to evening dinner about twice a week. He does on a snack or something when he's out because he hasn't got the time.

DC: Tell me about his scooter.

AF: We're dead wrong traffic-wise living here in the Glen in Ballyvolane with him having to go through town to get to College every day. Though I suppose every place is the wrong place nowadays with the traffic the way it is. It's for speed that he uses the scooter, though he's far too old to be on it. He has no patience, and with the scooter he can wiggle in and out of the traffic until he gets to the green light that says go. But if he's in the car and there are people ahead of him, I've seen him read the paper till the lights change! I was talking to him yesterday about the car and that it should be possible to organise things so that we could both use it.

'Why?' he said, 'I'll be on the scooter for the next 15 years!'

I said: 'Don't you realise you'll be 85 then?'

'What about it?' says he.

So where does that leave you!

MAIGREAD Ó MURCHADHA (CORK), Art Teacher, daughter of the sculptor Joseph Higgins, wife of the sculptor Seamus Murphy. Here are extracts from a conversation with Anne Fleischmann
My mother's people knew Aloys Fleischmann's grandparents, who

lived on the Mardyke with their nine children. That was way back in the 1890s. But in 1915 my mother married Joseph Higgins the sculptor and went off to live in Youghal, where I was brought up, so as a child I never had any contact with them. I met them again later on through my husband Seamus. He was very friendly with the MacSwineys, with Daniel Corkery and the Stockleys, and used to go to the Fleischmanns' recitals. Aloys and his parents were at that time living in the house I now live in: 6 Wellesley Terrace. The Herr (as we used to call him) planted young trees in the back garden: they grew to be enormous and by the time the Fleischmanns moved out the garden was very narrow and very dark. Seamus called it the Black Forest. Then the telephone and electricity people came along and because of the wires cut the tops off all the trees. Actually they grew better and greener afterwards and they are still there, though not growing up into the sky any more. So the Herr wasn't too upset. He loved trees. Bridget Doolan and myself had one planted in his memory in Fitzgerald's Park. There was a huge old one nearby that has since been knocked down in one of the gales.

Seamus became a good friend of Aloys'. Indeed so much so that when Aloys got engaged to Anne, he took Seamus along to help him choose the engagement ring! It was a square emerald. Seamus had never heard of anyone needing moral support on such an occasion and taking his butty along rather than the girl. When Aloys got married, they moved to the island house on Oileán Ruadh in Rochestown, and I visited them there with Seamus: we walked the seven miles as there were no buses during the war. They spent the war years there. Aloys' mother Tilly used to cycle into town to teach – I remember someone describing her on the bike in her long clothes and the stately air she managed to preserve.

I was a bit nervous of Tilly, but got on well with Aloys senior. I don't think he was a very happy man, and he didn't have a lot to say for himself, at least not to me. But then I was very young in those days. However, I will never forget one conversation I had with him as we walked up the road together. I was terrified of being buried alive, and I told him that it was an idea which scared me out of my wits. He told me not to worry, that one wouldn't notice as one would smother first. He could have laughed at me or said: 'For heaven's sake – what a thing to be thinking of!' but he was so nice about it. I was always grateful to him for understanding me: I had never mentioned this fear to Seamus, nor to anyone else. From then on I felt confident that it would not happen.

The Herr spent part of the last year of his life in St Patrick's hospice, just up the road from his home. Aloys junior used to bring him home regularly in a wheelchair: they had a handrail fitted on the steps to get him up into the house. He would be home for the afternoon and go back to the hospital at night. I remember once Seamus went to visit him at the hospital towards the end. When he came back he said 'The Herr is at the bottom of the cage'. This was one of Seamus' sayings – that when the bird goes down to the bottom of the cage, you know things aren't so good with that bird. He said that the old man across the ward from the Herr was on the way out, that screens had been put up, that the relatives were all there. And that Herr Fleischmann was not talking any more either. Seamus was worried and went back the next night. The screens were all down, the relatives gone, and the old man was sitting up in bed reading the *Echo*. Herr Fleischmann was sitting up in bed too and said to Seamus, pointing to his revived neighbour: 'See him now: he eats the apple without the knife'.

Seamus also liked Aloys junior very much. He was terribly good to us. His wife Anne didn't have an easy time being married to somebody with so many things on hand. I always believed in him, as she did, but like her, I felt he should have done a lot more composing. He took on too much. He had the ballet, and the orchestra, which he forced to play music that they sometimes resented, so he had to coach them endlessly. And there was the Choral Festival, which was great. Anne was obviously very fond of Aloys and very proud of him. She used always go to the concerts and stand at the side. She wore a lovely long red velvet cloak. She used to pretend she knew nothing about music, but I never believed her. She once told me her favourite composer was Gustav Mahler – a strange choice for somebody who knew nothing about it! I was very fond of her.

Aloys was one of the people who helped us a lot, like Denis Gwynn and Edmund Hayes. We used to be stuck for cash all the time. Whenever Seamus got a bit of money from his sculpture, he would go out and pay the gas bill, the rent, the electricity and anybody he owed anything to before he ever thought of buying a loaf of bread. I had two small children to feed. One day Aloys was here and he noticed a bust of Corkery that my father had done. It was in plaster, because my father never saw any of his works cast. It was the last thing my father did before he died. When Aloys saw the head of Corkery, who was professor of English at the university, he decided it should be cast and that it should be in the university. So he went to see Alfred O'Rahilly, the president, and they went walking in the grounds. Long before that there used to be a statue of Queen Victoria up on the roof of the library, and President O'Rahilly had decided to have it taken down. When Aloys and O'Rahilly were walking in the grounds, there she was lying in the grass, as nobody knew what to do with her. Aloys told us that

O'Rahilly gave her a slight kick and asked: 'Do you think Seamus Murphy could make a Virgin out of her?' But they buried her instead. Aloys persuaded O'Rahilly to commission Seamus to cast the head done by my father for the university.

That was the sort of thing Aloys did, and I think it was why a lot of people didn't like him. He was always interfering and making people do things: he was really very good at getting things done. When all the professors were motoring up and down in their cars, full of dignity, he would be tearing around on his motor-bike in all weathers. He fought for the right things and this is why we were all for him. Seamus thought the world of him. He was the salt of the earth.

MÁIRÍN O'ROURKE (CAMBRIDGE), UCC and Cambridge Graduate, until her retirement Tutor in the History Department at the University of Cambridge
My connection with Professor Fleischmann and his parents goes back over many years, both as a family friend, and as a piano pupil of Frau Fleischmann. My earliest recollection is of the day when I was brought to Cork from my boarding-school with another child to play for Frau Fleischmann. We were eight or nine years old and, needless to say, rather apprehensive. However, we were quickly put at our ease, mainly thanks to Professor Fleischmann, who happened to be there and who offered us a bowl of fruit, from which we each chose a banana – a rare treat at that time. We played our pieces and Frau Fleischmann was most encouraging, so we returned to school very pleased with ourselves.

Aloys Fleischmann and his wife Tilly were unworldly people and money had no dominion over them. Above all, they strove to be true to their art and to the high ideal of performance they had set themselves. I remember them both in Oileán Ruadh, Rochestown – a poetic place full of trees and birds, where Aloys senior seemed to be in his element with his dog Bran. The cathedral choir which Aloys Fleischmann directed was a valuable part of the musical life of Cork. The choir sometimes gave recitals of polyphonic music in the Honan Chapel. I recall two such memorable occasions, one in the 1930s and another in the 1950s, but it was probably the singing during the Holy Week ceremonies in the cathedral which made the most lasting impression on us all, as it was an annual event. It was indeed a unique experience to assist at these ceremonies, where the music and the devotion went hand in hand. Those of us who had the privilege of hearing it would always remember the intoning of the Good Friday 'Popule meus' and the jubilant singing of the High Mass on Easter Sunday.

Tilly's generous hospitality will never be forgotten. It remained constant, irrespective of how circumstances may have varied from time to time. She had an old-world graciousness which made her a delightful hostess. She was generous with her time, too. She was known on occasion to have given free tuition to a talented student, who would otherwise have been unable to have piano lessons. Tilly could also be quite amusing, for she had a lively imagination and a vivid way of telling a story. She once gave a most entertaining account of an incident which occurred when she was directing the cathedral choir in her husband's absence. She decided that the choirboys deserved a treat, so she arranged to take them to the cinema. To her disgust, she found that the film was based on a tale of love and betrayal, which was depicted in the crudest manner. However, she consoled herself by thinking that these innocent little fellows would not understand what it was all about, when to her confusion, she heard one of them saying to his friend: 'Look, the husband is watching!'

I studied with Tilly Fleischmann for three years as a teenager. I had done Grade 5 before I went to her, but I took no further examinations after that, as she preferred to follow her own syllabus rather than that of the Royal Irish Academy. Although most of her pupils were more mature than myself, she was able to 'descend' to the level of a fourteen year-old and to talk their language. For instance, in one of the Mozart sonatas where the sombre mood changes quite suddenly to a more cheerful one, I remember her conveying this to me by saying: 'You know, it's just like a child smiling through his tears.' Each piece was studied in its own context, be it personal or literary. Tilly would always introduce you to a piece by first describing the background of its composition, telling you, for example, that Schumann's 'Erinnerung' expresses the composer's grief on the death of his friend Mendelssohn, or that Chopin's *Prelude* No. 15 was written in a deserted monastery. Then there were the Playdays. These were informal performances which enabled us to appreciate a variety of musical talents in our fellow-students. Among my contemporaries was Denis Houlihan, the very gifted hunchback with the long fingers. Tilly would sometimes play a piece herself, which was invariably a great joy for the listeners. On one occasion, I recall her playing Brahms. I have no idea what the title of the piece was, but never since have I heard Brahms played with such artistry and discernment.

Aloys Óg – as he was known to many of us – was first and foremost a devoted son. When his father was terminally ill in hospital, he often took him out in his wheel chair for a change of scene. After his father's death, once a week regularly he would lunch in town with his mother. (The attachment was reciprocal and she usually referred to him simply as 'my son'.) He was also a loving husband and father, besides being a loyal and steadfast friend. Aloys saw the best in everyone and if any misunderstanding arose between mutual friends, he would do his utmost to clear it up. His kindness will always be remembered, as will his inclination to defend the weaker party. He had a natural trust in people which sometimes, however, had the effect of making him somewhat vulnerable. He was free from any kind of prejudice and took no personal credit for his great talents or achievements. Like his mother, he was able to get his message across clearly to the younger generation. His commentaries for school children on pieces such as *Peter and the Wolf* were dramatic and imaginative and were enjoyed alike by children and teachers. Aloys was undeniably serious-minded, but he had a quiet sense of humour which enabled him to see the funny side.

In my own recollection of Aloys, two moments stand out in my memory. One was when he and his wife, Anne, appeared at Cork railway-station to bid farewell to the bereaved Germaine Stockley, who was leaving Cork to go to live in Dublin. The other was much later, when I returned to Cork in rather sad circumstances. Aloys came to meet me at the station and brought me to his house for supper, where I spent a very pleasant evening with Anne and himself. It was marvellous the way he found time for everyone in spite of leading such a busy life. Aloys used his gifts and great energy to work for Ireland and in particular for Munster. He chose to remain in Ireland, whereas some Irishmen have preferred to leave their native land in search of better opportunities or more rewarding remuneration. In this he was single-minded, and in truth *Hibernior Hibernis multis*.

ANN QUAIN NÉE NEESON (CORK), *Member of the Cork Ballet Company*
Any one of the manifold activities of Professor Aloys Fleischmann would have required the full commitment of one ordinary man for a lifetime, but 'the Prof' was not an ordinary man: he managed to achieve the apparently unachievable.

He was well known to my family for as long as I can remember, and even longer than that. My father, Seán Neeson, sang in the choir of the Cork Cathedral of St Mary and St Anne under Aloys Fleischmann senior, who was the organist and choirmaster there. My mother, Geraldine Neeson, was a pupil of his wife's, of Frau Tilly, a pianist who had studied in Munich. The two couples lived quite near each other: Dad and Uncle Aloys strolled home together from choir practice; they were both men of good conversation, so they'd stop at our house to continue their discussions until late in the evening. Both my parents enjoyed these evenings with Uncle Aloys, who was a round cheery man with a twinkle in his eye. His wife was a straight woman always dressed in flowing garments who appeared very tall, and sailed through the streets of Cork.

Domestic life in those days was very different from now. A working mother was unusual but there was always domestic help, and fathers did very little in the home. One of my favourite stories about the young Aloys illustrates that. Once when he was a baby, Frau Tilly had to go out and instructed Uncle Aloys, who was working at home, to keep an eye on him as he was at the crawling stage. Frau Tilly arrived home to an unexpectedly quiet house and found Uncle Aloys deep in his composition with the baby nailed to the floor. Young Aloys had been showing all the signs of his future active life and had been crawling into everything, greatly disturbing his father's concentration. As all babies, boys and girls, wore long gowns, his father just nailed the baby's flowing gown to the floor, which still gave plenty of room for movement. Uncle Aloys thought it a most practical solution; he was surprised that Frau Tilly was not amused.

In 1914 young Aloys started school at Scoil Ita, the school run by the Misses MacSwiney, the sisters of Terence MacSwiney who was to die on hunger strike during the Troubles. It is on record there that when young Aloys injured his right hand, he immediately started to practice with his left hand – even in kindergarten he was not a person to sit back and let the work pass him by! He was an exceptional young man from the start. When a student in UCC, he became ill; in order to keep him at rest and entertained, Frau Tilly asked my mother to lend him some books which, however, were not to be 'too advanced'. With some apprehension as to the stipulation, Mum introduced him to the Russians – Gorki, Turgenev and Chekhov. In her own words: 'Anyone who saw the beauty in these books, and realised their relationship to music, was worth watching.'

I met the Professor in my own right when the Cork Symphony Orchestra and the Cork Ballet Company started their long and fruitful cooperation. He was a demon for work, who must have been maddened by the casual approach of some of the musicians. They often left their instruments in the Aula Max from one rehearsal to the next, but the conductor's calm politeness was always maintained. I can remember on one occasion, at dress rehearsal in the old Opera House, his quiet apology to us dancers: 'Do you mind if we practice a little?' He had very strong and definite views about music but his was not a closed mind. For instance, when ballet programmes were being prepared he was a bit reluctant to include Johann Strauss, the waltz king. Before the orchestra's involvement, when we performed to piano or tape, Strauss was a great favourite with dancers and audience but wasn't considered a serious musician in the classical mode. However the Prof agreed to the inclusion of the waltzes and the polkas and, watching him from the stage, you could see that they got the same attention as any other music and the orchestra had the true Viennese lilt. He also seemed to be enjoying himself.

When my mother became the Theatre and Music critic for both the *Cork Examiner*, as it was then known, and the *Irish Times*, she spent a very busy life attending concerts, recitals and plays, as well as teaching piano to university students, so she was still very much connected to the life of the Prof. She was not a young woman, she didn't drive and she was disturbingly independent. When she had a deadline she would get a taxi, or more often than not, she would walk home at all hours of the night. She had many concerned friends, including the Prof, who often collected her and brought her home. On one occasion she was anxious that she might be late and went down to the road to meet her lift. We took the opportunity to go out and, having locked up the house, we set off to have a pleasant evening. Arriving home before Mum, we didn't see her until the next morning, when everyone was flying out with no time for talk. During the morning the Prof phoned enquiring about Mum. I wondered at his concern. He then told me that he should have been her escort the previous night and that he had come to the back door as it was a shorter walk than from the house to the road. There was no reply to his ringing and he became concerned about my mother alone in the house, as he thought. So he climbed the wall, which was not too high on the outside, but had a very big drop on the inside, a fact of which he was not aware, and it emerged that he had injured his ankle, having misjudged the jump. He was unable to get into the house and had visions of my mother collapsed on the floor. I was now very upset about his injuries, he was really concerned about Mum, and she was off about her business totally unaware of the distress she had caused. This was a man who appeared reserved and aloof, but he was truly concerned about the welfare of others, something I had seen on more than one occasion.

He had a wonderful gift of language and his public speeches were well known and remembered for their insight and wit, but he could also express himself sparingly. When my mother died, he rang to offer his condolences and any help he could. I asked him about music for the funeral mass; he paused a moment and said quietly: 'The rule is you must have the resident choir and organist.' We had no music.

The Prof packed more into a fast and full life than a score of ordinary people. One of my last recollections of him was when my husband came home one evening and told me he had seen the Prof walking in town. I replied that he always walked everywhere, but Charlo said: 'No, he was *walking* – not racing.' We just looked at each other, realising that time was running out for Professor Aloys Fleischmann.

367

GERALD Y. GOLDBERG (CORK), UCC Arts Graduate, Lawyer, former Lord Mayor
of Cork, Patron of the Cork Orchestral Society[1]
It is only when one is concerned with writing that memories jostle and
clamour for liberation from the living past – in a sense a re-birth. Aloys
Fleischmann was indifferent to fame. Fame was something that followed him but he ignored it, was impervious to it and either shared it
with others or allowed it to pass him by. As a student, later as incumbent of the Chair of Music in UCC, he used his great scholarship and
his outstanding ability as teacher-writer to encourage the careers of his
many pupils. He caught and at times deeply and sincerely felt the
mood of people, their urgent urging for a living vibrant Ireland. So he
composed new music, encouraged other composers, brought some of
the world's greatest interpreters to work with him. Arnold Bax was
one from whom Aloys learned much and gave much in return. When
Bax died he paid a living tribute through Aloys to Ireland and Cork by
bequeathing his scores, his piano and other personal effects to the university. When it became necessary to create and advance the Cork
International Choral Festival, it was to Aloys that Der Breen, who initiated the Cork Tóstal, turned. These two collaborated for all the years
left to Breen, who died prematurely. Year after year Aloys travelled to
Europe enlisting the great European choirs. He had been alerted to the
possibility of advancing Irish ballet. This was a challenge. In this he
had, as collaborator, Miss Moriarty and her newly formed ballet school.
I have referred to this venture elsewhere and to the fact that for a short
time I was involved as her adviser while later my wife Sheila, Leslie
Horne, the solicitors John Coakley, Edmund Hayes, and James W.
O'Donovan and others were fellow workers.[2] We saw the advantages
which the dance and, especially, Irish dance offered to the nation. It
would have been tragic if we had allowed this grand collaboration to
collapse and fade away.

If one can make any criticism of Aloys Fleischmann it would be
that for years he over-taxed his strength and pressurised his every
instinct in the cause of Irish music. That is why at his call so many distinguished helpers and artists rallied to him. He lived at a time when
Ireland was emerging from darkness into light. The indebtedness
owed by Ireland to men of the calibre of Aloys Fleischmann cannot yet
be fully appreciated. When Ireland needed him most he answered the
call. His magnificent example, his skilled reorganisation and rebuilding of music throughout the country will go down in history. He did
not wait for people to come to him; he went to them. He did not
preach: he took action. He recognised the need and brought music and
the arts to the community. The greatest among the great in the world
of music found themselves in Cork under his aegis and never regret-

ted their coming. He recognised the 'call' and, fortunately for us, he answered it.

Aloys Fleischmann was an only child born to Herr Aloys and Frau Tilly Fleischmann, the one a choir master, the other a consummate pianist, and later teacher, who in her youth had been a pupil of a pupil of Liszt. Music and art was the milk upon which he was bred and fed. This made him – with the help and support of his wife Anne and a loving family – of a sensitivity like that which inspired the Irish poet William Edgar O'Shaughnessy to write:

> We are the music makers,
> We are the dreamers of dreams.

Aloys Fleischmann has, like other great men, been subjected to criticism. He believed in his ideas, and that what was true for him in his private heart was true for all men. Such was described by Edward Emerson as genius. Aloys was an upright man, a gentleman and an example to all good living men. How else, then, can I conclude but by once more turning to Emerson: 'Is it so bad, then, to be misunderstood? Pythagoras was misunderstood, and Socrates, and Jesus, and Luther and Copernicus and Galileo, and Newton, and every pure and wise spirit that ever took flesh. To be great is to be misunderstood'.

CATHERINE BURNS (CORK), *UCC Medicine Graduate, pupil of Tilly Fleischmann and her physician*
Professor Aloys Fleischmann is sadly missed by all who knew him. His contribution to both musical circles and culture in general was immense. I had the privilege of meeting him on several occasions when he came to visit his aged parents Herr and Frau Fleischmann. His concern for, his care of, his parents and his obvious admiration of them impressed one immediately. Professor Fleischmann was very popular with all his students at the university: many still speak of him with gratitude and affection. His 'end of term' parties at the College were always enjoyed. I knew quite a few of the members of the orchestra which he conducted so well, and for which he worked so hard. The players, some of whom were personal friends of mine, often spoke of his patience, dedication and the encouragement he gave them.

Professor Fleischmann was a humble gentleman, one with the humility of the great. It was a privilege to have known him. His music will always live on.

Ar deis Dé go raibh a h-anam.

JOAN BURKE (CORK), *formerly of the Burke Typing Service*
Throughout my years in business I had many dealings with the late

Professor Aloys Fleischmann. Though a person of great eminence and one held in the highest regard, he was a most humble man.

I also had many dealings with students of his. They spoke often of him and I wish I had taken notes of all their loving comments about him so that I could have passed them on to his family. I remember particularly they used to speak of Christmas parties in his home which they enjoyed so much. They didn't seem conscious of any generation gap and had such a good time. I am sure he enriched the lives of many people with whom he came in contact.

It was always a pleasure to see him coming through the door; he was always so appreciative of any work done for him. I feel very honoured to have known him.

JULIAN HART (DUBLIN), UCC Science Graduate
Aloys Fleischmann was a giant who galvanised the Cork people into appreciating culture. I became auditor of the Art Society during my studies at UCC, and once played in a Saturday lunchtime recital in the Aula Maxima with Máire McHenry. In those days we had Saturday lectures, so there were plenty of people around. I played first Chopin's *Military Polonaise*, followed by the delicate, gentle *La fille aux cheveux lisses* by Debussy. The professor commented afterwards that the order in which I had played the pieces showed a complete disregard for audience reactions.

He was an imaginative fundraiser. Once when he had to raise money for the Cork Symphony Orchestra, he had the original idea of inviting citizens to sponsor the different instruments: e.g., £50 for a first violin, £30 for a second violin, £20 for the flute and so on. The idea was copied a few years ago where I live in Dalkey by the parish priest, who was rebuilding the local church: £50 symbolised an organ pipe, £5 a slate, etc. Aloys had equally original ideas regarding the salaries of senior public servants. At a time of financial stringency in public expenditure, he had the courage to write to the newspapers stating that professors were overpaid and suggesting that they give a good example to the nation by voluntarily accepting a ten per cent cut in their salaries. I believe he put the same proposal to a meeting of UCC's Academic Council, where it found no support.

When my mother Mary V. Hart died in 1974, my two brothers and I founded the first prize in the Music department: the Mary V. Hart Memorial Prize, which is awarded yearly to the best BMus student. The Professor was pleased with this.

FINBARR DOWDALL (CORK)
The first time I saw a member of Cork's most distinguished musical

family was when I saw Herr Aloys Fleischmann walking his dutiful collie around the streets of the city. He was a delightful Bavarian gentleman, with a soft black hat, long hair, and coat sweeping to the ground, who trained and conducted the Choir at the Cathedral of St Mary and St Anne (the 'North Cathedral').

Some time later, his wife, Frau Tilly Fleischmann, requested my cousin and me to leave a piano lesson for the very obvious (and perfectly valid) reason that neither of us had done any practice since the previous lesson. Shortly thereafter, my mother hauled the pair of us off to a symphony concert at the City Hall – the first given by the Cork Symphony Orchestra, conducted by Aloys Fleischmann – son of the two Fleischmanns already mentioned, who was Professor of Music at University College Cork (UCC). The concert seemed long to a pair of fidgety urchins, though I do recall that the last piece was the one we liked best – and it was composed by the Professor. In the fullness of time, he and the CSO would enter the record books as the longest-lasting conductor/orchestra partnership in the world.

But that was 1939. Then came the war, which we got through to the strains of Vera Lynn, Gracie Fields, Joe Loss, Glenn Miller, Bing Crosby and the Andrew Sisters, and, towards the end of the conflict, a precocious upstart called Frank Sinatra. Having gone to boarding school in 1942, I persisted with piano lessons for some years. Frau Fleischmann had not produced another Franz Liszt, but she did teach me some useful lessons.

In 1945 there were Military Tattoos in Cork and Dublin to enable the wartime army to make a fitting exit before being stood down and, as it was the centennial of the death of the patriot, Thomas Davis, there was a concert on the *Clare's Dragoons* theme, from a commissioned work by the Professor, performed in Dublin and, subsequently, in Cork. He needed a piper and Joan Denise Moriarty agreed to perform if he would agree to provide his orchestra for her incipient Ballet Company. This well-documented cooperation was to last for the remainder of their lives.

In 1953, Seán Lemass, presumably in an effort to lighten the gloom generally prevailing in the 1950s, introduced 'An Tóstal' or spring festival. It met with mixed success throughout the country but, as Val Jago was to point out some years later when he was Lord Mayor of Cork, if An Tóstal had not been a countrywide success, neither had it been a failure, as it had produced the Cork Choral Festival, of which Professor Fleischmann was director (and the instigator). The director of the overall An Tóstal effort in Cork was Der Breen, a remarkable organiser with a background in dramatics. At this stage, my mother, Senator Mrs Jane Dowdall, who had become a member of Cork Corporation in 1950, was very involved in An Tóstal, and in its various Cork 'components'. The Choral Festival was initiated in 1954, but I believe that the most memorable Tóstal was in 1956 when the Film Festival was added. The Tóstal began with a Ballet Week in the City Hall (the century-old, and much loved old Opera House had burned down the previous year); then a visit by the Vienna Philharmonic Orchestra, then the Choral Festival, also in the City Hall, and, finally, the Film Festival in the Savoy Cinema. It was an exhausting three weeks, and the Professor seemed to be in the thick of everything!

The professional Ballet Company, Irish Theatre Ballet, was founded in 1959, and my mother, who was then Lord Mayor, had the honour of declaring it open. The Professor – known by some of the musical fraternity in Cork as Aloys Óg – continued to give tirelessly of his time and effort for the remainder of his life. He climbed Mount Brandon on his eightieth birthday!

He was extremely focused on the job in hand, but he was not narrow in his interests and he occasionally erupted into print in letters (always keen and perceptive) to the newspapers. In our last discussion he pointed out to me that, over the years, many countries had changed their national anthems, and I got the impression that he would have been happy if Ireland were to do the same, as he obviously could restrain his enthusiasm for 'Amhrán na bhFiain'. Having no competence to discuss the song's musical merits, I suggested that he might like to hear the Welsh anthem 'Land of my Fathers', of which he was unaware, but of which I knew through the Rugby connection. He died in the next few weeks and I don't know if he managed to hear the Welsh record I sent him. However, we may be sure that he now enjoys listening to all the choirs he brought to the Choral Festival over the years.

Ceol na bhFláitheais in a thimpeall go deó.

ISABEL HEALY (CORK), *Critic and Writer*
When I think of Professor Fleischmann I see a man running in a dinner jacket with a worn brown leather briefcase or a small figure on a 50 cc motor-bike dwarfed by a double bass strapped to the pillion seat. Professor Aloys Fleischmann was music, energy, kindness, tolerance and formality, to whom, even as a friend's daughter and a daughter's friend, I was always 'Miss Healy'.

In Cork, the world's largest village, peoples' lives are so interconnected that there is little differentiation between establishment, institution and family friend and over the years the distinctions become even more blurred. Professor Fleischmann was establishment and institution but he was also The Da, the father who was friend to his children's friends, offering the hospitality of his home or lifts on his motor-bike (up the hill on icy evenings and he wouldn't even notice, but carry on immune if the young passenger fell off at a corner). It was the 1960s and the music (not his music) was loud and there were always parties up in Fleischmann's, but such was the Prof's presence and importance that we lowered the good time decibels when he was working.

It was the 1960s and the music was loud and we were cool, oh yeah, but we still queued up like kids in a playground for a 'go off' the rocking horse in the hall of Glen House. We were so cool we had the nerve to stage our student revues in a city theatre, though Professor Fleischmann was so well known locally that the line 'Alloys make very good conductors' was probably one of the few in-jokes which was understood by both town and gown.

We were so cool that we invited Cork's most popular guitarist to play in UCC. Professor Fleischmann – whose permission had to be sought for such a ground (and possibly sound barrier) breaking event – asked: 'Roaring Gallagher? Who is this Roaring Gallagher?' but it was music and the Prof didn't stop Rory Gallagher playing in UCC. He was equally bemused by the request of the English Literature Society for the Aula Maxima as a venue for a group called Doctor Strangely Strange (supported, probably, by Supply, Demand and Curve) but those requests also were conceded. It may have been just noise to the Prof, but his tolerance was mighty. Without such tolerance, how could he, year after year, have blithely carried on conducting against the din – the racket, the thunder – of the entire capacity audience of the municipal auditorium opening sweet-paper wrappings and munching potato crisps during the annual orchestral concerts for schools?

Ballet dancers, as well as kids and students lived in worlds of which the Prof was innocent or didn't understand, but never censured. It is said that when he was trying to bring in an eminent international male ballet dancer to the city and somebody whispered that the dancer was gay and might find life in Cork lonely, the Prof replied that he would ensure the guest would be looked after!

Maybe it was a story, or maybe I really remember him taking a short nap in an armchair at his home during the Choral Festival, only to jump to his feet exclaiming 'The Russians are coming, the Russians are coming!' And they were. And they did, returning year after year with their high boots and long plaits and ribbons, their elastic knees and voices and their disciplined whoops because, no doubt, the Prof was also conscious of their needs and ensured that they too were looked after.

Cork is the largest village in the world, but every year it loses something more of its inherent infuriating unique charm and becomes more bland, more ordinary in the international mould called 'cosmopolitan'. It may be more open and more free, but it has lost a formality and dignity that raised it above the ordinary. Cork is a place of water, a small pond of correspondingly large fish. Maybe never again will it be blessed with a character so devoid of conceit or personal ambition but of such energy and altruism with cultural riches as to create such enduring ripples to reach the high water mark attained by Professor Fleischmann.

THEO DORGAN (DUBLIN), *Director of Poetry Ireland*
Man on a Motor-bike

Who is this curious man on a blue, black and silver Honda 175? Bald, with heavy-rimmed spectacles, a briefcase strapped on the pillion? He drives the bike upright, even around sharp corners, he drives altogether too fast for such an old fella. And even if old fellas are allowed ride motor-bikes, at least they should be wearing helmets. What if he falls off, bangs his baldy head? What a mess that would make. Romey Sullivan, two doors up from our house, rides a big Triumph 500, up and down to Dunlops every day. Doesn't ride it to matches, though. Does he ever ride it at the weekends? I don't think so. Mr Begley in school has a big Heinkel scooter but that's decently quiet, doesn't draw attention to itself. Romey and Begley wear helmets, they know they're old fellas and have a bit of cop on. And the comics are full of decent men riding motor-bikes to work. But this lad has a briefcase strapped to the saddle, I mean, Jesus, he often wears a long, belted brown overcoat.

You wear a leather jacket on a bike. Everyone knows that. And, old fellas shouldn't be allowed! Ruins the whole thing, doesn't it?

I draw bikes in the margins of schoolbooks, copybooks. Big, raked front forks, chopped-in saddles, wide swept handlebars. *Easy Rider* is only a year or so away when I spot this old lad first, but all teenagers have preternatural antennae for what's cool and hormone-driven and powerful and dangerous – which means fast big bikes, fast low-slung cars – and a righteous Darwinian aversion to old fellas bucking the natural order. Not acting their age.

He stood out, then. A place the size of Cork, where everything and everyone spirals down off the hills eventually, to roll round and round in the bowl of the city centre, what happens is you build a map by the body's instincts, you come to expect that people of fixed and settled habit will turn up, time after time, in the places you saw them last at that time. Friday afternoon, around 4.30, the baldy fella swings into

Daunt's Square, heading on down into Patrick Street. Where's he coming from? Doesn't matter. Doesn't matter where he's going. He's just there to mark the time and the place and even if you've just started talking to some young one who's making it hard for you to breathe or look at or think of anything else except her perfect small breasts inside the soft powder-blue sweater, you have a flick of an eye over her shoulder for the big specs and the baldy head, the exact bark of the engine falling satisfyingly into place. Here he comes, so you know the day and time and place or, you know the time and place and day so ... yes, here he comes.

Innocence is pattern, the comfort of fixed things coming round again and again and again.

I can't say I ever got to know Aloys. I found out all about him, eventually, when I got to university. Professor of Music, married with daughters, lived in that big rambly old house out in the Glen. A glittery eye for women, a restrained flirt, aware, playful, never predatory; a sharp eye for the erotic nuances of conversation between his students and their boyfriends and girlfriends. You had a strong hunch he knew who was sleeping with whom, that it amused him, that in some subtle and sardonic way Ireland renewing itself under the benign and bleary gaze of Eros was somehow a vindication of his complex, sophisticated ancestry. Even if, as I now suspect he did, he disapproved.

The young are cruel in their casual judgements. I knew from books what it meant, what it was, to be Professor of Music, bald, middle-aged, in a small, inconsequential, provincial university. With the world before us, the old and grey and boring to be swept aside, what should we feel but a low-key pity for someone whom history had so definitively passed by? And yet, we all liked him, noticed him, had a sense that the dull men of the right in the College administration did not like him, which made us like him all the more. If we didn't know exactly where he came from, and his fathers and mothers before him, we knew he was other, most likely Middle European; that the dust of the Habsburg Empire, of gaslit coffee-houses and passionate intellectual argument, arcane knowledge, immense worldweariness hung in the vaults of air behind him (and us) to the east, far to the east, in the plush and polished mahogany vaults of a vanishing and vanished Europe.

In that sense he was a sign to the unknown, had always behind him the gate to a world of immense significance we were too hurried and lustful and passionate to be curious about. Until, of course, life in the provinces being what it is, we knew him well enough to feel inhibited by the accretion of politeness, the empty knowingness of shallow acquaintance over time, and it never occurred to us to ask anything at all.

I was involved in the world of the arts and had published a bad poem or two; we would meet at one thing or another and I like to think he thought of me as someone who might, in a small kind of way, be civilised. I would always address him as Professor and he would, as invariably, address me as Mister Dorgan. He liked to address young men as Mister. I liked that in him, I liked the sense it gave me of some peripheral implication in an older, more formal world of good manners. We would speak of cultural matters with a certain ponderous reserve, ambassadors disposing of some minor matter in an evolving and complex situation. With a certain gravamen that hovered, very delicately, on the edge of being sly and mocking. I seem to remember that we would listen to each other with heads cocked to one side, may even have risen to the sardonic heights of nodding sagely at each other's more trenchant observations. It was a kind of ironic and subtle self-mockery, as if we could not possibly be expected to take life in this dead town seriously. As if some part of us was forever in exile, an exile to be borne stoically and from which we might, just might, expect someday to be delivered. Easy for me of course, with the world, as I so naively thought, before me. But I wonder now what kept Aloys going, doubly an exile since what he must have missed and mourned was already a generation away and the terrible chasm of the war and the holocaust stood forever between him and the redemption of family memories.

What I see in him now, reaching back tentatively to the ghost of a man I scarcely knew, is a kind of heroism. He was too intelligent not to have been sometimes lonely in his very soul, too deliberately kind to have permitted himself to bemoan his fate or despair of that dreary middle class who had adopted an idea of culture as a shield against self-knowledge. The truth is that in his class and generation the genuinely cultured were an embattled few, a race of solitaries who would never grow because context, the play of time and place and fate, was denied them. It would fall to a semi-barbarian generation, ours, to name into being that city forever beyond the reach of that handful of our elders. Was that what he saw in us? Was that why we seemed to bring out in him a kind of tart, regretful amusement? I am conscious now of the lost opportunities, the questions I might have put to him, the lessons he might have had to teach. But of course it is perfectly possible he might have had nothing to say to me, nothing, if I can put it like this, that I could not in any case have learned from books and from other people.

And yet, almost every day of my life I find myself startled for a moment by some dream of Cork, or perhaps only of my younger life, and sooner or later he comes round again, sweeping upright against the traffic, a small, indomitable baldy man on a motor-bike. I imagine sheet music bulging in the worn briefcase on the saddle, I see the head behind thick-rimmed glasses dignified and alert through the vertical windshield. I imagine him as he may or may not have been, a cosmopolitan man of middle Europe, exiled to the ragged fringe of the continent, forever *nella media del camino de vita sua.*

It is in any case beside the point whether or not he was really like that, whatever, in this context, 'really' means. Something about the man, something perhaps in the man, keeps on refusing to die in my mind, keeps coming round. Perhaps after all not so much the man himself as some necessary idea of the man. I salute him and thank him for his perpetual amusement, for the hint of ageless courtesy in his demeanour, for his small kindnesses to an awkward young poet. If I say of him 'here was a man', it is in the hope I may be understood.

ITA O'DONOVAN (CLIFDEN, CO GALWAY). The following poem remembers Aloys Fleischmann's mother, the pianist and teacher Tilly Fleischmann, who studied at the Royal Academy of Munich and took master classes in 1904–1905 with Liszt's last pupil Stavenhagen

The Music Lesson

A piano
in a tall slated
terraced house which languishes
out of its time.

I greet the maestro.
In stiff black silk and cameo,
she is a standard bearer in exile.
The metronome clicks.

Chords and Czerny,
Siegfried and legend,
notes like drops,
steady from an iron eave,

until,
like a cloud of starlings,
a melody interweaves and
swoops in intricate wing touches

from Liszt
to pupil,
from pupil
to Madame.

I hear the whirring breath
of a hundred wings
and fail to fly.

ORLA MURPHY (BALTIMORE, CO CORK), Writer, UCC Music Graduate
The Alabaster Buddha

During piano lessons, Frau Tilly Fleischmann, Aloys Fleischmann's mother, would sometimes talk about her son. Glimpses of this man, friend of my parents, father of my school friend Maeve, awe-inspiring Professor of Music, conductor of the orchestra which transformed the slog of ballet classes into the dream world of *Coppélia, Les Sylphides, Giselle*, made vivid sketches. I should have asked for more but to have spoken would have broken the spell shaped by her sibilant voice, her pearl-white hair, full length black velvet and silk dresses with flounced lace collars. Her house was four doors from ours on Wellesley Terrace (she and Herr Fleischmann moved first to no. 6 and then to no. 2 when my family went to live at no. 6), and every day Aloys visited them, often calling to speak to my parents about the Orchestral Society, the university, the Choral Festival, driving, walking, or guiding his father's wheelchair, always at enormous speed. He was, as parents' friends often are, at once familiar and distant, addressing us with an avuncular, peremptory friendliness, an extension of his faultless good manners. His politeness never failed, never altered and thus sustained a gap that it never seemed appropriate to bridge.

Frau Fleischmann rested her large hands on her lap below the keyboard of the grand piano and talked about the day Aloys had taken part in the Anglo-Irish War. She had been practising in the drawing-room of their house on the Western Road when suddenly the maid (she always had a maid), burst in shrieking and pointing towards the window. Outside, Aloys, then ten years old, was parading up and down the road, with a flag over his shoulder, singing a rebel song, in a very loud voice. They rushed out and dragged him in before a roving detachment of the Black and Tans might catch him. The mother reproved the boy. The maid burnt the flag. His part in the war was over. Frau Fleischmann dabbed her temples with 4711 from the bottle that always lay on the ledge beyond the last key of the treble clef. 'He had made the flag himself,' she said, with a trace of astonished pride in her voice. Next day I gathered with the other students around the piano in the Music department, our Professor, with his gown, his starched white shirt, black tie, horn-rimmed spectacles, cufflinks, not a hair out of place, analysing a piece of music, a rebel?

Frau Fleischmann continued to teach. Scraps of Schumann pecked their way down the stairs past the bust of Beethoven that stood, back to the world, in the fanlight of the front door, when I played. When she played, the pecking was smoothed into curved phrases of jointless song. Something, perhaps a performance of an Oratorio in the City Hall, perhaps a visit from the Jehovah's Witnesses reminded her of another incident: the finding of the alabaster Buddha. Wellesley Terrace is a quiet place, a suburban cul-de-sac with only its name and the Egyptian influenced design of the front door knobs to indicate connections with the greater world, but officers of the British army had been quartered there up to 1921. Small reminders of their presence: a cap badge, the bronze tip of a cane, turned up in the gardens from time to time and, once, the small carved head of a Buddha. Aloys had found it and wanted to keep it but she had told him to throw it away. He was an obedient child. Of course he did as he was told. One would not have contradicted her, much less disobeyed.

What would she have said if she had known that my sister, some thirty years later, had found the little head in the dark space behind the cold water cistern? It was smooth, polished, translucently white and had been roughly severed from its body. My father admired the skill of the carving. Bebhinn painted the mouth red. It lay around the house with toys, on windowsills, on bookcases, smiling its secret smile. One day, unnoticed, it vanished. The piano lessons continued until Frau Fleischmann died the next year. The Music department moved from the campus to the Western Road and the small boy disappeared behind the dauntingly energetic and brilliant professor.

He was unstoppable: snow brought the city to a halt but he wove his way to College on his motor-bike, pausing only to rescue a student who had fallen in the slimy wasteland of Bridge Street. Arriving late he still lingered to look out of the gothic window, smiled at the snowballing students and remarked that the Quad looked like a scene from Breughel. Unstoppable but not relentless: he drove himself without mercy but he often paused to enjoy the snow or the sun and encouraged us to remember that there were other things in life besides music. He climbed the cliffs at Ardmore to search for seagulls' nests with his family; he initiated, organised and nurtured much of the cultural life of the city, he gave parties, such parties with Anne, in their wonderful house in the Glen. He made time to listen to radio broadcasts and at home, in his study, at the curve of the staircase, he tuned into live concerts on BBC Radio Three. He encouraged us to do the same. We tried and found the reception too bad. How could he listen to Bach or Schubert, Messaien, Cage, or Ó Riada when his house was deep in that wooded hollow, beyond the reach of the most determined signal? Did his ears refuse to take in the static in the same way that his enthusiasm was unmuted by the repetitions of teaching, the obstructions of bureaucracy, the recurrent threat of fiscal famine, or the slowness of minds less brilliant than his own? Was it against all those impediments that he rebelled?

RTE recently played one of his chamber works: the *Piano Quintet*.

379

Written in 1938, this was its first broadcast, one of its few public performances. As students we were dimly aware of his work as a composer. *Clare's Dragoons* was occasionally played during the Choral Festival and at least one orchestral work had its premier performance in the Festival of Twentieth Century Music. If self-promotion now lies somewhere between a religion and a contractual obligation, Aloys Fleischmann had no taste for it but his reputation as a composer is growing. The work that he did to establish the study and practice of music (and the biography that must follow this book) will eventually secure his reputation. As the descendants of his own students play his music, the body of the Buddha will at last be reunited with its smiling head.

BRID DUGGAN NÉE LYNCH (INNISHANNON, CO CORK)
My memory of Professor Fleischmann is a very informal one, but nonetheless I think it illustrates his wonderful kindness and warmth. In my very early school life I was invited to several parties given in his house for his daughter Anne. The Professor contributed greatly to the enjoyment, and those occasions are still remembered by me as very happy childhood events. He encouraged each child to be involved and was generous in his praise and attention to each individual. Any time over the years that I have found myself in the Ballyvolane area I remember him with great affection.

SISTER PATRICIA DONOVAN of the Little Sisters of the Assumption Cork, who helped to nurse Aloys Fleischmann during his last days
Having grown up in Cork, I have memories of the Fleischmann name as being synonymous with music, since Herr Fleischmann senior had the beautiful choir in the North Cathedral, and the Professor ran music in the city.

I lived away from Cork for nearly thirty years, and did not encounter the Fleischmanns again until I helped to nurse Aloys' wife Anne and then himself during their short last illnesses at home. When he became ill, I was amazed at how very patient and calm he was. Of course, modern drugs, thankfully, help to maintain a person's dignity. Sometimes he would share a little of old Cork's history, but that was not often. He had been remarkably sprightly for his age, and he kept his car in the garage as if to say: 'I'll get up that hill again!'

The question struck me: 'Does he realise he is terminally ill?' But of course he did. He did not show much emotion or ask many questions. But then he had gathered around a family who embodied all that was needed. I felt that his intelligence and deep love of music helped him to retain his independence and inner freedom, and that these were qualities he had nurtured in his children too.

Nóirín Hurley (Cork), friend of the Fleischmann family

Professor Fleischmann was one of the most interesting, charming, exasperating and infuriating people I have ever known. I will leave it to those who are suitably qualified to write about his talents; I can only describe under these four categories my impressions of him as the father of a friend of mine.

Interesting: I cannot think of a subject that he was not willing to discuss, even if the conversation was about his lack of interest in the issue in question, for instance sport. When I say he was *charming*, I don't just mean that he was well-mannered: his charm lay in his lack of malice towards his fellow man. The most vitriolic attack I ever heard him make on anybody was to say: 'Well really, that man is quite hopeless.' But in describing the incident when he had trouble with the person in question, he would proceed to give you an explanation and an excuse as to why the 'poor fellow' was the way he was. The Prof was *exasperating*: this trait is linked with his charm. It could happen that he would gaily and insensitively trample on the feelings of the aforementioned fellow man (usually in the pursuit of one of his many Causes); when he realised or was made to realise what he had done, a bewildered hurt look would appear on his face which was so obviously genuine that it was impossible for victim or onlookers to maintain their sense of hurt or annoyance. He was *infuriating*: though comic to outsiders, I imagine the comedy must have palled for those who had to live with it. I am talking about the forgotten appointments, birthdays, anniversaries; the invitations to incompatible guests (i.e., incompatible to the rest of the household or to each other), the late arrivals for meals, the forgetting of domestic duties that did not involve one of the Muses. However, his lack of domesticity (excluding the garden) can be attributed at least partly to the fact that he was allowed, as they say, to get away with it. Most workaholic men do not realise that they are consumed by their work to the extent that their long-suffering wives allow them to be.

Which brings me to speak of the lady of the house, Mrs Fleischmann. In any other household Mrs Fleischmann's utterances would have been treated, if not as pearls of wisdom, then at the very least as the epitome of logic and common sense. There is a cleric who often sat at the Fleischmann table who will agree with me on this. I have sat in the dining-room of Glen House listening to the most fascinating arguments on subjects varying from Byzantine church music to potty-training of children, everybody listening to Papa and to each other, and nobody listening to Mother. Now, Dad might have been your man for an analysis of Wagner's *Ring*, but when it came to the Humanities, Mother was the sage. Did anybody see it? Only occasionally, and usually in hindsight. There were times when a comment or suggestion uttered by Mother (proffered in that laconic voice reserved for statements she knew would fall on deaf ears) was totally ignored but which, when later put forward by Himself or one of the offspring, was hailed as the utterance of the week. Logic in the Fleischmann household was never that of the cold, clear variety. Their logic was charged with intense emotion and feeling, stemming from the lame dog syndrome. They did not just give encouragement to the odd stray dog: they ran kennels. Lest I have painted a picture of Mrs Fleischmann as a saint, let me add that I heard her make the most delightfully outlandish statements ever spoken. But then, if you quietly tell people that the candle is burning and nobody listens, shouting that the house is on fire may be the only way to get them to take notice. I used often think that when the day came that her voice could no longer be heard, the warmth and colour would go from Glen House.

MAX FLEISCHMANN (CORK), *Aloys Fleischmann's grandson*
I was eleven when my grandfather died, and as his working hours never ended, I did not get to know him very well. I remember him of course as conductor of the orchestra, and as organiser of the concerts in the City Hall, which I was always taken to – I don't think I fell asleep at them either.

I used to meet him at mealtime in Glen House. I can still see him taking a brief nap after lunch having read the papers. He would support his head with his right hand, his thumb under his chin, the first two fingers at a right angle up against his cheekbone. After ten minutes he would dash off to college to work on his research project. When he wasn't in college, or upstairs in the study, he would be out doing hard labour in the garden. I remember him racing around with the lawn mower: he could get the large stretch of lawn cut faster than anybody else – faster even than my mother – and would often beat his own record. There was a row of ancient apple trees on one side of the back garden, one of which got knocked down by the wind one night during a severe storm. Granddad cut up all the wood for the fire with a heavy power saw. He didn't want to leave a stump, because that would have delayed him when he was doing the grass. I was too young to help but I remember watching him dig a deep pit down around the roots, tying a rope around them, the other end of which he attached to his waist; he then proceeded to drag that huge stump out of the earth like a horse. He almost had the strength of a horse too. He sometimes had to undertake excavation work in the stream that flowed under his house, which used to be a flax mill. Heavy rain tended to cause flooding, and once he tried to deepen the bed of the stream.

He filled bucket after bucket with stones and mud and dragged them up the ladder to the top of the eight-foot stream wall. They must have been an excruciating weight for anybody to carry, not to mind somebody of his age.

My main memories are of the disasters that hit him regularly. Or should I say, that he hit. He once drove into the big wrought-iron gates of Glen House – they were normally kept open, but one day we had to close them because of a herd of stray cows that were wandering around in the Glen and which might have destroyed his beloved lawn. Granddad didn't expect the gates to be closed when he came home, and simply didn't notice that they were. They were green, and blended into the grass of the front lawn, I suppose. But he must have been driving on automatic pilot. The car, which had been a wreck anyway, was now totally ruined; he himself escaped injury, though. But I remember him coming home seriously hurt once. He had been running around in town, in a hurry as usual, and had wanted to cross the road at the bottom of Patrick's Hill, where work was being done on the drains. The site wasn't properly secured: he fell into a manhole and cut his face badly. Where other people would have gone to court and obtained a fortune, he probably apologised to the men on the site for having damaged their manhole and caused them inconvenience.

There are two stories I didn't see for myself, but heard the people concerned telling my mother. One was about the days when my grandfather had a motor-bike. He had offered a woman student a lift to college on the back of the bike; she fell off; he failed to notice and continued his journey. When he arrived in college he was dismayed to find that he had lost his passenger – she arrived later on by bus. The other story is about what happened when he didn't keep on driving. A friend of my mother's was coming down from Sunday's Well and got into an endlessly long traffic jam on the quay. Eventually he reached the cause of the problem – and recognised my grandfather's car. Granddad had not found a parking space at the side of the road, so he parked in the middle, jumped out, ran down the street to do his messages, and left the traffic piling up after him. He was no doubt quite unaware of this. And the police wouldn't have been able to get through to give him a ticket.

I was at summer camp in West Cork when he died, and was told by the principal. The next activity on the programme was art, so I made a piece of sculpture of him as conductor. The form I gave it was of a very thin figure dressed in black. I missed him when he was gone: he was an unusual and interesting grandfather.

My perception of my father is that he was a good, hardworking man, but a man who lived in his own world. He was not worldly, yet if his cause required him to be so, he had remarkable business sense and organisational capability.

He was a good man in the sense that he was rarely unkind; he treated people with respect, with a rather old-world formal politeness. As a father he was more distant than one would expect these days and perhaps a little more distant than his peers. He was present for one if not two family meals each day where conversation was always lively and engaging. Apart from that and an occasional picnic or outing, he spent most of his time working and not involved with family affairs, which were the purview of our mother. She was the dominant influence in our lives – she was always there for us, always on our side and always ready to fight for us and for what was right. Needless to say, we often disagreed with her, but as I look back now, I realise that she had the irritating habit of being almost invariably right. She was a strong woman in a man's world, which was not an easy role to play and it was further complicated by her husband putting music first – playing second fiddle was not her forte. However, she was totally loyal to him, very proud of him, and always backed him up. I remember once, as we went backstage after the opening night of the ballet, our mother was thanked by Pat Murray, the designer of Irish National Ballet, for hosting the reception to which they would all be coming later that evening in Glen House. She said that it was her pleasure, gathered her daughters, Mrs Goldberg (the Lord Mayor's wife and a friend who was an amazing cook) and some other willing friends, dashed home, and by the time the guests arrived it was as though the event had been planned for weeks. The reality was that our father had omitted to tell her of his invitation! Mother retired to bed once the crisis had been resolved.

My father was, however, always in the background as a dependable father figure, always working, kind and gentle, devoted to his cause of music, to the arts and to his country. He provided for us well and gave us great educational opportunities. But due to his immersion in his world of the arts, he was utterly impractical and undomesticated. I don't think I ever saw him use any tool and I don't believe he was even able to boil an egg. He would drive round Cork on a motor-cycle or a scooter with briefcases and occasionally messages for Mother on the back. Not infrequently would he forget to strap them on properly and the streets of Cork would be littered with sheets of music, or letters, which would be gathered up and delivered to our home by kindly citizens. He was once cutting the lawn with a motorised lawn mower which got a bit choked, so he put his hand under the machine to free it, and the rotating blade almost removed the tip of his finger.

On the other hand, when he set out to put a music teacher into every school in Ireland to further the cause of 'good' music, he designed and implemented a strategy that was successful. He ran a huge international Choral and Folk Dance Festival with his loyal helpers. He created an orchestra which he ran for almost sixty years, for which he was entered in the *Guinness Book of World Records* as 'the most durable' orchestral conductor. It appears to me that he was extremely practical in things that benefited his cause and incapable only in areas that meant little to him. I feel that I was brought up with a powerful set of values, a strong work ethic and a devotion to family. Both parents contributed to his, my father in a more distant way and my mother with a more 'hands on' approach. I am proud to be my parents' child.

RAINER WÜRGAU (HERFORD, GERMANY), Aloys Fleischmann's son-in-law
I first met the man who was to become my father-in-law when in 1962 I came to work as a student demonstrator under the late Professor Mary Boyle at the UCC Department of German. He struck me as holding political views several degrees more conservative than those of the most conservative professors at my German home university. Our few exchanges at meetings of the Cork German Society did not bring us closer, and it seemed that we were to remain strangers. Not even music, which was part of my life, could bridge the gap, though I was intrigued by the concert atmosphere in the City Hall, which to me seemed duly music-centred (not glamour-centred). When I witnessed a fellow-student from UCC whom I knew as a sober scientist shedding enthusiastic tears over 'Freude schöner Götterfunken' – something unlikely to happen in a German concert hall – I was even awed. But the man who worked this wonder with his baton was nearly as remote to me as Beethoven himself. It took a more powerful force or *Himmelsmacht* to bring us closer.

The more regular my visits to Glen House became, the more I liked sitting opposite him, top left next to Anne Fleischmann, the lady of the house, who presided over teas and dinners with a liberal carving knife and sharp comments. While the knife was busy steadily filling the plates of friends and family, the remarks were thrown into her husband's discourse as spices. Aloys Fleischmann, like other successful men, enjoyed talking about how he tackled things and got them going against various odds: lack of funds, opposition of colleagues, inertia of bodies. But, as he observed three iron rules of good narrative

385

style, his accounts were never self-complacent or boring: he always spoke to the point, kept moral judgement in suspense, and challenged his listeners' preconceived notions of things that can happen. One of his rhetorical devices was: 'Would you believe what he did (or said) *then*?'

My hostess monitored his words from the perspective of a woman who had given up her professional career as a medical doctor to become a housewife and mother of five. She was proud of her husband and greatly respected his sphere, but insisted that works of art and learning were neither the only ones that counted nor scholars and artists superior human beings. 'Oh, *that* fellow!' was a frequent introduction to her snap-shot X-ray diagnoses of character and motive. Much later I came to realise how much he profited from her gift of seeing through people's masks and false pretences, and that he sought and took her advice in major decisions. But at table he often contested her words in quite unfleischmannerly terms ('psaw!', 'nonsense', 'the things you say!') while she coolly drove her point home, hear-heared by friends and family, who took her side whenever they felt that his high-mindedness required a down-to-earth corrective.

'To do him (or her) justice' was another household word of Aloys Fleischmann's. His evenhandedness was deeply rooted in his philosophy. Or should I call it *Weltanschauung*? He never proclaimed it, rather kept it locked up in the German department of his bosom. But to a certain extent I was able to reconstruct it from his conversations with me down the years.

Across the table when he was having his 'wine' (a sweet German cherry liqueur) he liked to challenge my philosophical views, which he understood to be materialist, because I proudly called them thus. He used the eighteenth-century version of an ancient argument: what would I think of a person who showed me an artifice, say a chronometer, claiming that it had sprung into being all by itself, without the labours of an ingenious watchmaker? I defended myself with Kant, who had found a flaw in this argument: if it was sound to conclude that somebody had created the watch, it was equally sound to conclude that somebody, an even more ingenious artifex, was the creator of the watchmaker, and so on forever. And this was what materialism was all about: the self-organising faculty of something, *deus sive natura*, that took the shape of a galaxy or an atom, a snow-flake crystal or a sunflower, a DNA-molecule or a human brain. This something, wonder of all wonders (though in no way supernatural), was what materialists referred to as *matter*, but the name did not really matter.

Of course the name mattered a great deal to *him*, and he would not hear of something as dear to him as *ideas* given a name synonymous with dust. I hadn't a hope of convincing him, but he kept utterances of disbelief at a low pitch, just enough to encourage me to continue. So I have reason to believe that he enjoyed my talk. After all I had the same curious thirst for the weird and wonderful as himself, but different sources on various naturalist subjects, from astronomy to biology, to quench it.

He was very quick at processing information and at making use of miscellaneous illustrations in putting his case for the arts. I remember once towards the end of the Ballet Week, when he had begun to relax, we had a discussion at supper about patterns of self-organisation in nature. I told him about a discovery by a German ethologist: that bees who have found a source of honey return to the hive to inform the others, and through a dance indicate the precise direction to be taken, sketching the position of the find in relation to the sun. The following evening he had to make a speech from the stage at the end of the performance, and as usual advocated that the powers that be give more support to the arts and in particular to dance. The central function of dance in ancient and modern human societies was touched on; the argument was capped with a reference to the essential role it plays in the world of organised insects, where it serves as a vital means of communication!

Aloys Fleischmann's *Weltanschauung* was artistic. Works of art circled around each other like celestial bodies, and the universe itself, of which universities were but faint and imperfect epitomes, was to him like a vast symphony created by an infinitely artful composer. There was, among finite artists, a hierarchy of masters. Fair and public competition for rank therein he considered wholesome and necessary. However, there was also dog-fighting and plotting for status and privilege, which he thought distasteful and unworthy of 'brethren in Apollo'. For the service of the muses he regarded as a self-rewarding obligation in which considerations of fame and material gain had no place. It was perhaps from this attitude that his remarkable politeness stemmed: if no artist or scholar could know the other's final rank in the hierarchy, and if it was the service to the arts that counted more than the ultimate result, then it behoved all those involved in the work for the arts to treat each other with the utmost respect and courtesy. I think it was this insight which rendered him immune to that disease so often endemic in artistic and academic circles: the blight of vanity.

I recall one story which vividly illustrates this acutely honest self-perception: it was a tale ruefully recounted by this respected academic in which he presented himself as an anti-hero. During a holiday in the Kerry Gaeltacht, not long after he had taken up his duties in UCC, he attended a session of traditional musicians from the area. After each of them had given proof of his musicianship, a fiddle was handed to the guest. When the visitor said he could not oblige, he was given an accordion; when he said he was unable to play that, a song was requested: the newly appointed Head of the UCC Department of Music had to admit that he did not sing. A loud voice was heard at the back of the room asking: 'What is the use of having a fellow like that made Professor of Music!' – I remember Aloys Fleischmann telling this story to a mixed table round of family and friends years before his retirement. He dwelt on his double embarrassment of not being able to play, and not being able to explain what, under these circumstances, he was doing as a professor. It might well be that this incident furnished a strong stimulus to embark on his huge research project on Irish traditional music, and it may also have spurred him on, given him the strength to complete it despite the serious illness of his last year.

He had an intriguing theory of the cyclical nature of folk music. He pointed out that folk music was 'discovered' in the drawing-rooms of the big houses, that there it was seen as the result of a collective creative process in which not individuality but traditional forms were of paramount importance. I had encountered something similar in the works of the Swiss novelist Gottfried Keller, who pointed out that there was a counter-movement: that an art form which may seem to the outsider to be the most genuine folk art had two or three centuries previously been art-music which had sunk down from the courtly sphere, been adapted by the people, integrated and assimilated. It can be shown that art-music, like literature and painting, continuously regenerates itself through contact with folk art. Aloys Fleischmann set himself the task of studying and documenting that two-way process discovered by the European Romantics. In so doing, he also supplied an answer to the question put by those traditional Kerry musicians.

REV. THOMAS HAMILL (DUNDALK), *Priest, Poet, friend of the Fleischmann family. The term* évkolos *was applied to Sophocles by Aristophanes in his comedy* The Frogs, *and means 'benign' or 'well-disposed'.*

ÉVKOLOS
strange & genial & earthly & elusive,
bright of Moshéh, & dark of Fionn
spangled hand-in-hand your fire,
fire not fire, but music's
Ganymede his flammant wings,
but music's albatross his near
& distant oceanic soul!

I realise your unrehearsable
irony, hearing this encomium

(there's a word we'd quickly explore!)
will nimbly antiphon, 'O my goodness,
Father Tom!' thus you'd welcome,
'O my goodness!', flights of fancy,
new ideas, even hirsute
theological tropes, shards
of half-exaggerated piety,
neums & names & nomes & nemonies!

you seemed to find the burning bush,
& struggle upward the mountain, & stand
at the tent-of-encounter, surelier than most!
Moshéh too (peace be upon him!),
would you agree, a very hidden,
whispering mouth-to-mouth with The Holy?
but steppt forth betimes, to shout
inspired intimations of love's
singultances! a most hidden!
Amergin too, singer
of earth's strange elusive genius!

& how the rush of heaven's honey
musst share your puissant amaze
with burgeons of projects & chores & dreams!
afoot & motor-bike & jaloppy!
one & two & three-way streets!
meals like Bede's hurrying bird,
through the nearest Harry Clarke,
pause for winks, out another,
down to Cork's fulacht fian!

& did the opus?
did the music?
did the honey?
did the questions?
did the sceptical?
& the labyrinthine?

always versatile you faced
the inscrutable mountain of God, a stoic
entrained in beauty's singularity!
peripatetic Orpheus, you chanted
the sombre land that yearns within
& beyond the sapful fireful tree ...

9: REQUIEM

To Celebrate the Life and Death and Many-Faceted Commitment of
ALOYS FLEISCHMANN
St Mary's Cathedral Cork 23 July 1992

REV. TOM HAMILL (DUNDALK, CO LOUTH), Mount Oliver Institute
Words of Welcome and Introduction
I welcome you all today to the Cathedral church in Cork City on behalf of the Fleischmann family, who have gathered here in this ancient
ritual to give Aloys Fleischmann back to the Lord and to the Earth. We
are happy that Bishop Michael Murphy of Cork and Ross is present to
honour this occasion, and that he has enabled me to be invited, from
far away in the other quarter of this island, to act as celebrant.

The variety of persons who are here, a variety of ages, colour, of
talent, of attainment, is a reflection of the many-sidedness of Aloys
Fleischmann himself. We often say, casually enough indeed, that each
person is a mystery. But perhaps, when we look at ourselves, we do
not always recognise this. Maybe we are taught too much to look out-
wards rather than inwards, to look at others rather than ourselves. But
at some point, however, I think that you look at yourself and you say:
'There's something mysterious about me. Will I ever find it out? Will
it ever deliver itself in reality?' I suppose it's part of our sadness that
we feel it won't happen, and part of our hope that we wonder over
and over: 'Will I ever get close to it? Will I ever be able to feed at that
cauldron, to drink at that spring?'

The mystery embodied in Aloys Fleischmann was reflected in his
many-sidedness. It could be said that he was like a Renaissance figure.
But I don't think that people realised that that many-sidedness which
they admired, or envied, or were in awe of, or whatever way they
responded to it – that such many-sidedness is also themselves. For this
reason too we assemble: to celebrate some of the many windows
through which you could glimpse something: in him, in his life.

We want to celebrate too in some way the mystery of ourselves;
and if I may say so, that is what he would have wanted. He would
have wanted each one to begin to wake up within, to glimpse their
own many-sidedness. It may be, as we build up this eucharistic ritual,
as you reminisce about him, whatever was special about him for you,
in whatever sense, that you will also see that there is something in
yourself that is reflected back to you as you contemplate Aloys Fleischmann.

In this ritual, we are presented with the ancient and venerable images and stories and prayers, appropriate for our celebration of his crossing-over from life to death. Through these, I want to evoke particularly four narrative characters that were important in his unfolding-as-a-man.

The first figure is Oisín. Oisín, a momentary glimpse, but a worthy glimpse too, some special region of the soul, someone who is born and lives and dies on this island. Listen carefully for this, as you hear *Oisín's Lament after the Fianna*.

The second figure I want to evoke (these are all male figures, all aspects of Aloys Fleischmann the man) is Socrates. I think there was something Socratic about Aloys Fleischmann. It was the way he interacted with people, the way he saw things, the way he would pursue something: that kind of classical mindset. Will you hear anything of this in *Socrates' Prayer for Beauty and Purity of Soul*?

The third figure, the third bridge he might sally forth on, represents another way of being a man: it is the figure of Moses (peace be upon him!). Moses, for various weighty reasons, has perhaps become remote in our galaxy, but he is an utterly central figure in the Jewish Christian Bible. You will hear the story of the death of Moses, his final time, when he stood in the company of the Blessed One on the threshold of the Land of Promise. This is, I think, one of the most moving moments in all Biblical narrative.

And finally: the fourth bridge that Aloys Fleischmann crossed back and forward on, as well as Oisín, and Socrates, and Moses: the figure of Jesus of Nazareth, who was always there, always dialectically. Not at all the simple straightforward devotional dialectic: but something that reached deep, and that was mixed through with these other figures. The interpenetration of archetypal figures is a function of the mystery of the individual being unfolded. It will no longer be simple. We will no longer be something obvious and pedestrian and run-of-the-mill, liable to be summed up in a few trite phrases. Any one of us, were our mystery effectively unveiled, would be unrecognisable indeed, vis-à-vis what we seem to be now. Would you agree that it is a matter for serious regret that invariably we are constrained, or at least encouraged, to be simple and safe rather than being complex, opened-out, and dangerous? Think of the four bridges!

Insofar as we can say, he made a choice between the pedestrian and the ebullient options, he chose to be complex, opened-out, deep, elusive in some ways, closely affectionate in other ways, essentially a soul person.

You have your own thoughts about this. But what you think about in him, what you find reflected in him is really yourself, it is your own potential. It is your own awakening to a unitedness of birth and death. Something like this was offered by Jesus: can you glimpse it? Something like that was offered by Moses, something uncanny that brought him over the threshold. Something like that was offered by Socrates: his own people actually killed him because of it: we are still ashamed about this. Something like that was offered by Oisín, as you hear in that poem: light and darkness, youth and old age.

We encourage each other in this ritual to interact and to offer back what he was. But also to ask what each one of us is. This is not at all simple, not as simple as we believe when we look in the mirror. Let us not be content to be the way we are, but let us strive as he did for excellence, for many-sidedness and for soul.

We are very happy to recognise in this Cathedral Church many modalities of the 'Christian', the 'Messianic'. The controversy and enthusiasm that swirled around Jesus of Nazareth over two thousand clamorous years are reflected here. As well as the Christian people of God, I am pleased that there are representatives here of the Jewish people of God. We will never know, as Christians, how much we are indebted to the Jewish people of God and how much we have rejected seeing this and admitting it. Most of all, the gift that the Jewish people have given us: one of their own sons, Jesus of Nazareth – the great Jewish gift.

The ancient Greeks, dare I say it, are represented here too: friends of soul, friends of the Earth. Dare I say pagans too. 'Pagans' in the best possible and most affectionate way, out in the little villages, out in the countryside. Then there are some people who have come with us: these are truly from the earlier home of soul which they called the Tuath de Danaan.

There are others here invisibly, the empty spaces, the dead. There is always an empty space for a light: there is always space for those who come back, who are always living with us. A few names: both for the Fleischmann family and for each one of us. Our dead always follow us around and look for remembrance, look for acknowledgement, be this but in retrospect. We think of Anne, his wife, and of Aloys Georg and Tilly, his parents. We think of Lal Reardon, his sister-in-law.

The final thought: let it be yours! What are you doing, what are you looking for here? What is the important value that this life and death carries for you? What is reflected back to you? – You are a woman, you are a man? You are young, you are old? You are orthodox, you are regular or you are not? You are unorthodox, you are non-regular? What is Aloys Fleischmann reflecting to you on this day when he goes away, back into the arms of the Lord and into the bosom of the Earth?

In the name of the Father, of the Son and of the Holy Ghost.

RUTH FLEISCHMANN, *eldest child:*

Oisín's Lament after the Fianna

Long, this night, the clouds delay,
And long to me was yesternight,
Long was the dreary day, this day,
Long, yesterday, the light.
Each day that comes to me is long –
Not thus our wont to be of old,
With never music, harp nor song,
Nor clang of battles bold.
No wooing soft, nor feats of might,
Nor cheer of chase, nor ancient lore,
Nor banquet gay, nor gallant fight –
All things beloved of yore.
No marching now with martial fire –
Alas, the tears that make me blind –
Far other was my heart's desire
A-hunting stag and hind.
Long this night the clouds delay –
No striving now as champions strove,
No run of hounds with mellow bay,
Nor leap in lakes we love.
No hero now where heroes hurled –
Long this night the clouds delay –
No man like me in all the world,
Alone with grief, and gray.
Long this night the clouds delay –
I raise their grave-cairn, stone on stone,
For Fionn and Fianna passed away –
I, Oisín, left alone.

(George Sigerson, *Bards of the Gael and Gall*, London 1907)

ALAN FLEISCHMANN, *youngest child:*
Phaedras – Socrates' Prayer For Beauty And Purity Of Soul
Dear Pan and all ye other gods that dwell in this place, grant that I
may become fair within, and that such outward things as I have may
not war against the spirit within me. May I count him rich who is wise,
and as for gold, may I possess so much of it as only a temperate man
might bear and carry with him.

(*Translated from the Greek in 1952 by R. Hackforth, Cambridge University Press*)

GERALD Y. GOLDBERG, family friend:

The Death of Moses – Deuteronomy 34

Then Moses went up from the lowlands of Moab to Mount Nebo, to the top of Pisgah, eastwards from Jericho, and the Lord showed him the whole land: Gilead as far as Dan; the whole of Naphtali; the territory of Ephraim and Manasseh, and all Judah as far as the western sea; the Negeb and the Plain; the valley of Jericho, the Vale of Palm Trees, as far as Zoar. The Lord said to him, 'This is the land which I swore to Abraham, Isaac and Jacob that I would give to their descendants. I have let you see it with your own eyes, but you shall not cross over into it.'

There in the land of Moab Moses the servant of the Lord died, as the Lord had said. He was buried in a valley in Moab opposite Beth-peor, but to this day no one knows his burial-place. Moses was a hundred and twenty years old when he died; his sight was not dimmed nor had his vigour failed. The Israelites wept for Moses in the lowlands of Moab for thirty days; then the time of mourning for Moses was ended. And Joshua son of Nun was filled with the spirit of wisdom, for Moses had laid his hands on him, and the Israelites listened to him and did what the Lord had commanded Moses.

There has never yet risen in Israel a prophet like Moses, whom the Lord knew face to face: remember all the signs and portents which the Lord sent him to show in Egypt to Pharaoh and all his servants and the whole land; remember the strong hand of Moses and the great deeds which Moses wrought in the sight of all Israel.

TOM HAMILL, family friend:

From the Holy Gospel of Mark

Jesus and his disciples set out for the village of Caesaria. On the way, he asked his disciples: 'Who do people say that I am?' They answered: 'Some say you are John the Baptiser, others that you are Eliza, others that you are one of the prophets.' 'And you,' he said, 'who do you say I am?' Peter, one of the twelve, said: 'You are the Messiah: you are the anointed one.' Then he gave strict orders not to tell anyone about him. And he began to teach them that the Son of Man had to undergo great sufferings and be rejected by the elders, chief priests and doctors of the law, to be put to death and to be raised again three days afterwards. At this Peter took him by the arm and began to rebuke him. But Jesus turned around, and looking at his disciples, he rebuked Peter. 'Away with you, Satan!' he said. 'You think in a human way, not as God thinks.' And he called the people to him as well as the disciples and he said: 'Anyone who wishes to be a follower must leave himself behind, must take up their cross and come with me. Whoever cares for their own safety is lost. But if someone will let themselves be lost for my sake and for the good news, that one is safe. What do you gain,' he said, 'by winning the whole world at the cost of your true self? What do you give to find that self back again? If anyone is ashamed of me in this wicked and godless age, the Son of Man will be ashamed of that person when he comes in the glory of his father and holy angels.'

Out of the readings we begin to build up the prayers of the faithful people. However each one is faithful, that is the way the prayer will come to that person. Let me invite those representative people who will be saying on your behalf the intercessions, but don't forget your own personal prayer too. Bear in mind the four bridges I mentioned that Aloys Fleischmann went back and forward on and across into the great mystery of soul as it transforms itself in human life. We will celebrate in these prayers some of the many-sidedness of the man. Each of you will notice that there is a particular side that is not specially mentioned. Make that a part of your own prayer then! We celebrate his many initiatives towards a peaceful advent of a European cultural renaissance.

We gather these prayers, which are but stammering hints towards the deep desire within ourselves to celebrate the human mystery in him and in ourselves and in these others here. We would like to gather the best words we can find within us; we try to gather the best feelings, the best memories, and the best hopes as we carry him here now deeper into the mystery of the divine. We carry him now through the bread and wine into another great story and through that again we will be carrying him back into the arms of the One who sent him onto the Earth. Our prayers go with him and his own prayers remain with us as a hope of further ramification and fruitfulness. His mantle has now fallen on us. Whoever you are and however he touched you, a portion of his mantle has fallen on you! Let us remember all those who are gone from us, and all your own dear dead people.

Music of the Requiem Mass
The choir consisted of past and present members of the University College Cork Choir and Madrigal 1975, and was conducted by Dr. Geoffrey Spratt, with Colin Nicholls (Organist and Master of the Choristers, St Fin Barre's Cathedral) Organ.

- *Funeral Sentence No. 1*: 'Man that is borne of a woman' by H. Purcell
- 'Kyrie' and 'Gloria' from the *Missa brevis* by G. da Palestrina
- *Funeral Sentence Nr. 2*: 'In the midst of life' by H. Purcell
- 'Ave Maria' by Séamas de Barra
- 'Memorial Acclamations' and 'The Great Amen' from the *Mass in honour of St Teresa* by John C. Murphy
- 'Ave verum corpus' by W. A. Mozart
- No. 1 of *Trí hAmhráin*: 'Marbhna Eoghan Rua Uí Néill' by Aloys Fleischmann, sung by Cara O'Sullivan (Soprano) with Patrick Zuk (Piano)
- Communion Hymn: 'As runs the thirsting deer' from the *Mass*

for Peace (1976) by Aloys Fleischmann
- *Funeral Sentence No. 3*: Thou knowest Lord, the secrets of our hearts by H. Purcell
- 'Lament' played by Dr Tomás Ó Canainn (Uillean pipes)

MARY LELAND (CORK), *Journalist, Critic, Novelist*
Obituary for Aloys Fleischmann: Sunday Independent *2 August 1992*
For the last 60 years Cork has been a divided city. The split was between a small group of people who saw, and sometimes even said, that Aloys Fleischmann was prophet and pilgrim, inimitable teacher, tireless advocate, dedicated musician – and generally a good thing. On the opposite side was that enormous body of opinion which noticed him only when forced to do so and then decided that he was an eccentric at best and a joke at worst.

These somewhat bitter thoughts surfaced last week as what passes in Cork for the great and the good assembled in robes and decorations, town and gown officially united for the occasion of the Requiem Mass for Dr Aloys Fleischmann, Emeritus Professor of Music at UCC. What a convenient thing is civic memory. Out of the hundreds there in the North Cathedral I could pick out the derisory voices of the past, the faces on which the smile with which he was greeted changed to a smirk of condescension as he passed on. In other words, Cork was not all songs and roses for Aloys Fleischmann. What rows there were, in the early days of the Orchestral Society, the Ballet Company, the Symphony Orchestra, the Choral Festival! And those were among his friends and followers! How often his stubborn insistence on the maintenance of standards – and thus the security of reputation – left the opposition gasping in his wake. How real his challenge was to the cosy cultural fellowship of the city – and of other cities.

Here his stage was small, and he was too big for it, but instead of seeking a platform elsewhere he endeavoured, all his persistent life, to make the local one bigger and stronger and more accommodating – and not just for himself. No one can be surprised that he got little thanks for this. His concentration made him remarkable to some, risible to others, but as he puttered on his motor-bike around the city the legend grew to cheer those of us who needed the sense of his invincibility.

Cork does not appreciate the uncomfortable commitment to the classical. During the Requiem the readings reflected his devotion to the imaginative lure of Ireland's legends: the echoing *Song of Oisín*, and then the *Prayer of Socrates* to remind us all of the provenance of his philosophy. But they were read in a city which in so many public ways has embraced the consoling dictum that there are no standards, only taste. Of course even those of us who valued him had some fun at his

396

expense. The absolutism had its inappropriate moments, his allegiances took precedence over everything else and although intellectually subtle he was not always socially sensitive. His passion remained predictable to the end.

We last met at UCC a month before his death. The occasion was a concert by soprano Cara O'Sullivan and the young composer and pianist Patrick Zuk – himself Dr Fleischmann's protégé – and it included a suite of songs written by the Professor. He was obviously ill, but stood sturdily for the applause, sharing it with the artists.

Now I reflect that I've never been to a Fleischmann event I was not writing about. The pen has always been between my affection and respect for him and an actual knowledge of the man whose father my father still remembers. It was to this very church – not one of Cork's finest – that Aloys Georg Fleischmann came as choirmaster and organist with his wife Tilly, the Cork-born concert pianist. They came nearly 100 years ago to set in train an association which has enriched the city. So this is my last Fleischmann event.

The Requiem Mass was a firm statement of the beliefs to which Dr Fleischmann held all his life: the finest possible music was performed by local artists. Church music has deteriorated in the appeasement of public taste and it is only by a huge effort that a Requiem such as this can now be offered. If the effort was a tribute to him, even more indicative of the significance of his life and work to Cork was the contribution that morning of Séamas de Barra and Patrick Zuk and the choir of graduates under Dr Geoffrey Spratt. They, like Cara O'Sullivan, know his worth and measure his loss even as they live out his legacy. For the rest of us there is the reminder by Fr Tom Hamill that in some ways the world is still ashamed of what happened to Socrates. His words ring true: Amid this public grief, there is a little shame.

Appendix A:

(1) An Annotated Catalogue of the Music of Aloys Fleischmann, Compiled by Séamas de Barra

Preface to 'Annotated Catalogue of the Music ... by Séamas de Barra
The student of Fleischmann's music will hitherto have had two principal published sources of information: A Catalogue of Contemporary Irish Composers, ed. Edgar M. Deale (Dublin: The Music Association of Ireland, 1968; 2nd ed. 1973) [referred to below as Deale, 1968 and Deale, 1973]; and Catalogue of Contemporary Irish Music, ed. Bernard Harrison (Dublin: Irish Composers Centre, 1982) [referred to below as Harrison, 1982]; with additional information in Fleischmann's own Music in Ireland (Cork and Oxford: Cork University Press/B. H. Blackwell Ltd, 1952) [referred to below as Fleischmann, 1952]. Anyone who may have had cause to read these carefully or to compare one with the other will have found that the information they contain is often contradictory, not only between the catalogues but also within each catalogue. The editors will of course have had to rely on information supplied by Fleischmann himself and naturally are not responsible for the omission of works or for the incompleteness or inaccuracy of the entries. Nevertheless, it is surprising to read in both editions of Deale, for example, that The Four Masters was composed in 1948 but first performed in 1944! And again in Harrison that the Three Songs for Tenor and Orchestra were first performed in 1935 but not composed until 1937! One may wonder how the respective editors could have allowed such anomalies to pass unquestioned. Needless to say this is very unsatisfactory for anyone needing reliably accurate information about Fleischmann's music and the present catalogue it is hoped will go some way towards remedying the situation. It is not presented as work completed however, but as work in progress. Some research remains to be done: there are still gaps, some of which hopefully may yet be filled, and there may of course be necessary modifications as new information comes to light. It is unlikely however that the profile of Fleischmann's output as it emerges here will require any substantial alteration, and the present catalogue certainly presents the most complete and detailed picture of his work so far available.

The works are listed in chronological order although in a few instances (indicated by a question mark) the precise placing is uncertain, or at least provisional. The information is presented as follows:

(1)   Title/subtitle [translations where necessary]
(2)   Author(s)/source(s) of text(s) [language of text where not obvi-

ously in English]
(3) Forces
(4) List of movements
(5) Details of the first performance (**F.p**:), or in the case of the ballets of the premier (**Prem**:)
(6) Details of publication (**Pub**:)
(7) Details of recordings (**Rec**:)
(8) Details of commissioning (**Com**:)
(9) Dedication (**Ded**:)
(10) (Explanatory notes where necessary)

Alternative versions or other adaptations are listed under the same catalogue number as the original work irrespective of when they were made.

All enquiries about the music of Aloys Fleischmann, including the availability of scores and performance material, should be directed to: The Contemporary Music Centre Ireland, 19 Fishamble Street, Temple Bar, Dublin 8.

1   *Cradle Song*
[E. J. Sheehy]
Voice and Piano
(The MS is undated but almost certainly composed during Fleischmann's years as a student in UCC (1927–1932): 'When I went to college … I wrote a number of songs and a *Movement for String Quartet*.' (Aloys Fleischmann in conversation with Tomás Ó Canainn, *The Cork Review*, Tomás Ó Canainn (ed). Cork, 1992.) This is the only song that has come to light. There is no record of a performance. For some reason Fleischmann's name does not appear on the MS, which reads 'music by 'Gerald Pierce'!)

2   *Movement for String Quartet*
(The MS is undated but composed during Fleischmann's years as a student in UCC (see above). The only performance appears to have been a private performance arranged by Fleischmann's father in Munich in 1932.)

3   *Sreath do Phiano* [*Suite for piano*]   **1933**
5 movements:
(i)   *Le líonrith* [*Agitato*]
(ii) *Mall sionsach* [*Andante espressivo*]
iii) *Mear anamúil* [*Allegro animato*]
(iv) *Mall calma, diaidh ar ndiaidh ag sírneartú* [*Largo resoluto, poco a poco sempre rin forzando*]
(v) *Gasta gealadhramach* [*Presto scherzando*]
F.p:?.?.1934; State Academy of Music, Munich (there is no record of who gave the first performance, but it is not impossible that it was Fleischmann himself).
Pub: J. & W. Chester Ltd., 1935 under the pseudonym 'Muiris Ó Rónáin'.
Rec: NIRC [New Irish Recording Company] NIR001 (1971); Charles Lynch (piano).

4   *Illumina Occulos Meos*   1934
     [Liturgical (Latin)]
     SATB Choir
     F.p:?.2.1934; Munich Cathedral Choir, Mons. Ludwig Berberich (cond); Munich
     Cathedral.

5   *Trí hAmhráin* [*Three Songs*]   1935
     [Turlogh Carolan (attrib) No. i, Mícheál Ó Murchú Nos. ii and iii (Irish)]
     High Voice and Piano
     (i)   Marbhana Eoghain Ruaidh Uí Néill [Lament for Owen Roe O'Neill]
     (ii)   Bíogadh [Away!]
     (iii) An Píobaire [The Piper]
     F.p: as *Amhráin* [Songs] 15.12.1935; Seán Cuirtéis (tenor), Gerard Shanahan
     (piano); Aula Maxima, University College Cork. Performed under pseudonym
     'Muiris Ó Rónáin'.
     Pub: An Gúm, n.d. under pseudonym 'Muiris Ó Rónáin'. Although the pub-
     lished title is *Trí hAmhráin le hAghaidh Guth Árd agus Ceol-Fhuireann* [Three Songs
     for High Voice and Orchestra] this is in fact the original version with piano. The
     title page however describes it as 'Scór Gléasta don bPiano' [Score arranged for
     piano] and the availability of orchestral material on hire is advertised. Fleisch-
     mann gives 1945 as the year of publication (Harrison, 1982).
     Rec: [No. i only] Black Box Music BBM 1022 (1998); Kathleen Tynan (soprano),
     Dearbhla Collins (piano).
     Ded: Carl Hardebeck.

a   *Trí hAmhráin* [Three Songs]   1937
     Orchestral Version
     High Voice and Orchestra [2(picc)222/4231/timp/perc/hp/str]
     F.p: as *Amhráin le Ceol-fhuireann* [Songs with Orchestra], 24.4.1938; Heddle Nash
     (tenor), Radio Éireann Symphony Orchestra, Aloys Fleischmann (cond); Gaiety
     Theatre, Dublin. Performed in English (translation by An t-Athair P. Mac
     Suibhne) under pseudonym 'Muiris Ó Rónáin'.
     (In all published catalogues of his music that appeared in Fleischmann's lifetime
     this work is entitled *Three Songs for Tenor and Orchestra*.)

6   *Four Old Italian Songs* (arr)   1937
     Mezzo-soprano, Orchestra [2222/2230/timp/str]
     (i)   Consolati e spera (Domenico Scarlatti)
     (ii)   Se tu m'ami (G.B. Pergolesi)
     (iii) O cessate di piagarmi (Alessandro Scarlatti)
     (iv)   Chi vuol la zingarella (G. Paisiello)
     F.p: 14.4.1937; Countess Tomacelli (mezzo-soprano), The University Orchestra,
     Aloys Fleischmann (cond); Aula Maxima, University College, Cork. Performed
     under the pseudonym 'Muiris Ó Rónáin'.

7   *Piano Quintet*   1938
     Piano and String Quartet
     4 movements:
     (i)   *Allegretto*
     (ii)   *Andante tranquillo*
     (iii) *Allegro scherzando*
     (iv)   *Allegro molto*

F.p: 28.4.1939; Tilly Fleischmann (piano), The Kutcher String Quartet; Clarence Hall (Imperial Hotel), Cork. Performed under his own name.
Rec: Marco Polo 8.223888 (1996); Hugh Tinney (piano), Vanbrugh String Quartet.

8   *Prelude and Dance*   1940
Orchestra [3(picc)222/4331/timp/perc/hp/str]
F.p: 11.12.1940; Cork Symphony Orchestra, Aloys Fleischmann (cond); City Hall, Cork. Performed under pseudonym 'Muiris Ó Rónáin'.
Ded: 'To Anne' (MS) [Anne Madden, later Mrs Fleischmann].

9   *The Humours of Carolan*   1941–1944?
Suite for String Orchestra
4 movements:
(i)   Carolan's Dowry
(ii) Elizabeth MacDermott Roe
(iii) Young Cusack
(iv) Carolan's Quarrel with the Landlady
F.p: As the history of this work is somewhat involved and the information in the published catalogues particularly contradictory, it is worth attempting a clarification:
(I) 6.11.1941: a broadcast performance as *A Carolan Suite* [3 movements: (i) Carolan's Dowry, (ii) Planxty Dodwell, (iii) Young Cusack]; Radio Éireann Symphony Orchestra, Michael Bowles (cond); performed under his own name.
(II) 10.12.1941: first concert performance as 'Three Movements from *A Carolan Suite*' [same as (I) above]; Strings of the Cork Symphony Orchestra, Aloys Fleischmann (cond); Aula Maxima, University College, Cork; performed under pseudonym 'Muiris Ó Rónáin'.
(III) 12.8.1942: a broadcast performance, the first performance as *The Humours of Carolan*. There is no information as to the number of movements or their titles, so it is not possible to say if this was a performance of the work in its final form; Radio Éireann Orchestra, Aloys Fleischmann (cond); performed under his own name.
(IV) 20.2.1944: as *The Humours of Carolan* in its final form; Radio Éireann Symphony Orchestra, Aloys Fleischmann (cond); Capitol Theatre, Dublin; performed under his own name.
Com: Radio Éireann (Fleischmann, 1952).
Ded: Mr and Mrs John Horgan.
(Fleischmann lists this work as having 4 movements in Deale, 1968 and Deale, 1973, but curiously as having only 3 in Harrison, 1982, omitting mention of No. iv 'Carolan's Quarrel with the Landlady'.)

a   *Eilís Nic Dhiarmada Rua*   1944?
Lamento per Strumenti a Corda/Caoineadh do Shreanganna
[*Elizabeth MacDermott Roe* Lament for Strings]
No. ii from *The Humours of Carolan*
F.p: (as independent piece) 13.9.1949; Radio Éireann Symphony Orchestra, Aloys Fleischmann (cond); Phoenix Hall, Dublin. Performed under his own name.
Pub: An Gúm, n.d., under his own name. Fleischmann gives 1952 as the year of publication (Harrison, 1982), but this seems to be incorrect.
Rec: Black Box Music BBM1103 (1997); Irish Chamber Orchestra, Fionnuala Hunt (dir).

(The performance of 'Three Movements from *A Carolan Suite*' in 1941 was the last occasion on which Fleischmann presented a work under the pseudonym 'Muiris Ó Rónáin'.)

10   *Cáit Ní Dhuibhir* (arr)   1943?
SAB Choir
(In 1943 Fleischmann revived the Choral Society of University College, Cork and it is likely that this arrangement was made for one of its concerts. There is no record of a performance but the new Choral Society gave its first concert on 24.3.1944 in the Dairy Science Theatre of the College and it is possible that it was part of the programme.)

11   *The Four Masters*   1944
Overture for Orchestra
Orchestra [2(picc)222/4231/timp/perc/hp/str]
F.p: 25.6.1944; Radio Éireann Symphony Orchestra, Aloys Fleischmann (cond); Gaiety Theatre, Dublin.
Com: by?, for the tercentenary of the death of Mícheál Ó Cléirigh O.F.M., Chief of the Four Masters.
Ded: 'To my father' (MS).

12   Song Cycle from *The Fountain of Magic*   1945
[Frank O'Connor (from the Irish)]
High Voice, Orchestra [2(picc)222/4231/timp/perc/hp/str]
4 movements:
(i)   Winter
(ii) Autumn
(iii) The Lover
(iv) The Student
F.p: there is some uncertainty about the exact date of the first performance which appears to have been radio broadcast as the 'first concert performance' (programme note), given on 2.3.1945, Violet Burne (soprano), Cork Symphony Orchestra, Aloys Fleischmann (cond); Aula Maxima, University College, Cork.
Ded: 'To my mother' (MS).

a   Song Cycle from *The Fountain of Magic*   1945
Version with Piano
F.p?: 4.6.1955, René Soames (tenor), Tilly Fleischmann (piano); concert promoted by the Cork Orchestral Society at Clontymon, Boreenmanna Road, Cork (by kind permission of Mr and Mrs Cornelius Murphy).

13   *Where Finbarr Taught*   1945
A Song for University College, Cork
[*Scoil Bharra Fhinn*
Amhrán don Choláiste Ollscoile, Corcaigh]
[J. J. Horgan (Irish translation by 'Torna')]
SATB Chorus and Piano
F.p:? (there is no record of a performance with piano accompaniment).
Pub: (anonymously at the request of Alfred O'Rahilly, President of UCC), *Cork University Record* 4 (Summer 1945): 42 – 48 (Irish and English versions printed separately).

a *Where Finbarr Taught*   **1946**
Orchestral Version
SATB Chorus, Orchestra [2(picc)222/4321/timp/perc/str]
F.p: 2.3.1946, University and Aeolian Choirs, Cork Symphony Orchestra, Aloys
Fleischmann (cond); Aula Maxima, University College, Cork.

14 *Clare's Dragoons*   **1945**
[Thomas Davis]
Baritone, SATB Chorus, War Pipes, Orchestra [2(picc)222/433 1timp/perc/ str]
F.p: 9.9.1945, Michael O'Higgins (baritone), choir?, Joan Denise Moriarty (war
pipes), Radio Éireann Symphony Orchestra, Aloys Fleischmann (cond); Capitol
Theatre, Dublin.
Com: by Radio Éireann for the centenary of the death of Thomas Davis, founder
of the 'Young Ireland' movement.
Ded: 'To Donal O'Sullivan' (MS) (Fleischmann lists Joan Denise Moriarty as
dedicatee in Harrison, 1982).

15 *The Golden Bell of Ko*   **1947**
Ballet in three scenes
Orchestra [2(picc)2(ca)22/4231/timp/perc/hp/str], SATB Choir
Scenario: Martin Cumberland (after a Chinese legend)
Choreography: Joan Denise Moriarty
Décor, Costumes: Marshall Hutson
Prem: 10.5.1948; Cork Ballet Group, Aeolian Choir, Cork Symphony Orchestra,
Aloys Fleischmann (cond); Opera House, Cork.
Ded: Joan Denise Moriarty
(Fleischmann lists a concert version of the score in Harrision, 1982. There is in
fact no such distinct version but the complete work was given a concert perfor-
mance on 12.10.1948 by the Radio Éireann Symphony Orchestra, Aloys Fleisch-
mann (cond), in a broadcast concert from the Phoenix Hall, Dublin.)

16 *An Cóitín Dearg* [*The Red Petticoat*]   **1951**
Ballet in three acts
Orchestra [3(picc)222/4231/timp/perc/hp/str]
Scenario: Mícheál MacLiammóir
Choreography: Joan Denise Moriarty
Décor, Costumes: Mícheál MacLiammóir
Prem: 28.5.1951; Cork Ballet Group, Cork Symphony Orchestra, Aloys Fleisch-
mann (cond); Opera House, Cork.

a *An Cóitín Dearg* [*The Red Petticoat*]   **1951**
Ballet Suite for Orchestra
Orchestra [3(picc)222/4231/timp/perc/hp/str]
7 movements:
(i)   Prelude
(ii) General Dance
(iii) Theme and Variations
(iv) Romance
(v)   Fughetta and Passacaglia
(vi) Intermezzo
(vii) Reel and Finale
F.p: 16.10.1951; Radio Éireann Symphony Orchestra, Aloys Fleischmann (cond);

Phoenix Hall, Dublin.

b   *An Cóitín Dearg* [*The Red Petticoat*]   1968?
     Irish Harp
     1 movement [adapted from the ballet music]
     F.p:?
     Pub: in *The Irish Harp Book: A Tutor and Companion*, ed. Sheila Larchet Cuthbert
     (Cork: Mercier Press, 1975) p. 86.
     Com: Cáirde na Cruite [Friends of the Harp] specially for the *Irish Harp Book*.

17   *Six Folk Song Arrangements*   1952
     [Traditional (Nos. i – v in Irish with English translations by Donal O'Sullivan)]
     SSA (TTB) Choir
     (i)   Eibhlín a Rúin [Eileen Aroon]
     (ii) Fáinne Geal an Lae [The Dawning of the Day]
     (iii) Cill Chais [Kilcash]
     (iv) Bán Chnuic Éireann Ó [The Fair Hill of Éire Ó]
     (v)   An Spailpín Fánach [The Itinerant Labourer]
     (vi) Kelly, the Boy from Killann
     F.p: (I) [Nos. i – iv] 28.6.1952; Cross and Passion College Choir, Maryfield?, Mary
     Keogh (cond); Dublin?
     (II) [Nos. i – iv and vi] 23.11.1952; Cross and Passion College Choir, Maryfield,
     Mary Keogh (cond); Gresham Hotel, Dublin.
     (III) (In a list of works compiled in 1958, Fleischmann mentions performances
     by Cór Laoigheogach, H. W. Rosen (cond) in 1952 and by the Radio Éireann
     Singers, H. W. Rosen (cond) in 1954. He gives no further details but it is possi-
     ble that the complete set was performed on either or both of these occasions.)
     Pub: [No. iii only] Cumann Náisiúnta na gCór [The Association of Irish Choirs],
     1983.
     Com: The Committee for Cultural Relations, Department of External Affairs.

a   *Kelly, the Boy from Killann*   1960
     [Traditional]
     TTBB Choir
     Version of No. vi above
     F.p:? (there is no record of a performance).
     Ded: 'for St Finbarr's Male Voice Choir' (MS)

18   *Four Fanfares for An Tóstal*   1952
     4hr / 3tpt / 3trb / tuba / timp / sdrm
     (i)   For an Opening Ceremony
     (ii) For a Solemn Ceremony
     (iii) For a Gay Event
     (iv) For a Closing Ceremony
     F.p:?.?.1952; No.1 Army Band? (cond); Tóstal Parade, Dublin
     (Awarded First Prize in a National Competition for fanfares organised by An
     Tóstal in 1952.)

a   *Tableau for An Tóstal III*   1953
     Version of No. iv above
     Orchestra [3(picc)222 / 4321 / timp / str]
     F.p: 6.4.1953; Cork Ballet Group, Cork Symphony Orchestra, Aloys Fleischmann

(cond), Opera House, Cork.

(This was the third of three pieces of music to an historical tableau staged by the Cork Ballet Group at the beginning of each evening of its 1953 season. Of the other two pieces all we know, from a pencilled note in the orchestra leader's part, is that they were '2 fanfares: 1 Drums, 2 Brass.')

19   *Macha Ruadh* [*Red (-haired) Macha*]   **1955**
Ballet in two scenes
Orchestra [2(picc)222/4231/timp/perc/hp/str]
Scenario: uncredited, but probably by Joan Denise Moriarty and Aloys Fleischmann in collaboration.
Choreography: Joan Denise Moriarty
Décor, Costumes: Marshall Hutson
Prem: 9.5.1955; Cork Ballet Company, Cork Symphony Orchestra, Aloys Fleischmann (cond); Opera House, Cork.

20   *Songs of Affection*   **1955?**
Five Irish Folk Songs arranged for Medium Voice and Piano
[Traditional (Donal O'Sullivan's translations into English, underlaid by the original Irish versions)]
    (i) I'd put you myself, my baby, to slumber [Do chuirfinn-se féin mo leanbh a
        chodla]
    (ii) The red-haired man's wife [Bean an fhir ruaidh]
    (iii) The fretful baby [An leanbh aimhréidh]
    (iv) You remember that night, love? [An cuimhin leat an oíche úd?]
    (v) Why, liquor of life, do I love you so? [A fhuisgí, croí na n-anamann]
F.p:?
('Some fifteen years ago I was asked by the late Donal O'Sullivan to write piano accompaniments to *Songs of the Irish*, a volume of Irish folk songs which he was producing. I set five as a sample and these were accepted, but the publishers found subsequently that the cost of printing the accompaniments was prohibitive, and the volume was produced with tunes only. The five settings were broadcast twice by RTÉ.' [Letter from Aloys Fleischmann to Alec Robertson, 2 Sept. 1974]. There is unfortunately no record of these performances. The year of composition, 1955, is Fleischmann's from a list of works complied in the 1980s. It is of course at variance with the date suggested by his letter to Robertson!)

21   *Na Trí Captaení Loinge*   **1956**
Sreath Rincí do Chór-Gutha
[*The Three Sea-Captains* Choral Dance Suite]
[Pilib Ó Laoighre, Diarmuid O'Driscoll (Irish)]
SATB Choir
3 movements:
    (i) *Allegretto*
    (ii) *Allegro commodo*
    (iii) *Molto vivace*
F.p: 18.5.1956; Cór Cois Laoi, Pilib Ó Laoighre (cond); Cork International Choral Festival, City Hall, Cork.
(This work, based on the rhythms of jig, reel and hornpipe and designed to allow the combination of choral singing and Irish dancing, was danced by the Lehane sisters.)

22   *Bata na bPlanndála* [*The Planting Stick*]   **1957**
Choral Dance Suite
[Pilib Ó Laoighre, Diarmuid O'Driscoll (Irish)]
SATB Choir, Chamber Ensemble [fl(picc), perc, hp, str quartet]
5 movements:
(i)   *Allegro moderato e poco pesante*
(ii) *Vivace*
(iii) *Allegro risoluto*
(iv) *Allegro grazioso*
(v)   *Allegro giovale e ritmico*
F.p: 22.5.1957; Cór Cois Laoi, *ad hoc* chamber ensemble?, Aloys Fleischmann
(cond); Cork International Choral Festival, City Hall, Cork.
(This work develops the idea of combining choral singing and Irish dancing
with which Fleischmann experimented in *Na Trí Captaení Loinge*, No. 21 above,
and was written for the Folk Dance Group of the Cork Ballet Company. The
dancing was choreographed by Joan Denise Moriarty.)

23   **Suite:** *The Cake Dance*   **1957?**
Chamber Ensemble [fl(picc), perc, hp, str quartet]
5 movements:
(i)   *Allegro commodo*
(ii) *Andante quasi recitativo*
(iii) *Moderato energico*
(iv) *Poco andante*
(v)   *Allegro moderato e ritmico*
F.p: 24.5.1957; *ad hoc* chamber ensemble?, Aloys Fleischmann (cond)?; Cork
International Choral Festival, City Hall, Cork.
(The Folk Dance Group of the Cork Ballet Company performed four times at the
1957 Cork International Choral Festival. Three of these performances are simply
listed in the festival programme as with 'Choir and Chamber Orchestra' and
clearly refer to *Bata na bPlanndála*, No. 22 above. That the second of the four performances, with chamber orchestra alone, refers to *The Cake Dance* is confirmed
by the list of the Folk Dance Group's repertoire in *Joan Denise Moriarty: Founder
of Irish National Ballet*, ed. Ruth Fleischmann (Cork: Mercier Press, 1998) p. 251.
The dancing was choreographed by Joan Denise Moriarty.)

24   *Toccata for Carillon*   **1958**
F.p:?.?.1958; Staf Gebruers, Cóbh International Carillon Festival, St Colman's
Cathedral, Cóbh, Co. Cork.
Pub: Cóbh Carillon Series, 1958.

25   *Nocturne for Carillon*   **1958**
F.p:?.?.1958; Staf Gebruers, Cóbh International Carillon Festival, St Colman's
Cathedral, Cóbh, Co. Cork.
Pub: Cóbh Carillon Series, 1958.

26   *Introduction and Funeral March*   **1960**
Orchestra [3(picc)2+ca2+bcl2+cbsn/4331/timp/perc/hp/str]
F.p: 28.2.1961; Radio Éireann Symphony Orchestra, Aloys Fleischmann (cond);
Phoenix Hall, Dublin.
Ded: 'In Memoriam E. J. S.' (MS) [Edward J. Sheehy].

27   *Amhrán na gCúigí* [*Song of the Provinces*]   **1963**
[Alfrid (attrib), trans from Old Irish by James Clarence Mangan]
SATB Choir, Orchestra [2(picc)222/4331/timp/perc/hp/str] with audience
participation
F.p: 29.6.1965; Radio Éireann Singers, Radio Éireann Choral Society, Radio Éire-
ann Symphony Orchestra, Aloys Fleischmann (cond); St Francis Xavier Hall,
Dublin.
Ded: Lady Dorothy Mayer.

28   *Songs of Colmcille*   **1964**
[Robert Farren]
Speaker, SATB Choir, Orchestra [1121/1000/timp/perc/pno/str]
5 movements:
(i)   Prelude
(ii) The Greatness of Colmcille
(iii) Murmur and Make Music
(iv) The Pets
(v)   The Bell Maker
F.p: (I) [Nos. i, iii and iv only as 'Three Excerpts from *Song of Colmcille*'] 2.12.1964;
The College Singers, The College Chamber Orchestra, Aloys Fleischmann (cond);
Public Theatre, Trinity College, Dublin.
(II) [complete] 3.1.1967; Frank O'Dwyer (speaker), Radio Telefís Éireann Singers,
Radio Telefís Éireann Symphony Orchestra, Aloys Fleischmann (cond); St Fran-
cis Xavier Hall, Dublin.
Com: by Trinity College, Dublin, for the bicentenary of the founding of the
School of Music.
Ded: 'To Brian Boydell' (MS).

29   *Ballinderry*   **1968?**
Irish Harp
F.p: 21.5.1992; Teresa Lawlor (Irish harp); John Field Room, National Concert
Hall, Dublin.
(In complying with Sheila Larchet-Cuthbert's request for a work to be included
in *The Irish Harp Book* which she was editing, Fleischmann produced at least two
pieces. 'Herewith another attempt at a suitable piece for your book. It may well
be less suitable than the last, and I would say it is certainly more difficult, as it
should go at a reasonable speed.' [Letter from Aloys Fleischmann to Sheila
Larchet, 2 July 1968] *An Cóitín Dearg*, No. 15b above, was of course one of these
pieces and it is not unlikely that this reference is to *Ballinderry*.)

30   *Cornucopia*   **1969**
Prelude and Rondo for Horn and Piano
F.p: 6.1.1970; The Melos Ensemble: Neil Saunders (horn), Lamar Crowson
(piano): Dublin Festival of Twentieth Century Music, The Examination Hall,
Trinity College, Dublin.
Com: Dublin Festival of Twentieth Century Music.

a   *Cornucopia*   **1970**
Orchestral Version
Solo Horn, Orchestra [2(picc)222/2200/timp/perc/hp/pno/str]
F.p: 11.6.1971; Victor Malirsh (horn), Radio Telefís Éireann Symphony Orchestra,
Aloys Fleischmann (cond); St Francis Xavier hall, Dublin.

31   *Le Balai de Plume* [*The Feather Mop*]   **1970**
      Essay for Pianist-Comedienne
      (Written as a send-up of the *avant-garde*, this work appears never to have been
      performed.)

32   *Cathal Mór of the Wine-Red Hand*   **1970?**
      [James Clarence Mangan]
      SATB Choir and Piano
      F.p?: 17.12.1995; UCC Chamber Choir, Michael Murphy (cond), John Davis
      (piano); Aula Maxima, University College, Cork.
      (At this stage in his career it is unlikely that Fleischmann would have written a
      work like this except for some specific occasion, the opening of the Cork Inter-
      national Choral Festival, possibly. There is no record, however, either of what
      the occasion might have been or of any performance in Fleischmann's lifetime.)

33   *The Bells of Shandon* (arr)   **1970?**
      [Sylvester O'Mahony (Fr Prout)]
      Arrangement of traditional melody
      Orchestra [3(picc)2+ca22/4331/timp/perc/str] with audience participation
      F.p?: 24.4.1970; Cork Symphony Orchestra, Aloys Fleischmann (cond); Cork
      International Choral Festival, City Hall, Cork.

34   *Kelly, the Boy from Killann* (arr)   **1971?**
      [Traditional]
      Arrangement of traditional melody
      Orchestra [2(picc)222/42[1]31/timp/perc/hp/str] with audience participation
      F.p?: 25.2.1971; Cork Symphony Orchestra, Aloys Fleischmann (cond); Schools'
      Concert, City Hall, Cork.

35   *Amhrán Dóchais* [*Song of Hope*] (arr)   **1971?**
      [Traditional (Irish)]
      Arrangement of traditional melody
      Orchestra [2222/4331/timp/perc/str] with audience participation
      F.p?: 25.2.1971; Cork Symphony Orchestra, Aloys Fleischmann (cond); Schools
      Concert, City Hall, Cork.

36   *The Poet's Circuits*   **1972**
      [Padraic Colum]
      Soprano and Irish Harp
      4 movements:
      (i)   The Crane
      (ii) Black Tassels
      (iii) Caoine
      (iv) Spring
      F.p: (I) [Nos. i – iii only] 27.6.1972; Gráinne Yeats (soprano, accompanying her-
      self on the Irish Harp).
      (II) [complete]?

37   *Mass*   **1972**
      for Juvenile or Female Voices and Organ
      [Liturgical (English)]
      SSA Choir, Organ

6 movements:
(i)   Entrance Hymn: Cry Out with Joy
(ii) Kyrie
(iii) Gloria
(iv) Sanctus
(v)   Agnus Dei
(vi) Communion Hymn: As Runs the Thirsting Deer
F.p: [Liturgical] 3.5.1973; South Presentation Convent Choir, Christopher Stembridge (organ), Sister Rosario (cond); South Presentation Convent Chapel, Cork.
Ded: 'for Sister Rosario and the South Presentation Convent Choir' (MS).

38   *Poet in the Suburbs*   1973
     [Thomas Kinsella]
     SATB Choir
     F.p: 24.4.1974; BBC Northern Singers, Stephen Wilkinson (cond); Cork Inter-
     national Choral Festival, City Hall, Cork.
     Pub: Oxford University Press, 1976.
     Ded: Stephen Wilkinson and the BBC Northern Singers.
     (The published score inaccurately states that this work was composed for the
     1975 Cork International Choral Festival. Fleischmann, in Harrison, 1982, says
     that the work was commissioned by the festival, and it is listed as having been
     commissioned in the Cork International Choral Festival's current literature, but
     this is also inaccurate.)

39   *The Boys of Wexford* (arr)   1973?
     [Traditional]
     Arrangement of traditional melody
     Orchestra [3(picc)333/4331/timp/perc/hp/str] with audience participation
     F.p?: 23.2.1973; Cork Symphony Orchestra, Aloys Fleischmann (cond), Schools'
     Concert, City Hall, Cork.

40   **Song Cycle from** *Tides*   1973
     [John Montague]
     Medium Voice and Piano
     4 movements:
     (i)   King and Queen
     (ii) North Sea
     (iii) A Dream of July
     (iv) Wine Dark Sea
     F.p: 10.1.1974; June Croker (mezzo-soprano), Gerard Shanahan (piano); Dublin
     Festival of Twentieth Century Music, Examination Hall, Trinity College, Dublin.

 a   **Song Cycle from** *Tides*   1974
     Orchestral Version
     Medium Voice, Orchestra [2121/2110/timp/perc/hpsd/hp/str]
     F.p: 31.10.1975; June Croker (mezzo-soprano), Radio Telefís Éireann Symphony
     Orchestra, Aloys Fleischmann (cond); St Francis Xavier Hall, Dublin.

41   *Mass for Peace*   1976
     [Liturgical (English)]
     Unison Choir, Orchestra [2(picc)222/4231/timp/perc/str]
     11 movements:

(i)   Entrance Hymn: Give Peace, Lord
(ii)   Kyrie
(iii) Gloria
(iv) Responsorial Psalm: The Lord God Speaks of Peace
(v)   Gospel Acclamation
(vi) Sanctus
(vii) Eucharistic Acclamation
(viii) Great Amen
(ix) Agnus Dei
(x)   Communion Hymn: As Runs the Thirsting Deer
(xi) Recessional Hymn: Peace of the Lord

F.p: [Liturgical] 13.3.1977; Massed Cork School Choirs, Cork Symphony Orchestra, Aloys Fleischmann (cond); St Francis Church, Cork.
Com: PEACE [Prayer Enterprise And Christian Effort].
Ded: 'Dedicated to my wife Anne' (MS).
(No. x, 'Communion Hymn: As Runs the Thirsting Deer', is borrowed from the *Mass* of 1972, No. 37 above.)

a *Mass for Peace*   **1976**
Version with Organ
(In Harrison, 1982, this work is listed as for 'unison chorus/org [=orch].' There never appears to have been a performance of this version.)

42 *Two Antiphons*   **1976?**
[Liturgical (English)]
Unison Choir and Organ
(i) Antiphon: I am the Living Bread
(ii) Antiphon: How Holy is this Feast
(There is no record of a performance of either of these pieces. It is possible that they were originally intended for either of the two masses, Nos. 37 and 41 above. The texts indicate that they were intended as communion hymns, and Sr Rosario, who was involved in the performance of both masses, writes: 'I know that he wrote other hymns either for the first mass or for the Mass for Peace but decided that "As Runs the Thirsting Deer" was either better or more suitable.' [Letter from Sr Rosario to Séamas de Barra, 5.2.1993])

43 *Sinfonia Votiva*   **1977**
Orchestra [3(picc)2+ca2+bcl2+cbsn/4331/timp/perc/hp/str]
This work incorporates No. 26 above, the addition of a third movement completing the original conception.
3 movements:
(i)   Introduction
(ii) Funeral March
(iii) Bacchanal
F.p: 6.1.1978; Radio Telefís Éireann Symphony Orchestra, Aloys Fleischmann (cond); Dublin Festival of Twentieth Century Music.
Ded: In memoriam Edward Sheehy.

44 *Festival Song*   **1978**
[John Montague]
SATB Choir, Orchestra [2(picc)222/4331/timp/perc/str]
F.p: 3.5.1978; Massed Festival Choirs, Cork Symphony Orchestra, Aloys Fleisch-

mann (cond); Cork International Choral Festival, City Hall, Cork.

Com: Cork International Choral Festival (Harrison, 1982). Whether an actual commission in the generally understood sense of that word or not, the work was certainly written to mark the twenty-fifth anniversary of the Festival in 1978.

45 *Omós don Phiarsach* [*Homage to Pádraig Pearse*]   **1979**
    [Pádraig Pearse (Nos. ii – v in Irish)]
    Mezzo-soprano, Speaker, Orchestra [3(picc)2+ca2+bcl2+cbsn/4331/timp/perc/hp/str]
    7 movements:
    (i)   Introduction
    (ii)   Cad chuige dhíbh dom' chiapadh? [Why do you torture me?]
    (iii) A chinn áluinn [O lovely head]
    (iv)   A mhic bhig na gcleas [Little lad of the tricks]
    (v)   Fornacht do chonac thú [Naked I saw thee]
    (vi)   – Pearse on Education
           – Pearse on Nationality
    (vii) The Mother
    F.p: 18.11.1979; Bernadette Greevy (mezzo-soprano), Bill Golding (speaker), Radio Telefís Éireann Symphony Orchestra, Colman Pearce (cond); Gaiety Theatre, Dublin.
    Com: by Radio Telefís Éireann, for the centenary of the birth of Pádraig Pearse.

46 *The Fool*   **1979**
    [Pádraig Pearse]
    Medium Voice and Piano
    (This song was originally intended as part of *Omós don Phiarsach* [*Homage to Pádraig Pearse*], No. 45 above, and remains unperformed.)

47 *The Táin*   **1981**
    Ballet in three acts
    Orchestra [2(picc)222/4231/timp/perc/hp/str]
    Scenario: uncredited, but probably by Joan Denise Moriarty and Aloys Fleischmann in collaboration.
    Choreography: Joan Denise Moriarty
    Décor, Costumes: Patrick Murray
    Prem: 6.10.1981; Irish Ballet Company, Radio Telefís Éireann Concert Orchestra, Prionnsias Ó Duinn (cond); Dublin Theatre Festival, Gaiety Theatre, Dublin.
    Com: Irish Ballet Company.
    Ded: Joan Denise Moriarty.

a   **Ballet Suite**: *The Táin*   **1982**
    Orchestra [2(picc)222/4231/timp/perc/hp/str]
    8 movements:
    (i)   Introduction – The Brown Bull of Cuailgne
    (ii)   Dance of Medb's Warriors and Dance of the Serving Girls
    (iii) Dance of Allegiance
    (iv)   Cúchulainn and Emer
    (v)   General Dance
    (vi)   Interlude
    (vii) Entry of the Armies

(viii)The Truce and Reconciliation
F.p: 15.10.1982; Radio Teleffs Éireann Concert Orchestra, Aloys Fleischmann (cond); National Concert Hall, Dublin.

b **Five Dances from** *The Táin* **1990?**
Orchestra [2(picc)222/4231/timp/perc/hp/str]
5 movements:
(i)   Prelude – The Brown Bull of Cuailgne
(ii) Dance of the Camp Maidens – Fanfare
(iii) Cúchulainn and Emer
(iv) Queen Medb's Warriors
(v)   Finale
F.p: 8.3.1991; National Symphony Orchestra, Kasper de Roo (cond); National Concert Hall, Dublin.

48   *Hymns and Magnificats for Knock*   1982
SATB Choir (Nos. i and vi) / Unison Choir (Nos. ii – v) and Piano (Organ)
(i)   Hymn to Our Lady of Knock I: Lady of Knock, You shone, a glowing vision [Tom Hamill]
(ii) Hymn to Our Lady of Knock II: Lady of Knock, You shone, a glowing vision [Tom Hamill] (second setting)
(iii) Hymn to Our Lady of Knock (III): A secret garden and a rose [Michael Hodgett]
(iv) Magnificat (1st version) [Liturgical (English)]
(v)   Magnificat (2nd version) [Liturgical (English)]
(vi) Magnificat (3rd version) [Liturgical (English)]
(These *Hymns and Magnificats* were written as entries in a competition organised by Fr Peter Waldron of Knock in 1982.)
F.p: There is no record of any of these being performed, except for No. vi (see below).
Pub: [No. vi only] in *Hymns of Knock*, Michael Casey (arr), Fr Peter Waldron (ed), Knock Shrine, Co. Mayo: Knock Publications, 1985, pp. 32 – 34.

a   *Magnificat for Knock*   1982
Version of No. vi above
SATB Choir, Orchestra [2(picc)121/3231/timp/perc/hp/str]
F.p: 7.8.1982; Our Lady's Choral Society, Radio Teleffs Éireann Concert Orchestra, Prionnsias Ó Duinn (cond); Knock Basilica, Knock, Co. Mayo.
(Of the six pieces that Fleischmann wrote for the competition, No. vi was awarded a prize, hence its publication and its subsequent orchestration for performance in a concert of the prize-winning entries. In Harrison, 1982, Fleischmann lists No. vi only, simply as *Magnificat*.)

49   *Song for a Festive Occasion*   1984
[Arthur William O'Shaughnessy]
Orchestra [3(picc)2+ca2+bcl2/4331/timp/perc/hp/str] with audience participation
F.p: 12.4.1984; Cork Symphony Orchestra, Aloys Fleischmann (cond), City Hall, Cork.
(Composed to mark the fiftieth anniversary of the Cork Symphony Orchestra in 1984.)

50   *Time's Offspring*   **1985**
A Cantata based on the writings of Bishop Berkeley
[Bishop Berkeley; supplemented by quotations from Lord Byron, T.H. Key,
Alexander Pope and the Bible (Jeremiah x, Amos v.8, Psalm LXV)]
Speaker, SATB Chorus, Orchestra [2(picc)222/4231/timp/perc/str]
5 movements:
(i)   Overture
(ii) The Principles of Human Knowledge
(iii) Chorus of Derision
(iv) The Querist
(v)   Finale
F.p: 25.8.1985; Canon H.G. Watts (speaker), East Cork Choral Society, Cork Symphony Orchestra, Aloys Fleischmann (cond); St Colman's Cathedral, Cloyne,
Co. Cork.
Com: by the Cloyne Literary and Historical Society, for the tercentenary of the
birth of George Berkeley, Bishop of Cloyne 1732–1753.

a   *Time's Offspring*   **1985**
Overture for Orchestra
No. i from *Time's Offspring*
Orchestra [2(picc)222/4231/timp/perc/str]
F.p (as independent piece): 13.11.1985; Radio Telefís Éireann Symphony
Orchestra, Bryden Thomson (cond), National Concert Hall, Dublin.

51   *Clonmacnoise*   **1986?**
[Frank O'Connor (from the Irish)]
SATB Choir, Orchestra [2(picc)222/2231/timp/perc/hp/str], with audience
participation
F.p: 3.5.1990; Choir of University College Cork, Radio Telefís Éireann Concert
Orchestra, Geoffrey Spratt (cond); Cork International Choral Festival, City Hall,
Cork.
Pub: Cumann Náisiúnta na gCór [The Association of Irish Choirs], 1989.
Com: by the Choir, Orchestra and Choral Society of University College, Cork, to
mark the occasion of Fleischmann's retirement from the Chair of Music in UCC
in 1980.
Ded: Geoffrey Spratt and the UCC Choir.

52   *Games*   **1990**
[Vasco Popa (translated from the Serbo-Croat by Anne Pennington)]
SATB Choir, Harp and Percussion
6 movements:
(i)   Before Play
(ii) The Nail
(iii) Hide and Seek
(iv) The Rose Thieves
(v)   He
(vi) Ashes
F.p: 6.5.1990; BBC Singers, Sheila Larchet-Cuthbert (hp), James Hynes, Noel
Heraty (perc), Simon Joly (cond); Cork International Choral Festival, City Hall,
Cork.
Com: by the Thirty-seventh Cork International Choral Festival, for the Twenty-seventh Seminar on Contemporary Choral Music.

Amhrán Dóchais [*Song of Hope*] (arranged), 1971?, cat. no. 35
Amhrán na gCúigí [*Song of the Provinces*], 1963, cat. no. 27
Balai de Plume, Le [*The Feather Mop*], 1970, cat. no. 31
Ballinderry, 1968?, cat. no. 29
Bata na bPlanndála [*The Planting Stick*], 1957, cat. no. 22
Bells of Shandon, The (arr), 1970?, cat. no. 33
Boys of Wexford, The (arr), 1973?, cat. no. 39
Cáit Ní Dhuibhir (arr), 1943?, cat. no. 10
Cathal Mór of the Wine-Red Hand, 1970?, cat. no. 32
Clare's Dragoons, 1945, cat. no. 14
Clonmacnoise, 1986?, cat. no. 51
Cóitín Dearg, An, 1951, cat. no. 16
Cornucopia, 1969, cat. no. 30
Cradle Song,? 1927–32, cat. no. 1
Eilís Nic Dhiarmada Rua, 1944?, cat. no. 9a
(*Elizabeth Mac Dermot Roe* – see: *Eilís Nic Dhiarmada Rua*)
Festival Song, 1978, cat. no. 44
Fool, The, 1979, cat. no. 46
Fountain of Magic – see: Song Cycle from *The Fountain of Magic*
Four Fanfares for An Tóstal, 1952, cat. no. 18
Four Masters, The, 1944, cat. no. 11
Four Old Italian Songs, 1937, cat. no. 6
Games, 1990, cat. no. 52
Golden Bell of Ko, The, 1947, cat. no. 15
(*Homage to Pádraig Pearse* – see: *Ómos don Phiarsach*)
Humours of Carolan, The,? 1941–44, cat. no. 9
Hymns and Magnificats for Knock, 1982, cat. no. 48
Illumina Occulos Meos, 1934, cat. no. 4
Introduction and Funeral March, 1960, cat. no. 26
Kelly, The Boy from Killan (arranged), 1971?, cat. no. 34
Macha Ruadh [*Red-Haired Macha*], 1955, cat. no. 19
Magnificat – see: *Hymns and Magnificats for Knock*
Mass for juvenile or female voices and organ, 1972, cat. no. 37
Mass for Peace, 1976, cat. no. 41
Movement for String Quartet, ? 1927–32, cat. no. 2
Nocturne for Carillon, 1958, cat. no. 25
Ómós don Phiarsach [*Homage to Pádraig Pearse*], 1979, cat. no. 45
Piano Quintet, 1938, cat. no. 7
(*Planting Stick, The* – see: *Bata na bPlanndála*)
Poet in the Suburbs, 1973, cat. no. 38
Poet's Circuits, The, 1972, cat. no. 36
Prelude and Dance, 1940, cat. no. 8
Sinfonia Votiva, 1977, cat. no. 43
Six Folk Song Arrangements, 1952, cat. no. 17
Songs of Colmcille, 1964, cat. no. 28
(*Song of the Provinces* – see: *Amhrán na gCuigí*)
Song Cycle from *The Fountain of Magic*, 1945, cat. no. 12
Song Cycle from *Tides*, 1973, cat. no. 40
Song for a Festive Occasion 1984, cat. no. 49
Songs of Affection, 1955?, cat. no. 20

Sreath do Phiano [*Suite for Piano*], 1933, cat. no. 3
Suite: *The Cake Dance*, 1957?, cat. no. 23
Táin, The, 1981, cat. no. 47
Three songs for Tenor and Orchestra – see: *Trí hAmhráin*
Tides – see: Song Cycle from *Tides*
Time's Offspring, 1985, cat. no. 50
Toccata for Carillon, 1958, cat. no. 54
Trí hAmhráin [*Three Songs*], 1935, cat. no. 5
Trí Captaení Loinge, Na [*The Three Sea-Captains*], 1956, cat. no. 21
Two Antiphons, 1976?, cat. no. 42
Where Finbarr Taught, 1945, cat. no. 13

(3) MISSING MANUSCRIPTS
The Fleischmann family does not know the whereabouts of the manuscripts listed
below; any information on the subject would be gratefully received by the editor, c/o
The English Department, University of Bielefeld, 33501 Bielefeld, Germany.

1. *Sreath do Phiano* [Suite for Piano], cat. no. 3
2. *Cáit Ní Dhuibhir*, cat. no. 10
3. *Clare's Dragoons* (full score), cat. no. 14
4. *The Golden Bell of Ko* (full score), cat. no. 15
5. *An Cóitín Dearg* [The Red Petticoat], Ballet Suite (full score), cat. no. 16a
6. *An Cóitín Dearg* [The Red Petticoat], for Irish Harp, cat. no. 16b
7. *Four Fanfares for An Tóstal* (score), cat. no. 18
8. *Songs of Affection*, cat. no. 20
9. *Na Trí Captaení Loinge* [The Three Sea Captains], cat. no. 21
10. *Toccata for Carillon*, cat. no. 24
11. *Nocturne for Carillon*, cat. no. 25
12. *Le Balai de Plume*, cat. no. 31
13. *Poet in the Suburbs*, cat. no. 38
14. *Mass for Peace* (Vocal / organ score), cat. no. 41a
15. *Ómós don Phiarsach* [Homage to Pádraig Pearse] (Vocal score), cat. no. 45
16. *Magnificat for Knock* (full score), cat. no. 48a
17. *Song for a Festive Occasion* (fullscore), cat. no. 49
18. *Clonmacnoise* (vocal score), cat. no. 51

APPENDIX B:

Writings by Aloys Fleischmann, Provisional List Compiled by Séamas de Barra and Ruth Fleischmann

Publications:
Die Iren in der Neumen- und Choralforschung, in: *Die Zeitschrift für Musikwissenschaft*, Jahrgang 16, Leipzig, July 1934
The Outlook of Music in Ireland, in: *Studies*, Vol. XXIV, March 1935
Ars Nova: Irish Music in the Shaping, in: *Ireland Today*, Vol. I, No. 2, June 1936
Composition and the Irish Folk Idiom, in: *Ireland Today*, Vol. I, No. 6, November 1936
Music in Munster in: *Irish Art Handbook*, Dublin, 1943
Music in University College Cork, in: *University College Cork Record*, No. 4, Summer 1945
Music and Its Public, in: *University College Cork Record*, No. 7, Summer 1946
Music in Ireland (with Brian Boydell and Michael Bowles), in: *The Bell*, Vol. XIV, No. I, April 1947
References to Chant in Early Irish MSS, in: *Féilschribhínn Tórna*, ed. Séamus Pender, Cork University Press, 1947
The Music of E. J. Moeran, in: *Envoy: An Irish Review of Literature and Art* Vol. 4 No 16, March 1951
The Future of Music in Ireland, in: *The Bell*, April 1951
Irish Music, in: *Encyclopaedia Americana*, New York, 1952
Music in Ireland: A Symposium (ed.) Cork and Oxford, (Cork University Press and Blackwell), 1952 (Two contributions by Fleischmann: 'Historical Survey' and 'The Organisation of the Profession')
Brian Boydell, in: *Groves Dictionary of Music and Musicians*, (5th. ed.) 1954
Dublin, in: *Groves Dictionary of Music and Musicians*, (5th. ed.) 1954
Music Criticism in Ireland (a series of three articles), in: *The Irish Times*, February 1954
The Arnold Bax Memorial, in: *UCC Record*, No. 31, Easter 1956
University Appointments, in: *University Review*, Vol. I, No. 11, 1957
Endowments for Music, in: *UCC Record*, No. 34. Easter 1959
Grants for the Music Department, in: *UCC Record*, No. 36, Easter 1961
Music in Ancient Munster and Monastic Cork (with Ryta Gleeson), in: *Journal of the Cork Historical and Archaeological Society*, Vol. LXX, 1965
Preface to Ita Hogan's *Anglo-Irish Music 1780–1830*, 1966
Amateur Music, in: *Encyclopaedia of Ireland*, Dublin, 1968
Musical Education, in: *Encyclopaedia of Ireland*, Dublin 1968
Brian Boydell, in: *Hibernia*, Vol. 32, No. 9. 1968
Musical Education, in: *Encyclopaedia of Ireland*, Dublin 1968
Arnold Bax, in: *Recorded Sound*, London, Nos. 29–30, January–April 1968
Music in Education, in: *Education in Ireland II: What should students learn?* ed. Michael W. Murphy, The Mercier Press, Cork, 1971
Seán Ó Riada, in: *Cork Evening Echo* Oct. 11 1971
Petrie's Contribution to Irish Music, in: *Proceedings of the Royal Irish Academy*, Vol. 72, Section C, No. 9, 1972
Seán Ó Riada's Nomos, No. II, in: *Éire–Ireland*, Vol. VII, No. 3. St Paul, USA, Autumn 1972
Musicians in Ireland: In Defence of the Kennedy Hall, in: *The Irish Press*, 16 September 1974

Church Music, in: *The Fold: The Cork Diocesan Magazine*

Music in Nineteenth-Century Ireland, in: *Four Centuries of Music in Ireland*, ed. Brian Boydell, BBC, London, 1979

A Munster Phidias, in: *The Cork Review on Séamus Murphy* (1907–75), No 4, ed. Paul Durcan, Triskel Arts Centre, Cork 1980

The Music of the Celtic Rite, in: *The New Grove Dictionary of Music*, 1980

The Music Critics Criticised, in: *The Irish Times*, 16 March 1988

Introduction to: Nóirín Ní Riain, *Stór Amhrán*, Cork 1988

Crisis in the Arts Council, in: *The Sunday Independent*, 30 October 1988

Seán O'Faoláin: A Personal Memoir, in: *The Cork Review*, ed. Seán Dunne, Triskel Arts Centre, Cork, 1991

A Key to Sources of Irish Traditional Music, *Ó Riada Memorial Lecture 6*, The Irish Traditional Music Society UCC, Cork 1991

Music and Society, 1850–1921, in: *A New History of Ireland Vol. VI, Ireland Under the Union*, Oxford (Clarendon Press) 1996

The Ballet in Cork, in: *Joan Denise Moriarty: Founder of Irish National Ballet*, ed. Ruth Fleischmann, Cork (Mercier Press) 1998

Sources of Irish Traditional Music c 1600–1855: An Annotated Catalogue of Prints and Manuscripts 1583–1855, 2 vols., New York (Garland) 1998

Unpublished Writings:

The Neumes in Irish Liturgical Manuscripts, M.A. Thesis, Music Department, University College Cork, 1932

A History of the Music Department at University College Cork
   (written in 1987 for a publication to celebrate the 150 anniversary of UCC, which was to be edited by Prof. Joseph Lee of the History Department but was abandoned.)

The Arts Council and the Dance, March 1989
   (The Arts Council, to whom it was shown, threatened legal proceedings unless some of the statements made were withdrawn)

A Thematic Index to the Sources of Irish Traditional Music

APPENDIX C:

Music Graduates of UCC 1916–1980, Compiled by Maura Jones and Conn Murphy

1916 Jeremiah O'Connor
1928 Ena P. Peggs-Hendrick
1931 Aloys G. Fleischmann
1933 Michael Bowman
1934 Anne O'Connor
1935 Joan Burke O'Callaghan, William Shanahan
1938 Rose A. Hennessey
1939 M. McSweeney-Crowley, Joseph A. Reade, Mary B. O'Mahoney
1940 M. Tubridy-Cummins, Patrick G. Spillane
1941 Edith C. Curran
1942 M. Jacobs-Shanahan
1943 Jane O'Brien
1944 Mary Horgan
1946 Sister Mary Crowley, Deirdre O'Sullivan, Eithne O'Sullivan Murray, Sister Julia Scollard
1947 Sister Colmcille Curnane, Shaun Hayes, Micheal Ó Ceallacháin, Proinsías Ó Ceallaigh
1949 Ryta Mulcahy-Gleeson, Annette de Foubert
1950 Eileen O'Donovan-Barry
1952 Seán Ó Riada
1953 Rev. A. Sanusi
1954 Bridget Doolan, Rev. Henry McCarney, Máire Ní Bhriain-Uí Chleirigh, Micheal Weedle
1955 Mary Garvey-Weedle, Mary O. Murphy, Patricia O'Sullivan
1956 Bernard Geary, Ita Hogan-Beausang
1957 Brendan O'Boyle, Louise Reidy-Verling
1958 Patricia Dowling-Campbell, Clement Garvey, Margaret M. O'Connor-O'Brien, Pilib Ó Laoghaire
1959 Sister Mercedes Considine, Declan Townsend, Donal Twomey
1960 Sister Rosario Allen, Gareth Crowley, Bernard Curtis
1961 Brother Malachy Breslin, Vera Jones-Kenny, Rev. J. McAuliffe, Leonard Sheridan, Anne Wallace
1962 Rev. Patrick Ahern, Sister Hilary Hurley, Sheila McDermott-Duffy, B. M. O'Connell-Rice, Rev. D. O'Driscoll

1963 Michael J. Hynes, Sister Mary O'Shaughnessy, Anne Warren-O'Reilly
1964 Michael Casey, Ailish Jones-Cassidy, Rev. Nicholas Motherway, Colum Ó Cléirigh
1965 William N. Kelly, Rev. Henry H. Keogh, Eithne O'Neill-Phelan
1966 Rosalind Gordon, Geraldine Kelly-Fletcher, Yvonne Ruttle
1967 Sister K. Finn, Elaine M. Gowan, Donagh S. Madden, Sister Finbarr Muckley, Rosemary Mulcahy, John C. Murphy, Marion Nevill, Sister de Lourdes Ní Chathain, Mary O'Driscoll-Fleming, Marie O'Shea-Murphy, Evelyn Tait, Brother Kevin Treacy
1968 Ethel Balfe, Esther Dunne-Greene, Sister Gerard Grisewood, Denise Lane-Murphy, Emelie Miles-FitzGibbon, Eleanor O'Loughlin, Elizabeth Wallace
1969 Tom Barry, Patrick Butler, Patrick Dermody, Mary S. Desmond, Patricia Moloney-Murphy, Neil O'Brien, Jane O'Dea Titley
1970 Josephine Barry, Eileen Burke, Orla Ní Mhurchadha, Marie O'Connell, Raymond O'Shea, Ellen M. Penny, Anne Willis
1971 Ann Buckley, Catherine Hogan-Dunlea, Breda McMeel-O'Toole, Máire Ní Cheallacháin, Tomás Ó Canainn, E. Mary Sheehan
1972 Maire Buckley, Hilary Carleton, Mary Carroll, Sister Cecilia Cotter, Anne B. Coughlan, Catherine Delaney, Rosita A. Doyle, John Fitzpatrick, Rev. J. J. Gannon, Eileen Gleeson-Ui Chathain, Richard Eugene Goodison, Patricia Murphy, Maire Ní Dhuibhir, Nóirín Ní Riain-Uí Shúilleabháin, Conchubhair Ó Ceallacháin, Míheál Ó Súilleabháin
1973 Meav Proinseas de Burca, Sister Rupert Corkery, Eilís Cranitch, Anne Dennison-Roche, Eric Dunlea, Cathal Dunne, Sister Carmel Flynn, Sister Jacinta

418

Kavanagh, Seán MacCiarnan, Máire Ní Cheallacháin, Kaye O'Gara, David O'Sullivan, Marie Sexton, Patricia Sheehan, Sister Marguerite Togher

1974 Mary Beattie, Emer Black, Brid Cranitch, Geraldine Fahy, Patricia Harrison, Patricia Kelleher, Katherine Kiely, Sister Máirín McDonogh, Brendan Power, Sister Nuala Reidy, Annette Tyrrell, Sister Teresa Walsh

1975 Elizabeth Barry-Moloney, Mary Black, Sister Teresa English, Anne Gartland, Sister Evelyn Glynn, Marjorie Golden, Mary Harrington, James Horgan, Sister Frances Hurley, Florence Linehan-Jansen, Ita McCarthy, Sister Mary McGrath, Seán MacLiam, Maura Manning-Jones, Conn Murphy, Aine Ní Ghabann, Jane O'Donovan, Frances Watters, John Joseph Williams

1976 Frank Buckley, Johanna Buckley, Matthew Cranitch, John Dunne, Catherine Egan, Gerard Hession, Patricia Horgan, Catherine Janeczek, Mary Kerin, Ellen Malone, Maura McGuire, Olive McMahon, Anne Moloney, Mary Murphy, Bebhinn Ní Mheara, Póilín Ní Shuibhne, Aidan O'Carroll, Patricia O'Connell, Margaret O'Donnell, Veronica O'Sullivan, John Reidy, Mary Ridge, Mary Ryan, Bridget Walsh, Eileen Walsh, Mary Ward

1977 James Barry, Mary Bracken, Hanora Casey, Valerie Cave, Elizabeth Cooper, Laura Cunningham, Jean Downey, Catherine Foley, Bridget Forde, Anne Higgins, Mary Hogan, Margaret Keating, Margaret Maher, Bernadette McCarthy, Mary Moylan, Gerard Moynihan, Eileen

Mulligan, Julia Murphy, Una Ní Conghaile, Donal O'Callaghan, Eugenie O'Connell, Basilia Okeke, Catherine O'Leary, Susan O'Regan, Ann Redmond, Monica Sheehan, Thomas Toomey, Anna Wasilewski

1978 Michael Bennett, Timothy Cotter, Geraldine Cotter, Michael Forde, Jennifer Furlong, Mary Hynes, Deirdre Jackson, Aiveen Kearney, John Kilgarriff, Finola Laide, Gabrielle Lee, Colm Long, Mary MacMahon, Sheila McCarthy, Gerrardine Mullarkey, John Francis Murphy, Majella Murphy, Juliet Neville, Maire Ní Laoghaire, Aodh Ó Tuama, Catherine O'Connell, Noel O'Regan, Karen O'Reilly, Carbry O'Sullivan, Louise Roche, Patricia Ruth, Eleanor Ryan, Jeremiah Sexton, Mary Shorten

1979 Deirdre Campbell, Juliette Cant, Mary Collins, Paschal Conroy, Richard Daly, Mary Devereux, Nora Flynn, Mary Gallagher, Thomas Guiry, Margaret Hallissey, Cliona Harding, Michael Hennessy, Mary Higgins, Mary Joyce, Catherine Leamy, Gerard McConnell, Ursula Muckley, Patrick Nolan, Margaret O'Brien, Gerard O'Connor, Maria O'Donoghue, Eve O'Kelly, Susan O'Neill, Annette O'Sullivan

1980 Padraig Carroll, Gregory Crosbie, Kathleen Dineen, Geraldine Fitzgerald, Susan Foley, Bernard Harrison, Mary Hayden, Angela Hayes, Mary Horan, Jerome Leonard, Mary Lucey, Catherine Lynch, John Lynch, Mary Lynch, Declan Martin, Ann McAuliffe, Johanna McNamara, Mary Mitchell, Margaret O'Flaherty, Catherine O'Sullivan, Nora O'Sullivan, Norma Rohan, Eleanor Willis

LIST OF CONTRIBUTORS

NOTES

CHAPTER 2: THE EDUCATOR OF TEACHERS

1 Aloys Fleischmann, 'The Outlook of Music in Ireland', in *Studies*, Vol. XXIV No. 93, March 1935, p. 130.

2. Aloys Fleischmann, 'Music in UCC', *Cork University Record*, No. 4, Summer 1945, p. 42.

3. *Ibid.*

4. 'Unflagging Energy – Michael Dervan talks to Aloys Fleischmann', *Music Ireland*, Vol.5, No. 5, May 1990, p. 7.

CHAPTER 4: THE ORGANISER

1 *Editor's note*: The silver baton did not get lost: it is a treasured family possession. Aloys Fleischmann often lost things he carried around with him, such as his free-travel pass, his glasses or keys; but presentations were always carefully deposited somewhere in his study. They often got buried for long periods under piles of papers, but there they were safe both from the various burglars who visited the house and from his own absent-mindedness, and all have survived.

2 *Editor's note*: Jimmy Hynes played the percussion part together with Noel Heraty in Fleischmann's last work *Games*, written for choir, harp and percussion, which was performed in 1990 by the BBC Singers under their conductor Simon Joly; the harpist was Sheila Cuthbert Larchet.

3 *Editor's note*: Michael McCarthy was over many years one of most reliable members of the Cork Symphony Orchestra, who regularly helped Aloys Fleischmann prepare the hall for rehearsal.

4 *Editor's note:* The other recipients of Honorary Life Membership of the Royal Dublin Society in June 1991 were Sybil Connolly, Professor Denis Crowley, Michael Dillon, Dr Patrick Hillary, and John B. Keane – information kindly supplied by Eileen Byrne, the RDS Assistant Registrar.

CHAPTER 5: THE COLLEAGUE

1 John A. Murphy was Professor of Irish History at University College Cork from 1971 to 1990, and an Independent member of Seanad Éireann in the National University of Ireland constituency from 1977 to 1983, and 1987 to 1993.

2 Fleischmann A., (ed); Ó Súilleabháin M., (assoc. ed); McGettrick, P., (assoc. ed) *Sources of Irish Traditional Music c.1600–1855: An Annotated Catalogue of Prints and Manuscripts 1583–1855*, Garland, New York, 1998.

3 Murphy John A., *The College, A History of Queen's College/University College Cork 1845 –1995*, Cork University Press, Cork, 1995, p. 221.

4 *Ibid.*

5 Moody T. W.; Martin F. X.; Byrne F. J.; (eds.), *A New History of Ireland, Vol. III*, Oxford: Claredon Press, 1976.

6 *Editor's note*: Kevin Roche did not originally mention these issues in his article: they were included at the request of the editor.

7 *Editor's note*: It was Professor Cox of the Music department of UCC who had the idea of celebrating the 60th anniversary of the Cork Symphony Orchestra's first concert by performing the same programme as was given in 1935.

8 The Music Association of Ireland was founded in 1949.

9 *Music in Ireland* , (ed.) Aloys Fleischmann, was published by the Cork University Press in 1952.

1 Her Excellency the President has very graciously allowed the editor to reproduce the speaking notes she used for her address when she launched Fleischmann's *Sources of Irish Traditional Music* at University College Cork in January 1999.

2 Mícheál Ó Súilleabháin's Preface to Aloys Fleischmann's posthumously published work *Sources of Irish Traditional Music* has been reproduced with kind permission of Garland of New York.

3 Tilly Fleischmann (edited by Michael O'Neill, 1986), *Aspects of the Liszt Tradition*, Cork, Adare Press; Roberton Publications, Wendover, Aylesbury/Bucks, and Theodore Presser Co., Brynmawr / Pennsylvania 1991, see 'Editor's Preface'.

4 Brian Boydell (1970), 'Fleischmann, Aloys (Georg)' in Stanley Sadie (ed.) *The New Grove Dictionary of Music and Musicians*, Volume 6, London, OUP, p. 635.

5. Aloys Fleischmann (1971), 'Music in Education', in Michael W Murphy (ed.) *Education in Ireland 2; What Should Students Learn?* Cork, The Mercier Press, p. 68–69

6 Aloys Fleischmann (1935), 'The Outlook of Music in Ireland' in *Studies*, Volume 24, March issue, pp.121–130.

7 Aloys Fleischmann (1936), 'Ars Nova', in *Ireland Today*, Volume 1, July issue, p. 46.

8 *Ibid.*, p. 46.

9 Aloys Fleischmann (1935), 'The Outlook of Music in Ireland' in *Studies*, Volume 24, March issue, pp. 125–126.

10 *Ibid.*, pp. 127–128.

11 Aloys Fleischmann (1951), 'Future of Music in Ireland' in *The Bell* edited by Peadar O'Donnell, Volume XVII, No.1, April issue, p. 8.

12 Aloys Fleischmann (1952) 'The Organisation of the Profession' in Aloys Fleischmann (ed.), *Music in Ireland; a Symposium*, Cork University Press, pp. 77ff.

13 Aloys Fleischmann (1951), 'Future of Music in Ireland', in *The Bell* edited by Peadar O'Donnell, Volume XVII, No. 1 April issue, p. 7.

14 Aloys Fleischmann (1971), 'Music in Education', in Michael W Murphy (ed.) *Education in Ireland 2; What Should Students Learn?* Cork, The Mercier Press, p. 71.

15 Aloys Fleischmann (1951), 'Future of Music in Ireland', in *The Bell* edited by Peadar O'Donnell, Volume XVII, No. 1, April issue, p. 7.

16 Aloys Fleischmann (1936), 'Ars Nova', in *Ireland Today*, Volume 1, July issue, pp. 43–44.

17 Aloys Fleischmann (ed.) (1952), *Music in Ireland; a Symposium*, Cork University Press; Aloys Fleischmann (1951), 'The Future of Music in Ireland', in *The Bell* edited by Peadar O'Donnell, Volume XVII, No.1, April issue, pp. 5–10; Aloys Fleischmann (1968), 'Amateur Music' and 'Musical Education' in Victor Meally (ed.) *Encyclopaedia of Ireland*, Dublin: A. Figgis, pp. 393–396; Aloys Fleischmann (1971) 'Music in Education', in Michael W. Murphy (ed.) *Education in Ireland 2; What Should Students Learn?* Cork, The Mercier Press, pp. 68–88.

18 Harry White (1998), *The Keeper's Recital: Music and Cultural History in Ireland 1770–1970*, Cork University Press, p. 134.

19 Aloys Fleischmann (1951), 'Future of Music in Ireland', in *The Bell* edited by Peadar O'Donnell, Volume XVII, No. 1, April issue, p. 5.

20 Aloys Fleischmann (1968), 'Music Education' in Victor Meally (ed.) *Encyclopaedia of Ireland*, Dublin: A.Figgis, p. 396.

21 See, for example, John Paynter and Peter Aston (1970), *Sound and Silence*, Cambridge University Press, an influential textbook on teaching children to compose, and Ronald B. Thomas' publications and reports of the Manhattanville School Music Project, an American initiative aiming to develop a more appropriate music curriculum for use in schools. These were widely known and used extensively during this period but, even in my own time in UCC, none were available in the

Music department library, although the works which he cited by Orff, Kodály and others were. Nor did Professor Fleischmann draw on the psychology of music education to improve his case although, by 1970, there was a considerable literature on the assessment of musical aptitude and ability using standardised tests, e.g., Arnold Bentley (1966), *Musical Ability in Children and its Measurement*, London, Harrap and Co. and Carl Seashore (1939), *Measures of Musical Talent*, Camden, N. J. and H. D. Wing (1957), 'The Measurement of Musical Aptitude' in *Occupational Psychology*, Volume 31, No. 1, not to mention Helmut Moog's ground-breaking study on musical development in early childhood, which was published in Germany in 1968, although the latter study was not generally disseminated prior to Claudia Clarke's 1976 translation, *The Musical Experience of the Pre-school Child*, published by Schott.

22 See The National Council for Curriculum and Assessment (1990), *Report of the Review Body on the Primary Curriculum*, NCCA, pp. 59–62 and Seán Mac Liam (1990, revised 1992), 'Position Paper on the Standing of Leaving Certificate Music', unpublished work undertaken for the NCCA, for reviews of the complex nature and the causes of failure at their respective levels .

23 Aloys Fleischmann (1971), 'Music in Education', in Michael W Murphy (ed.) *Education in Ireland 2; What Should Students Learn*? Cork, The Mercier Press, p. 74, citing the 'Introduction' in Frigyes Sandor (ed. 1966), *Musical Education in Hungary*, London.

24 See *Rialacha agus Clár do leith Meanscoile* 1976/77, Oifig an tSoláthair, p. 13 which contains a reprint of the rule cited by Professor Fleischmann in his 1971 article.

25 Aloys Fleischmann (1971), 'Music in Education', in Michael W Murphy (ed.) *Education in Ireland 2; What Should Students Learn?* Cork, The Mercier Press, p. 82.

26 See statistics cited in Aloys Fleischmann (1935), 'The Outlook of Music in Ireland' in *Studies*, Volume 24, March issue, p. 126 and Aloys Fleischmann (1971), 'Music in Education', in Michael W Murphy (ed.) *Education in Ireland 2; What Should Students Learn*? Cork, The Mercier Press, pp. 81–82.

27 Statistics supplied by the Department of Education and Science.

28 Aloys Fleischmann (1971), 'Music in Education', in Michael W Murphy (ed.) *Education in Ireland 2; What Should Students Learn?* Cork, The Mercier Press, pp. 83–84

29 Aloys Fleischmann (1936), 'Composition and the Folk Idiom' in *Ireland Today*, Volume 1, November issue, pp. 40–41.

30 Aloys Fleischmann (1936), 'Ars Nova', in *Ireland Today*, Volume 1, July issue, p. 43.

31 Aloys Fleischmann (1935), 'The Outlook of Music in Ireland' in *Studies*, Volume 24, March issue, p. 125.

32 Aloys Fleischmann (1971), 'Music in Education', in Michael W Murphy (ed.) *Education in Ireland 2; What Should Students Learn*? Cork, The Mercier Press, p. 82–83

33 Aloys Fleischmann (1951), 'Future of Music in Ireland', in *The Bell* edited by Peadar O'Donnell, Volume XVII, No. 1, April issue, p. 7.

34 Aloys Fleischmann (1971), 'Music in Education', in Michael W Murphy (ed.) *Education in Ireland 2; What Should Students Learn*? Cork, The Mercier Press, p. 83.

35 From my personal notes taken at lectures.

36 Aloys Fleischmann (1951), 'Future of Music in Ireland', in *The Bell* edited by Peadar O'Donnell, Volume XVII, No. 1, April issue, p. 6.

37 Harry White (1998), *The Keeper's Recital: Music and Cultural History in Ireland, 1770–1970*, Cork University Press, p. 130.

38 *Sean-nós* literally means 'old style' and refers to traditional songs in Irish. The *Déise* refers to the Co. Waterford Gaeltacht of An Rinn.

39 Introduction by Aloys Fleischmann to Nóirín Ní Riain's publication *Stór Amhrán*, Mercier Press, 1988.

1 Beausang, Ita: 'Obituary: Aloys Fleischmann MA, DMus, Hon MusD (Dubl), MRIA 13 April 1910–21 July 1992', *New Music News* (Sept. 1992), p. 5.

2 Donoghue, Denis: 'The Future of Irish Music', *Studies*, Vol. 44 (Spring 1955), p. 111.

3 Ryan, Joseph J.: 'Fleischmann: *Piano Quintet*', sleeve notes for CD Marco Polo 8.223888 1995 [1995].

4 Fleischmann, Aloys: 'The Outlook of Music in Ireland' *Studies* xxiv (March 1935), p. 124.

5 Ryan, Joseph J.: *Nationalism and Music in Ireland* (unpublished PhD diss., National University of Ireland [St Patrick's College, Maynooth], 1991) p. 440.

6 Klein, Axel: 'The Composer in the Academy (2) 1940–1990', *To Talent Alone: The Royal Irish Academy of Music*: 1848–1998, ed. Richard Pine and Charles Acton (Dublin: Gill & Macmillan, 1998), p. 426.

7 Composers in Conversation: Interview with Aloys Fleischmann on RTE; producer: Jerome de Bromhead (first broadcast FM3, 6/1988).

8 'Man spürt den Jig eher als daß man ihn hört', quoted from Klein, Axel: *Die Musik Irlands im 20. Jahrhundert* (Hildesheim: Georg Olms, 1996), p. 187, author's translation.

9 *The Hidden Ireland: A Study of Gaelic Munster* was a book by Daniel Corkery (1878–1964), professor of English at University College, Cork, from 1930 to his retirement in 1947. First published in 1924, this study of Irish poetry and culture in eighteenth-century Munster was a curious influence on Fleischmann; its espousal of a narrow sense of cultural separatism, as promulgated by the Irish Ireland movement, would seem to have flown in the face of his avowed pluralist approach to music. However, it is telling that Corkery was one of a considerable number of the contemporary cultural intelligensia to have frequented the Fleischmann family home during the composer's youth. (Dunne, Seán: 'A life given to music', *The Cork Examiner*, 15 January 1986.)

10 Quoted in de Barra, Séamas: 'Fleischmann the Composer', *New Music News* (September 1992) p. 7.

11 *Ibid.*, p. 7.

12 Ryan, Joseph J.: *Nationalism and Music in Ireland* (unpublished PhD diss., National University of Ireland 1991) 440.

13 *Ibid.*, p. 6.

14 De Barra, Séamas: 'Fleischmann the Composer', *New Music News* (September 1992) p. 7.

15 Klein, Axel: 'Aloys Fleischmann', *Komponisten der Gegenwart*, ed. Walter Wolfgang Sparrer and Hans Werner Heisker (1992 ff.), p. 9.

16 The ballet was named after the famous Irish mythological cycle of tales which came back to prominence following Thomas Kinsella's translation of 1969.

17 Leland, Mary: 'A lifetime spent in the service of music.' *The Irish Times*, 21 January, 1991.

18 Burn, Sarah, M.: 'Irish Musical Portraits: A Series of Performers, Composers and Collectors – 5. Aloys Fleischmann', *NCH Calendar*, May 1993 after Séamas de Barra: 'Fleischmann the Composer', *New Music News* (September 1992) p. 7.

19. *Ibid.*, p. 7.

20. *Ibid.*, p. 7.

21 *Editor's note*: Scott-Sutherland also reviewed the CD: Silver Apples of the Moon – Irish Classical Music, saying that of the works on the disc, Fleischmann's *Elizabeth McDermott Roe* is 'the most substantial', that it explores the 'darker aspects, evoking the bleaker side to that "land beneath the visiting moon".'

22 See my chapter 'The Composer and the Academy (2) 1940–1990', in: R. Pine & C.

Acton (eds.), *To Talent Alone – The Royal Irish Academy of Music 1848–1998,* Dublin 1998, pp. 419–428 (esp. p. 426) and my entry on Fleischmann in *Komponisten der Gegenwart* (KdG), ninth supplement, February 1996.

23 See editor's note in Ruth Fleischmann, ed., *Joan Denise Moriarty* (Cork, 1998), p. 30–1.

24 S. de Barra, 'Aloys Fleischmann's Ballet Music', in: *Joan Denise Moriarty,* p. 106.

25 A. Bax, *Farewell, My Youth* (London, 1943), p. 47.

26 A. Fleischmann, 'Composition and the Folk Idiom', *Ireland ToDay,* I (Dublin, Nov. 1936), p. 39.

27 Bunting attributes the poem to Carolan. See D. O'Sullivan, *Carolan: The Life, Times and Music of an Irish Harper,* 2 vols. (London, 1958), II, p. 134.

28 This analysis of the *Piano Quintet* is taken largely from this author's sleeve note for the fine Marco Polo recording of the work by Hugh Tinney and the Vanbrugh String Quartet issued in 1996. The quintet is paired with May's quartet.

29 D. O'Sullivan, *Carolan: The Life, Times and Music of an Irish Harper,* London, 1958, II, p. 134

30 Fleischmann's music for this form is discussed in Séamas de Barra's article 'Aloys Fleischmann's Ballet Music', in: Ruth Fleischmann ed., *Joan Denise Moriarty* Cork, 1998, p. 106.

31 'Aloys Fleischmann in conversation with Tomás Ó Canainn', *The Cork Review,* Tomás Ó Canainn, ed., Cork 1992, p.15.

32 *Ibid.,* p.16.

33 *Ibid.,* p.15.

34 'Unflagging Energy – Michael Dervan talks to Aloys Fleischmann', *Music Ireland,* Vol. 5 No. 5, May 1990, p. 7.

35 On the cover of the recent Marco Polo CD of Fleischmann's *Piano Quintet.*

36 Letter from Daniel Corkery to Aloys Fleischmann, undated (probably 1934), The Fleischmann Papers, UCC Archive.

37 'Michael Dawney concludes his conversation with Aloys Fleischmann', *Composer,* Spring 1976, p. 38.

38 Aloys Fleischmann, 'The Outlook for Music in Ireland', *Studies,* Vol. xxiv No. 93, March 1935, p. 124.

39 Aloys Fleischmann, 'Ars Nova', *Ireland Today,* Vol. 1 No. 2, July 1936, p. 45.

40 Aloys Fleischmann, 'Composition and the Folk Idiom', *Ireland Today,* Vol. 1 No. 6, November 1936, p. 43

41 Aloys Fleischmann, 'The Outlook for Music in Ireland', *Studies,* Vol. xxiv No. 93, March 1935, p. 125

42 Aloys Fleischmann, 'Composition and the Folk Idiom', *Ireland Today,* Vol. 1 No. 6, November 1936, p. 40 *ibid.*

43 *Ibid.*

44 Frederick May, 'The Music of Aloys Fleischmann', *The Father Mathew Record,* Vol. 42, No. 12, December 1949, p. 6

45 Letter fromE.J. Moeran to Tilly Fleischmann, 20 April 1934 [from the content it is clear that Moeran has mis-dated this letter and that the year is 1938], Fleischmann Papers, UCC Archive.

46 From Fleischmann's programme note for performances of the *Piano Quintet* by Una Hunt and the Vanbrugh String Quartet in Dublin, 24 June 1990, and Cork, 3 July 1990.

47 Frederick May, *op.cit.*

48 *Ibid.*

49 Seán Ó Riada, 'An Open Letter to Charles Acton', in: *Integrating Tradition: The Achievement of Seán Ó Riada,* Bernard Harris and Grattan Freyer, eds., Ballina 1982, p. 151

50 Frederick May, *op. cit.*

51 This account is taken from Joseph Gilmore, 'The Cork Ballet Company', *Threshold*, Vol. 1 , Autumn 1957.

52 Aloys Fleischmann, *Ballet in Cork*, typescript, pp. 14–15, the Fleischmann Papers, UCC Archive.

53 Letter from Donal O Sullivan to Aloys Fleischmann, 10 September 1945, The Fleischmann Papers, UCC Archive.

54 Letter from Seamus Murphy to Aloys Fleischmann, 10 October 1945, Fleischmann Papers, UCC Archive.

55 Frederick May, *op. cit.*

56 *Ibid.*

57 *The Standard*, 23 June 1944 (Review of *The Four Masters*).

58 Frederick May, *op.cit.*

59 From the programme booklet for the first performance.

60 Mícheál MacLiammóir, *et al.*, 'Design for a Ballet', *The Bell*, Vol. 4 No. 6, September 1942, p. 339.

61 *The Irish Times*, 29 February 1961.

62 *The Irish Times*, 12 February 1962.

63 Copy of a letter from Aloys Fleischmann to Robert Farren, 14 April 1964, Fleischmann Papers, UCC Archive.

64 *The Irish Times*, 4 January 1967.

65 Copy of a letter from Aloys Fleischmann to Gerard Victory, 8 November 1963, Fleischmann Papers, UCC Archive.

66 *The Irish Times*, 30 June 1965.

67 *The Cork Examiner*, 30 June 1965.

68 *The Irish Times*, 2 July 1960.

69 *Ibid.*

70 Aloys Fleischmann, script for radio broadcast, typescript, n.d., (probably for the weekly series *Composers at Work* broadcast by Radio Éireann in 1957), Fleischmann Papers, UCC Archive.

71 Aloys Fleischmann, summary of publication history of *Eilís Nic Dhiarmada Ruaidh*, MS, 1957 (?), (probably draft of a letter), Fleischmann Papers, UCC Archive.

72 *The Irish Times*, 19 April 1980.

73 *The Irish Times*, 23 July 1992.

74 Copy of letter from Aloys Fleischmann to Gerard Victory, 8 November 1963, Fleischmann Papers, UCC Archive.

75 Aloys Fleischmann, script for radio broadcast, typescript, n.d., (probably for weekly series *Composers at Work* broadcast by Radio Éireann in 1957), Fleischmann Papers, UCC Archive.

76 Copy of questionnaire completed by Aloys Fleischmann in 1990, Fleischmann Papers, UCC Archive.

77 Aloys Fleischmann, 'On Writing Music for Ballet', *Soundpost*, No. 4, October/November 1981, p. 11.

78 Copy of questionnaire completed by Aloys Fleischmann in 1990, Fleischmann Papers, UCC Archive.

79 Copy of letter from Aloys Fleischmann to Gay Byrne, 10 September 1985, Fleischmann Papers, UCC Archive.

80 Copy of letter from Aloys Fleischmann to Bill Skinner, 13 August 1970, Fleischmann Papers, UCC Archive.

81 Copy of letter from Aloys Fleischmann to Gráinne Yeats, 29 December 1971, Fleischmann Papers, UCC Archive.

82 Copy of letter from Aloys Fleischmann to Gráinne Yeats, 22 May 1972, Fleischmann Papers, UCC Archive.

83 *The Irish Times*, 26 April 1974.
84 *The Irish Times*, 26 April 1974.
85 *The Irish Times*, 11 January 1974.
86 *The Irish Times*, 7 January 1970.
87 *The Irish Times*, 28 June 1972.
88 *The Irish Times*, 11 January 1974.
89 Letter from Gerard Victory to Aloys Fleischmann, 19 October 1981, Fleischmann Papers, UCC Archive.
90 Copy of letter from Aloys Fleischmann to Gerard Victory, 11 February 1974, Fleischmann Papers, UCC Archive.
91 Aloys Fleischmann, 'Ballet in Cork', *Music Ireland*, Vol. 2 No. 10, November 1987, p. 15.
92 *The Irish Times*, 7 October 1981.
93 *Daily Telegraph*, 8 October 1981.
94 'Aloys Fleischmann in conversation with Tomás Ó Canainn', *The Cork Review*, Tomás Ó Canainn, ed., Cork 1992, p. 16.
95 Aloys Fleischmann, 'Ars Nova', *Ireland Today*, Vol. 1 No. 2, July 1936, p. 47.
96 Aloys Fleischmann, 'Composition and the Folk Idiom', *Ireland Today*, Vol. 1 No. 6, November 1936, p. 44.

CHAPTER 8: THE MAN

1 *Editor's note*: It was Gerald Goldberg who by his generous sponsorship made possible the visit to Cork of the Vienna Philharmonic Orchestra in the course of the Tóstal Festival of 1956. In 1962 he and his wife Sheila initiated, sponsored and organised a series of Lunchtime Recitals in the Crawford Art Gallery, which have continued ever since – the first series of recitals were dedicated to Aloys and Tilly Fleischmann. With Anne Fleischmann, Gerald Goldberg founded The Friends of the Orchestral Society: their most successful venture was bringing Micheál Mac Liammóir to Cork to perform his one-man show on Oscar Wilde: *The Importance of Being Oscar*. It was Gerald Goldberg who as Lord Mayor of Cork proposed to the Corporation that Aloys Fleischmann be made a Freeman of the city.
2 See Gerald Y. Goldberg's article in: *Joan Denise Moriarty, Founder of Irish National Ballet*, edited by Ruth Fleischmann, Cork 1998.

INDEX

Ireland), 20
Sources of Irish Traditional Music, 16, 132, 186, 252–9, 288
Fleischmann, Aloys senior, 22, 31, 38, 134, 199, 217, 263, 351–2, 353, 356, 362–2, 363, 365–6, 371
Fleischmann, Anne née Madden, 42, 51, 235, 285, 357–8, 362, 381–2, 384–5, 385–6
Fleischmann, Tilly, 22, 37, 41, 134, 135–6, 189–190, 228, 234, 349, 351, 353, 356, 361, 363–4, 377, 378
Flynn, Peter, 258
Foley, Dorothy, 97
Fota, 120–2, 142
Foubert, Annette de, 43, 113, 256
Goldberg, Gerald Y., 428 note 2 (chap. 8)
Goldberg, Sheila, 85, 260, 384
Gúm, An (Government Publications Office), 338
Gwynn, Denis, 362
Haas, Joseph, 298, 325
Hart, Mary V., 370
Harty, Hamilton, 132
Hayes, Edmund, 362
Healy, James N., 171
Healy, Joe, 194
Higgins, Joseph, 361
Honan Hostel UCC, 26
Horgan, John J., 349, 356
Horgan, Mary née Windle, 356
Horne, J. T., 52, 53
Houlihan, Denis, 364
Howell, Cissie, 153
Hughes, Anthony, 63, 121
Irish Harp Book, The, 236
Kavanagh, Kruger, 191
Kelly, Seamus (Quidnunc), 24
Killian, Peadar, 91, 129
Kinsella, Thomas, 342–3
Kodaly method, The, 92–3, 98
Lacy, St John, 249, 324
Larchet, John F., 130, 202, 235
Lynch, Charles, 62, 127, 212, 238, 260
Mac Liammóir, Micheál, 128, 165, 334
MacSwiney, Mary, 350, 366
McGettrick, Paul, 258
May, Frederick, 45, 135–6, 330, 332
Moeran, E. J., 304, 329
Montague, John, 343
Moriarty, Joan Denise, 13, 15, 105–6, 118, 127, 136, 157–171, 331
Mülhausen, Prof. von, 194
Munnelly, Adrian, 15
Murphy, Seamus, 41, 135, 332, 361–3
Murray, Patrick, 167, 384
Music Association of Ireland, 118, 238, 267
Music Teachers Association, 52, 69, 81, 84,

266–7
Neeson, Geraldine, 29, 104, 234, 365, 367
Neeson, Seán, 19, 355, 365
Ó Laoghaire, Pilib, 23, 177, 209, 256, 283, 284, 285
Ó Riada, Seán, 20, 42, 73, 130, 205, 210, 249, 256, 288
O'Donovan, James W., 183
O'Faoláin, Seán, 12, 13, 14
O'Rahilly, Alfred, 187, 194, 215, 362–3
O'Sullivan, Cara, 397
O'Sullivan, Donal (Cork), 188
O'Sullivan, Donal (Dublin), 332
Pyne, Moira, 351
Queens University of Belfast, 132
Reardon, Lal, 392
Reyghera, de, 154
Rosen, Waldemar, 191
Royal Dublin Society, 125, 172
Schmidt–Isserstet, Hans, 260
(Schools' concerts – see: Children's concerts)
Seminar on Contemporary Choral Music, UCC 19, 74, 80, 181, 187, 191–2, 197, 226, 234, 237, 238, 240, 298
Shanahan, Gerard, 349, 355
Sheehy, Edward, 22, 335
Siamsa Theatre, Tralee, 39, 104, 106
Spratt, Geoffrey, 397
Stavenhagen, 377
Stembridge, Christopher, 62, 67, 85, 89
Stockley, Germaine née Kolb, 353, 355, 365
Student Performances, 29, 32, 62, 66, 97, 112–3, 138, 270
Swertz, Maria née Rössler, 351, 352
Swift, Carolyn, 346
Terry, Father Seán, 57, 269
Tinney, Hugh, 123, 128, 234, 307
Tóstal, An, 13
Trinity College Dublin, 239
Tulloch, Davy, 259
University College Dublin, 130
University College Galway, 48, 63, 118
Vanbrugh String Quartet, 21, 122–3, 127, 227
Vaughan Williams, Ralph, 204
Victory, Gerard, 181, 344
Vocational Educational Committees, 90–2, 276
Walton, Sir William, 80, 180–1, 187–8
Walsh, Helen, 257
Wilson, James, 181
Windle, Bertram, 249, 356
Wulstan, David, 67, 78
Yeats, Gráinne, 342
Yeats, Michael, 336
Zuk, Patrick, 146, 189, 397

430